International Handbook
of Contemporary
Developments in
Criminology

International Handbook of Contemporary Developments in Criminology

EUROPE, AFRICA,
THE MIDDLE EAST,
AND ASIA

Edited by ELMER H. JOHNSON

Greenwood Press
Westport, Connecticut • London, England

Library of Congress Cataloging in Publication Data
Main entry under title:

International handbook of contemporary developments in
   criminology.

   Includes bibliographies and index.
   Contents: V. 1. General Issues and the Americas—
   V. 2. Europe, Africa, the Middle East, and Asia.
   1. Crime and criminals—Addresses, essays, lectures.
I. Johnson, Elmer Hubert.
HV6028.I53   364   83-1721
ISBN 0-313-21059-4 (set : lib. bdg.)   AACR2

Library of Congress Catalog Card Number: 83-1721
ISBN: 0-313-23803-0 (Vol. 2)

First published in 1983

Greenwood Press
A division of Congressional Information Service, Inc.
88 Post Road West
Westport, Connecticut 06881

Printed in the United States of America

10   9   8   7   6   5   4   3   2   1

To Carol Holmes Johnson
My inspiration and partner
for more than four decades

CONTENTS

FIGURE

TABLES

PREFACE

Comparative criminology has been handicapped by the insularity of attitudes, sometimes described as ethnocentricity—the tendency to be convinced without careful consideration that the beliefs of one's own ethnic group are superior to those of other groups. "Insularity" conveys a number of interrelated ideas: the isolation of a people from a broader social universe that has crucial impact on their lives; the separation of peoples that denies them the benefits of the joint actions characteristic of social relationships distinctive to human beings; excessively limited perspectives in trying to explain common human experiences; and a provinciality of customs and opinions that ignores promising solutions to those problems encountered in all societies.

The decades since the second World War have been ushered in by a renewal of contacts between peoples which some have heralded as an opportunity to extend the recognition that all of us share the world. Secular "evangelicalism" sometimes seizes on this development to argue that increased contacts are sufficient to impart a "moral purity" to relationships among peoples, but this oversimplistic view ignores the persistence of self-interests that have led to exploitation of one people by another possessing superior power and the tendency of people to cling to ingrained customs. It is necessary to examine the nature of the new contacts and the forces that impel them before we can conclude that they will be of ultimate benefit to all peoples. We must be prepared to find that greater familiarity among peoples will be a mixed blessing.

The caution is supported by the consequences of massive social, economic, and political changes in the decades since World War II. These changes have had the negative effect of increasing the magnitude of the crime problem but have also lent impetus to the development of international criminology. Since crime and reactions to it are symptomatic of broader developments within a given social system, the macro-changes of those decades have underscored the validity of the principle that both crime and criminology are international phenomena.

The economic interdependence and degree of communication among the world's peoples have greatly eroded the insularity of nations and of communities within nations. Both long-established and emergent nations have undertaken programs of economic development that have released the effects of industrialization; some of these societies were previously largely agrarian. Societies with a long history of industrialization are experiencing in new forms increased population mobility, greater scale of social organizations, heightened influence of subcultural divisions within a society, further decline of the viability of informal control institutions, and politicization of social issues.

A noteworthy paradox is found in many nations. In the face of the remarkably great need for public order in highly complex societies, urbanites are less capable of sustaining the moral consensus that traditionally has been seen as the foundation of the social order. Legalization is the process by which selected cultural norms are translated into the abstract language of laws and are made subject to official enforcement. This process is unlikely to capture fully the nuance of those norms, making the administration of legal norms less effective and more visible than informal controls. Yet, the urban paradox, mentioned above, has accelerated the growth of professionalized and bureaucratized systems of criminal justice.

The new possibility of an enriched criminology rests to an important extent on reducing the insularity separating and isolating the criminologists of various nations from one another. With the macro-forces decreasing the insularity of nations, criminologists should be able to take advantage of joint transnational efforts to understand the criminal phenomenon that crosses political boundaries. The provinciality of accepted but unsubstantiated beliefs and excessively narrow explanations can be exposed when criminologists are given greater opportunities to become familiar with the relevant knowledge and research findings of their foreign colleagues.

On several sojourns my search for criminological insights has taken me abroad for intellectually enrichening experiences. Along with many criminologists here and abroad, I have become convinced that transnational investigations are especially promising for disabusing us of the consequences of insularity and giving researchers access to data controlling for different environments. The universality of scientific concepts can be tested to an unprecedented degree. The claims of comparative criminology, however, have been more an expression of hope for the future than a record of tangible and widespread accomplishments.

The years since World War II have underscored the interdependence of nations, the difficulties of socioeconomic development for well-established and emergent nations, and the spread of conditions that contribute to criminality. In upsetting traditional social and cultural systems, these major trends have generated increased crime and new crime patterns that extend beyond national boundaries. These international dimensions are further illustrated by certain patterns found around the world: the apparent rise of crime among females of urbanized-industrialized countries, the overrepresentation of minority and underprivileged persons, the unprecedented recognition of the implications of white-collar offenses, and the growing involvement of the young.

Those considerations motivated me to undertake preparation of the *International Handbook of Contemporary Developments in Criminology*. There is a unique need for a review of the various "criminologies-in-societies." We cannot speak of a single model of criminology because in each country the work, status, and subject matter of the criminologists are determined by the peculiarities of political-legal history, the impact of recent developments, and the general institutional system. Since the patterns of crime, the reactions to crime, and the nature of criminology are creatures of the varying macro-sociocultural systems of nations, it is essential that we expect criminology to occur in a range of models.

Unfortunately, it was not possible for me to visit a great number of nations to experience directly the ideas, work settings, and products of foreign colleagues. As an alternative to such direct experiences, insights may be provided by reports from experts from an array of countries. Readers from many nations would benefit from such a rough equivalent of a sample of the differing versions of criminology.

As for an international conference, there is a need for a scheme to coordinate the reports into a conceptual whole. To that end, each contributor was asked to focus on those elements that characterize criminology as an occupational system. The authors were asked to answer a number of general questions: What is criminology? How are specialists in criminology recruited and educated? How do criminologists see themselves within the division of labor among the disciplines— law, biology, and the social and behavioral sciences—that are relevant to criminology? What are the regularized channels of communication among those persons who see themselves as criminologists? Is criminological research carried out regularly? If so, within what organizational setting is it typically carried out? What are the general parameters of the social, cultural, economic, and political setting within which criminology emerged in your country and is now practiced? What are the dimensions and nature of crime as the subject of criminological study in your country?

The answers make each chapter unique; yet, what also emerges in this book is the awareness of certain similarities that have excited the curiosity of comparative criminologists. In those respects, we are obliged to the contributors who agreed to undertake the assignment and to complete the challenging tasks of preparing their chapters. As editor, I have served as intermediary in assembling a cohort of authors, providing a platform through which each author could present the particular "criminology-in-society" in its own terms. As an additional resource, the authors were asked to prepare representative bibliographies on the criminological literature of the respective nations. Almost all authors compiled bibliographies, many of them annotated.

The decades since World War II have been marked by transnational developments of particular significance for criminology. Part I of the *International Handbook of Contemporary Criminology: General Issues and the Americas* deals specifically with these trends in some of the developing nations, the feminist movement, and radical criminology. Also singled out for special attention are those international organizations devoted to criminological activities on an international plane, especially the United Nations and the International Society for Criminology. The chapters on the two Americas comprise Part II of the volume, although the varieties of "criminology-in-society" are not limited to a particular continent. The chapters on other nations are presented in the *International Handbook of Contemporary Criminology: Europe, Africa, the Middle East, and Asia.*

This handbook represents a major contribution to the literature. The dedicated efforts of the contributors support this claim in a fashion that frees me of the charge of excessive audacity. My primary obligation is to those authors. Scarcely secondary is my obligation to Greenwood Press for originating the idea for a book of this kind.

Many of my fellow criminologists provided an indispensable service in suggesting persons who would be appropriate contributors. The Center for the Study of Crime, Delinquency, and Corrections, Southern Illinois University at Carbondale, has made it possible for me to carry out the time-consuming tasks of editing. A great volume of correspondence and other detailed tasks were accomplished through the support of Jacqueline Goepfert, Sandra Martin, Mary Joiner, and Terry O'Boyle. Dr. Virgil L. Williams and Cyril Robinson served me well in specific professional ways. Marilyn Brownstein, Cynthia Harris, and Arlene Belzer, members of the Greenwood Press staff, generously contributed their respective specialized competencies.

ELMER H. JOHNSON

ABBREVIATIONS

ABS	Australian Bureau of Statistics
ACPS	Australian Crime Prevention Council
ACT	Australian Capital Territory
AFP	Australian Federal Police
AIC	Australian Institute of Criminology
ANZ	Australian and New Zealand Society
ANZAAS	Australian and New Zealand Association for the Advancement of Science
ASC	American Society of Criminology
CCRC	Coordination Committee for Criminological Research
CEMS	Center for the Studies of Social Movements
CFR-ES	Centre de Formation et de recherche de l'education surveillée
CNERP	Centre national d'étude et de recherche pénitentiare
CTN	Centre technique national de l'enfance et de l'adolescence inadapté
DRGST	Delegation générale à la recherche scientifique et technique
GRA	Government Reservation Area
GRIJ	Groupe de Recherche sur l'Adaption Juvenile
HSRC	Human Sciences Research Council
INED	Institut national d'études démographique
INSERM	Institut national de la santé et de la recherche médicales
INTERPOL	International Criminal Police Organization
ISC	International Society for Criminology
NICRO	National Institute for Crime Prevention and Rehabilitation of Offenders
NISER	Nigerian Institute for Social and Economic Research
NRC	National Redemption Council
NSW	New South Wales
ONSER	Organisme national de securité routiere
PLA	People's Liberation Army

SANCA	South African National Council on Alcoholism and Drug Dependence
SEPC	Service d'études pénales et criminologiques
SDCR	Social Demographic and Criminological Research
SMC	Supreme Military Council
SUL	Special Unnumbered License
TRC	Terrorism Research Center
UNAFEI	United Nations Asia and Far East Institute
UNISA	University of South Africa
UNSDRI	United Nations Social Defense Research Institute

International Handbook
of Contemporary
Developments in
Criminology

AUSTRALIA

Duncan Chappell

The growth of criminology in Australia is an independent discipline worthy of academic and professional recognition has been both recent and slow. It was not until the 1950s that the two oldest tertiary institutions in the country, the universities of Melbourne and Sydney, established centers devoted to teaching and research in the field of crime and the treatment of offenders.[1] In each university, the creation of these centers was largely attributable to the activities of law teachers and practitioners with an interest in criminal law and the administration of criminal justice. These activities produced centers possessing close ties to the law and an affiliation between the study of criminal law and criminology. This affiliation has continued, criminology remaining a discipline taught primarily in Australian law schools, although an increasing number of sociology, social work, psychology, and related degree courses expose students to criminological issues and materials.

The primary academic alliance between law and criminology in Australia has tended to produce a conservative ideological perspective in regard to theories of crime causation, prevention, and control. The views of "new" or "radical" criminologists have not taken rapid hold in the tradition-oriented climate of Australian law schools and their environs.[2] Similarly, criminologists working in this legal setting, and in the criminal justice system at large, have experienced difficulty gaining recognition as professionals in their own right rather than as lawyers, or members of other disciplines, with special qualifications in criminology.

Yet change is occurring. In the past decade Australian governments, both federal and state, have exhibited a growing interest in criminology and the contribution it is believed it can make to alleviating the crime problem. Among important developments none has been more significant than the establishment, through the joint efforts of federal and state authorities, of the Australian Institute of Criminology (AIC).[3] The institute has become the focal point in Australia for applied criminological research and training. Staffed by a core of experts, called criminologists, the AIC has given fresh impetus to the development of criminology in Australia as an officially sanctioned and autonomous discipline.

A SOCIAL AND CULTURAL PRIMER

In Australia, crime and offenders have had special significance since the first European settlers landed and raised the British flag on the continent at Botany Bay in January 1788.[4] Of the settlers to follow most were convicts, transported as a punishment to the colony of New South Wales (NSW), and the balance mainly members of the military sent to guard the involuntary migrants.[5] This small group began the occupation of a land mass slightly larger than the continental United States and populated at the time by an estimated three hundred thousand native aboriginals.[6]

Until the abandonment of transportation in 1868, some 166,000 convicts made the hazardous voyage from England. A growing flow of free settlers was stimulated, among other things, by access to cheap convict labor.[7] Initially, some convicts were imprisoned under exceedingly harsh conditions in notorious places like Port Arthur in Van Diemens Land (now Tasmania) and Norfolk Island. Most were obliged to work on public projects or for private individuals under conditions of a "ticket of leave." Through these precursors of modern work release and parole programs, convict labor contributed substantially to the early economic development of the new nation.

Modern Australia

Today the 14 million Australians enjoy one of the highest standards of living in the world. Rich in natural resources, Australia has a thriving export industry in minerals and agricultural products. Its largest trading partners are the countries of the Pacific Rim, particularly Japan. Although remaining a member of the British Commonwealth, Australia has achieved a large measure of independence from its former colonial mentor and, especially since World War II, has grown correspondingly closer to the United States.[8] Linked to the United States by a series of defense and trade treaties, Australia has in general been a strong supporter of American foreign policy, including participation in the Vietnam War. At the same time, Australia has increasingly involved itself with neighboring Southeast Asian countries, including the People's Republic of China.

Overseas, the popular image of Australia tends to be that of the last great frontier, sparsely populated by rather brash and rugged souls who spend their time in the vast Outback grappling with the problems of survival.[9] Australia is, in fact, a highly urbanized society with the bulk of the population residing in a small proportion of the total land area. Most of the land mass is inhospitable and largely uninhabitable desert. Other areas suitable for rural development remain sparsely settled.

For historical, climatic and economic reasons the population of Australia is concentrated in capital cities and other major towns, mainly on the South and East coast of the Continent. In June 1976, 69.7 percent of the population lived in the six state capital cities and five other major towns of 100,000 or more persons. . . . Of these, only Canberra (the national capital) is located inland. The percentage of the population living in rural areas has declined over the years as the major cities and towns have attracted most of the population growth; there have been periods when the rural population has actually declined in numbers. This trend, however, appears to have slowed considerably since 1971.[10]

TABLE 1-1
ESTIMATED POPULATION OF AUSTRALIAN STATES, TERRITORIES, AND CAPITAL CITIES, JUNE 30, 1976

Area	Population (Thousands)
NSW	4,914
Sydney	3,094
Victoria	3,746
Melbourne	2,672
Queensland	2,111
Brisbane	985
South Australia	1,261
Adelaide	912
Northern Australia	1,169
Perth	820
Tasmania	407
Hobart	164
ACT	203
Canberra	201
Western Territory	101
Darwin	45

Source: Australian Bureau of Statistics.

Table 1-1 shows the general distribution of population among the states and territories as well as the number of people living in the various capital cities. Table 1-2 shows the estimated age and sex distribution of the population at large. Since World War II an extensive immigration program has increased the population and changed its profile. The preponderance of British settlers has been partly balanced by an influx of new settlers drawn primarily from other Northern and

TABLE 1-2
ESTIMATED AGE DISTRIBUTION OF AUSTRALIAN POPULATION,
JUNE 30, 1976 (THOUSANDS)

Age Group (Years)	Males	Females	Persons
0- 4	630	602	1,232
5- 9	654	621	1,275
10-14	646	610	1,256
15-19	638	610	1,248
20-24	588	576	1,164
25-29	594	579	1,173
30-34	499	468	967
35-39	430	406	836
40-44	382	360	742
45-49	407	379	786
50-54	389	377	766
55-59	319	324	643
60-64	278	300	578
65-69	215	244	459
70-74	148	188	336
75 +	155	284	439
All ages	6,972	6,928	13,910

Source: Australian Bureau of Statistics.

Southern European countries. In 1976, people born overseas made up 20 percent of the Australian population. In the same year, some 115,000 aboriginals made up less than 1 percent of the population.

During the past decade, there has been a reduction in the rate of natural increase in the Australian population because of a decline in the birth rate and lower levels of net migration. If we assume that these trends will continue, the Australian population can be projected to be about 18 million in the year 2000. However, there are recent indications that the traditional migration patterns to Australia are changing, with emphasis now being given to the admittance of new settlers from Asian countries.[11] If, as seems likely, this development continues, Australia should by the turn of the century become a much larger and more racially diverse society than it is at present.

THE CRIMINAL JUSTICE SYSTEM

Australia's origin as a penal colony is a constant source of academic, cultural, and social interest now, without the bitterness and embarrassment often exhibited in former years.[12] Historians and political scientists have, in particular, long been concerned with the impact of the convict days upon the development of the nation's institutions and the attitudes of its citizens. For instance, it has been asserted that this past accounts for the scant respect Australians tend to have for the symbols of authority, such as the police.[13]

The convict past played a part in the organization of the criminal justice system when Australia adopted a federal system of government (1901) modeled, in large part, upon that of the United States. There were difficulties in maintaining law and order in the years when the population contained large numbers of former convicts and when control was being established over vast areas of land occupied by hostile aborigines. Strong and centrally controlled police forces were formed in each of the six colonies that ultimately joined together in the new Commonwealth of Australia.[14] Under the terms of the Australian constitution these colonies, which now became states, were made responsible for the enactment and enforcement of criminal laws.

The Criminal Law

The present Australian criminal justice system reflects these historical and constitutional developments. While retaining the English common law as the basis of the legal system, three states—Tasmania, Queensland, and Western Australia—have codified their major criminal laws.[15] The remaining states and the two territories established since federation—the Australian Capital Territory (ACT) and the Northern Territory—have opted to rely upon a mixture of statutory and common law provisions to delineate the boundaries of their criminal laws.[16] The federal government has also enacted a wide range of penal provisions within the sphere of its constitutional responsibilities.[17] However, under what has been termed an "autochthonous expedient" the administration of these federal criminal laws has largely been carried out by the states and territories on behalf of the federal authorities.[18]

Much of Australian criminal law is at present in need of major substantive and procedural reform.[19] Attempts to develop a uniform criminal law for the entire country have met with little success.[20] In general, such reform as has occurred has been of an *ad hoc* and spasmodic form.[21]

Law Enforcement

There are eight police forces in Australia—one in each of the six states, one in the Northern Territory, and one federal agency responsible for the enforcement of federal statutes and the policing of the ACT. The respective strength of these forces is shown in Table 1-3. Although drawing mainly upon British traditions of policing, the head of the Australian Federal Police (AFP) is, for instance, a former senior officer from the London Metropolitan Police Force. Australian law enforcement agencies have increasingly taken on American police trappings, including the wearing of guns.[22] Entry standards to most Australian police forces require less than the completion of a high school education, while career ad-

TABLE 1-3
STRENGTH OF AUSTRALIAN POLICE FORCES, JUNE 30, 1977

Jurisdiction	Number
NSW	8,959
Victoria	6,663
Queensland	4,230
South Australia	3,216
Western Australia	2,345
Tasmania	1,026
Northern Territory	451
Federal[a]	2,054

Source: Australian Bureau of Statistics.

[a] The Federal police figures represent an amalgamation of the strengths of the Commonwealth and ACT police forces. These two agencies were merged into the Australian Federal Police in 1979.

vancement within the forces is determined largely by seniority.[23] Police officers with tertiary educational qualifications remain rarities in Australian police forces.[24]

Prosecution and Defense

The prosecution of summary (minor) offenses in Australia is almost exclusively a police responsibility.[25] Summary offenses account for more than 90 percent of all criminal prosecutions. Indictable (serious) offenses are prosecuted by legally trained Crown law officers employed by various departments of justice and/or attorneys general in the states and territories.[26] Decisions as to whether or not a prosecution should be instituted for an indictable offense are made primarily by Crown law officers; grand juries were abolished in Australia in 1828.[27] A review of decisions to prosecute is made by magistrates in preliminary hearings (or committal proceedings).[28] The scope of these hearings is restricted in a number of Australian jurisdictions, including such provisions as the substitution, with the consent of the accused, of written depositions for oral testimony.[29]

In prosecution of summary offenses, most accused persons go unrepresented, although limited legal aid schemes, funded by government monies, exist in all Australian jurisidictions.[30] In indictable proceedings, accused persons are more likely to be represented by private counsel or, if indigent, by public defenders. Even so, no right to counsel exists in Australia by virtue of constitutional or judicial decree.[31]

Adjudication

The Australian constitution, while lacking in general bill of rights provisions akin to its U.S. counterpart, requires that indictable offenses be tried by jury.[32] In practice, very few jury trials occur, for most prosecutions for indictable offenses result in guilty pleas.[33] Jury trials, when they do take place, are conducted before judges of one of the courts of superior jurisdiction, while nonjury trials are heard before magistrates in each Australian jurisdiction,[34] as are almost all criminal proceedings involving juveniles.[35] The latter proceedings are conducted in special children's courts which are closed to the public. The entire system of child welfare, including the involvement of juveniles with the criminal justice system, is currently being reviewed in a number of Australian jurisdictions.[36]

Of the approximately 550 judicial officers in the country, 300 are magistrates and 250 judges. All judicial officers are appointed, not elected. The appointment of judges, a responsibility of the queen acting on the advice of the government of the day, is made from among the ranks of practicing barristers; magistrates are appointed either from within the ranks of the public service or from among members of the legal profession.[37]

All Australian jurisdictions allow appeals by offenders against their conviction in criminal cases. In most instances, such appeals are as of right in matters of law and at the discretion of the court in matters of fact. Appeals against sentence by both the defense and prosecution are also allowed.[38] The hierarchy of appeals courts varies from jurisdiction to jurisdiction, but in general the ultimate court of appeal is the high court of Australia.[39]

Corrections

Each Australian government, with the exception of the federal, maintains its own correctional system for adult and juvenile offenders.[40] These systems provide a range of facilities and services for persons convicted of state, territorial, or federal offenses. The states and territories are obliged under the Australian constitution to provide prison accommodation and allied noncustodial services, including parole, for all offenders convicted under the laws of the Commonwealth.[41]

The nature and scope of available correctional services differ among the jurisdictions.[42] The quality of custodial facilities also varies markedly from place to place.[43] Many of the maximum security prisons in Australia date from the late 1800s; one or two institutions still in use were built when convicts were being transported to Australia.[44] Some jurisdictions have recently begun a program either to update existing facilities or to build new institutions. For instance, the Northern Territory, which has by far the highest per capita rate of imprisonment in the country, has recently completed a new prison complex in Darwin.[45] The Victorian government is involved in a major prison construction program. Western Australia is undertaking an official inquiry into the adequacy of its custodial facilities and the need for more institutions.[46]

Australian jurisdictions vary widely in their use of both custodial and noncustodial punishments. As Table 1-4 illustrates, the rates of imprisonment range from a high of about 170 per 100,000 in the Northern Territory to 19 per 100,000 in the ACT; similar disparities exist in the use of probation and parole.[47] There

TABLE 1-4
ADULT PRISONERS, PROBATIONERS, AND PAROLEES, AUSTRALIAN STATES AND TERRITORIES, NOVEMBER 1, 1978

Jurisdiction	Prisoners		Probationers		Parolees	
	No.	*Rates*	*No.*	*Rates*	*No.*	*Rates*
NSW	3,837	76.5	8,089	161.2	2,255	44.9
Victoria	1,569	40.9	2,821	73.6	837	21.8
Queensland	1,600	73.6	2,413	110.9	398	18.3
South Australia	808	62.4	2,428	187.6	164	12.7
Western Australia	1,253	101.8	1,758	142.8	496	40.3
Tasmania	328	79.0	1,815	437.3	59	14.2
Northern Territory	193	170.8	74	65.5	41	36.3
ACT	41	18.9	182	83.9	15	6.9
Australia	9,629	67.4	19,580	137.0	4,265	29.8

Source: Australian Institute of Criminology.

has been substantial conjecture as to the reason for these variations, particularly in the use of imprisonment. One explanation calls attention to the varying proportion of aboriginals in the general population in different parts of Australia.[48] The claim has been made that aboriginals, in contrast to whites, are discriminated against from the initial point of contact with police to their ultimate disposition by the courts. Aboriginals, it is said, are therefore more likely than white Australians to be charged with offenses, more likely to be arrested and then proceeded against by summons, less likely to be granted bail, and, if found guilty, more likely to be sentenced to imprisonment than to a form of noncustodial punishment.[49] Although the empirical data are incomplete, there appears to be some justification for this claim. For example, in Western Australia in 1977 aboriginals represented 2.1 percent of the state's population, but 36 percent of the prison population.

Because this explanation does not account for all the variations in the rates of imprisonment, other factors must be considered. Other explanations refer to differences in geographic and social isolation, the availability and access to mental hospitals, the relative efficiency of the police forces, and variations in the rates and seriousness of crime.[50] Far more research is required for final conclusions.

PATTERNS OF CRIMINALITY

A continuing lament of criminologists, criminal justice administrators, and others concerned with the examination of crime trends in Australia has been the absence of accurate, reliable, and uniform criminal statistics.[51] Only since 1964 has the Australian Bureau of Statistics (ABS) collected and published figures concerning offenses known to Australian police under seven categories—homicide; serious assault; robbery; rape; breaking and entering; motor vehicle theft; and fraud, forgery, and false pretenses.[52] In compiling data for the ABS, the participating law enforcement agencies are supposed to comply with certain standard classification and accounting rules. However, the published data suggest that these rules are not always being followed; consequently, much of the information is of limited interpretive value.[53]

Government is slowly recognizing these deficiencies. After almost two decades of discussion among state and federal agencies, there are prospects for more adequate data.[54] ABS under its constitutional mandate is seeking agreement on the types of statistics to be gathered and the form of their publication.[55] The first national crime victim survey in Australia, conducted by ABS in 1975, obtained information from more than 18,500 people in all Australia, except the Northern Territory and remote rural areas. The results of the survey, published in June 1979, provided a first assessment of the reliability of the limited police statistics incomes and estimated the rates of nonreporting of different types of crime.[56]

Major Crime Trends

In spite of the current deficiencies in Australian criminal statistics, there is reason to believe that most of the seven categories of crime included in the uniform crime series have recorded significant increases.[57] For the seven categories combined, the crime rate in Australia increased from about 756 per 100,000 of population in 1964-1965 to about 1,952 per 100,000 in 1977-1978. The increase was especially steep during the 1960s, but the growth of serious crime tailed off throughout most of the 1970s. One commentator notes:

Even though some crime rates, particularly for robbery and breaking and entering, increased dramatically in the 1960s, it seems that rates for most serious offenses have been relatively stable for most of the 1970s. It should also be borne in mind that violent crime rates in Australia are generally low by international standards.[58]

Dr. S. Mukherjee of the Australian Institute of Criminology has undertaken a long-term analysis of crime trends between 1900 and 1976. His analysis is expected to provide a more comprehensive picture of Australian crime throughout this century. This major study, based primarily on the number of charges and convictions in the courts of all Australian jurisdictions, relates criminal justice data to a number of social and economic factors.[59]

Homicide

Among violent crimes, homicide rates seem to have been relatively stable in Australia since 1945 and remain among the lowest in the Western world, according to World Health Organization estimates.[60] These estimates indicate that the Australian rate of deaths by homicide and injury purposely inflicted by other persons (illegal intervention) per 100,000 population was 1.6 in 1975. In contrast, the rate in that year in the United States was 10.0 and in England and Wales 1.1. The low homicide rate in Australia may be accounted for, in part, by the quite stringent gun controls in most Australian jurisdictions. The possession of handguns is prohibited by all Australian governments, except for special purposes like competitive pistol shooting or for official use by police, private security organizations, and others involved directly in criminal justice activities. Control of long guns is less rigorous, but a number of jurisdictions are implementing registration for owners of all guns.[61]

Terrorism

At a time when terrorist violence deeply concerns much of the Western world, Australia remains remarkably free of this form of violent crime. The most publicized and serious terrorist act took place in 1978 when an unidentified person or organization exploded a bomb in front of the Hilton Hotel in Sydney when a number of political leaders from Southeast Asian countries were holding a high-level international conference.[62] The deaths of a number of people, including a police officer, shocked Australia, and the federal government declared a state of emergency.[63] The federal government instituted a special inquiry, chaired by former chief commissioner of the London Metropolitan Police Force, Sir Robert Mark, into Australian security measures against terrorism. The Mark Report recommended a number of major changes in the structure and organization of federal law enforcement agencies.[64]

Rape

Rape rates increased sharply in Australia from about 2.2 per 100,000 in 1964-1965 to 6.9 per 100,000 in 1977-1978. It is not clear whether this increase reflects an actual growth in the incidence of rape or only reflects other factors such as changes in the reporting behavior of rape victims. Particularly since the 1970s, with international attention focused on rape by the women's movement, including the women's movement in Australia, many changes have taken place in the official handling of rape complaints. For instance, a number of Australian police forces have revised their investigative practices to ameliorate the trauma experienced by the rape victim, and hospitals have improved procedures for examining victims of rape and other sexual offenses.[65]

Robbery

The number of robberies increased dramatically between 1964-1965 and 1977-1978. Between 1964-1965 and 1971-1972, the rate of robbery rose from

5.7 to 24.0 per 100,000. In 1977-1978, the robbery rate reached 25.3 per 100,000. The rate of increase in the 1960s produced substantial concern among law enforcement agencies and among the victims who were, in the main, businesses rather than individuals.[66] Among the more frequent robbery targets were banks, drugstores, betting shops, and gasoline stations. These businesses improved their security measures. Unlike many urban centers in North America and other parts of the world, Australian cities, the Australian police believe, are generally free of muggings and related violent crimes in public places that are frequently associated with drug abuse.

Drug Offenses

Despite the presence of safe streets, the growing prevalence of drug-related offenses in Australia became the subject of a number of major official inquiries during the 1970s, with the most prominent being the Australian Royal Commission of Inquiry into Drugs jointly sponsored by federal and state governments.[67] The Royal Commission, which reported its findings early in 1980 following several years of extensive investigations, concluded that:

Illegal drug abuse is a most serious problem in Australia. It is a problem which shows definite signs of increasing in magnitude. For the last decade there has been no sufficiently coordinated Australian approach to its suppression. There is no doubt that the problem is much greater today than it would have been had there been a coherent national policy against illegal drug abuse during that decade....Although exact quantification is not possible, the Commission has no doubt that huge sums flow out of Australia every year to pay for drugs produced overseas. This movement of money has a significant effect on Australia's balance of payments.[68]

The commission made more than two hundred detailed recommendations for a change in the national policy towards drugs, including extensive increases in police powers and the enactment of national and uniform laws to deal with drug-related matters.[69]

White-collar Crime

The nature and extent of white-collar crime in Australia drew marked official concern in the 1970s. From a topic rarely discussed in public and receiving only peripheral attention from law enforcement agencies, white-collar offenses and offenders began to gain prominence in the media and a far higher priority among investigative targets of police and related bodies.[70] Much of a perceived increase in white-collar crime in Australia over recent years was believed to be associated with a series of economic booms in the early and late 1970s. These booms brought with them not only massive international investment in Australian share markets and resources, but also a spate of fraudulent schemes to manipulate stock prices and reap other illegal economic gains. Another possible factor in the perceived increase of white-collar crime is the expanded role played by the federal government in the field of social welfare. Federal police, who investigated and prosecuted more than two-thirds of all fraud and allied offenses in Australia, reported sharp increases in frauds upon health insurance and social security programs.[71] To combat these developments both state and federal governments have strengthened their security and corporate laws and bolstered the investigative units of police and corporate affairs bodies.[72]

Young Offenders

Crime committed by young Australians, particularly those under the age of eighteen, came under official scrutiny in several Australian jurisdictions as the number of juveniles appearing before children's courts grew apace.[73] Of offenders convicted in Australian courts, both adult and children's, for breaking and entering and theft, more than two-thirds were under the age of twenty-one and more than half under eighteen.[74] Throughout the 1970s, a number of jurisdictions considered, and sometimes implemented, major procedural changes for handling juvenile offenders, defined in most jurisdictions as persons under the age of eighteen.[75]

Aboriginals and Migrants

As noted earlier, aboriginals are represented disproportionately in Australian crime statistics, especially for prison admissions. Most aborigines continue to reside in semirural and rural areas, but a pronounced movement into cities commenced in the 1950s. As for similar minority groups in other countries, the urban aboriginal population has suffered discrimination in access to adequate housing, medical care, employment, and other services.[76] Most aborigines residing in cities like Sydney and Brisbane, or in larger country towns, live in "ghetto-like" conditions that are related to crime, much of it linked to excessive drinking. A growing number of young aborigines have known no life-style other than that of urban poverty; their future appears bleak. Interracial violence has been virtually nonexistent historically in Australia, but these conditions for young aboriginals hold potential for violence in coming years.[77]

Migrant groups, too, possess the potential for violence in the future. Australia, the beneficiary of one of the Western world's largest voluntary migration programs since World War II, is now a multi-ethnic, if not multiracial, society. For instance, over one-quarter million Australians are Muslims, many of them recent arrivals from Turkey, Lebanon, and other Middle Eastern countries. The "cultural shock" produced by the migration from these areas is severe but has not raised major difficulties for the criminal justice system.[78] Studies show that in general migrants have much lower rates of crime than native-born Australians.[79] Experience from elsewhere, and especially in the United States, suggests that, while first-generation migrants have crime rates usually well below those of the host nation, the second generation of migrants becomes "better" assimilated. One effect is that their crime rates become similar or higher than those of the locally born population.[80] There is no substantial evidence that this pattern is occurring in Australia. While the media frequently give prominence to crimes committed by members of ethnic groups, such as the alleged cultivation of major quantities of marijuana by Italians possessing "Mafia-type" connections to their former place of residence, or fraudulent social security claims made by Greek migrants, no serious studies have been made of recent patterns of migrant crime in Australia.[81] The paucity of such research illustrates the urgent need for criminological investigations into many issues associated with crime and justice in Australia.[82]

DISCIPLINARY AND OCCUPATIONAL PERSPECTIVES

From its inception, Australian criminology has had a close academic affiliation with the law, as made evident by the first department of criminology in the country established in 1951 at the University of Melbourne.[83] Two "modern" pioneers in the field—the late Sir John Barry, a judge of the Victorian supreme court and a historian of note, and Dr. Norval Morris, a member of the Faculty of Law of the university, were instrumental in establishing the department.[84] The department was set up under a board of studies chaired by Sir John Barry. The first head of the department, appointed on a part-time basis, was Dr. Morris, who also retained his association with the Faculty of Law. The department began teaching a single elective subject on criminology in 1953 within the Arts Faculty of the University of Melbourne, with students drawn predominantly from arts and law.

Following Dr. Morris's departure overseas, Stanley Johnston, another lawyer, was appointed head of the department in 1958 on a full-time basis. The department introduced a postgraduate diploma in criminology in 1960. In 1963, Johnston assessed the curriculum as follows:

Outside one Indian university, we were the first university in the British Commonwealth to take this step [introduce a criminology diploma]. Universities in Britain and Canada have since followed suit. However, a rich variety of precedents have been set for decades by universities in Europe and the U.S.A. One person has completed the diploma—the Deputy Director of Prisons in Victoria. At least a dozen other candidates are currently pursuing the diploma. The department teaches three of the seven subjects in the diploma: Criminology A, Criminology B and Criminology C. Criminology A is basically an undergraduate subject, since it is also taken by arts, law and social studies students. . . . It is worth noting that some of the diploma candidates are professionals on salaries many hundreds of pounds higher than that of the head of the department. . . . The department's teaching staff comprises two persons, a senior lecturer (head of department) and a lecturer, with some provision to hire part-time and casual assistance. A staff-student ratio of one to 44 is very poor, and in a graduate school surely amazing.[85]

In 1971, about 150 students were enrolled in the undergraduate program administered by the department and about 120 students in the diploma program, most of them on a part-time basis. Application for admission to the diploma program, which appears to have changed little in its basic structure since the early 1960s, was open to

graduates in approved fields, and. . . undergraduates in combination with any approved degree. Under approved circumstances, candidates who have a professional qualification at the tertiary level together with extensive relevant experience may be admitted to the course. . . . The diploma course is closely related to courses in law, psychiatry, psychology, social work and education. But it is of interest to candidates in many fields—whether simply as an exercise in a modern discipline, or as a preparation for a professional career in the field of crime control.[86]

By 1980, the department had a full-time staff of six, including one reader, Johnston, one senior lecturer, and four lecturers. In addition, a number of part-time and occasional lecturers were providing services to the department. In 1976, the department became part of the Faculty of Arts, and in 1979 for the first time offered an honors major in criminology at the undergraduate level which could be taken as a part of an arts degree.

Criminology has now been taught at the University of Melbourne at the undergraduate level for almost thirty years and at the graduate level for twenty. The main student bodies exposed to this academic involvement with criminology have been arts and law students at the undergraduate level, and lawyers and criminal justice practitioners at the graduate level.[87] Many of these students now occupy senior positions within the criminal justice system in Victoria and, to a much lesser degree, in other parts of Australia.[88] No criminal justice agency requires completion of the diploma course in criminology as a condition for employment, but it is believed to be a useful qualification for employment or promotion in most areas of the criminal justice system.[89]

An unfulfilled need is a strong M.A. and Ph.D. program. In 1979, eight persons were enrolled for an M.A. by thesis within the department and three for a Ph.D., but even fewer have completed these programs.[90] In fact, any Australian wishing to obtain an M.A. or Ph.D. involving substantial and full-time course work in the field of criminology or criminal justice must, almost as a matter of course, travel overseas.[91]

University of Sydney

In 1962, when he was the newly appointed head of the University of Melbourne's department of criminology, Johnston indicated the need to match the standards of institutes abroad:

Criminology is a new department in Melbourne and a new discipline throughout the world. The sum of knowledge in criminology is expanding more rapidly than in most disciplines. . . . Melbourne has assumed leadership in criminology amongst Australasian universities and has some obligation to match its standards not with weaker ventures in this part of the world, but with established institutes of criminology in Britain and America.[92]

At that time, an institute of criminology was being established within the Faculty of Law at the University of Sydney. This institute seems to have been the culmination of almost a decade of discussions involving the dean of the University of Sydney's law school, Professor K. O. Shatwell, and a number of senior and influential persons in the judiciary, government, academia, and various criminal justice agencies.[93] The first official approach to the University of Sydney about the possibility of establishing "serious studies in criminology within the framework of the faculty of law" came in a letter in April 1953, addressed to Shatwell, from the then NSW attorney general and minister of justice.[94] In his reply, Shatwell noted that he was "very interested in the development of such studies and that for some years the Australasian University Law Schools Association had been pressing on Australian law faculties the desirability of establishing departments of criminology but that there were some practical problems to be considered, particularly in relation to finance, administration, and the place of the work of such a department in the university curriculum."[95]

Despite this official interest, discussions seem to have borne no fruit until 1958 when, as a result of potential competition in the criminological field from a newly established Department of Sociology at the University of NSW, they gained a new momentum. The then attorney general and minister of justice, the Honorable R. R. Downing, was strongly of the view that criminology should be developed "within the ambit of a law school on lines which make provision for the participation of some persons trained in other disciplines."[96] He accordingly offered a special government grant to the University of Sydney to assist with the establishment of a criminological institute within the Faculty of Law. Following further discussions and negotiations between Shatwell and other persons involved with the study of criminology both in Australia and overseas, an agreement was reached during 1959 between the University of Sydney and the NSW government about the financial arrangements necessary for setting up the institute.[97] Shatwell, as dean of the Faculty of Law, was to become its first director. In addition, four core staffing positions at the lecturer and senior lecturer level were agreed to, with priorities going to recruitment of one person with formal training in criminal law, one in a social science other than law, one in psychiatry, and one in statistics. The first academic appointment made within this agreed framework was that of Gordon Hawkins, who was made a senior lecturer in criminology in February 1961.[98] Other staff members were appointed during the next four years, including a psychiatrist and a statistician.[99]

The teaching of criminology as a section in a first-year course on criminal law within the law school curriculum began immediately upon Hawkins's appointment. An elective subject on penology also was included in the law degree program. In 1965, four postgraduate courses in criminology leading to the degree of L.L.M. and four diploma courses in criminology were established.[100] The latter diploma was intended mainly for persons lacking degree or other tertiary qualifications who were members of the police force, or other sections of the public service involved in criminal justice including officers from the departments of justice, corrective services, and child welfare. The development of a diploma course seems to have been one of the unofficial *quid pro quos* demanded by the NSW government in recognition of its financial and allied support for the establishment of the Institute of Criminology.[101] According to Shatwell:

There was general agreement that the teaching and research would be greatly benefited by the admission of suitable diploma students actively involved in various aspects of criminal law inforcement, whether as police, magistrates (present or future), prison officers or child welfare officers, and this was recognized by the faculty in the by-laws governing the admission to candidature for the diploma. [These by-laws] provide that admission may be granted to any person who furnishes evidence of special fitness which satisfies the faculty of law that such a person is qualified to enter upon systematic courses of study in criminology.[102]

The first diplomas in criminology were awarded in 1967, and since then 369 candidates have successfully completed the course.[103] Of these, the largest group comprised officers from the NSW police force, most of them possessing no previous tertiary education qualifications and admitted under the special bylaw provisions of the Faculty of Law. Of the remainder, most persons had law qualifications, many of them magistrates from throughout NSW. By 1980, following some fifteen years of teaching within the diploma program, a significant proportion of those in senior management positions within the criminal justice system in NSW had attended the diploma course and, in most instances, successfully completed it.[104] The impact of this diploma experience is difficult to evaluate.[105] Although no NSW criminal justice agency has made possession of the diploma a condition for promotion, exposure to the literature and research methodologies of criminology is believed to have been beneficial.[106]

It is estimated that about ten persons per year enroll in criminology courses within the L.L.M. program in criminology, and many of these specialize in this subject area. The majority of these students are part-time, most of them being practitioners working in a criminal justice agency.

Other Tertiary Institutions

Until recently, the teaching of criminology in Australia has been mainly confined to law schools. Each of the major law schools in the country continues to offer criminology as part of a criminal law course and/or as an elective subject in a law degree program.[107] In addition, a number of departments of sociology, psychology, social work, and anthropology offer various courses in criminology as part of more general degree programs within these respective disciplines.[108]

A significant development in the late 1970s was a move away from the teaching of criminology solely in these settings through the establishment of a number of applied college-based programs designed to service particular groups and agencies within the criminal justice system.[109] For example, Mitchell College of Advanced Education at Bathhurse in NSW offers an associate diploma in justice administration based upon a two-year full-time or longer external studies program. The requirements for the award include the passing of units in organizational studies, personnel management and public administration, as well as psychology and sociology.[110] The diploma has attracted substantial interest from persons working in criminal justice agencies, particularly police, who are able to combine their studies with their employment. It remains to be seen whether the obtaining of this associate diploma will become a requirement for future promotion within criminal justice agencies like the NSW police force.[111]

At the State College of Victoria at Coburg, a suburb of Melbourne, a two-year full-time associate diploma of criminal justice and welfare administration has been offered during the past five years. The diploma is directed at persons working in the criminal justice and welfare administration field and caters particularly to the needs of police, correctional officers, and those working in probation and parole.[112] The course seeks to equip middle-management personnel with skills necessary to their work, and it is a prerequisite for admission to the course that students work in one of the above fields. The State College of Victoria and Deakin University at Geelong in Victoria are considering the expansion of the diploma course into a full degree program that could be taken either externally or on a full-time basis.[113]

Australian Institute of Criminology

At the government level, no development has been of greater significance in the field of criminology in Australia than the establishment of the AIC in 1971. The original idea that led to the creation of the institute seems to have flowed from the fertile mind of Sir John Barry, who in 1960 proposed the establishment in Australia of an institute of criminal and penal science.[114] At that time, Australian authorities were considering the possibility of locating in Australia the proposed United Nations Asia and Far East Institute for the Prevention of Crime and the Treatment of Offenders. Sir John, who was leader of the Australian delegation to the First and Second United Nations Congresses on the Prevention of Crime and the Treatment of Offenders, favored such a development, but eventually the United Nations Institute was established at Fuchu in Japan.[115] Following a personal visit to the Fuchu institute, Sir John continued to press for the formation of an Australian institute to be funded, maintained, and administered by the federal government of Australia. Sir John believed that the main functions of such an institute would be first a training and instruction of senior law enforcement officials and social workers and correctional officers from Asian, African and Pacific countries and from Australia, New Zealand, United Kingdom and Canada. Secondly, the institute would conduct research into problems of youthful delinquency and of their criminal or aberrant conduct, with a view to prevention or diminution of crime in all those countries.[116]

In a major address to the Third National Conference of the Australian Prison and Aftercare Council (now the Australian Crime Prevention Council) in January 1965, Sir John pressed these views further and urged the federal government to act upon them.[117] Later in the same year, the Australian delegation to the Third United Nations Congress on the Prevention of Crime and the Treatment of Offenders held in Stockholm was asked to give specific consideration to the proposal for the establishment of an Australian institute of criminology.

In the succeeding five years, extensive discussions took place at the highest levels of government concerning formation of an institute. It was envisaged that such an institute would be controlled by a board or committee upon which the federal and state governments of Australia, and also the government of New Zealand, would be represented. Loof explains:

Governmental control was...thought desirable to insure that priorities in research were observed which would be most likely to bring practical results in areas of greatest need. An important factor was that much of the source material for research was contained in State departments and it was anticipated that State departments would be more willing to permit access to this material to official researchers than to individuals from a university or independent institute, who might publish material without due sympathy for departmental problems. It was noted that governmental bodies have been established in a number of other countries and the establishment of the Home Office Research Unit in the United Kingdom to conduct research on a national basis and provide grants of money for research activities, was referred to in particular.[118]

These general considerations, which were aimed at maintaining governmental influence over the operations of the institute, particularly its research activities, were subsequently adopted in the Criminology Research Act of 1971.[119] To alleviate state government fears that the new institute would be no more than a component of the federal government, the AIC was established not as a unit within a federal government department but as an independent government instrumentality controlled by a board of management consisting of three federal and three state representatives with the chairman, a federal government member, having a casting as well as a deliberative vote. In addition, the legislation established a criminology research fund comprising contributions from both the federal and state governments to finance nongovernmental research. A criminology research council was set up to administer this fund and, among other things, to determine the relative importance and urgency of projects for which the expenditures of governmental monies might be authorized. The research council consisted of six state representatives and one Commonwealth representative.

The first full-time director of the institute was appointed in 1975.[120] He was William Clifford, formerly director of the Social Defense Section of the United Nations and a person with wide-ranging international experience in research and training in the field of criminology. A core staff of professional criminologists was recruited together with support staff. The institute now operates with an annual budget of more than $1 million (all dollar amounts in this chapter are in Australian dollars) and employs some forty persons on a full-time basis.[121] It functions as both a research and training facility as well as being a clearinghouse for all information relating to criminal justice in Australia. In the latter capacity, the institute has accumulated by far the most comprehensive library of criminological literature in the country and disseminates on a regular basis information about its acquisitions, and ongoing research and allied activities.[122]

Assistant directors of research and training at the institute control its day-to-day work activities.[123] In the training field, the institute has conducted an extensive range of courses, seminars, and conferences which have brought together people in all areas of criminal justice from around Australia as well as from the South Pacific and Southeast Asian regions.[124]

Institute research carried out "in house" has tended to follow academic rather than applied research traditions. In the main, individual professional staff members have been able to pursue their own research interests without having to follow any comprehensive research goals and objectives set for them by either the board of management or the director of the research division.[125] This system has produced some significant, if eclectic, publications in areas such as sentencing, women offenders, motor vehicle theft, and the impact of long-term imprisonment.[126] This academic approach to research has not found favor with some criminal justice agency personnel who believe that the institute has failed to meet its original mandate to provide an applied research resource for people working in the field in the criminal justice system. Despite these criticisms, the AIC has become a widely recognized and accepted institution among federal and state government instrumentalities.

The criminology research council, which was formed at the same time as the institute, has also had some impact through its funding of a range of external research projects, conducted mainly by university-based researchers. A limited amount of money is available for external research. The annual operating budget of the council has rarely exceeded $100,000 and more recently has been as low as $60,000.[127] Hence, the external projects have been restricted in scope.[128]

State Government Criminological Research Activities

Although supporting the establishment of the AIC, state governments in Australia have not been content to rely solely upon that body for applied criminological research assistance. Perhaps partly because of dissatisfaction with the applied research resources being made available by the AIC, as well as a desire to remain independent of what has been perceived to be primarily a federal government initiative in the criminological arena, a number of states have now established their own criminological research institutes. In 1971, a bureau of crime statistics and research was set up in NSW with a dual mandate to furnish crime statistics and applied research facilities.[129] The NSW bureau rapidly established a reputation for undertaking thorough, comprehensive, high-quality research, the results of which received widespread circulation.[130] In addition, the bureau was able to develop an excellent statistical series dealing with the handling of criminal offenses by the NSW court system. This series, which is the first of its kind in any Australian jurisdiction, represents a most useful prototype for any future national statistics relating to the activities of criminal courts.

Following the NSW model, South Australia established an office of crime statistics in 1978.[131] This office has commenced the publication of comprehensive court statistics for that jurisdiction as well as working towards the preparation of the first offender-based transaction statistics in Australia. Meanwhile, the remaining state and territorial governments have preferred to use existing general research facilities available in their respective jurisdictions for criminal justice studies rather than creating specialized units.[132]

Private Organizations

Foundations and other private, nongovernmental, and nonprofit organizations have played only a limited role in the development of Australian criminology. The relatively limited criminological research has been supported largely from government or quasi-government sources and has been performed in either universities or governmental bodies. However, a number of recent research projects have been supported by nongovernmental monies from Australian and overseas foundations.[133] This form of funding became more important during the 1970s following the establishment in a number of jurisdictions in Australia of foundations associated with the legal professions.[134] For instance, in 1967 the government and the law society of NSW established a law foundation with a charter to "further legal education, legal research, law reform and the establishment, maintenance and operation of law libraries." The Law Foundation of NSW has been active in sponsoring and conducting research on a range of topics, including issues affecting the criminal justice system.[135] The foundation staff has investigated such matters as bail and pretrial release, measures to deal with drinking drivers, alternatives to imprisonment, and the effectiveness of public defender programs.[136] In 1979, the structure of the foundation was changed to permit it to receive more substantial and assured funding, and it now has about $1 million in disposable research funds each year. The foundation is the largest potential private sponsor of criminological research in Australia, but the board of governors has not set policy on the proportion of available funds to be used for this purpose.[137]

A similar foundation has been established in Victoria, but it has fewer disposable funds available for research and has not taken similar initiatives in developing criminological studies.[138] However, as the principal nongovernmental resource, foundations could become important sources of funding for research and an employment base for personnel in the field of criminology.[139]

CRIMINOLOGICAL MILLING

Despite their relatively meager numbers and the vast distances involved in traveling between different parts of the country, Australian criminologists have devised a number of significant communication networks.

The Australian and New Zealand Society of Criminology

Foremost among these networks has been the Australian and New Zealand Society of Criminology (ANZ Society) which, together with its journal, was established in 1967. Sir John Barry was the first president of the ANZ Society. In a foreword to the first issue, Sir John said the *ANZ Journal of Criminology* was intended to offer

A common market for Australia and New Zealand for the formulation and presentation of ideas and hypotheses, and, where it is available, verified knowledge upon criminological topics. One test (though it is by no means infallible) of the truth of a proposition is its ability to gain acceptance in the marketplace frequented by persons knowledgeable in the particular field to which the proposition belongs, and it is hoped that the society and its journal will provide such a marketplace.[140]

Dr. A. A. Bartholomew, a Melbourne psychiatrist, has been the editor of the journal for more than a decade. Prior to its appearance, the main source for the publication of Australian and New Zealand criminological material tended to be law and social science journals. These journals were, in many cases, reluctant to devote substantial space to a discipline viewed as being somewhat esoteric and unimportant. In filling this void, the *ANZ Journal* has become the predominant criminological publication in both countries.[141]

A recent analysis of its contents during the first ten years suggests that the *ANZ Journal* has adopted a consistent approach to the discipline: "Stressing correctionalism, treatment and the need to increase the efficiency of the criminal justice system. . . . This view of criminology has all the hallmarks of positive criminology, an approach that has dominated the field."[142]

In rank order frequency, the principal topics covered in the articles were corrections, juvenile delinquency, law and legal issues, social control, punishment, deterrence, rehabilitation, and treatment. Generally, the content analysis revealed a range of topics similar to that identified in *Federal Probation* in the United States and the *British Journal of Criminology*.[143] As O'Connor, the author of the content analysis, noted:

Such similarities are not unexpected, considering the heavy dependence on American and British developments in criminology by Australian criminologists/sociologists. What is interesting is that particular American and British developments, for example, labelling, conflict theory and radical deviance theory, which occurred prior to and during the decade of publication were ignored.[144]

O'Connor was pessimistic about the possibility of change in the future in the direction of the *ANZ Journal*, believing that the persons working in the criminological field in Australia were predominantly proponents of the positivist school. Nonetheless, O'Connor believes the appearance of the *Alternative Criminology Journal* presents a possible influential challenge to the positivists in Australia in the 1980s. The activities of the ANZ Society have been less influential and expansive than those of its journal. The ANZ Society has remained mainly a Melbourne-based and -operated organization. Occasional meetings of the executive board are conducted in other parts of the country, but the rank-and-file members have little active involvement. Even the biennial lecture series established to commemorate the memory of the foundation president, Sir John Barry, who died in 1969, has continued to be held in Melbourne. A number of distinguished criminologists and prominent public figures from Australia and overseas have been invited to participate in the lecture series.[145]

Sydney Institute of Criminology Seminars

A far more active forum for meetings by Australian criminologists has been the regular seminar series conducted by the University of Sydney's Institute of Criminology. Academicians and criminal justice practitioners from different parts of Australia have been brought together in seminars on a wide variety of criminological issues. The published proceedings of the seminars are widely circulated in Australia and overseas.[146]

Academy of Forensic Sciences

Another active forum for the discussion of criminological matters has been the Australian Academy of Forensic Sciences.[147] As its title suggests, the academy has a special interest in forensic issues. In addition to regular meetings in Sydney, occasional seminars on topics of special significance are held.[148] The academy publishes the *Australian Journal of Forensic Sciences*.[149]

Australian and New Zealand Association for the Advancement of Science (ANZAAS)

Another important meeting place for criminologists has been ANZAAS. Since the mid-1970s, it has included a division devoted to criminology at its biennial congresses.[150] ANZAAS, through its congresses, represents the principal multidisciplinary gathering place for physical, biological, and social scientists in Australia and New Zealand. It is a voluntary organization which celebrated its fiftieth anniversary at meetings held in Adelaide in South Australia in May 1980 under a general theme of "Science for a Sustainable Society for Us by 2000 A.D. Why? How?" Most of the active criminologists in Australia and New Zealand attended the sessions of the criminology division.

Australian Crime Prevention Council

Since World War II, the Australian Crime Prevention Council (ACPC) has made a significant contribution to the development of citizen interest in the work of criminal justice agencies.[151] ACPC consists of a loosely knit organization of private individuals and governmental and semigovernmental bodies that brings together, on a periodic basis, criminal justice practitioners and private citizens to discuss issues related to crime and the treatment of offenders.

THE FUTURE OF AUSTRALIAN CRIMINOLOGY

From modest beginnings in the early 1950s, Australian criminology presents evidence of a strong vitality that augurs well for its continuing growth in the 1980s. An "indigenous brand" of criminology remains to be developed in the Antipodes because Australian criminology continues to reflect its original domination by law and lawyers and its strong alignment with the positive school. Those criminologists who possess graduate degrees in the subject have been trained almost exclusively in overseas institutions, primarily in the United Kingdom, but increasingly in the United States and Canada.[152] The noted absence of a strong Australian-based graduate degree in criminology has made it almost inevitable that persons wishing to further their academic careers within the discipline have had to travel abroad. It is to be hoped that, at one of the existing centers for research and teaching in criminology, or at a new location, a quality program will be created in the future leading to a master's or Ph.D. degree in the discipline.

Financial and other support for independent criminological research remains sparse in Australia. It is difficult to undertake objective evaluations of programs of criminal justice agencies and to develop the institutional prerequisites for criminology as a discipline and an occupational system. If these difficulties are to be overcome, the governments in Australia will have to become more active in supporting independent criminological research and raise their standards for entry to, and promotion within, criminal justice agencies under their direction and control. Without demand for tertiary qualifications in criminology in the occupational marketplace, the potential for further growth in university and colleged-based criminology programs remains slim.

The last word should go to the most significant figure in Australian criminology, Sir John Barry. "There are in Australia and New Zealand," said Sir John in

1968, "a goodly number of persons who are capable of making contributions to criminal science worthy of comparison with work done elsewhere."[153] The 1980s may well reveal whether or not this contribution will be significant and lasting.

NOTES

1. Radzinowicz, in the course of his far-reaching travels "in search of criminology," noted that "the recent advance in criminology in certain parts of the Commonwealth should not pass unnoticed, particularly the work done in Melbourne under the direction of Mr. Justice Barry and Dr. Norval Morris." Surprisingly, Radzinowicz made no mention of the development of criminological studies at the University of Sydney. The development of the centers at both these universities is discussed in detail below. L. Radzinowicz, *In Search of Criminology* (Cambridge, Mass.: Harvard University Press, 1962), p. 170.

2. A noted exception to this general rule is to be found in the University of New South Wales (NSW) where a number of "radical" criminologists have been active within the law school. For a general critique of the conservative ideological perspective to be found in Australian criminology, see D. Brown, "Criminal Justice Reform: A Critique," in D. Chappell and P. R. Wilson (eds.), *The Australian Criminal Justice System*, 2d ed. (Sydney: Butterworth's, 1977), pp. 471-491 (hereafter cited as Chappell and Wilson, *Australian Criminal Justice System*). These University of NSW-based criminologists, together with members of the Prisoners' Action Group in NSW, have recently begun to publish an *Alternative Criminology Journal*.

3. The AIC was established under the provisions of the Criminology Research Act, 1971 (Cwlth). The formation of the institute and its subsequent contributions are discussed below.

4. Although sightings were made of the west coast by Dutch seamen during the sixteenth and seventeenth centuries, the official discovery of the eastern seaboard of the continent and its annexation for the British Crown was made during an epic voyage of discovery by Captain James Cook in April 1770. Cook had landed at Botany Bay. His reports led the English government sixteen years later to select Australia as the site for the first British settlement in the Pacific. See G. Blainey, *The Tyranny of Distance* (Melbourne: Sun Books, 1966).

5. The first fleet of eleven ships took over eight months to reach Australia from England on a voyage of some 14,000 miles. The ships contained just over one thousand people, three-quarters of them convicts and the remaining members officers and marines, wives and children. Blainey, *The Tyranny of Distance*, p. 33.

6. For a general account of this period, see A.G.L. Shaw, *Convicts and the Colonies* (London: Faber and Faber, 1966).

7. The estimated population of Australia in 1870 was 1.6 million. See Australian Bureau of Statistics (ABS), *Yearbook Australia. 1977 and 1978* (Canberra: Australian Government Publishing Service), p. 99.

8. Many U.S. military personnel, including General Douglas MacArthur, were stationed in Australia during the course of the war, and Australian troops fought in the Pacific alongside Americans. This contact helped to develop later political and associated ties between the two countries.

9. This image has been stimulated by such popular movies as *The Sundowners* and novels like *The Thornbirds*.

10. ABS, *Yearbook Australia. 1977 and 1978*, p. 100. Other demographic data presented below are drawn from this source.

11. For many years, the so-called white Australia policy restricted migration to peoples of Caucasian origin, but the federal government officially abandoned the policy at the beginning of the 1970s. The result has been a striking growth in the number of non-Caucasians arriving in the country.

12. The change in public attitudes toward the convict past is reflected in the recent formation of a First Fleet Society consisting of Australians who can trace their origins back to the initial group of convicts and military in 1788.

13. It has been said that the average Australian citizen views the "police as enemies, army officers as traitors to democracy...the boss as a barely necessary evil and anyone who gives an order as deeply suspect." C. McGregor, *Profile of Australia* (London: Hodder and Stoughton, 1966), p. 43.

14. NSW, for instance, had a centrally controlled police force as early as 1862. For a general description of the historical development of police forces in Australia, see D. Chappell and P. R. Wilson, *The Police and the Public in Australia and New Zealand* (St. Lucia, Queensland: University of Queensland Press, 1969), pp. 1-36 (hereafter cited as Chappell and Wilson, *The Police and the Public*).

15. See Criminal Code Act 1924 (Tas); Criminal Code Act 1899 (Qld); and Criminal Code Act 1913 (WA).

16. See Crimes Act 1900 (NSW); Crimes Act 1958 (Vic); Criminal Law Consolidation 1935 (SA): Crimes Act 1900 (NSW) as amended by ordinance in its application to the ACT; Criminal Law Consolidation Act (NT). As to the general criminal law in Australia, see C. Howard, *Criminal Law*, 3d ed. (Sydney: Law Book Co., 1977).

17. Under the Australian constitution, the administration of criminal justice is substantially but not exclusively a state and territorial responsibility. The federal government enacted the Crimes Act of 1914, but the term is something of a misnomer for the legislation deals only with a range of somewhat specialized offenses against the Commonwealth and is in no way intended as a general criminal law statute akin to those referred to in other Australian jurisdictions. In general as to the scope of federal criminal jurisdiction, see Sydney University Institute of Criminology, Proceedings, "The Problem of Crime in a Federal System," 41 (September 1979); Australian Law Reform Commission, *Sentencing Federal Offenders* 15 (1980), Chapter 3 (hereafter cited as ALRC, *Sentencing Federal Offenders*).

18. This expedient seems to have been adopted largely for pragmatic reasons. In 1901, the fledgling federal government lacked criminal justice facilities and services to deal with those who committed offenses against its laws. It was, therefore, decided to rely on the existing resources of the state and territories to provide these facilities and services, rather than incurring the expense of creating a duplicate federal criminal justice system.

19. Only in South Australia has any recent attempt been made to undertake a sweeping revision of the criminal law. Under the chairmanship of Justice R. Mitchell, a law reform committee met for a number of years during the 1970s and issued a series of reports recommending major changes to the criminal law in that jurisdiction. However, to date only a very small portion of these recommendations have been adopted. See South Australia, Criminal Law and Penal Methods Reform Committee, *Reports 1 - 4* (Adelaide: Government Printer of South Australia, 1973-1977).

20. A draft of a Uniform Criminal Code was prepared during the 1960s under the auspices of a committee of the Law Council of Australia. However, the committee's

work was not taken up at the government level. In the 1970s, the federal government sponsored a review of the criminal law of the ACT with a view to developing a draft code that might be adopted not only in the ACT but also in the Northern Territory which, at that time, was administered by the federal authorities. However, the draft code prepared by this committee was never introduced in legislative form to the Australian Parliament. See Australia, Attorney General's Department, *Report of the Working Party on Territorial Criminal Law* (Canberra: Australian Government Publishing Service, 1975).

21. For example, a number of Australian jurisdictions have recently revised their rape laws, largely as a result of pressures coming from women's groups. For an overview of these reforms, see D. O'Connor, "Rape Law Reform—the Australian Experience," *Criminal Law Journal* 1 (1977):305.

22. The arming of the Australian police has been gradual; even now, not all forces require officers to carry weapons when on duty.

23. As to the general requirements concerning entry to Australian police forces, see Chappell and Wilson, *The Police and the Public*, Chapter 7.

24. In the Victorian police force, for example, in 1977 only about twenty officers had degrees from a tertiary institution. See D. Chappell, "Tertiary Education and the Policeman: Prospects for the Future," *Australian Police Journal* 32 (October 1978):220.

25. Only the ACT has abandoned the practice of allowing police to prosecute in summary offenses. See ALRC, *Sentencing Federal Offenders*, p. 62.

26. As to the prosecution process in general in Australia, see ALRC, *Sentencing Federal Offenders*, Chapter 4.

27. This abolition is said to have occurred because there were not at that time sufficient numbers of free men in the colony to permit the formation of grand juries.

28. See in general J. Seymour, *Committal for Trial* (Canberra: AIC, 1978).

29. In two jurisdictions, South Australia and Victoria, special provisions have been made in regard to committal proceedings in rape cases that allow for handup briefs to be provided of a complainant's testimony without the specific consent of the accused. Only in special circumstances will oral testimony be permitted. In general, see Victoria, Law Reform Commissioner, *Rape Prosecutions. Court Procedures and Rules of Evidence*, 5:18-20; South Australia, Criminal Law and Penal Methods Reform Committee, *Special Report on Rape and Other Sexual Offences* (Adelaide: Government Printer of South Australia, 1976), p. 45.

30. As to legal aid in Australia generally, see Commonwealth Legal Aid Commission, *Annotated Bibliography on Legal Aid* (Canberra: Australian Government Publishing Service, 1979); S. Bothmann and R. Gordon, *Practicing Poverty Law* (Melbourne: Fitzroy Legal Service, 1979).

31. For a recent discussion of the relevant principles and authorities as to the right of an accused in Australia to legal representation, especially in a trial on serious charges, see *McInnis* v. *The Queen* (1979) 54 ALJR:122.

32. This requirement extends, however, only to offenses against the laws of the Commonwealth. Thus, Section 80 of the constitution provides that "the trial on indictment of any offense against any law of the Commonwealth shall be by jury, and every such trial shall be held in the State where the offense was committed, and if the offense was not committed within any State, the trial shall be held at such place or places as the Parliament prescribes."

33. For instance, in NSW in 1976, of the defendants dealt with in the higher courts

more than two-thirds pleaded guilty. See NSW, Department of the Attorney General and Justice, Bureau of Crime Statistics and Research, *Court Statistics 1976*, 8:50.

34. Magistrates' courts account for more than 90 percent of all criminal business dealt with in each Australian jurisdiction.

35. Discretionary powers exist in each Australian jurisdiction to permit the trial of juveniles for serious offenses like homicide and rape in adult courts.

36. See in general Australia, Discussion Paper, Topic 2, Sixth United Nations Congress on the Prevention of Crime and the Treatment of Offenders, "Juvenile Justice: Before and After the Onset of Delinquency" (Canberra: Australian Government Publishing Service, 1979).

37. In some states, like Tasmania and South Australia, there is not a split profession, and thus an appointment to the bench can be made from among members of the practicing legal profession who may be both barristers and solicitors. In the case of magistrates, the majority are appointed from public service positions, having first served as clerks of court.

38. As to sentencing appeals in general, see South Australia, Criminal Law and Penal Methods Committee, First Report, *Sentencing and Corrections* (Adelaide: Government Printer of South Australia):29-37; ALRC, *Sentencing Federal Offenders*, pp. 260-267.

39. A restricted right of appeal to the Privy Council in London still exists, but this avenue of review is likely to be abolished in the near future.

40. Because of its small size and the limited number of offenders convicted before its courts, the ACT has relied heavily upon NSW for its correctional services, including the provision of custodial facilities for both adults and juveniles. See ALRC, Discussion Paper, "Sentencing: Reform Options," 10 (1979), pp. 17-33.

41. Australian Constitution, Section 120.

42. As to the situation in the ACT in regard to juveniles, see ALRC, Discussion Paper, "Child Welfare. Child Abuse and Day Care," 12 (1980).

43. See ALRC, *Sentencing Federal Offenders*, Chapter 7.

44. As, for example, the main prison in Fremantle in Western Australia.

45. This complex includes minimum, medium, and maximum security facilities as well as a work release center.

46. Extensive prison construction is also being undertaken or planned in NSW. The NSW correctional system was the subject of a comprehensive investigation by a Royal Commission in the mid-1970s following widespread allegations of brutality and sordid conditions within the state's jails. See NSW, *Report of the Royal Commission into N.S.W. Prisons* (Sydney: Government Printer of New South Wales, 1978).

47. For comment upon these variations, see ALRC, *Sentencing Federal Offenders*, Chapter 6.

48. By far the highest proportion of aboriginals reside in the Northern Territory. There are also significant numbers resident in the more remote parts of Western Australia and Queensland.

49. See E. Eggleston, *Fear, Favour or Affection. Aborigines and the Criminal Law in Victoria, South Australia and Western Australia* (Canberra: Australia National University Press, 1976); NSW, Department of the Attorney General and of Justice, Bureau of Crime Statistics and Research, "Aboriginal People and N.S.W.'s Criminal Justice System: A Review of Existing Information" (Sydney: Government Printer of NSW, 1979).

50. See Australia, Discussion Paper, Topic 4, Sixth United Nations Congress on the

Prevention of Crime and Treatment of Offenders, "De-institutionalisation of Corrections and Its Implications for the Residual Prisoners" (Canberra: Australian Government Publishing Service, 1979), pp. 4-5.

51. For a critical account of the present situation in Australia in regard to criminal statistics, see ALRC, *Sentencing Federal Offenders*, Chapter 3.

52. These categories do not include offenses like theft, which is by far the most common form of serious crime in Australia, and arson.

53. The published data are particularly suspect in the field of serious assault. Statistics, for instance, from the two most populous states of NSW and Victoria indicate that the rate of assault in Victoria is almost twice that of NSW, even though the populations are much the same.

54. Most of the discussions have taken place between the various police forces. Police leaders have been reluctant to join in past efforts to produce uniform law enforcement statistics, in part because of fears that they would be used to make interjurisdictional comparisons of efficiency.

55. Pointing to its constitutional role, the ALRC recommended recently that "the A.B.S. should, as a matter of priority, institute, collect and publish national and uniform statistics which permit the tracing of Federal, State and Territorial cases through the criminal justice system from the point of reporting to their ultimate disposition." ALRC, *Sentencing Federal Offenders*, Recommendation 8.

56. Australia, ABS, *General Social Survey of Crime Victims—May 1975* (Canberra: ABS, 1979). J. Braithwaite and D. Biles, "Overview of Findings from the First Australian National Crime Victims Survey," *ANZ Journal of Criminology* 13 (1980):41.

57. See D. Biles (ed.), *Crime and Justice in Australia* (Canberra: AIC, 1977); D. Biles, *The Size of the Crime Problem in Australia* (Canberra: AIC, 1977) (hereafter cited as Biles, *Crime Problem*).

58. Biles, *Crime Problem*, p. 21.

59. For a more comprehensive description of this study, see Australia, Discussion Paper, Topic 1, Sixth United Nations Congress on the Prevention of Crime and the Treatment of Offenders, "Crime Trends and Crime Prevention Strategies" (Canberra: Australian Government Publishing Service, 1979), pp. 8-13.

60. See South Australia, Office of Crime Statistics, "Homicide in South Australia. Rates and Trends in Comparative Perspective" (Adelaide: Law Department, 1980), p. 10.

61. Both Western Australia and South Australia possess stringent gun control measures for all types of weapons.

62. The leaders were present in Sydney for the Commonwealth Regional Heads of Government Meeting.

63. The Australian prime minister called out the Commonwealth Defense Force, prompting subsequent legal and constitutional debate regarding protective security arrangements against terrorist activity in Australia. See Comment, "Legal and Constitutional Problems of Protective Security Arrangement in Australia," *Australian Law Journal* 52 (1978):296-297.

64. R. Mark, *Report to the Minister for Administrative Services on the Organization of Police Resources in the Commonwealth Area and Other Related Matters* (Canberra: Australian Government Publishing Services, 1978).

65. For a description of some of these developments, see D. Chappell, "Investigating Rape: A New Approach," *Legal Service Bulletin* 5 (1980):19.

66. For a study of Australian trends in robbery, particularly those occurring in the

state of Victoria, see S. I. Miller and K. L. Milte, *Operational Planning Against Patrol Preventable Crime: Armed Robbery* (Melbourne: Government Printer of Victoria, 1978).

67. The governments of Victoria, Queensland, Western Australia, and Tasmania cooperated with the federal government in establishing the commission that was chaired by Mr. Justice E. S. Williams.

68. Australia, Royal Commission of Inquiry into Drugs, *Report Book D* (Canberra: Australian Government Publishing Service, 1980), p. 9.

69. The commission's recommendations are summarized in *Report Book D*.

70. For a general description of the legal and investigative issues associated with white-collar crime in Australia, see A. Hopkins, "A Working Paper on White Collar Crime in Australia" (Canberra: AIC, 1977); Australia, Discussion Paper, Topic 3, Sixth United Nations Congress on the Prevention of Crime and the Treatment of Offenders, "Crime and the Abuse of Power: Offences and Offenders Beyond the Reach of the Law?" (Canberra: Australian Government Publishing Service, 1979); Sydney University Institute of Criminology, Proceedings, "White Collar Crime—Can the Courts Handle It?" 23 (1975); Proceedings, "White Collar Crime (No. 2)" 37 (1979).

71. See ALRC, *Sentencing Federal Offenders*, p. 55.

72. The ALRC, as well as a number of law reform bodies in other Australian jurisdictions, have been reviewing existing penalty structures and legal provisions relating to white-collar offenses.

73. Government inquiries were instituted in NSW, Queensland, South Australia, Victoria, and Western Australia during the 1970s into the problems associated with the increase in juvenile crime. See generally Australia, Discussion Paper, Topic 2, Sixth United Nations Congress on the Prevention of Crime and the Treatment of Offenders, "Juvenile Justice: Before and After the Onset of Delinquency" (Canberra: Australian Government Publishing Service, 1979), p. 29.

74. For a general review of trends in the rates of juvenile crime during the period 1959-1969, see J. Krause, "Trends and the Rates of Non-capital Offenses among Male Juveniles in New South Wales, 1959-1969," in Chappell and Wilson, *Australian Criminal Justice System*, 1st ed., p. 123.

75. Western Australia and South Australia have implemented the most significant changes in procedures affecting the handling of juveniles. See Australia, Discussion Paper, Topic 2, Sixth United Nations Congress.

76. See, in particular, C. D. Rowley, *Outcasts in White Australia* (Canberra: Australian National University Press, 1970).

77. Such violence as has occurred in the immediate past between white and black Australians seems largely to have been the product of insensitive behavior on the part of police and criminal justice officials towards aboriginals and their customs. See F. G. Cohen, D. Chappell, and P. R. Wilson, "Aboriginal and American Indian Relations with Police. A Study of the Australian and North American Experiences," in Chappell and Wilson, *Australian Criminal Justice System*, 2d ed., pp. 112, 115-117.

78. R. Francis, "Contemporary Issues Concerning Migration and Crime in Australia," in Chappel and Wilson, *Australian Criminal Justice System*, 2d ed., p. 100.

79. Ibid., pp. 103-104.

80. Ibid., p. 104.

81. Francis has undertaken the most comprehensive studies to date of migrant crime in Australia, but his work has relied upon official records. It is well recognized that certain crimes committed by migrants may not reach the attention of law enforcement officials,

being dealt with informally within migrant communities. A study is required of this nonreported crime before any significant assessment can be made of the dimensions of criminal behavior by migrants within Australia.

82. Research needs and issues are dealt with in greater detail below.

83. The author is indebted to Mrs. Deidre Greig and Dr. Austin Lovegrove, lecturers in criminology at the University of Melbourne, for their invaluable assistance in preparing this section of the chapter.

84. Sir John Barry is perhaps best known internationally for his writing about Alexander McConochie and his work on Norfolk Island. For a current review of Barry's contribution to criminology in Australia, see M. D. Kirby, "John Barry and Sentencing: A Contemporary Appraisal," *ANZ Journal of Criminology* 12 (1979):195. Norval Morris has since achieved international recognition as a criminologist. He is presently a member of the faculty at the University of Chicago Law School and formerly dean of that institution.

85. Extract from an untitled report written by Johnston in 1963.

86. University of Melbourne, Department of Criminology, *Diploma in Criminology Handbook* (1980), p. 5.

87. Regrettably, no detailed study had been made of the students passing through the graduate program, so the comments made here are impressionistic.

88. The lack of opportunities for career mobility across state boundaries in Australia within criminal justice agencies probably accounts for this situation. It is only in the academic area that graduates from the University of Melbourne's program have been able readily to move further afield.

89. The most active supporters of the diploma course seem to have been persons working in the correctional field. It is because of this aspect of criminal justice work that the diploma has gained the greatest recognition as an entrance and promotional advantage.

90. It should be noted, however, that in 1978 only one person was enrolled for a Ph.D. and four for an M.A.

91. Most travel to Europe, particularly to the United Kingdom. Quite a significant number of Australian students have completed the diploma course in criminology (now a master's degree) at the University of Cambridge.

92. Excerpt from an untitled report, 1962.

93. The author is indebted to Professor G. Hawkins and Dr. W. Lucas, both members of the University of Sydney's Institute of Criminology, for their assistance in preparing this section of the chapter.

94. University of Sydney, Faculty of Law, "A Memorandum by Professor K. O. Shatwell on the Institute of Criminology and the Faculty of Law at the University of Sydney" (unpublished and undated), pp. 4-5 (hereafter cited as Shatwell memorandum).

95. Shatwell memorandum, p. 5.

96. Ibid.

97. Ibid., pp. 6-7.

98. Hawkins had previously been involved in the training of prison officers in the United Kingdom. He has since gained an international reputation for his writings in fields such as deterrence and has been closely associated with the Center for Studies in Criminal Law at the University of Chicago Law School.

99. In the case of the psychiatric position, the opportunity was also provided for its occupant to undertake clinical work in the correctional field in NSW.

100. The courses covered the areas of theories of crime, the administration of justice, psychiatry and the criminal law, and statistics and research methods.

101. In addition to the diploma, the institute established a short course for senior police officers, consisting of twenty two-hour lectures.

102. Shatwell memorandum, p. 9.

103. University of Sydney, Faculty of Law, "A Memorandum on Diplomas in the Faculty of Law" (unpublished, 1980), p. 7.

104. The completion rate for the diploma course was about 80 percent. "A Memorandum on Diplomas in the Faculty of Law," p. 10.

105. It has been said that

the major educational benefit accruing...from the diploma in criminology...appears to lie in the mixed nature of the groups which the classes bring together....[T]he course brings into one class people from both sides in the adversary system of criminal justice. Policemen especially tend to talk only to other policemen and one of the most frequent unsolicited comments received by teachers in that diploma from successful students is how much benefit they have obtained from being in a class where they can discuss their views and hear the often opposing views of other students and/or the lecturers.

"A Memorandum on Diplomas in the Faculty of Law," p. 9.

106. It is unfortunate that no external agency has conducted an evaluation of these benefits. As it is, an internal review of the diploma course by the faculty of law has concluded that "the diplomas provide a valuable educational, professional and community service which is not to be found anywhere else in the State." "A Memorandum on Diplomas in the Faculty of Law," p. 11.

107. In addition to law schools, the Department of Legal Studies at LaTrobe University in Melbourne offers criminology and criminal justice subjects as electives in a B.A. degree.

108. For instance, criminology is taught as part of a sociology and anthropology degree program at the University of Queensland and in a graduate degree program in social work at LaTrobe University in Victoria.

109. The development of these programs came as part of a national expansion of college-based education in the 1970s which followed federal government assumption of responsibility for funding all tertiary education in Australia.

110. Mitchell College of Advanced Education, *Handbook* (1980).

111. At the time of writing, a committee of inquiry appointed by the NSW government was considering the educational and allied requirements of the state's police force. As part of its investigation, it was believed to be examining the possibility of requiring some tertiary qualifications for promotion to senior ranks within the NSW police force.

112. State College of Victoria at Coburg, *Handbook* (1977).

113. Deakin University, the most recently established tertiary institution in Victoria, has begun to develop a comprehensive series of external degree programs for targeted professional groups like criminal justice practitioners.

114. P. R. Loof, "Establishment of the Australian Institute of Criminology and the Criminology Research Council. Proposals, Criteria and Negotiations Associated with the Establishment of the Institute and the Council" (Canberra: Attorney General's Department, 1979), p. 1 (hereafter cited as Loof, "Establishment of the A.I.C.").

115. The federal government offered the United Nations a site in Sydney for the institute, but it was decided ultimately to locate it in Japan. It has been said that "Japan made a better offer and the U.N., slightly embarrassed at having to decline such a

generous Australian proposal, made the first director of the U.N. institute in Japan an Australian—Dr. Norval Morris." W. C. Clifford, "Director's Digest," *Criminology Newsletter* 5 (December 1977):6.

116. Loof, "Establishment of the A.I.C.," p. 5.

117. Sir John's speech is attached as an appendix to the Loof report on the establishment of the AIC.

118. Loof, "Establishment of the A.I.C.," pp. 11-12.

119. Although participating in a number of the preliminary discussions concerned with the establishment of the AIC, the government of New Zealand decided ultimately not to join with the other governments in sponsoring its development. This decision seems to have been based upon the feeling that adequate research facilities already existed in the criminological field in New Zealand and that training needs could, in large part, also be met in that country rather than Australia. See Loof, "Establishment of the A.I.C.," p. 15.

120. Prior to the appointment of a full-time director, Mr. Justice J. Muirhead, a judge of the district court in South Australia and now a member of the supreme court in the Northern Territory, was appointed director on an interim basis.

121. Over the period July 1977 to June 1978, the AIC's approved staff ceiling was reduced from fifty-four to forty-four positions, and then further reduced to forty positions in June 1979. These reductions were made as part of a broader cutback in federal government spending. AIC, *Interim Annual Report 1978* (Canberra: AIC, 1979), p. 1.

122. See in particular the *Information Bulletin of Australian Criminology* which is published quarterly by the AIC.

123. These activities are at present conducted in temporary facilities, but in the near future a new building is to be constructed for the institute in a prime location in Canberra.

124. In collaboration with the Australian Development Assistance Bureau, the training division of the AIC has conducted a regular series of training programs for officials in criminal justice agencies from many parts of the world.

125. Research projects by staff members of the AIC are still subject to approval by the board of management.

126. A current list of the various publications of the AIC is contained in its quarterly journal *Reporter*.

127. Both state and federal governments make contributions to the Criminology Research Council's funds. These contributions are cumulative, unspent monies being carried forward into succeeding years. In 1978, for example, the Criminology Research Fund received a total of $63,700, of which almost half was contributed by the federal government and the balance by the states at an agreed level on a pro rata population basis. The Criminology Research Council noted that

the income to the Criminology Research Fund in 1977-78...was higher than in the previous year, but still considerably lower than the income received in each of its first three years of operation. This financial constraint has forced the council to restrict its funding to projects which it considered to have the highest priority....In its report for the previous year the council stated that its income was "inadequate to fund research to meet the challenge of the increasing cost of crime to the community." The council regretfully reports that this continues to be the case.

Criminology Research Council, *Sixth Annual Report, 1978* (Canberra: AIC, 1979), p. 11.

128. The majority of grants made by the Criminology Research Council are for sums less than $5,000.

129. The bureau, established under the control of the Department of the Attorney General and of Justice, issued its first statistical report in March 1972 on the subject of drug offenses.

130. The foundation director of the bureau was Dr. T. Vinson, an academic who had also previously had experience in the field of probation and parole. Dr. Vinson has since become the chairman of the NSW Corrective Services Commission.

131. The foundation director of this office of crime statistics was Dr. P. Grabosky, a political scientist trained at Northwestern University in the United States.

132. For example, there is a research center within the Department of Social Welfare in Victoria which undertakes studies in the area of criminal justice.

133. For example, the British-based Nuffield Foundation has provided funding for a variety of studies related to criminal justice, including the work carried out on police and public attitudes by Chappell and Wilson in the late 1960s. Within Australia the Myer Foundation, based in Melbourne, and the Utah Foundation in Queensland have provided funds for criminological research.

134. These foundations were created to receive funds obtained from interest accruing on trust funds in solicitors' offices. Rather than allowing these interest payments to be of benefit to individual legal practitioners, it was decided to accumulate them and use them for broader public purposes.

135. One of the first research studies approved by the foundation's board of governors involved an examination of bail and pretrial release procedures in New South Wales. The foundation's own full-time research staff conducted the study. See R. Tomasic, *Bail and Pretrial Release—Strategies and Issues* (Sydney: Law Foundation of NSW, 1976).

136. The foundation has also provided research support to a variety of official government inquiries such as the Royal Commission into NSW's Prisons and the ALRC, *Sentencing Federal Offenders*.

137. The executive director of the foundation since its creation, T. Purcell, has been an influential force in moving the foundation's research towards the area of criminology.

138. A series of defalcations by legal practitioners in Victoria has largely accounted for the lack of available research funds. Unlike the Law Foundation of NSW, which now has a guaranteed income, the Law Foundation of Victoria has had to rely upon the residual monies available after provision has been made for the repayment of losses resulting from defalcations.

139. Because of the absence of adequate M.A. and Ph.D. programs in the field of criminology, foundations like the Law Foundation of NSW have experienced difficulty recruiting qualified staff.

140. J. V. Barry, "The President's Foreword," *ANZ Journal of Criminology* 1 (1968):3.

141. Other journals such as the *Australian Law Journal, Australian Journal of Social Issues*, and *Australian Social Work* continue to publish occasional articles dealing with criminological subjects, but in the main the *ANZ Journal of Criminology* has taken over the field.

142. M. E. O'Connor, "A Decade of the Australian and New Zealand Journal of Criminology 1968-1977," *ANZ Journal of Criminology* 13 (1980):11, 13.

143. Ibid., p. 16.

144. Ibid.

145. This John Barry memorial lecture is jointly sponsored by the University of Mel-

bourne and the ANZ Society of Criminology. In addition, the university has awarded medals bearing his name to the outstanding criminology students graduating from the university's Department of Criminology.

146. The Institute of Criminology at the University of Sydney conducts about five seminars each year, and they represent by far the most widely attended regular criminological meetings held in Australia.

147. The academy, entrance to which is secured through nomination and election by its current membership, has among its fellows many judges and persons holding senior positions in government and criminal justice agencies. It represents a distinct "establishment wing" of Australian criminologists.

148. The academy also sponsors an annual national symposium on the forensic sciences.

149. The editor of the journal since its inception has been a psychiatrist, Dr. O. R. Schmalzbach.

150. The acceptance by ANZAAS of a specific division at its meetings devoted to criminology represents an important mark of recognition for Australian criminology. (ANZAAS is regarded as the most prestigious joint meeting place for natural and social scientists in Australia and New Zealand.)

151. A substantial overlap exists in the membership of ACPC, the ANZ Society of Criminology, and, to a lesser degree, the Academy of Forensic Sciences. However, the ACPC members also include many more private citizens who have no specific qualifications in the field of criminology but who are interested in and concerned about issues associated with the treatment of offenders.

152. A long-standing connection has existed between Canadian and Australian criminologists through the Center of Criminology at the University of Toronto. Richard Fox, a criminologist and criminal lawyer at Monash University Law School in Melbourne, has spent substantial periods working at the Toronto center.

153. Barry, "President's Foreword," p. 4.

BIBLIOGRAPHY*

Bates, Allan. *The System of Criminal Law: Cases and Materials in New South Wales, Victoria and South Australia.* Sydney: Butterworths, 1979.
For an understanding of the substantive criminal law and its administration in New South Wales, Victoria, and South Australia, this book reports on cases and offers extracts from statutes, articles, and Law Reform Commission reports. Practical treatment of offenses is a feature unusual among Australian criminal law texts.

Biles, David. *Background Paper on Crime in the Geelong Region.* Canberra: Australian Institute of Criminology, 1976.
Basic information is provided about crime trends in the Geelong region, a major growth center in Australia.

---

*The author is indebted to the librarians at the Australian Institute of Criminology for the preparation of this bibliography.

Biles, David. *The Size of the Crime Problem in Australia*. Canberra: Australian Institute of Criminology, 1979.
The analysis of data covers homicide, serious assaults, robbery, rape, breaking and entering, motor vehicle theft and fraud, forgery, and false pretenses.

Biles, David (ed.). *Crime and Justice in Australia*. Canberra: Australian Institute of Criminology, 1977.
The functions of the criminal justice system in the states of Australia on a national basis are discussed, and basic facts on crime are presented to shed light on the peculiar problems arising from the disparate histories of the states.

Campbell, Enid. *Freedom in Australia*. Rev. ed. Sydney: Sydney University Press, 1973.
In examining facets of Australian law as it affects the liberty of the individual, the book pinpoints problems for the layman as well as for various experts.

Chappell, Duncan. *The Police and the Public in Australia and New Zealand*. St. Lucia: University of Queensland Press, 1969.
This book examines public attitudes toward the police and police attitudes toward the public in all Australian states and New Zealand. Other topics are the development of the Australasian police forces, their training methods and efficiency, and means of improving police-public relations.

Chappell, Duncan (ed.). *The Australian Criminal Justice System*. Sydney: Butterworths, 1972.
This book is designed as an integrated Australian information source, a resource for those who have an interest in the area of crime and criminal justice at the academic level.

Chappell, Duncan (ed.). *The Australian Criminal Justice System*. 2d ed. Sydney: Butterworths, 1977.
This second edition of a basic sourcebook contains new materials on trends in crime and criminal justice, minority groups in the criminal justice system, juvenile delinquency, police and police powers, sentencing, prisons, semi- and noncustodial sentences, victims of crime, and criminal justice reform.

Dunphy, D. C. *Cliques, Crowds and Gangs: Group Life of Sydney Adolescents*. Melbourne: Cheshire, 1969.
Theories of adolescence are related to a participant-observational study of adolescent group life in Sydney that considers varying size of groups at different stages, the nature of leadership, the criteria for membership, and the group processes favoring conformity.

Edwards, Anne R. (ed.). *Social Deviance in Australia*. Melbourne: Cheshire, 1975.
A number of social and moral dilemmas of deviance are explored within an Australian context.

Eggleston, Elizabeth. *Fear, Favour or Affection: Aborigines and the Criminal Law in Victoria, South Australia and Western Australia*. Canberra: ANU Press, 1976.
The administration of the criminal law is assessed in regard to its impact on aborigines within the framework of legal institutions in three states.

Fox, Richard G. *Research Guide to Criminology Material.* 2d ed. Canberra: Australian
     Institute of Criminology, 1977.
This guide for librarians, researchers, practitioners, and students promotes access to basic
sources of criminological material.

Freiberg, Arie. *The Meaning of "Life" : A Study of Life Sentences in Australia.* Canberra:
     Australian Institute of Criminology, 1975.
The subsequent history is traced for persons whose death sentences have been commuted,
who received life sentences in courts, or were found not guilty on grounds of insanity. The
report also examines the criteria and procedures for release in each jurisdiction.

Grabosky, Peter N. *Sydney in Ferment. Crime, Dissent and Official Reaction, 1788 to
     1973.* Canberra: ANU Press, 1977.
The evolution of criminality and official reaction is traced through the course of Sydney's
history. The extent of criminality appears to have been influenced by population growth,
immigration and ethnic diversity, short-term fluctuations in the level of material well-
being, and changes in the economic structure.

Headlam, Freya. *Deviance Research Bibliography: A Bibliography of Australian Studies
     from 1960 to Date.* Melbourne: Department of Sociology, School of Social Sci-
     ences, LaTrobe University, 1977.
This bibliography, including a variety of theoretical approaches to deviance, covers crime
and criminals, self-destructive behavior, mental illness, sexual deviance, social dropouts,
radical politics, and protest.

Hopkins, Andrew. *Crime, Law and Business: The Sociological Sources of Australian
     Monopoly Law.* Canberra: Australian Institute of Criminology, 1978.
The book investigates the social and political processes that lie behind the decision to
prohibit restrictive trade practices in Australia.

Hopkins Andrew. *A Working Paper on White-Collar Crime in Australia.* Canberra:
     Australian Institute of Criminology, 1977.
This appreciation of the varieties of white-collar crime also considers the Australian
responses to it.

Kelly, David St. Leger. *Probation and Parole: Interstate Supervision and Enforcement.*
     Canberra: Australian Institute of Criminology, 1975.
Comparison is made of the differing arrangements among the states for managing the
movement of probationers and parolees from one Australian state to another while under
supervision.

Kononewsky, Anatole. *The Costs of Criminal Justice: An Analysis.* Canberra: Australian
     Institute of Criminology, 1976.
Details of expenditures of the various components of the criminal justice system for
1963-1964 and 1973-1974 are compared according to the categories of law, order and
public safety, education, and health.

Milte, Kerry L. *Police in Australia: Development, Functions, and Procedures.* Sydney:
     Butterworths, 1977.

The development of law enforcement and related problems are explored within an Australian historical and social perspective.

Newton, John Elwell. *Factors Affecting Sentencing Decisions in Rape Cases*. Canberra: Australian Institute of Criminology, 1976.
Current Australian court decisions regarding rape are reviewed to determine factors affecting the sentencing of rape offenders.

O'Brien, G. M. *The Australian Police Forces*. Melbourne: Oxford University Press, 1960.
The development of the police in Australia from the colonial period provides background for discussion of changes in the police role.

Potas, Ivan Leslie. *The Legal Basis of Probation*. Canberra: Australian Institute of Criminology, 1976.
The legal bases upon which Australian courts are empowered to place offenders on probation are analyzed.

Rinaldi, Fiori. *Australian Prisons*. Canberra: F and M Publishers, 1977.
Contemporary information on prisons is given the general public.

Ward, Paul. *Law and Order in Australia*. Sydney: Angus and Robertson, 1972.
The main issues considered by politicians campaigning on a "law and order" platform are reviewed, including violent crime, police powers, drugs, demonstrations, pornography, and punishment.

Wardlaw, Grant. *Drug Use and Crime: An Examination of Drug Users and Associated Persons and Their Influence on Crime Patterns in Australia*. Canberra: Australian Institute of Criminology, 1978.
The report investigates the relationship between illicit drug use and crime. It deals specifically with crime directly attributable to the effects of a particular drug and to demands for money to support expensive drug habits.

White, Stephen. *Criminological Materials in the Parliamentary Papers of Australia and New Zealand from 1901*. Canberra: Australian National University, 1977.
All the Parliamentary Papers of Australia and New Zealand from 1901 onwards are identified, and their location in documents is described.

Wilson, Paul R. *Crime and the Community*. St. Lucia: University of Queensland Press, 1973.
Public attitudes are described in regard to police forces generally, police powers, prisons, prison reform, and other criminal matters. Crime from the victim's point of view and a profile of victimization situations are examined.

Wilson, Paul R. *The Sexual Dilemma: Abortion, Homosexuality, Prostitution, and the Criminal Threshold*. St. Lucia: University of Queensland Press, 1971.
Abortion, homosexuality, and prostitution are discussed. The purpose is to assist the general public, and their legislators, to arrive at a rational decision as to whether these activities should remain illegal.

Wilson, Paul R. (ed.). *Delinquency in Australia*. St. Lucia: University of Queensland Press, 1977.
A number of authors assess the academic and practical advances made by employees of government agencies and staffs of universities who are concerned about delinquency in Australia. New developments are tested for their intellectual and practical adequacy.

Wilson, Paul R. (ed.). *Two Faces of Deviance: Crimes of the Powerless and the Powerful*. St. Lucia: Queensland University Press, 1978.
This book assesses the exploitation of the powerless by those in power. A number of studies illustrate how certain behavior becomes defined as illegal. The second part of the book considers the methods and mechanics of the powerful in using their positions for exploitative or illegal acts.

Inquiries and Commissions

Australia, Committee on Computerisation of Criminal Data. *Report*. Canberra: 1974.
Australia, Law Reform Commission. Reports.
Australia, Royal Commissions. *Human Relationships*. Reports. Canberra: 1977. Commissioners: Elizabeth Evatt; Felix Arnott; Anne Deveson.
Australia, Royal Commissions. *Intelligence and Security*. Reports. Canberra; 1977. Commissioner: Robert Maraden Hope.
Australia, Royal Commissions. *Drugs*. Reports. Canberra: 1980. Commissioner: Mr. Justice E. S. Williams.
Australia, Sixth United Nations Congress on the Prevention of Crime and the Treatment of Offenders. Discussion Papers. Canberra: 1979.
New South Wales, Law Reform Commission. Reports.
New South Wales, Parliament, Joint Committee on Drugs. *Progress Report*. Sydney: Government Printer, 1976. Chairman: A.E.A. Viney.
New South Wales, Royal Commissions. *Prisons*. Sydney: 1978. Commissioner: Mr. Justice Nagle.
Queensland, Law Reform Commission. Reports and Working Papers.
Queensland, Legislative Assembly. Select Committee on Punishment of Crimes of Violence. *Report*. Brisbane: Government Printer, 1975.
South Australia, Criminal Law and Penal Methods Reform Committee. Reports. Adelaide: Government Printer.
South Australia, Royal Commissions. *Administration of the Adelaide Juvenile Courts and Other Associated Matters*. Report. Adelaide: 1976. Commissioner: R. F. Mohr.
South Australia, Royal Commissions. *Allegations Made by Prisoners at Yatala Labour Prison*. Report. Adelaide: Government Printer, 1975.
South Australia, Royal Commissions. *The Dismissal of Harold Hubert Salisbury*. Report. Adelaide: 1978. Commissioner: Roma Flinders Mitchell.
South Australia, Royal Commissions. *Non-medical Use of Drugs, 1977*. Adelaide: 1977. Chairman: Ronald Sackville.
Tasmania, Law Reform Commission. Reports.
Tasmania, Prisons Administration Inquiry. *Report*. Government Printer, 1977.
Victoria, Board of Inquiry into Allegations Against Members of the Victoria Police Force. *Report*. Melbourne: Government Printer, 1976. Chairman: B. W. Beach.
Victoria, Board of Inquiry into Allegations of Brutality and Ill Treatment of H. M. Prison Pentridge. *Report*. Melbourne: Government Printer, 1973.

Victoria, Chief Justices, Law Reform Committee. Reports.
Victoria, Law Reform Commission. Reports and Working Papers.
Western Australia, Law Reform Commission. Reports and Working Papers.
Western Australia, Royal Commission. *Report Upon Various Allegations of Assaults on or Brutality to Prisoners in Fremantle Prison.* Perth: Government Printer, 1973. Commissioner: R. E. Jones.
Western Australia, Royal Commissions. *Gambling.* Report. Perth: Government Printer, 1974. Chairman: P. R. Adams.
Western Australia, Royal Commissions. *Homosexuality.* Report. Perth: Government Printer, 1974. Chairman: R.J.L.Williams.
Western Australia, Royal Commissions. *Laverton, 1975-76.* Report. Perth: Government Printer, 1976. Chairman: G. D. Clarkson.
Western Australia, Royal Commissions. *Prostitution, 1975-76.* Report. Perth: Government Printer, 1976. Commissioner: J. G. Norris.

2

AUSTRIA

János Fehérváry

Fundamental disagreements exist in Austria, as elsewhere, on the content, significance, and problems of criminology as a field of study. These differences obviously affect theory, research, practice, and public attitudes.

GENERAL DIMENSIONS OF AUSTRIAN CRIMINOLOGY

As in other European countries, the academic content and scientific foundation of Austrian criminology are intimately related to the penal law. The concept of crime rests on criminal law, and scientific considerations are expected to be framed within the terminology of criminal law rather than providing opportunities to utilize a sociological perspective in its own terms.

From the Austrian perspective, criminology presents two major elements. First, it includes the phenomenology, etiology, psychology, and sociology of criminal behavior. Second, the administration of criminal justice can be studied as reactions to criminals through prosecution and prevention. In the second element criminalistics is a very important part of criminology, a point of view that distinguishes Austrian criminology from West German criminology. This difference is apparent in the organization and identification of tasks of the criminological institutes at Austrian universities and in the attitude of most practitioners who see criminology as the equivalent of criminalistics or police science.

The emphasis in Austrian criminology is on traditional beliefs supporting the prosecution and adjudication of criminals and their management by correctional agencies rather than on exploration of the many factors inherent in the patterning of offenses. Most practitioners believe that biology, psychology, and criminalistics are the subject matter of criminology. Criminology is seen as an auxiliary of law enforcement and adjudication and, therefore, to be adapted to the requirements of criminal law. It is expected to assist the courts in decision-making through forensic psychology and to assist the police through criminalistics and to be a source of information rather than to be part of policymaking. When sociological approaches are emphasized in research, the findings are not translated into empirical practice.

Although Austrians have a high level of education, the people do not have a reliable understanding of the phenomenon of crime and of the real tasks and aims of criminology. Public opinion tends to be shaped by newspapers whose accounts of crime and criminals correspond more to the messages of detective novels and the fiction of crime motion pictures than to the reliable findings of scientific research. There are exchanges of information between sectors of public opinion, but constructive discussion is impeded by biased views and failure to carefully examine the merits of opposing arguments.

PRECEDENTS FOR CONTEMPORARY STUDIES

Austria has provided crucial impulses for the development of European criminology, particularly in regard to the development of the law as an institution and of the orientation of judicial practice. In prewar Germany, Franz Von Liszt, a dedicated Austrian, lectured on criminal law at many of the German universities, attributing crime to both heredity and social surrounding. He thought that criminology consisted of the disciplines of criminal biology and criminal sociology. Liszt was a co-founder of the journal of the science of criminal law[1] which published articles of authors from all over the world.

The direction for institutionalization of criminology, as proposed by Liszt, was provided by Hans Gross who has been called the founder of Austrian criminology. Gross founded the first criminological institute at the University of Graz in 1912. His principal works—*Handbook for the Examining Magistrate*[2] and *Criminal Psychology*[3]—were influential in shaping developments in Austria. Gross founded the journal *Archives of Criminology*[4] which has specialized in exploring the themes emphasized by traditional criminology.

Another pioneer at the turn of the century was Julius Vargha. In his principal work, *Abolition of Penal Servitude*,[5] he anticipated some of the ideas of the labeling approach but, since his development of these ideas was incomplete, his ideas were not appreciated until the last few years.[6] Other well-known Austrian criminologists—Wenzoslaus Gleispach, Adolf Lenz, Hubert Streicher, Ernst Sellig,[7] Hanns Bellavic, and Roland Grassberger[8]—appeared on the scene later, and they adhered to the doctrine of Hans Gross, including his emphasis on criminalistics as the core of criminology. Representatives of the multiple-factor approach, they placed the criminal in the center of their interest as they sought to extend their reliable knowledge through the systematic observation of science. The heredity of the criminal received primary attention, making the social environment only a secondary consideration. The net result has been a tradition of narrowing criminological questions to themes related to the personality of the offender, thereby largely ruling out a persistent investigation of the sociocultural reality within which personality is shaped. The legal institutions have been developed and continue to operate in this tradition. Anticrime programs also follow the tradition in striving to achieve successful outcomes.

While the enthusiasm for this orientation has ebbed in Austrian criminology, the traditions persist and weaken efforts to develop criminology as an independent branch of science—so much so that Austria may remain a blank on the international map of criminology.[9] This pessimistic prognosis rests on the fact that Austria continues to adhere to outmoded traditions in a time when sweeping social changes since 1945 throughout the world have stimulated remarkable progress in international criminology. Although the appearance of radical criminology signals the growth of skepticism of traditional beliefs—a skepticism not limited to those who identify themselves primarily as "radicals"—Austrian criminology continues to accept the principles of prewar penology and to avoid searching criticism of established criminal policy.

Austria's unquestioning acceptance of traditions, regardless of whether they are relevant to the contemporary scene, is revealed in the narrow definition of the subject matter of criminology, the absence of institutionalized means for preparing students as criminologists, the identification of criminology with the criminal law, and the isolation of experienced practitioners from new developments in criminology. The problem of Austrian criminology then is not the management of criminality, but the management of traditions.[10]

INFLUENCES FROM ABROAD

Its common language, cultural traditions, and geographical proximity have made the Federal Republic of Germany particularly influential in exposing Austrian criminology to world developments in that field. Although Austria, unlike West Germany, emphasizes criminalistics in its definition of criminology, the scientists and practitioners of the two countries do carry out an active exchange of ideas. Within his or her own extensive literature in contemporary criminology and criminalistics, the Austrian scholar depends on West Germany's criminological resources. Research findings are imported regularly to lend support to empirical analyses of Austrian issues and to help undertake indigenous research in light of limited financial resources.

West Germany's criminologists are a conduit for the transmission of new theoretical approaches and new research findings coming from other nations. The contributions to Austrian thought do not rest primarily on the original work of the West Germans. There are direct contacts with intellectual developments in the United States, Canada, Scandinavia, and England, but these theoretical ideas and research findings find their way to Austria mostly via the Federal Republic of Germany.

Some scientists and practitioners have strongly resisted the influences of West Germany. They believe that the Germans tend to advocate extreme positions in scientific debates, to engage in theoretical abstractions that diverge excessively from practical realities, and to color their doctrines with thinly veiled nationalistic chauvinism. Perhaps these beliefs stimulate an objective assessment of West German literature. Unfortunately, the weaknesses that purportedly exist among West German criminologists are inherent in the partisanship of certain Austrians who discount foreign criminology.

For their part, West German criminologists have recognized the potential importance of their Austrian colleagues through their contributions to the theoretical strength of German criminology. This recognition has been useful in communicating the insights of criminal sociology to Austria, particularly in regard to research. Modern criminologists, especially those with a sociological perspective, have presented lectures in Austria as well as in West Germany, illustrating the intensive contacts of scientists of both countries.

This intellectual interchange has produced ideological controversies and conflicts. Sometimes advocates of a particular perspective have defended a given specialized discipline to the detriment of multidisciplinary inquiry and have taken their analyses to such a level of theoretical abstraction that linkages with practical issues have been lost. This one-sided partisanship of extreme positions clearly weakens appreciation of opposing points of view. Of far more benefit to Austrian criminology would be critical analysis of German criminology.

In spite of its proximity to the socialist countries of Eastern Europe, Austria has not apparently been influenced by criminological developments there.

OTHER SOCIOCULTURAL CONDITIONS

According to its constitution, Austria is a democratic republic with a separation of legislative, executive, and judicial authority. Substantial and fundamental laws guarantee civil rights, and law enforcement is monitored by independent courts. The principles of political equality, freedom of speech, and the independence of science are fundamental to the establishment of criminology and other scientific activities.

A pluralism of scientific ideas without legal restrictions is possible because of the liberty of science. In reality, this liberty is limited, first, by the organization of science within the structure of the society as a reflection of the distribution of power and, second, by the ingrained moves of the scientific community that employ informal controls to defend currently favored concepts and theoretical models against new and opposing ideas. The new approaches that are contrary to dominant theories are thrust into the position of aliens. Therefore, their adherents have difficulty recruiting new followers and gaining the rewards of the recognized scholar.

These resistances can be overcome only if the errors of invalid theories are generally recognized or if the new theories gain substantial support in other countries. Since resistance is formidable in Austria, many scientists of various disciplines have left the country to be able to lecture on new doctrines and to gain the benefits of a more stimulating dialogue. Since these conditions are present for criminology, we can understand why modern conceptions of criminal sociology are not seriously considered at Austrian universities.

The principles of social equality, expressed in the Austrian constitution, have not been realized in many fields of life because the economy is still in the late capitalism stage, because political parties tend to protect their narrow interests, and because discriminatory practices persist. The announced political agenda calls for economic equity and social equality. The Social Democratic party, in power for the last ten years, is striving to reduce the discrepancy between social-political reality and the principles of the constitution. To lend legitimacy to reform proposals and new laws, social scientists are urged to analyze socio-economic conditions as they exist and, if feasible, to support public policy.

Clearly, injustice exists in the areas of prosecution and adjudication. To promote greater social justice, a new penal code was enacted in 1975, and a new procedural system for managing criminals is now in preparation. The Ludwig Boltzmann Institute for Criminal Sociology has been called upon to undertake research of a criminal sociological nature to lend greater relevance of the new laws to the realities of contemporary life.

Austria's government and administration are dominated by jurists who are not necessarily professionally competent in their central positions. As jurists, they tend to be conservative. They generally cling to traditional value judgments in their approach to present issues, without giving due recognition to changed social conditions. They view sociological analyses and the application of modern police sciences as a threat to their authority. Sociologists are not employed in governmental offices. Even within Austria's scientific community, the social sciences are at the lower rungs of the ladder of prestige. Criminology is dominated by the legalistic perspective, and the jurists are prepared to defend their dominant position against the sociologists who want to change Austrian criminology.

One recurrent theme in comparative criminology is that a viable criminology is more likely to develop when the society has experienced a serious crime problem. During the last two decades, Austria has had no political, economic, social, or religious crises. Drastic social changes and threats to internal security have not been present. To the contrary, Austria has demonstrated a high degree of social consensus, full employment, apparently broadly based social satisfaction, an absence of student protest, and amity in democratic establishment of public policy. Austria has escaped much of the radical extremism that West Germany has experienced as a stimulus for granting resources and political support to criminological research there. Few foreign terrorists have appeared in Austria.

TRADITIONAL AND SOCIOLOGICAL MODELS OF CRIMINOLOGY

A discussion of Austria's criminological activities must distinguish between, first, the traditional version, described above, that is presented in lectures at law schools and, second, a modern tendency represented by the response to developments in international criminology by the Ludwig Boltzmann Institute for Criminal Sociology in Vienna.

A clear delineation of contemporary criminology in Austria is complicated by the scientists' lack of general agreement as to the proper boundaries of each of the disciplines within an overall division of labor. There is no common discourse for dealing with manifold ideas and relating fundamental arguments to one another. Inherent in this lack of systematic debate is the intolerance which adherents of the traditional, law-dominated Austrian criminology have displayed towards modern sociological theories. Conversely, the criminal sociologists impede communication with the traditional criminologists by excluding individual approaches, by refusing to grant a place to criminalistics in their conception of criminology, and by employing technical language which the jurists do not comprehend. The opposing groups aggravate the situation by their unwillingness to undertake self-criticism.

The competition has seeped into the political process because the ruling political party employs the research of the criminal sociologists to legitimatize its crime policies and programs. The conservative opposition has called this research into question.[11] Politicians compare the results of research without considering the theoretical positions that are being tested, without considering important scientific questions, and without assessing the validity of the research methods employed.

The traditionalists perceive a crisis resulting from new challenges to their grounding criminology in the legal definition of crime. New premises are raising questions about the validity of the traditional idea that crime is defined by criminal law. The traditional definition is that crime is behavior harmful to society that is prohibited specifically by criminal law.[12] The definition is penal in that it implies elements of guilt, illegality, and responsibility as legal matters of fact.

Opponents of the legalistic approach reject the implication that criminology is only an auxiliary science (although in practical applications to the administration of justice, it may serve criminal law) and insist that it is an independent branch of criminal law.[13] Crime is seen to be as natural as conventional behavior, being the consequence of biological, sociological, and psychological phenomena. Dependence on the law per se is considered to be inconsistent with the neutrality of science, which ideally makes no value judgments about actions whether or not they oppose the public welfare or are harmful to the community. Basic to this argument is the differentiation of criminal law as a "normative science" and criminology as an empirical science that strives to describe and analyze without normative evaluation, if possible, of the facts and problems. In this sense, criminal law and criminology deal with different aspects of the same subject.

According to the traditional perspective, crime is the objectionable human misconduct of a manifoldly inadequate person. In this viewpoint, research should concentrate on the criminal personality and associated behavior. The social and cultural genesis of the definition of certain misconduct as criminal is not considered. Attention is concentrated on the personal defects and social deficiencies of individuals that are supposed to be behind the misconduct that is punishable under criminal law. Answers are supposed to be provided by consulting psychology, psychopathological explanations, biology, forensic medicine, behaviorism, and similar bodies of theory. Multifactor analysis is used to interrelate a host of basic conditions for criminogenesis explanations.

The jurists and criminalists favor multifactor analysis because it comes rather close to their perceptions of the causes of crime. The traditional criminologists try to find new causes to capture the many-layered occurrences of crime, but their search is futile because of the unlimited number of possible causal relationships. Actually, their approach is antitheoretical because variables are selected for examination in order to directly explain punishable offenses, not on the basis of carefully delineated theories of fundamental cause-effect relationships. In fact, a theoretical order is overlooked as a framework for fitting biological, semantical, psychological, and social causes into a conceptual whole.

Austrian criminology distinguishes itself by a close connection to practice,[14] but, when subjected to the realities of practice, a "science" without theory offers little guidance beyond so-called common sense. A further risk is that, when traditional criminology devotes primary attention to the individual offender and to promoting the efficiency of prosecution and adjudication, criminology becomes an instrument of penal social control and a defender of the status quo. These considerations help explain the favored position of criminalistics in Austria's traditional criminology.

The new direction of criminology in Austria may be described as criminal sociology to distinguish it from the traditional version. Crime is seen neither as simple pathology nor as the sum of offenses by individuals. Instead, the emphasis is on rejection of selected forms of deviants—formally expressed in a content of law that implements and limits the rejection—through applications to single individuals that are socially organized and politically authorized.[15] Criminology would not follow the previously accepted terms and conceptions of criminal law. Instead it would explore three aspects of the involvement of the social structure in criminal phenomena: first, the selection of certain kinds of misconduct as targets for the penalization of criminal sanctions; second, the process of defining given forms of misconduct as appropriate targets; and, third, the implementation of criminal justice actions against those forms of misconduct. It is not sufficient to regard crime simply as criminal behavior because value judgments are implied in the definition of a given behavior as a crime. The labeling of the misconduct as a crime is, in itself, subject to investigation because the crime is a subjective creation in the course of interaction between the individuals so labeled and the control system that reacts against them. The social genesis of delinquent behavior would be evaluated as part of this process of definition.

This labeling approach was taken up in West Germany before it appeared in Austria. It has been significant in raising questions in Austria that are challenging the dominance of the traditional criminology which was previously taken for granted. As a result of the theoretical considerations summarized above, the focus of interest has shifted from punishment of the individual criminal to social control systems, their sets of sanctions, the selection among cultural norms for legalization, and the genesis of norms. Furthermore, problems with criminal statistics previously unrecognized have been revealed. For example, the failure of official data to count white-collar crimes is receiving more attention.

PREPARATION FOR CRIMINOLOGICAL TASKS

Austria has no professional training programs designed to prepare specialists in criminological work. Even those who are lecturers and assistants at criminological institutes at the universities and regard themselves as criminologists have been educated in the law and identify themselves as specialists in law. Criminology is not an independent subject nor an optional subject for the examinations that conclude the educational program of law schools. Regulations for the conduct of examinations place criminology in conjunction with criminal law; specifically, the examination is likely to be identified as "criminal law and criminal procedures, considered in reference to criminological aspects."

Lectures on criminology are offered, but few students are interested because the topic is not required for examinations. As a result, law school graduates leave the university with little comprehension of crime and criminality. Their knowledge of criminology is limited to interpretations of laws.

The training of practitioners, whether police, prosecutors, or prison officials, is almost exclusively limited to their orientation by more experienced colleagues. They are seldom exposed to the expertise of specialists who are not members of the particular organization. Obligatory in-service training is dedicated to serving the purposes of the employing organization. The title of "criminology" loses its precise meaning. For example, applied criminalistics taught to policemen goes under the title "criminology." As a consequence, persons who continuously confront criminals and the difficulties of dealing with problems related to crime are unlikely to have learned much about the body of reliable criminological principles that have been carefully accumulated by generations of criminological scientists. Their practical learning is more of a form of indoctrination into the folkways of their agency and the senior personnel. Socialization to work is oriented more toward satisfying the interests of the given agency or of one's occupational peers than toward gaining genuine professional insights.

Because law school education and practical training produce respect for traditional ways and offer little information on more recent developments in criminology, criminal justice administrators believe that criminal sociology will lead to excessive permissiveness in the face of a rising tide of crime. Through their skepticism about modern science and their unfriendly reception of new research, practitioners add to the unlikelihood that criminological principles, no matter how valid and relevant, will become part of the consciousness of practitioners and transform the realities of criminal justice administration.

Prospects for introducing criminology into professional education vary among the occupational fields. It is seriously discussed in all proposals to modernize the education of judges and public prosecutors. Members of the parole board, whose status is rather inferior among criminal justice officials, are exposed to the latest points of view, including the doctrines of criminology and criminal sociology. The police are particularly resistant to changes in their training; the introduction of traditional psychology is regarded as major progress, but criminal sociology continues to confront diehard opposition.

CRIMINOLOGICAL INSTITUTES IN AUSTRIA

In the criminological institutes at the University of Graz (founded in 1912) and the University of Vienna (founded in 1923), lecturers and assistants carry out minor research projects in addition to their instructional responsibilities. They are also involved in making expert judgments in criminalistics, especially in the field of graphology, and in providing scientific evidence. This work takes up approximately half of their time; the remaining half is divided equally between teaching and research.

The demand for criminalistic expertise has equipped the institutes with technical instruments and laboratories that resemble those of police departments. Criminalistics is so popular that the university has been unable to keep up with the demand. The institutes' equipment tends to be obsolete, probably very appropriate for museum display. At both institutes, the orientation is legalistic and full-fledged criminological inquiry is not undertaken. The limited financial resources are channeled exclusively into penal or criminalistic research.

The research situation is altogether different at the Ludwig Boltzmann Institute for Criminal Sociology (founded in 1973). This institute has a close relationship with the Ministry of Justice, for the ministry requests that certain research projects be undertaken and the institute's budget is partly supported by the ministry. Accordingly, empirical investigations of issues important to the administration of justice and relevant to penal legislation are included in the institute's activities. Furthermore, efforts are made to test the rationales for proposals to reform laws and to test the effectiveness of innovations already implemented. It should be emphasized that the institute has the freedom to carry out its research independently of the ministry and to reach conclusions regardless of outcomes that might be preferred in advance. That research freedom does exist is indicated by the fact that the research team—including sociologists, psychologists, and lawyers in its membership—has produced several research publications that have been favorably received in other countries.

This does not, of course, mean that the perspective of criminal sociology has gained acceptance in Austria. The scientific director of the institute has not been invited to lecture at Austrian universities, although he has done so in West Germany. In recent years, penologists from abroad, who do have a grasp of modern criminology, have been appointed to the faculties of the University of Linz and the University of Salzburg. It remains to be seen whether or not these appointments indicate a strengthening in the position of criminology at the universities.

The Austrian Society of Criminal Law and Criminology has a distinguished membership of scientist practitioners who come together to exchange ideas. Through the society penologists and criminologists keep abreast of recurrent problems of criminal prosecution and adjudication, and practitioners can learn the results of scientific endeavors. Legal issues, developments in the incidence of crime, and the concerns of traditional criminology are the topics of lectures, discussions, and seminars. The subject matter and concepts of modern criminology, however, are not included.

THE LITERATURE OF BOOKS AND PERIODICALS

Austria has few publications in criminology compared with the United States, England, or West Germany. One person who has been quite active in this field is Roland Grassberger, the retired director of the Criminological Institute at the University of Vienna. He has edited eleven volumes of *Criminological Treatise* in the last fifteen years.[16] His books deal mainly with legal problems, however; the few criminological studies follow the phenomenological-ethnological approach.

The publications of the Ludwig Boltzmann Institute of Criminal Sociology emphasize research reports that are criminological in their formulation of questions.[17] Since 1974, the institute has published a periodical called *Criminal Sociological Bibliography*.[18] It has developed into a reputable publication, surveying a variety of thoughts and problems in each number. Other publications of the institute have expanded the readership for contributions to the criminal sociology and modern criminology fields.

Providing a bridge of understanding among penologists, psychologists, and medical specialists is *Forensia: Interdisciplinary Periodical for Law, Neurology, Psychiatry and Psychologists*, founded in 1975. Its articles deal with criminology, criminal prognosis, criminal therapy, and forensic psychology. The appearance of this journal demonstrates the strong demand among penal jurists for practical assistance in reaching decisions through scientifically validated methods. When committed to the traditional perspective and prepared only to lend apparent legitimacy to established practices in the administration of the law, traditional Austrian criminology has difficulty in meeting this demand. Because this new clinical periodical relies upon these traditionalists, it has not yet realized its potential.

PATTERNS OF CRIMINALITY IN AUSTRIA

Criminality statistics for Austria are not very reliable, for a number of reasons: the public does not report all crimes to the police; the extent of offenses is sometimes exaggerated by those groups who feel great insecurity in the face of evidence of urban disorder; administrative units differ in their management of anticrime activities; the fact of the "dark figure" of undetected offenses; appearance of unprecedented opportunities for law violations; and so on. In short, the changing patterns of criminality are not reflected by the crime statistics. Nevertheless, variations in the incidence of crime are usually measured according to official statistics.[19]

Some dedicated efforts have been made to determine the dimensions of crime through empirical research, but the data collected are for such short time spans and such narrow geographical areas that the estimates cannot be considered reliable. Inasmuch as this present analysis of crime patterns is derived from official statistics, it must therefore be emphasized that these data are only approximations of the true extent of criminality.

In Austria as elsewhere, the sources of reported offenses are police registers and court reports on convictions. Additional information may be acquired through the public prosecutors. These three primary sources follow different registration practices and different choices of units of count. These sets of data describe only known crimes and the patterns of interaction among the components of the criminal justice organization.

Since World War II, the official data have shown a consistent increase in crime rates. The first year that the police reported crime was 1953. Between 1953 and 1978, the number of all crimes known to the police increased from 194,916 to 313,233. Meanwhile, the population of Austria rose from 6.95 million to 7.5 million. The crime rate climbed from 2,801 to 4,160 per 100,000 inhabitants, an increase of 48 percent. The increase was approximately 2.1 percent per year on the average. The greatest increases occurred in the 1953-1960 and 1965-1970 periods.

The greatest increases were for crimes against property. Of all punishable acts, 42 percent were crimes against property in 1953 and 67 percent in 1978. The absolute number of property offenses rose 158 percent, whereas total crimes increased 137 percent. In comparison, acts of violence and assault declined from 14 percent to 9 percent of all offenses. Bodily injuries attributed to reckless driving have become more important, representing 12 percent of all offenses in 1978. The rate for assaults was 100 per 100,000 inhabitants in 1953 but only 43 per 100,000 in 1978.

Of all crimes known to the police in 1953, 85 percent resulted in apprehension, compared to only 56 percent in 1978, largely because of the increasing share of property offenses among all offenses. In 1978, only 37 percent of all property offenses resulted in arrests. In 1953, there were 2,550 persons per 100,000 inhabitants accused by the police of punishable offenses, compared to only 2,159 in 1978, or a decline of 15 percent. In 1953, there were 1,547 persons per 100,000 inhabitants sentenced by courts, or about 57 percent of all accused persons. In 1978, the rate declined to 1,130, or 52 percent of all suspects.

Austria strictly follows the principle of legality. All punishable acts known to the security authorities must be investigated and reported to the public prosecutor. The police are not allowed to dismiss a reported case, and the public prosecutor serves the filtering function. Investigations fail to turn up the offender in 50 percent of all cases. Another 20 percent of the cases are dismissed for lack of sufficient evidence. Of the remaining 30 percent, about 20 percent result in acquittals. Of those cases resulting in sanctions, 75 percent draw fines, 25 percent result in prison sentences, and 21 percent involve probation. On an average day in 1978, there were 8,024 convicted persons, or 107 prisoners per 100,000 inhabitants. During recent years, these figures have not changed significantly.

Newspapers and political debates repeatedly lament the continual increase in juvenile delinquency among persons fourteen to eighteen years of age. In 1953, juveniles represented 4.7 percent of all suspects, whereas in 1978 they held a 10.9-percent share. Some of this increase can be attributed to the growth of the juvenile population as a whole. Among adults, the eighteen to twenty-five year olds represent 27 percent of all suspects, a significant proportion of all adult offenders.

There is a general impression of increasing violence associated with particularly sensational crimes or the short-term appearance of particular types of criminality. "Rockerism," bank robberies, and terrorism loom large in the impressions of escalating violence, but the crime statistics do not lend credence to the impression.

The police statistics issued by the Ministry of Interior reveal increasing drug offenses to be a threat to public security. Austria has long been identified as an important transit country for drugs coming from the Orient. This trade has also become serious for Austria itself because of increased consumption of drugs there. There were only forty-nine drug-related arrests in 1978, but one can suppose that the "dark figure" problem is especially relevant to drug crimes because of ineffective laws and law enforcement.

FINAL COMMENT

Today, a traditional criminology clings tenaciously to the norms of criminal law, to the legalistic orientation, and to a concentration on the individual offender. The inadequacies of this traditional criminology have brought Austria to a deadend.

To escape this situation, Austrian criminology has made tentative overtures— although still to be institutionalized—toward accepting modern criminology as a new theoretical base. These ideas are being expressed through criminal sociology which appears to be an apt framework for the systematic research and instruction that would supply the ingredients of an institutionalized modern criminology. At present, interaction between the adherents of traditional criminology and criminal sociology is weak, with each group opposing the possibility of effective integration. Can traditions be overcome and can Austrian criminology adapt to more modern perspectives? This is the crux of the problem.

NOTES

1. *Zeitschrift für die gesamte Strafrechtswissenschaft* [Periodical for All the Penal Sciences], edited by Max Planck Institute for Foreign and International Criminal Law (Berlin: De Gruyter).

2. Hans Gross, *Handbuch für den Untersuchungsrichter* [Handbook for the Examining Magistrate] (Graz: Leuschner Lubensky, 1893); *Criminal Investigation*, 3d ed. (London: 1934).

3. Hans Gross, *Criminalpsychologie* [Criminal Psychology] (Leipzig: F.C.W. Vogel, 1905).

4. *Archiv für Kriminologie* [Archives for Criminology] (Lübeck: Verlag Georg Schmidt-Römhild).

5. Julius Vargha, *Die Abschaffung der Strafknechtschaft* [The Abolition of Penal Servitude] (Graz: Leuschner Lubensky, 1896, Vol. 1; 1897, Vol. 2).

6. Karlheinz Probst, "Die moderne Kriminologie und Julius Vargha" [New Criminology and Julius Vargha], *Monatsschrift für Kriminologie und Strafrechtsreform* 59, no. 86 (1976):335-351; Karlheinz Probst, "Der Labeling-approach eine österreichische kriminologische Theorie" [Labeling Approach: An Austrian Criminological Approach], *Österreichische Richterzeitung*, 55, no. 3 (1977):45-51.

7. Ernst Seeling, *Lehrbuch der Kriminologie* [Textbook for Criminology] (Graz: Verlag Josef Kienreich, 1950).

8. Roland Grassberger, "Österreich und die Entwicklung der Kriminologie zur selbständigen Wissenschaft" [Austria and the Development of Criminology to an Independent Science], *Wissenschaft und Weltbild* 18, no. 3 (1965):277-289; Roland Grassberger, "Hundert Jahr reformierter Strafprozess und die Entwicklung der Kriminologie in Österreich" [Hundred Years of Criminal Procedure and Development of Criminology in Austria], in Viktor Liebscher and Otto F. Müller (eds.), *Hundert Jahr Österreichische Strafprozessordnung* [Hundred Years of Austrian Criminal Procedure] (Vienna: Springer Verlag, 1973); Roland Grassberger, "Pioneers in Criminology—Hans Gross," *Journal of Criminal Law, Criminology and Police Science* 47, no. 3 (1956):398.

9. Reinhard Moos, "Hundert Jahre österreichische Strafprozessordnung. Betrachtungen zu einer Festschrift" [Hundred Years of Austrian Criminal Procedure. Reflections to a Celebrating Publication], *Österreichische Richterzeitung* 53, no. 6 (1975):77-86.

10. Fritz Sack, "Kriminalität al gesellschaftliche Legitimierungsproblematik—Kriminologie als Legitimationswissenschaft" [Crime as a Problem of Legitimization—Criminology as a Science of Legitimization], in *Recht und Politik* [Law and Policy], edited by the Institute for Social Science and Ludwig Boltzmann Institute for Criminal Sociology, Vienna, 1975.

11. Mechthild Tumpel and Gertrude Edlinger, *Kriminalität in Wien—Jugendkriminalität in Stadtrandsiedlungen* [Crime in Vienna—Juvenile Delinquency in the Suburbs] (Vienna: Ludwig Boltzmann Institute for Criminal Sociology, 1975); Franz Csaszar, "Kinder und Jugendkriminalität in Wien" [Juvenile Delinquency in Vienna], *Österreichische Juristenzeitung* 33, no. 3 (1978):62-70.

12. Roland Grassberger, "Versuch eines kriminologischen Systems zur Klassifizierung der strafbaren Handlungen" [Attempts of a Criminological System to Classify Punishable Offenses], *Kriminalistik* 15, no. 11 (1961):469-478.

13. Roland Grassberger, "Österreich und die Entwicklung der Kriminologie zur

selbständigen Wissenschaft" [Austria and the Development of Criminology to an Independent Science], *Wissenschaft und Weltbild* 18, no. 3 (1965):277-289.

14. Konrad Schima, "Die österreichische Kriminologie—etwas anders gesehen" [Austrian Criminology—Seen from Another Position], *Österreichische Richterzeitung* 54, no. 8 (1976):130-131.

15. Heinz Steinert, *Der Prozess der Kriminalisierung* [Process of Criminalization] (München: Juventa Verlag, 1973), p. 1.

16. These books are examples: Konrad Schima, *Erpressung und Nötigung* [Blackmail and Coercion] (Vienna: Springer Verlag, 1973); and Franz Csaszar, *Der Überfall auf Geldinstitute* [Bank Robbery] (Vienna: Springer Verlag, 1976).

17. Examples of research reports edited by the Ludwig Boltzmann Institute for Criminal Sociology are the following: Stefan Mikinovic and Wolfgang Stangl, *Das Rechtsmittel im Strafprozess, Eine empirische Studie richterlicher Entscheidungsfindung* [Legal Remedy in Criminal Procedure: An Empirical Study of Judicial Sentences] (1977); Arnold Pilgram and Heinz Steinert, *Zur Soziologie der Rechts- und Kriminalitätsentwichlung* [Sociology of Development of Law and Crime] (1974); Irmtraud Gössler-Leirer and Heinz Steinert, *Kriminalität der Frau in Österreich* [Crime by Females in Austria] (1975); Arnold Pilgram, *Kriminalität in Österreich 1953-1974* [Crime in Austria 1953-1974] (1976).

18. *Kriminalsoziologische Bibliografie* [Criminal Sociological Bibliography], edited by the Ludwig Boltzmann Institute for Criminal Sociology in Vienna.

19. Arnold Pilgram, *Kriminalstatistiken als Quellenmaterial für eine Geschichte der Kriminalitätsentwichlung* [Criminal Statistics as a Source for a History of the Development of Crime] (Vienna: Ludwig Boltzmann Institute for Criminal Sociology, 1977).

BIBLIOGRAPHY

Csaszar, Franz. "Kinder und Jugendkriminalität in Wien" [Juvenile Delinquency in Vienna]. *Österreiche Juristenzeitung* 33, no. 3 (1978):62-70.

Exner, Franz. *Krieg und Kriminalität in Österreich* [War and Crime in Austria]. Vienna: Holder-Pichler-Tempsky, 1927.

Frassine, I., K. Piska, and H. Zeisel. *Die Rolle der Schoeften in der osterreichischen Strafgerichtbarkeit* [The Role of Lay Judges in Austrian Criminal Justice]. Vienna: Forschungsbericht Nr. 47, Institute fuer holhere Studien und Wissenschafliche Forschung, 1970.

Grassberger, Roland. "Hundert Jahr reformierter Strafprozess und die Entwicklung der Kriminologie in Österreich" [Hundred Years of Criminal Procedure and Development of Criminology in Austria]. In Viktor Liebscher and Otto F. Müller (eds.). *Hundert Jahr Österreichische Strafprozessordnung* [Hundred Years of Austrian Criminal Procedure]. Vienna: Springer Verlag, 1973.

Grassberger, Roland. "Osterreich und die Entwicklung der Kriminologie zur selfstandigen Wissenschaft" [Austria and the Development of Criminology to an Independent Science]. *Wissenschaft und Weltbild* 18, no. 3 (1965):277-289.

Gross, Hans. *Criminalpsychologie* [Criminal Psychology]. Leipzig: F.C.W. Bogel, 1965.

Gross, Hans. *Handbuch für den Untersuchungsrichter* [Handbook for the Examining Magistrate]. Graz: Leuschner Lubensky, 1893.

Hackler, Jim, Joan Brockman, and Eva Luczynska. "The Comparison of Role Interrelationships in Two Juvenile Courts: Vienna and Boston." *International Journal of Criminology and Penology* 5 (November 1977):367-397.

Johnson, Elmer H., and Johannes Driendl. "Police Prosecutor and Police Prison: A Note on Summary Justice in Austria." *International Journal of Comparative and Applied Criminal Justice* 4 (Winter 1980):125-130.

Moos, Reinhard. "Hundert Jahr österreichische Strafprozessordnung. Betrachtungen zu einer Festschrift" [Hundred Years of Austrian Criminal Procedure. Reflections to a Celebrating Publication]. *Österreichische Richterzeitung* 53, no. 6 (1975):77-86.

Pilgram, Arnold. *Kriminalität in Österreich 1953-1974* [Crime in Austria 1953-1974]. Vienna: Ludwig Boltzmann Institute for Criminal Sociology, 1976.

Probst, Karlheinz. "Die moderne Kriminologie und Julius Vargha" [New Criminology and Julius Vargha]. *Monatsschrift für Kriminologie und Strafrechtsreform* 59, no. 6 (1976):335-351.

Schima, Konrad. "Die österreichesche Kriminologie—etwas anders geschen" [Austrian Criminology—Seen from Another Position]. *Österreichische Richterzeitung* 54, no. 8 (1976):130-131.

Seelig, Ernst. *Lehrbuch der Kriminologie* [Textbook for Criminology]. Graz: Verlag Josef Kienreich, 1950.

Steinert, Heinz. *Der Prozess der Kriminalisierung* [Process of Criminalization]. München: Juventa Verlag, 1973.

Tumpel, Mechthild, and Gertrude Edlinger. *Kriminalitat in Wien—Jugendkriminalität in Stadtrandsiedlungen* [Crime in Vienna—Juvenile Delinquency in the Suburbs]. Vienna: Ludwig Boltzmann Institute for Criminal Sociology, 1975.

3

BELGIUM

Lode Van Outrive and Danielle Quanten

At the turn of the century, a new science—the so-called criminal anthropology associated especially with the work of the Italian physician, C. Lombroso[1] —developed in various countries of Western Europe. In Belgium, this approach was the first theoretical theme in the appearance of criminology. From this beginning, Belgian criminology has moved through several theoretical orientations to evolve into the multi- or interdisciplinary orientation it has today. This chapter begins by tracing the movement through the several orientations.

DEVELOPMENT OUT OF CRIMINAL ANTHROPOLOGY

Criminal anthropology flourished for a time in Belgium. The works of the Dutch professors A. Aletrino and Dr. M.S.L. Vervaeck, director of the anthropological service of the penitentiary administration, contributed to the popularity and success of this science. At international congresses on criminal anthropology, other Belgians such as A. Prins, H. Semal, and L. Dallemagne were also actively involved in debates about the theory and applications of the Italian biological and French sociological views.[2] In Belgium one did not have to wait long for the effects. In the 1920s, criminal anthropology influenced Belgian administration to such an extent that institutes which originated then still have a function today.

Already at the end of the nineteenth century, the views on treatment of delinquency started to change. At first, the whole problem was looked upon from the perspective of classical penal law theories that had dominated the Belgian penal code of 1867. Magistrates, politicians, and officials gradually ascertained that the application of these classical views could not meet their expectations. The belief in free will and in the effectiveness of punishment decreased. Instead, criminality from then on was regarded as a social illness that had to be cured by society, by means of the most efficient remedies.[3] This view was defended especially by A. Prins, inspector-general of penitentiary administration, and by influential foreigners such as G. Van Hamel and F. Von Liszt. In their opinion, the administration of justice had to be oriented to the moral correction and readaptation of the delinquent. In those days, ministers of justice A. Lejeune and E. Vandervelde, Attorney General L. Servais, Professor A. Prins, L. Vervaeck, and Professor L. Braffort took a number of measures to guarantee the security and protection of certain categories of detainees.

These "measures of social defense," the juridical translation of these penal law theories, were given concrete form in Minister E. Vandervelde's criminal justice policy. The foundation of the anthropological service of penitentiary administration, the psychiatric annexes, the sanatoriums, the special sections of the prisons, and the central labor office were the most important reforms in the administration of justice that supported this treatment ideology.[4]

In this context, criminology acquired an important function. In 1929, L. Braffort, barrister at the court of appeal in Brussels and professor at the Faculty of Law in Louvain, defined criminology as the study of the physical and social causes of criminality. He would use direct observation, scientific induction, and deduction as the most important methods of investigation for achieving a more humane approach to delinquency.[5]

In 1937, Professor A. De Greef published his *Introduction à la Criminologie* in the periodical called *l'Ecrou* in which he defined criminology as the scientific study of crime, not as a legal concept but as a complex phenomenon arising in a human being.[6] Very important is his contribution to the formulation of the theory of criminal psychology, in which he made clear the notion of criminogenesis.[7]

Since then, the area of criminology has not been restricted to the study of the conventional criminal, not even to the study of the criminal as such. Nowadays, there is a growing belief that the concepts of "order," "criminality," and "deviance" can be applied, not only to traditional criminality and penal law, but also to the social areas of health, labor, taxes, social security, economy, environment, and so on. In addition to those concepts, "irregularity," "abuse," "corruption," and "defrauding" are also the result of intricate individual and social processes of meaning and control. One becomes aware that these processes are linked up with various conditions of origin and also that they are tied essentially to political, social, and economic power structures, institutions, and ideologies.[8] From this point of view, criminology cannot remain a mere neutral kind of occupation. Because in essence it is involved in social life, education in criminology will participate in social renovation by structuring new perspectives within society.[9]

In former days, criminology was split up according to the different basic sciences, such as sociology and psychiatry. Nowadays one considers the possible working areas of the criminologist—police, the judiciary, psychosocial guidance, and so on—as subdivisions and specializations within criminology.[10]

CRIMINOLOGY AS THE SERVANT OF PENAL LAW

Within the framework of the criminal justice policy of the 1920s, the abstract and absolute approach to delinquency became partly obsolete. One could not solve everything by means of repression. Therefore, one aimed at the individual-ization of punishment that pointed to the physical and psychic readaptation of the delinquent, whereas resocialization aimed at social readaptation. This was the kernel idea of the "movement of social defense" that dominated the Belgian criminal justice policy in those days. In 1929, Professor L. Braffort stressed the importance of a training in criminology for future lawyers. To realize the views of social defense, they had to approach delinquency as a complex phenomenon in which the legal aspect was only of partial importance, along with psychological, psychiatric, and moral aspects.[11]

From this basic idea, academic preparation for criminology has evolved into a multi- or interdisciplinary encounter in which various human sciences are in-volved in the study of a wider range of problems—namely, social deviance—that can be punishable or not. At first psychiatry and psychology were the most important disciplines, along with the dominating penal law, but in the further development of criminology there has been a growing participation of sociology and a certain decline of psychiatry. Although those disciplines are part of the academic approaches in the various schools for criminology, some schools em-phasize the more clinical approach, whereas others pay more attention to the sociological approach.

After about sixty years of history, it can be stated that criminology has become chiefly an academic enterprise involving theoretical studies. In the beginning, these studies were inspired especially by the clinical approach. From this view the prison was to be used as a laboratory. This practice was well received in Belgium because it had been an important tradition in the criminal-anthropological approach.[12] Moreover, the clinical approach inspired a diffuse assistance ap-proach that entails a variety of educational and psychological methods for deal-ing with personal deficits believed to be the sources of criminality.

There have been two remarkable features of this evolution. First, analytical and systematic research has developed rather late, especially research into the institutions for administration of criminal justice. Second, criminology has not been professionalized within the administration of justice, with the exception of the Gendarmerie (national police) where criminology is part of the training of all officers.

SETTING FOR THE NATION'S CRIMINOLOGY

Academic studies in criminology originated in the 1920-1940 period. A school of criminology and scientific police work was founded by the Ministry of Justice, and six schools of criminology came into being at the university level.

School voor Criminologie en Criminalistiek in Brussels

The foundation of this school was part of the renewed criminal justice policy of Minister E. Vandervelde. By royal warrant of October 15, 1920, he estab-lished it as a unit of the Ministry of Justice, under the leadership of eminent magistrates and officials. The training involves the study of criminal anthropology and police science. The police officers and magistrates were given a notion of criminology to enable them to participate in the reforms of the administration of justice instigated by E. Vandervelde.[13]

Therefore, the first Belgian criminologists were practitioners who sought pragmatic solutions to the crime problem. They were taught an etiological criminology based on concepts of clinical and social pathology and directed toward investigation of biological and social causes of criminality. The police made full use of anthropometrics. Within penitentiary administration, treatment was oriented toward readaptation of prisoners. Because this kind of criminology was practiced by officers engaged in the administration of justice, the work of these first criminologists mirrored the Belgian criminal justice of those days that fully approved of this type of criminology.

Developments on University Level

In the 1930-1940 period, four schools of criminology on the university level were established: the School for Criminology of the Université Catholique de Louvain in 1929, the one of the Université Libre de Bruxelles in 1936, and finally the schools at the Rijksuniversiteit van Gent and at the Université de Liège in 1938.

The establishment of four schools at the university level within this decade was more than mere coincidence. Moreover, the schools of Louvain and Brussels split afterwards, and Dutch-speaking departments were established. Since the end of 1978, the French-speaking Ecole de Criminologie de l'Université Catholique de Louvain has been situated at Louvain-la-Neuve in Wavre-Ottignies. At the moment there are six schools in Belgium. The number of schools can be explained by the existence of Flemish and Walloon communities and the political and sociological cleavages in contemporary Belgium.

Ecole des Sciences Criminelles of Louvain

At the opening of the academic year 1929-1930, Rector Magnificus Monseigneur Ladeuze established the Ecole des Sciences Criminelles.[14] In establishing this school, professors and students emphasized the protection of society or social defense against criminals.

The study of anthropological and psychiatric sciences was an essential part of the education. Physicians, lawyers, and criminologists were confronted daily with the problem of criminality. In keeping with the emphasis on defense, those professionals needed expertise in their judgments about normality versus abnormality and responsibility versus irresponsibility.

To present that kind of education, the School of Criminology depended on the professors in the faculties of law, medicine, and philosophy. Moreover, an active cooperation was engendered among the school, the central prison of Louvain, the psychiatric clinic of Lovenjoel, and the scientific laboratories of the university. The program of the school consisted of the following subjects: criminal sciences, penal law and criminal procedure, the notion of "free will," psychology, youth criminality, psychiatry, criminal anthropology, and forensic medicine.[15]

L'Ecole des Sciences Criminologiques of Brussels

Within the Faculty of Law of the Université Libre de Bruxelles, the Ecole des Sciences Criminologiques was opened on October 13, 1936. In their inaugural addresses, Professor L. Cornil, solicitor-general at the court of Cassation, and E. De Craene, vice-president of the school, emphasized the importance of the school. The establishment of L'Ecole des Sciences Criminologiques Leon Cornil was a result of the reorganization of education. L. Cornil and E. De Craene directed the reorganization along the lines earlier followed by L. Braffort in emphasizing measures of social defense. The program of this school was almost identical with that of Louvain, with courses in criminal prophylaxis and scientific policy added to the curriculum.[16]

Schools in Gent and Liège

On December 19, 1936, Dean Professor N. Gunzburg and Professor J. Simon proposed the establishment of an Instituut voor Criminologie within the Faculty of Law in Gent. Together they drew up the plan and organization of the program of which they wanted to take charge.[17]

The details of the program clearly reveal the intention to create a specialization for those who would be involved in a range of criminality problems: magistrates, higher officials in the Ministry of Justice, and directors of prisons and psychiatric institutes in penitentiaries.[18] After prolonged discussions and after approval and acceptance of the project through the royal warrant of May 10, 1938, a school of criminology at the universities of Gent and Liège, respectively, was established.[19]

In 1938, the program included the following subjects: penal law, penal procedure, criminology, penology, metaphysics, philosophy, forensic medicine, toxicology, sociology, encyclopedia of law, criminal prophylaxis, psychiatry, criminal anthropology and pathology, youth defense, and criminalistics.

Influence of the Unique Conditions of Belgium

In general, the frameworks of those schools in that period hardly differed from one another. It is necessary to understand Belgian politics to explain the establishment of four institutes and the later addition of two more—Dutch-speaking departments in Leuven and Brussels, respectively.

From the very beginning, Belgian democracy has faced three important sources of potential conflict: the ideological area, the social-economic area, and the opposition between the linguistic communities. First, the country is characterized by a vertical segmentation into three ideological-political blocs—each with its own unions, professional organizations, health services, cultural organizations, schools, and newspapers—which is part and parcel of the political and social infrastructure of the country.[20] Each Belgian, sooner or later, confronts this vertical segmentation. He is obliged to take a political option because his social life is closely linked with institutions that have political labels. As J. Billiet says: "When people vote, join a trade union, send their children to school and to youth organizations, they generally follow a consistent pattern."[21]

The ideological duality, Catholic versus liberal, also influenced the organization within which education was established. Different educational systems emerged. Furthermore, each of the linguistic communities—the Dutch-speaking and the French-speaking communities—demanded an equal place in the expansion of universities.

The establishment of the six schools of criminology operated within this attitudinal climate. The question that arises is whether or not the schools of criminology were established mainly as a means of keeping the ideological-linguistic factions well balanced. If this purpose was central, the expansion policy has been an expensive solution that has not offered the best guarantee of a high-quality education.

DEVELOPMENT OF CRIMINOLOGICAL RESEARCH

It is remarkable that criminological research has always been initiated through a political stimulus. Indeed, important initiatives were taken by three socialist ministers of justice: E. Vandervelde, P. Vermeylen, and A. Vranckx.

The policy of E. Vandervelde is discussed above. The introduction of medical anthropology, especially in penitentiary administration, was a great innovation in those days. The first anthropological services were established in the prisons of Saint Gillis and Leuven. In 1907, L. Vervaeck initiated anthropological research to realize the organization of a systematic classification of prisoners.[22]

Through P. Vermeylen, a penitentiary observation center was created at the prison of Saint Gillis on October 31, 1963. "This center has to make contributions to scientification of the convicts," L. Van Outrive explains, "whose case causes specific problems to officers who have to point out the institution where the punishment has to be undergone and on what level of treatment is to be applied."[23]

The second important initiative was the establishment of the Studiecentrum voor Jeugdmisdadigheld—Centre d'Etude de la Délinquance Juvénile in Brussels. This interuniversity organization was established in 1957 under the auspices and financial support of the Ministry of Justice. The center has explicit objectives in carrying out scientific research and providing information:

1. To conduct research on youth crime with social action in view.

2. To be a national documentary center about youth criminality and related problems.

3. To provide coordination between individuals and institutions with responsibilities in dealing with the problems.

4. To publish a monograph at set times about youth criminality in Belgium.

5. To evaluate the efficiency of the present methods of prevention and treatment.[24]

Another initiative of Minister P. Vermeylen was the establishment of the National Centrum voor Criminologie-Centre National de Criminologie on March 8, 1965. The center is subsidized yearly by the Ministry of Justice and is controlled by a director and board. Moreover, the center is guided by a scientific council of representatives of the schools of criminology and of public institutions with special interest in criminological research. The institute has a team that is responsible for the research.[25]

As required by Minister A. Vranckx, research on the treatment of prisoners was begun in the prisons of Verviers, Saint Gillis-Brussels, Gent, and Leuven in January 1970. Within the six universities, interdisciplinary research teams were created with the assistance of the director of prisons.[26]

On the basis of this brief review of developments, several interpretative comments can be offered. The above initiatives were taken by a few interested and involved political leaders. A rather traditional view on crime was taken. Their actions did not imply a real commitment to academic research from the side of penitentiary administrators.

An important issue is whether or not criminological research occupies only a marginal position in respect to its impact on policy. The marginal position is suggested by the very passive participation of officials, administrators, and magistrates in the Belgian Association for Criminology and the presence of only one criminologist on the commission for reform of Belgian penal law. Of course, there are a few contacts with the penitentiary administration, with youth defense agencies, the courts, and so on; those contacts are not systematic, but they are personal and sometimes entail many difficulties.

Even the limited opportunities for research are further restricted because a good part of research can be characterized increasingly, not by a juridical and psychiatric perspective, but by a psychological and sociological approach to criminology that slowly has become more oriented to the analysis of the institutionalized administration of justice than to the analysis of the criminal personality. More and more, some aspects of the functions of criminology reflect the administration of justice. As such, the relationship between researchers and criminal justice policy and administrators has become rather controversial.

Of course, some research continues to serve the interests of the established administration of justice, but the situation is changing. Within certain political parties, commissions have been established: the Commission for Human Rights in the Socialist party and the Commission on Prisons in the Christian party. Along with the reestablishment of the High Council for Penitentiary Administration, those commissions of the political parties show a gradually increasing sensitivity in political circles to the quality of the administration of justice.

Members of university communities have played a part in that growing political sensitivity. However, events other than the findings of scientific research have stimulated the political interest: recent revolts by prisoners, scandals of police corruption, the conviction of a high magistrate, accusations made against an important lawyer, increased concern about the political appointments of police officers and magistrates, and so on.

NOTEWORTHY PATTERNS OF CRIME STATISTICS

In Belgium criminal, judicial, and penitentiary statistics are published yearly. Although these data offer basic information, it is very difficult to give a correct interpretation of the mass of figures collected, processed, and published each year because the scheme of each set of data is not explained. Even the most general and simplest count is derived from premises about the nature of crime and how its appearance may be explained. For example, in Belgian criminal statistics, the convicts are classified according to sex, kind of crime, judicial past, matrimonial status, profession, social status, age, and geographical residence. These elements are counted and grouped into categories to serve certain purposes. Then, although the rationale for choosing these variables produces some uncertainty, the emphasis on certain kinds of information suggests something about the underlying views on the subject matter of criminology.

The Belgian criminal statistics imply a vague social-deterministic view, following either a social or psychological model, as drafted by A. Quetelet and A. M. Guerry in their time.[27] Those statistics cannot capture the evolution of the phenomenon of delinquency over time, but they do reveal the capacity of the administration of justice to react to various types of crime during a certain period. What is revealed is the familiar pattern of crime statistics in Western societies: a high prevalence of crimes against property, many crimes of violence, increasing road offenses, and relatively fewer sexual delicts and murders. Until recently, there were no acts of terrorism and very few incidents of kidnapping and hostage-taking.

With regard to the number of accused in criminal cases, several patterns are discernible: At the lowest level of court jurisdiction—police courts—the number of accused persons has increased since World War II. At the next highest level—the correctional court—the number of accused persons has remained about the same. The number of people prosecuted by the grand jury increased after World War II, but to a much smaller extent than for the first-level courts. The number of cases heard by appellate courts has increased at a rather constant rate, although the war interrupted the trend. The high court (Cassation) has followed the same pattern, with the increase of criminal cases more marked than that for civil cases.[28] When we look at convictions and new cases, two exceptions to ascending trends are revealed. The grand jury and the high court are less active.[29]

Because of the many possible interpretations of criminal statistics, one cannot flatly state that criminality has increased. Although the statistics point to an increasing activity of the administration of justice, it is necessary to recognize that the size and composition of the population have changed considerably. Moreover, certain factors have increased the propensity to denounce the law-breaker. The report of certain crimes against property, for example, is a condition favored by the insurance companies. In addition, one may not lose sight of the fact that the number of criminal justice agents has increased generally, although more in one category than in another.[30] Striking in the Belgian situation is the rather strong extension of the National Gendarmerie in the 1970s to eighteen thousand men[31] to produce one policeman per 295 inhabitants.[32] This rate is rather high compared to those of neighboring countries; it is only surpassed by France. Of course, staffing, and especially expansion of staff, influences the registration of criminality.

Finally, these figures must be interpreted within the context of a growing tendency to expand the area of application of Belgian penal law. This expansion is particularly striking in the areas of protection of the environment, protection of the consumer, price fixing, and social law. Punishments for aggressive and organized crimes against property have been made more severe. However, within these areas more and more possibilities have been created for handling matters with methods other than penal sentencing.[33]

EDUCATION AND OCCUPATION OF CRIMINOLOGISTS

Education in criminology at first was meant to be relevant training for criminal justice agents, especially for lawyers. The establishment of schools for criminology was felt to be necessary because training in criminology was considered to be the finishing touch in the education of criminal justice agents. Today there is more mistrust and skepticism about the actual type of education among the personnel of the justice establishment.

At this time, the institutions of higher learning no longer concentrate exclusively on the training of personnel of criminal justice agencies as a means of improving the quality of their performance of duties in regard to delinquent persons. Instead, some schools have taken a direction other than the preparation of practitioners for professional careers in fields of criminal justice administration. In academic models of a multi- or interdisciplinary character, students are prepared for scientific study and research, instruction in high schools and colleges, and public and private (welfare) administration—careers that are not necessarily in the administration of justice.[34]

In Belgium, criminology is often studied in combination with another academic specialization—law, sociology, psychology, pedagogy, medicine—or in addition to preparation for another career field, such as social worker and therapist. In Louvain it is possible to begin studies immediately after high school; in that case, the education takes four years (two "candidatures" and two "licenses").[35]

Students of criminology often specialize in sociology, psychology, law, or medicine. Graduates of special schools for higher education have access to the program of the "license" as well, through an entrance examination or through one preparative year of "candidature." Generally, this form of access concerns so-called A1 graduates (social workers, nurses, educators, assistant psychologists) and officers of the judiciary police, the municipal police, and the Gendarmerie.

It is striking that in the period 1920-1940 all the academic schools of criminology were established within the faculties of law of the universities. The legal orientation of the founders of these programs colored the choice of courses: penal law, penal procedure, a few additional law subjects, psychiatry, psychology, forensic medicine, juvenile delinquency, criminalistics, and criminology.[36] In examining these curricula now, it can be seen that the heavy emphasis on the law has disappeared and that they show significant differences. For one thing, the number of hours of lectures varies among the schools from 877 hours in Leuven to 660 in Gent.

Law and psychiatry were the central subjects when the programs were first established. They are still dominant at the Rijksuniversiteit van Gent, the Université Libre de Bruxelles, and the Vrije Universiteit te Brussel. The Rijksuniversiteit te Gent has a tradition of emphasizing education in and practice of legal medicine. The psychological approach is emphasized at the Université Catholique de Louvain-la-Neuve, whereas the sociological approach is most developed at the Katholieke Universiteit te Leuven. The Université de Liège has a major interest in general criminology and youth protection. The programs of the Université Catholique de Louvain, the Katholieke Universiteit te Leuven, and the Vrije Universiteit te Brussel provide a "probation term" (internship) in the field. The writing of a thesis has become obligatory at all academic schools.[37]

The officers of the Gendarmerie are awarded the degree of "licencié" in criminology only at the state schools of criminology of Gent and Liège. All officials of the Gendarmerie are obliged to study criminology after completing their education at the Royal Military School. They are not allowed to go to the Catholic or liberal universities.

The Brussels Ecole de Criminologie et de Police Scientifique (Ministry of Justice) offers a program at the intermediate level for all lower ranks of the police, the Gendarmerie, the Sûreté de l'Etat (State Security Service), and the Haute Comité de Surveillance (Higher Committee of Inspection). The advanced program is accessible to all police officers and magistrates. The School of Criminology and Scientific Police of Brussels was established as a unit of the Ministry of Justice. As far as organization and management are concerned, the high magistrates and officials of the higher judicial administration still have jurisdiction over this school. It is possible to get a diploma at this school, but its value is rather uncertain. In the advanced classes, people refuse to take examinations because there is little chance of valorization of the training. The school has had scanty development since it was established. Along with a few technical courses on criminal investigation, there are studies in criminal anthropology, psychiatry, and penal law. In general, the training has failed to keep up with recent knowledge.[38] This is difficult to understand because this school is the only institution where Belgian magistrates are educated. It may be noted in passing that the Belgian magistracy does not have a professional consensus; therefore, there is no universal opinion on criminal justice policy and professional matters.[39]

As far as employment is concerned, criminologists are considered for some vacancies at the Ministry of Justice, but it must be noted that many agents of justice have had no training in criminology, in fact no manner of specialized training at all. Within the frame of "youth defense" criminologists are considered for functions in borstals, as social workers at the juvenile courts, and as social workers employed by the Committee for Youth Defense. For probation or resocialization work, they can serve as assistants on guidance teams. In prison, they can have the function of director or of member of the staff. Moreover, they can be employed as officers in the judiciary police or as officials in central administration. Sometimes they are considered for provincial and municipal services. Some functions of the municipal police are accessible to criminologists, sometimes on the condition that they receive short additional training. Few criminologists have been employed in the private sector and in research. Finally, there are some vacancies for criminologists in high schools and colleges, especially if they have another academic degree.

HOW CRIMINOLOGISTS ASSOCIATE
WITH ONE ANOTHER

Established in 1966, the Belgian Association for Criminology has regularly organized conferences. In 1968, the Belgian Association started organizing congresses that are held every three years. The following themes have already been treated: 1971 (Leuven) methods for criminological research in prisons; 1974 (Liège) the Belgian system of the administration of justice: professions, functions, and policy; and 1977 (Gent) administration of justice and scientific research. The 1980 congress in Brussels examined the training of agents of the administration of justice.

These assemblies offer the opportunity for interaction among various categories of specialists, including practitioners and scientists. Because few of the real policymakers participate, however, these assemblies have little significance beyond the opportunities for discussion.

A few alumni associations in Gent, Louvain-la-Neuve, and Leuven regularly organize lectures, outings, and so on. So far they have not been oriented primarily to advancing professional and occupational interests.

Four years ago, the schools for criminology started meeting each other systematically. Standards for admitting students, uniformity in programs, and specialization in education are being especially discussed. In the future, the goal is to realize a better and more intense coordination between the schools concerning scientific research.

Periodicals provide a forum for exchange of information about the administration of justice, criminology, and forensic social work. Through them, systematic discussion and confrontation of opposing viewpoints become possible.[40] Unfortunately, the present Belgian journals do not meet these objectives. The *Revue de Droit Pénal et de Criminologie*, which was very famous in the past, is now almost completely controlled by lawyers. The *Bulletin der Strafinrichtingen— Revue Pénitentiaire* is nearly limited to discussions of problems of penitentiary administration.

As a consequence, most worthy works, especially those prepared in academic circles, are published in foreign reviews, especially Dutch journals such as *Delikt en Delinkwent, Tijdschrift voor Criminologie*, and the international *Déviance et Société*. At present, Belgium has no proper channel through which, in a systematic and continuous way, multidisciplinary ideas can flow from one administration of justice field to another.[41] Therefore, *Panoptican*, a new review, was undertaken in 1980 by the School of Criminology of Leuven, in collaboration with members of other universities and agencies, to fill the gap for the Dutch part of Belgium.

A few colloquia have been meritorious. In 1976 the topic, research on the police, was dealt with in Leuven. In 1979, a congress was organized on the subject of "dangerousness"; the occasion was the fiftieth anniversary of the School of Criminology at the Université Catholique de Louvain-la-Neuve. Finally, along with the congresses of the Belgian Association for Criminology, are the colloquia of the Centre d'Etudes de Délinquance Juvénile of Brussels which are held every two years on a topic related to youth protection.

The number of international contacts has increased during the last few years. There is participation in the traditional International Society for Criminology and a growing interest in the English-speaking European Group for the Study of Deviance and Social Control. The latter is the international meeting place of criminologists, lawyers, social scientists, and economists who concentrate on the processes of social control and on all forms of deviance-control. Belgian researchers also participate in the French-speaking Interlabo, a group of European criminological institutes that publish the review *Déviance et Société*, edited in Geneva.

LEVEL AND DIRECTION OF RESEARCH

Criminological research in Belgium is conducted mainly by the academic and para-academic institutions. The orientation of the research at those centers primarily follows the interactional approach. Only in the Penitentiare Orientatie Centrum—Centre d'Orientation Pénitentiaire (Brussels) and in the national centers is the etiological approach still important. The applied methods and techniques actually remain rather classic. Mostly, one makes use of attitude scales, statistics, and population censuses, structured interviews, direct observation, and analysis of documents and files. The more radical approach of institutional and historical analysis is employed in Leuven, but action research scarcely exists in Belgium.

Para-Academic Centers

The Penitentiaire Orientatie Centrum—Centre d'Orientation Pénitentiaire conducts some worthy research, although it still is inspired by an etiological criminology. The center is involved in continued routine research as well as in specific studies, for example, about homicide and training of prison-warders. The Gendarmerie organizes research but only in the operation of its own police system. The results are not published.

The National Centrum voor Criminologie is subsidized by the Ministry of Justice and therefore conducts research relevant to the ministry. In the past, its research team has had representatives of various disciplines, such as law, psychology, criminology, and sociology. The research has been almost exclusively in cooperation with the schools of criminology of the Brussels universities. A few publications have appeared, dealing with shoplifting, armed robbery, violence in prisons, and sexual assaults.[42]

The Studiecentrum voor Jeugdmisdadigheid—Centre d'Etude de la Délinquance Juvénile is also subsized by the Ministry of Justice. A multidisciplinary research team—composed of a psychologist, sociologist, criminologist, and lawyer—is able to approach the problems from various angles. The research is not restricted to juvenile delinquency, in spite of the name of the center. Indeed, the center has enlarged its scope to youth problems in general, juvenile institutions, and so on.[43] Since 1957, much research has been done with or without the cooperation of the universities. Moreover, this center has published some monographs, reports on workshops, and colloquia and research reports.

Research at Universities

In the last few years, scientific research has developed especially at the Department of Penal Law and Criminology of Leuven, although it is scarcely mentioned.[44] The research is interactional as well as structural and institutional in orientation, and is related to the following topics: principles for a fair administration of justice; decision-making of public defenders; unequal conditions of detention at the Central Prison of Leuven; problems concerning alcohol, administration of justice, and assistance; evaluation of the seriousness of juvenile delinquency; history of youth protection; history of the police system as a political institution; legal aspects of expertise and the problem of contest in the penal process; and psychosocial consequences of imprisonment.

Projects now under way are concerned with the following themes: alternatives for detention; public inspection agencies with police authority; the functioning of the municipal police; the making of practicing lawyers; influences of the school on the knowledge and opinion about criminality and administration of justice; and sentencing. Various working papers and research reports have been published.

The research at the School of Criminology of Louvain-la-Neuve has become famous through the publication of seventeen volumes of the *Cahiers de Criminologie et de Pathologie Sociale*. At the moment, in the prison of Namur, research is being conducted on the resocialization of inmates, as well as on special institutions for youth protection.

The School of Criminology of the Rijksuniversiteit van Gent has specialized in investigations of youth problems, forensic medicine, and toxicology.

The School of Criminology at Liège has organized research on penitentiary leaves and has a certain tradition of research on economic crime.

Problems for Researchers

In general, public policy in Belgium is not attuned to criminological research. The Ministry of Justice is concerned primarily with its own staff services, and, with justification, it may be asked whether this orientation is conducive to sound criminological research.

Research projects in Belgium have to settle a series of problems. Contacts with the judicial authorities are difficult for researchers seeking access to files and other data. These authorities have little interest in research and present many legal and other objections. With agencies other than those of criminal justice, contacts are less difficult. As indicated above, the official data suffer from inadequacies found throughout the world. Research is falling behind because financial support is diminishing.

The relationship between research and criminal justice policy is problematic because the impact of research on policy is nonexistent. Belgium's justice system continues to be sustained by "principles" and "doctrines," and not by the findings of research in the human sciences.

Some problems concerning administration of justice and criminology are beginning to be revealed, although not sufficiently, by the scientific research disseminated by the media. Nongovernmental research is increasing. A greater interest in criminology is indicated by the growing number of students. Finally, more international contacts are contributing to the growth of criminological research in Belgium, but teachers and researchers in Belgium continue to receive more esteem abroad than in their own country.

NOTES

1. R. J. Landman and Jac Van Weringh, "De Wereld van Aletrino" [The World of Aletrino], *Nederlands Tijdschrift voor Criminologie* (June 1977):133-144.

2. A. Aletrino, *Handleiding bij de studie der Criminele Anthropologie*, 2 delen. [Handbook for Study of Criminal Anthropology, 2 vols.] Amsterdam: Tierie en Kruyt, 1902-1904); L. Vervaeck, *La Théorie Lombrosiènne et L'Evolution de l'Anthropologie Criminelle* [The Lombrosian Theory and Evolution of Criminal Anthropology] (Brussels: 1910); and "Cours d'Anthropologie Criminelle et Notions de Psychiatrie élémentaire" [Courses in Criminal Anthropology and Notions of Psychiatry] in *Syllabus des cours du degré inférieur de l'Ecole de Criminologie et de Police Scientifique* [College Handbook of Middle Degree at the School of Criminology and Police Science] (Brussels: 1937).

3. *Revue de droit pénal et de criminologie*, no. 8 (1921):201.

4. E. Vandervelde, *Réalisations socialistes. Notre action d'après-guerre* [Socialist Realizations: Our Postwar Action] (Brussels: L'Eglantine, 1923), pp. 10-65.

5. L. Braffort, "Mémoire pour la fondation d'une Ecole des Sciences Criminelles à l'Université de Louvain" [In Commemoration of the Founding of the School of Criminal Sciences at the University of Louvain], in *Essai de contribution à l'evolution du droit pénal* [Essay on the Evolution of Penal Law] (Brussels: Ferdinand Larcier, 1929), pp. 7-63.

6. E. De Greaff, *Introduction à la Criminologie* [Introduction to Criminology], in *L'Ecrou* [Commitment to Prison] (Louvain: 1937), pp. 176ff.

7. P. Lieven, "Allocution à la Séance Académique du Cinquantenaire de l'Ecole de Criminologie de Louvain-là-Neuve" [Speech at the Academic Session on Occasion of the Fiftieth Anniversary of the School of Criminology of Louvain-la-Neuve], May 22, 1979, p. 3 (unpublished paper).

8. *Criminologie* [Criminology], brochure on the educational programs at the University of Louvain, Office of Student Advisement, Leuven, p. 2.

9. Mgr. Massaux, "Allocution à la Séance du Cinquantenaire de l'Ecole de Criminologie de Louvain-la-Neuve" [Speech at the Academic Session on Occasion of the Fiftieth Anniversary of the School of Criminology of Louvain-la-Neuve], May 22, 1979 (unpublished paper).

10. Lievens, "Speech at the Academic Session."

11. Braffort, "In Commemoration of the Founding."

12. Ch. Andersen, "National Chronicles: Belgium," *Annales Internationales de Criminologie* 1, no. 2 (1962):471-473.

13. Vandervelde, *Socialist Realizations: Our Postwar Action.*

14. Braffort, "In Commemoration of the Founding."

15. Ibid.

16. "Ouverture de l'Ecole des Sciences Criminologiques de l'Université de Bruxelles" [Opening Session of the School of Criminal Sciences at the University of Brussels], *Revue de droit pénal et de criminologie* (1936):1209-1219.

17. "Voorstel san de Rechtsfaculteit. Nota" [Proposal to the Faculty of Law. Note], Universiteit te Gent, December 19, 1936 (unpublished paper).

18. Ibid.

19. K. D. Clerck, "Veertig jaar School voor Criminologie aan de R.U.B. Uit het verleden van de R.U.G. door 'Lombrosiana' Oud-Studenten Criminologie R.U.G." [Forty Years of the School of Criminology of the University of Gent (RUG). The Past of the University of Gent by "Lombrosian" Old Students of the Department of Criminology of the University of Gent], *Archives of University of Gent* 3 (1978):5.

20. L. Huyse, "Sociologie" [Sociology], in *Handleiding biji de colleges* [Course Handbook] (Leuven: Acco, 1976), p. 85.

21. J. Billiet, "Secularization and Compartmentalization in the Belgian Educational System," *Social Compass* 20 (1973-1974):569-591. An analysis of the problems relevant to the revision of the school pact.

22. L. Van Outrive, *De Gevangenis: een systeem op drift* [The Prison: A System Out of Control] (Leuven: Davidsfonds, 1978), p. 33; G. Kellens, "National Chronicles: Belgium," *Annales Internationales de Criminologie* 12, 1-2 (1973):132.

23. Van Outrive, *The Prison: A System Out of Control*, p. 48.

24. *Studiecentrum voor Jeugdmisdadigheid* [Center for the Study of Juvenile Delin-

quency], brochure, Brussels, undated.

25. *Nationaal Centrum voor Criminologie. Nota* [National Center of Criminology. Note], Brussels.

26. Kellens, "National Chronicles: Belgium," p. 132.

27. T. Peters, *Criminografie voor een Interactionistische Criminologie* [Criminography: For an Interactionist Criminology] (Leuven: Acco, 1974), pp. 86-88.

28. E. Langerwerf and J. Van Houtte, *Sociografische gegevens voor de studie van het gerechtelijk systeem. Juristen, Activieeiten van Hoven en Rechtbanken* [Sociographical Facts for the Study of the Judicial System: Lawyers, Activities of the Courts] (Antwerp: Kluwer, 1977), pp. 60-66.

29. *Basistatistieken over de aktiviteiten van Hoven en Rechtbanken, Deel I, Jaarlijkse gegevens over burgerlijke en strafrechtbanken 1831-1969* [Basic Statistics of the Activities of Courts, Part I, Annual Figures on the Civil and Penal Courts] (Antwerpen: Centrum voor Rechtssociologie, Universitaire Faculteiten St. Ignatius, Department en Sociaal Beleid, 1977).

30. Langerwerf and Van Houtte, *Sociographical Facts for the Study of the Judicial System*, pp. 2-40.

31. L. Huyse, L. Van Outrive, C. Fijnaut, L. Dupont, and T. Peters, "Justitiebeleid in de jaren zeventig" [Administration of Justice in the Seventies], *Tijdschrift van het Belgisch Instituut voor Wetenschap der Politiek* 21, no. 2 (1979):343-369.

32. E. Perrick, "Taakaanbod en politiesterkte" [Tasks in Police Work], *Nederlands Tijdschrift voor Politie* 4 (October 10, 1979):552.

33. Huyse, et al., "Administration of Justice in the Seventies," pp. 360-361.

34. *Criminology*, brochure of University of Louvain, 17.

35. Ibid. and G. Kellens, "Note sur l'emploi des criminologues" [Note on the Activities of Criminologists] (unpublished paper).

36. See *Criminology*, brochure of University of Louvain, p. 17; Braffort, "In Commemoration of the Founding"; "Opening Session of the School of Criminal Sciences"; and De Clerck, "Forty Years of the School of Criminology."

37. T. Peters, *Nota. Een vergelijkende analyse van de programma's van de Schol en voor Criminologie R.U.G., U.L. B., U.C.L., U. Lg., K.U.L.* [A Comparative Analysis of the Programs of the Schools of Criminology: School of the Rijksuniversiteit van Gent, of Vrije Université Libre te Bruxelles, of Université Catholique de Louvain, of Université de Liège, and of Katholieke Universiteit van Leuven] (unpublished paper).

38. D. Quanten, "De School voor Criminologie en Criminalistiek als onderdeel van politieen justitiebeleid in de jaren twintig" [The School of Criminology and Scientific Police as a Part of Police Administration and Administration of Justice], thesis submitted in fulfillment of requirements for degree of Licentiate in Criminology (Leuven, September 1979).

39. A. Vandeplas, "Les organisations professionelles des magistrate belges" [The Professional Organizations of Belgian Magistrates], *Déviance et Société* 2, no. 4 (December 1978):388.

40. See Note 36.

41. "Panopticon," *Tijdschrift voor Strafrecht, Criminologie en Forensisch Welzijnswerk*, (June-July 1979):1-2.

42. *National Center of Criminology. Note.*

43. *Center for the Study of Juvenile Delinquency.*

44. Kellens, "National Chronicles: Belgium," pp. 129-134.

BIBLIOGRAPHY

Bosly, H. *Les sanctions en droit pénal social belge* [The Sanctions in Belgian Social Penal Law]. Gent-Leuven: Story-Scientia, 1979.
The author presents a very complete overview of the general principles of Belgian penal law; control of the applications of social legislation; the actions of the public prosecutor; competent jurisdiction; and the civil effects of penal repression. Finally, the book considers the application of social penal laws and the relationships between penal sanctions and administrative sanctions.

Boydens, J., J. Casselman, M. Decnop, et al. *Strafuitvoering in Close-up* [Penal Measures in Closeup]. Leuven: Acco, 1978.
This reader deals with the execution of prison sentences, the psychological effects of detention, the problems of incarcerating alcoholics, selective treatment, decision-making in provisionary liberation, probation, after-care, and penitentiary policy. Most chapters treat Belgian situations.

Dupont, L. *Beginselen van behoorlijke strafrechtsbedeling* [Principles of a Fair Administration of Justice]. Antwerpen: Kluwer, 1979.
This study of the fundamentals of penal law describes the history of normative theories of penal law, beginning with the *ratio more gemetrico* of the eighteenth century, through the *cahiers of doleances*, to the codification of penal law in the liberal state. Finally, the principles of penal law in the modern social state (Belgium) are analyzed.

Dupont, L., and T. Peters. *Hold-Up: beeldvorming en beleid* [Hold-Up: Image and Policy]. Leuven: Acco, 1975.
In examining the qualities of this crime, the authors also analyze the reactions of victims and the police. The Belgian judicial policy towards hold-ups is summarized and criticized.

Fijnaut, C. *Opdat de macht een toevlucht zij? Een historische studie van het politieapparaat als een politieke instelling* [That Power Is a Resource? A Historical Study of the Police Apparatus as a Political Institution]. Antwerpen-Deurne: Kluwer, Rechtswetenschappen, 1979.
The political history of the police apparatus is studied for Austria, France, Germany, Great Britain, and the Netherlands from the seventeenth century through the cold war period. Particular emphasis is placed on the description and analysis of the reorganization of various police systems in past centuries under the influence of wars, revolutions, and coups and how they were drastically overhauled—between the periods of repetitive changes of regimes—in order to deal with politically important disturbances and politically extremist groups. These analyses are intended to be the basis of a model to be constructed for the study of the political history of the Belgian police system.

Junger-Tas, J. *Verborgen Jeugddelinkewentie en gerechtelijke selektie. Een onderzoek in een stadsmilieu* [Dark Figure Juvenile Delinquency and Judicial Selection. A Research in an Urban Area]. Brussels: Studiecentrum voor Jeugdmisdadigheld, 1976.
First, the research report compares the "dark figure" (those crimes not visible to official agencies) with registered crimes and finds property crime normally distributed through the

youth population. Second, the causes of delinquent behavior are treated in regard to relationships with significant others, involvement in subsystems, and acceptance of generally preferred values and norms. Third, the following criteria of the selective processes of the administration of justice are examined: frequency and seriousness of delinquent acts, sex, race, class, and broken homes. Finally, the processes of prevention are discussed critically.

Kellens, G. "Crise économique et criminalité économique" [Economic Crisis and Economic Delinquency]. *L'année sociologique* 29 (1978):191-221.
First, the author synthesizes the present state of knowledge linking criminality and economic conditions. Next, he specifies the meanings of the terms "economic criminality" and "economic crisis." He describes as "statistical temptations" the efforts to correlate quantitatively these terms as variables. His preference is to examine the administration of justice generally and specifically as an element for understanding the social climate of a crisis. In studying the salient features of crisis-economic criminality, he recommends research into a new legitimacy of economic activities.

Lafinneur, G. *Police Communale, Gendarmerie, Police Judiciaire des parquets* [Municipal Police, National Police, Judicial Police of the Public Attorney]. UCA, Heule, 1979.
Legislation, jurisprudence, and doctrine are synthesized in this study of the three important components of Belgian police forces. The first part deals with the municipal and national police: their tasks, organization, recruitment, statutory dispositions, attributes, execution of duties, use of their competencies, and the consequences of irregular and delinquent behavior. The second part treats the judiciary police of the public prosecutor, who have only judicial and not administrative functions, in regard to the unique features of this kind of police work.

Lahaye, N. *L'outrage aux moeurs* [Outrage to Morals]. Brussels: Bruylandt, Centre National de Criminologie, 1980.
First, there is a phenomenological analysis of morals: the contingencies and limits of the approach, the terminological lags, the protected values, the variability of content, the unity or pluralism of the material facts, the intentional elements, and public opinion. The second part treats the evolution of the notion of "outrage to morals" in the law, in the sociocultural environment, in the doctrine of law, and in jurisprudence. The third part presents results of relevant public opinion surveys. After an overview of polls in Belgium and other countries, the author describes the results of her own sampling (N = 500) of magistrates and other groups of Belgians.

Ponsaers, P., and R. De Cuyper. *Arbeidsinspektie: overheidszaak of privé-aangelegenheid* [Labor-Inspectorate: Public Concern or Private Affair?]. Antwerpen: Kluwer, Interuniversitaire Reeks Criminologie en Strafwetwenschappen, 1980.
This book presents the preliminary findings of a larger investigation of police agencies specializing in the control of so-called economic crime. The first part is an inventory of those agencies in the Belgian central government that exist in addition to the traditional police units. Special attention is devoted to those regulating labor conditions and circumstances. The second part deals with the origins and development of the labor inspectorates, including a historic shift from the public to the private domain. The third part is

intended to reveal the consequences of the privatization of the control of labor in the course of an analysis of the functions of private and public control on production relationships. The general theoretical framework of the study is structural; Louis Althusser's views on the functions of the capitalist state are broadly discussed. An extensive introduction by L. Van Outrive and C. Fijnaut places the study generally within the criminological field and specifically within police research.

Walgrave, L. *Bescherming voorbij. Ontwerp voor een emanciperende jeugdkriminologie* [Beyond Protection. A Draft for an Emancipatory Criminology of Youth]. Antwerpen: Kluwer, Interuniversitaire Reeks Criminologie en Strafwetenschappen, 1980.
The etiological direction still dominant in the investigation of youth criminality is subjected to systematic criticism. Similarly, the classical model of judicial protection of youth is found unsatisfactory. The author argues for a more emancipatory approach to theory and practice that views deviance not primarily as a danger to society but rather as an opportunity for individual emancipation and as an element of societal renewal. The contributions of an emancipatory criminology of youth, it is said, are to point out the redundant forms of power in society and to seek theories and practices furthering individual and collective emancipation.

4

BRITAIN

Richard F. Sparks

This chapter describes the development of criminology in Great Britain[1] since the end of World War II. In order to provide background information, I begin with a brief description of the experience—the data base, if you will—from which the chapter is written.

Sent to England by the U.S. Air Force at the time of the Suez adventure, I remained there eighteen years, spending most of that time as a student, researcher, and teacher of criminology. I left England in 1974. Although, since then, I have tried to keep abreast of developments within the profession in England, my perspective on those developments has necessarily been that of an American criminologist. We all have our personal ideograms—pictures by means of which we interpret history, including our own. When I think of my years in English criminology, the pictures I see come from Robert Bresson's film *Un Condamné à Mort s'est Echappé*, which I first saw shortly after arriving in England in 1956.

I mention these biographical facts so that the reader can discount any traces of cynicism, which he or she may find in my account. While I believe there is much about British criminology since the late 1940s that can be criticized, I also think there is much to be commended. There are precisely the affinities that one might expect between British criminology of the past thirty years or so and American criminology on the one hand and criminology of the Nordic countries on the other. Both the strengths and the weaknesses (as I see them) of British criminology are related to the situation which Gibbons[2] has called the "criminological enterprise" within British society, and to the myriad changes that have taken place in that society in the last thirty years or so. Those years were characterized by the rapid, complex, and fascinating transformation not only of British society in general, but also of British scientific and educational institutions in particular. Crime, and the public's perception of "the crime problem," also changed during that period, although not necessarily in ways that any criminologist might predict. These changes necessarily affected the study of crime and of the criminal justice system in Britain.

MAIN TRENDS OF CRIME, 1945-1970

For reasons that will be given shortly, it is convenient to divide this account of criminology in postwar Britain into two periods: 1946-1970[3] and the 1970s. In dealing with the earlier years, I shall begin by briefly summarizing the main trends in crime and criminal policy in Britain. I shall then describe the organization of the teaching and research in criminology, and indicate some of the main themes with which researchers were concerned.

Section 77 of the Criminal Justice Act of 1948 authorized the home secretary to conduct, or support financially, research into "the causes of delinquency and the treatment of offenders, and matters connected therewith." But since very little research took place in the years immediately following this act, it is reasonable to begin the present chronicle somewhat later. For two reasons, the year 1955 is a suitable starting point. First, 1955 marked the beginning of a steady and virtually continuous upturn in recorded crime in Britain, which undoubtedly stimulated much government, academic, and even popular interest in criminology. Second, 1955 was the year which saw the publication of Mannheim and Wilkins's *Prediction Methods in Relation to Borstal Training*.[4] This work, one of the most influential books of its kind, in many ways marks a transition from "traditional" to "modern" criminal research in Britain.

In 1955, the police in England and Wales[5] recorded a total of 438,085 known indictable crimes. The crime rate had oscillated fairly regularly in the years since the end of the war, alternately rising and falling in two- to three-year periods. Halfway through the 1950s, the level of known indictable crimes was in fact slightly lower than it had been ten years previously. But in 1955 the graph turned upward, and known crimes rose steadily, at an average rate of about 8 percent a year. By 1970, according to *Criminal Statistics*, the total number of known indictable offenses recorded by the police had reached 1,555,995, that is, over three times the number recorded only fifteen years before. In addition, there were 970,598 persons found guilty of motoring offenses and 380,560 persons convicted of other nonindictable offenses in 1970. These figures represent increases of 139 percent and 208 percent, respectively, over 1955.

The general pattern of types of known indictable crime remained broadly the same over the years 1955-1970, with property crimes of various kinds making up over nine-tenths of the total. But in this period the number of recorded crimes of violence against the person grew at a much greater rate than that of all indictable offenses: the 41,088 violent crimes (of all kinds) recorded in 1970 represented an increase of about 450 percent over 1955, or an average annual increase of about 10 percent compound. Yet, within the broad and heterogeneous category of "violent crime," the bulk of the increase was in the less serious offenses of malicious wounding. The rates of murder and attempted murder, and of felonious (that is, more serious) woundings, were much more stable.[6]

It is far from clear, of course, how far the apparent rise in crime revealed by official statistics in this period was a real one. It is probable that, even now, only a small proportion of conventional crimes against both property and persons are actually recorded in police statistics in Britain. In 1973, together with my colleagues Hazel Genn and David Dodd, I carried out a victimization survey in three inner London areas. We found evidence that the volume of indictable crimes against individuals residing in those areas was over eleven times as great as police statistics suggested.[7] Given a "dark figure" of unrecorded crime of that magnitude, it is clear that only slight changes in the perception, definition, reporting, and recording of crime would be needed in order to account fully for the statistical increase of the years since 1955. Moreover, some account must be taken of the great increase in opportunities for crime in Britain in that period.

Even if the official criminal statistics of this period are accepted at face value, however, it is difficult to argue that crime was a major social problem in Britain in the years 1955-1970. I use the expression "major social problem" as it might be used by a Bethamite philanthropist trying to find the area of social life that would most benefit from his money. Of course, this concept is necessarily a vague one, and there is room for some dispute about the relative seriousness of social ills. But by any objective criteria that might reasonably be used to evaluate the seriousness of "social problems," it is plain in retrospect that crime would go far down the list. It would be well behind problems concerning unemployment, technological change, poverty, education, health, race relations, or the treatment of the aged, all of which were important postwar concerns of British society. In comparison to these problems, crime was really a nonissue. Nor was there much evidence of widespread public concern about crime in those years, though admittedly the subject was not much studied. Certainly, the level of public concern was nowhere as near as great in Britain as it was in the United States.

BRITISH CRIMINAL POLICY, 1945-1970

Given these facts, the statements made by the shapers of British criminal policy in this period may seem striking. In 1959, for example, an important White Paper on *Penal Practice in a Changing Society* began by remarking that "[i]t is a disquieting feature of our society that, in the years since the war, rising standards in material prosperity, education and social welfare have brought no decrease in the high crime rate reached during the war; on the contrary, crime has increased and is still increasing."[8] This fact, the White Paper continued, gave "cause for grave concern." The increase in offenses against persons and in convictions of young men aged sixteen to twenty-one were also said to be "disturbing."[9] Yet, at this time, the level of recorded indictable crime had been rising for only three years, and in the preceding three-year period the numbers had actually fallen by about 6 percent a year.

Five years later, another White Paper—*The War Against Crime in England and Wales, 1959-64*—took a similar view. While allowing that some of the apparent increase may have been due to improved reporting and recording of crime, it stated that "even so, the actual volume of crime has increased substantially."[10] There was, in fact, little evidence for this or any other claim about the "actual volume" of crime. Nonetheless, both of these White Papers, especially the first, announced substantial expenditures of public money on the police and the penal system. They set up government machinery for the continued revision of the criminal law and criminal procedure, and the review of penal methods.[11] Finally, as we shall see, they gave a strong impetus to criminological research in Britain. These steps were justified by the Home Office, in part, by a concern for "the moral health of the nation" which, though no doubt sincere, must, in retrospect, seem rather unrealistic.

Despite these official expressions of concern about crime, British criminal policy in the period went in a relatively liberal direction. Thus, suicide ceased to be a crime in 1961;[12] the definition of murder was narrowed somewhat in scope;[13] the legal test of insanity was supplemented by the wider concept of "diminished responsibility";[14] capital punishment was first restricted, then abolished;[15] the law on abortion was liberalized;[16] most acts of homosexual behavior between consenting adults in private were legalized;[17] most forms of gambling were legalized;[18] and the law on obscene publications was liberalized.[19]

Concurrently, substantial changes took place in many areas of the criminal justice system in Britain. To give but a few examples, there was a reorganization of the police in 1964, which saw a dramatic reduction in the number of separate police forces;[20] the Criminal Justice Act of 1967 introduced, among other things, the suspended sentence and parole for adult offenders;[21] and majority jury verdicts were introduced by the same statute, replacing the former requirement of unanimity. With regard to adult offenders, there was something of a retreat (no doubt more important symbolically than in terms of practical effects) from the notion of social defense which had been manifested in such things as preventive detention for habitual offenders.[22]

The situation concerning juvenile offenders was in marked contrast, however. During the years 1955-1970, there was continued pressure to deal with young offenders on some kind of "welfare" basis, thus abolishing or at least limiting the jurisdiction of juvenile courts. The most radical proposals of this kind were undoubtedly made by the Kilbrandon Committee in Scotland.[23] In England, the minimum "age of criminal responsibility" was raised from eight to ten in 1963. Then, in 1965, a White Paper advocated the complete abolition of the juvenile court and its replacement by a system of "family councils" and family courts.[24] While this proposal was dropped after extensive debate, a series of less extreme changes announced in another White Paper in 1968 were subsequently enacted by the Children and Young Persons Act of 1969.[25] In short, during the period under review, British criminal policy regarding juvenile offenders moved quite sharply away from judicial control toward a "welfare" orientation—at a time when the United States and some Nordic countries were moving in exactly the opposite direction.[26]

INVESTMENT IN CRIMINOLOGICAL RESEARCH, 1945-1970

Against this briefly sketched background of crime and criminal policy in the years 1955-1970, we may turn now to the history of criminology in Britain in that period. I have already noted that Parliament had authorized financial support for criminological research in 1948. The first grants under the 1948 act were made in 1951, but the total number of projects supported by the Home Office in the early years was small and had probably not exceeded twenty by 1961. The Home Office Research Unit, set up in 1957, has since that time administered grants to universities or other bodies under the 1948 act, as well as carrying out its own research (described in more detail in a later section of this chapter). By the mid-1960s, support for research at universities had increased to more than £80,000 a year; by 1970, no fewer than fifty-one separate research projects were being carried out by the Home Office Research Unit and the Home Office Statistical Division, with another forty-nine in progress at universities (including some on child care and race relations, which also fall within the purview of the Home Office).[27] By the early 1970s, total Home Office support for criminological research was in the neighborhood of £500,000 a year. In addition, there were substantial projects being supported by other agencies such as the Medical Research Council, the Social Science Research Council, and the National Foundation for Educational Research, as well as by private sources such as the Nuffield Foundation. In summary, within a period of fifteen years or so, there had been a substantial and increasing investment in criminological research in Britain.

This increase needs to be put into perspective, however. To begin with, the figures for expenditure given here (which were obtained from Home Office reports) are in current prices and so take no account of inflation—which, even in the years before 1970, was substantial. To some extent, too, the increase in expenditures on social research must reflect the increased cost of computing and electronic data processing in that period. In any case, it surely cannot be said that research on crime and the criminal justice system accounted, even by 1970, for more than a small fraction of the total amount government and nongovernment sources spent on social research. To take but one example, the Social Science Research Council, set up by the Science and Technology Act of 1965 to "encourage and support" research in the social sciences, had only supported a few small projects that related in any way to criminology during its first five years. Its largest field of activity was economics.

Finally, of course, the level of expenditure on research on crime and criminal justice in Britain in the years up to 1970 was minute in comparison to that in the

United States in that period. Comparisons of this kind are obviously very difficult to make sense of. Do we, for example, compare research expenditures in relation to gross national product per capita in the two countries? Yet, whatever the basis for comparison, in the years in question the level of expenditure on criminological research in Britain was not at all like that in the United States. In particular, the U.S. President's Commission on Law Enforcement and Administration of Justice, which reported in 1967, had probably commissioned far more research during the preceding two years than had been done in Britain during the whole of the twentieth century. A Royal Commission on the Penal System was set up in England in 1964. This commission, which self-destructed (without having produced a report) in 1966, actually did initiate some original criminological research, including a medium-sized survey of the adult population of England and Wales which included some questions on respondents' experiences of victimization.[28] This research was insignificant, however, compared to the small library of articles and research reports which the U.S. President's Commission produced at the same time.[29]

RESEARCH AND CRIMINAL POLICY

In part, of course, this difference reflects a basic difference in the two countries' social organization of social research in relation to social policy. In England, academic researchers have played, and still do play, a large part in formulating policy relating to crime and criminal justice through membership in the Parole Board, the Advisory Committee on the Penal System, the occasional Royal Commission, and the like. Analogous roles, though certainly not unheard of in the United States, are much less prevalent there. But social scientists in England are not usually paid for this kind of work; generally, the most that is offered is the promise of a knighthood or similar recognition. In contrast, in the United States, both federal and state governments and their agencies habitually commission criminologists and other social scientists to carry out research designed to produce data on which policies can be based.

It is not clear which country gets the best value for its money. On that ground alone, cost comparisons like those given above need to be treated with reserve.[30] But this points to a larger issue which the contributions to this volume may help to illuminate: which is the best method for using the knowledge obtained from research in criminology and other social sciences to inform social policy. Comparisons between Britain, the United States, and the Nordic countries would be especially illuminating in this respect.

A further point of interest is how important the expressed concern about crime in Britain (for example, in the 1959 and 1964 White Papers) was in justifying both the changes in the law and the increases in criminological research that took place in the years up to 1970. What would have happened, for example, if the level of recorded crime in Britain had remained constant, or had declined, in the years 1955-1970? Almost certainly, criminology would not have developed as rapidly as it did in those years. Yet, it may well be that things would also have been different in Britain if levels of recorded crime had risen even faster or had attained American levels. As mentioned earlier, English criminal policy in the postwar era moved in a relatively liberal direction. It is doubtful whether this trend would have developed if either Parliament or the general public had feared "crime in the streets." I shall return to this point below.

The 1959 White Paper pointed out that at that time there was not "any agency outside the Home Office which can keep the whole problem of crime under constant and critical survey; which can keep track of what is being done; and which can serve as a focus of constructive thinking about delinquency in all of its aspects." This was a reference to plans that were then afoot to set up the Institute of Criminology at Cambridge, which opened the following year. During the next decade, the Cambridge Institute was the only university department wholly devoted to research and teaching in criminology. A small Penal Research Unit was subsequently created at Oxford. Similarly, a Centre for Criminological Studies was created in the mid-1970s in the Law Faculty at the University of Sheffield, and a Department of Criminal Law and Criminology was created at the University of Edinburgh. There were, of course, several places—for example, the London School of Economics, part of London University—in which a number of people were engaged in teaching and research in criminology, even though formally housed in different university departments.

Even in this period of rapid expansion in the practice of academic criminology in Britain, its practitioners were relatively isolated. The general picture was of individuals carrying out research and teaching, very much on their own, within university departments or other institutions that were devoted primarily to other subjects. (As a rough indicator of this diversification, no fewer than twenty-six British universities and polytechnics were represented at the Fourth National Conference on Teaching and Research in Criminology, held in Cambridge in July 1970. The number of separate university departments involved was even greater.)

The academic orientation of the discipline during this period was even more diverse. As is well known, criminology has tended to be associated with law faculties in Continental Europe and with social science, especially sociology, faculties in American universities.[31] In England, criminology has been taught in both law and social science departments. At a rough estimate, by 1970, at least ten law departments in British universities offered criminology courses. A much larger number of departments of sociology or social administration taught courses in criminology, penology, and the sociology of crime and deviance. Some aspects of the subject were also taught, of course, in courses in psychology and psychiatry, especially in London. This last fact doubtless reflects the predominance of psychiatry and clinical psychology in the study of crime in Britain in the earlier years of this century: the influence of Cyril Burt, H. J. Eysenck, Peter Scott, and T.C.N. Gibbens was still evident in the period under review, for example, in the British Society of Criminology.

KINDS OF RESEARCH CONDUCTED, 1955-1970

Any short summary of fifteen years of research done by scholars as dispersed and heterogeneous as British criminologists is bound to be misleadingly oversimple. Nonetheless, the substantial number of projects done in the 1955-1970 period can be divided into five broad areas.

(1) *Descriptions of patterns of officially recorded crimes and officially defined criminals.* "Crime" and "criminals" can be linked together here, since many of the studies in this category dealt both with patterns of behavior and with the persons who displayed them. This is true, for example, of the Cambridge studies of sexual offenses and crimes of violence;[32] of the work by Hammond, West, and others on persistent offenders;[33] and of research such as that by Gibbens and Prince on shoplifting, West on murder-suicide, and Willett on motoring offenses.[34] Almost all of the studies in this group focus on crimes and criminals already defined as such by the police and the courts; most of the samples of offenders studied were drawn from penal institutions.[35] The term "description" also needs emphasis, since fact-finding in a broad sense of that term was the main object of most of these studies. Most were completely untheoretical.

(2) *Studies of the content and effectiveness of punishments and treatments.* In quantitative terms, this category is easily the largest of the five categories of British criminological research in this period. Although many of the studies done, both by the Home Office Research Unit and by academics, were relatively unsophisticated in design (control groups were seldom used and genuine experiments were unheard of), between them, they did amass a great deal of basic data on the subsequent conduct of offenders dealt with in different ways.[36] The general finding that there was little difference in outcomes probably contributed to the general disenchantment with the "rehabilitative ideal" which came in the next decade (and to which I shall return below).

(3) *Studies of prediction methods.* This research was to some extent a spin-off of that described in category 2. It deserves separate mention in part because of its methodological character and in part because so much of it was carried out. In Britain (as in California), the impetus for this kind of research, especially in the earlier years, came almost entirely from the pioneering work of Leslie Wilkins. The methodological impact of the original Mannheim-Wilkins study on subsequent research has clearly been enormous. The prediction methods thus developed had some operational use in the English penal system, but their main use was in estimating prior probabilities of recidivism, in connection with research on the effectiveness of penal measures.[37]

(4) *Studies of the regimes and organization of penal institutions.* In this category belong not only studies of prison and borstal regimes, but also a variety of smaller scale projects on inmate interaction and informal social systems; the inmate's (and his family's) experience of institutional treatment and its consequences; and a number of institutionally based projects done by the Home Office Research Unit and the Prison Department.[38]

(5) *Studies of decision-making by agents of the penal system.* Last but not least were a number of projects done in these early years of discretionary decision-making—by the courts in sentencing, as well as by the police and institutional bodies such as the Parole Board and the Preventive Detention Advisory Board. There were also a few studies on related topics such as the provision of information in relation to decision-making.[39]

The basis of this grouping is a purely quantitative one, with no element of evaluation. Moreover, while these five categories comprise the majority of empirical studies done in the years 1955-1970, they still leave out a good deal of important criminological research conducted in England in that period. Mention should be made, for example, of the ecological and subcultural work done by sociologists such as Mays, Morris, Downes, and Willmott; of studies of the police by Banton and Cain; and of the long-term cohort studies done by West and Farrington, and J.W.B. Douglas.[40]

The pragmatic character of the bulk of this research should be obvious: in this period, criminological research was regarded primarily as a weapon in the "war against crime." Less obvious from this brief summary is the profoundly untheoretical character of most of English criminological research during this period. There can be no doubt that this characteristic was largely due to the influence of Leon Radzinowicz, the first Wolfson Professor of Criminology and director of the Institute of Criminology at Cambridge. In his account of the history and present state of criminology, Radzinowicz asserted that "in the present state of knowledge, the very attempt to elucidate the causes of crime would be better put aside,"[41] and that is precisely what most British criminologists did. It was also true, however, that in the period in question the administrators responsible for supporting most of the research done in Britain simply had other priorities.

IMPACT OF NATIONAL DEVIANCY CONFERENCE

By the late 1960s, things were beginning to change, and they went on changing, with a vengeance, throughout most of the next decade. As noted earlier, crime had received relatively little attention from sociologists up to that time. The profession of sociology had grown exponentially in that period, as new universities were opened; there were forty chairs of sociology in 1967 compared with only one before the war. Yet, while there had been a few distinguished sociological contributions to criminology, these constituted only a tiny fraction of the output of the rapidly growing discipline.

It was partly in reaction to this relative professional neglect that a group of younger British sociologists founded the National Deviancy Conference (NDC), an organization that held a number of symposia on aspects of the sociology of deviance, most of them at York University. But the founders of the NDC had other motives as well. To begin with, the sociology of deviant behavior had become fashionable in the United States, as had the "labeling theory" espoused by American sociologists such as Howard Becker and Edwin Lemert. For reasons that in retrospect are difficult to understand, the writings of David Matza were also influential with the NDC group.[42] Then, too, there was a widely held feeling among that group that "establishment" criminology in Britain, as represented by the Home Office Research Unit and the Cambridge Institute, was too interested in "correcting" offenders rather than (as Matza had put it) "appreciating" them. I have already suggested that there was considerable justification for this feeling. I have also noted elsewhere that the NDC sociologists probably also felt that most of British criminology of the day was just plain boring.[43] I would add that there was substantial justification for that view too.

The NDC was by no means a purely academic group. On the contrary, its membership rapidly came to include a number of "radicalized" social workers, prisoners and ex-prisoners, trans-sexuals, and the like. At some of its symposia, the academic element was occasionally rather difficult to find among the plethora of self-confessed deviants and other amateurs eager for a chance to denounce "the system." A popular pastime in those heady days in the late 1960s was the advocacy of "radical" prison reform. There was much sympathy, and even a little support, in the NDC for the inmate organization known as PROP (Preservation of the Rights of Prisoners), which had recently been formed.[44] Perhaps because of their deliberately "oppositional" stance, few of those researchers associated with the NDC sought research support from the Home Office.[45]

Yet, those sociologists associated with the NDC, at least in its early days, did manage to create a valuable forum for a perspective on crime and the criminal justice system which, at that time, had been conspicuous by its absence in Britain. For the first time, not only the sociology of crime and deviance, but also the sociology of law, received the serious attention of able researchers.[46] The NDC group attained its greatest prominence in 1971, when the Annual Meeting of the British Sociological Association was devoted primarily to the sociology of deviance. A major speaker at one of the plenary sessions of these meetings was Howard Becker. Somewhat ironically, it was in this address that Becker conceded that some of his earlier notions about labeling theory had been mistaken.[47]

Despite its undeniable influence on British criminology, the NDC was shortly to experience serious internal conflicts. A schism began to develop in the early 1970s between those sociologists whose theoretical orientations were toward interactionist and other traditional sociological as opposed to criminological theories[48] (prominent examples included Stanley Cohen, David Downes, Paul Rock, Laurie Taylor, and Mary McIntosh) and those who, presumably determined to "outradicalize" their colleagues, eventually declared themselves to be Marxist criminologists. The most prominent representatives of this second group were Ian Taylor, Paul Walton, and Jock Young, whose book *The New Criminology* was published in 1973.

I will not repeat here the criticisms that I and others have made of contemporary British and American "Marxist" criminology.[49] It is sufficient to note that the work of Taylor, Walton, and Young and others of this school had a tremendous impact on the teaching of criminology in both Britain and the United States during the 1970s. Whatever the theoretical shortcomings of this group's work may be, it did introduce into Britain's academic criminology a number of ideas and points of view that were completely ignored in the earlier period. No matter that part of the motivation of the group may have been a desire to *épater* the Cambridge and Whitehall *bourgeoisie*. One result of the intellectual ferment they helped create was an undoubted broadening of the subject matter of academic criminology in Britain in the 1970s.[50]

It would be most premature to attempt to assess the impact, even in the short term, of the academic turmoil in British criminology. Indeed, perhaps "turmoil" is not the right word. It is not, after all, as if the "pragmatic" types in Cambridge and elsewhere had been taken out and shot. Predictably, there has been some reaction against the "Marxist" criminology popularized by Taylor, Walton, and Young—not least from some of those sociologists, founders of the NDC, who continue to approach the study of crime and deviance from within more traditional (many would say, better founded) theoretical perspectives.[51] At this point I would also remind the reader that my own perspective is a relatively distant one. It is difficult, at least in the near term, to assess the effect of such intellectual changes without witnessing and hearing about them on a face-to-face and day-to-day basis.[52] Yet, it seems clear that British criminology has been greatly enriched by the events of the past decade. The skeptical reader is invited to test this claim by comparing a random sample of books and articles by British criminologists of the 1950s with a similar sample drawn two decades later. A brief list of sources for this exercise is given in the bibliography at the end of this chapter.

"MAINSTREAM" CRIMINOLOGY: ALIVE AND WELL

The events just described were not the only important ones in the development of criminology in Great Britain in the past decade. On the contrary, what may be called "mainstream" criminology is still alive and well in that country, though it, too, has changed, for a variety of reasons in addition to the stimuli provided by the sociology of the 1960s. In part, some of these changes reflect nothing more profound than the passage of time. The older order has been replaced by a newer one which, in criminology as in other sciences, including social sciences, is better trained and possessed of a bigger stock of knowledge, including that produced by its immediate predecessors. In part, however, the changes in "mainstream" (that is, non-Marxist, non-phenomenological, and so on) British criminology are due to changes in the levels and patterns of crime and the criminal justice system which have taken place during the past decade.

Two changes, one of them ideological and the other distressingly practical, seem of particular importance. On the one hand, the past few years have witnessed the development of a near-total disillusionment with the "rehabilitative ideal" which dominated British penology following the publication of the Gladstone Report in 1895. Of course, there had been a good deal of skepticism about this "ideal" even earlier, partly as a result of the research findings to which I have already referred, which seemed to show that none of the available "treatments" for offenders was much better or worse than any other. The disillusionment seems to have spread with increasing rapidity in the last three or four years, however. It is now difficult to find a British criminologist who is prepared to adhere to the "treatment model," at least without substantial qualifications and reservations.[53]

Two aspects of this ideological change are important. The first is that empirically it means considerable dismantling of established practices, including obtaining vast amounts of information on convicted offenders in order to prepare presentence investigations and recruiting prison staff under the pretense that they are to be "change agents" rather than mere turnkeys, a notion that is probably immensely useful in screening out the more florid sadists, psychopaths, and imbeciles among those who tend to apply for jobs in prison services throughout the world. A shift away from the pious hypocrisy that correctional systems aim to provide moral "treatment" and pure happiness means a drastic alteration of the rhetoric by which those who actually do the thankless work of the criminal justice system justify (to themselves and others) the ways in which they earn their daily bread. This can in turn entail not only radical reorganization of the content of those persons' work, but also changes in recruitment, selection, training, and measures of successful job performance. It may even entail the dismemberment of entire subsystems, such as the probation service, which in Britain has been under attack in recent years.[54]

WHAT ALTERNATIVE TO "REHABILITATION"?

The second aspect of the ideological change is that this disillusion with "rehabilitation" has been a little late in coming in comparison with the United States and the Nordic countries. (As noted earlier, in the case of juveniles both the English and Scottish systems were moving toward a "welfare" approach, at the same time that American and Nordic systems were abolishing that approach in favor of more justice for children.) The problem raised by the collapse of so long established an ideology, however, is that, in this case, at least, *there is nothing handy to put in its place.* That is, there is little by way of well-articulated philosophy or principle that can guide the reorganization of the criminal justice system in the wake of the abandonment of the "rehabilitative ideal." I would not wish to suggest that the theoretical and philosophical alternatives to rehabilitation so far proffered by American thinkers are as clear or cogent as they might be. This drastic change in social policy has entailed many issues, which have probably not been been adequately dealt with in any country, if indeed they have been clearly perceived at all. Yet, in the past six or seven years, American legal theorists, criminologists, and philosophers have made numerous attempts to deal with these problems. In contrast, my impression from a reading of the British literature on this topic is that until very recently there has been a reluctance even to recognize the existence of these problems.[55]

It is important to emphasize that these problems are philosophical or theoretical rather than practical. As always, changes in penal practice are likely to have a marginal or incremental impact rather than a drastic one. A strong case can be made for saying that the effects of the "rehabilitative ideal" have in fact been very slight, both in Britain and elsewhere, for some time now. As it happens, the history of British penal practice furnishes a striking analogue here, where the notion of crime prevention through incapacitation of "dangerous" offenders is concerned. Lip service was paid to the worth of this damnable piece of oppression, beginning with its introduction, through the sentence of "preventive detention," by the Prevention of Crime Act, 1907. Yet, it was clear almost immediately that this measure—whatever its impeccable credentials in "positivist" criminology— was almost never used and, when used, permitted the incapacitation of incompetent petty criminals rather than the arch-fiends for whom it was devised.

The demise of this penological monstrosity in the mid-1960s was largely the result of two of the kinds of empirical research which I catalogued in the preceding section of this chapter: (1) the studies by Hammond and Chayen, West, and others demonstrating the extent to which the law was in practical desuetude; and (2) the research on prediction methods showing the virtual impossibility of identifying potentially dangerous offenders with an acceptable degree of precision.[56] It is striking, however, that the policy reformulations offered (for example, in the reports of the Advisory Council on the Penal System, and similar bodies) were both simplistic and confused in their analysis of the issues involved and the costs and benefits of various options for their resolution.[57]

There is danger of a similar situation now, as the more general problems of replacing a penal system aimed at "treatment" are confronted in Britain (and, to be fair, in other countries in which such a change seems in the offing). The issues have been discussed in a number of recent writings by British criminologists; most of them, of course, are a part of the liberal "mainstream" so excoriated by the NDC and its Marxist offspring. Even so, it does not seem that a satisfactory resolution of those issues is yet in sight.[58] It is precisely here, in the clarification of issues, the impartial analysis of evidence, and a historically informed reflection upon the range of possible solutions, that academic criminologists should make an important contribution to the complex process of formulating public policy.

Even at the beginning of the period with which this paper is concerned, several criminologists in Britain, including Hermann Mannheim, Radzinowicz, and the late Max Grünhut, were thoroughly familiar with the intricately argued and voluminous debates that characterized *politique criminelle* in Continental countries from about 1870 onward. Most of the problems now confronting the criminal justice system of Great Britain and other Western countries were at least identified, if not solved, in that corpus of writing. But none of that body of social and political theory seems to have received any attention in Britain, perhaps because of the peculiar "pragmatic" tradition of social reform found in Britain and perhaps for other reasons.[59]

The "distressingly practical" change referred to above concerns the drastic overburdening of the resources of the English penal system which has taken place in the past few years. By 1980, the prison population in England stood at about 42,000, compared with 11,000 before World War II. In contrast to what appears to have happened in many jurisdictions in the United States, this increase was not the result of an increase in the average length of sentence. Nor was it the result of an increase in the use of imprisonment by the courts. Actually, the average prison term in Britain declined during the 1970s; so, too, did the probability of imprisonment, in part because new forms of noncustodial sentences were introduced. (In fact, the prison population in England and Wales had passed the 40,000 mark in 1970; the increase in the succeeding decade was thus less than the system had experienced in the years since 1955.[60]) The primary cause of the continued increase, from 1955 onward, was the increase in the number of adults convicted.

Nonetheless, the consequences of this increase have been grave. Not only is the prison system itself overcrowded, but also the resources of the probation and after-care services, which are also responsible for parole supervision, are badly strained. These facts have led many criminologists and many of those in government charged with the administration of the criminal justice system in Britain to talk of a "coming penal crisis."[61] The response to this talk may be rephrased: the penal crisis has already arrived.

THE KEY ROLE OF THE HOME OFFICE

Contributors to this volume were asked by the editor to address a number of questions concerning the organization, context, and training associated with the "criminological enterprise" in the country under review. In the section, I shall try to address those questions on which I have not already touched and to describe some central facts about the organization of the profession of criminology in contemporary Britain.

As I observed earlier, until about 1970, criminology in Britain was characterized by the relative isolation of its practitioners. With the exception of the Cambridge Institute, it consisted mostly of one or two people teaching a course or two. Graduate programs were subsequently established at the universities of Keele, Sheffield, and Edinburgh. With these exceptions, anyone wishing to undertake graduate-level training or research at the doctoral level had to do so in a university department (for example, of sociology) which was not primarily oriented to the study of crime and criminal justice.[62]

So far as academic criminology is concerned, this pattern still seems to obtain. Any account of criminology in Great Britain must take into account the role of the Home Office Research Unit, especially the way the unit has developed over the past decade. Although it was officially created in 1957, the unit had only a small number of professional staff during its first ten years. After that, however, it grew steadily. The report on its research program for fiscal year 1979-1980 lists a total of no less than forty-two professional staff members, which was about equal to (if not indeed greater than) the total number of persons holding comparable positions and engaged in criminological research in all of the universities in Britain in that year. Certainly, it was greater than the total number of university teachers in Britain whose teaching and research interests were primarily in criminology. The Home Office Research Unit is thus the most important single locus of research on crime and the criminal justice system in Great Britain today and thus the primary job opportunity for someone aspiring to do research in this field. In other words, if you are told that a person is earning his living by engaging in research on crime in Britain at the present day, you probably would have at least an even-money bet that that person was in the employ of the agency of central government charged with the prevention and control of crime and the treatment of offenders.[63]

One can of course "be a criminologist" without doing any research, or at least not much research, or research of the kind that costs money. Nor am I suggesting that research should be the criminologist's only activity. On the contrary, one role of the profession involves the communication of knowledge about crime and kindred phenomena, not only through the higher education of those whose professional or occupational careers will be concerned with other things, but also directly to what some book and magazine publishers pompously call the "enlightened general public."[64]

To the extent that being a criminologist means or implies carrying out scientific research on crime, the Home Office Research Unit clearly occupies a central role in criminology. The unit's perceptions of research are of great importance to the "criminological enterprise." Those perceptions are necessarily influenced by the statutory mandate under which the unit operates. That mandate necessitates that the research conducted, or supported, by the unit should have at least some relevance for criminal policy. This notion of "relevance" has not, in practice, been construed narrowly, at least in recent years. Those in charge of the Research Unit's activities, particularly I. J. Croft, who has been head of the unit since 1972, are well aware of the complex association between "research" and "policy" in relation to crime and criminal justice.[65] Moreover, there are good grounds for thinking that the views of the NDC sociologists, which regarded the whole of the criminological establishment in Britain as monolithically "correctionalist" in its attitude toward research, are and always were a gross oversimplification.

First, however, I describe the work of the Research Unit. It involves both a program of in-house research, and the administration of grants and contracts to externally based researchers, almost all of whom are in British universities.[66] The budget figures which I quoted earlier in this chapter suggest that, even in the earlier years, the in-house component of the Research Unit's program bulked rather larger than its support for external research. This has continued to be the case. The report on the Research Unit's program for fiscal 1979-1980 estimated that a total of £868,000 would be spent on internal research in that year, as compared with £334,000 for external research supported by grants. When estimating the proportions of Home Office financial support allocated to internal and external research, these relative magnitudes, like those quoted earlier, need to be treated with caution. The internal figures include some overhead costs and some salaries that are borne by universities in the case of external research.[67] The 1979-1980 figures show that the internal research done by the unit has grown at a much more rapid rate over the past decade than the external research which the Home Office supports. The internal figure is over three times its 1971 counterpart, whereas that for external research is only a little over twice as large.[68]

The tangible output of the Research Unit's internal research program has been impressive. At the time of this writing (early 1982), a total of over eighty-five research reports had been published by Her Majesty's Stationery Office, for the Home Office, in which the results of in-house research by members of the unit's staff were described.[69] In addition, members of the unit staff have contributed about 150 articles to professional journals since 1957.[70] It is probably fair to say that in the unit's early years, its research was primarily descriptive and narrowly focused. Thus, it had little importance in terms of its contribution to the wider body of criminological knowledge.[71]

By the middle 1970s, however, a notable change became evident in the focus of the work of the unit's staff, as judged by the titles of its reports as well as by their content. As would be expected, much of this work still focuses on the workings of the criminal justice system, notably on the evaluation of various penal measures (compensation orders, junior attendance centers, and so on), and on penological topics such as absconding from institutions, the operation of the Parole Board, and the "careers" of prisoners serving life sentences. But the unit's in-house research has broadened to include such things as opportunity structures in relation to crime, the possible roles of the police in relation to crime prevention, and the position of ethnic minorities in Britain.[72] Moreover, the internal research done by unit staff members has long since ceased to be done in a vacuum, as if theory and research produced by academics in Britain and elsewhere did not exist. On the contrary, the research reports and articles produced by Research Unit members consistently show a high degree of professionalism in the sense of methodological skill and sophistication, and awareness of relevant theoretical and empirical work done by criminologists in British universities and elsewhere in the Western World.

Reasonable persons may reasonably disagree about the value of research of this kind, even if it displays the high technical quality which the internal work produced by the Research Unit has shown in recent years. Would it not in some sense be better to show that capitalism inevitably destroys Christianity, which in turn promotes crime, or to describe in intricate detail the theoretical implications of inadvertent erotic thoughts in a nudist colony?[73] Perhaps so, but criminologists in Britain have never thought that way. The traditions of the subject in that country seem always to have been firmly rooted in a humane determination to minimize the social problems of crime and the criminal justice system. From the kind of external research lately supported by the Home Office, it seems evident that this does not entail a narrow-minded "correctionalist" view of what criminology may legitimately be about. For example, the 1979-1980 program description from which I have already quoted indicates that support is to be given to external projects dealing with irregular payments obtained under the agricultural support scheme of the European Economic Community, the attitudes of black youth toward social and statutory agencies, arranged marriages among immigrants, and the ways in which visual and voice identifications of suspects are made. Those topics may be policy-relevant, but they are not as narrow as some critics have made the Research Unit's perspective seem.[74]

Moreover, the Home Office, at least in recent years, has not taken a partisan or uncritical view of the rest of the machinery of social control in Britain. It has not accepted without question the perceptions of those in authority of what "the crime problem" really is. To give but one example: I have lately been informed[75] that in the near future, a national survey of criminal victimization will be conducted in Britain in which a sample of about 30,000 persons will be interviewed on their experiences of victimization, perceptions of crime, and life-styles, among other things. This survey, if carried out, will almost certainly find much evidence that discredits the *Criminal Statistics* which the Home Office compiles and publishes each year. Since 1895, this publication has formed the sole basis of official estimates of the state of crime in England and Wales.[76] By way of analogy, one might imagine the Federal Bureau of Investigation in the United States planning research that would similarly discredit the *Uniform Crime Reports* which that agency has used in the past fifty years to justify its annual budgetary appropriations. Those unfamiliar with the FBI might prefer to imagine first that pigs will fly.

CONCLUSIONS: EFFECTS OF GREAT CHANGES

Criminology in Britain has obviously undergone great changes in the past twenty-five years. The profession has expanded rapidly, and the character of research and teaching has changed significantly from that of the immediate postwar years.

The central element in this growth and change has clearly been the support given to criminological research by the Home Office, under the provisions of the Criminal Justice Act of 1948. This support led to the development of a government research organization—the Home Office Research Unit—as well as the funding of most of the research done in British universities in the period. There has been an increasing recognition of the importance of research for policy-making in relation to criminal justice, and of the complex interrelations between research and policy. There has also been a recognition of the difficulties of carrying out research in a university setting that will be relevant for decision-making purposes. The proper lines of demarcation between "internal" and "external" research are slowly being drawn.

In this respect, the British experience may provide an instructive contrast to that of other countries described in this text. In the United States, for example, there has been massive federal support for research on crime and criminal justice, but very little in-house research has been done like that performed by the Home Office Research Unit. By contrast, in Finland, most criminological research is done in the Research Institute of Legal Policy (formerly called the Institute of Criminology). Very little is carried out in universities.[77] Other chapters in this work will no doubt illustrate other models.

In academic terms, there has also been much change in British criminology, though much less, perhaps, than might have been expected in the circumstances. British criminology still remains predominantly eclectic, pragmatic, and multi-disciplinary. It has no dominant intellectual orientation and is virtually unconcerned with explanatory theory. The hopes of the founders of the National Deviancy Conference that the study of crime might be brought nearer to the mainstream of sociology seem not to have materialized to any great degree. (This is not to say that there has been no progress in this direction. For example, the sociological research on crime in relation to work done by Mars, McIntosh, Henry, Mack, Ditton, and Levi is equal to the best research on that subject that has been done anywhere.[78])

It is doubtful that the next twenty-five years will see the same amount of expansion and change in British criminology as have taken place in the last twenty-five. Current levels of crime, as well as the pressing problems that currently confront the penal system in Britain, seem likely to persist for at least the near future, however. The criminological profession in Britain is much better qualified to provide an understanding of those problems than before, even if it cannot provide solutions to them. It may also be that their work will in future have a greater influence on the thinking of criminologists in other countries than it has so far.

NOTES

1. Including Scotland as well as England and Wales. However, as will be seen, much of what is described refers specifically to England. It should be borne in mind that in some respects Scotland needs to be considered separately, for example, where certain legislative and administrative matters relating to crime are concerned.

2. Don M. Gibbons, *The Criminological Enterprise* (Englewood Cliffs, N.J.: Prentice-

Hall, 1979). Another useful historical account is Leon Radzinowicz, *In Search of Criminology* (London: Heinemann, 1961).

3. Portions of this section are based on my paper "Crime, Criminal Policy and Criminology, 1955-70," presented at the first British/Nordic Research Seminar in Criminology in Oslo in 1971.

4. Hermann Mannheim and Leslie T. Wilkins, *Prediction Methods in Relation to Borstal Training*, Studies in the Causes of Delinquency and the Treatment of Offenders No. 1 (London: Her Majesty's Stationery Office, 1955). Further developments in criminological prediction are critiqued in Frances Simon, *Prediction Methods in Criminology Including a Prediction Study of Young Men on Probation*, Home Office Research Study No. 7 (London: Her Majesty's Stationery Office, 1971). In more recent years the impact of the same methodology can be seen in the development in several U.S. jurisdictions of sentencing guidelines. See L. T. Wilkins et al., *Sentencing Guidelines: Structuring Judicial Discretion. Final Report of the Feasibility Study* (Washington, D.C.: U.S. Government Printing Office, 1976). Wilkins is one of the very few British criminologists whose work has had this kind of transatlantic influence.

5. For a detailed description of crime trends in Britain to 1965, see F. H. McClintock and N. H. Avison, *Crime in England and Wales* (London: Heinemann, 1968). Comparisons with later years are complicated by legislative changes, for example, in 1968; for a discussion see the *Criminal Statistics* for 1969.

6. McClintock and Avison, *Crime in England and Wales*. But on the changes in the law of homicide on the murder rate, cf. Andrew Ashworth, "A Short Note on the English Murder Rate," *Criminal Law Review* (December 1969): 645-653.

7. R. F. Sparks, Hazel G. Genn, and David J. Dodd, *Surveying Victims: A Study of the Measurement of Criminal Victimization, Perceptions of Crime and Attitudes to Criminal Justice* (London: John Wiley, 1977). Further developments in victimization surveying in Britain are described in a later section.

8. Cmnd. 645, para. 1.

9. Ibid., paras. 3-4.

10. Cmnd. 2296 (1964), para. 7.

11. These included the Criminal Law Revision Committee and the Advisory Council (later Advisory Committee) on the Penal System. For an account of later developments, see John Croft, *Crime and Comparative Research*, Home Office Research Study No. 44 (London: Her Majesty's Stationery Office, 1979).

12. Suicide Act, 1961.

13. Homicide Act, 1957, s. 1. An invaluable background reference to this statute is the *Report of the Royal Commission on Capital Punishment, 1949-1953* (Cmnd. 8932).

14. Homicide Act, 1957, s. 2. For data on the operation of this section, see E. Gibson and S. Klein, *Murder 1957 to 1968. A Home Office Statistical Division Report on Murder in England and Wales*, Home Office Research Study No. 3 (London: Her Majesty's Stationery Office, 1968), and R. F. Sparks, "'Diminished Responsibility' in Theory and Practice," *Modern Law Review* 27 (January 1964): 9-33, but note that the author now regards the latter paper as conceptually muddled on some points.

15. Homicide Act, 1957; and Murder (Abolition of Death Penalty) Act, 1965. The latter statute was made permanent by a resolution of Parliament on December 31, 1968. It seems likely to remain permanent, even given the "law'n'order" platform of the present Conservative government.

16. Abortion Act, 1967, s. 1.

17. Sexual Offenses Act, 1967.

18. By the Betting, Gaming and Lotteries Acts of 1960 and 1963. However, these laws led to such a substantial increase in gambling that more restrictive legislation, limiting the number of gaming clubs and setting up a board of control, was later passed: the Gaming Act, 1968.

19. Obscene Publications Act, 1959. A judicial reaction was the revival of the ancient offense of "conspiring to corrupt public morality": *Shaw v. Director of Public Prosecutions* (1962) A.C. 220. This issue inspired extensive debate; see, for example, H.L.A. Hart, *Law, Liberty and Morality* (Oxford: Oxford University Press, 1968); and Patrick Devlin, *The Enforcement of Morals* (Oxford: Oxford University Press, 1970).

20. Police Act, 1964.

21. The early effects of this statute were counterproductive; see Sparks, "Crime, Criminal Policy and Criminology, 1955-1970."

22. Criminal Justice Act, 1967. A similar measure, with more restrictive conditions, was introduced by the same law, but this measure (known as the "extended sentence") has been even less used. This matter is discussed further below.

23. *Report of the Committee on Children and Young Persons* (Scotland), 1964: Cmnd. 2306; and see the Social Work (Scotland) Act, 1968.

24. *The Child, the Family and the Young Offender*, Cmnd. 2742.

25. For the background to this statute, see the White Paper *Children in Trouble*, Cmnd. 3601 (1968).

26. In the United States, since the case of *In re Gault* (1966); for the situation in the Nordic countries, see Inkere Anttila, "Conservative and Radical Criminal Policy in the Nordic Countries," in Nils Christie (ed.), *Scandinavian Studies in Criminology*, Vol. 3 (London: Tavistock, 1971).

27. However, there were fairly substantial year-to-year fluctuations. In 1971, for example, the figures were forty-nine projects being done in the Home Office and only twenty-two at universities. In later years, the position has been more stable; see the next section of this chapter.

28. Mary Durant, Margaret Thomas, and H. D. Willcock, *Crime, Criminals and the Law* (London: Her Majesty's Stationery Office, 1972), report some findings of this research.

29. However, the British situation seems to have improved in recent years. A recent Royal Commission on Criminal Procedure commissioned (and got) no less than nine volumes of research in the course of its deliberations. See Croft, *Crime and Comparative Research*.

30. This issue is further discussed below. In Britain, much fact-finding for policy purposes is done by a government agency (the Home Office Research Unit) which has no analogue in the United States.

31. Leon Radzinowicz, *In Search of Criminology* (London: Heinemann, 1961). There appears to be no analogue in Britain of schools of "criminal justice" now found in the United States.

32. Leon Radzinowicz, *Sex Offenses* (London: Macmillan, 1956); F. H. McClintock and Evelyn Gibson, *Robbery in London* (London: Macmillan, 1961); and F. H. McClintock, *Crimes of Violence* (London: Macmillan, 1963).

33. W. H. Hammond and Edna Chayen, *Persistent Criminals: A Study of All Offenders Liable to Preventive Detention in 1956*, Studies in the Causes of Delinquency and the Treatment of Offenders No. 5 (London: Her Majesty's Stationery Office, 1963); D. J. West, *The Habitual Prisoner* (London: Macmillan, 1963).

34. T.C.N. Gibbens and Joyce Prince, *Shoplifting* (London: Institute for the Study and Treatment of Delinquency, 1962); D. J. West, *Murder Followed by Suicide* (London: Heinemann, 1965); T. Willett, *Criminal on the Road* (London: Tavistock, 1964).

35. See, for example, T.C.N. Gibbens, *Psychiatric Studies of Borstal Lads* (London: Tavistock, 1963); D. J. West, *The Habitual Prisoner* (London: Macmillan, 1963); R. G. Andry, *The Short-Term Prisoner* (London: Tavistock, 1962); and John Mack, "Full-Time Miscreants, Delinquent Neighborhoods, and Criminal Networks," *British Journal of Sociology* 15 (March 1964):38-53.

36. For a full review and critique of this research, see Simon, *Prediction Methods in Criminology*.

37. As was the case with the Base Expectancy Scores developed in California by Leslie T. Wilkins and Don M. Gottfredson. For a recent and comprehensive assessment, see Michael R. Gottfredson and Don M. Gottfredson, *Prediction in Criminal Justice* (Cambridge, Mass.: Ballinger, 1980).

38. The Prison Department of the Home Office has (or at least had, during the period under review) its own research staff, most of whom carried out research on the regimes of various institutions as well as assessments of inmates. Research of this kind was also carried out by the Home Office Research Unit, as well as by academic researchers. See, for example, Nancy Goodman and Jean Price, *Studies of Female Offenders*, Studies in the Causes of Delinquency and Treatment of Offenders No. 11 (London: Her Majesty's Stationery Office, 1967); Terence Morris and Pauline Morris, *Pentonville* (London: Routledge and Kegan Paul, 1963).

39. For example, Hammond and Chayen, *Persistent Criminals*; R. G. Hood, *Sentencing in Magistrates' Courts* (London: Stevens, 1962); and on the use of information, L. T. Wilkins and Ann Chandler, "Confidence and Competence in Decision Making," *British Journal of Criminology* 5 (January 1965):22-35.

40. John Barron Mays, *Growing Up in the City* (Longon: Macmillan, 1954); Terence Morris, *The Criminal Area* (London: Routledge and Kegan Paul, 1958); David M. Downes, *The Delinquent Solution* (London: Routledge and Kegan Paul, 1966); Peter Willmott, *Adolescent Boys in East London* (London: Tavistock, 1966); D. J. West, *Present Conduct and Future Delinquency* (London: Heinemann, 1969); J.W.B. Douglas, et al., "Delinquency and Social Class," *British Journal of Criminology* 6 (July 1966):294-315; Michael Banton, *The Policeman and the Community* (New York: Basic Books, 1964); Maureen E. Cain, *Society and the Policeman's Role* (London: Routledge and Kegan Paul, 1973); David P. Farrington and D. J. West, "A Comparison Between Early Delinquents and Young Aggressives," *British Journal of Criminology* 11 (October 1971):341-358; David P. Farrington, "Self-Reports on Deviant Behavior: Predictive and Stable?" *Journal of Criminal Law and Criminology* 64 (March 1973):99-110.

41. Radzinowicz, *In Search of Criminology*; a somewhat different view—roughly that causal studies are a kind of middle-class spectator sport—was at one time expressed by Radzinowicz's successor as Wolfson Professor, Nigel Walker, *Crime and Punishment in Britain*, 2d ed. (Edinburgh: Edinburgh University Press, 1968).

42. In particular, David Matza, *Becoming Delinquent* (Englewood Cliffs, N.J.: Prentice-Hall, 1969). Matza had spent a year in England at about this time, and it seems fair to say that his personal influence on the NDC founders was considerable.

43. See R. F. Sparks, "A Critique of Marxist Criminology," in Norval Morris and Michael Tonry (eds.), *Crime and Justice: An Annual Review of Research*, Vol. 2 (Chicago: University of Chicago Press, 1980), for a somewhat more detailed history of the

NDC. See also Stanley Cohen, "Criminology and the Sociology of Deviance in Britain," paper presented at the 1981 Annual Meeting of the British Sociological Association, London (mimeo). Subsequently, the paper was published in Paul Rock and Mary McIntosh (eds.), *Deviance and Social Control* (London: Tavistock, 1974), pp. 1-40.

44. I do not know if this organization still exists. It drew in part on the Scandinavian prison reform organizations and on the writings of Thomas Mathisen, *The Defenses of the Weak: A Study of a Norwegian Correctional Institution* (London: Tavistock, 1965), among others. See also Stanley Cohen and Laurie Taylor, *Psychological Survival* (Harmondsworth, Middlesex: Penguin Books, 1972).

45. It may also be, however, that most of this group distrusted large-scale quantitative research because it was thought to be too "positivistic." Many American studies of deviance, of course, use ethnography and participant-observation.

46. See, for example, W. G. Carson, "White-Collar Crime and the Enforcement of Factory Legislation," *British Journal of Criminology* 10 (October 1970):383-398; and W. G. Carson and P.N.P. Wiles, *The Sociology of Crime and Delinquency in Britain* (London: Martin Robertson, 1974).

47. This address is reprinted in Howard S. Becker, *Outsiders: Studies in the Sociology of Deviance* (New York: Free Press, 1973). Compare the earlier statement in the 1963 edition of his book.

48. See the papers in David Downes and Paul Rock (eds.), *Deviant Interpretations* (London: Martin Robertson, 1979), for example.

49. Sparks, "A Critique of Marxist Criminology." See also David Greenberg, *Crime and Capitalism* (Palo Alto, Calif.: Mayfield Press, 1980), for a much more careful statement of Marxist theories, and a critique of earlier versions including that of Ian Taylor, Paul Walton, and Jock Young, *The New Criminology* (London: Routledge and Kegan Paul, 1973); and Ian Taylor, Paul Walton, and Jock Young (eds.), *Critical Criminology* (London: Routledge and Kegan Paul, 1975).

50. Of particular importance was the emphasis many Marxist criminologists placed on historical studies. The works of E. P. Thompson, *Whigs and Hunters: The Origins of the Black Act* (New York: Pantheon Books, 1973), and Douglas Hay et al., *Albion's Fatal Tree: Crime and Society in Eighteenth-Century England* (New York: Pantheon Books, 1975), are also highly relevant here.

51. Downes and Rock, *Deviant Interpretations*; Mary McIntosh, *The Organization of Crime* (London: Macmillan, 1975).

52. Although British criminologists rarely attend professional meetings in the United States, they seem to have done so rather more frequently in recent years. Perhaps this itself is a symptom of something apart from cheaper transatlantic air fares.

53. See, for example, Nigel Walker, "Release by Executive Discretion: A Defense," *Criminal Law Review* (October 1975):540-544; Nigel Walker, *Treatment and Justice in Penology and Psychiatry* (Edinburgh: Edinburgh University Press, 1976); and the discussion by Anthony Bottoms, "Introduction," to A. E. Bottoms and R. H. Preston (eds.), *The Coming Penal Crisis* (Edinburgh: Scottish Academic Press, 1979). Hood's views seem more representative of recent thought in Britain on this subject; see R. R. Hood, "Some Fundamental Dilemmas of the English Parole System and a Suggestion for an Alternative Structure," in D. A. Thomas (ed.), *Parole: Its Implications for the Criminal Justice and Penal Systems* (Cambridge: University of Cambridge Institute of Criminology, 1974), and R. G. Hood, *Tolerance and the Tariff: Some Reflections on Fixing the*

Time Prisoners Spend in Custody, NACRO papers and Reprints No. 11 (London: National Association for the Care and Resettlement of Offenders, 1974).

54. See Ken Pease, "The Future of the Community Treatment of Offenders in Britain," in Bottoms and Preston, *The Coming Penal Crisis*.

55. Or to understand what the problems are. For a striking example of noncomprehension in recent American writings on this subject, see L. Radzinowicz and R. G. Hood, "The American Volte-Face in Sentencing Thought and Practice," in R. G. Hood (ed.), *Crime, Proof and Punishment: Essays in Memory of Sir Rupert Cross* (Oxford: Oxford University Press, 1979).

56. Hammond and Chayen, *Persistent Criminals*; D. J. West, *Who Becomes Delinquent?* (London: Heinemann, 1973); and on the prediction problem, see Simon, *Prediction Methods in Criminology*. Many of the same findings and the same points had been made much earlier in Britain by Norval Morris, *The Habitual Criminal* (London: Oxford University Press, 1948).

57. See, for example, the White Paper on *The Adult Offender* (Cmnd. 2852 of 1965); and the report of the Advisory Council on the Penal System on Preventive Detention (1964).

58. The paper by Bottoms, "Introduction," in *The Coming Penal Crisis*, presents the clearest statement of what the problems are by any contemporary British criminologist. But even Bottoms states no convincing solutions. He is not alone in this failure, of course; the solutions adopted in many American jurisdictions are far from satisfactory. For an overview, see Andrew von Hirsch and Katherine Hanrahan, *Abolish Parole?* (Cambridge, Mass.: Ballinger, 1980).

59. Indeed, both Max Grünhut, *Penal Reform* (Oxford: Oxford University Press, 1948), and Radzinowicz, *In Search of Criminology*, went out of their way to deride Continental *politique criminelle*, treating it as "conceptualism" or worse. Radzinowicz's views were influential in the Advisory Council report cited in note 58 above.

60. See R. F. Sparks, *Local Prisons and the Crises in the English Penal System* (London: Heinemann, 1971), for a discussion of earlier years.

61. Bottoms and Preston, *The Coming Penal Crisis*, use this phrase, indicating that it is now commonly heard. Variants of it have appeared, of course, in many White Papers over the past thirty years.

62. I am informed by Dr. R. W. Burnham, formerly Reader in Criminology at Keele, that the M.A. program there has been abolished and the one at Sheffield substantially reduced since 1981.

63. I have not included in this head-count those persons employed in research work in British penal institutions (prisons, borstals, and so on). These, too, are, of course, the responsibility of the Home Office.

64. This phrase was often heard, for example, at *The Economist* newspaper when I was a member of its editorial staff in the late 1950s. I am not using it cynically. The dissemination of criminological knowledge to the general public is not something that most criminologists (in Britain or anywhere else) know much about.

65. See, for example, John Croft, *Crime and Comparative Research*, Home Office Research Study No. 57 (London: Her Majesty's Stationery Office, 1979); Croft, *Research and Criminal Policy*, Home Office Research Bulletin No. 10 (1978).

66. Research institutes, either nonprofit or for-profit, are much rarer in Britain than in the United States.

67. There is no such thing in Britain as the "nine-month contract" which American professors commonly have, enabling them to make extra money from their research during the summer months. Universities in Britain are state institutions, so that they are expected to absorb many overhead expenses that are necessarily directly budgeted for and included in the Home Office "internal" figures.

68. Again, the increase in real terms is difficult to calculate; inflation reached as high as 18 percent in the late 1970s.

69. Information on these and other Home Office publications is given in the bibliography at the end of this chapter.

70. An estimate based on data in Croft, *Research and Criminal Policy.*

71. An exception is Mannheim and Wilkins, *Prediction Methods.*

72. See, for example, R.V.G. Clarke, *Tackling Vandalism*, Home Office Research Study No. 47 (London: Her Majesty's Stationery Office, 1978); P. Mayhew, et al., *Crime in Public View*, Home Office Research Study No. 49 (London: Her Majesty's Stationery Office, 1979); John Burrows, et al., *Crime Prevention and the Police*, Home Office Research Study No. 55 (London: Her Majesty's Home Office, 1979); Phillip Stevens and Carole F. Willis, *Race, Crime and Arrests*, Home Office Research Study No. 58 (London: Her Majesty's Home Office, 1979).

73. I take the first of these topics to be the theme of Richard Quinney, *Class, State and Crime*, 2d ed. (New York: Longmans, 1980), although I may be mistaken. The second is illustrated by the writings of Martin Weinberg, "The Nudist Management of Respectability," in Jack D. Douglas (ed.), *Deviance and Respectability* (New York: Basic Books, 1970).

74. There is now a special unit within the Home Office which reviews criminal justice policy and its relation to research. See Croft, *Research and Criminal Policy.* For an earlier statement of critics of the Home Office's definition of research, see Cohen, "Criminology and Sociology of Deviance in Britain."

75. By I. J. Croft and Dr. R.V.G. Clarke of the Home Office, in a personal communication. Another source (who must be nameless) informs me that, ironically, cabinet-level approval for the funding of the victimization survey would probably not have been forthcoming, except for the riots that took place in several British cities in 1981!

76. And of almost all of the research described in this paper; see, for example, McClintock and Avison, *Crime in England and Wales.*

77. Inkere Anttila, "A Report from Finland," in the Home Office Research Unit *Research Bulletin*, No. 6 (1978), p. 19.

78. Gerald Mars, "Dock Pilferage," in Rock and McIntosh, *Deviance and Control*; Jason Ditton, *Part-Time Crime: An Ethnography of Fiddling and Pilferage* (London: Macmillan, 1977); Stuart Henry, *The Hidden Economy* (London: Martin Robertson, 1978); Mary McIntosh, "Changes in the Social Organization of Theft," in S. Cohen (ed.), *Images of Deviance* (Harmondsworth, Middlesex: Penguin Books, 1971); Mary McIntosh, *The Organization of Crime* (London: Macmillan, 1975); John Mack, *The Crime Industry* (London: Saxon House, 1975); Mack, "Full-Time Miscreants"; Michael Levi, *The Phantom Capitalists: The Organization and Control of Long-Term Fraud* (London: Heinemann Educational Books, 1981).

BIBLIOGRAPHY

The literature on criminology in Britain, although not even remotely as large as that of the United States, is nonetheless substantial and diverse. Inevitably, the relative accessibility of American books and learned journals to British scholars had an impact, especially in the earlier years of the period reviewed above, not only on teaching and research in criminology but also on the volume and quality of writing on the subject. There is still no British criminology textbook of the stature of those written by Sutherland and Cressey and other American authors. However, within the past decade or so, there has developed a solid and still-growing British professional literature on crime, deviance, and social control. The short list of works given below is intended to provide no more than a broad overview of contemporary British writing on these topics, giving as little regard as possible to my own interests and prejudices. Although I have naturally had to be selective, I hope that I have not been unfairly so.

The main professional journal is the *British Journal of Criminology* (formerly the *British Journal of Delinquency*), published by Sweet and Maxwell in London. It should be noted, however, that a fair proportion (roughly half) of the articles, research reports, and book reviews that appear in this journal are by non-British authors. Criminological articles also appear with some frequency in the *British Journal of Sociology* and in *Sociology* (the journal of the British Sociological Association), as well as in professional journals in fields such as psychiatry. Among legal periodicals, the *Criminal Law Review* contains many articles of criminological interest, especially on topics relating to sentencing, criminal policy, and proposed criminal legislation.

In addition to the large volume of official reports of advisory committees, Royal commissions, and other government agencies (such as the Prison Department of the Home Office), official publications on criminological topics are numerous. The annual *Criminal Statistics* (collated and published by the Home Office, from data recorded by police forces throughout England and Wales) is of high quality, as are many of the other statistical series relating to crime and the penal system.

In addition, as noted earlier, the Home Office Research Unit publishes a large number of research reports and bulletins describing its in-house research and projects carried out at universities, and so on, which it funds. Between 1955 and 1969, thirteen reports were published in the series of Studies in the Causes of Delinquency and the Treatment of Offenders. Although a few of these are now out of print, photostat copies can be obtained. In 1969, these reports became known as Home Office Research Studies; since that time, over seventy further reports, most of them describing research by the unit's staff, have appeared. (All of these reports can be obtained from government bookshops throughout Britain or from overseas agents in many countries. They may also be obtained directly by writing to the London address of Her Majesty's Stationery Office: The Government Bookshop, P.O. Box 569, London, SE1 9NH.) Finally, a small number of Research and Planning Unit Papers can be obtained from the Research and Planning Unit, Information Section, 50 Queen Anne's Gate, London, SW1H 9AT, as can the *Research Bulletin* published twice a year. The *Research Bulletin* consists mainly of short articles describing the unit's work, new research grants, and the like.

Here is a small, nonrandom sample of contemporary books on criminological topics, written by British authors.

Bottomley, A. K., *Decisions in the Penal Process*. London: Martin Robertson, 1973.
    This work is a systematic summary of the available evidence, from British and other research, on discretionary decision-making in connection with arrest, prosecution, sentencing, parole release, and other points in the criminal justice process.

Cross, Rupert. *The English Sentencing System*. 2d ed. London: Butterworth, 1975.

Cross presents an overview of the principles governing sentencing in Britain in recent years. His work should be read in conjunction with David Thomas's book cited below.

Downes, David, and Paul Rock. *Deviant Interpretations*. London: Martin Robertson, 1979.
This collection of papers by a number of English sociologists deals with a variety of issues in deviance theory. It is written mostly from an interactionist perspective that is somewhat critical of recent "critical" criminologists.

Eysenck, H. J. *Crime and Personality*. London: Paladin, 1971.
The author applies his theories of clinical psychology to problems of personality development and criminal behavior. The work is a stalking-horse for many other British theorists.

McClintock, F. H., and N. J. Avison. *Crime in England and Wales*. London: Heinemann Educational Books, 1968.
The authors present a thoroughgoing description of patterns of crime, based on police statistics of "crimes known." The work provides a sort of benchmark for the more recent history of crime in Britain.

Mack, John. *The Crime Industry*. London: Saxon House, 1975.
This collection of writings is by one of the leading British writers on "professional" crime.

McIntosh, Mary. *The Organization of Crime*. London: Macmillan, 1975.
This short but incisive analysis of the forms of criminal organization is based on extensive historical data. It contains an excellent bibliography.

Rock, Paul. *Deviant Behavior*. London: Hutchinson, 1973.
Rock provides an introduction to contemporary sociological theorizing about deviance and crime, including critiques of British and non-British writers.

Rock, Paul, and Mary McIntosh. *Deviance and Social Control*. London: Tavistock, 1974.
This collection of papers was originally presented to the meetings of the British Sociological Association in 1971.

Taylor, Ian, Paul Walton, and Jock Young. *The New Criminology*. London: Routledge and Kegan Paul, 1973.
As well as being the sourcebook of many students' understanding of contemporary "Marxist" criminology in Britain and elsewhere, this book contains a detailed, if sometimes tendentious, critique of almost every other criminological theory imaginable.

Thomas, David. *Principles of Sentencing*. 2d ed. London: Heinemann, 1979.
Thomas presents a thoroughgoing analysis of the decisions, in appeals against sentences in the higher courts, of the Court of Appeal (Criminal Division). His book is the starting-point for those who want an understanding of the distinctive techniques of control of discretion in sentencing used in Britain.

Walker, Nigel. *Crime and Punishment in Britain.* 2d ed. Edinburgh: Edinburgh University Press, 1968.

Walker, the present Wolfson Professor of Criminology at Cambridge University, has written the closest thing to a textbook in contemporary British criminology.

5

PEOPLE'S REPUBLIC OF CHINA

James P. Brady

The general rationale of this handbook is nowhere better confirmed than in the People's Republic of China. The criminological phenomena and reactions to them operate within the contours of a sociocultural and political system. The analysis below is necessarily wide ranging in attempting to grasp criminology and legal policy at their contemporary economic and historical roots. The examination of those roots in the People's Republic provides opportunities for criminologists to compare the evolution and operation of a criminal justice system in the sociocultural and political system most familiar to them. Here is a distinctive alternative to the common assumption that Western Europe and North America afford the exclusive model for international criminology.

WILL THE REAL CRIMINOLOGIST STAND UP?

Searching out criminology in the People's Republic of China is no simple task. Western criminologists must locate and deal with the clues that, properly assembled, indicate what their field of investigation and action is in a context that differs markedly from that of their own country. We must also disregard the *wrong* clues. This can be particularly difficult when confronting the great mass of Western political propaganda that has often passed for journalism and scholarship in accounts of the People's Republic since the end of World War II.

The clues that we have seem outdated and unconvincing. It is not only that we are so distant from the Orient and from its very different traditions of law, academy, and government. It is also that, for decades now, we have been fed little more than caricatures about that country. From 1949 until the Richard Nixon visit of 1972, "Red China" was insistently portrayed as an outlaw state with totalitarian government, Maoist hate for social theory, and terror and brainwashing in a system of social control and corrections. Since the blooming of China's unofficial alliance with the West, China has been "rehabilitated" in the American media. It is now described as a hard-working and friendly nation, with a government striving toward industrial progress and legal modernization. Cold war politics cultivated an almost incredible public ignorance and confusion about China.

Given this general situation, it is hardly surprising that most criminologists in the West know almost nothing about the largest and most active criminal justice system in the world. Even those who look beyond media portrayals to study more detailed materials on China will encounter difficulties. The literature compiled by our comparative law scholars reads rather like an encyclopedia of mirrors. It reveals more about the loyalties and assumptions of Western "experts" than the actual basis of policy and research in China.[1] The Chinese themselves have provided only a few short-lived law codes, constitutions, fragmentary crime statistics, sporadic professional publications, and terse descriptions of legal institutions and research facilities which have been frequently reorganized, abolished, and resurrected. (See the Bibliography at the end of this chapter.)

The three decades of socialism since 1949 have been marked by sharp conflicts in virtually every aspect of culture, politics, and production, but nowhere have controversies raged more intensely than around the institutions of justice and the learned academy. Although the present Peking leadership now informs us that it has (since 1976) erected a permanent new legal system and social science establishment, it would be foolish indeed to accept these rather Westernized arrangements as final. Rather than describe the current situation in misleadingly static terms, it seems more useful to identify the contending forces and ideas that have so enlivened justice, socio-policy, legal theory, and research over the stormy course of China's socialist transformation.[2]

TERMINOLOGY AND CONTRADICTION: CAUTIONS FOR THE WESTERN READER

The following discussion describes in brief the Chinese cultural context and is of necessity broadly sociological and historical in scope, since it must correct our layered misunderstandings. The main body of the chapter considers in some detail the specifics of crime, justice, and "criminology" in the People's Republic. First, however, there is need of some preliminary observations on terminology in order to highlight important nuances of language and to avoid some of the traps of ethnocentricism.

Linguists have well demonstrated that language both reflects and structures each conception of the world. In the West, the title "criminologist" identifies one as ostensibly a scientist, guided by rational dictates in the study of what is adjudicated as criminal under law. In recent years, theorists of conflict or Marxist persuasion have challenged the legalism and value-free pretensions of traditional criminology. They point to its implicit political conservatism and insist that the invisible issues of class and power are central to an understanding of crime and justice. Nevertheless, the dubious claims to "objective detachment" in research continue, and positivism remains entrenched in nearly every aspect of justice planning and administration.[3]

It is quite significant that the Chinese have no equivalent to the term "criminology" in their language. Instead, they use the words *"cheng fa"* which are best translated as "political legal." Police officers, judges, lawyers, justice planners, law professors, and research scientists are all described as political legal specialists or "cadre." Justice bureaus, such as courts or police stations, as well as specialized training or research facilities, are all considered to be political legal institutions. The juxtaposition of these two concepts *cheng* (political) and *fa* (legal) does most accurately convey the Chinese conception of this field as one of dynamic duality. Political issues such as class, power, and ideology are explicitly addressed alongside the more technical questions of law, social control, and administration.

The fusion of politics and law in the Chinese terminology provides some clue to the intense conflicts that have so strained justice policy and often disrupted the careers of those whom we might (rather incorrectly) describe as criminologists. One effect of political contest over the direction of government and economy (which will be discussed later) has been to blur the lines of responsibility between trained legal specialists, other political authorities, and volunteer activists in community organizations. The degree of special expertise deemed necessary to make arrests, judge cases, and prepare research varies greatly, depending in no small way on the current lineup of competing forces and ideologies. A "political legal" scholar, official, or institution may draw its legitimacy and guidance from either legal statutes or ideological principles, or both.

The definition of crime likewise varies from overt acts proscribed by criminal laws to general attitudes that violate widely recognized (but uncodified) political ethics. The object of justice may be individual offenders, entire social classes, or deviant thought patterns themselves. The role of justice has shifted between a legalistic protection of the social order and a highly politicized concern for social justice and egalitarian reform.

UNCERTAINTY OF "CRIMINOLOGIST" AS OCCUPATION

Legal scholars and teachers may work in universities and specialized institutions, or they may be "sent down" (*hsia fang*) into the villages and factories to engage in manual labor and learn about conflict resolution through practical experience at the grass roots. Sociological theory and commentary on justice policy may be carried in academic law journals or in newspapers and pamphlets or even "wall posters" on the streets. Finally, the political legal scholars and officials, as well as the institutions of law and justice, have themselves been targets of sometimes violent political struggle, with dramatic demotions and advancements following in rapid succession.

These almost dizzying reversals make political legal affairs an unsettling occupation both for the Chinese practitioner and for observers in the West. There are, however, recognizable reference points that make sense out of the twisting course of justice policy and legal scholarship. But these points are found in a reading of the political economic contradictions that lie behind the conflicts over jurisdiction, professional roles, and social theory. The connections between political legal policy or scholarship and conflicts over modernization economics and ideology are the central theme of this chapter, to which reference will be made again and again.

Such an integrated analysis of justice, academy, and political economy is not, however, common in Western writings on China. Most of our "experts" are lawyers who teach comparative law courses at a handful of elite law schools in the United States and Europe. They have generally interpreted the instability of Chinese justice and the uneven growth of legal scholarship and professionalism there as an indication of underdevelopment or totalitarianism. Such characterizations are essentially syllogisms, resting on the unexamined assumption that the Western capitalist mode is the *sine qua non* of justice and modern social science. While our comparative law specialists have contributed much detailed information, they have in many cases also contributed to the general misunderstanding of China. Elsewhere the evolution of Western writings is described as "three generalizations of scholarly misunderstanding."[4] Space limitations preclude a serious critique here, save to note that in the evolution from cold warriors to legalists to functionalists our scholars have come closer to a sensitive and less ethnocentric view of Chinese justice.[5]

SOCIALIST TRANSFORMATION AND POLITICAL CONTEST

Chairman Mao used to say that the Chinese people emerged from the Liberation Victory of 1949 as "a people poor and blank." Certainly the widespread famine, primitive agriculture, and miniscule industrial base left China the poorest of nations; economic modernization has been the constant aim of the socialist government. The central question has been, of course, how best to proceed toward national development, and in this area of political economic theory the Chinese were certainly not "blank" even in 1949.

Indeed, not one but two sets of ideological principles have emerged over the stormy process of China's socialist transformation. One cannot read very far in the story of modern China before encountering mention of the "two-line struggle." This central conflict has set the weaving course of political legal affairs, along with virtually every other social institution. These ideologies are known by many names in Chinese and Western literature, but here they are termed the revolutionary and the revisionist lines to call attention to their social consequences and the relationship to the Maoist heritage.

The revolutionary line and its leading adherents developed over three eras of sweeping social reforms and powerful mass movements: the Civil War (1927-1949), the Great Leap Forward (1957-1961), and the Cultural Revolution (1966-1968).

During the long Civil War, the communists formed a shadow government and organized the peasants for class struggle (against the landlords) and defense (against the Japanese and the Kuomintang dictatorship).[6] The Great Leap Forward pressed collectivization in the rural areas, attempting to improve peasant opportunities by bringing industry, technology, and higher education down to the village level in the countryside.[7] The Cultural Revolution was set chiefly in urban zones where the administration of schools, factories, and government was challenged and reorganized along more egalitarian and participatory lines.[8]

The revolutionary line rests on three key principles: the "mass line" in political leadership, the "continuing revolution" in social development, and "red and expert" for the role of educated specialists. The mass line was created as a means of galvanizing peasant support during the Civil War, and in the emphasis on volunteer citizen activism within strong community organizations it continues both to assist and to counterbalance the government bureaucracy. Virtually the entire adult population is involved in these mass organizations, which include trade unions, agricultural communes and cooperatives, urban neighborhood committees, the national women's association, and the communist youth league.

The mass line requires that officials, party members, and administrators work closely with these grass roots associations, consult with them in decision-making, and avoid elitist or bureaucratic leadership styles.[9] The continuing revolution calls for ongoing reforms to eliminate the feudal cultural influences and to close gaps in wages and prestige between city and rural zones, workers and farmers, mental and manual laborers, men and women. Finally, the principle of red and expert demands that those with higher education develop their specialized skills while foreswearing material privileges and elevated status.[10] Political leaders, administrators, and intellectuals are required to submit to public examination and criticism in the periodic rectification campaigns that have repeatedly mobilized the populace to challenge corruption and elitism.[11]

The competing revisionist line can be traced back to three different historic periods: postwar Reconstruction (1949-1956), recovery from the failures of the Great Leap Forward (1961-1965), and the Thermidorean Reaction to the Cultural Revolution (1976-present). During the Reconstruction era, Soviet advisers were most influential in educating Chinese specialists and in pointing Chinese planning in the Soviet direction of sharp material and political stratification. In the mid-1960s, the excessive dislocations of the Great Leap Forward prompted a reassessment of radical reforms, a restoration of material incentives, and more centralized decision-making.[12] Since Mao's death, the conservatives of the Communist party and government have mounted a third and by far most powerful push, resulting in steeper wage scales, more rigid hierarchies of authority, and a reduced role for community organizations vis-à-vis the strengthened bureaucracy.

The ideas and policies advocated by the right have been fairly consistent, although advanced with more boldness at each resurgence. Initially, conservatives such as Liu Shao Chi[13] justified their policies with selected excerpts from Mao's (generally radical) writings. In most recent years, Teng Hsiao Ping and others have begun to cite what they call "the objective laws of socialist development."[14] The new conservatives are pledged to rapid modernization through the most expedient concentration of available capital and technology, even if this causes rural zones to lag further behind.[15] In the countryside, conservative policy has allowed private plots and free market exchange to expand, with the result that economic differences between peasant families have widened and allegiance to collectives has declined. Similarly, they have implemented strictly objective academic standards for university admissions, although this has meant that youth from poorer rural schools have far less chance than the graduates of better urban schools or the children of intellectuals and officials.[16] Modernization, say the revisionists, should be led by technical specialists and bureaucratic administrators working in stable hierarchies free of interference from mass supervision by community organizations, or the obligation to engage in periodic manual labor. Material incentives, bonuses, and prestigious titles are seen as necessary to spur individual effort and to clearly distinguish the contributions of essential specialists from the less crucial efforts of ordinary workers and farmers.

SOCIAL VERSUS ECONOMIC NECESSITIES

The two lines and their repeated conflicts arise from a contradiction between social and economic necessities. The margin of survival is still thin, and the country must have a closely coordinated economy to marshal scarce material and technological resources. At the same time, the fiscal limits of the state and the labor-intensive nature of production make the morale of worker and citizen especially important. The state must continue to depend upon volunteer citizen activists in community organizations to help in virtually every aspect of social service, including crime control and correction. Worker motivation is also essential to ensure adequate harvests and the achievement of industrial production quotas. Thus, in the long run, China cannot choose between the two lines; both are necessary and even ultimately interdependent.

In the short run, however, the two lines are certainly at odds. Historically, public activism and worker morale have been highest in times of wage leveling, political decentralization and rectification campaigns. Such reform eras have also disrupted production routines and undermined the stability of social and administrative hierarchies. Adherents of the two lines can, and have, claimed that their approach offers the greatest hopes for the modernization of China.

Their disagreements are based not only on differences of perception but also, and increasingly, on different material interests. The revolutionary line and its radical policies have been most strongly supported by unskilled and semiskilled workers, poorer peasants, women, and youth, especially students and lower level cadres from the poorer social classes. These are precisely the groups that have benefited most from radical reform policies. Middle-level bureaucrats, intellectuals, technicians, wealthier peasants, and those from "bad" class origins (especially former landlords, capitalists, and their offspring) have most stoutly defended the conservative positions. All of the latter groups have a personal stake in the maintenance of social hierarchies and material inequalities, and in the relaxation of class struggle and political rectification movements. More pointedly still, these elites are most often the targets of criticism and sanction in the rectification campaigns and ongoing mass supervision efforts.[17] The coalescence of these elite class interests around conservative ideology and modernization policy makes the term "revisionist line" an appropriate description now, although it would not have been perhaps ten years ago.

As argued elsewhere,[18] justice policy, institutional jurisdiction, and the definition of crime itself have been strained and tossed between these two lines. China has in fact developed two justice systems: a bureaucratic justice based on formal legal agencies and operated by more or less specialized professions; and the popular justice institutions sponsored by the vast national network of community organizations and activated by millions of volunteer activists. The discussion now turns to this dialectic of justice institutions and to the shadow of the two-line struggle.

BUREAUCRATIC JUSTICE:
ORDER AND PROFESSIONALISM

The bureaucratic justice system is a natural consequence of the conservative notion that the Chinese revolution has been completed. Advocates argue that law is vital to consolidate past gains, regulate future changes, ensure production and protect state authority.[19] A set of multitiered bureaucracies is entrusted, under China's constitution, with the legal powers in a check and balance arrangement which in theory is designed to protect due process and maintain social order[20] as follows:

1. *People's courts* are a hierarchy of three-judge courts that decide cases at law and hear appeals. Law-trained professionals and lay judges ("assessors") serve together with equal voting rights.

2. The *procurate* is charged with preparing evidence for prosecution at trials and with systematic review of legal procedures in other bureaus (especially the police). The procurate has been the most professional of the justice agencies, and its regular staff includes many law-trained specialists.

3. The *Ministry of Public Security* serves as local and national police and is responsible for arrests, investigation, the operation of walled prisons and the more numerous labor reform brigades, and the supervision of citizens placed under mass control (roughly analogous to probation). The police ranks include many ex-soldiers and former citizen activists, but there are comparatively few trained specialists.

4. *Ministry of Control or Party Control Commissions* are internal investigation bureaus that hear complaints and prepare charges against government

or party officials who have violated the law. The ministry was abolished in 1959, but the commissions have taken on this task since their rebuilding in the early 1970s.

The justice bureaucracies, especially the courts and procurate, have pressed for complete codification of criminal laws, procedures, and jurisdictional guidelines. They have asserted, in a manner not unlike Western or Soviet justice officials, that legal authority should be concentrated in the hands of trained specialists, who would themselves be regulated by law, bureaucratic routines, and professional ethics. Justice and freedom would be defined in terms of individual rights, and its dimensions set by law and guaranteed by a system of checks and balances between the three legal bureaucracies. The correction of abuses by government officials or administrators would be entrusted to the procurate and the Control Ministry, later the Control Commission. This system seeks to manage and control the process of social change and to put an end to the more revolutionary upheavals of the past.[21]

POPULAR JUSTICE: INTEGRATIVE AND COMBATIVE

The popular justice system has been historically linked to revolutionary-line ideals. Popular institutions do contribute to the protection of social order, but there is also an explicit commitment to social justice and egalitarian reform. The mass organizations at local workplaces and residential communities sponsor their own internal peacekeeping bodies which function as auxiliaries to the regular police and as lay representatives in the people's courts. The mass organizations have also mobilized the populace for political struggle against erring individual officials, intellectuals, and administrations, or against whole social classes (such as landlords or capitalists), or against general political problems within the government, Communist party, or the academy (such as the errors of bureaucratism, elitism, or corruption).

Such an ambitious and wide-ranging plan of action is not easily incorporated into law. Indeed, the Chinese radicals have been generally lukewarm or even hostile to codified law, even as they have resisted the professionalization of justice as advocated by the leading conservatives. Popular justice has instead been guided by Maoist ideological principles which are widely understood and discussed in the community and workplace. The mass line requires close working relations and mutual consultation between justice professionals and citizen activists in the mass organizations. The ideal of self-reliance encourages the informal resolution of social conflicts within the confines of the community organization and without formal legal proceedings.

While the bureaucratic ideal defines crime as a specific act proscribed and sanctioned by law, the popular justice approach emphasizes the offender's social background and motivations. The mass organizations play a crucial role in this process. Study, criticism, self-criticism, and correction within millions of intimate small groups are so continuous and ubiquitous that one hesitates to call it by such formal terms as "investigation, classification, and sanction." Only when a deviant fails to respond to informal pressures (in which virtually everyone has a turn as both subject and object of correction), or when the offense is considered extremely serious, does the state intervene with the formal agencies of control: the police and courts.[22]

Probably the most difficult aspect of popular justice for Westerners to understand (or Chinese conservatives to accept) has been the mass campaigns and ongoing rectification that arise from the ideology of the continuing revolution. In these tumultuous campaigns and in the less intense rectifications between campaigns, the public has been mobilized for direct political and legal action in their various local mass organizations. The general direction of a specific campaign of rectification is set by the central leadership in Peking, but the actual application of "line" into policy is a local affair, one that circumvents the regular channels of government and that often provides a vehicle for airing public grievances, the "great debates," and open "struggle" meetings. Erring officials or intellectuals have been frequently obliged to make humiliating self-criticism, and demotions, transfers, or even the scrapping of entire departments and policies have resulted.[23]

In sum, popular justice has both an integrative and a combative function in China, the main elements of which may be summarized as follows:

1. The mass organizations sponsor internal peacekeeping bodies that include security defense teams and militia forces (volunteer police) and also mediation teams (to arbitrate quarrels). These bodies serve as auxiliaries to the justice professionals.

2. The local small groups involve perhaps a dozen co-workers or neighbors in weekly meetings to discuss politics and local problems, and to correct conflicts, misunderstandings, and egotistic attitudes through the process of criticism and self-criticism.

3. Representatives of mass organizations participate within the bureaucratic justice agencies, most notably as people's assessors who sit alongside professional jurists in the courts.

4. Systematic monitoring of government officials at the local level is handled by the people's supervisory committees and at other levels by the rectification committees, both of which are charged to compile and forward accusations against leadership.

5. The public has been repeatedly mobilized for mass campaigns which have been directed at the correction of major social inequalities and fundamental political problems resulting in massive changes in social policy and reorganization of government.

6. The suppression of class enemies, political corruption, and bureaucratic abuse has been entrusted to temporary nonprofessional judges sitting in

people's tribunals. Such tribunals systematically involve mass organizations as both witnesses and as judges, but the tribunals are usually disbanded when the given mass campaign passes.

Between bureaucratic and popular justice there has been compromise, coexistence, and conflict, but no steady amalgam of the two. The bureaucrats have sought to make popular justice a reliable auxiliary, discarding the more combative functions of mass campaigns, rectification, and the people's tribunals, while maintaining the peacekeeping elements under the tight control of the regular courts, police, and procurate. The radicals, for their part, have sought to popularize the bureaucratic agencies, through the infusion of critics and activists into the ranks of the police; through anti-elitist political education of judges, police, and procurators at "May 7th Schools"; and through the incorporation of the mass line principles into the national constitution of 1975 and the procedural guidelines of the justice bureaus. At present, of course, the conservatives are very much dominant in China, and as might be expected they have pressed for extensive codification, legal professionalism, and expansion of the justice bureaus, while limiting and containing popular justice. It remains to be seen whether the more combative aspects of popular justice can be laid to rest without sacrificing public support and volunteer participation in the peacekeeping auxiliaries.[24]

Crime patterns, crime control, the development of political legal theory, and professionalism bear the marks of the two-line dialectic. Unfortunately, only fragmentary criminal statistics are available, but these are supplemented by numerous local accounts of journalists and scholars, both Western and Chinese. There is also a considerable body of theoretical material and reports on academic associations and the training and research programs of political legal institutions. All of these matters, like the agencies of justice and the larger social context, are best understood historically.[25]

EARLY YEARS: A TIME FOR GENERALISTS (1927-1954)

The long Civil War (1927-1949) and the Liberation period (1949-1953) were most formative for popular justice institutions and for the political side of political legal theory and professionalism. The revolutionary transformation of political economy and social relations would require a new sort of justice system to resolve both interclass and intraclass conflicts. Interclass reforms meant the dispossession, and sometimes punishment, of rural landlords and capitalists, as well as the suppression of organized crime syndicates and counterrevolution activities. Intraclass reforms included the remaking of the notoriously sexist marriage institution, controlling drug addiction and rampant street crime, and the inculcation of new socialist ethics among the population as a whole.

The Chinese approach differed not only from the bourgeoisie revolution of the eighteenth century but also from those of other socialist nations. The central Chinese leadership, then as now, did not include a single lawyer, while by contrast Lenin, Castro, Robespierre, and Patrick Henry (to name but a few) were all from that profession. Mao, Chou en Lai, and most of their important colleagues were trained as classical scholars of history and the humanities. Lawyers were regarded with contempt in traditional China, litigations were strongly discouraged, and formal proceedings commonly involved extensive bribery, torture, and unpredictability.[26] During the first decades of war and reconstruction, the communists did little to reverse this antiprofessionalism.

The communists built a range of model institutions, including mobile university departments, in the large base areas, but they did not organize law schools or legal research facilities during the Civil War. For political legal officials, training was limited to a few months' study of Marxist texts and the half dozen brief revolutionary laws.[27] Most of these laws were intended to guide dispossession and/or punishment of landlords, counterrevolutionaries, and (later) capitalists, while other laws specified new rights for women within a reformed marriage institution.[28] There was no criminal code applicable to what we in the West call ordinary street crime.[29]

Class analysis and the mass line were at the heart of training for political legal cadres, or any other officials for that matter. The aim of the fledgling courts, police, and procurate was not so much to enforce the letter of the law, which was rather imprecise in any case, as to assist in the process of transforming class relations, overcoming feudal thinking, and mobilizing the populace. Thus, training was very practice-oriented, and individual cases were studied to point out underlying issues of class conflict or ideology. The importance of working closely with mass organizations was stressed, along with the dangers of bureaucratic isolation. Not infrequently, cadres were expected to grow their own food and engage in periodic manual labor, both to relieve the state's burden for their support and to deepen understanding of local conditions.[30] Since most political legal cadres were recruited either from the mass organizations or from the People's Liberation Army (PLA), there were already strong links between officials and public. Legal procedures were generally informal and participatory, nor did theory develop far as a specialized discipline.[31]

CONCEPTIONS OF CRIMINALS AND ACTIONS TAKEN

As revolutionaries, the communists considered the feudal system of peasant exploitation to be the germinal crime in Chinese society. Landlords and, to a lesser extent, rich peasants were regarded as parasitic, although sanctions against any one individual depended not only upon that landlord's past action, but also on the general line at that moment. The peasant associations played a central role in investigation and judgment of local tyrants. The moderate punishments and rent reductions of the Civil War era gave way to much more severe treatment after 1949 and especially during the Korean War. For example, in one six-month period of 1951, there were 143,761 proceedings against landlords, with thousands shot and tens of thousands imprisoned in Central South China alone. Mao later revealed that some 800,000 landlords and counterrevolutionaries were executed over the course of the decade (1945-1954).[32] Truly, this revolution was "not a dinner party."

Similar policies were adopted against the well-entrenched secret gangster societies (the *T'angs*), who controlled an enormous urban racketeering based on smuggling, prostitution, opium, extortion, labor monopolies, and corruption. A network of urban "residential committees" was formed to mobilize the public and to expose and investigate the *T'ang* leadership. Some three million Chinese citizens participated in over twenty-five thousand mass meetings held to denounce local gangsters, hundreds of whom were executed while thousands more were sent to labor reform camps. Western travelers, journalists, and visiting scholars have reported with consistent astonishment on the effective curtailment of organized crime activities within a few years of the communists' arrival in the crime-ridden coastal cities.[33]

Capitalists were not, on the whole, considered an "enemy" class. Those few who had enjoyed monopoly privileges by virtue of special ties to the old regime or the foreign corporations were singled out for stiff punishment, but the remaining majority faced only restrictions on profit-taking in the first years. However, in 1951-1952, a national campaign ("Three/Five Antis") was launched to investigate bribery, corruption, and illegal profiteering within both the people's government and the major capitalist firms. As in earlier struggles against landlords and gangsters, the campaign against illicit profits involved millions of citizens. The new trade unions took a leading role in examining company account books, publicly criticizing and denouncing those found guilty of malfeasance. Political legal cadres, Communist party members, and some special procedural legislation provided a degree of national coordination, but there was considerable room for local initiative. Very few executions resulted, but heavy fines were levied which drained private capital and accelerated the state's takeover of enterprises.[34]

The new political legal system was also concerned with a second dimension of social conflict—those conflicts arising among the people (peasants, workers, and cadres). Most prominent was the torrent of discontent released when married couples were invited to dissolve unhappy or arranged marriages maintained under the constraints of the old society. So intense were the cross-pressures from spouse and relatives that communist sources document over seventy thousand suicides or murders of women seeking divorce in each of the first few years after 1948.[35] The local mass organizations formed mediation teams to resolve domestic conflict wherever possible through directed discussion and compromise, but still more than four million divorce petitions were heard during 1950-1956 in people's courts.[36]

Hundreds of thousands of opium addicts were sought out by the urban neighborhood committees and strongly encouraged to come forward, make self-criticism, and abandon their drug habits. In great open rallies, opium smoking was discussed as a vestige of Chinese humiliation by Western nations which had forced this profitable drug on the population as a means of balancing trade deficits.

Rallies were followed by mass destruction of pipes and opium and the reading of pledges by former addicts.[37] The combination of police suppression, severe penalties for recalcitrants, and extensive community involvement was also employed in dealing with thieves, prostitutes, and other minor criminals. The minister of public security reported that in 1950 the police and mass organizations tracked down some 2,197 robberies, 31,729 thefts, and 1,856 opium and drug violations.[38] The purpose of ideological examination was "to cure the disease to save the patient"—that is, to identify the historic roots of deviance and to direct informal social pressure toward the reform of former outcasts within the community. Within prisons and labor reform camps, hard labor was combined with political education and the criticism and self-criticism process as carried out within prisoners' small groups.[39]

The Chinese were able to handle all of these various social conflicts with less than eighty thousand police and a few hundred courts in the entire country.[40] This accomplishment was possible only because the political legal cadres relied upon activists of the mass organizations. It would be inaccurate, however, to speak of anything like a criminological profession or of a discrete body of legal theory at that time. The mass organizations were multipurpose associations, responsible for almost everything from food production and manufacture to the formation of militias and public health services. A highly specialized political-legal profession or a formalized legal process would have been inappropriate to mass line politics and self-isolation in these first formative decades. As Mao noted in describing justice policy, social change, and the mass mobilizations in Hunan province:

Even if ten thousand schools of law and political science had been opened, could they have brought as much political education to the people, men and women, young and old, all the way into the remotest corners of the countryside, as the peasant associations have done in so short a time? I don't think they could.[41]

CONSOLIDATION AND UPHEAVAL IN THE MIDDLE YEARS (1954-1976)

Once the old ruling classes were displaced and the Korean War danger passed, China could concentrate on developing the economy and the new socialist state. The mid-1950s were the high point of Sino-Soviet relations, but it was natural that the Chinese would look to the Soviets for both technological assistance and political counsel. The Soviets stressed material incentives, industrial concentration, and a system of centralized planning and administration, with the whole regulated by law and entrusted to professional specialists. Many Chinese agreed, and the ideas and adherents of what would become the revisionist line and the accompanying bureaucratic justice trace back to this period. The remarks of the conservative (later vilified) Liu Shao Chi were:

Now the period of revolutionary storm and stress is past, new relations of production have been set up, and the aim of our struggle is changed into one of the productive forces of the society. A corresponding change in the methods of struggle will consequently follow, and a complete legal system becomes an absolute necessity.[42]

The political legal system became increasingly legal as the first constitution[43] was passed along with a sheaf of laws and procedural guidelines. The three multitiered legal bureaus were filled with increased staff and empowered by the new organic laws. Chiefs of police, courts, and procurates complained, however, that subordinates were inadequately prepared for their more formalized roles. They also worried about the public's continuing distrust of lawyers and formal procedures. The chief justice of the supreme court spoke for many legal officials when he insisted that the new professionals needed further training but also deserved greater status:

Jurisprudence is an important branch of social science. We have more than fifty institutes in our Academy of Science, but the Institute of Jurisprudence is only in the stage of consideration and preparation. Legal work is a kind of specialized work, but the personnel engaged in legal work have not yet been given the kind of treatment that should be given to personnel working in a specialized field.[44]

The new justice administrators (especially in the courts and procurate) clearly regarded themselves as reformers. The new legal procedures and institutions would have to overcome not only the traditional Chinese antipathy toward law and lawyers, but also the Maoist preference for informal processes, community self-reliance, and mass line leadership methods. Although the legal professionals did not directly confront Maoist principles, their emphasis on law and professionalism contradicted the revolutionary emphasis on class analysis and mass participation. Thus, for example, the new court and procurate officials criticized the police for taking the "poor man's viewpoint" rather than the law into account when they sympathized with a poorer thief whose victim was more affluent.[45] The strengthened legal bureaucracies sought to restrict and subordinate popular justice bodies, as in the court controls on neighborhood mediation teams and the virtual proscription of the tumultuous mass rectification campaigns.[46] They preferred to handle political corruption on a case-by-case basis through the offices of the procurate, and they concentrated on the maintenance of social order.

Chinese academics were drawn into the process of consolidating state administration, and particularly remaking justice along more regular bureaucratic and legalistic lines. Most intellectuals, it will be recalled, had not taken an active part in either the revolution or the Kuomintang dictatorship of Chiang Kai-shek, but had instead chosen the moribund "third force" represented by the China Democratic League. The communists described them as a wavering element whose elitist subculture was at odds with a generally meager income and so led to vascillating politics. However, when called upon in the mid-1950s, the intellectuals joined the Communist party in large numbers and played an especially significant role in drafting laws and training political-legal cadres.[47]

BUREAUCRATIC PROFESSIONALISM VERSUS
CONTINUING REVOLUTION

Professionalism was considerably advanced in the period 1952-1957, with the opening of a half dozen new law departments at regional universities and the creation of several political legal institutes. Law students were enrolled in a five-year course, including principles of criminal law, organic laws of state agencies, legal history, comparative socialist and capitalist law, and both Maoist and Marxist theory. The national institutes had a slightly more vocational orientation. Indeed, some programs were specifically designed to train managerial personnel for the police bureau. Other institutes offered shorter courses for in-service personnel at the regional level.

Intellectual exchange was accelerated by the establishment of the Chinese Political Legal Association and the Institute of Law of the Academy of Sciences. Both of these organizations published prominent journals, sponsored professional conferences, and managed research and teaching efforts at the various law schools and institutes. The number of professional publications increased dramatically in 1953-1958, with concentration of articles on such themes as theory of state and law, roles of the various legal bureaus, and international and comparative law. Neverthless, the overall dimension and status accorded the profession were still very modest. Most law school or institute graduates could not find work as legal professionals, but would be obliged to take administrative positions in finance, production, or trade.[48]

The impatience of some bureaucrats and intellectuals to consolidate society through law and (not incidentally) to improve their own personal positions in terms of pay and prestige exploded in the "Hundred Flowers" events of 1957.[49] Intellectuals and bureaucrat conservatives alike deplored the continuing interference of nonspecialists from the party or the mass organizations in legal affairs. Academics also complained about the intrusion of irrelevant political ideology in all aspects of education. They were especially resentful of the Maoist notion that intellectuals need engage in criticism/self-criticism to rectify their historic tendencies toward arrogance and elitism.[50]

The radical counterattack on conservative policies began with the anti-rightist campaign of 1957-1958 and continued with the Great Leap Forward and the Cultural Revolution of 1965-1969. Chinese admiration for the USSR and the Soviet path to socialism waned as the two nations found themselves at odds over foreign policy. Ironically, it was the Chinese who then insisted on a more aggressive confrontation strategy against the West. More to the point, Chinese revolutionaries worried about the erosion of popular political participation and the deepening of social stratification that followed pragmatic conservative policies. The new professionalized legal order only confirmed and reproduced these problems of bureaucratic stagnation and social inequality. In forming their strategy against the conservatives, the Maoists could count on the public's traditional antipathy for litigation and the mounting resentments of official highhandedness and intellectual elitism.[51]

When the mass rectification movements struck government, party, and university in 1958-1969, legal bureaus and law schools were especially hard hit. Indeed, the entire political legal sphere itself became an object for investigation, sanction, and correction in upheavals involving millions of citizens. Within the universities, students newly recruited from peasant and worker backgrounds resented tradition-bound professors whose mandarin notions of the educational process had been largely unchanged by the advent of socialism. By 1966, student Red Guard units within the law schools openly confronted academic authorities, seized classroom buildings, and began publishing their own short-lived revolutionary law manifestos. They subjected many professors and administrators to criticism/self-criticism before street audiences. Western visitors in the mid-1970s found most law schools still closed, long after other departments reopened. Law school faculty were among the last academics to return from "May 7th Schools" where they were assigned to farming, political study, and criticism/self-criticism sessions in order to overcome elitism.[52]

The legal bureaus were equally besieged and disrupted. National and local newspapers published a long series of articles exposing abusive behavior by judges, police, and procurators in order both to criticize individual officials and to illustrate the general problems of bureaucratic complacency and the independent kingdom mentality among legal professionals. The anti-rightist movement led to the demotion and transfer of many ranking officials; and the Cultural Revolution featured Red Guard seizures of police stations and courthouses. Legal officials angered both youths and Maoist leaders in Peking by attempting to suppress the young protesters, first openly with arrests and beatings and later in raids by secretive groups such as the "One Million Warriors" (who were mainly Wuhan area political legal officials acting out of uniform). Ultimately, thousands of legal cadres were either packed off to May 7th Schools or sent down to manual labor at factories or communes. Although a great many, probably most, would eventually return to legal work, demotions and transfers were common. Some, like the national police chief Lo Jui Ching, would be permanently stripped of all authority, while others, like the chief justice of the Peking High Court, could not stand the humiliation of mass criticism and chose to commit suicide.[53]

After the 1960s decade of protest, law school curricula were shortened to three years and made more relevant as students demanded. Specialized courses were cut down to make room for more courses on political philosophy, agricultural and industrial production, and military training. This shift toward a more general preparation coincided with the reduction in specialized legal work that followed the retrenchment of the courts and the virtual elimination of the procurate. Indeed, by 1975, the director of the Tienstin High People's Court noted[54] that most of the law-trained professionals "do ordinary factory or office work until asked to defend an accused person." Law school departments were broken up, and students and faculty scattered to local communes and factories where they often conducted part-time university courses for peasants and workers. Legal research was increasingly tailored to meet local needs, and the publication of scholarly articles on grander macroscopic themes declined, with an accompanying fall in the number of professional journals and in the activities of the Political Legal Association and the Institute of Law at the Chinese Academy.[55] Within the remaining law schools, most textbooks were discarded, and shorter mimeographed materials were preferred for the more practical case study teaching methods. Exchange of concrete experience among students was accorded greater importance as they returned from their studies and work experience at the local level.[56] Even after the tempest of Cultural Revolution was long past, this emphasis on "open door education" remained, as radical academic Cheng Shi Yi noted:

The old college system harmed the youngster's ability. Students learned a lot of empty theories. Still more serious was the fact that long years of corruption by bourgeois ideas led the students to seek comfort and enjoyment and fear hardship....They gradually became divorced from proletarian politics, from productive labor, and from the worker and peasant masses. Open door education's main purpose is to promote the teachers' remolding of this world outlook and training student into new socialist people....We have organized teachers and students to take part in physical labor and to study, work, and live together with the workers.[57]

The drive toward professionalization and codification within the legal bureaus was effectively checked from 1957 to 1976. Legal officials joined law school students and faculty in manual work assignments and especially at the May 7th Schools. Remaining judges and police were enjoined to work more closely with mass organizations; indeed, their scope of independent action was diminished in relation to the resurgent institutions of popular justice. New recruits to the police were drawn from the ranks of activists in the mass organizations, even as peasant and working-class students were recruited into the law schools in greatly increased numbers after the Great Leap Forward.[58] Officials increasingly relied upon ideological principles and informal methods in resolving conflicts.[59] Maoist political legal theorists argued that was to be avoided as an essentially conservative institution ill fitted to the needs of the continuing revolution. Wu Tu Peng, for example, noted:

A time of radical social change is not the time to codify laws. Law is the armor of the social system. If, for example, laws pertaining to property had been finalized during the cooperative state of agriculture, they would now be quite out of date, since the commune movement has alerted the whole basis of property.[60]

THEORETICAL LINCHPIN FOR POPULAR JUSTICE POLICY

While the "red and expert" ideal was to guide the reform of the university and the resocialization of intellectuals, the principles of "Handling Contradictions" were advanced as the theoretical linchpin for justice policy. This theory, which essentially displaced reliance on codified law, begins with the observation that social conflict (or contradiction) is essential to social progress and socialist democracy. Thus, it could call for future mass rectification movements, even though they are disruptive and have no legal standing. The role of the political legal system, then, is not to prevent or contain conflict but to distinguish between those contradictions which are rooted in class conflicts (that is, antagonistic) among the working classes. While the essentially nonpunitive means of peer pressure, mediation, and criticism are appropriate to handling nonantagonistic conflicts, the more severe and formal measures of the legal system are reserved for antagonistic contradictions. This theory and the related principle of continuing revolution hold that class conflict is a continuing phenomenon in China, hence the origin of crime as discussed by theorist Ts'ao Tsu Tan:

Crime and class struggle form two mutually dependent and closely related social phenomena that exist objectively in class society. The pre-requisite for the emergence of crime is the appearance and conflict of class interests.

We must aim the sharp point of our law against the reactionary classes, the landlords, Kuomintang counter-revolutionaries, and comprador capitalists.

The exploiting class has been overthrown, but it will be impossible to consider that the exploiting class has been already eliminated. At the same time, in the protracted, complex class struggle during the period of transition, there is the possibility that certain wavering elements among the people will degenerate into bourgeois elements.[61]

The contradictions theory is the conceptual link between justice practice and radical social policy, but the problem is that the class categories here are essentially meaningless. Former landlords and capitalists, of course, exist, but they have not functioned as a class for generations now. The Maoists are unwilling to describe the bureaucracy or the Communist party or the intellectuals as a potentially exploiting class. Likewise, they are unwilling to incorporate as important those intraclass differences among peasants, workers, or intellectuals. Rather than come to grips with the political and economic roots of modern class conflicts in China, the Maoists insist that the new contradictions arise from the degeneration of individuals whose socialist ethics have gone sour. The theory, then, is essentially a tautology: crimes are committed by members of the exploiting classes or the "bad elements"; therefore, anyone who commits such an offense must have adopted enemy class identity and consciousness.[62]

The theory does contain an essential optimism, since it argues that criminals are reformable, if only they can throw off their "bad class" consciousness. Thus, the Maoists make a point of "curing the disease to save the patient" and share the traditional Confucian confidence in the power of reflection and criticism to work a change of heart. However, the theory leaves the Maoists unable to account for patterns of crime and corruption which are greater than the individual deviant (even if they criticize whole agencies of government). Moreover, the theory may be quite easily twisted for opportunist purpose, as in the Red Guard practice of branding their opponents (usually other students) as enemies or bad elements because they had another interpretation of Maoist thought, or, worse still, simply because they were competitors in the same campus or community. The brutal savagery of Red Guard "justice" during 1966-1969 was justified as class struggle by the most convenient application of this rather un-Marxist theory.[63]

Crime and crime control during this middle period were decisively influenced by political events. During the early years of bureaucratic dominance (1953-1957 and 1960-1963), the emphasis was on supervising those with "bad class histories" (that is, landlords and Kuomintang officials) as well as the maintenance of order. The Great Leap Forward produced its share of conflicts, especially in the urban commune experiment which temporarily collectivized whole neighborhoods and led to turmoil over sudden new arrangements for shared cooking, housing, and child care. Likewise the Leap's communization of agriculture led to bitter, sometimes violent, disputes over property (personal versus collective and also between communes). The Maoists, however, were prepared to accept a measure of such conflicts as the price of continuing revolution, while the conservative bureaucrats were not.

The Cultural Revolution and the anti-rightist movement, of course, created a whole new set of conflicts. Mass movements, as Bennett[64] has shown so well, often expose considerable elite corruption as a byproduct of mass mobilization. Moreover, the mass movements, by raising new standards of ethics and ideology against the performance, especially of political and technical elites, do actually generate deviants among those who were at least technically law-abiding. The anarchist mob-rule runaway of Red Guard units constituted yet another new form of crime, which had to be controlled by the army (PLA) since by that time (1968) the regular justice agencies were defunct. Against these problems must be weighed the gains of egalitarian advance and renewed community activism. Although one would not dare to project from this a quantitative crime reduction quotient, the control of political corruption and the easing of social alienation have been described by a number of observers.[65]

In the mid-1970s, with Mao's death imminent, there was a discernible effort to work out some sort of compromise between the radical Maoists, led by the so-called Gang of Four, and their conservative opposition. The new constitution of 1975 attempted to combine the two, as in its resurrection of the procurate along with its stricture that the procurate conduct its work "in accordance with the mass line." The police and courts were likewise restored, and a goodly number of former chiefs resumed their posts in organizations that were now filled with new recruits often drawn from the ranks of the critics of agencies. These efforts and even the naming of a centrist and former national police chief, Hau Kuo Feng, as new chairman did not result in a stable compromise. Within weeks after Mao's death in 1976, the Gang of Four was captured by a special police unit and imprisoned to await their now famous trial. A new period in political legal development had begun.[66]

PATTERNS OF THE POST-MAO ERA (1976-1981)

China watchers in the West, both academics and journalists, have generally applauded the downfall of the radical Gang of Four and the rise of the new pragmatic leadership in Peking. Unfortunately, our experts have defined the latest round of struggle in Western terms, as a conflict between competing leadership cliques and political personalities. In fact, the conflict goes much deeper, to the very structure of Chinese government and society. The new revisionist line policies, led by Teng Hsiao Ping, have tremendously widened inter- and intraclass stratification within the country, while also reducing citizen participation in a decision-making process that is now increasingly dominated by a privileged bureaucrat and intellectual elite. The exploitation of temporary rural labor in urban enterprises, the concentration of industry in the cities, and the new policy of regional autonomy have caused poorer regions and the countryside in particular to lag farther behind the cities in terms of cultural and economic opportunity. The emphasis on material incentives bonuses, free market agriculture, steep wage scales, and the dismantling of the Revolutionary Committees are all aspects of this present turning away from revolutionary egalitarianism.[67]

In this time of increasing social inequality, the newly emergent social theory and the reorganized justice system alike start from the assertion that the basic contradictions of socialist transformation have been resolved. Like the Chinese conservatives of the 1950s, the present Peking leadership and the dominant voices within the social science establishment inform us that class conflict and continuing revolution are past. There is no need for direct mass action and shakedowns as in the past rectification campaigns. As Shang Zhe noted: "There is no basic conflict of economic interests among the people although there are partial contradictions....These kinds of contradictions can be resolved by self regulation of the socialist system."[68]

Even more than the conservatives of the 1950s, the present Peking leadership has stressed the need to stabilize and regulate society through a complete legal system. They count heavily on the law to legitimate social and economic policies, as well as to guide centralization of power and the suppression of political dissent. Discounting China's centuries-long antipathy toward law and lawyers, the current regime claims a mass mandate to codify and professionalize: "Having had enough of turmoil caused by Lin Hiao and the Gang of Four, the people want law and order more than anything else. Democratization and legalization, which the Chinese people have long been yearning for, are now gradually becoming a reality."[69]

CONSERVATIVE DOMINANCE IN THE UNIVERSITIES

The universities, perhaps more than any institution, show the marks of the new pragmatism. Past policies designed to encourage the admission of students from poorer rural communes and working-class districts have been scrapped in place of an objective examination system that will inevitably favor the offspring of bureaucrats and intellectuals who attend the better schools in the city centers. The curricula have been reformalized, with longer and more specialized courses and a return to more hierarchical student-faculty relationships. The "red and expert" ideal has been discarded, along with the obligation of intellectuals to engage in periodic manual labor. The wages of scholars and teachers have been substantially increased, well above those of ordinary skilled workers.[70] The Peking leadership has declared China's historical intellectual arrogance and elitism solved:

In the wake of our Party's work being shifted to modernization, it has become increasingly important and urgent for a comprehensive and accurate understanding of the Party's policy toward intellectuals and from bringing their role into full play.... Some comrades, however, do not have a corresponding understanding.... Some ask if the Party's policy of uniting, educating, and remolding the intellectuals still applies, now that the overwhelming majority are part of the working class. The intellectuals are no longer objects to be united with, educated and remolded.[71]

Social scientists and law faculty in particular have been enlisted by the new regime in the conservative remaking of Chinese society. The important place of social scientists in policy planning is evident in the selection of Hu Chia Mu, a close associate of Ten Hsiao Ping, to head the newly revitalized Academy of Social Sciences.[72] Social scientists have supported the regime's claims that objective laws of development dictate the shape of current policies, and so provide an alternative to the ideological currency of Maoism. Law faculty and social science researchers have been called together for a series of National Propaganda Work Conferences designed to "mobilize social science research work in support of the Four Modernizations"[73] (as the new conservative policies are called). Other conferences, both regional and national, have been called with increased frequency to bring together law faculty, social scientists, court, procurate, and police administrators.[74] Law faculty and officers of the Academy of Social Sciences have blamed uneven codification of the "Gang's evil influence" and have unreservedly supported the expansion and formalization of bureaucratic justice.[75]

The law schools and the legal institutes have undergone dramatic expansion as the legal bureaus have become professionalized. Courses at the law schools have been lengthened, with emphasis on procedural law, criminal law, contracts, and international law. Most of the texts now in use were written by the earlier legalist generation in 1952-1957 or are translations of Soviet law texts.[76] In 1980, five new independent law colleges were established, as well as six university-based law departments and many more political legal institutes for the in-service training of legal officials. More than four thousand students were enrolled in these specialized law programs, and more than twenty thousand cadres rotated through the one-year training cycles at the institutes. These numbers are still small by

Western standards, as China has only 3,100 courthouses, 16,000 lawyers, and altogether 1 million political legal cadres for its total population of 975 million people (1978 population estimate). However, this represents a very considerable increase over the 1975 level, and already surpasses the highwater mark of professionalism in 1957.[77]

A tremendous increase in specialized legal publications is under way. One clear effect of professionalism is to remove the political level cadre from mass supervision. Instead, a new benevolent legalist elite is envisioned, in a style of government quite different from the mass line tradition and more in keeping with the Confucian ideals of the scholar-bureaucrat elite. This is typified in the following official orientation recently delivered to cadres in Peking (lectures, 1980):

The leading cadres at all levels of the judiciary organs must make themselves specialists in the understanding of law, experts at implementing the law, and models of acting according to law. If the political legal cadre makes himself a selfless, upright, and unyielding judicial warrior, we will be able to fulfill the sacred mission given to him by the party and the people.

GROWTH OF CODIFIED LAW AND ITS IMPLICATIONS

Legal professionalism and the accompanying rapid growth of codified law have been highly touted by the Peking regime as the foundation for a new national unity free of the bitter strife that has been frequent in the Maoist era. Indeed, there has been a great deal of lawmaking, with a new constitution,[78] organic laws for the various legal bureaus,[79] and a new criminal code.[80] However, a closer look at these documents and law enforcement priorities reveals that the new legal order is, in fact, more an expression of social conflict and an instrument of political repression than a guarantee of human rights and democratic expression.[81]

Many of the statutes pointedly criminalize those very forms of political activism that were of such importance in the last three decades. For example, the new criminal code stipulates a term of imprisonment for anyone who "obstructs a state functionary," or "disturbs public order by any means," or "gathers a crowd which seriously disturbs public order at a railroad, bus station, or any public site." Additional laws and police directives have made it a prisonable offense to "put up slogans, posters on public buildings, and the printing and selling of reactionary books, journals are prohibited."[82] The criminal law claims to "defend the right to criticism," but it outlaws "use of big character posters, or small character posters" if they are used "to insult another person." In justifying the criminalization of dissent, China's leading justice official, Zhou Zheng, said that these outlawed forms of expression "have nothing in common with freedom of speech in the general sense of the expression as people understand it. . . . In the hands of the Conspirator (Gang of Four) it became an instrument for usurping Party and State leadership."[83]

Recent Western journalist's reports of dissident trials in China[84] certainly do not indicate that the new legal system protects the democratic rights of individual dissent. In the Chinese press, there are also many references to the necessary punishment of "people abusing their democratic rights," both in the protests that followed the arrest of the Gang of Four and in more recent demonstrations.[85] Aside from criminal statutes, new laws governing labor have created criminal penalties for violation of work standards as in "seriously defective or shoddy work, neglect of duty, embezzlement, or other offenses involving heavy economic loss or breaches of authority."[86] The right to strike, expressly granted in the compromise constitution of 1975, is nowhere mentioned in the 1978 constitution, but the new work regulations imply that it would be considered criminal.[87]

UPSURGE IN CRIME AND DELINQUENCY

It is not surprising that the new social and economic policies have been accompanied by a rise in crime so serious that it is now openly acknowledged by worried officials. Marxists would argue that crime is a result of social alienation and social inequality. Both of these problems have recently intensified in China. By every measure of wages, living standards, and opportunities, China is becoming a much more sharply stratified class society. The erosion of mass participation exemplified by the abolished Revolutionary Committees and the weakened mass organization cannot but increase alienation, as does the rigidification of social hierarchies in party, government, academy, and workplace. As one Western journalist and resident in China observes: "The country appears to be caught in the grip of a general malaise...a marked decline in public morale, growing cynicism and apathy, a breakdown in law and order and a sensational increase in crime and prostitution."[88]

Already mentioned are the continuing problem of political unrest and the government's use of law to criminalize and control dissent. There has also been a considerable increase in ordinary street crime. Shanghai radio broadcasts report increasing patterns of smuggling, gambling, black marketeering, and illegal speculation.[89] Reports of large-scale embezzlement schemes involving officials at the local and provincial levels are frequent in Chinese and Hong Kong newspapers.[90] Reappearing are descriptions of organized prostitution and even opium use in Peking, Shanghai, and Canton.[91] The trials of robbers in Peking were recently televised to arouse public indignation, and wide publicity was given to police crackdowns on robbers and pickpockets in Shanghai.[92] The police report that urban crime has become increasingly a gang phenomenon, and reports of looting during the recent earthquake in North China have also upset images of the country as a crime-free society.[93] It does not appear that any of these patterns even approaches those found in, say, Western Europe, to say nothing of Third World nations or the United States. Still, these are serious matters, as even nonviolent crimes like black marketeering undercut the whole basis of a socialist economy and further break down community solidarity.

Probably most threatening is the alarming increase in juvenile delinquency. Socialist nations are always particularly concerned about the ethics and behavior of their youth, since the process of transformation depends so much upon the kind of human values and social relations instilled in youth. Mao in part supported the Cultural Revolution as a way to build a revolutionary tradition for young people unborn at the time of the Long March. Recently, a high political legal official[94] announced that national statistics indicated at 300-percent increase in juvenile delinquency from 1950 to 1980, with most of the increase coming in the last few years in China's major cities. Shanghai's steady decreases in the first decades after 1949 were followed by an extraordinary increase in delinquency since 1965.

The explanations advanced by political legal officials and social scientists in China are a mixture of functionalism and conspiracy theory. Xiu Jian informs us that "China has a huge work force, and in most families both parents work, so that it easily happens that scientific education and strict supervision of children are neglected."[95] He also adds that, "during the Cultural Revolution they [the present-day delinquents] were in the growth process and the Gang of Four's influence weakened the authority of government, police, parents, elders, and teachers." Another Chinese scholar says:

Our opinion is that, aside from their own immaturity and the effects of the class struggle that is still continuing in this country, the ten year period of unrest (1965-1976) caused them to take a wrong turn and destroyed the beautiful vision in their minds. They answered the call from above (Mao) to participate in the "Great Proletarian Revolution" in the mistaken belief that they could create a brave new world colored in red in one stroke. What resulted, instead, was one havoc after another.[96]

The textbook used by Peking University law students concurs and emphasizes the negative economic effects of the Cultural Revolution and the impact of "remnant supporters of the Gang of Four."[97] High rates of unemployment among urban youth are also cited as a cause of delinquency, and this, too, is attributed to the Gang of Four whose leadership wrecked the national economy.[98]

FINAL COMMENT: COMPETING CRIMINOLOGIES

The trial of the Gang of Four was intended to be a showcase for the new professional legal system and criminal code, as well as a means of discrediting the radical leaders and their followers. Of course, few serious people could actually believe the charges that the Four were personally responsible for all of the tumultuous upheavals of 1965-1969. By attaching all blame to them, the current Peking leaders can more easily discredit and caricature the whole Cultural Revolution, its destruction as well as its progressive reforms. The prosecuting procurator and presiding judges at the trial repeatedly stressed that the Four were not on trial for their ideals, but only for their overt criminal acts. In fact,

Chiang Ching was absolutely right when she screamed from the witness stand that this was indeed a trial of Maoism itself.

The passing of Maoist ideology and the substitution of rule by law may indeed smooth China's relations with the West. It may even bring substantial industrial progress in a few cities and considerable material improvement for some Chinese. It will not, however, restore the sort of ongoing reforms and community activism that are essential to the prevention and control of crime. The whole notion of individual rights is itself borrowed from bourgeois legal traditions and stands in sharp contrast to the more ambitious socialist ideal of freedom as a social condition, measured by economic opportunity and the degree of control which citizens enjoy vis-à-vis the institutions of government and justice. It remains to be seen whether the political legal system now dominant can survive the buffeting of future conflicts born of increasing stratification. Professionalism, codified law, and the conservative theories of state and society have yet to bury the ghost of Maoism and may yet be challenged by what might be called China's "other" criminology.

NOTES

1. For support of his criticism, see James Brady, *Justice and Politics in People's Republic of China: Legal Order or Continuing Revolution?* (London: Academy Press, 1981); James Brady, "Political Contradictions and Justice Policy in People's China," *Contemporary Crises* 1 (April 1977):127-162; Victor Li, "Human Rights in a Chinese Context," in Ross Terrill (ed.), *The China Difference* (New York: Harper and Row, 1979), pp. 219-236; and Richard Pfeffer, "Crime and Punishment: China and the United States," in Jerome Cohen (ed.), *Contemporary Chinese Law* (Cambridge, Mass.: Harvard University Press, 1970), pp. 261-281.

2. This point is made by James Brady, "Season of Startling Alliance—Law and Politics in the Making of a New Order in China," *International Journal of Sociology of Law* 9 (January 1981):41-67; see rejoinder by Harold E. Pepinsky, "A Season of Disillusionment," *International Journal of Sociology of Law* 10, in press, and Brady's counter-response in the same issue.

3. The critique has been offered by Herman and Julia Schwendinger, "Defenders of Order or Guardians of Human Rights?" *Issues in Criminology* 5 (Summer 1970):123-157; Steven Spitzer, "Toward a Marxian Theory of Deviance," *Social Problems* 22 (June 1975):638-651; Anthony Platt, "Prospects for a Radical Criminology in the United States," *Crime and Social Justice* 1 (Spring-Summer 1974):2-10; Sheila Balkan, Ronald Berger, and Janet Schmidt, *Crime and Deviance in America* (Belmont, Calif.: Wadsworth Publishers, 1980); and Ian Taylor, Paul Walton, and Jock Young, *The New Criminology* (New York: Harper and Row, 1973).

4. Brady, "Political Contradictions and Justice Policy," and Brady, *Justice and Politics in People's China.*

5. As examples of cold warriors: Richard Walker, *China Under Communism* (New Haven, Conn.: Yale University Press, 1955); A. D. Barnett, *Communist China: The Early Years* (New York: Praeger Publications, 1964); and Hungdah Chin, "Criminal Punishment in Mainland China," *Journal of Criminal Law and Criminology* 68 (Septem-

ber 1977): 374-398. As examples of legalists: Jerome Cohen, *The Criminal Process in the People's Republic of China: An Introduction* (Cambridge, Mass.: Harvard University Press, 1968); Shao-Chuan Leng, *Justice in Communist China* (Dobbs Ferry, N.Y.: Oceana Publications, 1967). As examples of functionalists: Victor Li, "Law and Penology: Systems of Reform and Correction," in Michel Oskenberg (ed.), *China's Developmental Experience* (New York: Praeger, 1973); Stanley Lubman, "Form and Function in the Chinese Civil Process," *Columbia Law Review* 69, no. 4 (1969):532-575; Harold E. Pepinsky, "The People as the Principle of Legality in the People's Republic of China," *Journal of Criminal Justice* 1 (March 1973):51-60; Harold E. Pepinsky, "Reliance on Formal Written Law and Freedom and Social Control in the United States and the People's Republic of China," *British Journal of Sociology* 26 (September 1975):330-342; Pepinsky, "A Season of Disillusionment."

6. Mark Selden, *The Yenan Way* (New York: Doubleday, 1969).

7. V. S. Dutt, *China's Cultural Revolution* (New York: Asia Publishing House, 1970), pp. 90-97; Janet Salaff, "Urban Social Structure in the Wake of the Cultural Revolution," *China Quarterly*, no. 29 (January-March 1967):82-110; Immanuel C.Y. Hsu, "The Reorganization of Higher Education in Communist China, 1949-1961," *China Quarterly*, no. 19 (July-September 1964):128-160.

8. Victor Nee, "Revolution and Bureaucracy: Shanghai," in Victor Nee and James Peck (eds.), *China's Uninterrupted Revolution* (New York: Pantheon, 1973), pp. 322-414; Richard Pfeffer, "Serving the People and Continuing the Revolution," *China Quarterly*, no. 52 (October-December 1972):620-653; Richard Pfeffer, "Leaders and Masses," *Academy of Political Science Proceedings* 31, no. 1 (1973):157-174.

9. Mao Tse Tung, "Some Questions Concerning Methods of Leadership," in *Selected Works* (Peking: Foreign Language Press, 1943); Selden, *The Yenan Way*; and John Starr, *Continuing the Revolution* (Princeton, N.J.: Princeton University Press, 1979), pp. 72-98.

10. Mao Tse Tung, "Red and Expert," in T. Chew (ed.), *Mao Papers* (New York: Oxford University Press, 1970); Mao Tse Tung, "Some Questions Concerning Methods of Leadership"; Martin Whyte, "Inequality and Stratification in China," *China Quarterly*, no. 64 (September 1975):684-711; and Stuart Schram, "Mao Tse Tung and the Theory of the Permanent Revolution," *China Quarterly*, no. 46 (April-June 1971):221-244.

11. Gordon Bennett, "China's Mass Campaigns and Social Control," in A. R. Wilson, S. Greenblatt, and R. Wilson (eds.), *Deviance and Control in Chinese Society* (New York: Praeger, 1976), pp. 121-139; Gordon Bennett, *Yundong: Mass Campaigns in Chinese Communist Leadership* (Berkeley, Calif.: University of California, Center for Chinese Studies, 1976).

12. Charles Hoffman, "Work Incentive Policy in Communist China," *China Quarterly*, no. 17 (January-March 1964):92-110; Audrey Donnithone, "Centralized Economic Control in China," unpublished paper delivered at China Conference, Chicago, May 1966; Dutt, *China's Cultural Revolution*, pp. 9-19.

13. Liu Shao Chi, "Address to Eighth Party Congress," *Documents of Eighth Party Congress* (Peking: Foreign Language Press, 1956).

14. Teng Hsiao Ping, "Speech at National Education Conference," *Peking Review* 5 (May 1978):1-2.

15. *Jen Min Jih Pao*, February 2, 1979; this is the official daily of the Chinese Communist party as translated in *The Survey of China Mainland Press* and *Peking Review*, a foreign language weekly published by the Foreign Language Press of Peking.

16. Fred Pincus, "Higher Education and Socialist Transformation in China since 1970," *Review of Radical Political Economics* 11, no. 1 (1979):24-37.

17. Gordon Bennett, "China's Continuing Revolution: Will It Be Permanent?" *Asian Survey* 10, no. 1 (1970):2-17.

18. James Brady, *Conflict and Community in the Chinese Legal System* (Ph.D dissertation, 1974, University of California, Berkeley); Brady, "Political Contradictions and Justice Policy in People's China"; Brady, "Season of Startling Alliance"; Brady, *Justice and Politics in People's Republic of China*.

19. Tung Pi Wu, *Report to the Eighth Party Congress* (Peking: Foreign Language Press, 1956); Peng Zhen, "Report on the Draft Criminal Code," *Peking Review*, July 13, 1979, pp. 2-3.

20. People's Republic of China—National People's Congress, Constitutions of 1954, 1975, and 1978.

21. Victor Li, "The Role of Law in Communist China," *China Quarterly*, no. 44 (October-December 1970):71-111; Cohen, *Contemporary Chinese Law;* George Ginsburgs and Arthur Stahnke, "The People's Procurate in China—The Institutions in the Descendant—1954-1957," *China Quarterly*, no. 34 (April-June 1968):82-132; George Ginsburgs and Arthur Stahnke, "The Genesis of the People's Procurate: 1949-1951," *China Quarterly*, no. 20 (October-December 1964):1-37.

22. Victor Li, "Law and Penology"; Victor Li, "The Role of Law in Communist China"; Randle Edwards, "Reflections on Crime and Punishment in China, with Appended Sentencing Documents," *Columbia Journal of Transnational Law* 16, no. 1 (1977):44-103; Stanley Lubman, "Mao and Mediation: Politics and Dispute Settlement in Communist China," *California Law Review* 55, no. 5 (1967):1284-1325.

23. Gordon Bennett, "Mass Campaigns and Social Control," in Wilson, Greenblatt, and Wilson (eds.), *Deviance and Control in Chinese Society*; Tung Pi Wu, *Report to the Eighth Party Congress*; Cohen, *The Criminal Process in the People's Republic of China*; Jerome Cohen, "The Chinese Communist Party and Judicial Independence," *Harvard Law Review* 82, no. 5 (1970):967-1006; Teng Hsiao Ping, "Report on the Rectification Campaign," *Documents of Eighth Party Congress* (Peking: Foreign Language Press, 1965).

24. Brady, "Political Contradictions and Justice Policy in People's China"; Brady, "Season of Startling Alliance"; Pfeffer, "Serving the People and Continuing the Revolution"; Salaff, "Urban Social Structure in the Wake of the Cultural Revolution."

25. *Kuang Ming Hih Pao* (Chinese regional press, as translated in Survey of China Mainland Press), July 12, 1956; Shao-Chuan Leng, *Justice in Communist China*, pp. 90-92; Jerome Cohen, "Chinese Mediation on the Eve of Modernization," *California Law Review* 54, no. 3 (1973):1211-1226; Lubman, "Mao and Mediation."

26. Tung Tsu Ch'u, *Local Government in China Under the Ch'ing* (Palo Alto, Calif.: Stanford University Press, 1962), pp. 116-130; Phillip Chen, *Law and Justice: The Legal System in China* (New York: Danellen Publishers, 1973), pp. 8-24; Sybille Van Der Sprenkel, *Legal Institutions in Manchu China* (London: Athlone Press, 1962); John Watt, *The District Magistrate in Late Imperial China* (New York: Columbia University Press, 1972), pp. 210-225; Derek Bodde and Clarence Morris, *Law in Imperial China* (Cambridge, Mass.: Harvard University Press, 1967), pp. 160-184.

27. Bela Kun (ed.) and Chinese Soviet Republic, *Fundamental Laws of the Chinese Soviet Republic* (New York: International Publishers, 1934).

28. M. J. Meijer, *Marriage, Law and Policy* (Hong Kong: Hong Kong University Press, 1971), pp. 5-157; Albert Blaustein, *Fundamental Elements of Communist China* (South Hackensack, N.J.: F. B. Rothman, 1962).

29. Kun, *Fundamental Laws of the Chinese Soviet Republic*.

30. Theodore White and Annalee Jacoby, *Thunder Out of China* (New York: William Sloane Association, 1946), pp. 226-232.

31. Selden, *The Yenan Way*; Mao Tse Tung, "The Struggle in the Chingpang Mountains," *Selected Works* (Peking: Foreign Language Press, 1928); Richard Solomon, *Mao's Revolution and Chinese Political Culture* (Berkeley, Calif.: University of California Press, 1971), pp. 191-209.

32. Wen Hui Chen, "Wartime Mass Campaigns in Communist China" (Maxwell Air Force Base, Ala.: Human Resource Research Institute, 1955).

33. Ken Liberthal, "Post Liberation Suppression of Secret Societies in Tientsin," *China Quarterly*, no. 54 (June 1973):242-266; Edgar Snow, *The Other Side of the River* (New York: Hutchinson, 1964); Ezra Vogel, *Canton Under Communism* (Cambridge, Mass.: Harvard University Press, 1969), pp. 62-67; Lloyd Shearer, "Rewi Alley—50 Years in China," *Parade*, November 14, 1976.

34. Barnett, *Communist China: The Early Years*; Vogel, *Canton Under Communism*, pp. 80-83; T. J. Hughes, *Economic Development of Communist China* (London: Oxford University Press, 1959), pp. 81-86; Gene Hsiao, "Basic Legal Institutions in Communist China" (Berkeley, Calif.: Comparative Studies in Communist Societies Project, 1965), unpublished paper; Lynn White, "Corruption Redefined in Liberated Shanghai" (Berkeley, Calif.: Regional Seminar of Center for Chinese Studies, 1973); H. Franz Schurman, *Ideology and Organization in Communist China* (Berkeley, Calif.: University of California Press, 1966), pp. 315-319.

35. Ch'en Shao Yu, "Propaganda for Implementations of the Marriage Laws," *Jen Min Jih Pao*, February 25, 1953.

36. Meijer, *Marriage, Law and Policy*, pp. 112-113, 123-127.

37. Nancy Southwell, "Kicking the Habit," *New China* (Fall 1975):24-26.

38. *Kuang Ming Jih Pao*, August 8, 1950; *Hung Wing Ji Pao* (Chinese regional newspaper, translated in *Survey of China Mainland Press*), 1951, pp. 512-513.

39. Alyn and Adele Rickett, *Prisoners of Liberation* (New York: Doubleday, 1973), pp. 125-239; Jean Pasqualini, *Prisoner of Mao* (New York: Doubleday, 1977).

40. *Jen Min Jih Pao*, September 7, 1950.

41. Mao Tse Tung, "Investigation of the Peasant Movement in Hunan," in *Selected Works*, Vol. 1 (Peking: Foreign Language Press, 1927), p. 47.

42. Liu Shao Chi, "Address to Eighth Party Congress," pp. 82-83.

43. People's Republic of China, "Constitution of the People's Republic of China," 1954.

44. Tung Pi Wu, "Report to the Eighth Party Congress," pp. 94-95.

45. *Nan Fang Jih Pao*, September 7, 1951; *Jen Min Jih Pao*, September 7, 1950; Shen Chun Ju, "Report on Work of People's Courts," *Hsin Hua Yueh Pao* (HHYP) 2 (July 1950):500-502.

46. Cohen, "Chinese Mediation on the Eve of Modernization."

47. Ch'en Chin, "Training of Political Legal Cadres," *Chinese Law and Government* 17 (1981).

48. Tao-Tai Hsia, "Chinese Legal Publications: An Appraisal," in Jerome Cohen (ed.), *Contemporary Chinese Law* (Cambridge, Mass.: Harvard University Press, 1970).

49. Roderick McFarquahar, *The Hundred Flowers Campaign and the Chinese Intellectuals* (New York: Praeger, 1960).

50. T'ao Ta-yung, "The Flowers in Bloom Are Too Few," *Jen Min Jih Pao*, April 20, 1957.

51. Hughes, *Economic Development of Communist China*, E. L. Wheelwright and Bruce McFarlane, *The Chinese Road to Socialism* (New York: Monthly Review Press, 1970), pp. 31-98.

52. Gerd Ruge, "An Interview with Chinese Legal Officials," *China Quarterly*, no. 61 (March 1975):118-126; Alexander Casella, "The Nanniwan May 7th Cadre School," *China Quarterly*, no. 53 (January-February 1973):153-157; Pfeffer, "Serving the People and Continuing the Revolution."

53. Hsieh Fu Chih, "Speech Before Public Security Cadres," in *Samples of Red Guard Literature*, Vol. 2 (1967), Joint Publications Research Services (translations of political and social information on Communist China); Stephen Pan and Raymond J. de Jaegher, *Peking's Red Guards* (New York: Twin Circle Publishers, 1968), pp. 36-53; *Hung Win Ji Pao*, December 22, 1966; *Jen Min Jih Pao*, June 1, 1966; Thomas Robinson, "The Wuhan Incident: Local Strife and Provincial Rebellion During the Cultural Revolution," *China Quarterly*, no. 47 (July-September 1971):413-430.

54. Hai Shuan Lu, "Interview," *New York Times*, August 13, 1975; see also Ruge, "Interview with Chinese Legal Officials."

55. Cohen, "Notes on Legal Education in the People's Republic of China."

56. Franklin Lamb, "Interview with Chinese Legal Officials," *China Quarterly*, no. 66 (June 1976):323-327; Ruge, "Interview with Chinese Legal Officials."

57. Cheng Shih Yi, "Open Door Education," *Peking Review*, January 2, 1976, pp. 3-4.

58. Salaff, "Urban Social Structure in the Wake of the Cultural Revolution."

59. *Cheng Fa Yen Chiu* (Legal Research), 1959; leading national law journal published in Peking; Institute of Criminal Law Research, 1958.

60. Felix Greene, *The Wall Has Two Sides* (London: Jonathan Cape Publishers, 1962), p. 187.

61. Ts'ao Tsu Tan, "On the Relationship Between Crime and Class Struggle," *Cheng fa Yen Chiu*, 1964, as translated in *Chinese Law and Government* 1, no. 1 (1968):80-91.

62. Richard Kraus, "Class Conflict and the Vocabulary of Social Analysis in China," *China Quarterly*, no. 69 (March 1977):54-74.

63. Pan and Jaegher, *Peking's Red Guards*, pp. 130-140.

64. Bennett, "China's Mass Campaigns and Social Control" and Bennett, *Yundong*.

65. Sidney Greenblatt, "Campaigns and the Manufacture of Deviance in Chinese Society," in Wilson, Greenblatt, and Wilson (eds.), *Deviance and Control in Chinese Society*.

66. Wang Hsiao T'ing, "An Evaluation and Analysis of China's Revised Constitutions," *Chinese Law and Government* 9, nos. 2-3 (1978):34-53; Edwards, "Reflections on Crime and Punishment in China, with Appended Sentencing Documents"; Pfeffer, "Serving the People and Continuing the Revolution"; Fredrick Teiwes, "Before and After the Cultural Revolution," *China Quarterly*, no. 58 (April-May 1974):332-348.

67. Teiwes, "Before and After the Cultural Revolution"; Hua Tuo Feng, "Report to the Eleventh Party Congress," *Documents of the 11th Party Congress* (Peking: Foreign Language Press, 1979); Li Hong Rin, "What Sort of Socialism Should We Uphold?"; H. J. Lee, *The Politics of the Chinese Cultural Revolution* (Berkeley, Calif.: University of

California Press, 1978), pp. 81-87, 142-148; and Charles Bettleheim, "The Great Leap Backward," in *China Since Mao* (New York: Monthly Review, 1980).

68. Shang Zhe, "Persistently Carry Forward Proletarian Democracy," *Hung Chi* (New China News Agency), June 1, 1979.

69. Editorial, *Jen Jim Jih Pao*, July 20, 1979.

70. Pincus, "Higher Education and Socialist Transformation in China Since 1970"; Hua Tuo Feng, "Report to the Eleventh Party Congress"; Suzanne Pepper, "An Interview on Changes in Chinese Education After the Gang of Four," *China Quarterly*, no. 72 (December 1977):815-824; Teng Hsiao Ping, "Speech at National Education."

71. *Kuang Ming Jih Pao*, February 2, 1979.

72. *New York Times*, February 28, 1978.

73. Chou Hsun, "Present State of Future Outlook of Social Science Research in Communist China," *Chi shih mien tai*, no. 103, as found in *Chinese Law and Government* 12, no. 4 (1978):86.

74. *Joint Publications Research Services*, 1979.

75. Ronald C. Keith, "Transcript of Discussion with Wu Daying and Zhang Honglin Concerning Legal Changes and Civil Rights," *China Quarterly*, no. 81 (March 1980):111-121; Hua Tu Feng, "Report to the Eleventh Party Congress"; Editorial, *Hung Chi*, June 1, 1979.

76. William Butler, "China in the Family of Socialist Legal Systems," *China Now*, no. 91 (1980):11-14.

77. Ch'en Chin, "Training of Political Legal Cadres"; *Jen Min Jih Pao*, May 1, 1980; New China News Agency, July 31, 1980; Lie Jiegiong, "Complete in Four Modernizations and the People's Democratic Legal System," *Peking Review*, July 20, 1979.

78. National People's Congress, *Constitution of the People's Republic of China* (Peking: Foreign Language Press, 1978); see commentary by Jerome Cohen, "China's Changing Constitution," *China Quarterly*, no. 76 (December 1978):794-840.

79. National People's Congress, "Law on Criminal Procedure of People's Republic of China," New China News Agency, July 4, 1979; National People's Congress, "Organic Law for People's Procurate of People's Republic of China," New China News Agency, July 5, 1979.

80. National People's Congress, "Criminal Law of People's Republic of China," New China News Agency, July 7, 1979.

81. *Peking Review*, June 8, 1979; Peng Zhen, "Report on the Draft Criminal Code."

82. *Jen Min Jih Pao*, April 6, 1979.

83. Zhou Zheng, "The Dazibao (Wall Posters): Its Rise and Fall," *Peking Review*, October 6, 1980.

84. Fox Butterfield, "China Dissident Likens Present to Repressive Past," *New York Times*, November 15, 1979; Fox Butterfield, "Another Dissident on Trial in Peking," *New York Times*, October 13, 1979; Barrie and Emilie Chi, "Crime and Punishment in China," *New York Times Magazine*, October 7, 1979, pp. 48-70.

85. Brady, "Political Contradictions and Justice Policy in People's China"; Jürgen Domes, "The 'Gang of Four' and Hua Tuo Feng: Analysis of Political Events in 1975-1976," *China Quarterly*, no. 71 (September 1977):473-487; *Peking Review*, July 13, 1978.

86. *Peking Review*, August 10, 1979.

87. National People's Congress, "Constitution of the People's Republic of China," New China News Agency, 1975 (1st Revision), 1978 (2d Revision).

88. Keyes Beech, "Crime Comes to China," *Boston Globe*, November 24, 1976, p. 1.

89. *Jen Min Jih Pao*, 1979.

90. *New York Times*, January 10, 1980; *Peking Review*, May 18, 1979; Bangzi Mao, et al., "Elements Violating Law and Discipline Cannot Be Shown Softheartedness," Hangehow Radio, as found in *Chinese Broadcasts*, Joint Publications Research Services, no. 76883, 1980; *Peking Review*, April 14, 1978.

91. Marian London and John London, "Prostitution in Canton," *Worldview*, May 1977; Fox Butterfield, "An Upsurge of Crime in China," *New York Times*, November 15, 1979.

92. Joint Publications Research Services, 1979; Union Research Institute, Hong Kong, 1978; United Press-International, "Peking Using Television in Drive Against Crime," *Boston Globe*, March 12, 1980; James Sterba, "China Entering New Legal Era," *New York Times*, September 13, 1979, p. A2.

93. *New York Times*, February 26, 1980; Butterfield, "An Upsurge of Crime in China."

94. Xiu Jian, "Research on Juvenile Deliquency Problem," *Shehui Kexue* (Social Science), no. 47, as found in *China Report*, Joint Publications Research Services, no. 76971, 1980.

95. Ibid.

96. Tan Tao tuo, "Young People Need Understanding," Peking Kuangming Radio broadcast, August 28, 1980, as found in *China Report*, no. 76883, p. 55.

97. Chinese Research Group, Law Institute of Chinese Academy of Social Sciences (CRG-CASS), *Lectures on Criminal Law*, as found in *Chinese Law and Government* 13, no. 2 (1980):7, 26-27; also see Bangzi Mao, "Elements Violating Law."

98. CRG-CASS, *Lectures on Criminal Law*.

BIBLIOGRAPHY

To a remarkable degree, Western literature on developments in China—certainly that literature in the United States—has expanded recently both quantitatively and qualitatively. The following items are of necessity only a selection among the books and articles that would be useful to readers who want to know more about criminology and its background in the People's Republic of China. For each of the selected references, the central function it will serve for the reader is summarized.

Barnett, A. D. *Communist China: The Early Years*. New York: Praeger Publications, 1964.
This work focuses on socialist transition justice and land-urban reform in China—a treatment from the perspective of anticommunist "cold warriors."

Blaustein, Albert. *Fundamental Documents of Communist China*. South Hackensack, N.J.: F. B. Rothman, 1962.
This is an important collection of organic laws, criminal codes, and early constitutions from 1949 to 1960.

Boddie, Derek, and Clarence Morris. *Law in Imperial China*. Cambridge, Mass.: Harvard University Press, 1967.
This major treatise is on precommunity legal heritage.

Brady, James. *Justice and Politics in People's Republic of China: Legal Order or Continuing Revolution?* London: Academic Press, 1981.
This historical study details the evolution of legal theory and institutions in modern China, utilizing political-economic methods and developing a Marxist perspective.

Brady, James. "Political Contradictions and Justice Policy in People's China." *Contemporary Crises* 1 (April 1977):127-162.
Brady discusses popular and bureaucratic justice systems and political conflicts from 1949 to 1976.

Brady, James. "Season of Startling Alliance—Law and Politics in the Making of a New Order in China." *International Journal of Law* 9 (January 1981):41-67.
Brady describes the professionalization of justice and the conservative transformation of the state and society since 1976.

Chen, Phillip. *Law and Justice: The Legal System in China.* New York: Danellen Publishers, 1973.
Written from the legalist perspective, the book includes historical materials on the Imperial Era as well as brief discussions of laws and legal bureaucracies up to 1960.

Chin, Hungdah. "Criminal Punishment in Mainland China." *Journal of Criminal Law and Criminology* 68 (September 1977):374-398.
An essentially cold war perspective considers the totalitarian aspect of Chinese justice: denial of the due process, and so on.

Cohen, Jerome. "China's Changing Constitution." *China Quarterly*, no. 76 (December 1978):794-840.
Cohen traces textual changes in China's successive socialist constitutions, with critical commentary from the legalist perspective.

Cohen, Jerome. *Contemporary Chinese Law, Research Problems and Perspectives.* Cambridge, Mass.: Harvard University Press, 1970.
This eclectic collection of papers, both European and American, focuses on the methodology of comparative law and on the development of studies on Chinese law in China, the United States, Europe, the USSR, and Japan.

Cohen, Jerome. *The Criminal Process in the People's Republic of China: An Introduction.* Cambridge, Mass.: Harvard University Press, 1968.
The most important work among early legalist writings, this book includes brief historical analyses of justice institutions, a study of the Security Administration and Punishment Act, and a great mass of illustrative criminal cases from the Chinese press.

Edwards, Randle. "Reflections on Crime and Punishment in China, with Appended Sentencing Documents." *Columbia Journal of Transnational Law* 16, no. 1 (1977):44-103.
This functionalist analysis of justice procedures in China is supplemented by a series of cases drawn from newly translated Chinese sources.

Ginsburgs, George, and Art Stahnka. "The Genesis of the People's Procurate in Commu-
    nist China, 1949-1951." *China Quarterly* 20 (October-December 1964):1-37.
Early legalist writings trace the rise and fall of the most professional of China's legal
bureaus from 1949 to 1964.

Gudoshnikov, L. M. *Legal Organs of the People's Republic of China.* Moscow, 1957,
    and translated by Joint Publications Research Services, 1959.
Written during the era of good feelings between China and the USSR, this work glows
with the pride of "parents" over China's progress toward codification and professionalism.

Hsiang, Shih. "New Problems in the Realm of Legal Studies." Reprinted in *Chinese Law
    and Government* 1, no. 2 (1968).
An important Maoist theoretician examines the place of law and the mass line in the
continuing revolution.

Kun, Bela (ed.). *Fundamental Laws of the Chinese Soviet Republic.* New York: Interna-
    tional Publishers, 1934.
Kun presents early pre-Liberation materials and the laws of the Civil War era.

Leng, Shao-Chuan. *Justice in Communist China.* Dobbs Ferry, N.Y.: Oceana Publica-
    tions, 1967.
This cold war analysis of the historical development of the Chinese legal system from
1927 to 1965 focuses on the lack of judicial independence and formal procedure safe-
guards in describing the society as a "totalitarian dictatorship."

Li, Victor. "Law and Penology: Systems of Reform and Corrections." In Michel Oskenberg
    (ed.). *China's Developmental Experience.* New York: Praeger, 1973.
One of the classic "functionalist" articles, written by the foremost spokesman of the
school, this work emphasizes the importance of the informal processes in dispute resolution, crime control, prevention, and—more importantly—the ongoing correctional process within "small groups" in Chinese mass organizations.

Li, Victor. "The Public Security Bureau of Political Legal Work in Hu-yang 1952-1964."
    In Robert Lindbeck (ed.). *Management of a Revolutionary Society.* New York:
    Praeger, 1972.
This is the best study available of Chinese police organization and practice in a rural
county.

Li, Victor. "The Role of Law in Communist China." *China Quarterly,* no. 44 (October-
    December 1970):77-111.
Li traces the Chinese preference for the internal model back to precommunist philosophical traditions and discusses the cultural and political issues that mitigate against and limit
the application of the external legalistic model.

Lifton, Robert. *Thought Reform and the Psychology of Totalism.* New York: Norton, 1963.
Lifton studies the treatment of American prisoners-of-war by the Chinese during the
Korean War.

Lubman, Stanley. "Mao and Mediation: Politics and Dispute Settlement in Communist China." *California Law Review* 55, no. 5 (1967):1284-1325.
Lubman has written probably the finest work on the mediation process and the relationship of mass organizations to popular justice.

Mao Tse Tung. "On the Correct Handling of Contradictions among the People." Peking: Foreign Language Press, 1975.
This crucial article forms the basis for Maoist criminal process in regard to the distinction between antagonistic and nonantagonistic contradictions.

Mao Tse Tung. "On the Investigations of the Peasant Movement in Hunao." Peking: Foreign Language Press, 1929.
This important early work is on mass line in justice and class conflict.

Meyer, M. J. *Marriage, Law and Policy*. Hong Kong: Hong Kong University Press, 1971.
Meyer has produced a fine study of the marriage laws, implementation of these laws, and social consequences in the early years of Chinese communism.

Pepinsky, Harold E. *Crime and Conflict: A Study of Law and Society*. New York: Academic Press, 1976.
The Chinese justice process—especially in regard to the informal aspects—is used as a foil for comparison with American justice.

Pepinsky, Harold E. "Reliance on Formal Written Law and Freedom and Social Control in the United States and the People's Republic of China." *British Journal of Sociology* 26 (September 1975):330-342.
An essentially functional approach is applied to the informal aspects of social control.

Pepinsky, Harold E. "A Season of Disillusionment." *International Journal of the Sociology of Law*, in press.
An anarchist position on law and the state is taken in this reply to and critique of Brady, "Season of Startling Alliance..." (listed above).

Pfeffer, Richard. "Serving the People and Continuing the Revolution." *China Quarterly*, no. 52 (October-December 1972):620-653.
Pfeffer presents a Marxist assessment of post-Cultural Revolution reforms, including May 7th Schools, revolutionary committees, and the process of ongoing rectification.

Selden, Mark. *The Yenan Way*. New York: Doubleday, 1969.
Selden's book is a fundamentally important work on the germination and development of mass line ideology and government institutions during the Civil War era.

Van Der Sprenkel, Sybille. *Legal Institutions in Manchu China*. London: Athlone Press, 1962.
This important assessment of justice policy and law under the Manchu government in China clearly demonstrates the brutal, unpredictable nature of imperial justice.

Vogel, Ezra. *Canton Under Communism*. Cambridge, Mass.: Harvard University Press, 1969.
Vogel has written one of the best portrayals of the socialist transition process in the urban setting. It has a few scattered but useful passages on social control and crime.

Walker, Richard. *China Under Communism*. New Haven, Conn.: Yale University Press, 1955.
A prominent anticommunist cold warrior develops "thought control" ideas as basic for social policy in China.

Wilson, Amy, Sidney Greenblatt, and Richard Wilson (eds.). *Deviance and Control in Chinese Society*. New York: Praeger Publications, 1977.
This work offers some excellent studies on the small group structure, deviance and control, as well as the process of mass rectification campaigns and their consequences for political and social elites.

6

CZECHOSLOVAKIA

Oldřich Suchý and Jiří Nezkusil

In order to understand Czechoslovakia's criminology, one must examine its subject matter, methodology, and place in the system of science. Criminology is usually conceived in either a narrow or broad sense. In the narrow sense, the subject matter of criminology is thought to be limited to the etiology of criminality, its methodology to deal with only a restricted array of scientific findings, and its place to be within the scope of the criminal law. In the broad sense, the subject matter takes in all forms of antisocial conduct, the methodology involves rigorous use of all forms of scientific investigation, and its place is to draw on the knowledge of all branches of science.

The discussion in this chapter follows this format. Thus, first, we must cope with the issues of subject matter, methods, and scientific foundations as a basis for pointing out the close interrelationships of the three aspects of criminology. Then, it will be possible to summarize the conception of scientific criminology in concrete terms.

Since the late 1950s when Czechoslovakian criminology originated, the three aspects of criminology have been debated in deliberations through which the contemporary perceptions of criminology crystalized.[1] The general emphasis was that those organizations engaged in the struggle against criminality should act consistently with the findings of scientific research. Of particular importance are the findings of the science of criminal law, procedural law, criminalistics, penology, and, above all, criminology. In these terms, criminology is identified as a branch of science dealing with the nature of criminality (its structure and its dynamics), with its causes and conditions, with the qualities of the offender's personality, and with all the measures and means applied in the struggle against those phenomena that are undesirable in a socialist society.

THE SUBJECT MATTER OF CRIMINOLOGY

In its structural and dynamic dimensions, criminality is the subject matter of criminology. Investigation of questions about the nature of criminality is an essential prerequisite to probing how it is caused and to effectively draft preventive measures whereby criminology can be a means for society to cope with this undesirable phenomenon.

Here criminality is understood to be a complex of socially conditioned acts which in their relatively wholesale character seriously menace society so that valid legislation declares them to be either major crimes or petty offenses. Criminology deals with criminality, both as a mass social phenomenon and as the misconduct of individuals, in all the fundamental circumstances connected with it. Investigation takes in criminality as social-class conditioned misconduct, but, unlike the conceptions of criminality in bourgeois society, criminality is perceived from the perspective of socialist morals and legal principles.

Investigation of criminality begins with prosecuted or condemned offenders, but a more complete and profound understanding of criminality—including the mastering of detailed questions latent in this misconduct—calls for expanding the groups that are studied. Depending on the kind of criminal activity, the prosecuted or convicted offenders are only a part of real criminality, although the share captured by official data differs according to the type of offense. Ideally, the research data would include the number of known crimes whether or not they are prosecuted and, when feasible, the latent criminality that eludes the official registration of offenders. Because socialist society is interested in the eventual uprooting of all criminality, both apparent and latent criminality must be considered in order to reach more precise and accurate conclusions on its causes and to elaborate effective measures for its suppression.

Another important obligation of criminology is to avoid limiting the sphere of research to that criminality defined according to legal norms. In keeping with the circumstances encountered, criminology must move beyond crimes as defined by narrow legal norms and deal with socially harmful behaviors particularly relevant to administrative law. Attention must be given to so-called coherent sociopathological behavior even though not touched by law. With what sociopathologies and to what extent does criminology deal? Such phenomena as alcoholism and drug abuse are relevant to the degree that they inevitably involve explanations that also apply to the criminality defined by criminal law. Sometimes sociopathology, even when expressed in minor antisocial acts, can be an early stage of the manifestation of criminality. Reactions to sociopathology are important for prevention of broadly defined deviance, but they can also strike at the roots of criminality as a particular form of deviance.

In these ways, a broad definition of the scope of criminology is vital to the development of penal policy and the appropriate modification of the legal foundations of policy. Within this scope are criminality as defined specifically by penal law, the petty deviance covered by administrative law, and other forms of rule-breaking that otherwise would not be considered law violations. Above we have referred to drinking and drug abuse, but parasitism and other immoral acts would also be included. The misconduct of children, when it constitutes predelinquency, is included when it can lead to activities that are subject to prosecution under the criminal law.

Criminological investigations may follow the course of either "pure" or empirical research, depending on the viewpoint adopted, the level of abstraction taken, the time available, the territorial expanse covered, and similar considerations. Regardless of the course followed, the quality of data sources must be improved and the methodology strengthened for effective management of criminality. Special attention must be devoted to improving uniform penal statistics, to maximum utilization of modern computer techniques, and to broader application of statistical methods.

The prognosis of the development of criminality as a mass phenomenon also constitutes a vital aspect of criminological investigation. Only with the availability of valid and reliable knowledge can there be intelligent planning and meaningful implementation of a systematic struggle against violation of the legal rules of the socialist society generally and against criminality in particular. The knowledge must encompass the central tendencies and complex interrelations among tendencies that characterize the various forms of violation. Czechoslovakian criminology recognizes that the prognosis of the development of mass criminality must be dealt with in planning the battle against crime. Within the investigative framework, there must also be a prognosis of the antisocial behavior of individuals so that appropriate measures can be taken to deal effectively with the particular perpetrator.

The etiology of criminality and the conditions favoring its appearance are also key parts of the subject matter of criminology. The elaboration of necessary measures raises especially complicated difficulties for researchers. Accomplishments have fallen short of the ideal because of overly simplistic perspectives on the causes and conditions of criminality in a socialist state. There has been excessive optimism that the conditions of the socialist state will automatically eliminate criminality. Gradually, Czechoslovakians have overcome such deficiencies through the development of socialist criminology.

Fundamental social changes that have taken place in the Czechoslovak Socialist Republic have raised the possibility of drastically reducing the incidence of crime. To take advantage of the possibility, well-directed effort must be concentrated on suppressing the causes and associated conditions of criminality. At a most general level, criminology can provide insights into the causes of crime under the conditions of a socialist state, but a full and exhaustive explanation for all concrete manifestations cannot be given. Even if such an explanation were feasible, the research responsibilities are formidable when different territorial units and time periods are considered in the search for explanations of particular classes of crime. Yet, without the undergirding of generalized principles, the detailed exploration of crimes in concrete reality offers only limited knowledge of the general causes of criminality.

The offender's personality is an important part of the investigation of criminality because personality and environmental factors interlock in ways that are crucial to explaining criminality as a social phenomenon, to detecting its causes, and to determining how to prevent it. The accomplishment of those three purposes, Shlyapochnikov says, "is not possible without the disclosure of the mechanism of the offender's antisocial conduct, without the deep investigation of everything that characterizes his personality as a social individual."[2]

Czechoslovakian criminology deals with the offender's personality at different levels, depending on which of the branches of science is drawn upon for concepts and a reservoir of established facts. The level may be that of the personality in general, that of a particular class of offender (for instance, recidivists or juvenile delinquents), or that of a single perpetrator of a crime. Victimology also enters into a consideration of the offender's personality because of the interplay of the personality qualities of the perpetrator and the victim in the criminal incident.

The field of criminology is not limited to etiology because the prevention of crime—including its suppression and management—is crucial to socialist criminology as a science. The incorporation of prevention is justified by close connection of the understanding of crime causation with the effectiveness of preventive measures. From this standpoint, Czechoslovakian criminology regards crime prevention as a special aspect of social regulation and the management of social processes.

General crime prevention is related to those general social measures that are designed to strengthen Czechoslovakian society and, as a byproduct, to remove the conditions favorable to the appearance of crime. Criminological research plays a part by alerting public agencies to the criminogenic implications of the general social processes that are relevant to crime prevention. In addition, there is special crime prevention that focuses on concrete criminogenic factors. Special preventive measures may target a certain territorial unit, particular types of crime, reduction of recidivism, or otherwise have specialized purposes. The target may be criminals whose behavior is to be changed through reeducation, or the target may be deviants who have the potentiality for engaging in crime.

Criminological research has produced useful suggestions for crime prevention, but Czechoslovakian criminology has yet to work out in sufficient detail the answers to the problems related to crime prevention. Planning and coordination are essential to implementing the myriad elements of systematic crime prevention. The elements must be synchronized so that they are employed appropriately at each of the time stages over the period of implementation. Crime prevention operates at different levels in respect to either environmental or psychological factors. The implementation of preventive measures in a time sequence is closely connected with the level of preventive actions. All of this indicates that the planning of crime prevention is a challenge for the criminologist. Within the broad framework of general planning, criminological research has the task of clarifying the role of the many specialists carrying out preventive programs, identifying the points of their interaction, and specifying their particular functions in the overall preventive enterprise.

METHODS OF CZECHOSLOVAK
SOCIALIST CRIMINOLOGY

Czechoslovakian criminology is based on the premise that criminality is a social phenomenon intimately interrelated with and conditioned by other social phenomena. Marxist principles are crucial to understanding criminality which stems from the economic qualities and intrastructure of a given socioeconomic system. Criminality and its causes are investigated in terms of their historical development through the course of change viewed as a transition of quantity into quality. Czechoslovakian criminology understands the implementation of preventive measures against criminality to be a manifestation of the broader contradictions of the struggle of the new and progressive against the old and obsolete.

The basic propositions and principles of dialectic and historical materialism, of course, call for special methods of criminological investigation. There is a special interest in the application of the methods of mathematical and analytical statistics, sociology, psychology, and social psychology, but the cybernetic techniques and methods are also employed. The character of the particular research objective determines the choice of methodology.

The statistical and sociological methods are oriented toward research into large-scale social phenomena, into the sources of criminality that are external to the individual offender, and into the conflicts generated by the social contradictions. Among the sociological methods are the historic, comparative, typological, monographic, experimental, and genetic methods. Especially useful are the structural and generic methods recently employed for investigating the origin and development of phenomena as wholes in terms of structure and functions. Related to these methods are the statistical, experimental, monographic, historical, and typological procedures, as well as the techniques of direct observation, field inquiry, and interviews. Analysis of various kinds of documents is employed, especially reports of criminal proceedings and files on convicted offenders under supervision.

Those methods are fundamental to criminology in permitting more or less complete descriptions of criminological phenomena and other phenomena occurring concurrently in time and place (criminography). The descriptive analyses are grounded in theoretical concepts and are supplemented by careful and exacting exploration of correlations. The conclusions are also derived from relevant analyses of the broader structures within which criminality occurs to determine the regularities and dynamics of criminality as it develops within a framework of underlying causes and conditions.

In the past, investigations of mass phenomena were limited to partial use of statistical charts and diagrams to illustrate the parallel occurrence of various factors with the incidence of crime. A prime example would be the classical investigation of corn prices and crimes against property. Modern statistical analyses promise to disclose the strength or quality of relationships beyond a gross relationship, especially with the help of computers and cybernetic models. Nevertheless, criminologists have made only a beginning in taking advantage of modern techniques. In addition, the current quality of official statistics raises major difficulties. Recent development of uniform statistics of prosecutors and courts has not been fully implemented. Furthermore, there has been insufficient improvement of research design, particularly in sociological and statistical research.

Other methods used to study the personality structure of individuals as individuals are psychological and psychiatric methods which present a complex of clinical approaches for observation, field investigation, and complex examination of subjects.

Scientific investigation of criminality is impossible without considering the offender's personality as a product of the dynamic development of the psyche and human consciousness. Personality is essentially shaped by a complex of all social relationships. The individual's values depend on an understanding of the patterns and needs that go with development of the society as a whole. His or her values are also related to understanding the significance of his or her conduct to the entire society. To understand the personality and associated conduct, primary attention is directed to those social relations that are present during development of the individual's psyche. This form of examination gives some insight into the mind of the criminal since it shows the effects of linkages between misconduct and early social relationships. For some offenders, the psyche is such that certain individuals are vulnerable to negative social factors and are disposed to antisocial conduct.

There are two extreme types of offenders: those who engage in crime only under quite extraordinary and special conditions; and those who commit crimes even when subject to anticriminogenic conditions. Multiple recidivists are characterized by seriously inadequate socialization, usually restricted intellectual capacities, inadequate vocational qualifications, and so on. Their major social deficits favor recidivism. Because transformation of the whole personality structure is involved—including their consciousness—the multiple recidivists pose great difficulties for the struggle against criminality.

The individual-oriented research is the basis for preventive measures, primarily using reeducation methods that rely on pedagogical, vocational, psychological, and psychiatric approaches. Psychotherapy is generally employed, particularly group psychotherapy and psychodrama. Nevertheless, even when the emphasis is on the individual offender, the research draws on modern analytic methods, especially those of social psychology which is methodologically linked closely with sociology.[3]

The range of applied methods gives a character to criminology that demands teamwork and the representation of many branches of science in the knowledge the criminologists master. Those who are involved in criminology in the Czechoslovak Socialist Republic necessarily are recruited from different professions in which they were originally educated. They bring to the field different academic preparations and professional orientations that may block their common understanding. Their common task—to contribute to the complex elucidation of the differing facets of criminal behavior—is to promote the integration of scientific findings with the prevention of criminality.

SCIENTIFIC FOUNDATIONS OF CRIMINOLOGY

From the perspective of Marxist philosophy, the starting point for criminological theory is the premise that criminality is a social phenomenon that can only be overcome as such. This view is of basic importance for all scientific branches. The investigation of the concrete social relations proceeds on the basis of historical materialism, with the association between criminology and sociology being prominent. Criminological investigation also relies on psychology, economics, pedagogics, and a number of juridical branches of which jurisprudence is especially noteworthy. These disciplines make criminology a branch of science.

Czechoslovakian literature conveys the theme that criminology stands on the borders of the disciplines, and overall, as a branch of science, criminology is a borderline scientific branch. Criminology is a synthetic science that presents the findings of those sciences relevant to criminality, but at present this is more of an ideal than an accomplishment. It cannot be stated absolutely that knowledge of only some branches of science is connected with criminology and to apply them as though that portion were sufficient to deal with the greater part of criminality. Similarly, recommendations drawn from only selected branches would produce only partial means of crime prevention. These tendencies would overemphasize fragmentary linkages betweeen criminogenic conditions and overly narrow approaches to crime prevention.

Accordingly, research, even when it apparently deals only tangentially with criminology, can have great importance for the choice of preventive measures. The relative importance of various findings can be evaluated reliably only when the full scope of the branches of science contributing to criminology is considered. While partial means of prevention have their place, successful forestalling of potential crime ultimately depends on the integration of the elements that make up the overall comprehensive effort. Thus, a full range of the relevant branches of science must be included within the theoretical resources of criminology.

Criminology developed in the Czechoslovak Republic within the framework of criminal law. With the further development of criminology, opinions as to its place in the social sciences have changed. Finally, it is recognized as an independent science, side by side with jurisprudence, because criminology approaches the investigation of criminality to deal with other aspects and to employ methods other than those of criminal law. Criminal law views the crime and its perpetrator as phenomena subject to penal sanctions, and it investigates mostly through the logical, deductive, normative, and juridic methods. Scientific criminology understands crime to be a collection of facts that are to be investigated through inductive methods, especially those of statistics and sociology. Criminology also extends its attention to check on the effectiveness of all means of dealing with crime, of which penal methods are a part, and to find new ways for gradually reducing and then liquidating criminality.

The independence of criminology does not oppose the continuance of investigation into criminal law. On the contrary, criminal investigations must proceed through a close partnership of criminology and jurisprudence. Along with the science of criminal law, criminal proceedings, criminalistics, and other branches that have been included under the term "penal sciences," criminology deals with criminality. In this respect, criminology is related to criminal law through its place in shaping penal policy. In drawing on research into penal practices, criminology extends the range and contents and more precisely defines the findings of the science of criminal law. Vice versa, scholars of criminal law make similar contributions to criminology. In short, each field of study conditions and completes the other.

There is a close connection between criminology and the science on the penal policy of the socialist state. The penal policy generally agreed on is dedicated to the task of eliminating criminality. Penal science is a relatively independent branch that is not a mere appendage of applied criminology. Penal policy draws from criminology as does criminal law. The criminological findings are a certain "specific part of the scientific basis of penal policy."[4] At the same time, through its interventions penal policy influences the subject matter investigated by criminologists, especially for the unanticipated negative effects of legislation of a criminogenic nature. Penal policy primarily studies and recommends what misconduct should be declared punishable or unpunishable at a given time. The recommendations may lead to revision of laws, new laws, or changes stemming from reinterpretation of laws and their applications. Criminology investigates the consequences of implemented recommendations on penal policy. The mutual interaction and the reciprocity of penal policy and criminology are, of course, of great variety and very numerous.[5]

ORIGIN AND DEVELOPMENT OF THE INSTITUTE

As mentioned earlier, criminology in Czechoslovakia is now viewed as an independent entity rather than as an element within the science of criminal law. In 1959, this attitude resulted in the emergence of the central institutional base of criminology in Czechoslovakia—the Criminological Research Institute which is attached to the Office of the Prosecutor General of the Republic. It was originally known as the Criminalistic Institute because fundamental questions about its mission were not clarified. In 1965, the name was changed to the Criminological Research Institute when its research activities were fully directed toward the causes and prevention of criminality.

The early period of the development of Czechoslovakian criminology established the subject matter and personnel that, it was agreed, are prerequisites for criminological research. The research staff received training in concepts, methodology, and techniques that gave a sense of direction to their investigations. Meanwhile, lengthy discussions were held concerning the character of criminological science and its place among the sciences and concerning its relationships with the science of criminal law.

From the "speculative" stage, broad-range empirical investigations were to emerge. Among the forerunners of more substantial research was the investigation of the stealing of property under socialist ownership in the machine industry in one district and preliminary inquiries into juvenile delinquency. In the years 1967-1970, there already was evidence of a well-developed program of empirical research. The social and personality qualities of juvenile delinquents have been examined extensively. A wide array of projects have expanded the data resources of state and social agencies. Research has guided policy on preventing juvenile delinquency and on the Governmental Commission for the Care of Endangered Youth. A substantial portion of the research findings on juvenile criminality has been published in books.

Particularly valuable results have been obtained from research in more effectively identifying criminality as a mass social phenomenon. Methods have been adopted for more penetrating analysis of crime data. Initial work has been done on crime trends in the Czechoslovak Socialist Republic. The topography of crime in Prague has been developed, and the influence of environmental constraints in large cities has been traced. Investigations of recidivism and its prevention include works on probation and after-care.

In 1971, the conception that had shaped the Criminological Research Institute was changed and influenced its activities in the years 1971-1975. The new conception was that too few empirical investigations based only on fragmentary theoretical rationales would produce only modest progress against criminality. Until 1971, the institute's research had not been sufficiently connected to the questions of chief concern to the prosecutor's office. The theoretical level employed was insufficient, and there was no clear delineation of the part the institute could play in answering these questions in carrying out its statutory mission of conducting research on the causes and prevention of crime. In dealing with these faults, the new conception stressed international cooperation, especially with criminological institutions of other socialist countries.

The new conception has given new force to research activities that have covered all main problems. Research into juvenile delinquency and recidivism has been performed over the longest period of time, with the projects based reasonably well on sound theories. Investigations have been initiated into the personality of the offender, especially in regard to youth, young adults, and recidivists; predelinquency and crimes of children; post-release care of prisoners; the prediction of criminality; crime patterns in large cities; alcoholism; and the reporting of crimes to the police.

Legal cognizance—the reporting of crimes to the police—has been of great interest because, along with investigations into the causes of crime, research into that topic has been central to the long-term responsibilities of the Criminological Research Institute. Increased attention has been devoted to the tendencies among citizens to initiate official reactions when they witness delinquent behavior. With a steady growth of citizen participation in the management of society, active reporting of the criminal incidents is an extraordinarily significant element in the struggle against criminality. Without the public's active support, even the best and most rigorous administration of the security and judicial apparatus will have inadequate effect on crime. Optimum conditions for motivating citizen reporting of crimes may be created if research reveals the regularities and social correlates of active participation.

Further development of the socialist society is contingent upon reliable forecasting of the tendencies likely to emerge, and the quality of forecasting depends on scientific mastering of the concrete elements and their relationships that shape likely future trends. Reliable prediction of future criminality falls within the scope of those responsibilities of scientific research that have been assigned to the Criminological Research Institute, the pioneer in this sphere of research for the Czechoslovak Socialist Republic. Reliable and valid information on tendencies and social correlates of criminality is essential to managing the complex system of reactions against violations of the normative rules of the socialist society generally and against crime in particular. The institute has achieved initial results in the prognostication of crime trends and has gained valuable experience in this area.

Recidivism has been a cardinal problem, highlighting the necessity to improve the after-care of released prisoners. The institute, encouraged by the establishment of a national commission for Prague, has conducted experimental research on after-care. The research has dealt with factors influencing the resocialization of former prisoners, prediction of their possible continued delinquency, and appropriate methods of reeducation. The research has contributed to the establishment throughout Czechoslovakia of a system of professional social-care specialists who assist released prisoners.

TEACHING OF CRIMINOLOGY AND EDUCATION OF CRIMINOLOGISTS

For a number of years, the teaching of criminology has been part of the instruction in criminal law by law faculties in Czechoslovakia. It is taught mostly within the framework of judicial specialization but also in courses in criminalistics, forensic psychiatry, and psychology.

The requirements of the struggle against criminal activity have necessitated instruction in criminology. Those requirements would not be satisfied if law students were taught only the conditions of criminal liability, the legal categorization of crimes, individualization of punishment, criminalistic techniques for detecting crimes and their perpetrators, and procedures of crime investigation and trials. The struggle against criminality strongly brings to the fore the questions of the causation and prevention of crime.

Faculties are charged with responsibility for preparing the future experts in criminal investigation, prosecution, judicial tasks, and working reform institutions. They must be prepared in both criminological knowledge and juridical matters.

In recent years, the law faculty of Charles University in Prague has focused on the teaching of criminology. Selected fundamentals of criminology are presented in optional lectures and are given more intensive treatment in a specialized study block. The teaching is closely related to empirical research, which is the inevitable foundation for both theoretical work and teaching in criminology. The linkage between empirical research and teaching is assured by selected workers in the Criminological Research Institute attached to the Office of the Prosecutor General. That linkage guarantees that the orientation of teaching will be toward the most important and topical issues of the struggle against criminality in the Czechoslovak Socialist Republic.

The first all-state textbook of criminology, published in 1978, is available for the teaching of criminology. For deeper study, there are the research reports of the Criminological Research Institute.

For the study of criminology, the specialized study block will probably be the dominant form of instruction, and the question is how that teaching strategy can be improved. A block of subjects could be developed to prepare for work in the penal sector. Criminologists are still debating the proper connections between the teaching of criminology and teaching in related disciplines: criminal law, procedural law, criminalistics, forensic psychiatry, and so on. The objective is to integrate all these branches of learning into a single unit that will collectively give the students an image of all problems involved in criminality. Knowledge of the criminal law continues to be the inevitable precondition to the study of criminology because the student becomes acquainted with the concepts applied to criminality. Nevertheless, juridical interpretations cannot be offered separate from the criminological aspects. The study of criminology thus continues to deepen the insights gained in the study of criminal law in terms of both crime causation and societal reactions to crime. In the course of studying criminology, students also become acquainted with the principles of sociology, statistics, and research methods.

The instructional method used is that of the lecture. Students also learn in seminars, training courses, or pro-seminars where the subject matter is further explained and practical habits are acquired. In these ways, students cultivate practical skills for conducting research and engaging in preventive activities.

Even after graduation from universities, specialists in fields of practice may obtain a criminological education through postgraduate studies under the guidance of law faculties. Specialists with the appropriate prerequisites can take postgraduate studies. The Criminological Research Institute is the training institution for preparing specialists for research in criminology as a field within criminal law. This educational program assures a regular system for recruiting new criminological professionals.

FUTURE COURSE OF CRIMINOLOGICAL ACTIVITIES

Other organizations, in addition to the Criminological Research Institute, show promise for Czechoslovakia's socialist criminology. The Criminological Cabinet is the common workplace of the Law Faculty of Charles University and of the Institute of State and Law of the Czechoslovak Academy of Science which have been very active since 1965. The Institute of State and Law seeks to unite the workers of different professions and the leading representatives of practice.

Attached to the Czechoslovak Sociological Association is the Section on Social Pathology which brings together criminologists, penologists, psychologists, psychiatrists, and others who deal with criminality for a broader exchange of information. The newly established College of the National Security Courts offers an important place to scientific criminology. The chair of criminal law in Bratislava has produced reputable work even though only a few people are involved in criminology. Palacky's University in Olomouc also has been active.

The research tasks of the Criminological Research Institute, attached to the Office of the Prosecutor General, have recently been and will continue to be concentrated on these main research topics:

1. Problems of planning and the organization of the battle against crime as past of the mission of the Office of the Prosecutor General to assure coordination. These problems entail the difficulties of achieving the essential cooperation and accord of different agencies.
2. Investigation of criminality as a mass social phenomenon, including long-term forecasting of crime trends. These areas of research are prerequisites for further exploration of the causes of criminality and the further development of necessary preventive activities. The tasks are to strengthen the perspectives and methodologies already employed and to explore issues not previously given necessary attention. Therefore, it is of special contemporary interest to discover the interrelationships of the nature, regularities, and associated social phenomena of criminality. The research would probe forms of crime, categories of offenders, and appropriate kinds and relative effective forms of reactions to criminality under the conditions of some selected districts. Prediction of the trends of crime as a mass phenomenon is an important field of research that has the secondary function of revealing more exacting tasks for future research.
3. Legal cognizance in the sense of improving official awareness of the perpetration of crimes. To understand the causes of criminality and how to prevent it, the full dimensions of criminal activity must be subject to research and to decision-making in the field of penal policy.
4. Preventive and educational functions of those agencies involved in criminal proceedings, with particular attention to juridical education and public education.
5. The personality of offenders, including juvenile offenders, and the problems of their reeducation. Investigation of the offender's personality entails uncovering the mechanisms associated with antisocial conduct. The characteristics of the offender's personality, the structure of the individual's criminal conduct, and the classification of offenders—all of these are instruments for discovering the sources of criminal activity and the means of preventing it. Thereby, continued study of recidivists and of juvenile delinquents' personalities is of major importance.

6. Development of a complex system of prisoner after-care. The effort to eliminate criminality is intimately connected to reduction of recidivism, making postpenitentiary care an aspect of penal policy that must be further developed.

7. To continue to deal with the basic theoretical and methodological questions of Czechoslovakian criminology. Although it has successfully coped with many of these questions, other theoretical and methodological questions of special import to criminology remain to be worked out.

CRIME IN THE REPUBLIC: PATTERNS AND CORRELATES

In contemporary Czechoslovakia, the following patterns of criminality are apparent: a gradual reduction in the extent of crime; simplification of its forms; and the disappearance of those crimes most endangering society. An absolute comparison with criminality found in highly developed capitalist countries is inappropriate in light of these patterns. In the Czechoslovak Socialist Republic, organized criminality does not exist at all, and crimes against the state are very exceptional. There is no mass violation of the public order. The most numerous crimes are murder, robbery, rape, and similar offenses and they occur with relative infrequency.

The absolute number of persons prosecuted for crimes has been declining: 157,130 in 1975 and 125,369 in 1978, or a decline of 20 percent. For prosecutions of petty offenses, there were 87,684 cases in 1975 and 66,182 in 1978, or a decline of almost 25 percent. If the comparison is between 1971 and 1978, the decline is even more significant. During this period, the number of persons prosecuted for crimes dropped by 25 percent and for petty crimes by 31 percent. Since there is no reason why the sum of disclosed and latent criminality would expand to decrease disclosed criminality—although some kinds of crime are hidden to a considerable extent—the decline of the number of prosecuted classes of crime indicates a drop of overall criminality.

The reduced number of prosecuted persons is an index of the continued trend of decreasing criminality described above. The next section of this chapter will deal with general prevention and special prevention measures that have been undertaken in the Czechoslovak Socialist Republic. Here it is sufficient to note that the decline in criminal prosecutions undoubtedly can be attributed to coordinated actions against criminality and the gradually increasing willingness of citizens to report offenses.

The emphasis is on prevention in the criminological research and penal policy of the Czechoslovak Socialist Republic. This emphasis is justified because, among many reasons, the demographic processes affect the relative incidence of crimes that make the measures of general prevention very relevant. The demographic processes entail changes in the relative importance of subcategories of persons as differentiated according to a particular demographic variable. The age and sex characteristics of persons committing crimes and petty offenses are very useful in determining the probable patterns in the nature, characteristics, and dynamics of criminality. By knowing likely demographic trends of the future, it is feasible to deduce the probable rate of particular crimes that is influenced by the sex and age of offenders. Age and sex statuses are differentiating factors in likelihood of criminal behavior because criminogenic influences—such as industrialization and migration—have different import for persons in various statuses.

In the Czechoslovak Socialist Republic, the sex ratio among criminals has been rather constant over the years, with women representing a relatively low 13 percent of all criminals. Physiological and psychological differences between the sexes have influence, but social variables are decisive because sex roles cannot be attributed to the inherent nature of either sex. An important implication is that sex roles will have effects in the socialist society that are not found in a capitalist society. Crimes that are more characteristic of males are, first of all, connected with transport, whether the offenses be drunken driving, unauthorized use of motor vehicles, or inflicting bodily injury. Violent and sexual criminality is also characteristic. Typical crimes committed by females tend to involve some form of property and economic criminality. Also remarkably prevalent among women are offenses linked to the role of mother: child abandonment, failing to follow official regulations on education of minors, endangering the moral education of juveniles, and similar offenses. Women also are peculiarly involved in deceptions such as false accusation, defamation of character, and false testimony.

Age, of course, marks juvenile offenders from other offenders, but age status has importance in other ways because it carries with it distinctive social conditions. Although ages are distinctive in biological terms, their differential crime rates reflect the varying criminogenic influences. Offenders less than thirty years of age constitute over half of the perpetrators of crimes and petty offenses. The ages from fifteen to eighteen years bring emotional problems stemming from conflict situations. In the ages between twenty and twenty-nine years, criminal activity is most frequent because at this point in the life cycle vital problems are faced in employment and establishing a family. In ages over thirty years, persons are more likely to have found their places in the social establishment and to have sufficient experience to manage the complexities of life. The probability of antisocial conduct is considerably reduced.

Crimes are unevenly distributed among the administrative, economic, geographical, ethnic, and other units associated with the territory of the Czechoslovak Socialist Republic. There are significant differences in the prevalence of criminalities in large cities and the countryside, and among the regions and districts. These variations usually reflect differences among economic structures in terms of the achieved level of industrialization. Within the economic framework, other variables operate: degree of population density, population composition, cultural distinctions, living standards, prevalent working activities of the population, and so on. Inherent to industrialization is the many-sided process of scientific and technical development that has some effect in all countries, but the character of the given social order shapes the particular course of scientific and technical development. Within the context of the given order, the technical and economic aspects of industrialization are supplemented by the consequences of a spectrum of social phenomena: increased population mobility, demand for new manpower, concentration of population growth in industrial centers, the creation of stable living in cultural environments, changes in family life especially stimulated by employment of women, expansion of income, and so on.

In socialist countries, the many implications of the scientific-technical revolution cannot in themselves produce increased antisocial conduct because this revolution has the positive effect of leading to both material and cultural growth of the population in terms that eliminate criminality. This general consequence is a matter of managing the secondary effects of scientific-technical changes in the course of the struggle against criminality. The success of this management is indicated by a 10-percent decline in the incidence of crimes for the 1971-1978 period in both the Czech Socialist Republic and the Slovak Socialist Republic.

Slovakia holds one-third of the total population and one-third of the total number of crimes in the Czechoslovak Socialist Republic. But the two regions present different structures of criminality; the Slovak Socialist Republic shows a greater prevalence of some violent crimes and some crimes committed under the influence of alcohol. Among the districts of the Czechoslovak Socialist Republic, crimes occur more often and for a longer time where industrial production is concentrated.

Criminality in large cities continues to be a problem. Gains have been scored, especially by reducing the participation of juveniles and their victimization in crimes, but there still are concentrations of dangerous recidivists and defective persons in large cities. With the increased anonymity of metropolitan life, residents enter into a large number of interactions with other persons; yet, the dependence of one person on another is decreasing. The impersonal and transitory character of secondary relations undermines the informal controls and primary groups that can only be partially replaced by the formal control system sustained by a variety of bodies and institutions. The formal control mechanisms are less effective, when compared with informal controls, because they are specific in application and are not interchangeable when differing situations are encountered.

With lessened public resistance to criminality and other normative violations, the urban population becomes somewhat acclimated to deviance. In addition, large cities provide opportunities for unearned profit and irregular subsistence, the possible support of deviants by a relatively extensive delinquent subculture, and decreased chances that criminality will be penalized by either insufficient formal control or nonexisting informal control. Offenders are insulated from observation by the anonymity of interpersonal relations and run less risk of detection. For these reasons, the large cities attract persons from distant vicinities to obtain opportunities for crime. Juvenile delinquency also finds a more fertile soil in big cities where both parents have a great number of activities and multifaceted interests, some of which may be socially undesirable. Decreased parental care, weakened social control, and greater free time find expression in greater group criminal activity among the youth.

Anticriminogenic factors also operate in the large cities. The higher units of agencies active in coping with crime and a variety of cultural and educational institutions are located there. Free time can be used constructively in cultural pastimes, educational activities, sports, and so on. Large cities offer superior resocialization services for offenders and after-care facilities for released prisoners. With progress in the scientific-technical revolution, the population structure of metropolises is changing to the advantage of anticriminogenic forces. This progress does not have uniform effect on all sections of the large cities. On one hand, the complexity and multifaceted nature of criminality in the socialist society are demonstrated. On the other hand, the potentialities of the socialist society are revealed by the successes that have been achieved and the relatively low level of criminality in the Czechoslovak Socialist Republic as compared with the level in other countries.

PREVENTION: THE STRUGGLE AGAINST CRIMINALITY

In spite of the comparatively favorable situation in regard to crime, the need for an active struggle against it cannot be dismissed. Concrete social reality determines the character of penal policy and preventive measures. The reality, recognized through experience, is that the process of building a socialist society will not automatically terminate criminality. To the contrary, a more resolute elimination of criminality will accompany the strengthening and developing of the socialist society through planned and purposeful elaboration of the ideological, political, social, and organizational prerequisites for the ending of criminality. It is necessary, of course, to regard a well-developed socialist society as the means of achieving the gradual limitation of criminality as a mass phenomenon. Solution of the complicated problems of building the developed socialist society— including the education of the new man—is unthinkable without a stable legal order and without application of legality in proceedings against criminality. Meanwhile, the most effective means of dealing with crime now must not be relaxed, and all potentialities of the socialist social order should be systematically exploited to that end.

Penal sanctions have their place where no other means of social influence are sufficient. But the penal policy of the states is far from being dependent mostly on measures of repressive character, even when implemented through bodies of criminal law. The main and decisive strategy is to uncover and remove sources of criminality and the conditions associated with it. A wide variety of organizations are involved: central state agencies (especially the Ministry of Interior, the Office of the Prosecutor General, and the courts), regulatory agencies, commissions for protecting the public order attached to various national committees, social service workers, social organizations, economic organizations, and various bodies involved in anti-alcoholism, educational and psychological counseling, and other forms of intervention.

Crime prevention is regarded as an inseparable part of planned management of social processes by state agencies, economic organizations, social organizations—in fact, the whole society. General prevention of crime encompasses the planning, management, prognostication, and organization of society. This broad conception of crime prevention includes prediction of the possible negative side-effects of essential processes that are inherently constructive.

General prevention as discussed above is closely connected with special prevention directed specifically against criminality. As carried out by the Ministry of Interior, the Office of the General Prosecutor, and the courts, special prevention is oriented to the detection, investigation, and assessment of crimes and petty offenses; the adjudication of offenders; the supervision of convicted offenders; and the conducting of research (as previously discussed) and preventive activities.

The two categories of prevention complete one another because they are directed against antisocial phenomena whether regarded as a whole or in terms of individual manifestations. The several functions related to general prevention are brought to bear on the causes and conditions of criminality and other forms of antisocial behavior. The measures serve young people, these difficulties impeding education, socially inadequate families, alcoholics, released prisoners, and other socially unintegrated persons. Such groups of persons are symptomatic of the difficulties—urbanization and migration, for example—that accompany the transitional phases of socioeconomic development when social control is weakened.

In 1971, the upper level party and state agencies took advantage of research analyses to mount a significant attack on criminality in both senses of prevention. The effectiveness of the programs rests ultimately on the increased participation of the working masses and social organizations. The manifold activities must be coordinated and be oriented toward long-term measures. On June 30, 1972, the Federal Assembly considered the report on the state of social legality prepared by the prosecutor general and the chairman of the supreme court of the Czechoslovak Socialist Republic. The Federal Assembly issued an urgent appeal to all state, economic, and social organizations to increase their enforcement efforts and to obtain public support in condemning acts contradicting socialist legality and morals.

During the last five years, the government has adopted twelve policy statements on crime prevention, which were discussed by branch departments and national committees at all levels. These statements were concerned with increased inhibition of economic criminality, reduction of recidivism, greater production of juveniles against antisocial activities, observance of legality in operations of the socialist economy, protection of the economy against criminal activities, the struggle against alcoholism, and so on. The government has implemented a number of measures since 1971 that comprise a complex system of crime prevention. The regions and districts have adopted their long-range plans for general and special prevention.

In conclusion, it may be said that the future development of Czechoslovakia's socialist criminology requires further elaboration of its theory and methodology, although progress has been made in dealing with those questions. The growing significance of scientific criminology stems from the heavy stress in recent years on the penal and political implications of criminological research. The translation of research results has been tailored to practical objectives tied to the struggle against criminality. Research themes have been chosen for their appropriateness to the needs of practice and their harmony with the state's overall scheme for science and research. It is becoming increasingly important that the research be as complex as the scope of the tasks required.

NOTES

1. The summary is included in the textbook by Jiří Nezkusil, et al., *Československá kriminologie* [Czechoslovak Criminology] (Praha: Panorama, 1969).
2. A. S. Shlyapochnikov, *Sovetskaya kriminologia na sovremennom etape rozvitia* [Soviet Criminology at the Present State of Development] (Moscow: Yuridicheskaya literatura, 1973).
3. See, in more detail, *Československá kriminologie: aktuální problémy* [Czechoslovak Criminology: Topical Problems] (Praha: Orbis, 1971), pp. 25-26.
4. *Osnovnye napravlenie borby s prestupnostyu* [Fundamental Orientation of the Struggle Against Criminality] (Moscow: Yuridicheskaya literatura, 1975), p. 27.
5. G. Přenosil, *K pojmu a funkcím socialistické trestní politiky. Sborník prací z trestního práva k sedmdesátým narozeninám prof.dr.Vladimíra Solnaře* [Memorial Volume of Works from the Sphere of Criminal Law at the Occasion of the 70th Birth-day of Professor Dr. Vladimír Solnař] (Praha: Universita Karlova, 1969), p. 95.

BIBLIOGRAPHY

Československá kriminologie [Czechoslovak Criminology]. Praha: Orbis, 1971.
Description and analysis of the system and the state of criminology in Czechoslovakia.

Nezkusil, Jiří. *Československá kriminologie* [Czechoslovak Criminology]. Praha: Panorama, 1978.
Detailed description of the system of criminology in Czechoslovakia with regard to its general as well as specific aspects.

Nezkusil, Jiří. *Příčiny a prevence zločinnosti v ČSSR* [Criminality Causes and Prevention in the Czechoslovak Socialist Republic]. Praha: Panorama, 1978.
Results of the investigation of criminality causes and preventive measures in Czechoslovakia.

Suchý, Oldřich. *Mládež a kriminalita* [Youth and Criminality]. Praha: Melantrich, 1972.
Detailed description and analysis of the causes of juvenile criminality.

Suchý, Oldřich. *Podmíněné propuštění a postpenitenciární péče* [Parole and After-care]. Praha: Research Institute of Criminology, 1970.
A comparative study dealing with the function and purpose of parole and after-care, with their criminological aspects and legal adjustments in individual countries.

Suchý, Oldřich. *Recidiva* [Recidivism]. Praha: Criminological Research Institute, 1971.
A comparative study dealing with the conceptions of recidivism in their historical sequence, from the classical conception of recidivism up to the present legislative adjustment and developmental tendencies. In the forefront of the study are the questions of social response to the phenomenon of recidivism and the questions of recidivism prevention.

Vítek, Karel. *Zločin a prevence. I. část* [Crime and Prevention. 1st part]. Praha: Státní pedagogické nakladatelství, 1972; *II. část [2d part]*. Praha: Státní pedagogické nakladatelství, 1974.
Analysis of criminality phenomena and prevention, mainly from different historical aspects.

7

DENMARK

Preben Wolf

The year 1945 may be considered an appropriate point of departure for a description of developments in the criminology of Denmark. Although it did not exactly mark the beginning of scientific criminology for the country, it certainly saw the opening of new perspectives for the study of crime and criminal policies. Chronologically speaking, it became the approximate midpoint of a most fertile decade for criminological pioneering of outstanding scholars from different academic disciplines, scholars like Karl Otto Christiansen (1908-1976) in sociology, Stephan Hurwitz (1901-   ) in law, and Georg K. Stürup (1905-   ) in psychiatry.

POSTWAR DEVELOPMENTS
IN DANISH CRIMINOLOGY

Here is not the place or time to trace the history of Danish criminology much earlier than World War II. Like the rest of the civilized world, Denmark has had its "precriminologists" as well as some early criminological studies by specialists from other fields or by practitioners within the areas of criminalistics, criminal policy, and treatment of offenders.

Karl Otto Christiansen's unpublished thesis for a master's degree in philosophy, "What Is the Contribution of Sociology to the Ethical Discussion of Crime and Punishment?" (1937),[1] was noted and appreciated by Stephan Hurwitz, then professor of procedural law, who encouraged him to pursue his empirical interests through actual criminological research.

Among Christiansen's most important early empirical studies was his work with Georg K. Stürup on 335 state prisoners completed in 1946 but, for some unknown reason, never published in its entirety. The results have been made known mainly from frequent quotations in other books and articles and from three articles by Christiansen in *Nordisk Tidsskrift for Strafferet* (1942, 1943, 1945).[2]

Also in 1945, Christiansen could openly start on his venture into the etiology of various forms of criminalized collaboration with the enemy during the occupation of Danish territory by German forces from 1940 to 1945. Of several books and articles stemming from this research, the most important is his doctoral dissertation (1955) and his "Follow-up Study of 2,946 Danish Men Convicted of Collaboration with the Germans During World War II," pp. 245-283, in Marvin E. Wolfgang (ed.), *Crime and Culture: Essays in Honor of Thorsten Sellin.*[3]

The first scientific criminological society (Kriminologisk Selskab) was founded in 1943 as a subdivision of the older and more open Association of Danish Criminalists (Dansk Kriminalistforening), and a readership in criminology was established at the University of Copenhagen in 1944. Christiansen became the first occupant of that post. He also obtained the first full professorship in criminology in Denmark in 1967 at the same university.

Most of what happened during the early phases of the criminological development in Denmark up to 1945 was the result of initiatives taken by Stephan Hurwitz, who was professor of civil procedure and administration of justice at the University of Copenhagen from 1935 and in penal law from 1942. Hurwitz also wrote the first, and so far probably the best, criminological textbook in Scandinavia (1948).[4] It is true that Christiansen had previously published an extended article in a Danish legal journal on "The Fundamental Problems of Criminology" in 1942[5] and that Hans Chr. Kjarsgaard in 1940 also published a popular book, *The Causes of Crime,*[6] but neither could serve as a textbook for the teaching of criminology at the university level. Hurwitz's *Criminology* from 1948 has been translated and published in various countries, and a completely revised and extended edition with Karl Otto Christiansen as co-author was issued in two volumes in 1968 and 1971, respectively. An English language edition of this later work appeared in 1979.[7]

DEFINING THE FIELD OF CRIMINOLOGY

In their textbook (1968-1971), Hurwitz and Christiansen see criminology in a narrow sense as one among other sciences concerned with criminality and various penal problems. The term refers to that "part of criminal science which empirically describes criminal behavior and explores individual and social factors associated with—or potentially associated with—such behavior."[8]

This demarcation of the field of criminology does not differ greatly from the one applied by Hurwitz in the first edition of his textbook. Here he defined criminology as "that part of criminal science which through empirical research throws light on the factors of crime, i.e. the individual and social factors which determined criminal behavior." This 1968 formulation of the definition of the field of criminology appears in almost identical form in the 1979 English edition of Hurwitz's and Christiansen's book.

But this does not mean that all those in Denmark who call themselves criminologists will accept such a narrow definition of the field. In formulating their definitions of criminology, the two senior criminologists were well aware that criminology might legitimately be granted a much wider field of activity, includ-ing not just the etiology and the phenomenology of crime but also penology, penal policy, police science, and perhaps even forensic medicine and forensic psychiatry. However, their contention is that if this is done, the subject matter of criminology may become too diffuse. On the other hand, both are quite willing to include within the scope of criminology a more general science of prediction and the special studies of victimization and victimology.

So from the beginning the founders of modern scientific criminology in Den-mark considered criminology to be a branch of a more comprehensive science of criminality (the criminal sciences), with criminology itself branching off into a number of main areas, such as descriptive criminology (criminography), crimi-nal sociology, and criminal biology, which may be further subdivided into crim-inal somatology, criminal psychology, and psychiatry. Hurwitz and Christiansen consider social psychological treatment of the crime problem to be just another branch of criminology, as are the fields of criminal genetics, prognostics or prediction research, and victimology.

In spite of Christiansen's early and important efforts to treat criminological problems mainly from a sociological point of view, the long predominant influ-ence of jurisprudence—in cooperation and at times in competition with psychiatry—has had an impact on the study of criminology in Denmark.

In their textbook, Hurwitz and Christiansen have used the greater part of Volume 1 (1968) to discuss the biological bases of criminality, and they reserve about one-quarter of the volume for a treatment of psychiatric questions concern-ing criminality. The whole of Chapter 2 is devoted to the relationship between criminology and criminal law and advocacy of the legal definition of criminal behavior. Attempts to define a concept of crime independently of the penal laws (that is, the Penal Code and/or special penal legislation, such as traffic laws and tax laws) have not been successful. This view seems to have been accepted by most criminologists in Denmark to such an extent that it is now hardly a matter for discussion at all. Hurwitz and Christiansen (1968) viewed criminology as an empirical science based on a gathering of facts about crimes and criminals for description (criminography), classification, and analysis. The aim of criminol-ogy, according to them, is to formulate laws concerning the relationship between criminal data and other data (middle range generalizations) as well as more general theories. Both authors advocate a combination of inductive procedures with a hypothetical-deductive method in criminological research.

Most young Danish criminologists have been brought up in this spirit. Some have reacted against the so-called positivist attitudes of the older generation, but their reactions have been few and rather meek compared with the reactions since 1968 of those in sociology, psychology, and other academic fields.

Most Danish criminologists have avoided the often futile discussions of whether or not criminology should be considered a science in its own right or rather be seen as a special problem field, where researchers from various disciplines can meet and fight each other or join forces. Opinions will differ among Danish criminologists in this regard, but such divergencies are rarely brought out into the open.

The fashions, fads, and foibles of various mother disciplines have had some contaminating effects on criminology but never to such an extent that it has gone completely off its hinges. This comparatively balanced state of criminology in Denmark may be explained, at least in part, by the organizational and structural setting for the study of criminology where it is placed mainly, but not exclusively, within the law faculties of the two older universities in Copenhagen and Århus. Men like Christiansen, Hurwitz, and Stürup, assisted by Karen Berntsen, the psychologist, have formed a tradition of cooperation among representatives from different academic fields. Then, too, in the Scandinavian countries criminological theory and research have always been closely connected with practice.[9]

Expressively normative and/or critical forms of "New Criminology" are represented among young criminologists in Denmark, most of them inspired by and trying to follow in the footsteps of the two Norwegian sociologists Nils Christie and Thomas Mathiesen.

The theoretical aspects of Danish criminology are still rather vague. Like Christiansen, the younger generation of criminologists are predominantly empirically minded and/or oriented toward the practice of crime policy. Nevertheless, they may be opposed to the so-called positivist tendency which is more or less the heritage from the founding fathers of present-day Danish criminology. Among the reactions against the older generation of criminologists are found legalistically dominated trends toward a neo-classical attitude to penology and crime policy. One theme of this trend is the redefinition of criminology as a social science subordinate to or forming only a part of the sociology of law. Instead of making an original Danish contribution to this theme, those supporting it are only following the lead of other Scandinavian countries and of wider international circles.

Some older Danish criminologists and some of those belonging to psychiatric or other therapeutic schools of thought express apprehensions with what they consider to be punitive and reactionary overtones in the neo-classical, predominantly anti-treatment movement. The new, humanitarian neo-classicists and the legal sociologists, including the Marxists and the critical schools, on the other hand, will not be too pleased with the apparent revival of a biosocial and/or genetic approach to criminology which may be the latest fashion introduced to Danish criminal science.

If we judge from actual research, all branches of criminology defined above are now represented in Danish criminology. There seems to be a certain division of labor between those who prefer to define criminology in terms of the sociology of law and those who want to concentrate their efforts on the phenomena of crime, criminal behavior, recidivism, and victimology. This division of labor is not seriously disruptive among Danish criminologists; rather, different preferences reflect an effort to cover as many aspects of criminal science, penal policy, and preventive practice as possible.

SETTING OF DANISH CRIMINOLOGY

Denmark comprises the peninsula of Jylland (Jutland) with its northernmost point, Skagens Odde, situated at 57° 44' 55" north and its westernmost point at Blavandshuk at 8° 4' 36" east, and 428 islands of which only 99 are inhabited. The southernmost point is at Gedser Odde on the island of Falster at 54° 33' 31" north, its easternmost point on the islet group of AErthol-mene east of the island of Bornholm in the Baltic at 15° 11' 59" east.

The distance north-south is about 360 kilometers (225 miles), and east-west it is about 400 kilometers (250 miles). The total area of Denmark is 43,043 square kilometers (16,619 square miles). The total population is just over 5 million, or a little less than 120 to the square kilometer (just over 300 to the square mile). The metropolitan area of Copenhagen comprises 2,853 square kilometers (1,107 square miles) and about 1,758,000 inhabitants, or just over 600 to the square kilometer (1,588 to the square mile). Next to Copenhagen, the city of Århus in Jutland is the largest Danish city with about 250,000 inhabitants; third comes Odense on the island of Fyn (Funen) with 142,000; and fourth is Ålborg in North Jutland with almost 130,000 inhabitants.

Denmark proper is a low-lying country surrounded by the sea except for a short land frontier with Germany of 67.7 kilometers (42 miles). The total coast-line is 7,474 kilometers (4,645 miles). In the Sound (Øresund) the distance to Sweden is only 4 kilometers (2.5 miles) at the narrowest point. The climate is characterized by prevailing western winds, mild winters, and summers that are not excessively hot. The weather is changeable and fairly humid; mean annual precipitation is 60 centimeters (23.6 inches).

Both the Faroe Islands in the North Atlantic and Greenland close to the North Pole are part of Denmark, but they are usually treated separately with regard to crime and punishment. Both now have home rule; furthermore, Greenland has a separate penal law altogether. Of the limited criminological research conducted since 1945 in these areas, most has been in Greenland.

With regard to religion, almost all native Danes belong to the Lutheran Church (the Danish National Church) which is state supported. It is confessionally bound by the three symbols of the primitive church, Confessio Angustana, and the Shorter Catechism of Luther.

Denmark has been a monarchy for as long as there have been written records, although royal powers were very limited at first. Later growth of the king's powers was supported by the Church and the lords of the manors. Increasingly, the kings were given authority to maintain peace and order and to punish crimi-nals. In 1660, the royal powers became absolute, and in 1849 strictly constitu-tional. The latest revision of the constitution in 1953 conferred authority to the Danish Parliament to appoint a public affairs commissioner (the ombudsman). In March 1955, Parliament unanimously appointed one of the founding fathers of modern Danish criminology, Professor Stephan Hurwitz, as the first ombudsman.

The judicial system and police are organized into two high court districts, eighty-five legal districts, and fifty-four police districts (not including the Faroe Islands and Greenland). The highest court is the supreme court which functions only as a court of appeal. It has jurisdiction in civil, criminal, and administrative cases. While the courts are independent of the government, the prosecution is subordinate to the minister of justice and subject to the minister's oversight in discharge of its functions. The supreme prosecuting authority for the country as a whole is the chief public prosecutor. In most criminal cases, the decision to prosecute is made by fewer than ten local public prosecutors. All preliminary inquiries are carried out under the authority of the local chief of police, one for each police district.

An accused or prosecuted person has the right to defense counsel who may be privately engaged or appointed by the court. The costs are paid out of public funds. To ensure the liberty of the individual, the constitution provides that any person arrested shall be brought before a court within twenty-four hours. The court may then set the arrested person free or rule that the detention period may be extended to a total of not more than three full days, or pass sentence of imprisonment which may be appealed to the appropriate high court.

REVIEW OF HISTORY OF CORRECTIONS

Danish prisons were studied and described by John Howard in the eighteenth century. Beccaria's famous book on crime and punishment was translated into Danish only a few years after it was first published in French. Furthermore, decisive penal reforms were initiated early in the nineteenth century, inspired directly by Elizabeth Fry, Alexis de Tocqueville, and other European students of the American penal and penitentiary system.

The leading figure in Danish prison reform was C. N. David (1793-1874), a former professor of political economy at the University of Copenhagen and an active liberal member of the first constitutional assembly during the late 1840s. He was also active in the official Prison Reform Committee of 1840 which submitted its final report in 1842. In addition, he organized the first systematic Danish criminal statistics on a national basis from 1832 (published in 1847).[10] Two new prisons were established in direct consequence of the work of the Prison Reform Committee: one in the city of Horsens in Jutland in 1853, according to the Auburn system; and the other at Vridsløselille just outside of Copenhagen in 1859, according to the Pennsylvania system of absolute isolation. The buildings of these institutions still function as a kind of maximum security prison, although the systems according to which they were originally established have long since been abandoned. The old closed prison at Horsens was the scene of an experiment in the late nineteenth century which provided valuable experience for later prison reforms. Selected prisoners were housed under completely open and free conditions in camps or huts (so-called colonies) during the summer months. Under a few prison officers, they worked at cultivation of the Jutland moors. The next decisive reform was carried through at the introduction of a new Penal Code in 1930 which, as amended after World War II, is still in force.

Among the important changes introduced in 1930 were the abolishment of capital punishment for civil offenses and an extension of the use of open institutions, and a treatment-oriented acceptance of indefinite sentences with or without fixed maximums.

The German occupational forces (1940-1945) during World War II seized a number of the old prison buildings for their own purposes. Danish authorities had to find room elsewhere for an increasing number of ordinary criminal convicts. Accordingly, a number of new open institutions were established. Since 1945, open institutions have been increasingly used; in 1977, more than half the prisoners were in open institutions. Local prisons and detention houses are not counted as penal institutions. They are all closed prisons but are used mainly for short periods of time while prisoners are awaiting trial or transfer to a penal institution after sentencing. Bail is authorized by Danish constitutional law but seldom used. Consequently, the number of people in pretrial custody constitutes a comparatively high proportion of the average daily prison population—23 percent of the average of 2,747 total prisoners in 1977.[11]

The Prisons and Probation Administration is centralized under the minister of justice in Copenhagen with sixteen penal institutions and some fifty local jails distributed around the country, including five in Copenhagen. By 1976, the Probation and After-care Section supervised just over 4,500 clients, mainly persons on probation or parole.[12]

SOURCES OF CRIMINAL STATISTICS

The main sources of information about criminality in Denmark are the official criminal statistics dating back as far as 1828 when the first annual surveys were published for the years to 1831 in a government report. When the thirteenth volume of the *Collection of Statistical Tables* (Statistisk Tabelvoerk) was published in 1847, it contained for the first time detailed crime tables for the years 1832-1840.[13] Since 1933, such tables have been published in the *Statistical Reports* (Statistiske Heddelelser) by the Danish Bureau of Census—now, Danmarks Statistik.[14]

In Denmark, only infringements of the Penal Code (from 1930) are normally considered criminal acts. By and large, the violations of the Penal Code comprise the traditional crimes against the state, against persons or property, and sex crimes.

The punishable violations of special laws are mainly traffic and driving offenses, offenses against price regulations, rationing laws, various other economic regulations, tariff laws, police regulations, and so forth. During recent years, there has been an increasing awareness in Denmark of the importance of offenses against the special laws and of the apparent fact that such offenses are often much more costly to society than are the more traditional crimes. One consequence of this awareness has been serious discussions among experts and politicians in Denmark of redefining, for example, tax evasion as a "real crime" by making it part of the Penal Code, and not just an act punishable according to some special law. Another consequence has been the inclusion since 1974 of a selection of special law offense figures in the tables of the official publications of crime statistics.[15]

Other official publications contain statistical information which more or less overlaps the criminal statistics. The most important of such statistics are in the annual reports of the police[16] and of the Prisons and Probation Administration. Both reports contain statistical information over and above that given by the ordinary criminal statistics. For example, the table concerning persons questioned and/or charged for violation of the Penal Code published in the Annual Report of the Police is the only source of reasonable statistical information about police contacts with offenders and potential offenders under the age of criminal responsibility (age fifteen). Other means than crime statistics to provide data on criminality in Denmark are found in special counts and investigations done by the appropriate agencies and/or individual researchers. Such activities have consisted mainly of victimization studies carried out over a number of years.[17] The first survey of that type was actually carried out in the city of Århus in 1730.[18]

CRIMINALITY IN DENMARK: OFFICIAL DATA

The following outline of the state of criminality in Denmark for 1945-1978 is based on police statistics showing the incidence of Penal Code offenses (traditional crimes) known to the police during the period under study, supplemented by information from certain years about the prevalence of registered offenders in the adult Danish population in the particular years. Information derived from self-report studies and from victimization studies will be left out of this description.

Danish criminologists customarily choose 1933 as a starting point for describing trends in crime because the current Penal Code went into force that year. In the latest English language edition of their *Criminology* (1979), Hurwitz and Christiansen calculate a crime index using 1933 as a base.

In 1933, the total Danish population numbered about 3.6 million; a total of 78,078 criminal offenses were registered according to police statistics. That is a rate of 2,169 offenses per 100,000 of the total Danish population. This rate was fairly constant up to 1939. In 1940, the rate increased 15 percent to 2,498 per 100,000. The increase continued during the years of German occupation to a temporary peak of 4,216 per 100,000 in 1943. No police statistics are available for 1944 and 1945 because the German occupying authorities dissolved the total Danish police force in September 1944.

After 1945, offenses known to the police declined markedly. In 1946, the rate of 2,980 represented a decline of almost 30 percent compared with the 1943 rate. The decline may be especially attributed to fewer crimes of violence and against property. Continuing through the late 1940s and most of the 1950s, the decline reached bottom in 1954 at a rate of 2,524, only 15 to 16 percent above the prewar level.

On the whole, crime frequency stabilized during the 1950s at this level. From 1959 to 1960, the figure increased by 5 percent; the increase hovered between 2.5 and 5 percent per year until 1965. After a slight drop from 1965 to 1966, the rate rose in the 1966 to 1974 period at an annual increase of about 10 percent. The rate was more than doubled from 3,180 per 100,000 in 1966 to 6,465 in 1974, which exceeds the rate of the most disorganized years of the war. For reasons that are not clear[19] the rate dropped to 5,747 per 100,00 in 1975 and to 5,456 in 1976; there was an increase to 6,040 in 1977 and 6,672 in 1978, the highest official crime rate since 1921 in Denmark.

Of the 340,647 crimes known to the police in 1978, 34 were homicides, 110 attempted homicides, and 235 unintentional killings. Of the 235 unintentional killings, 223 involved traffic accidents. Of 335 unintentional woundings, 325 were connected with traffic accidents. Assaults totaled 4,357, or 1 percent of all reported crimes. The rate for registered rapes has been very low (between 200 and 300 per year) during a fairly long period of time, but the number increased suddenly from 280 in 1977 to 484 in 1978. This jump is probably due to an increased tendency among women to report rapes, and not so much a result of an increase of the number of rapes. Other sex crimes total less than 2,000. The total number of sex crimes is less than 1 percent of all registered Penal Code offenses. More than 90 percent of the offenses reported to and registered by the police in 1978 are offenses against property, including 1,182 robberies or thefts with violence.

As far as special law offenses are concerned, the information given in the official crime statistics is not comparable to that given with regard to Penal Code offenses, but it is quite clear that by far the largest number of special law offenses registered are traffic offenses.

The police statistics also contain information on the number of crimes solved. The percentage of offenses reported which have been solved decreased from 45 to 50 percent in the 1940s and early 1950s to 20 to 25 percent in the 1970s. In general, rising crime rates are accompanied by a decreasing share of cases that are solved. The two trends appear to be reflections of conditions released by increasing urbanization. The percentage of crimes solved differs among categories of crime. In 1970, the percentage of solved crimes was 100 for homicides, about 70 for attempted homicides, and less than 20 for thefts.

As elsewhere, Danish crime statistics indicate that the majority (89 percent) of offenders are male, 36 percent are between fifteen and twenty-one years of age, and less than 10 percent are forty years old or more. Of those questioned and charged by the police in 1978, 10 percent were younger than fifteen and 40 percent younger than twenty years (both sexes). Registered offenders tend to be drawn largely from the cities, especially from the metropolitan areas, and to be unskilled urban workers to a great extent.

The latest available crime statistics show that in 1977, of a total of 19,636 sanctions imposed, 89 percent were imposed on male offenders and 11 percent on female offenders. Fifty-five percent of the sanctions were more severe than fines.

COMPARISONS WITH THE TOTAL POPULATION

Up to this point, the amount of criminality has been expressed in the absolute numbers of reported crimes, of persons questioned and charged, and of offenders sanctioned. Information has also been given about the development over time of the incidence of crime, defined as the ratio of the number of offenses registered within a certain period to the number of persons in the corresponding population—in this case, the number of registered offenses per year per 100,000 inhabitants in the same year.

The prevalence of crime is another numerical expression of the amount of crime or criminals in a population. Here it is defined as the ratio of the total number of registered persons at a given time to the number of persons in the total population at the same time. The prevalence of crime is ascertained by finding the number of persons over fourteen years of age and the number of sanctioned people in the same age categories; the second figure is divided by the first. But the calculation is complicated by the lack of precise information on the number of sanctioned persons in the population at a certain point of time. The statistic may be estimated either through use of population and mortality statistics or through a random sample of the population under examination.

In Denmark, L. Kallestrup[20] made an informed guess that Penal Code offenders made up about 8 percent of the male population. Christiansen and Nielsen[21] calculated the frequency of criminals in the population aged fifteen years and more. They found about 8 percent sanctioned Penal Code offenders in the Danish male population aged fifteen and more. In a random sample of 3,032 men and 606 women twenty-one years of age or older in 1953-1954, Wolf et al.[22] (1958) found 569 men (18.8 percent) and 14 women (2.3 percent) registered by the police. The number of women was too small to warrant further statistical analysis. The males, however, comprised 292 (9.6 percent) offenders against the Penal Code and 277 (9.2 percent) violators of special laws. The fact that there were more Penal Code offenders in this study than estimated by Kallestrup and computed by Christiansen and Nielsen for the same time period appears to be a matter of methodological differences. Wolf et al. took a different approach by including those Penal Code offenders who had experienced waiver of prosecution, warnings, and/or fines only. After adjustments to correspond to the definitions of Kallestrup and Christiansen and Nielsen, the same frequency of 8 percent of all adult males in Denmark at the time was found.[23]

A number of studies have attempted to get behind the official registrations of crimes and criminals and to reach some assessment of the volume of the "dark field" of actual crime as opposed to registered crime in Denmark.[24] However, such studies have been confined to certain types of crime only and to no more than two or three points in time during recent years. Thus, they have been considered less appropriate for a general description of the development of criminality in Denmark from 1945 to 1978.

In concluding this description of criminal developments in Denmark from 1945 to 1978, it should be mentioned that another random sample was drawn in 1975 and used by Høgh and Wolf[25] for a new assessment of the prevalence of criminals in the adult population. Results show an increase over the years from the mid-1950s to the mid-1970s of about 5 percent in the adult criminal population—from about 19 percent in the 1950s to about 24 percent in the 1970s.

EDUCATION AND STATUS
OF DANISH CRIMINOLOGISTS

The particular version of Danish criminology may be a function of the country's small size, medium population density, geographical situation, climate, history of independence, religion, constitutional arrangements, economic policies, and so forth, but it is more than anything a function of the history and development of crime and criminal policies in Denmark over the years.

The German occupation and its aftermath made drastic changes in the traditional penal practice in Denmark up to 1945 and several years thereafter. It was also the beginning of new and more systematic criminological research activity. All this aside, criminological research originated from those practitioners who were active in the field of crime statistics and/or in prison reform; for example, C. N. David is one outstanding precursor of theoretical criminology.[26]

The present *Scandinavian Journal of Criminal Sciences* originated a bit more than a hundred years ago under the name *Journal of Prison Services and Practical Penal Law*, through the initiative and editorship of Frederik Stuckenberg who was the educational chief at the old prison at Vridsløselille. The Danish Association of Criminalists was founded in 1899 and is still active. It has collective membership in the Northern Association of Criminalists which published a yearbook until 1963 (issued in 1968). This organization is still publishing the *Scandinavian Journal of Criminal Sciences (Nordisk Tidsskrift for Kriminalvidenskab)* under the editorship of a number of Scandinavian researchers and practitioners in the field headed by the Danish professor of penal law, Knud Waaben.

Danish universities did not play any important part in the development of criminology until Hurwitz and Christiansen became influential in the field around 1945. They were both active at the University of Copenhagen, Faculty of Law, but Knud Waaben had succeeded Hurwitz in the chair of penal law when the Institute of Criminal Sciences was founded in 1957. There is no equivalent institute at any other university in Denmark, although similar activity is going on in a smaller scale at the Institute for Procedural and Criminal Sciences at the University of Århus. It is somewhat obscure when the latter institute was really founded. It has been said that it started around 1950 as a drawer in the desk of the late professor of penal law, Dr. Louis le Maire.

No Danish university awards a degree of criminology. It is an optional subject for law students at the universities of Århus and Copenhagen only. Teaching takes place at the two institutes mentioned above. Criminology may also be taught by departments of psychology and sociology as parts of their general curricula, and it enters into parts of the teaching at lower level schools such as the social workers' colleges and the professional schools for police and prison personnel.

Criminologists have no occupational status outside the small number of teachers allocated to the subject of criminology at the two university institutes mentioned. Even they belong professionally to their respective general fields of knowledge or faculty such as law, medicine (psychiatry), psychology, and sociology. This pluralistic attitude is also characteristic of the various criminological associations all over Scandinavia.

TRENDS IN DANISH CRIMINOLOGICAL RESEARCH

Criminological research is being conducted at other institutes and under faculties of other universities, but the two just mentioned are the main centers for much research and international cooperation, including the Scandinavian Research Council for Criminology (Nordisk Samarbejdaråd for Kriminologi). However, two agencies outside the universities are particularly important here. One is the Permanent Ministry of Justice Committee for Research Concerning Criminal Policy, established in 1973 by the Prison and Probation Administration and extended in 1975 to other sectors of the Ministry of Justice's jurisdiction. The other is the National Crime Prevention Board, established by the Ministry of Justice in 1971 but working exclusively as an independent advisory board. Both agencies are important coordinators and initiators of criminological research.

Most Danish criminological studies are based on empirical data. Pure theory, model construction, and methodological innovations are rarely presented in Danish criminological publications. Normative attitudes of both practitioners and theoreticians are in general moderately liberal and humane, and most research is explicitly policy oriented.

It may be appropriate, in concluding this review of criminology in Denmark, to mention some projects under way now. They cannot be discussed in detail. A characteristic of Scandinavian criminology, which is particularly emphasized by Danish researchers, is an interest in comparative studies in an international and, especially, inter-Scandinavian context. A number of these activities have been sponsored by the Scandinavian Research Council for Criminology and sometimes published in the council's series, Scandinavian Studies in Criminology.

Especially noteworthy are a series of victimization studies, police studies, and various interdisciplinary studies. Some projects are conducted over a considerable period of time in a longitudinal design. Among them are twin studies which the late Professor Karl Otto Christiansen developed in close cooperation with colleagues from other scientific disciplines. Another important longitudinal study is the inter-Scandinavian Project Metropolitan[27] which started in 1965 as an inter-Scandinavian comparison of the life chances and educational and occupational careers of a cohort of boys born in the metropolitan areas of Scandinavia. The members of the cohort are now in their twenties and are being followed up with regard to their criminal as well as conventional careers.

While Berl Kutchinsky's studies on knowledge and opinion about law and on pornography and sex crimes are well known internationally, it is probably characteristic of a new spirit that a team of feminine criminologists took up both extensive and intensive studies of rape in the late 1970s and that others are concentrating on the social and psychological situation of female prisoners. A number of studies encouraged by the National Crime Prevention Board deal with the preventative activities of small communities. Jørn Vestergaard, a legal scholar at Kriminalistisk Institut in Copenhagen has undertaken a large-scale study of sanctioning practice over a number of years. His colleague, Henning Koch, is analyzing the efficiency of police practices by examining about twenty thousand police reports, interviews, and direct observation. At the Institute for Proces-og Kriminalvidenskab at Århus, Jørgen Jepsen is concentrating on the difficult and sensitive field of large-scale economic crimes.

This brief summary may serve as an indicator of the kinds of Danish research in criminology that will be reported in the future as further evidence of the vitality that has come to this field since 1945.

NOTES

1. K. O. Christiansen, *Hvilket bidrag yder sociologien til den etiske diskussion om forbrydelse og straf?* [What Is the Contribution of Sociology to the Ethical Discussion of Crime and Punishment?] (Master's Thesis in philosophy, University of Copenhagen, Copenhagen, 1937).

2. K. O. Christiansen, "Kriminelle levnedsløb" [Criminal Careers], *Nordisk Tidsskrift for Strafferet* 30 (1942):1-40; K. O. Christiansen, "Forbryderen og hans milieu" [The Criminal and His Environment], *Nordisk Tidsskrift for Strafferet* 31 (1943):41-68; and K. O. Christiansen, "Tillidsbrud og tillidsbrydere" [Breach of Confidence and Those Who Break It], *Nordisk Tidsskrift for Strafferet* 33 (1945):27-51.

3. K. O. Christiansen, "Recidivism Among Collaborators...," in Marvin E. Wolfgang (ed.), *Crime and Culture. Essays in Honor of Thorsten Sellin* (New York: John Wiley and Sons, 1968), pp. 245-283.

4. Stephan Hurwitz, *Kriminologi* [Criminology] (Copenhagen: 1948).

5. K. O. Christiansen, "Fundamentale problemer i kriminologien" [The Fundamental Problems of Criminology], *Juristen* 22 (1942):449-501.

6. H. Chr. Kjærsgaard, *Forbrydelsens Aarsager* [The Causes of Crime] (Copenhagen: 1940).

7. St. Hurwitz and K. O. Christiansen, *Kriminologi I & II* [Criminology I and II] (Copenhagen: 1968 & 1971). English translation, 1979.

8. Ibid., 1968 edition, p. 11.

9. P. Wolf, "Apparent Tendencies in Scandinavian Criminology During Recent Years," *International Annals of Criminology* 15 (1977):217-225.

10. Det statistiske Bureau, *Statistisk Tabelværk* [Statistical Tables] (Copenhagen: 1847).

11. *Kriminalforsorgen* [Annual Report of the Prisons and Probation Administration], several years, Copenhagen.

12. Ibid.

13. *Statistisk Tabelværk.*

14. Danmarks Statistik, *Kriminalstatistikken* [Criminal Statistics], Statistiske Meddelelser, several years, and *Statistisk Årbog* [Statistical Yearbook], several years, Copenhagen.

15. *Kriminalstatistikken*, 1976, 1977.

16. *Politiets Årsberetninger* [Annual Reports of the Police], several years, Copenhagen.

17. P. Wolf, "Victimization Research and Means Other than Crime Statistics to Provide Data on Criminality," in Council of Europe, *Means of Improving Information on Crime, Collected Studies in Criminological Research*, Vol. 14 (Strasbourg: European Committee on Crime Problems, 1976), p. 64.

18. Ibid., p. 62; and F. H. Lauridsen, "Tyveri i 1720' erne" [Thefts in the 1720s], in Århus Byhistorisk Udvalg (ed.), *Ulykke, Nød, Brøde. Begivenheder i Århus* (Århus: 1969).

19. Fl. Balvig, "Bidrag til belysning af tyveriernes udbredelse og udvikling i Danmark 1970-1975" [A Contribution to an Elucidation of the Extension and Development of Thefts in Denmark 1970-1975], *Det kriminalpræventive Råd* (Copenhagen: 1977).

20. L. R. Kallestrup, "Straffefrekvensen i forskellige sociale grupper" [The Frequency of Punishment in Various Social Groups], *Nordisk Tidsskrift for Kriminalvidenskab* (1954):30-34.

21. K. O. Christiansen and A. Nielsen, "Nulevende straffede mænd i Danmark" [Punished Men in Denmark Today], *Nordisk Tidsskrift for Kriminalvidenskab* (1959):30-34.

22. P. Wolf, J. Kaarsen, and E. Høgh, "Kriminalitetshyppigheden i Danmark" [The Frequency of Crime in Denmark], *Nordisk Tidsskrift for Kriminalvidenskab* (1958):113-119.

23. P. Wolf, "Crime and Social Class in Denmark," *British Journal of Criminology* 3 (1962):5-17; and P. Wolf, "A Contribution to the Topology of Crime in Denmark," in K. O. Christiansen (ed.), *Scandinavian Studies in Criminology*, Vol. 1 (Oslo/London: 1965), pp. 201-226.

24. Wolf, "Victimization Research and Means Other than Crime Statistics to Provide Data on Criminality."

25. E. Høgh and P. Wolf, "Project Metropolitan: A Longitudinal Study of 12,270 Boys from the Metropolitan Area of Copenhagen, Denmark 1953-1977," in Mednick and Baert (eds.), *Prospective Longitudinal Research in Europe* (London: Oxford University Press, 1977).

26. C. N. David, "Ere vi beføiede til at anklage Civilisationen for Forbrydelsernes Tilvæxt?" [Are We Justified in Blaming Civilization for the Increase in Crimes?], *Statsoeconomisk Archiv* 2 (1829):431-492.

27. K. Svalastoga, "Longitudinal Research Designs," *International Journal of Comparative Sociology* (1970):283-291; and Høgh and Wolf, "Project Metropolitan: A Longitudinal Study of 12,270 Boys from the Metropolitan Area of Copenhagen, Denmark 1953-1977."

BIBLIOGRAPHY

Selection of items for this bibliography has followed a fairly narrow definition of criminology, in keeping with the Danish tradition since 1945. The bibliography does not include literature predominantly of a jurisprudential character or mainly concerned with the sociology of law and practical penal policy. Included are only books or parts of books amounting to fifty pages or more, written by Danish authors. The thirty-one works chosen are classified into categories and subcategories according to level of generality, beginning with theory and descriptions of crime including methodology and ending with treatment of offenders and its evaluation.

Criminology in General, Theory and Methodology

Hurwitz, Stephan. *Kriminologi* [Criminology]. Copenhagen: G.E.C. Gad, 1948; 2d ed. 1951. Edition in English, London: Allen and Unwin, 1952. Translated into other languages as well.
The first Scandinavian textbook for studies at the university level.

Wolf, Preben, and Erik Høgh. *Kriminalitet i Velferdssamfundet* [Crime in a Welfare Society]. Copenhagen: Jørgen Paludans Forlag, 1966; 4th ed., revised and extended, 1975.
Based mainly on sociological theory and its own research, this textbook deals with topics such as registered criminality in relation to social status; hidden crime (victimization studies); the influence of the court system, police, and prison systems; recidivism; prediction; and comparison of Danish criminality with data from other countries.

Hurwitz, Stephan, and Karl O. Christiansen. *Kriminologi*. I and II [Criminology]. Copenhagen: Gyldendal, 1968 and 1971; New English edition, London: Allen and Unwin, 1979.
This greatly revised and extended edition of Hurwitz's first work serves as a textbook and as a useful handbook as well.

Jepsen, Jørgen. *Lighed for Loven* [Equality Before the Law]. Copenhagen: 1970. Published in a Dutch translation as *Gelijkheid voor de Wet*. 's Gravenhage: Neederlandse vertaling stichting uitgeverij, NVSH, 1972.
This book attempts a critical perspective on crime policy, based on recent criminological, psychological, and sociological theory and research.

Moe, Mogens, *Straffesystemet* [The Penal System]. Copenhagen: Akademisk Forlag, 1975; 2nd revised edition, 1978.
This criminological textbook describes and analyzes criminality in close relation to criminal justice processing from commission and detection of the delinquent act to the postpenitentiary period.

Petersen, Eggert. *A Reassessment of the Concept of Criminality. An Analysis of Criminal Behavior in Terms of Individual and Current Environment Interaction. The Application of a Stochastic Model*. Copenhagen: Munksgaard; and New York-Toronto: Halstead Press, 1977.
From a psychological perspective, the author sees the concept of "criminal" as an effect of the interaction between the person and the current environment. From results of his research at the Institute of Military Psychology and Mental Health Research Institute in Copenhagen, he formulates a "dialectic-Lewinian" model of criminality.

Criminality in Specific Population Categories

YOUTH

Christensen, Erik. *Unge Lovovertraedere: En Undersøgelse af de Kriminalretlige Reaktioner Overfor Unge Lovovertraedere i Århus 1954-1955* [Young Delinquents: A Study of Legal Penal Sanctions Against Young Delinquents in Århus 1954-1955]. Acta Jutlandica. Aarsskrift for Åarhus Universitet (Publications of the University of Århus) XXIX Supplementum. Samfundsvidenskabeling serie 8 (Social Science Series), Universitetsforlaget i Århus. Copenhagen: Ejnar Munksgaard, 1957.

As one of the few relevant criminographic descriptions of juvenile crime in Denmark, this study includes studies of recidivism combined with a tentative evaluation of actual measures applied against juvenile crime and of the possibility of using other measures instead. Questions put by the then Permanent Committee on Penal Reform are applied to a sample of adolescents.

WOMEN

Sander, Inge. *Kvindekriminalitet* [The Criminality of Women]. Copenhagen: Jørgen Paludans Forlag, 1976.

Using data including the files of 320 women sanctioned in 1955 and 1963 in Copenhagen for Penal Code offenses, the author discusses the criminality of women as a separate social phenomenon. The author finds that female criminals differ more and are involved in greater varieties of criminality than has been hitherto supposed.

TWINS

Christiansen, Karl O. "A Review of Studies of Criminality Among Twins" and "A Preliminary Study of Criminality Among Twins," Chapters 4 and 5 in S. Mednick and K. O. Christiansen. *Biosocial Bases of Criminal Behavior*. New York: Gardner Press, 1977.

In reviewing criminological twin research, the author concludes that "in general, it must be maintained that criminality, defined as a sociolegal concept, can only be studied from a genetic point of view as long as it is closely associated with a well-defined somatic or psychological state." Second, he brings his own very important research up to date just before his death in 1976.

Self-Reported Crime

Greve, Vagn. *Kriminalitet som Normalitet. En Studie i den Ikke-registrerede Kriminalitet i Danmark* [Criminality as Normality. A Study in the Non-registered Criminality in Denmark]. Copenhagen: Juristforbundets Forlag, 1972.

This first—and so far the only—major Danish study of self-reported crime deals with nonregistered delinquency among 7,265 young men liable for military service coming up for examination in 1964.

Images of Crime and Criminals in the Population

Kutchinsky, Berl. "Sociological Aspects of the Perception of Deviance and Criminality. Report Presented to the Ninth Conference of Directors of Criminological Research Institutes (1971)." In *Collected Studies Criminological Research*. Vol. IX. Strasbourg: Council of Europe, 1972. Pp. 8-99.

As a comprehensive and informative survey of empirical research in a large number of countries, the study concentrates on knowledge and opinion about law. The author contends "that it is becoming increasingly clear that most criminals are created through a process of discriminating selection, ostracizing stigmatization, and dehumanizing punishments."

Balvig, Flemming. *Angst for Kriminalitet. Lov-og-Orden Tendenser i en Dansk Provinsby* [Fear of Crime. Tendencies of Law-and-Order in a Danish Provincial City]. Copenhagen: Gyldendal, 1978.

This handbook on the fear of crime and on attitudes about crime and criminals in general also presents the author's previous study of "a wave of Law-and-order" and its aftermath in a Danish city in Jutland with less than fifty-five thousand inhabitants.

Specific Types of Crime

HOMICIDE

Hansen, J. P. Hart. *Drab i Danmark 1946-1970. En Retsmedicinsk Undersøgelse* [Homicides in Denmark 1946-1970. A Medico-Legal Investigation]. Summary in English. Doctoral dissertation. Copenhagen: Munksgaard, 1977.

This phenomenological, medico-legal description and analysis of criminal homicide begins with the victimological characteristics of the victim and the offender. Also treated are the offender's motives, social and mental states, potential intoxication, and methods of homicide. Medical, juridical, and criminological aspects are discussed, but without realizing definite criminological conclusions.

THEFT

Balvig, Flemming. *Bidrag til Belysning af Tyveriernes Udredelse og Udvikling i Danmark 1970-1975* [Contribution to the Illumination of the Extension and Development of Thefts in Denmark 1970-1975]. Copenhagen: Det Kriminal Preventive Rad, 1977.

Information from police districts and insurance companies and from victimization surveys is used for tentative explanations for an allegedly unique situation in Denmark: a stagnating larceny rate in the first half of the 1970s with a sudden decrease from 1974 through 1976. The author cites changes in situational temptation; opportunities for alternative activities among the young; changes in the age distribution; a change of attitudes among the young from a more hedonistic or adventurous, shortsighted style of life to a greater political awareness, more farsightedness, and less materialistic attitudes; and increasing institutionalization of youth in educational establishments, new organizations and movements, and so on.

SEXUAL CRIMES

Le Maire, Louis. *Legal Kastration i Strafferetling Belysning* [Legal Castration in the
    Light of Penal Law]. Copenhagen: E. Munksgaard, 1946.
This doctoral dissertation contains jurisprudential discussions of the phenomenon of legal
castration of certain sexual criminals in Denmark, criminographic descriptions, and criminological discussions of various forms of sex crimes and of their determinants, based on
previous literature as well as on Le Maire's own research. The author suggests that
voluntary therapeutic castration will eventually take the place of compulsory castration as
part of a wider application of biologically founded therapeutic means in the general
struggle against criminality.

Jersild, Jens. *De Paedofile. Børneelskere* [The Paedophiliacs. Lovers of Children]. Co-
    penhagen: Nyt Nordisk Forlag Arnold Busck, 1964. English summaries after each
    chapter. English language edition, *The Normal Homosexual Male Versus the Boy
    Molester*. Copenhagen: Nyt Nordisk Forlag Arnold Busck, 1967.
The author draws on his experience as a chief of the Copenhagen Morality Police since
1950 and his series of minor studies of male prostitution, and so on. He follows up his
previous investigations with this study of men sexually attracted to children. These men
seem to differ from both heterosexual and ordinary homosexual men. The author presents
a new typology of paedophiliacs. The book's conclusions amount to a draft of a criminal
code.

Kutchinsky, Berl. *Studies on Pornography and Sex Crimes in Denmark. A Report to the
    U.S. President's Commission on Obscenity and Pornography*. Copenhagen: New
    Social Science Monographs, E.5, 1970.
In 1967, the Danish Parliament repealed the penal law ban on pornographic literature. In
1969, the repeal was extended to include erotic pictures and objects. This preliminary
study of some of the effects reaches the tentative conclusion that exhibitionism, peeping,
and physical indecency toward girls has decreased due to the influence on either the
victims or the potential offenders of the increased availability of pornography. The
general liberalization of sexual behavior and of Danish attitudes may have contributed.

COLLABORATION WITH THE ENEMY

Christiansen, Karl O. *Landssvigerkriminaliteten i Sociologisk Belysning* [Danish Collab-
    orators with the Enemy During World War II in the Light of Sociology]. Ph.D.
    Dissertation, Copenhagen: G.E.C. Gads Forlag, 1955. Summary in English.
Of 5,152 sentenced male collaborators, 2,967 were interviewed personally. The subjects
were 40 percent of all males sentenced for collaboration, excluding pure profiteers. The
results agreed with Thorsten Sellin's hypothesis that criminals "who have overcome the
greatest and most pervasive group resistance probably exhibit more clearly than others the
personality types which have significance for our research purposes."

Alcohol, Drugs, and Crime

ALCOHOL AND CRIME IN GENERAL

Christensen, Erik, Erik Jacobsen, Alvar Nielson, and Max Schmidt. *Alkoholvaner og
    Kriminalitet. En Empirisk Undersøgelse af Sammenhaenger Mellem Lovovertraedelser*

og Spiritus misbrug [Alcohol Habits and Criminality. An Empirical Study of the Association of Law Offenses with Alcohol Abuse]. Copenhagen: Landsforeningen Den Personlige Friheds Vern. Bilag til Nordisk Tidsskrift for Kriminalvidenskab, 1957.

This thorough analysis of alcohol use and recorded criminality among 1,565 male and 150 female offenders is based on documentary and interview data from selected police districts in Denmark between 1947 and 1950.

DRUNKEN DRIVING

Nielsen, Kirsten. *Spritbilisters Sociale Problemer—en Undersegelse Blandt Afsonere af Spiritdomme, Efteraret 1976* [Social Problems of Drunken Drivers—A Study of Some Prisoners Serving Time for Driving under the Influence of Alcohol, Autumn 1976]. Copenhagen: Kontaktudvalget Vedrørende Alkohol—og Narkotikaspørgsmål, 1978.

The main social problems, apart from the actual sentence, experienced by 127 men and two women are mapped. The major conclusions are that these prisoners have more persistent alcohol problems and that treatments other than imprisonment are both possible and warranted for this clientele.

DRUGS AND CRIME

Boolsen, Merete Watt. *Narkotika—Kriminelle—og Andre Afyigere—et Sociologisk/Kriminologisk Studie* [Narcotics—Criminals—and Other Deviants—A Sociological-Criminological Study]. Copenhagen: Kontaktudvalget Vedrorende Ungdomsnar-komanien, 1971.

A representative sample of 282 prisoners in the Copenhagen prisons in 1969, who had violated the antidrug act at some time in their criminal career, was compared with a control group of 161 prisoners not registered for such violations. The results are discussed in light of Robert K. Merton's anomie theory and classifications. Some drug violators were innovators, and others merely followed behavioral patterns previously developed by drug violators. The average drug-act violator in 1970-1971 did not possess innovative characteristics to the same degree as those of the late 1960s.

Prediction

FORECASTING OF CRIME RATES

Jepsen, Jørgen, and Lone Pál. "Forecasting the Volume and Structure of Future Criminality." In *Collected Studies in Criminological Research, Reports Presented to the Fourth European Conference of Directors of Criminological Research Institutes (1966).* Vol. 4. Strasbourg: Council of Europe, 1969. Pp. 23-209.

This pilot study was part of a larger project sponsored by the Scandinavian Research Council for Criminology. Its primary aim was to explore problems involved in forecasting national crime trends for periods of five to ten years and to examine materials available for such a task.

PREDICTION OF PERSONAL ADJUSTMENT WITH REGARD TO CRIMINALITY

Iversen, Lis Verena. *Forudsigelser Inden for Kriminologi* [Predictions Within the Scope of Criminology]. Copenhagen: Kriminalforsorgen, Forskningsgruppen, Forskningsrapport, Nr. 3, May 1974.
In this comprehensive review and evaluation of seventy American and European criminological prediction studies, 1931 to 1972, the author discusses the practical value of various predictors and the functions and dysfunctions for criminal policy of using prediction instruments at all.

Andersen, Ole E. *Social Tilpasning Efter Udstaelse af Faengselsstraf* [Social Adjustment After Having Served a Prison Sentence]. Forskningsrapport Nr. 5. Copenhagen: Justitsministeriet, Kriminalpolitisk Forskningsgruppe, September 1976.
A prediction model is constructed from a followup study of 190 men released from Danish penal institutions during the second half of 1973 (followup period, minimum ten months, maximum sixteen months). Best predictors: (1) length of latent crime-free period before actual sentence, (2) family life, (3) employment, (4) identifications, operationalized as number of leaves of absence during imprisonment, (5) adjustment to institutional life, operationalized as number of disciplinary sanctions, and (6) adjustment to sanction, operationalized as incidence of new criminality while serving time.

Studies of Inmates and Staff of Correctional Institutions

PRISONS

Balvig, Flemming, Ole Dalå, Svend Poulsen-Hansen, Harald Rømer, and Preben Wolf. *Faengsler og Fanger* [Prisons and Prisoners]. Copenhagen: Jørgen Paludans Forlag, 1969.
This first comprehensive sociological study of the Danish prison system is based on a secondary analysis of the Danish part of Stanton Wheeler's study of prisons in Scandinavia (1961-1962) and supplemented by documentary evidence and field studies carried out by one or more of the authors. The development of penal reforms in Denmark is shown to have corresponded with Neil Smelser's model for "structural differentiation" (*Structural Change in the Industrial Revolution*, London, 1959). Among their conclusions, the authors suggest that deprivation of freedom, leave of absence arrangements, and so on, combined with an increasing distrust of imprisonment among experts and the public.

Petersen, Eggert, Elisa Dall, et al. *I Varetaegt—I Faengsel* [In Custody—In Prison]. Copenhagen: Mentalhygiejnisk Forskningsinstitut, 1972.
Eggert Petersen has developed a stochastic criminality model and model of mental well-being. Based on these models, the authors describe in three aspects that part of the Danish prison system which consists of local detention houses (jails) of Copenhagen and five different provincial cities in Denmark. The three aspects are the formal aspect, the psychological aspect, and the sociological aspect. The authors' final diagnosis of the system is so devastating that reform appears impossible; nevertheless, they suggest various remedies.

OTHER INSTITUTIONS

Blegvad, Britt-Mari. *Brikker i et Spil Eller: Om Behandling på Institution* [Pieces in a
    Game or: On Institutional Treatment]. Copenhagen: Gyldendals Paedagogiske
    Bibliotek, 1972.
Interviews, documents, and participant observation were used in a study of an old and a
new Danish treatment institution for young delinquents and/or otherwise asocial or antisocial youth. The author suggests that treatment in closed institutions should be abandoned,
that these institutions should be turned into diagnostic centers, and that the centers should
operate in support of small treatment units outside the institutions proper.

Treatment of Offenders, Description, and Evaluation

Berntsen, Karen, and Karl O. Christiansen. *Mandlige Arresthusfanger i Københavns
    Faengsler. En Undersøgelse og et Experiment* [Male Short-Term Prisoners in the
    Prisons of Copenhagen. An Investigation and an Experiment]. Copenhagen:
    Direktoratet for Faengselsvaesenet, 1955.
Carried out in 1952-1953 through the Danish Prison Service, the study involved 126
randomly selected male prisoners and 126 controls, all serving less than five months. A
prediction score was calculated, compared with an intuitive prognosis, and tested against
actual recidivism. The results seem to show that personal investigation and resocialization
efforts are more important than are the sentence, the serving of time, and the external
framework of the prison.

Stürup, Georg K. *Treating the "Untreatable." Chronic Criminals at Herstedvester. The
    Isaac Ray Award Lectures.* Baltimore: Johns Hopkins Press, 1968.
The author was superintendent of the renowned Herstedvester Detention Center in Denmark. He gives an account of the methods he developed for treatment of emotionally
disturbed criminals, illustrated with case histories. His approach is sociopsychiatric,
humanitarian, and constructive. The chronic criminal is to be his own therapist. Stürup
emphasizes that humane treatment is possible within the limits of security and that it can
shorten the average detention considerably.

Christiansen, Karl O., Mogens Moe, et al. *Effektiviteten af Forvaring og Saerfaengsel...En
    Kriminologisk Efterundersogelse...* [The Effectiveness of Indefinite Detention and
    Special Imprisonment for Mentally Deviant Criminals etc. A Criminological Follow-
    Up Study...]. Copenhagen: Straffelovradets Betaenkning, Nr. 644. Statens
    Trykningskontor, 1972.
Sponsored by the Danish Permanent Committee on Penal Reform (Chairman: Professor
Knud Waaben), this study concludes that there are no significant differences between the
effects of indefinite and of comparable definite sentences with regard to recidivism, but a
significant difference for the number of relapses over time. Those released from an
indefinite sentence performed better over time than those released after a definite sentence, especially for characterologically deviant offenders (typical for Herstedvester inmates). Partly as a result of this report, the Danish Parliament in 1975 abolished indefinite
sentences except for a narrowly defined "dangerous" category of the typical Herstedvester
clientele.

Holstein, Bjorn E., and Torben Jersild. *932 Kriminelle Stofmisbrugere—fem ar senere*, Forskningsrapport Nr. 2 [932 Criminal Drug Abusers—Five Years Later]. Copenhagen: Justitsministeriet. Kriminalpolitisk Forskningsgruppe, 1976.

This is a sociomedical followup of 932 drug users and abusers who passed through the Copenhagen prisons in the years 1967-1969. The study favors a labeling theory approach illustrated by an escalating drug abuse which seems to be furthered by antinarco treatment, criminal registration, and psychiatric hospitalization. Forty percent of the subjects who had undergone any treatment had stopped drug use spontaneously between 1968 and 1973, while only 11 percent of those treated were not using drugs in 1973.

8

EGYPT

Saied Ewies

The social sciences in Egypt cannot be discussed in isolation from the country's main social problems, and the main social problems cannot be understood without a study of the political scene. These principles were as true in the past as they are today, and certainly they applied before 1936.

INDEPENDENCE AND NEW PROBLEM SENSITIVITY

Egypt was under the complete control of the British from 1882 until 1922, even though the country was supposed to be independent. Foreign influence persisted, although a constitution had been announced, a parliament of two houses had been established, and a democratic government had taken responsibilities.

A significant aspect of foreign control was the privileges accorded foreigners in Egypt through the mechanism of "capitulation"—"the privileges which foreigners in Egypt, whether their domicile is permanent or temporary, have been claiming and enjoying."[1] British control and the privileges conferred through capitulation crippled the Egyptian government and weakened the Egyptians' capacity to meet serious economic problems, to mobilize resources vital to national development, and to serve the welfare of the people.

As a self-respecting people, the Egyptians resented foreign interference. The struggle for independence involved violence and counterviolence before a treaty of friendship and alliance was concluded in 1936. With the signing of the 1936 treaty with the British, a period of active social reform began in Egypt. The Cairo School of Social Work was established by the Egyptian Association for Social Studies in October 1937 as a vehicle for developing a corps of urgently needed social workers. Through them, Egypt would be able to implement social projects and to spread knowledge of the aims and methods of social work.

The association's second project was a survey undertaken in 1938 to investigate the causes of poverty in Egypt in urban and rural districts. The methodology used was careful study of individual cases.

The third project, "village reconstruction," was launched in October 1939. The Social Services Bureau of the juvenile court in Cairo, the fourth project of the association, was inaugurated in June 1940 as an experiment. The bureau's services were directed toward psychological, medical, and social studies of delinquent children, followed by sympathetic advice and supervision as a means of promoting their readjustment in their home environments. Because of the demonstrated value of the bureau's services, the Ministry of Justice on March 22, 1941, officially recognized the bureau, designated detention homes, and made the bureau a definite part of the juvenile court system.

As the fifth project, the Boys' Club was established in 1941 to further the development of children and young men as cooperative members of their community for improvement of conditions. Over time, the services of the club have been extended to girls in the district. This club also serves as a training center for leaders who would administer similar clubs.[2]

The philosophy underlying these activities was that of "social engineering" through gradual reform of existing social institutions rather than the creation of new institutions. The unit of analysis was the local community rather than the total Egyptian society.

EGYPTIANS ADOPT AN APPLIED PERSPECTIVE

Through these projects, Egyptian sociologists gained their first opportunity to apply the principles of the social sciences to seek solutions for the social problems facing their society. The field of "social work" has been identified as a platform for the conjunction of social research and social services. The underlying rationale has been that withholding services only for the sake of advancing research into the process of social disintegration would be unethical in Egypt.

An especially important figure in the establishment of sociology in Egypt was Wendell Cleland,[3] an American sociologist who lectured in 1938 at the Cairo School of Social Work. In orienting his teaching toward developing a corps of social workers for Egypt, his emphasis was on Egypt's sociology rather than on general sociology proper. Cleland illustrated his lectures on the concepts and topics of sociology with examples drawn from Egyptian life.

By applied sociology Cleland meant practical sociology relevant to social work functions in dealing with poverty, disease, unemployment, insanity, race hatred, war, crime, and so on. In Cleland's view, social workers are "social engineers" who know the causes of social difficulties and the means of removing them. He regards hospitals, orphanages, prisons, and other institutions as only temporary devices.

Immediately after the signing of the treaty with Britain, the first generation of Egyptian sociologists, trained in the French and British traditions, began to replace foreign scholars. In a blend of French and British functionalism, their work was devoted largely to exposition of the works of the French and British founders of the discipline. Rarely did they succeed in freeing themselves from

the philosophies of Comte, Durkheim, and Spencer whose works were introduced as closed systems taken out of their contexts.[4]

Among the books on sociology in Arabic that soon appeared was Mostafa
Fahmy's book published in May 1938. It was welcomed by Egyptian and foreign
scholars such as Mansour Fahmy, Cleland, and Mohamed Abd El Moneim
Riad.[5] Mostafa Fahmy was concerned with such subjects as the emergence of
sociology, social doctrines, the structure of society, social functions, principles
of general sociology, and social scientific definitions. His bibliography included
such scholars as Bouglé, Challay, Déat, Durkheim, Giddings, Montesquieu,
Sorokin, and Spencer. Fahmy related his topic of social functions to the sociology of law in discussions of primitive societies, totem and taboo, responsibility
and its evolution, blood feud, blood money, retribution, the impact of ethics
upon legislation, and criminal and civil law.[6]

The sociology of law and criminal psychology were taught in the Faculty of
Law at Cairo University in the early 1930s. Mohamed El-Bably and Counsellor
Mohamed Fathy were the eminent pioneers of their time in these two fields.
El-Bably was the author of *Criminality in Egypt: Its Causes and Methods of Its
Treatment* published in 1941.[7] His book was a step towards the emergence of
criminology in Egypt. The contents were based primarily upon personal experience. A heavy emphasis was given to criminal statistics. His explanations for
criminality were traditional for that time in references to physical, individual,
and social factors. Criminality among women and juveniles in urban and rural
areas was given particular attention. As the dean of the Police College, El-Bably
was also concerned with police functions in crime prevention, detective work,
apprehension of criminals, and corrective measures. Finally, he was critical of
the criminal legislation of his day.

In addition to the work of El-Bably, juvenile delinquency was given concentrated attention in the lectures of Fath-Allah-El-Marsfy, Abd-El-Moneim Riad,
Elsa Tabet, and Yacoub Fam[8] during 1937-1938 at the Cairo School of Social Work.

As early as 1882, Egyptian law required that delinquent children receive
special treatment. The first boys' reformatory, established in 1907, housed eight
hundred boys in prison-like cubicles but provided them with adequate paraphernalia. In a militaristic environment, they had traditional activities: lessons, industrial education, music, drill, games, and the like. The reformatory had a mosque,
and the facilities were kept clean.

The lecturers at the Cairo School of Social Work in 1937-1938 advocated
basic changes in the reformatories and orphanages to improve chances that the
inmates would not become criminals. The lecturers proposed that the government make it possible for the Egyptian Association for Social Studies to extend
its investigations to include the reformatories and orphanages so that their environment would resemble the life to which the inmates returned rather than
continuing the prison spirit prevailing in these institutions. They also proposed
that a committee, formed by the association, study criminal legislation that
would call for reformatory—not punitive—treatment of the inmates.

Counsellor Mohamed Fathy was among the first to be appointed to the Executive Committee of the Social Services Bureau of the Cairo juvenile court in June 1940. Fathy's major contributions, however, have been in criminal psychology. He began lecturing on this subject in 1933 in the Faculty of Law at Cairo University. Among his important books is *Criminal Psychology: Theory and Practice* in three volumes.[9] These volumes were derived from his lectures, which ended in 1960, and from some of his published articles and studies.

An ardent advocate of psychoanalytic theory, Fathy sought to interpret criminal behavior from this perspective through field studies on the detection of criminals, the behavior of police investigators, and the behavior of judges. His activities were extended into reform of prisons, juvenile reformatories, and orphanages through criminal and social legislation. He was a member of various committees formed by the Ministries of Health, Justice, and Social Affairs. Since the National Institute of Criminology at Cairo was established in 1955, Counselor Fathy has been a member of its board of directors.

ESTABLISHMENT OF THE RESEARCH INSTITUTE

The National Institute of Criminology was founded in 1955 in accordance with Act 632 of 1955, but it was called the National Center for Social and Criminological Research under Act 221 of 1959. The establishment of the institute was a product of the 1952 Revolution and constituted an important event in the institutionalization of criminological research. The government was keenly interested in establishing this institute because of growing recognition that crime menaces the very structure of a nation and undermines its political, economic, and social welfare. Crime endangers rights, life, and property, but, even more significantly, it exacts a great toll on the productive capacity of society.

An independent organization endowed with a juridical personality and presided over by the minister of social affairs and labour, the institute was concerned with:

1. Research and surveys in crime, delinquency, and punishment.

2. Teaching, training, and orientation in the theoretical and practical aspects of these subjects.

3. Coordination of government and private agencies in combatting crime by preventive and corrective measures.

4. Setting down scientific bases for criminal and correctional policies in harmony with national conditions.

The institute was established to face the problem of crime as a whole rather than to deal with only one or a few aspects of the problem. The lone researcher of previous criminology was to be replaced with teams of trained researchers in established units concerned with particular problems in the field of crime. This organizational mode marked the beginning of criminological research as a newly born profession that would lead to official recognition of criminology as a discipline in Egypt.

Ahmed M. Khalifa was the architect of the National Institute of Criminology. As one of the many disciples of Counsellor Fathy, he was interested in criminal psychology. He is the author of *The Genesis of Criminal and Judicial Psychology* published in 1949.[10] His second book, *The Genesis of Social Criminology*, was published in 1954.[11] To earn a doctorate in criminal law, Khalifa prepared a dissertation on *The General Theory of Criminalization* in 1959.[12] Another of his books, *Introduction to the Study of Criminal Behavior*, was published in 1962.[13]

The vitalization of criminological research in 1956 attracted other persons, some of whom were connected in some way with criminology. Hassan El-Saaty, now a university professor, was among the pioneers concerned with juvenile delinquency in Egypt, as witnessed by his dissertation "Juvenile Delinquency in Egypt" in 1946 for a doctorate in sociology. As an instructor of sociology, El-Saaty wrote *About Criminal Sociology* in 1951[14] and *Sociology of Law* in 1952.[15]

Yassin El-Refaie and Mahmoud El-Sebaie, two police officers attracted by the new profession, joined the institute from the start. El-Refaie was an authority in penology. El-Sebaie had an A.M. degree in police administration and was interested in the detection of criminals.[16]

I had just been awarded a doctorate in criminology when I was invited to join the institute in 1956. Since 1939 I had been working in the fields of prevention and treatment and had served in the fields of institutional care and probation.[17]

From preliminary work carried out when it was called the National Institute of Criminology, the National Center for Social and Criminological Research has expanded the scope of its responsibilities. Act 221 of 1959 decreed that the center should further scientific research and the investigation of social affairs related to the different aspects of Arab society and attendant problems. This work was supposed to provide bases for social policies intended to deal with problematic conditions from preventive, protective, and correctional orientations.

These policies have never been established, but the center has endeavored to carry out its responsibilities through scientific activities in the general field of social affairs and in the more limited field of criminology. These activities may be broadly classified as research projects, conferences, and symposia, training programs, and scientific publications.

The criminological research projects may be roughly categorized. First, research of criminal behavior systems has investigated prostitution, hashish addiction, juvenile vagrancy, homicide, and pickpocketing. Second, juvenile delinquency has been studied in terms of family configurations, thefts by juveniles, pickpocketing by juveniles, the volume of juvenile delinquency and its types, trends, and factors. Third, research into the social effects of imprisonment pending trial, probation, and short-term imprisonment is but a sample of studies in the field of penology. Fourth, among projects on criminalistics are organic phosphorus insecticides, cannabis active constituents, barbiturates, analysis and identification of writing materials, and activation analysis for identification of hair.[18]

Experience accumulated through criminological research since 1956 has influenced criminology in Egypt. Questions have been raised about the status and functions of contemporary criminology in and of itself, but the focus of research has been on practical problems. Criminological research projects have been shrinking, however, since the center came into being in 1959. Criminology has expanded as an Egyptian branch of learning in the faculties of law, social work, and the arts, and in the Police Academy. Criminology, like sociology, is greatly affected by Western criminological thinking, but Islamic teachings influence many Egyptian criminologists.

The *Sharia* (the Islamic law), as interpreted by the *ulama* (the Muslim clergy), who are the most influential religious group, has great impact on the workings of the law in reality. The definition of juvenile delinquency, not included in the law until 1974, illustrates the impact of Islamic law. Islamic teachings set responsibility at the onset of puberty which may be the age of fourteen for males and thirteen for females. Experience in juvenile delinquency work and the findings of socio-criminological research have pressed for a raising of the age of responsibility under law to eighteen years. Although this reform was accomplished in 1974, the change continues to be opposed as a violation of Islamic teaching. Among the opponents, in addition to the *ulama*, are some legislators, policemen, and penologists.

DEMANDS PLACED ON SCIENTIFIC CRIMINOLOGY

Criminology may have several meanings. First, it may be confined to the science that deals with the etiology of crime. Second, it may deal with the treatment of criminals (penology) and the detection of criminals (criminalistics). Egypt has adopted a third meaning which includes the etiology of crime, the treatment of criminals, and the detection of criminals.

Some people assert that criminology, especially at the present stage of its development, is not a science. They claim that contemporary criminology, like social work, is generally dependent upon other sciences and in itself is not a science. Criminology deals with social phenomena because criminal behavior is but human behavior that is found only among men in society. Natural matter can be manipulated, but man, as a social being influenced by both nature and society, is not easy to manipulate.

The researcher in criminology is aware that the "criminal code" is only one of many codes of behavior found in society. Persons who violate the criminal law are not necessarily different, and should not be considered different, from those who violate other behavioral codes. That is, they are not a different species.

The diversity of behavioral codes is one reason why crime and delinquency remain vague concepts loosely defined. The multidisciplinary nature of criminology produces social, psychological, legal, anthropological, religious, and administrative definitions of the concepts. The legal definitions vary from society to society and even among jurisdictions in the same society. Inherent in these difficulties for reaching agreement on a definition is that "crime" and "delinquency" are based on legal norms variously selected from the broader body of cultural norms.

Many interrelated and dynamic factors may bring about criminal or delinquent behavior. Understanding the phenomenon calls for studying the criminal act, the criminal actor, and the victim. Study of the criminal act involves its type, the time and place it was committed, and the method with which it was committed. Study of the criminal actor involves his or her family background, social milieu, value system, state of health, motives, and personality as a whole. The study of the act and the actor alone, however, is not enough. The victim plays a definite role—or roles—in certain obvious crimes and delinquencies, such as sexual crimes, homicide, bribery, and various types of theft.

The research worker in the field of criminology must adopt an objective and scientific outlook or philosophy and clearly define his or her purpose and methodology.

If criminology in Egypt is to flourish, it should follow what medical scientists have done. One type of crime, or of delinquency, such as rape, begging, homicide, or prostitution, may be studied. Homogeneous groups of offenders, such as students, workers, girls, young men, mothers, and civil servants, are also appropriate subjects for investigation.

As in the physical sciences, scientific experiments in the field of social phenomena are tedious and expensive. The experiment of Edwin Powers, the American criminologist, in the prevention of juvenile delinquency[19] illustrates the difficulties. Ideological considerations inhibit social experimentation; for example, there are ethical constraints on twin studies as a device for testing the relative importance of nature and nurture in the development of criminality.

CONDITIONS FOR INSTITUTIONALIZATION

If criminology is to be institutionalized in Egypt, at least four major conditions must be satisfied: increased availability of well-trained and motivated research workers, development of a reliable data base, strengthening the quality of social service delivery, and, of course, provision of adequate resources for research and practice.

Availability of Researchers

As explained above, the National Center for Social and Criminological Research has followed the principle that team research is essential to criminology. This principle places a premium on the capacities of specialists, each competent in a particular sphere of criminology, to coordinate their separate contributions to the joint project.

Comparative studies among different societies have great potential, but they present great difficulties for establishing control and experimental groups. The choice of a special kind of research worker is a necessity. Training must be up to date, continuous, and of high quality. Every effort should be made to retain this brand of researcher and to avoid his or her transfer to professions in other fields.[20]

Reliable Data Base

The institutionalization of criminological research awaits reliable knowledge of fundamental facts about Egyptian society: the structure of the population (sex, age, professions, standard of living, cost of living, and so on); size and trends of the family institution and child-rearing practices; impact of mental and physical diseases; and correlates with social status, economic standards, and levels of education.

Official Egyptian statistics are misleading and have many shortcomings as measurements of the volume and trends of crime. As criminologists of all countries know, the "dark" figure of crime is especially problematic, and especially so for crimes connected with sex, bribery, drug traffic, drug addiction, and theft. As in other nations, the measurement and evaluation of recidivism is another major methodological issue.

Social surveys show promise for mapping the variance of criminality within the structure of Egyptian society. The descriptions generated would be useful for mobilizing the mass media and persuading opposing public opinion categories to support criminal policies and reform measures. Of course, the success of these measures and the development of needed policies pivot on the elasticity of values dominant in Egypt.

Strengthening Social Service Delivery

In keeping with the applied nature of criminology in Egypt, the quality of criminological practitioners is of great importance. These practitioners work in courts, jails, prisons, police agencies, schools, social centers, and hospitals. Their thinking is the product of direct experience. Their empirical logic persuades them that they are the best judges of what should be done. Faced with new developments outside the traditional sphere of their familiar experiences, they are likely to resist tenaciously new ideas coming from outside their limited universe.

A special program of training is needed to increase the impact of programs relevant to reducing crime. The design of these programs must take into account the opposition to training in new ideas and practices that many practitioners will demonstrate. Training of existing personnel is vital because it is not practical to create new staffs through recruitment. Training must be oriented to altering staff behaviors over the long term because radical and immediate revision of practices cannot be anticipated.

Provision of Resources

As in all nations, the institutionalization of criminology in Egypt is impeded by lack of money. In order to flourish, research and practice require quality staff members, time for implementation, and sufficient financial resources. Without such investment, human effort and precious time will be wasted, which will prove an acute disaster in this developing society.[21]

Egyptian criminologists already have accumulated more knowledge of the field than their predecessors. They owe much to students of criminology such as El-Bably and to his book, *Criminality in Egypt: Its Causes and Methods of Its Treatment*. Through this accumulated knowledge, together with proper investment of essential resources, contemporary criminologists can further expand the body of known principles.

NOTES

1. League of Nations, *Report and Proceedings of the World Economic Conference*, Vol. 1 (Geneva: May 23, 1927), p. 238.

2. Mohamed M. Shalaby, *Rural Reconstruction in Egypt* (Cairo: Egyptian Association for Social Studies, 1950), pp. 53-54.

3. Wendell Cleland, *Sociology and Its Human Services* (in Arabic) (Cairo: Enahda Bookshop, 1938).

4. Ezzat Hegazy, "Contemporary Sociology in Egypt," in Raj P. Mohan and Don Martindale (eds.), *Handbook of Contemporary Developments in World Sociology* (Westport, Conn.: Greenwood Press, 1975), pp. 379-390.

5. These are some of the eminent social reformers of the time.

6. Mostapha Fahmy, *Sociology* (in Arabic) (Cairo: Enahda Bookshop, 1938), pp. 167-169.

7. Mohamed El-Bably, *Criminality in Egypt: Its Causes and Methods of Its Treatment* (in Arabic) (Cairo: Dar El-Kotob El-Amearia, 1941).

8. The first person was the director of education in the reformatory schools, Riad was a prominent reformer (see note 5), Tabet was a Swiss social worker who had been a probation officer in Paris, and Fam was a YMCA secretary in Cairo.

9. Mohamed Fathy, *Criminal Psychology: Theory and Practice* (in Arabic) (Cairo: Enahda Bookshop, 1943, 1950, and 1974).

10. Ahmed M. Khalifa, *The Genesis of Criminal and Judicial Psychology* (in Arabic) (Cairo: Dar El-Fikr El-Arabi, 1949).

11. Ahmed M. Khalifa, *The Genesis of Social Criminology* (in Arabic) (Cairo: Lagnet El-Taaleef Wa-El-Targama Wa-El-Nashr, 1954).

12. Ahmed M. Khalifa. *The General Theory of Criminalization* (in Arabic) (Cairo: Dar El-Maaref, 1959).

13. Ahmed M. Khalifa, *An Introduction to the Study of Criminal Behavior* (in Arabic) (Cairo: Dar El-Maaref, 1962).

14. Hassan El-Saaty, *About Criminal Sociology* (in Arabic) (Cairo: Enahda Bookshop, 1951).

15. Hassan El-Saaty, *Sociology of Law* (in Arabic) (Cairo: Egyptian Anglo Bookshop, 1952).

16. Yassin El-Refaie was appointed head of the Correction Research Section and El-Sebaie head of the Criminalistics Research Section.

17. Some of my major works are: "Observation Homes for Underprivileged Juveniles" (1940), "The Probation System in Modern Egypt" (1954), and "The Application of the Delinquency Area Concept to a Non-Western Society." I have written articles and supervised various research in criminology. A new source of "dark" crime in Egyptian society was revealed in my book, *Some Features of the Contemporary Egyptian Society: The Phenomenon of Sending Letters to the Tomb of the Imam El Shafie* (in Arbaic) (Cairo: Dar Matabie El Shaab, 1965).

18. National Center for Social and Criminological Research, *Annual Report* (Cairo: 1967), pp. 4-7.

19. Edwin Powers, "An Experiment in Prevention of Delinquency," *Annals of American Academy of Political and Social Science* 261 (January 1949):77-88.

20. Several colleagues, who were excellent criminological researchers, have already left the center to work in other professions. Among them are El-Saied Yassin, Ahmed El-Alfy, and Samir El-Ganzory. Other colleagues still at the center have been attracted by social fields other than criminology; among them are Ezzat Hegazy, Hoda Megahed, Nahed Saleh, and Noha Fahmy.

21. Saied Ewies, "Some Basic Problems in Criminology," *National Review of Criminal Sciences* 7 (July 1964):306-314.

BIBLIOGRAPHY

Abu-Zied, Ahmed. "Vendetta: An Anthropological Study in an Upper Egyptian Village."
    National Review of Criminal Sciences 6 (November 1963):301-364 (in Arabic).
This pioneer study employs the anthropological method to investigate a form of institutionalized violence that has persistently weakened Egypt's social fabric.

El-Magdoub, Ahmed. "Incest in the Islamic Criminal Jurisprudence and the Positive
    Law." *National Review of Criminal Sciences* 21 (July-November 1978):3-91 (in
    Arabic).
A comparative law analysis concludes that Islamic *sharia* (Islamic law) is the appropriate response to incest.

Ewies, Saied. "A Comparative Study of Two Delinquency Areas: Roxbury of Boston,
    Mass., and Boulac of Cairo." *National Review of Criminal Sciences* 2 (November
    1959):433-448.
This work presents a cross-cultural examination of delinquency correlates in two satellites of major metropolises.

Ewies, Saied. "Juvenile Delinquency: Its Definitions, Types and Ecological Distribu-
    tion." *National Review of Criminal Sciences* 12 (March 1969):257-286.
This theoretical review of concepts of delinquency is drawn from a range of juvenile misconduct and their application to varieties and distributions of juvenile delinquency.

Ewies, Saied. "On Capital Punishment in Egypt." *National Review of Criminal Sciences*
    21 (July-November 1978):93-117 (in Arabic).

This pioneer study surveys those who were sentenced to death during the period of 1923 (the beginning of official registration) to 1973. The major conclusion is that a more humanitarian approach should be substituted for this sanction.

Hafez, Nagwa. "School Status and Delinquent Behavior Among Youth in the Arab
    Republic of Egypt." *National Review of Criminal Sciences* 21 (March 1978):3-15.
The relationships between educational experience and performance among juveniles and delinquency are placed in an Egyptian context.

Khalifa, M. Ahmed. "New Frontiers of Social Defense." *International Annals of Crimi-
    nology* 12, nos. 1 and 2 (1973):333-342.
The United Nations' adoption of the concept of social defense is traced through three phases: initial phase up to 1957; the conflict phase, 1957-1965; and the takeover phase beginning in 1965.

Khalifa, M. Ahmed. "Socio-Legal Considerations of Drug Abuse." *International Annals
    of Criminology* 11, no. 2 (1972):363-371.
For thousands of years, drug substances have been used by human beings for spiritual, ritualistic, and secular purposes. Only the choice of which substance is used, its availability, and the general purpose of use have changed.

Khalifa, M. Ahmed. "Some Social Aspects of Drug Abuse." *International Review of
    Criminal Policy*, no. 30 (1972):94-97.
The author emphasizes the necessity for caution in explaining the extent and future trends of drug abuse because of the diversity of causal factors and the grounding of drug abuse in regular sociocultural patterns.

Mobarak, Z., and N. Zaki. "Identification of Cannabis Constituent and Some Synthetic
    Thio-Cannabinoids by Gas Chromatography." *National Review of Criminal Sci-
    ences* 21 (July-November 1978):3-10.
This report illustrates Egyptian efforts to expand technical resources for dealing with crime-related problems.

National Center for Social and Criminological Research. *Brief Report on a Statistical
    Study on Juvenile Vagrancy*. Cairo: Government Printing Office, 1963.
Crucial variables are interrelated to provide basic information for policymaking in regard to juvenile vagrancy as an issue related to socioeconomic development.

National Center for Social and Criminological Research. *Brief Report on Prostitution in
    Cairo: A Social Survey and Clinical Study*. Cairo: Government Printing Office,
    1964.
The qualities of prostitution are related to the community setting of this social problem.

National Center for Social and Criminological Research. *Report I, Hashish Consumption
    in the Egyptian Region, U.A.R.: The Interviewing Schedule, Construction, Reli-
    ability and Validity*. Cairo: Government Printing Office, 1960.
As a sample of the National Center's research activities, this publication illustrates the development of methodological resources.

National Center for Social and Criminological Research. *Report II, Hashish Con-sumption in Cairo City: A Pilot Survey*. Cairo: Government Printing Office, 1963.
Patterns of hashish use are related to ecological variables.

9

FINLAND

Inkeri Anttila

In Finland, as elsewhere in Europe, criminology has developed on the basis of two sources: criminal statistics which indicate the level and trend of criminality; and psychological and psychiatric research which concentrates on individual factors. The first approach has been dominant in Finland.

REORIENTATION OF FINNISH CRIMINOLOGY

Previously, Finnish criminology tended to separate "true" criminology from the study of the official crime control system and from the investigation of the effects of sanctions. This same tendency was common to most European criminology. However, the situation in Finland changed after World War II, and especially since the beginning of the 1960s attention has been given to the crime control system.

Criminological research in Finland has always had close connections to research carried out in the other Scandinavian countries. In all these countries, research has been based on a sociological conception of criminology. But Finland has done more than the other Scandinavian countries in using an applied or problem-oriented approach to criminological research.

In Finland, the term "criminologist" expressly refers to a researcher, and not to a practitioner. Criminal policy, on the other hand, refers primarily to the activity of decision-makers connected to the criminal justice system. For example, the police or prison administration personnel would not be called criminologists in Finland.

SETTING FOR FINLAND'S CRIMINOLOGY

As is clear from the above discussion, in Finland a criminologist is a researcher interested in offenses, offenders, and the crime control system. There are conflicting opinions, however, on the position of the researcher. Some researchers emphasize the objectiveness of research and insist that research be separated from decision-making. They believe that the researcher should never say what should be done; instead, he or she should only study the effects of different alternatives and leave the decision-making to the authorities. Other researchers contend that even a researcher is continuously making decisions—for example, when he chooses what and how to study. In so doing, the researcher's own values and interests have a great effect on his work. Those who follow this line of thinking have concluded that no distinction should be made between the researcher and decision-maker. Still other researchers take a compromise position. They maintain that research can be separated from decision-making by having the researcher deliberately document the relevant value dimensions, including his or her own position, and thus produce "value-conscious" research.

Most Finnish criminologists believe that the ultimate aim of crime control policy is to keep the societal costs related to crime at a tolerable level. But equal importance is placed on another aim, the aim of effecting a just distribution of the cost Xand suff —ing caused by criminality. This goal can be achieved by making changes in the criminal sanction system. Even though the quality and quantity of criminality in a society depend above all on its social structure—for example, on how many opportunities there are for committing certain offenses—penal legislation is frequently the most effective tool for allocating the costs and suffering among different possible sectors: the victim, the offender, and the rest of society. An example can be taken from the field of property offenses. In order to reduce the number of car thefts, we may (1) increase the penalties so that the increased "costs," at least in a limited sense, are concentrated on the offenders; (2) intensify the control so that the increased costs are carried by society along with the increase in police expenditures; and (3) demand that the potential victim, in addition to taking out theft insurance, equip his vehicle with a truly effective lock so that the increased costs are paid by the car owners.

During the last few years, criminologists have also repeatedly emphasized that in order to reduce the harmful consequences of criminality it may be much easier to control the number of crime opportunities or change the penal legislation rather than to attempt to "cure" or "change" the offenders. Finnish criminologists in the 1960s rejected the so-called treatment ideology, which holds that certain personal characteristics cause criminality and that such persons can be "cured" of criminality through treatment. Instead, Finnish criminologists see criminality as a societal phenomenon.

PATTERNS OF CRIME

Surveys of Scandinavian crime trends[1] usually deal with one of two statistical series: crime known to the police and court statistics on sentenced persons. These statistical data suffer from certain basic shortcomings, such as variations in the proportion of unrecorded crime, variations in the reporting procedure, and lack of sufficient contextual information for the correct interpretation of crime figures. However, Finnish statistics probably compare favorably with other crime reporting systems. They reflect the European bureaucratic tradition with its detailed rules, rigid systems of control, and internalized standards of conduct. Finnish efforts to check the crime statistics against independent data, such as cause-of-death statistics, self-reported crime surveys, and victim-reported victimization data, have by no means shown a very high degree of agreement. Generally, however, the statistics are seldom entirely in error, for example, in indications of the annual increase or decrease in criminality (Table 9-1).

TABLE 9-1
CRIMES REPORTED TO THE POLICE PER 100,000 INHABITANTS
AGED 15 AND OVER (ANNUAL AVERAGE), 1950-1979

Offense Category	1950–1954	1955–1959	1960–1964	1965–1969	1970–1974	1975–1979
All offenses[a]	3,738[b]	3,296	3,724	4,706	6,168	7,285
Violence against an official	18	15	14	17	32	36
Perjury	6	6	7	6	5	8
Breaking the peace	46	41	41	46	49	55
Forgery	28	34	44	53	154	173
Forcible rape	6	5	7	10	9	9
Homicide	6	5	4	4	5[c]	6[c]
Assault offenses	208	180	177	205	350	329
Larceny offenses	680	812	1,099	1,373	2,166	2,649
Embezzlement	70	67	68	56	38	38
Robbery	7	6	9	16	41	52
Fraud	178	190	182	201	276	262
Illegal distillation of alcohol	47	42	25	20	16	16
Drug offenses	—	—	—	—	319	330
Drunken driving	66	80	168	209	342	503

Source: Patrik Törnudd, *Crime Trends in Finland*, p. 2.

[a]All reported offenses except drunkenness and traffic offenses involving motor vehicles.
[b]Prior to 1955, the total includes violations of local regulations and ordinances.
[c]From 1970 on, the homicide figures do not include assault which caused the victim's death.

Annual statistical reports show that the volume of crime has increased since World War II. They reveal a uniform pattern in many offense categories. Finland saw a marked crime wave in the years immediately after the war. This crime wave swiftly subsided, but at least some of the offenders continued their careers in crime. Thus, the impact of the wave can still be seen in later years.

After the peaceful 1950s, the 1960s brought tremendous changes: the large age cohorts born after the war reached the age of crime, economic growth accelerated, and the country saw vast demographic changes as young people moved to the cities in the South and exchanged agricultural employment for industrial and service occupations. From 1960 to 1970, the number of larcenies increased by 91 percent, the number of assaults by 101 percent, and the number of robberies by 222 percent. The 1960s was also the decade of much reform activity; some people have linked the increase in crime with these reforms and to the "tendency towards too lenient punishments." However, it would be more natural to see the changes in criminality of the 1960s as primarily the product of vast societal changes that increased crime opportunities and dissolved earlier systems of social control.

Larceny

Since World War II, larceny has been a predominantly urban crime. In 1950, one-third of all offenses were registered in rural communes, and by 1975 this proportion had diminished to one-fifth. This statistic illustrates one important structural change: a significant part of the increase in crime can be explained by the migration of people into high-crime areas. However, recently the difference between the urban and the rural crime rate has steadily diminished. This shift may be a consequence of the urbanization of the countryside; it can perhaps also be explained to some extent by the increase in car ownership and general mobility.

In addition to demographic changes, other explanations must be sought, especially as far as the 1970s are concerned. Urbanization increases the opportunities of committing crime, but, in addition, economic cycles would be expected to have an impact on the crime rate within a given community. There is no satisfactory economic indicator of the total amount of potential objects of larceny, including not only all goods manufactured, transported, and stored, but also goods offered for sale in shops and department stores and the objects of value kept in homes and in summer cottages—popular targets of burglary in Finland. The channels of distribution of merchandise have also undergone substantial changes, with supermarkets and large shopping centers accounting for a growing share of retail sales. This structural change was particularly rapid in Finland at the end of the 1960s and the beginning of the 1970s. Such a development could be expected to bring about a visible increase in the number of petty larcenies, and this was indeed the case.

Unemployment is traditionally considered a contributory factor in crime. However, the relation between the employment situation and the crime rate may be more complex. In times of unemployment, internal mobility is low; young people tend to remain in school or attend vocational courses; and business activity may be slower than usual. On the other hand, the amount of leisure time is increased, a major part of the industrial enterprises may adopt shortened working weeks, and the authorities responsible for employment may arrange special temporary work opportunities, such as road-building jobs for young males in the crime-prone age. Obviously, an understanding of how economic cycles have affected the Finnish larceny rate calls for more penetrating and ecologically differentiated analysis, taking into account alternative assumptions of causality.

The police authorities on several occasions associated the increase in larceny during the 1970s with an increased professionalization among offenders. Certainly, there is every reason to believe that the opportunities for professionalization have increased with the growth of the urban population, higher population density, better communication facilities, higher levels of education, and so on. The crime peak produced by the large age cohorts in the 1960s can also be expected to have later indirect effects as many of the first offenders then sent to prison will continue their careers in crime. The larger crime volume, the offenders' higher average age and educational status, and their greater sophistication—as well as their greater awareness of their own legal position—might also contribute to the subjective impression that criminals have become more professionalized. There is no satisfactory means of investigating the degree of professionalization.

Assault Offenses

Assaults, like larceny, increased sharply at the end of the 1960s. Unlike the trend in larceny, however, the assault rate (as well as the absolute number of assaults) decreased and reached a low point in 1958, then remained at a low level for most of the 1960s, and increased rapidly in 1967 and 1968, jumping upwards by 38 percent in a single year (1969).

Any Finnish interpretation of statistics on crimes of violence must take into account the alcohol factor. The majority of all assault offenders are intoxicated at the time of the offense; the more serious the crime, the higher the percentage of intoxicated offenders. Even the assault victims seem to be under the influence of alcohol in most instances.

After World War II, Finland's alcohol policy underwent great changes. During the 1950s, consumption was kept under tight reins and consumers were encouraged to drink wine rather than spirits. The thesis according to which such a consumption pattern would be beneficial from the point of view of criminal policy has been questioned, but crimes of violence certainly remained on a fairly steady level up to the middle of the 1960s. Pressures to liberalize the strict alcohol legislation rapidly grew stronger during the 1960s, and in 1967 the government introduced a bill to effect a radical change. The new law came into force in 1969. The results were explosive: the amount of alcohol consumed (measured as 100 percent alcohol) rose 42 percent in one year. The easier availability of alcohol and the general spirit of liberalization affected public behavior. Heavy drinking aimed at intoxication has become much more frequent. It can be no coincidence that the assault rate jumped up 38 percent in the first year the new legislation was in force.

The causal mechanism involved should by no means be assumed to involve only the perpetrators of assault offenses. Alcohol habits as well as changes in these habits pattern a whole subculture, where violence-prone people interact and may end up either as victims or perpetrators. The thesis concerning the importance of the alcohol law reform in 1968 cannot be invalidated by the finding that the number of nonintoxicated offenders increased almost as much as the number of intoxicated offenders.

Homicide

From an international perspective, Finland has a high rate of homicide. This is not a new phenomenon: it is apparent from the very first statistical series on homicide, the cause-of-death statistics compiled by the authorities in Sweden (of which Finland then was a part) from 1754.

Judicial statistics on murder and other intentional homicide indicate that the number of persons sentenced for this offense rose during the 1970s. However, the absolute number of persons sentenced does not match the postwar peak years of 1945 and 1946, not to mention the Prohibition years (1919-1932) when the homicide rate was exceptionally high. During the last years of Prohibition, smuggling was widespread and strong spirits were consumed in immoderate amounts under circumstances where the normal barriers against overintoxication did not work. Conflicts between the authorities and the smugglers and drinkers of smuggled alcohol were often violent.

In the long run, however, the rate of homicide has remained on a fairly steady, high level. The perpetrators tend to be not only older (median age over thirty-five) but also generally less homogeneous as to primary characteristics than other offender groups. In addition, demographic changes will seldom visibly affect the homicide rate. Most homicides in Finland are committed against victims who knew the perpetrator, either as a family member, friend, or casual acquaintance.

Drunken Driving

The number of cases of drunken driving has increased along with the increase in the number of cars. Any small variations left unaccounted for can be explained by variations in alcohol consumption. At the end of the 1960s and during the 1970s, the picture became more complicated. A law amendment which came into force in 1977 introduced blood alcohol levels as a criterion of drunken driving and aggravated drunken driving (0.5 and 1.5 percent, respectively). This has led to an apparent increase in criminality, as drunken driving with a blood alcohol level of less than 1.0 percent was rarely punished earlier.

Modern Crimes

Crime trend commentators tend to be preoccupied with so-called traditional crimes, as the available statistics concentrate on these. To balance the situation, the Finnish Research Institute of Legal Policy includes in its annual report on crime and crime control occasional bits of information about, for example, tax offenses and offenses against working safety regulations. The comments accompanying the statistics frequently complain that the available data are too sketchy and unreliable to allow any serious analysis of the situation.

CHARACTERISTICS OF OFFENDERS

Age

As observed above, the large population cohorts born after the war reached the age of intensive criminality during the 1960s. The implications of this fact can be seen in the trends of those crimes that are predominantly committed by young people. The general increase in juvenile crime at the end of the 1960s (Table 9-2) can also be attributed to the particular susceptibility of the young to those societal changes that increase the opportunities for crime and that weaken the effect of earlier forms of social control.

TABLE 9-2
PERSONS SENTENCED IN COURTS OF FIRST INSTANCE,
PER 100,000 OF THE SAME SEX, 1950-1975

Offense		1950	1955	1960	1965	1970	1975
Larceny							
	Males	182	131	165	213	269	668
	Females	36	24	24	42	52	117
Assault							
	Males	154	149	112	122	167	302
	Females	6	4	3	2	4	10
Drunken driving							
	Males	68	75	88	228	623	628
	Females	0	0	1	1	3	11
Perjury							
	Males	5	7	7	4	4	6
	Females	1	1	2	1	2	1

Source: Patrik Törnudd, *Crime Trends in Finland*, p. 35.

During the 1970s, the situation returned to normal as far as juvenile criminality is concerned; the trends generally follow the trends of adult criminality.

Sex

Both males and females engaged in more larceny crimes during the 1970s, but the increase in male criminality was somewhat steeper. The societal changes that began during the 1960s may well have had their strongest impact on young men.

Assault offenses and drunken driving show a somewhat different pattern. Drunken driving in particular has increased more steeply among women. It would seem natural to connect this phenomenon with the changing attitude towards alcohol among women. Finnish attitudes towards alcohol have traditionally been polarized, with most women advocating abstention. Recent years have witnessed a dramatic change: the idea of total abstinence is growing less popular, and the increase in drinking, particularly heavy drinking, has been more rapid among women.

CHARACTERISTICS OF CRIMINOLOGY AS AN OCCUPATION

Since the term "occupation" clearly refers to a full-time job, it must be observed that in Finland professional criminologists are to be found almost exclusively within the Ministry of Justice, in the Research Institute of Legal Policy. This situation differs from that found in the other Scandinavian countries. It means in practice that the bulk of criminological research takes place outside of the universities. There are no full-time teachers of criminology in Finnish universities. In addition, as has been noted earlier, people who work in the practical sectors of the criminal justice system are never referred to as criminologists. For example, a psychologist in a juvenile prison would be called a prison psychologist, and a physician in a mental hospital defines his professional sector as forensic psychiatry or criminal psychiatry.

Association among Criminologists

As early as the end of the 1950s, cooperation among criminologists was very active, primarily because of Scandinavian contacts. Since 1959, the official cooperative organ of the ministers of justice of the various Scandinavian countries, the Scandinavian Research Council for Criminology, has arranged one or two annual seminars for criminological researchers or for contacts between criminologists and decision-makers. In addition, the council annually publishes *Scandinavian Studies in Criminology* as well as a newsletter with a current bibliography. The council also arranges and funds smaller working groups every year and provides research and travel grants.

The international participation of Finnish criminologists has been extended by the establishment of the Helsinki Institute for Crime Prevention and Control, affiliated with the United Nations, in the Autumn of 1982. The institute is under the direction of Inkeri Anttila and was created by an agreement signed December 23, 1981, between the United Nations and the government of Finland. The functions of the institute are to conduct research and to cultivate regular exchange of information and expertise in crime prevention and control among countries of Europe. It is primarily funded by the government of Finland but also receives support from Denmark, Norway, and Sweden.

Recruitment and Education

In Finland, criminology is taught on the university level only in connection with other subjects. In the law schools, a one-semester course is offered for all law students in connection with criminal law. In addition, special elective courses are provided for advanced students. Departments of education give one course for all students who intend to enter the fields of social welfare or probation and parole. The police college offers one course every year. The Education Center for Prison Officials has three courses annually for guards, senior guards, and senior prison officials. Finally, the School for Social Studies offers an annual course. The Research Institute of Legal Policy gives on-the-job training to its staff, which generally has a background in either law or sociology and sometimes also in statistics.

LEVEL AND DIRECTION OF RESEARCH

As already mentioned, most Finnish criminological research is carried out by the Criminological Unit of the Research Institute of Legal Policy. The institute functions midway between research carried out in universities and research carried out by administrative agencies. Thus, for example, the institute does not undertake followup studies of legislative reforms unless such studies can be seen to have theoretical or other general interest. Such studies can be carried out just as well by researchers in the different ministries. However, attempts are made to relate all research activities in one way or another with decision-making.

Because the Research Institute is semi-independent under the Ministry of Justice—in other words it has its own board to take care of appointments and to establish the research program—it can evaluate the policy of the Ministry of Justice. In practice, much Finnish criminological research aims at making surveys of the present system, revealing its weaknesses and suggesting new solutions. Alternatives to proposed changes are often included in the work, and the pros and cons of competing alternatives are analyzed.

The following gives some examples of research projects through which Finnish criminologists have influenced or tried to influence decision-making.

A study on drunkenness fines was connected with public discussion during the 1960s on the appropriateness of the practice of punishing public drunkenness with fines. The discussion arose because of a concern over the high annual number of such fines and because, later, the person fined was often imprisoned for unpaid fines. In the two-part study, the general preventive and the individual preventive effects of the drunkenness fine system were examined. The study had a role in the later decriminalization of public drunkenness, which reduced the annual number of fines by seventy thousand and nearly emptied the prisons of people serving sentences for unpaid fines.

A study concerning the use of criminal records showed that the records, which were kept for the benefit of the prosecuting authorities and courts, had started to provide information on job applicants not only to state authorities, but also at times even to private companies. This practice was stopped.

A few years ago, a law was passed in Finland on compensation to victims of crimes. The law was preceded by research on, among other topics, how much damages were caused by crime. The information on the extent and type of crime damages has been used to sharpen the public's conception of the crime situation, which previously had been based primarily on data on the number of crimes.

At the beginning of the 1970s, Finland's "yellow press" grew rapidly, and strong demands arose for protecting the individual's right to privacy. A study was carried out on how members of different professions and social classes were "victimized." The preamble to the government bill leading to the new law on the subject improved the individual's right to privacy.

A few years ago, the question arose as to the utility of supervision of prisoners released on parole. A study was carried out, and on the basis of its results the Committee on Probation and Parole unanimously proposed that the mandatory supervision of paroled prisoners (which in Finland is carried out both by the police and by a special semi-official association) be terminated and that the resources thus saved be transferred to social services, especially in order to find employment and housing for released prisoners. The proposal was not realized as such, but the parole time was considerably shortened and the system remains a subject of public debate.

In 1971, a Working Group of Cabinet Ministers asked for the expert opinion of the Research Institute as to what to do about the "rising tide of violent crime" depicted by the mass media. The Research Institute offered a number of concrete suggestions, including the suggestion that the public be provided with more precise and balanced information on crime and its background and that efforts be made to improve the quality of crime statistics. These suggestions were, by and large, accepted.

During the last few years, criminologists have repeatedly stressed the point that in order to reduce the harmful consequences of criminality it may be much easier to control the number of opportunities for crime or change the penal legislation rather than to attempt to "cure" or "reform" the offenders. As the final item in this list of influential projects, therefore, the Research Institute has published a report on the extent to which firearms and knives are used in assaults. The goal was to have legislation passed prohibiting the possession of such weapons in public places without acceptable reasons. Since then, such legislation has been passed on the possession of knives, and a reform of the Firearms Act is being considered.

Besides planning and carrying out research work, criminologists in Finland participate in the modernization of legislation, as members of state committees, in working groups of the Legislation Department of the Ministry of Justice, and as experts before the law committee of the Finnish Parliament.

The Research Institute is frequently asked to evaluate committee reports, law proposals, and so on, and it responds in the form of written expert statements.

These statements usually contain both general evaluations of the proposal in question and a number of concrete suggestions on the details.

The impact of research cannot be evaluated independently of the impact of the researchers. This is particularly true in a small country, where key decisions may be made within a fairly small group of politicians, administrators, and scientific experts.

NOTE

1. This presentation of crime trends is with minor alterations an excerpt from Patrik Törnudd, *Crime Trends in Finland 1950-1977* (Helsinki: Research Institute of Legal Policy, 1978).

BIBLIOGRAPHY

This bibliography contains recent publications in the English language only. Because most Finnish criminological publications are written in Finnish—and sometimes also in Swedish—the collection is not altogether representative. Books and articles on psychiatry are not included.

Anttila, Inkeri. "Conservative and Radical Criminal Policy in the Nordic Countries." *Scandinavian Studies in Criminology* (Oslo), 3 (1974):9-21.
Major criticisms of treatment ideologies are presented. Spokesmen for individualization, treatment, and the conception of the criminal as an invalid have been pictured as radicals within the field of criminal policy, but actually they have been rather conservative. The article predicts that future criminal policy will be based on a sociological view that criminality emerges from conflict as the visible expression of a certain balance between opposing social pressures.

Anttila, Inkeri. "Victimology—A New Trend in Criminology." *Scandinavian Studies in Criminology* (Oslo) 5 (1974):7-10.
"Victim-centered" research explores criminality by using information concerning victims of crimes. Its outlook may be more balanced than offender-based analysis, but victims should not be placed in the new role of scapegoats in crime explanations. The dangers of atomistic thinking should be avoided.

Anttila, Inkeri. *Incarceration for Crimes Never Committed*. Helsinki: Research Institute of Legal Policy, no. 9, 1975.
This report describes the different stages which preventive detention institutions have gone through in Scandinavian countries. A primary purpose is to correct misconceptions about the prevailing system and the reform plans. Particular emphasis is given the point that the Scandinavian countries no longer favor indeterminant sanctions for dangerous recidivists.

Anttila, Inkeri. *Papers on Crime Control 1977-1978*. Helsinki: Research Institute of Legal Policy, no. 26, 1978.
This book presents a collection of unpublished articles on long-time incarceration, scope

of crime control, assessment of different approaches to traffic offenses, alternatives to the death penalty, searching for clinical criminology in Scandinavia, plans for a new penal code in Finland, changing ideologies of control of youth criminality in Scandinavia, offenses of sexual interference, relationship between research and criminal justice policy, and the limits of diversion.

Anttila, Inkeri, and Risto Jaakkola. *Unrecorded Criminality in Finland.* Helsinki: Institute of Criminology, 1966.
This report presents the Finnish results of the joint Scandinavian study of unrecorded criminality. The first part is a general presentation and discussion of results from the views of criminology and criminal policy. The second part examines the relationship between social background, criminality, and detection risk.

Anttila, Inkeri, and Achilles Westling. "A Study in the Pardoning of and Recidivism Among Criminals Sentenced to Life Imprisonment." *Scandinavian Studies in Criminology* (Oslo), 1 (1965):13-34.
Records of all life prisoners in Finland in the years 1929-1958 are examined. Of the males sentenced for homicide, ten committed another homicide while serving the sentence, and ten after release. For both groups, the rate for new homicides was 0.23 per one hundred years. Half of the prisoners were released after 13.2 years in prison. The law amendment of 1932 replaced parole with a pardon, resulting in a more differentiated pardoning practice. Several factors related to release and recidivism are examined.

Aromaa, Kauko. "Our Violence." *Scandinavian Studies on Criminology* (Oslo), 5 (1974):35-46.
Only official statistics are used in this analysis of the recent increase in the number of violent crimes in Finland. The characteristics of violent offenders are also delineated. Some basic findings of a recent Finnish victimization survey—later replicated in other Scandinavian countries—are described. The problems of measuring crime damages are considered.

Aromaa, Kauko. *The Replication of a Survey on Victimization to Violence.* Helsinki: Institute of Criminology, M:36, 1974.
The results of two national Gallup surveys dealing with victimization to violence in Finland (one in December 1970, the other in November and December 1973) are compared. The data measure victim percentage, not victimization risks. Conclusions are limited to changes in risks only if changes in habits (going out at night and other factors affecting risk) are also measured.

Aromaa, Kauko, Patrik Törnudd, and Kirsti Vartiovaara. *Department Store Shoplifters.* Helsinki: Institute of Criminology, M:6, 1970.
For four major department stores in Helsinki, a twenty-nine-item questionnaire was completed for each of the 803 shoplifters apprehended between October 1, 1964, and September 30, 1965. Data refer to offenders (age, sex, social background, motive, and so on), offenses (number of stolen objects, their worth, when stolen, and so on), the stores' control systems and sanction policy, and judicial consequences.

Blom, Raimo. *Contentual Differentiation of Penalty Demands and Exceptions with Re-*

gard to Justice. Tampere: Institute of Sociology, University of Tampere, no. 2, 1968.
Punitive demands and confidence in courts are analyzed in light of the crimes committed and of the population groups which the accused represent.

Joutsen, Matti. *Young Offenders in the Criminal Justice System of Finland*. Helsinki: Research Institute of Legal Policy, no. 14, 1976.
Finnish legislation concerning young offenders and statistics on them are the topics of this publication.

Joutsen, Matti. *Dealing with Child Offenders in Finland*. Helsinki: Research Institute of Legal Policy, no. 39, 1980.
The topics of this work include the incidence of offenses in Finland committed by children less than fifteen years of age, measures taken by the authorities to deal with them, development of the child welfare board, and the possible future direction of the system.

Lahti, Raimo. "Criminal Sanctions in Finland: A System in Transition." *Scandinavian Studies in Law* (Stockholm), 21 (1977):121-157.
This paper describes the background and effects of the development of the Finnish system of criminal sanctions from the late nineteenth century to 1976. The arguments advanced in the legislative history of reforms and the ideological and cultural circumstances are discussed.

Mäkelä, Klaus. "Public Sense of Justice and Judicial Practice." *Acta Sociologica* 10 (1966):42-67.
In this report, (1) a comparison is made between different segments of the population and their punitive demands for certain crimes; (2) the influence of a particular judge on sentencing variation is estimated; (3) judicial practices of categories of judges are analyzed; and (4) the punitive demands of the public are compared with prevailing judicial practice.

Mäkelä, Klaus. "The Societal Tasks of the System of Penal Law." *Scandinavian Studies in Criminology* (Oslo), 5 (1974):47-65.
The author discusses functional and Marxist approaches to criminality and criminal law.

Takala, Hannu. "Drinking and Driving in Scandinavia." *Scandinavian Studies in Criminology* (Oslo), 6 (1978):11-19.
The Research Institute of Legal Policy studied the effects of a seventeen-day police strike in 1976 on drunken driving by using three data sources: routinely taken blood tests in suspected cases, an anonymous questionnaire administered to restaurant patrons who had their cars with them, and an anonymous questionnaire given to drivers at gasoline stations.

Törnudd, Patrik. "The Preventive Effect of Fines for Drunkenness." *Scandinavian Studies in Criminology* (Oslo), 2 (1968):109-124.
Prosecution policy on public drunkenness was changed by agreement with the police in three middle-sized towns. Drunken persons were arrested as before, but the average rate of prosecution was reduced from 40-50 percent to 9-24 percent. Drunkenness arrest trends were compared among three experimental towns and three control towns of the same size

over a three-year period. Police officers in the experimental towns were interviewed anonymously about their opinions concerning the policy change. Through participant observation and interviews of policemen, it was investigated whether or not drunkenness offenders had noticed the policy change. The implications for criminology and criminal policy are discussed.

Törnudd, Patrik. "Forecasting the Trend of Criminality." *Collected Studies in Criminological Research*. Strasbourg: Council of Europe, 1969. Pp. 213-241.
A pilot study assesses the possibility of predicting crime trends through use of various socioeconomic indicators.

Törnudd, Patrik. "The Futility of Searching for Causes of Crime." *Scandinavian Studies in Criminology* (Oslo), 3 (1971):23-33.
The low utility of most present-day criminological research is attributed to the failure of criminologists to see crime as a necessary social phenomenon upheld by vital social forces. In place of a search for the so-called causes of crime, research strategy and communication of results should be in terms of estimates and predictions of (1) fluctuations in the total level of criminality, or (2) the process determining the selection of offenses and offenders to be punished. Formal research models for value-conscious criminological research must be developed.

Törnudd, Patrik. *Crime Trends in Finland 1950-1977*. Helsinki: Research Institute of Legal Policy, no. 29, 1978.
Trends of crimes known to the police, 1950-1977, are examined in association with social change in Finland. Comments on "explaining away crime problems" are offered.

Uusitalo, Paavo. "White-Collar Crimes and Status Selectivity in the Law Enforcement System." *Research Reports*, no. 120. Helsinki: Institute of Sociology, University of Helsinki, 1969.
This project investigates how the socioeconomic status of persons being reported for frauds, embezzlement, or forgeries, committed by occupants of the two highest social strata, affects the decisions of police, public prosecutors, and courts. Gathered in 1962, the data were on 145 offenses reported to the police in 1955 in Helsinki.

Uusitalo, Paavo. "Recidivism After Release from Closed and Open Penal Institutions." *British Journal of Criminology* (London), 3 (1972):211-229.
The article assesses the effect on post-release recidivism of relatively radical changes in the conditions and programs of penal institutions. Two types of penal institutions in Finland—conventional closed prisons and open labor colonies—are compared. The author recommends decreased use of closed prisons and replacement of them with open labor colonies.

10

FRANCE

Philippe Robert

The state of criminology in France is rather paradoxical. On the one hand, a recent and significant scientific growth may be observed; on the other hand, the term itself is rarely employed. Its usage is decreasing at the same time that the scientific reality underlying it is increasing in importance. The term "criminology" has no meaning from the standpoint of professional or administrative activity; it enjoys limited and relatively ancillary usage in the area of academic teaching. Even in research—where it corresponds to a vigorous and rapidly evolving reality—"criminology" has been progressively abandoned in favor of expressions such as "deviance and control," "deviance and social reaction," or "social control of deviance."

The best way of grasping the essence of criminology in present-day France is to regard it basically as a field of research, which while in full growth, is less and less identified with the term "criminology." In addition, in this widening field penal questions have come to constitute no more than a particular case in point. Doubtless they are the most extensively explored but not the only questions, still less an aspect that might be studied in isolation.

This chapter is divided into two sections. The first indicates the state of French criminology from the standpoint of professional and administrative practice, academic teaching, and research. This discussion also furnishes a detailed explanation of why French criminology constitutes a domain of research. The second section of the chapter points out the principal directions of the research.

STATE OF CRIMINOLOGY IN FRANCE

This section explains why criminology has no real place in professional or administrative practice; describes the limited role it plays in academic teaching; shows that in the research area criminology corresponds to a vigorous, rapidly evolving reality; and describes the coordination structures available to criminologists in France.

Professional and Administrative Practice

From this first point of view, criminology has no place whatsoever in France. No professionals exist who might be specifically designated by this term. No course of study has ever been set up for the purpose of training criminologists per se, probably because of the lack of a potential market. All the categories of agents intervening in the criminal justice system constitute bodies of officials determined by conditions of recruitment and career. Such is the case for the judges and the Department of Public Prosecution, which together comprise a single body, the magistrature; the police; court employees; penitentiary personnel; probation establishments; and personnel specializing in the area of delinquent minors. In this last instance, in addition to certain officials in probationary education (*éducation surveillée*), there are other educators who depend not on the state but on private associations to run services or establishments with the authorization of the Ministry of Justice. But these exceptions scarcely modify the situation under discussion. Access to jobs in these bodies has been reorganized by the widespread replacement of competitive examinations by professional schools. The graduates of these schools enter upon the scene, depending on the recruitment level, either at the end of pre-university studies (or even earlier for certain categories) or at the end of a university program of shorter or longer duration, depending upon the job category.

In any event, therefore, it did not seem useful to create a special channel for professional training for the criminal justice system. Each of the participating bodies has, in fact, set up its own professional training school for basic training or for specialization. Then too, the present decade has witnessed the development of more or less elaborate programs for on-the-job training and for periodic "brushing up" of professionals. These programs are fairly sophisticated for the magistrature and for personnel specializing in the juvenile delinquency field, but this on-the-job training remains at a simple level for the penitentiary personnel and the police.

In short, the sole prerequisite of each personnel category is a general education of higher or lower level depending upon the occupation. To these entrance requirements is grafted specialized professional training and on-the-job training conceived and instituted within the context of the given job category.

All or part of these professional schools may ultimately lead to the making of bona fide criminologists, but this trend has not appeared. Most of the schools that provide access to employment in official bodies do not develop specialized competence oriented only to the criminal justice system. This is, first of all, true for the police because their functions extend beyond the tasks of police administration and maintenance of order. In France, the magistrature handles both civil and penal affairs, thus eliminating any real and permanent specialization in criminal matters to justify intensive training in criminology. Similarly, the personnel of juvenile justice deal with both juvenile delinquents and with other children who require protection. Only penitentiary and probation personnel could adopt a true training program in criminology, but here professional training remains the most rudimentary.

Outside the penal sector, social work or a similar aspect of education would be of interest to criminologists, but the training programs are so generalized that criminologists are unlikely to be found among the broad array of social workers. Nevertheless, in various professional schools rather diffusive instruction may be characterized *de facto* as criminological. This is especially true in the schools attended by probation workers, the national school of penitentiary administration, the school of police commissioners, and that of *gendarmerie* officials. But the situation is altogether different for the school of secretary-clerks and for those who are geared towards the lesser police or *gendarmerie* personnel. As for the most important of these schools—the only one that belongs to the category referred to in France as the *grandes écoles*—the national school of magistrature, the situation is less clear. The school has no systematic elements of criminology because the curriculum is oriented more toward juridical problems, judiciary practices, and general instruction in social problems. But, in keeping with fluctuations in policy interests, sometimes criminological offerings may be found there.

The scattered interest in criminological training found in these professional schools is also present in the private schools for training social service personnel and in on-the-job training for criminal justice personnel to "brush up" on their knowledge. Other topics that may be considered criminological appear under other course titles: juvenile delinquency, protection of youth, sociology of penal justice, and, above all, deviance or control of deviance. This pattern suggests a rejection of instruction that is openly in the classic criminology mold.

The Committee for Coordination of Criminological Research (Comité de coordination des recherches criminologiques or CCRC) (its key role in French criminology is discussed later in this section) attempts to keep constantly abreast of the status of these professional teaching programs and to coordinate them to whatever extent possible.

Criminology and Academic Teaching

Criminology is found more in academic teaching than in professional or administrative practice, but here too the discipline finds only fragmentary and ancillary representation. Perhaps an indication of the rather secondary place of criminology is that only the Committee for Coordination of Criminological Research attempts to keep an up-to-date count of those programs and courses that qualify as criminological to a reasonable extent.

Certain law schools offer general courses in criminology geared for undergraduates and sponsor institutes with names that include the phrases "of criminology" or "of criminal sciences"—for example, the Institute of Criminology of the University of Law, Economics, and Social Sciences of Paris (Paris 2), the Institute of Criminology and Penal Sciences of the University of Aix-Marseille 3, and the Institute of Penal Sciences of the University of Bordeaux 1. These institutes do not deliver regular diplomas but simply additional certificates or credits towards a diploma that is a prerequisite for entrance examinations for the previously cited professional schools or for admission to the bar. Most courses have a juridical content. Certain of them, however, offer a sufficiently complete and varied range of teachings and teachers that they qualify as instruction in criminology.

In addition to various specialties in criminal law, legal medicine, and psychiatry, the institutes frequently offer courses in general criminology, which are often taught by penal jurists, and in criminal sociology, which are taught by the sociologists specializing in criminological research.

In a few instances, the law faculties offer a doctorate in criminology. Although the doctoral programs are often highly juridical, some of the diplomas in intensive studies (DEA)—at the University of Bordeaux 1, for instance—are veritable doctorates in criminology. The majority of them, however, are doctorates in penal sciences.

Criminology also serves as an accessory to medicine, particularly legal medicine or psychiatry. Some elements of criminology that are essentially clinical exist in the programs of institutes of legal medicine. The Institute Alexandre Lacassagne of the Université Claude Bernard of Lyon offers the most extensively developed program.

Very little teaching of criminology per se appears except in connection with penal law or legal medicine and psychiatry. However, the subject matter of criminology is taught in human sciences departments fairly often under a different appellation such as "deviance sociology" (at the Ecole de hautes études en sciences sociales with its seminar on social control of crime and deviance, for instance), or "psychology of socialization" (at the University of Lille 3), or "psychopathology" (at the Université René Descartes, at the Ecole des hautes études en sciences sociales, or at the University of Nice).

CRIMINOLOGY AND RESEARCH

Although criminology fails to qualify as an autonomous field in administrative and professional practice and has only a marginal status in academic teaching, it represents a significant field in contemporary social science research in France. This statement best characterizes the situation of French criminology.

The expression "field of study" is used here rather than "discipline" because the progressively stronger tendency is away from applying the term "criminology" as though it is an autonomous branch of knowledge. Rather, the trend is toward considering the study of penal questions—crime, the criminal, the social reaction applied to it—as part of a broader *ensemble* generally called deviance and social control. Two altogether recent events illustrate this assertion. When the General Delegation for Scientific and Technical Research (Délégation générale à la recherche scientifique et technique, or DGRST) sought to identify priorities for investigation in this sector, the group referred to the field as "social control of deviance."[1] When the National Center for Scientific Research (Centre national de la recherche scientifique, or CNRS) wanted to identify this field for evaluation purposes, it called the field "deviance and social control."[2]

These terms have international, and not simply national, popularity. However, the traditions of English-speaking and French-speaking sociologies differ in this regard. In the French-speaking tradition, these concepts are a relatively recent acquisition, at least in regard to their widespread use, borrowed from English-speaking practice, a source of some difficulty.

The concept of deviance has enjoyed considerably greater development than the concept of crime for a variety of reasons. Some scholars believe "deviance" is the superior term because it avoids the stigmatizing effects of "crime," which also is seen to be too heavily laden with common beliefs. Other persons prefer the term "deviance" because it avoids the excessively juridical approach. Still others are likely to follow a new terminology which has become fashionable. Whatever the motivation, the concept of deviance is understood in two ways. For some researchers, it sets itself apart from crime and designates behaviors which, while not indictable, are nonetheless regarded to be outside the legitimate norms; for others, it includes crime but extends beyond it. It is in the latter sense that "deviance" is generally accepted today in France.

The expression "social control" was fairly widely ignored in the French-speaking sociological tradition which has preferred the concept of social regulation inherited from Comte. The first attempt to introduce social control came in the mid-1960s and was rejected on the grounds that the already existing notion of social regulation made it redundant. This position was in accord with the traditional functionalist interpretation of social control. However, social control has on the whole lost this functionalist identification with social regulation. Now it means more specifically, first, the control and taking charge of acts of deviance and deviant persons by specialized agencies and, second, providing these agencies with referral processes. Social control has become differentiated from social regulation in general.

For a time in the mid-1970s, the expression "social reaction" was preferred to "social control," but "social reaction" is used less now because it appears to limit its attention to intervention after behavior occurs, whereas "social control" includes a prior proactive aspect. Whether we speak of criminology in the broader sense of its traditional scope or whether we place it within the sphere of deviance and social control, the fact remains that an important and vital field of research has emerged fairly recently.

In the nineteenth and early twentieth centuries, the study of penal questions (or problems of deviance) occupied a significant place in the body of French social sciences which were then taking shape. At least three important currents may be noted. First, the so-called moral statistics movement was, for the major part, a sociology of deviance. Second, the so-called social milieu current grouped around the *Archives d'anthropologie criminelle* with Lacassagne, Tarde, Joly, and so on. Third, of course, Durkheim and his disciples represented the *Année sociologique*.

World War I interrupted these lines of development in France and the majority of neighboring countries. Research activities entered into a period of sharp decline between the two wars. The end of World War II failed to awaken French research significantly, unlike the situation in certain European countries such as the United Kingdom or the Scandinavian nations, despite the holding of an international congress on criminology in 1950 in Paris and despite the choice of France as the seat of the International Society for Criminology. A revival of research in criminology, albeit a timid and exceedingly slow one, did not appear until the 1960s. The revival concentrated in general upon work in juvenile delinquency with, in particular, the studies of the Centre de formation et de recherche de l'éducation surveillée (CFR-ES).

The real thaw did not begin until the present decade when an unprecedented diversity of new paradigms appeared. The formerly dominant theoretical models, whether Durkheimian, psychological, or functionalist, have lost their impact, although they have not disappeared. The increasingly varied themes have reached beyond the study of crime, the criminal, and criminality. The concept of crime has been broadened to include it within the notion of deviance. The center of interest has moved towards an examination of social control processes. Finally, research productivity itself has become increasingly varied. Certain studies of high quality have occasionally emanated from scientists or research units not specializing in the field of deviance and social control, even from disciplines—such as history, economics, and linguistics—that previously showed only slight interest in the study of these questions. Within this newfound abundance, the quality of research has ranged from inferior to eligible for international recognition.

This research has several marked characteristics. First, the size of the research unit varies greatly. Two large units represent a significant share of the French scientific potential in this area. The rest of the research activities are distributed among small units and isolated researchers. Second, historical accidents—particularly the perennial indifference of universities towards this research sector—have placed the two chief units under the minister of justice. A third research unit under the minister that specializes in penology also exists, but, although created in 1964, the National Center for Penitentiary Study and Research (Centre national d'étude et de recherche pénitentiaire, or CNERP) has not achieved sustained production.

The first of the large units—the CFR-ES—has specialized in research in juvenile delinquency and judiciary protection of youth for the past twenty years. The most important French laboratory in the criminological field, it was created by H. Michard and is now under the direction of J. Selosse.

The second of the large units—the Service for Penal and Criminological Studies (Service d'études penales et criminologiques, or SEPC)—has existed for about ten years and specializes in the sociology of social control of crime and deviance. It has played a significant role in the successive introduction of the concepts of social reaction and social control. It differs from the CFR-ES by its association with the minister of justice and simultaneously with the CNRS.

The minister of health and family also supports a research center—the National Technical Center for Maladjusted Children and Adolescents (Centre technique national de l'enfance et de l'adolescence inadaptée, or CTN)—which operates on the rim of criminological research.

A few studies touch *lato sensu* upon criminological questions in certain major public research centers. The National Institute for Health and Medical Research (Institut national de la santé et de la recherche médicale, or INSERM) has conducted, for example, studies on student drug abuse. The National Institute for Demographic Study (Institut national d'études démographiques, or INED) has investigated divorces and violent deaths. The National Organization for Traffic Safety (Organisme national de sécurité routière, or ONSER) has examined social factors in traffic safety and accidents. But all this research is fairly scattered and has only a marginal place in criminological research even when broadly defined.

The CNRS includes within its own laboratories a few units devoted to criminological research (such as the research unit in criminal sociology directed by A. Davidovitch at the Center for Sociological Studies, or the cooperative research on Program 399 on women and criminality), or again researchers working in isolated fashion on these themes.

But the most numerous participation of the CNRS in this research sector comes, not from its own laboratory network, but from its associated network, in other words, research units that depend upon the CNRS and on a university or ministry. Examples of units in this associated network are the SEPC under the Justice Ministry, the Criminology Institute of the University of Law, Economy and Social Sciences of Paris (Paris 2), and the Institute of Criminology and Penal Sciences of the University of Aix-Marseille 3. Because of some common characteristics, we can also add the Institute of History of Ancient Lands with Written Law of the University of Montpellier 1 and the Center for Innovation Sociology of the School of Mines. If we accept a very broad definition of criminological research, we might also add the group that conducts analyses of medical institutions under Michel Foucault at the Collège de France, the Institute for Comparative Law of Paris (with M. Ancel's criminal sciences section), a part of the Center for Studies of Social Movements (Centre d'études mouvements sociaux or CEMS) under the leadership of A. Touraine at the Ecole des hautes études en sciences sociales.

Within the major teaching establishments are the group for analysis of medical institutions at the Collège de France, the CEMS at the Ecole des hautes études en sciences sociales and their seminar on social psychopathology, the Center for Innovation Sociology at the School of Mines, and, finally, the penal department of the Institute for Comparative Law of Paris.

Among the universities the following should be mentioned: at the University of Law, Economics, and Social Sciences of Paris (Paris 2), the criminal sociology laboratory and the Institute of Criminology; at the University of Paris 7, the study and research unit in human clinical sciences, the history of criminality group, and certain elements within the Sociology Department; at Paris-Vincennes, the quantitative ethnomethodology group; at Aix Marseille 3, the Institute of Criminology and Penal Sciences; at Nice, the chair in psychopathology; at Bordeaux 1, Toulouse 1, Poitiers, and at the University of Law and Health of Lille, their institutes of criminal sciences; at Lille 3, P. Deyon's history seminar; the Institute Alexandre Lacassagne at the Université Claude Bernard in Lyon and the Institute for Judiciary Studies at the Université Jean Moulin in Lyon; the Institute of Ancient Lands with Written Law of the University of Montpellier 1; and, finally, certain sociology departments at Strasbourg.

Several private associations may be added to this list, such as the Center for Institutional Study, Research and Training, the Study Group on Social Functions, or the Association for the Safeguard of Children and Adolescents of the Pays Basque.

ORGANIZATION OF CRIMINOLOGY IN FRANCE

It should be clear that no unique and unified channel of vocational training exists for those individuals who in France might be referred to as criminologists, that is, for those who regularly carry out research in this field of study. There are a few doctors in criminology, but too few to be of any real significance. The researchers specializing in this sector come from a variety of disciplinary routes, principally law, sociology, and psychology. Increasingly, they are combining several basic training programs. This characteristic is reinforced by the policy of certain research unit directors who require their beginning researchers to possess a multifaceted background. Although there are frequent cases of multidisciplinary orientations, it may be said that the dominant discipline tends to be psychology at the CFR-ES and sociology at the SEPC. In other settings, the emphases are variable.

A French criminological association does exist, but the basis of its cohesion is not clear. It is not a scientific society in the usual sense because it apparently includes more professional practitioners than scientists. There is evidence that many young researchers in criminology do not belong to the association, and even for those who do belong, it is not a point of primary identification. Its activity consists rather in organizing congresses, the themes and structure of which are geared more towards practitioners. Then too, criminological researchers tend to identify with associations corresponding to their main disciplines of origin (the French sociological society, the French psychological association, and so on); no work group on "criminology" or "deviance" is to be found within them, or in the international scientific societies, such as the International Society for Criminology, the International Society of Sociology, and the association of French-speaking sociologists.

An important French criminological organization, the Coordination Committee for Criminological Research (CCRC),[3] is a consultative committee created by the minister of justice in 1968. Under the presidency of P. Amor, the former director of social defense at the United Nations, it groups high officials concerned with questions of criminological research, a few magistrates, and the principal directors of research in this sector. The committee keeps a count,[4] via a network of regional representatives, of teaching, means of documentation, research centers, and ongoing research. It attempts to follow the complex problems of criminological training in the professional schools and in the "brush up" programs for professionals. It handles certain international relations (bilateral scientific exchange and Europe Council grants for research in criminology). Each year it awards a French-speaking criminology prize, the Prix Gabriel Tarde. Lastly, it selects those research projects that are to be financed by contract with DGRST funds. The research reports undergo an international evaluation procedure. In this way, the CCRC has become the geometrical center of criminological research in France. In addition, it constitutes the only place where complete information is available on the state of a sector undergoing rapid transformation.

MAIN DIRECTIONS OF CONTEMPORARY RESEARCH

How can we make sense out of the criminological research to pick the most significant contributions? One of the usual ways is to employ an international descriptive model that is overwhelmingly American and to classify the different studies by its criteria. If such an analysis is to be concrete, the point of departure must be a fairly detailed examination of the international-American descriptive model, avoiding simplistic dichotomizing interactionists and postinteractionists or, worse, consensus and conflict approaches.

A preliminary effort quickly reveals that such a diagram, even when oversimplification is kept to a minimum, is highly inadequate. Without doubt, certain interactionist tendencies may be located in Europe, particularly in the United Kingdom and West Germany. Certain radical currents may also be observed in the same two countries. But such remarks do not constitute a complete analysis. The picture of a Europe offering nothing more than latter-day replicas of paradigms imported from across the Atlantic is becoming very inadequate. In fact, interesting and often original attempts for a new paradigm are emerging in countries such as the United Kingdom, West Germany, the Scandinavian countries, the Netherlands, Belgium, France, and Italy. Then too, certain philosophers who have particularly inspired American criminological studies in the last two decades have had little impact in countries like France. The thinking of G. H. Mead, for instance, has had little influence, and R. Dahrendorf scarcely more. On the contrary, recent French work in criminology often calls upon very different philosophies; to cite a single example among others, we might mention the influence of M. Foucault.

Otherwise, the dominant trait of French work in criminology, at least for the present decade, is probably a diversification of inspirations and orientations. This remark is just as valid for the reference paradigms as for the sites of scientific production or the disciplines of origin. In short, we must abandon a descriptive diagram that is purely reductionist. The simplest approach consists in distinguishing according to the explicit or implicit agreement on the object of study.

It is doubtless reasonable to center the analysis on the production of the 1970s. Granted, the scope of this book adopts the post-World War II period as its point of departure. But as already mentioned, criminological research remained languid in France until at least the end of the 1950s, and throughout all of the following decade, the awakening remained slow and partial. In actual fact, as J. Pinatel pointed out in a résumé of the situation several years ago[5] and as corroborated by subsequent analyses,[6] problems of juvenile delinquency preoccupied French researchers until the end of the 1960s. Since this is the case, the main works of this period are listed in the bibliography, and the analysis in the chapter is limited to the contemporary period.

Along with the diversification pointed out above and a sort of all-out effervescence which contrasts with the languid nature of the previous scientific production, another characteristic of this research sector should probably be sought out in a shifting of interest from crime and deviance towards an analysis of social control phenomena.

Admittedly, this is a current of mingled tendencies: participation is not total, far from it, and this shift in accent is more of a tendency than an absolute change. Certain investigations give the impression that presenting research results is more important than holding deeply felt convictions. Still others pursue the dual ambition of elucidating two study objects at once: crime and its control. Finally, some researchers concentrate on the study of social control phenomena, employing a wide variety of theoretical orientations in the process.

Research on Crime and Deviance

Although crime and deviance are no longer popular study objects, this classical orientation has, nonetheless, not fallen entirely by the wayside. Crime or deviance is immediately attainable as a study object. The concern is either with simply describing some modality or other of crime or with explaining the processes that have permitted its development.

Such an approach to the field of study is inherent in the so-called clinical disciplines. Works with a psychiatric bent are encountered here; an example would be the study of the link between criminality and mental illness in general or with schizophrenia or aggressiveness. Psychoanalytic contributions are also to be found, particularly with a Lacanian orientation, in the studies carried out at the Institut A. Lacassagne of the Université Claude Bernard in Lyon. The psychological contribution is certainly the most marked with research on the delinquent's evolution and future and his self-image, incest, the application of J. Pinatel's theory of the core of the criminal personality, not to mention the contributions of criminal anthropology.

This output calls for three principal comments. First, the work is often painstakingly accomplished, following a tradition that has remained relatively constant despite the overall crumbling of the French criminological research edifice during a half-century period. Second, a certain slowing of such an orientation must be noted in the past few years, especially since the middle of the 1970s. Finally, the most recent research reveals frequent contamination by a symbolic interactionism orientation, although this conversion is less clear-cut in France than in the various neighboring countries (Belgium, for example, because of the reformulations roughed out by C. Debuyst[7] or L. Walgrave[8]).

Alongside these "clinical " contributions, room must be made in this first group for a genuinely sociological contribution which, while it may be more abundant, also appears to be more disjointed. Three types of work are encountered here. First, some work applies criminology paradigms of general sociology, ranging from one of the Durkheimian formulations of anomie to the project concept of A. Touraine's actionalist sociology. Second, other works, more modestly epistemological in nature, seek to describe a certain form of criminality or deviance. Third, certain other works take on a dimension of urban or regional ecology that is particularly characteristic of the production of the criminology institutes set up within the law faculties, for instance, at the University of Law, Economy and Social Sciences of Paris (Paris 2), at the University of Aix-Marseille 3, at the Université Jean Moulin in Lyon, or at the universities of Rouen or Pau.

Research on Deviance or Crime and Social Control Simultaneously

One way the dualistic approach can be accomplished is to consider social control as an explanatory variable of crime or deviance. This fundamentally interactionist disposition is encountered, for example, in several pieces of research concerning violence. It may not, however, be considered highly developed in present-day France, although countless works on juvenile delinquency, notably those carried out at the CFR-ES in Vaucresson, apparently hope to link up with such a view of the problem.

The more frequent approach, however, is to give crime and its control equal status as a research problematic. Several theses or studies on the most varied of subjects (concerning, in particular, criminality among foreigners or women) illustrate this trend where certain operational research and choice optimization studies bearing upon criminality or upon prevention may also be classified.

A frequent problem encountered in these dualistic studies is the availability of only a single data base for the elucidation of the two objects.

Research on Social Control

A third approach, research on social control, is probably the most productive one in French criminological research. This approach, however, is used more for the sake of convenience than specifically to advance research on social control.

Certain studies are concerned primarily with the problem of creating social norms, whether penal or otherwise. This investigation offers the opportunity to get some historical perspective where research in criminology broadly converges with the sociology of law, the history of law, and certain branches of general history, particularly social history or the history of poverty. Unfortunately, sociology and the history of law in France are far more concerned with questions of civil law than of penal law. Nonetheless, these sociological or historical works have made a number of contributions, with a borderline concern for the field of criminology, specifically deviance. This statement is concretely true for research on educative aid to minors or on divorce. Then too, various sections of general history are abundant—because history enjoys a solid position among the areas of scholarship in France—organized elements that may contribute to criminological research in the same manner as social history does in the British Isles.

Posing the problem of creating norms also implies, for criminological research, the study of their ingestion by society. From this standpoint, French works are distinguished by their use of the sociology of collective representations. Although the most important studies have dealt above all with representations of institutions for intervention or follow-through (criminal justice, for instance), a fair number of studies have focused on norms, crime, and deviance. In the last few years, some interesting theoretical contributions have been made to the solution of the highly complex problem of the reception of norms in a given society.

The importance of the establishment and reception of norms in the society notwithstanding, it is obvious that criminological research cannot limit itself to this consideration. It must also deal with the effectiveness of the normative prescriptions. This second side of the question constitutes the principal theme of present-day French criminological research: the specialized social control agencies with emphasis given to those that comprise the criminal justice system. The output in this research area is fairly sizable.

First, we have those historical works that seek to retrace the progressive establishment of the control networks. Historians specializing in the eighteenth and nineteenth centuries have made important contributions. Along with these studies, we may note the whole trend, more or less directly inspired by Foucault, involved with retracing the genealogies of institutions or networks of institutions such as penitentiary administration, social services, prevention, and psychiatry. Such works represent an extremely interesting, highly developed contribution of French research.

Systematic examination of the output of each agency or group of agencies, and, above all, that of the specific target populations, is also indebted to certain historical contributions. Studies of a more purely sociological nature do exist, but they are less numerous and less systematic than expected. They presuppose a capacity for constituting and managing large data bases, a possibility that is attainable only by fairly sizable research units.

The study of how these agencies function constitutes the most thoroughly explored domain, quantitatively speaking. A number of piecemeal studies treat a particular agency or institution (jury, preventive detention, partially suspended sentence, sentencing, collegiality, or singleness of judges). Others concentrate on a strategic mechanism of internal regulation (the discretionary powers of the public prosecutor, for example). Only a small number deal with a system in its entirety; such efforts are feasible only in large research units. A few studies, all too rare, center on the processes of target population reconstruction through which a social control system progressively remodels its raw material in order to make it comply with the necessities of its social function. The situation is the same for an examination of the agents' professional ideologies (existing studies concern the magistrature and educators for young delinquents) and of the inter-faces between the various social control networks (efforts are still fledgling here). Evaluation or impact studies are plentiful only in the juvenile delinquency area. On the contrary, French research has granted a special place to the study of ideological-symbolic phenomena through an examination of the collective repre-sentations of these social control agencies within French society.

The multiplicity of systems that specialize in the control of deviance and devi-ants does not mean that social control usually is not operative prior to the systems' eventual intervention. The process of control may be divided roughly into two phases: the first consists in increased pressure to conform and lies within the sphere of general social regulation. The second is initiated at the moment of the exclusion of the deviants from regular interaction and their referral to specialized control agencies that are supposed to intervene for the purpose of including them again in regular interaction within conventional groups. This noninstitutionalized sector is just beginning to reveal itself and is less accessible to study than the networks of specialized agencies. French research, however, is beginning to discover the importance of areas that precede the eventual intervention of special-ized agencies: studies on youth gangs, on marginal groups and the trajectories of their members, and on referral processes.

From a more general point of view, there are also more methodological works which examine production conditions—and therefore the limits of utilization—of administrative data used in secondary analysis, such as police, court, or file statistics. There are examples of such works in economics (on the costs of crime) and demography (on violent deaths), which make possible comparisons with penal data such as criminal statistics. French research is just beginning to approach studies of victimization. Significant development of this research line may be expected in the future.

FINAL COMMENTS

French criminological research has exhibited a number of characteristics in past years.

1. There is a diversity of the theoretical paradigms employed and of searches for new theoretical constructions capable of reaching beyond the limits of both the classical theories and the attempts of the last two decades.

2. Extended borrowing is being done, not only from sociology and social psychology, but also from history, economics, linguistics, demography, political science, and ethnology. On the other hand, there has been less recourse to the psychological approach.

3. Along with clearly criminological research, there are strong fields (such as application of representations sociology and of systems analysis and history) with less structured and less effective applications.

4. International networks of cooperation and diffusion have been established, particularly by organizations on the French-speaking level rather than only on a level limited to France.

The fluidity of present-day situations makes it difficult to strike a balance—a balance which, if excessively rigid, runs the risk of presenting an immobile picture of a state of events which is actually in rapid evolution.

NOTES

1. DGRST, *Le contrôle social de la déviance* [Social Control of Deviance] (Paris: Centre de documentation de la Maison des sciences de l'homme, 1979).

2. The following articles are from *La recherche en sciences humaines* [Research in the Human Sciences] (Paris: Editions du Centre national de la recherche scientifique, 1978): Pierre Arpaillange and Annick Percheron, "Déviance et contrôle social" [Deviance and Social Control], pp. 220-223; Philippe Robert, "Déviance et contrôle social" [Deviance and Social Control], pp. 191-201; and Victor Scardigli, "Modes de vie, déviance et contrôle social" [Modes of Life, Deviance and Social Control], pp. 201-209.

3. *Le Comité de Coordination des Recherches Criminologiques* [Committee for the Coordination of Criminological Research] (Paris: Ministère de la Justice, 1979).

4. Comité de Coordination des Recherches Criminologiques, *Criminologie en France, unités d'enseignement, centres de recherche, recherches en cours, centres de documentation* [Criminology in France, Instructional Units, Centers of Research, Ongoing Research, Centers of Documentation] (Paris: Ministère de la Justice, 1978).

5. Jean Pinatel, "Aperçu général de la recherche criminologique en France" [General Perception of Criminological Research in France], in *Orientations actuelles de la recherche criminologique* [Contemporary Orientations of Criminological Research] (Strasbourg: Council of Europe, 1970), pp. 161-194.

6. Philippe Robert, "Une unité de recherche criminologique, le Centre de Vaucresson" [Criminological Research Unit, The Center at Vaucresson], *Année sociologique* 19 (1968):481-512; Philippe Robert, "A propos de recherches récentes en criminologie juvénile" [Regarding Recent Research in Juvenile Delinquency], *Année sociologique* 22 (1971):499-526.

7. Christian Debuyst, "Le concept de dangerosité et un de ses éléments constitutifs: la personnalité (criminelle)" [The Concept of Dangerousness and One of Its Constituent Elements: The Criminal Personality], *Déviance et Société* 1, no. 4 (1977):363-387.

8. Lode Walgrave, "Considérations sur l'orientation de la psychologie dans la criminologie actuelle" [Considerations on the Orientation of Psychology in Contemporary Criminology], *Déviance et Société* 4, no. 4 (1980):305-330.

BIBLIOGRAPHY

The following bibliography, although only a selection of a small number of works published since the end of World War II, provides a good overall view of French works in this scientific sector. The following guidelines were adopted:

First, since this chapter appears in an international volume, omitted are works that are relatively inaccessible, particularly those documents not published in book or periodical form, notably all studies in mimeograph or offset.

Second, special attention is accorded to publications released after 1970. For the 1945-1970 period, a period of far less research productivity in French criminology, only the few works demonstrating fundamental value are included.

Third, whenever possible, preference is given to books over articles, considering their presumably greater accessibility. It is assumed that it would not be useful to cite all articles of interest in periodicals mentioned as such in the bibliography.

Fourth, given the reduced number of items resulting from stringent selection, the items in this bibliography are given in alphabetical order without subdivisions. Works of particular significance are denoted with an asterisk.

Abbiatecci, André. *Crime et criminalité en France aux XVII° et au XVIII° siècles* [Crime and Criminality in France in the 17th and 18th Centuries]. Paris: Colin, 1971.

Administration pénitentiaire. *Rapport annuel* [Annual Reports of the Penitentiary Administration]. Paris: Ministry of Justice.

Algan, Andrée, Marie-Thérèse Mazerol, et al. *Vols et voleurs de véhicules à moteur* [Motor Vehicular Thefts and Thieves]. Paris: Cujas, 1965.

*Ancel, Marc. *La défense sociale nouvelle* [The New Social Defense]. Paris: Cujas, 1966.
A classic work on criminal policy.

Ancel, Marc, and Henri Donnedieu de Vabres (eds.). *Le problème de l'enfance délinquante* [The Problem of the Delinquent Child]. Paris: Sirey, 1947.

Ancel, Marc, Louis Hugueney, and Henry Donnedieu de Vabres. *Les grands systèmes pénitentiaires actuels* [Today's Principal Penitentiary Systems]. Paris: Sirey, 1950.

Ancel, Marc, and Jacques Bernard Herzog. *L'individualisation des mesures prises à l'égard du délinquant* [The Individualization of Measures Taken with Respect to the Delinquent]. Paris: Cujas, 1954.

Ancel, Marc, and Louis Hugueney. *Les grands systèmes pénitentiaires actuels* [Today's Principal Penitentiary Systems]. Paris: Sirey, 1955.

Ancel, Marc, and Antonin Besson. *La prévention des infractions contre la vie humaine et l'intégrité de la personne* [The Prevention of Infringements on Human Life and Body Integrity]. Paris: Cujas, 1956.

Annales de Vaucresson. Periodical published yearly by the Center for Training and Research in Probationary Education of Vaucresson; an important journal on problems of juvenile maladjustment.

Armand, Marie-France, and Pierre Lascoumes. "Malaise et occultation: perceptions et pratiques du contrôle social de la délinquance d'affaires" [Malaise and Concealment: Perceptions and Practices in Social Control of Business Delinquency]. *Déviance et Société* 1, no. 2 (1977):135-170.

Aufusson de Cavarlay, Bruno, and Philippe Robert. "La recherche prévisionnelle en criminologie" [Forecasting Research in Criminology]. *Annales internationales de criminologie* 13, nos. 1-2 (1974):83-125.

Ballé, Catherine. *La menace, un langage de violence* [The Threat, Language of Violence]. Paris: Editions du Centre national de la recherche scientifique, 1975.

Barberger, Cécile. "Le choix des jurés [The Selection of Jurors]. *Annales internationales de criminologie* 15, no. 1 (1975):63-96.

*Boudon, Raymond, and André Davidovitch. "Les méchanismes sociaux des abandons de poursuite" [The Social Mechanisms Behind Dropping Charges]. *Année Sociologique* (1964):111-244.
A classic work in criminal justice systems analysis.

*Bouzat, Pierre, and Jean Pinatel. *Traité de droit pénal et de criminologie* [Treatise on Penal Law and Criminology]. Paris: Dalloz, 1967.
The most classic of all French criminological handbooks.

*Breuvart, Josse, et al. *Que deviennent-ils?* [What Becomes of Them?]. Vaucresson: Centre de Formation et de Recherche de l'Education Surveillée, 1974.
Evaluative research on youth establishments.

Briguet Lamarre, Marguerite. *L'adolescent meurtrier* [The Adolescent Murderer]. Toulouse: Privat, 1969.

Buffard, Simone. *Le froid pénitentiaire* [The Cold World of the Penitentiary]. Paris: Seuil, 1973.

Centre de Formation et de Recherche de l'Education Surveillée. *Cinq cent jeunes délinquants* [500 Young Delinquents]. Paris: Cujas, 1968.

*Chamboredon, Jean-Claude. La délinquance juvénile, essai de construction d'objet" [Juvenile Delinquency, An Attempt at Object Construction]. *Revue française de sociologie* 12, no. 3 (1971):355-377.
An application to criminology of P. Bourdieu's procedure.

Charrier, Yves, and Jacques Ellul. *Jeunesse délinquante: des blousons noirs aux hippies*. [Delinquent Youth: From the Hoods to the Hippies]. Paris: Mercure de France, 1971.

Chauvière, Michel. *Enfance inadaptée: l'héritage de Vichy* [Maladjusted Youth: The Vichy Legacy]. Paris: Editions Ouvrières, 1980.

Chazal, Jean. *Etudes de criminologie juvénile* [Studies in Criminology]. Paris: Presses Universitaires de France, 1952.

*Chesnais, Jean-Claude. *Les morts violentes en France depuis 1926; comparaisons internationales* [Deaths by Violence in France Since 1926; International Comparisons]. Paris: Presses Universitaires de France, 1976.
Application to criminology of demographic data and methods.

*Chevalier, Louis. *Classes laborieuses et classes dangereuses* [Working Classes and Dangerous Classes]. Paris: Plon, 1958.
One of the most famous works of criminological history.

Chirol, Yves, et al. *Délinquance juvénile et développement socio-économique* [Juvenile Delinquency and Socioeconomic Development]. La Haye-Paris: Mouton, 1975.

Chombart de Lauwe, Marie-Jose. *Psychopathologie sociale de l'enfance inadaptée* [Social Psychopathology of Maladjusted Youth]. Paris: Editions du Centre National de la Recherche Scientifique, 1959.

Colin, Marcel. *Etudes de criminologie clinique* [Studies in Clinical Criminology]. Paris: Masson, 1963.

Compte Général de l'administration de la Justice [General Accounts of the Justice Administration]. Paris: Documentation française, annual since 1825.
One of the oldest series of criminal statistics in the world, generously annotated.

*Coll. *Connaissance et fonctionnement de la justice pénale: perspectives sociologiques et criminologiques* [Awareness and Functioning of Penal Justice: Sociological and Criminological Perspectives]. Paris: Editions du Centre National de la Recherche Scientifique, no. 571, 1979.
An assessment of recent orientations in French criminological research.

Coll. *Les marginaux et les exclus dans l'histoire* [History's Marginals and Outcasts]. Paris: U.G.E., 1979.

Congrès (2°) *international de criminologie* [Second International Congress of Criminology]. Paris: Presses Universitaires de France, 1951.

Congrès français de criminologie. *Examen de personnalité et criminologie.* [Personality Testing and Criminology]. Paris: Masson, 1961.

Congrès (9°) français de criminologie. *Le fonctionnement de la justice pénale* [The Functioning of Penal Justice]. Montpellier: Faculté de droit et des sciences économiques, 1971.

Congrès (13°) français de criminologie. *Recherche criminologique et inadaptation juvénile* [Criminological Research and Juvenile Maladjustment]. Melun: Imprimerie administrative, 1971.

Cosson, Jean. *Les industriels de la fraude fiscale* [The Big Businessmen of Fiscal Fraud]. Paris: Seuil, 1971.

Davidovitch, André. "L'escroquerie et l'émission de chèques sans provision" [Swindling and Rubber Checks]. *Année Sociologique* 6 (1955-1956):3-130.

*Délégation générale à la recherche scientifique et technique. *Le contrôle social de la déviance* [Social Control of Deviance]. Paris: Centre de documentation de la Maison des Sciences de l'Homme, 1979.
Very fine synthesis of recent orientations in French criminology.

*Delumeau, Jean. *La peur en occident* [Fear in the Western World]. Paris: Fayard, 1978.
A monumental work in the history of mentalities.

Déviance et Société. Published trimonthly by M. & H., C.P. 229, CH 1211, Geneva, 4, in collaboration with the National Center of Scientific Research.
The only international French-speaking periodical in the field of deviance.

Deyon, Pierre. *Le temps des prisons* [Doing Time]. Lille: Editions Universitaires, 1975.

Dubet, François. "L'inadaptation sociale des jeunes à travers le projet" [Social Maladjustment in Youth Seen Through the Plan]. *Revue française de sociologie* 14, no. 2 (1973):221-244.

Dutrenit, Jean-Marc. "Ethos du service social et enfance en danger" [Ethos of Social Services and Children in Peril]. *Revue française de sociologie* 17, no. 4 (1976):6l5-632.

Education Surveillée. *Rapport annuel* [Annual Report]. Paris: Ministère de la Justice, annuel.

Farge, Arlette. *Le vol d'aliments à Paris au XVIII° siècle* [Food-Stealing in 18th Century Paris]. Paris: Plon, 1974.

Farge, Arlette. *Vivre dans la rue à Paris au XVIII° siècle* [Life in the Street in 18th Century Paris]. Paris: Gallimard-Julliard, 1979.

Faugeron, Claude, and Dominique Poggi. "Les femmes, les infractions, la justice pénale: une analyse d'attitudes" [Women, Infractions, Penal Justice: An Analysis of Attitudes]. *Revue de l'Institut de sociologie* (Université libre de Bruxelles) 3-4 (1975):369-385.

Faugeron, Claude, and Philippe Robert. "Les représentations sociales de la justice pénale" [Social Representations of Penal Justice]. *Cahiers internationaux de sociologie* 61 (1961):341-366.

Foucault, Michel. *Moi Pierre Rivière...* [I, Pierre Rivière...]. Paris: Gallimard, 1973.

*Foucault, Michel. *Surveiller et punir, naissance de la prison* [Surveillance and Punishment: Birth of the Prison]. Paris: Gallimard, 1975.
World-renowned work on the emergence of prisons.

*Gaillac, Henri. *Les maisons de correction, 1830-1945* [Reform Schools, 1830-1945]. Paris: Cujas, 1971.
Fine historical study of institutions for youth.

Geremek, Bonrislaw. *Les marginaux parisiens aux XIV° et XV° siècles* [Marginal Parisians in the 14th and 15th Centuries]. Paris: Flammarion, 1976.

Goglin, Jean-Louis. *Les misérables dans l'occident médiéval* [The Poor of the Western World in the Middle Ages]. Paris: Seuil, 1976.

Gonin, Daniel. *Psychothérapie de groupe du délinquant adulte en milieu pénitentiaire* [Group Psychotherapy of the Adult Delinquent Inside the Penitentiary]. Paris: Masson, 1967.

Gorphe, François. *L'appréciation des preuves en justice* [Evaluation of Evidence in the Justice System]. Paris: Sirey, 1947.

Gorphe, François. *Les décisions de justice* [Decision-making in the Justice System]. Paris: Presses Universitaires de France, 1952.

Grapin, Pierre. *L'anthropologie criminelle* [Criminal Anthropology]. Paris: Presses Universitaires de France, 1973.

Gruner, Simone, Marie-Thérèse Mazerol, and Jacques Selosse. *Etudes de peintures d'adolescents délinquants* [Studies of Paintings by Adolescent Delinquents]. Paris: Cujas, 1967.

*Gutton, Jean-Pierre. *La société et les pauvres en Europe (XVI-XVIII°siècles)* [Society and Its Poor in Europe from the 16th to 18th Century]. Paris: Presses Universitaires de France, 1974.
Excellent synthesis of the history of poverty.

Henry, Michel, and G. Laurent. *Les adolescents criminels et la justice* [Adolescent Criminals and Justice]. Vaucresson: Centre de formation et de recherche de l'Education Surveillée, 1974.

Herpin, Nicolas. *Les sociologues américains et le siècle* [American Sociologists and the Century]. Paris: Presses Universitaires de France, 1973.

Herpin, Nicolas. *L'application de la loi* [Applying the Law]. Paris: Seuil, 1977.

Hesnard, André. *Psychologie du crime* [The Psychology of Crime]. Paris: Payot, 1963.

Heuyer, Georges. *Les troubles mentaux, étude criminologique* [Mental Disorders, A Criminological Study]. Paris: Presses Universitaires de France, 1968.

Heuyer, Georges, and Georges Levasseur. *Les enfants et les adolescents socialement inadaptés* [Socially Maladjusted Children and Adolescents]. Paris: Cujas, 1958.

Hijazi, Mustafa. *Délinquance juvénile et réalisation de soi* [Juvenile Delinquency and Self-Realization]. Paris: Masson, 1966.

Hochman, Jacques. *La relation clinique en milieu pénitentiaire* [The Doctor-Patient Relationship Inside the Penitentiary]. Paris: Masson, 1964.

Institut de sciences criminelles et pénitentiaire de Strasbourg. *Recherches sur l'infanticide (1955-1965)* [Research on Infanticide, 1955-1965]. Paris: Dalloz, 1968.

Jacob, Pierre. *Schizophrénie et délinquance juvénile* [Schizophrenia and Juvenile Delinquency]. Toulouse: Privat, 1973.

Jorda, Michel. *Les délinquants aliénés et anormaux mentaux* [Mentally Disturbed and Abnormal Delinquents]. Paris: Montchrestien, 1966.

Laingui, André, and Arlette Lebigre. *Histoire du droit pénal* [History of Penal Law]. 2 vols. Paris: Cujas, 1979.

*Lascoumes, Pierre. *Prévention et contrôle social* [Prevention and Social Control]. Genève-Paris: Médecine et Hygiène-Masson, 1977.
Characteristics of the French current of thought on social control.

Lascoumes, Pierre, and Ghislaine Moreau Capdevielle. "La presse et la justice pénale, un cas de diffusion idéologique" [The Press and Penal Justice, A Case of Ideological Diffusion). *Revue française de science politique* 26, no. 1 (1976):41-69.

Lazerges Rothe, Catherine. *La cour d'assises des mineurs et son fonctionnement*. [The Juvenile Criminal Court and Its Functioning]. Paris: Librairie générale de droit et de jurisprudence, 1973.

Lemay, Michel. *Le groupe de jeunes inadaptés, rôle du jeune meneur*. [The Maladjusted Youth Group, Role of the Young Leader]. Paris: Presses Universitaires de France, 1961.

Lemay, Michel. *Psychopathologie juvénile* [Juvenile Psychopathology]. Paris: Fleurus, 1974.

Levade, Michel, and Jacqueline Costa-Lascoux. *La délinquance des jeunes en France, 1825-1965* [Youth Delinquency in France, 1825-1965]. 4 vols. Paris: Cujas, 1972.

Levasseur, Georges (ed.). *Les délinquants anormaux mentaux* [Mentally Abnormal Delinquents]. Paris: Cujas, 1959.

*Malewska, Hanna, and Vincent Peyre. *Délinquance juvénile, famille, école et société* [Juvenile Delinquency, Family, School and Society]. Vaucresson: Centre de formation et de recherche de l'Education Surveillée, 1973.
Characteristics of CFR-ES research on juvenile delinquency.

Malewska, Hanna, Vincent Peyre, and Hubert Bonerandi. *Attitudes envers les délits des jeunes* [Attitudes Towards Youth Offenses]. Vaucresson: Centre de formation et de recherche de l'Education Surveillée, 1973.

Mathé, André G. *Psychothérapie en prison* [Psychotherapy in Prison]. Paris: Denoël, 1976.

Mauger, Gerard, and Claude Fossé. *La vie buissonnière* [Living as Truant]. Paris: Maspéro, 1976.

Michard, Henry, Jacques Selosse, et al. *La délinquance des jeunes en groupe* [Youth Group Delinquency]. Paris: Cujas, 1963.

Michaud, Yves. *Violence et politique* [Violence and Politics]. Paris: Gallimard, 1978.

Ministère de la Santé. *La prévention des inadaptations sociales* [The Prevention of Social Maladjustment]. Paris: Documentation Française, 1973.

Mollat, Michel. *Les pauvres au moyen-age, étude sociale* [The Poor in the Middle Ages, A Social Study]. Paris: Hachette, 1978.

Monod, Jacques. *Les barjots* [The Kooks]. Paris: Julliard, 1968.

Parrot, Philippe, and Monique Queneau. *Les gangs d'adolescents* [Adolescent Gangs]. Paris: Presses Universitaires de France, 1959.

*Perrot, Michèle. "Délinquance et système pénitentiaire en France au XIX° siècle" [Delinquency and the Penitentiary System in 19th Century France]. *Annales E.S.C.* 30, no. 1 (1975):67-91.
"Fresco" of historical criminology covering the nineteenth century.

Perrot, Michèle (ed.). *L'impossible prison: recherche sur le système pénitentiaire au XIX° siècle* [Prison Impossible; Research on the 19th Century Penitentiary System]. Paris: Seuil, 1980.

Peyre, Vincent, and Michel Jacquey. *Clubs de prévention* [Prevention Clubs]. Paris: Cujas, 1964.

Pinatel, Jean. *Traité élémentaire de science pénitentiaire et de défense sociale* [Elementary Penitentiary Science and Social Defense]. Paris: Sirey, 1950.

Pinatel, Jean. *La criminologie* [Criminology]. Paris: Spes, 1978.

Pouget de Nadaillac, Bruno. *Adolescents de banlieue* [Suburban Adolescents]. Lyon: Fédérop, 1976.

Raymondis, Louis-Marie, and Michel Le Guern. *Le langage de la justice pénale* [The Language of Penal Justice]. Paris: Editions du Centre national de la recherche scientifique, 1977.

*Revue de science criminelle et de droit pénal comparé. Published every three months in cooperation with the Centre national de la recherche scientifique (especially the accounts by Jean Pinatel).
A review of penal law containing frequent articles of criminological interest.

Robert, Philippe. "La sociologie entre une criminologie du passage à l'acte et une criminologie de la réaction sociale" [Sociology Between a Criminology of the Deed and a Criminology of Social Reaction]. *Année sociologique* 17 (1973):441-504.

Robert, Philippe. "Les statistiques criminelles et la recherche, réflexions conceptuelles" [Criminal Statistics and Research, Some Conceptual Considerations]. *Déviance et Société* 1 (1977):1-27.

Robert, Philippe, Bruno Aubusson de Cavarlay, and Thibault Lambert. "Condamnations, classes d'âge et catégories socio-professionnelles; analyse et prévision" [Convictions, Age Brackets and Socio-professional Categories; Analysis and Prediction]. *Population* 31, no. 1 (1976):87-110.

Robert, Philippe, and Claude Faugeron. "Analyse d'une représentation sociale, les images de la justice pénale" [Analysis of a Social Representation, the Images of Penal Justice]. *Revue de l'Institut de sociologie* (Université libre de Bruxelles) 1 (1973):31-85.

**Robert, Philippe, and Claude Faugeron. *La justice et son public ou les représentations sociales de la justice pénale* [Justice and Its Public or the Social Representations of Penal Justice]. Genève-Paris: Médecine et Hygiène-Masson, 1978.
A synthesis of studies on the problems of representations, images, attitudes, and public opinion in criminology.

Robert, Philippe, Claude Faugeron, and Georges Kellens. "Les attitudes des juges à propos des prises de décision" [Judges' Attitudes with Regard to Decision-making]. *Annales de la faculté de droit de Liège* 20, nos. 1-2 (1975):23-152.

**Robert, Philippe, and Thierry Godefroy. *Le coût du crime ou l'économie poursuivant le crime* [The Cost of Crime or the Economy in Pursuit of Crime]. Genève-Paris: Médecine et Hygiène-Masson, 1978.
A synthesis of modern studies in criminological economics.

**Robert, Philippe, Thibault Lambert, and Claude Faugeron. *Image du viol collectif et reconstruction d'objet* [The Image of Collective Rape and Object Reconstruction]. Genève-Paris: Médecine et Hygiène-Masson, 1976.
A classic in the French consideration of social control.

**Robert, Philippe, and Pierre Lascoumes. *Les bandes d'adolescents, une théorie de la*

ségrégation [Adolescent Gangs, A Theory of Segregation]. Paris: Editions Ouvrières, 1974.
One of the French classics on youth gangs.

Robert, Philippe, and Ghislaine Moreau Capdevielle. "La presse française et la justice pénale" [The French Press and Penal Justice]. *Sociologia del diritto* 2 (1975):359-383.

Robert, Philippe, Jacques Toiser, and Bruno Aubusson de Cavarlay. "Recherches prévisionnelles en criminologie; application d'une méthode à élasticité spatiale" [Predictive Research in Criminology; Application of a Spatial Elasticity Method]. *Compte Général de l'administration de la justice pour 1973*. Paris: Documentation Française, 1977.

Robert, Philippe, and Claude Faugeron. *Les forces cachées de la justice, la crise de la justice pénale* [The Hidden Forces of Justice, the Crisis in Penal Justice]. Paris: Centurion, 1980.

Schmelck, Robert, and Georges Picca. *Pénologie et droit pénitentiaire* [Penology and Penitentiary Law]. Paris: Cujas, 1967.

*Selosse, Jacques, et al. *L'internat de rééducation* [Reformatories]. Vaucresson: Centre de formation et de recherche de l'Education Surveillée, 1972.
One of the best studies on establishments for youth.

Serverin, Evelyne. "De l'avortement à l'interruption volontaire de grossesse: L'histoire d'une requalification sociale" [From Abortion to Voluntary Interruption of Pregnancy: The History of a Social Redesignation]. *Déviance et Société* 4, no. 1 (1980):1-18.

Szabo, Denis. *Crimes et villes* [Crimes and Cities]. Paris: Cujas, 1960.

Vexliard, André. *Introduction à la sociologie du vagabondage* [Introduction to the Sociology of Bumming]. Paris: Librairie Michel Rivière, 1956.

*Vexliard, André. *Le clochard* [The Bum]. Bruges-Paris: Desclée de Brouwer, 1957.
A classic in the sociology of deviance in the use of observation-participation.

Weinberger, Jean-Claude, et al. "Il declino del diritto come strumento di controllo sociale" [The Decline of Law as an Instrument of Social Control]. *Questione criminale* 2, no. 1 (1976):73-96.

Weinberger, Jean-Claude, et al. "Société et gravité des infractions" [Society and Seriousness of Offenses]. *Revue de science criminelle* 4 (1976):915-930.

11

GERMAN DEMOCRATIC REPUBLIC

Guenter Lehmann

In the German Democratic Republic (GDR), criminology evolved as part of the development of socialist society and science. Around the beginning of the 1960s, there appeared the new sociopolitical and theoretical prerequisites and requirements for criminology, which was generally acknowledged as a new, independent discipline of socialist science based on Marxism-Leninism. The theoretical views and practical experiences of the Soviet Union and other socialist countries also played an eminent part in its development.

DEVELOPMENT AND OBJECT
OF SOCIALIST CRIMINOLOGY

The development of criminology as an independent discipline in the GDR is closely connected, historically and materially, with the Socialist Unity party of Germany's goal of gradually pushing back criminality in the process of development of socialism through joint endeavors by the entire socialist society, its state, and all the citizens. On the one hand, complete consolidation of socialist power and production relations, the considerable strengthening of the economic basis of socialism, the further spreading of socialist ideology, and the impressive increase in the working people's intellectual-cultural living standard have created real and favorable conditions, leading to a provable decline in delinquency. On the other hand, new and greater demands emerged to effectively combat and prevent criminality. With the transition to the advanced socialist society and the realizing of its aims under the changed international and national conditions these demands even gained in significance.

Against this social background, it became increasingly necessary to make a systematic analysis of criminality in order to penetrate to its sources and to disclose the interrelationships among social processes, personality development, and punishable modes of conduct. Such an analysis must be performed with a view to widening the scientific foundations for the management, planning, and organization of crime prevention throughout the whole state and society and thus to giving a new impetus to pushing back criminality.

Knowledge of the sources of criminality and their functioning brought the realization that combating and preventing criminality require a complex approach. This realization in turn gave rise to the social need for an independent scientific discipline of criminology, the very concept itself bearing a complex character. This separate discipline takes up the partial results of the disciplines of law and the other social sciences that are relevant to criminality and its sources, lifting them to a higher level of generalization. Thus, criminology can submit to the leading organs of the party and of the socialist state scientifically founded proposals and recommendations for liquidating, paralyzing, and neutralizing the sources of criminality and for effectively combating and preventing criminality as part of the management and planning of political, economic, social, and intellectual-cultural development.

Thus, socialist criminology was born out of the revolutionary process of transforming society in its systematic advancement toward socialism. In its practical efficiency, socialist criminology is oriented toward, and obliged to, this social reality. Simultaneously, socialist criminology emerged from a break with bourgeois criminology. In the face of the explosion of delinquency in the capitalist countries, bourgeois criminology was not in a position to offer real solutions, and, in its biological version, it was abused by the Nazi regime in Germany which used it as a theoretical instrument for exculpating mass annihilation. Drawing, on principle, a demarcation line to separate itself from bourgeois criminology, however, socialist criminology takes a stand that is quite different than that of the sociological conception, on one hand, and that of the biological one, on the other. Socialist criminology had to build on a new theoretical groundwork, enabling it to fulfill its social function. Its scientific basis is Marxism-Leninism as a world outlook, theory, and methodology. Thus, it is rooted in the Marxist-Leninist theory of society and makes use of the material-dialectical approach to social processes and appearances.

That is why socialist criminology is in a position to explain the real nature of criminality and its sources and to predict their historical destiny. It rests on the basic theories of Marxism-Leninism and applies them creatively to concrete historical conditions. At the same time, it also assimilates dialectically all the progressive findings of the pre-Marxist theorists of society concerning criminality as a social phenomenon. In summary, socialist criminology is an original discipline, compared with bourgeois criminology, and differs from the latter in its genesis, tasks, theoretical groundwork, and methodology.

The development of socialist criminology was linked with the definition of its object and its relationship to and distinction from other branches of science. Thus, there are universal, acknowledged basic positions in regard to the relationship of criminology to criminal law science, criminalistics, sociology, sociopsychology, and other sciences dealing with social problems.[1] The definition of criminology's object was essentially favored by its developmental process and by the social function assigned to it.

The object of socialist criminology is dictated by the sources of criminality—all those material and ideological conditions, relations, circumstances, and factors that determine the emergence and existence of criminality (both as a negative social phenomenon and as the concrete culpable misconduct of an individual human being) and their quality, structure, and functioning. It is also dictated by the processes, measures, subjects, and methods for abolishing, paralyzing, or neutralizing those conditions. Thus, the object of socialist criminology is to be seen in the laws underlying the emergence, development, pushing back, and surmounting of criminality as a historically conditioned, social mass phenomenon within the international historic process of the revolutionary overthrow of the old system of exploitation that has existed for thousands of years, and the buildup of the socialist and, finally, the communist society, in accord with respective international and national conditions.

Socialist criminology analyzes the actual appearance of the given socioeconomic order, reveals its developmental tendencies, and indicates the direction in which, first, social reality has to be progressively changed and, second, the material and intellectual-cultural advancement that has to be achieved. Thus, the determinants causing men to commit punishable acts are to be liquidated or their sphere confined. By no means is it merely a registering or retrospective discipline; rather, it is an active, demanding one. Its findings and results contribute to improving the complex management and planning of social development with a view to providing (by increasing the efficiency of the national economy, further improving the working people's material working and living conditions, and raising their ideological and intellectual-cultural standard) more favorable conditions for the responsible conduct of individuals toward society. In this way, society meets its own responsibility to the individual, with a view to providing socialist personalities a full opportunity to unfold and develop. Through criminology, then, the possibilities inherent in the socialist society for eliminating the sources of criminality can be translated into practice. Investigation into the sources destroys the functioning of criminality and banishes it from life in the socialist society. This does not occur automatically, but only as the result of diverse state and social activities performed by the whole socialist political system.

Since at the present stage of development of the socialist society it is not yet possible to eradicate criminality completely, a more effective prevention of criminality takes priority. This understanding has led, particularly during the last few years, to an extension of the object of socialist criminology. There has been an increased effort to use studies on the sources, structure, and functioning of criminality in combating the problem. Thus, criminology has embarked upon an integrated elaboration of the theoretical bases of a practically functioning system of crime prevention.

With the emergence of the criminological theory of crime prevention, socialist criminology began to embrace the theory of crime determination and the theory of crime prevention as two mutually conditioned and mutually enriching, but also relatively independent, constituent parts. With the unity of these two elements, socialist criminology has developed new theoretical and practical powers, as well as the typically socialist qualitative features of that discipline. The extension of socialist criminology's object, however, requires some elaboration here.

Socialist criminology must not be considered to be a general theory of the sources and prevention of legal conflicts or modes of conduct contrary to the morals and norms of social life. Criminology takes an interest, however, in the "process of escalation" whereby generally immoral and illegal conduct is translated into criminal conduct, although criminology does not mean to label all those persons who infringe moral norms as potential criminal offenders or to consider all violations of moral norms as examples of criminality. Socialist criminology neither can be nor desires to be a substitute for other legal branches or social disciplines responsible for investigating the theoretical aspects of social conflicts. But the findings of those disciplines constitute essential sources of generalizations serving the complex approach to pushing back criminality. Finally, from the point of view of its object, socialist criminology is only able to submit proposals and suggestions as to the initiatives and activities to be taken by state and social management organs in realizing their competencies. Still, socialist criminology makes an important contribution to legislation. Its findings broaden the bases for the legislator's decisions concerning (1) conduct that, in the interest of protecting both the socialist order of society, state, and law and the citizens' rights, must be declared a punishable act, and (2) conduct that need not be considered a punishable act because of the existence of other state and social forms of legal response. At the same time, criminology helps define more precisely the legal responsibility of all subjects engaged in preventing and combating crime. Thus, the tasks of criminology derive from and have developed with its objects.

There is general agreement that socialist criminology belongs to the social sciences. Criminology is a discipline of law, since it deals with sociolegal phenomena, particularly with conduct relevant to criminal law. Taking the partial results of other disciplines relevant to the sources and prevention of crimes, socialist criminology generalizes and enriches those results through its own research, thereby exercising a stimulating and promoting influence. In close connection with this task, it analyzes the practical efficiency of the struggle waged by the whole state and society for gradually eliminating criminality. Since socialist criminology, as a legal discipline, integrates itself in this way into the social sciences and bases itself on socialist practice, the danger of a hampering absolutism or isolation, hence a dogmatic numbness, is immediately excluded and its creative development furthered.

Socialist criminology bears class character. It investigates criminality exclusively from the point of view of the producing, working masses. It bears this character because the only criterion for the criminalization of certain modes of conduct in socialist criminal law lies in the interest that the working class, as the overall social subject, takes in safeguarding its social achievements, the growth of social wealth, the protection of social property, the maintenance of the rights of the individual members of society, and the development of educated and civilized men. Socialist criminology makes its specific contribution to implementing the working class's historic mission, which in its essence includes freeing itself from criminality.

This class character simultaneously expresses the human character of socialist criminology. It is directed at the well-being and security of the working people and at conditions that do not bring the individual into conflict with society but enable him to be fully integrated into that society.

CRIMINALITY AND ITS RELATIONSHIP TO SOCIETY

Socialist criminology proceeds from the basic views of Marx, Engels, and Lenin on criminality and its relationship to society. These views, arrived at through a scientific analysis of the laws governing the motion of the socioeconomic formation of society, particularly capitalism and its imperialist phase, are as follows:[2]

1. Criminality is a historically conditioned, negative social phenomenon. It arose at a certain stage in the development of the productive forces and productive relations and of the political and power structures corresponding to that stage. Historically, criminality originated with the development of private ownership of the means of production which gave rise to man's exploitation of man and led to the splitting of society into classes—exploiting and exploited classes. The exploiting relationships resting on the private ownership of the means of production create a deep antagonism not only between the exploiting and exploited classes, with regard to the differences in their living conditions and basic interests, but also between single members of a class and their class as a whole. Hence, the contradiction between the individual and society. The emergence of private ownership has brought about the material alienation of the producing masses from the means and results of production, together with the social consequences of the alienation of man from his work, his environment, other men, and his own social being.

There is an advancing transformation of all human values into commodities, and this transformation unavoidably exerts a demoralizing and destructive influence on the quality of social relations and creates a struggle of all against all. In the course of that struggle, the individual tries to or is compelled to pit his actual or alleged vital interests against that of his fellow men. Thus, individualism, selfishness, isolation and loneliness, carelessness, recklessness, and brutality spread and become increasingly consolidated into basic patterns of conduct which in the extreme expression is criminality.

Realizing the historical-social character of criminality is of fundamental importance. Recognizing its historical character means taking the clear position that criminality does not represent an eternal phenomenon, a fatal attribute of each social order that will inevitably accompany general human development into the future. The disclosure of the social conditions for the origin and existence of criminality justifies the conclusion that criminality, in principle, can be excluded from social life by liquidating those conditions that force it on society. It is this historical reflection on criminality that makes it possible to surmount criminality in a planned and systematic way and allows criminologists to set such a strategic objective free of defeatism and voluntarism.

2. The material-dialectical characterization of criminality as a social phenomenon not only consistently excludes its eternity and unchangeability but also uncovers the social nature of its sources. Ultimately, a social manifestation always has social roots. The most important socioeconomic sources of criminality are the exploitative relations based on the private ownership of the means of production. Those relationships—by dint of multiple mediating links that are sources of the paralysis of social relations, the destruction of social ties, the distortion of ideas of value and a person's way of life, and the deformation of the personality—provoke the individual's decision to commit punishable acts. A principal line of distinction between socialist and capitalist criminology lies in the latter's inhuman views that displace the sources of criminality to the individual, ascribe one's becoming an offender to the general nature of man, particularly to his biological and psychical structure, his "lower psychical layers" or his basic "nihilistic" disposition, or that regard man's genetic code as the essential exciting agent of criminality. These views end in the concept of the clinical treatment of socially conditioned behavior, a concept representing a violation of human rights.

The general basic source of criminality also explains the increase in criminality in the capitalist society. This increase assumes dimensions resembling an explosion in the course of that society's transition to imperialism, for in that transition the antagonisms in all spheres and at all levels of social life sharpen, and the motivation to perform criminal acts intensifies because of the economic, political, social, and moral effects of crises. Not even the development of the productive forces, the remarkable increase in labor productivity, and the growth of social wealth in capitalism bring about a decline in the crime rate. Under the conditions of imperialist power relations, historically relative, objective progressiveness changes into anachronist, subjectivist destruction of human creativeness with a gross expansion and solidifying of antisocial patterns of conduct. The capitalist reproduction process turns out to be a reproduction process of criminality. The laws governing the extended reproduction of capitalism to imperialism also lead to an extended reproduction of criminality. This statement is presently being verified in the major imperialist countries. Thus, criminality is immanent in the exploiting order of capitalism.

This social order itself—because of its nature, and not single deficiencies—conditions the existence and growth of criminality, which is its unavoidable product. The ruling exploiting class and its monopolist groupings, therefore, are not interested in revealing the genuine roots of criminality, for if they did so, they would question their own raison d'être and show their historical outdatedness. It is, therefore, of high topicality that Marx called on men to think seriously about a change in the system that rears crime with the "regularity of natural phenomena."

3. These views on the historical character and the social conditionality of criminality imply as a consequence that only through the revolutionary overthrow of the exploiting order and the establishment of socialist power and production relations by the working class and the allies will it be possible to eliminate the main political, class-conditioned, and socioeconomic sources of criminality and thus to create the prerequisites for dislodging criminality from society. This task can only be accomplished if the conditions of the social alienation of man are abolished, the contradiction between individual and society is brought to a progressive solution, the antagonism of interests is replaced by a basic uniformity of interests, and relations among the working people come to include friendly cooperation and mutual assistance and respect.

According to its historical-social character, criminality is deeply alien to socialism. However, it still exists unavoidably, in the socialist order of society, as a relative mass phenomenon that does not disappear automatically with the abolition of its basic socioeconomic sources. Its complete abolition calls for changing, in a planned way, the complex of social living conditions determined by exploitation and the human personality shaped by those conditions. However, criminality is not the product of the socialist society.

Criminality in socialism is not identical with criminality in the exploitative social order, particularly capitalism; nor are the two comparable as to their essence. Rather, criminality in socialism is conditioned, on the one hand, by the external activities of the imperialist system and its attacks on socialism, which threaten peace and bear counterrevolutionary and interventionary character, and, on the other hand, by the lasting impact of relics of the exploitative order. Not only are these relics still inherent in the social reality of socialism, intellectually and materially, but they can be steadily infiltrated, preserved, and stimulated by surrounding capitalism.

Thus, criminality in socialism is extraordinarily tenacious. Surmounting it will not be possible "at one blow," or even within a few decades during which socialism is being constructed. Still, historically, criminality has tended to decline in socialist countries—although, of course, the trend is not a linear one. This decline shows that the maturing of socialist society brings about the political and economic, social and intellectual powers and conditions necessary for the liquidation of criminality in the classless communist society. The laws governing the all-round liberation and self-liberation of the working class and all working people from exploitation, oppression, and manipulation determine the laws underlying the combating and overcoming of criminality.

The politically organized working class is the only class that takes an interest in revealing unconditionally the sources and nature of criminality. Because of its historical role and position within society, the working class is the only class able to counteract criminality successfully because it carries in itself the strongest motive forces. With the socialist state, the working class has an outstanding instrument for organizing and planning, in the interest of all working people, the prevention and combating of criminality at the scale of the whole state and society. Through a coordinated effort, following a uniform concept and common directions, the organs of the socialist state power, the judicial and security authorities, the institutions of economic management, the social mass organizations, and the various honorary organizations of socialist democracy, built a broad democratic basis and social mass movement to drive back criminality. This process is considered a revolutionary change of social relations as well as of the way of life and the human personality.

In the German Democratic Republic, basic views that have been proved by history form the theoretical foundations for the strategy and tactics of the Marxist-Leninist party and the socialist state in preventing and combating criminality. These basic views determine the main direction of criminological research during the present stage in the shaping of the advanced socialist society.

STRUCTURE AND SOURCES OF CRIMINALITY

Although certain categories of crime, which are prototypical of the capitalist order of society, have been liquidated or considerably reduced and criminality as a social mass phenomenon has substantially declined, criminality continues to be a critical negative social phenomenon. In the past few years, more than 125,000 offenses were recorded on the average.[3] Criminality inflicts considerable material and ideological damage on society, represents a severe disturbance of the processes of social reproduction, and impedes the development of the socialist way of life and the creative powers of the people. Presently, the efforts made by the socialist society and its state power are directed against two main kinds of criminality which differ with respect to political, class, and socioeconomic aspects.

First, socialist society is struggling against so-called general criminality, which includes offenses against social and personal property, against the person, and against public order and safety, and other offenses that are considered "traditional" ones. Their main social source consists in the entirety of socially negative, selfish-individualistic, spontaneous-anarchic modes of conduct in differentiated solidification that are felt afterwards in society. These modes of conduct, which find certain material vestigial conditions for operation within the socialist society, are fostered by the external influence exerted by imperialism. These vestiges, particularly in the sphere of consciousness and conduct, include the appearance of individualism and selfishness, which find expression in greediness, a rage for enrichment and other excesses of bourgeois mentality, consumption fetishism, and anarchic practices for acquiring private property and speculative profit-making. Other vestiges include indifference, recklessness, and lack of cultural and educational needs, bureaucratic pathologies, and inattentiveness to the citizens.

The social weight and persistence of such relics of the liquidated social order ensue from various interrelated factors. Not only are these relics unpleasant consequences of capitalism, but also they emerged as a product and heritage of an exploitative society that lasted for centuries. During this long historical process, individualism, egoism, and the anarchic maintenance of one's own existence came to be considered basic and "eternal human" patterns of social conduct. These patterns deeply penetrated the consciousness, feelings, and customs of a lot of people, as well as practical social conduct and empirical living conditions. In this way, they are passed on socially and "transmitted," and thus have been regenerated and reproduced. In addition, these relics exist primarily as vestigial elements in man's everyday consciousness. This everyday consciousness has a special inertia. Particularly as far as its socially conservative and reactionary components are concerned, everyday consciousness largely has an elementary effect, develops without a more thorough intellectual processing, and is marked by no longer consciously reflected traditions, prejudices, ideas of value, and maxims of action, by the concrete empirical living conditions and experiences of individuals and social groups, by their everyday impressions and similar spontaneous-empirical influences. These historical, socio-psychological connections also explain the "relative independence" of vestigial elements of consciousness and conduct in the face of the developing socialist being.

In addition, the eradication of these relics is and will continue to be considerably hampered by influences originating with the imperialist system. The antisocialist policies of the ruling imperialist forces are aimed directly at preserving and stimulating these modes of thinking and conduct that are alien and hostile to socialism in order to disturb and undermine the socialist development politically, ideologically, and economically. With a tremendous economic and technological expenditure and the use of all means and forms of mass manipulation, these forces try to rear anticommunist feelings, denigrate the achievements of socialism, poison the socialist ideology and morale that are unavoidably spreading, and prevent the development of the socialist way of life. This ideological and psychological subversion continues without interruption through open and secretive methods that are regularly modified and adjusted. Mass communication, tourist and visitor traffic, and economic relations are deliberately used to extenuate demagogically the inhuman reality of the imperialist system. Indeed, they are used to conjure up the outer picture of a desirable "sound world" and to infiltrate the deteriorations of the bourgeois "quality of living" as ideals of conduct, thereby burdening and softening the new socialist forms of consciousness and living.

Second, socialist society is resolutely struggling against criminality of a peace-endangering and counterrevolutionary character. This criminality includes crimes that, according to international law, are punished as crimes against peace, war crimes, and crimes against humanity, as well as crimes of a counterrevolutionary-interventionist character committed against the workers' and peasants' power. This criminality is the most dangerous form of expression of imperialism itself. It aims at suppressing the worldwide struggle waged by the peoples for national and social liberation and self-determination, and at restoring the domination of monopoly capital in the states of socialism. This criminality expresses itself in political, economic, ideological, psychological, military, and other activities aimed at undermining, prejudicing, and hampering the socialist development of the state, as well as weakening the international prestige and position of the socialist community of states.

This criminality has its roots in monopoly capital's reckless race for super profit, a race that is regularly connected with expansion and aggression. Thus, crimes against the socialist order are instigated and launched from outside. In advanced socialist society, the internal social class foundations for such crimes have disappeared. Nevertheless, imperialism, by using its power apparatus, its secret services, agencies, and hacks, and by scrupulously undermining the positive results of relaxed tensions, tries to win the antisocialist elements that still exist here and there in the socialist society and to encourage them to perform counterrevolutionary actions. These elements create internal points of attack and support and, in doing so, use other criminal elements and criminogenic factors of general criminality.

This kind of criminality is vigorously rejected by the German Democratic Republic. Thus, she makes a valuable contribution to maintaining and developing productive relations, based on peaceful coexistence between states with different social orders; these relations are exraordinarily burdened by such crimes. She has to reject this criminality under the particularly difficult conditions, resulting from the fact that the two independent German-speaking states—the German Democratic Republic and the Federal Republic of Germany—confront each other with basically different social orders, and their frontiers represent the frontier between the two world systems—socialism and imperialism.

TASKS OF CRIMINOLOGISTS IN THE GDR

Criminologists, therefore, have the task of formulating more concretely and precisely those generally acknowledged findings on the sources of criminality under socialism and the conditions shaping the advanced socialist society in the German Democratic Republic.

In the first place, criminologists must investigate more thoroughly the dialectic between the basic processes of the development of the socialist society and the development of the socialist personality, and throw more light on the mediating links and spheres. From the criminological point of view, this means analyzing the concrete changing of the relics of a selfish-individualistic, spontaneous-anarchic character in the offenders' living conditions, mode of living, and personality, as well as the situations of conflict connected with those relics, disclosing the connection between the changing social conditions and the existence and effectiveness of these relics, and revealing the mechanisms whereby these relics are reactivated, reproduced, and transmitted to the rising generation.[4]

Criminal acts, like every empirical act, are socially mediated and determined in multiple ways. Three levels of mediation must be examined retroactively in time from the moment of the commission of the crime. One is the decision to commit a crime, connected with the personality of the offender as the point of transformation of the causes and conditions of criminality into concrete crimes. The second level is made up by the direct real social ties of the personality within the concrete historical social conditions, the channels by which social reality affects the personality in a more or less complete, differentiated, modified, or contradictory way. Finally, there is the entirety of the social and living conditions as objects of acquisition in their politico-ideological, socioeconomic, intellectual-cultural, and demographic relations; this level by no means must be left aside.

Research must be continued in two directions at the same time. The point is, first, to investigate all social processes and appearances that are both of criminogenic significance and of an anticriminogenic character, as well as the interrelation of these processes and appearances and the mechanism of their influencing criminality. Second, it is necessary to reveal the contradictory mechanism of anticriminogenic and criminogenic effects of social processes and appearances on the personality of the offender, and by means of them on the probability of criminality.

Such a differentiated criminological investigation into the operation of social and personal determinants of criminality, particularly with regard to some of the main phenomena, provides valuable points for starting a more purposive, differentiated program for preventing and combating criminality. These points consolidate the theoretical and practical foundations of a functioning stable system of crime prevention. That system is to be brought to bear on the general social and special criminological levels as well as on demographic structures and structures relating to specific relics.

MAIN DIRECTIONS OF PREVENTION

The advantage inherent in the nature of socialism—that is, the complex management and planning of the development of the whole society—lends a scientifically founded, planned, and organized character (based on practically proved findings as to the causes of criminality) to the process of pushing back criminality. It is possible to stipulate strategies and tactics to lend direction to the joint efforts of the society, state, and citizens, so that tasks with the greatest priority are accomplished with the greatest chance of success. In addition, the socialist society can specify the politico-ideological, economic, social, intellectual-cultural, technological, organizational, and legal measures that have to be taken in both a comprehensive and differentiated manner, either individually or in a favorable combination, at the generally social or specially criminological level, as well as the state or social organs that have to bear joint or specific responsibilities and the institution that is responsible for coordinating efforts.

The general basic directions of prevention also result from the basic structure of criminality in its two major groups. These general directions are inseparably linked to each other, condition each other, and grade into each other. They are the directions in which all state and social activities must be directed. What matters is for one to break up all hostile attacks against the socialist social, state, and legal order, to unmask indefatigably the destructive influences and subversive activities of the imperialist system, to expose and thus make people aware of the variants and modifications of imperialism's attempts at intervention and infiltration in order to strengthen vigilance, and to oppose the reactionary endeavors through a closed front of condemnation, disapproval, and rejection by the working people. At the same time, with the material and intellectual-cultural living standard rising, it is necessary further to increase socialist legal consciousness as an element of socialist ideology, to make safeguarding legality a firm part of all management activities, to develop social mass initiatives that will not only create an atmosphere of intolerance for violations of law and discipline, but also consolidate social relations and ties, strengthen friendly cooperation and the feeling of mutual responsibility, and encourage people to lend a helping hand to all men and leave nobody alone, particularly in situations of conflicts.

A more effective crime prevention calls for defining these general basic directions and their content more exactly, in order to focus energies on the "main links of the chain of prevention." Material problems with long-term character that go beyond one single sphere are:

1. To make the quality of the plans appropriate for developing the whole society, and to improve and enrich the uniform economic and social planning, by taking the effects of crime prevention into account when investigating the social consequences of economic and social decisions.

2. To surmount "subjectivism," resulting from the violation of democratic centralism and the principles of socialist economy and management, within the process of planning and fulfilling the plan, particularly in the lower economic units, and thus to overcome all of the negative consequences and destructive attitudes toward the plan, and as a result toward law, legality, security, order, and discipline, as well as toward one's own behavior.

3. To realize a many-sided and stringent accounting and control, as well as to safeguard the functioning of the control system, in the first place by means of utilizing effectively the material and financial funds of socialist property.

4. To eliminate certain phenomena encouraged by still existing limitations in the satisfaction of material needs; that is, the phenomena of unjustified granting or subreption of advantage and the abuse of bottlenecks in production, trade, and services.

5. To implement without compromising legality in the state and economic apparatus through a relentless stopping of all instances of bureaucracy and looseness vis-à-vis the rights of the citizens.

6. To develop socialist characteristics in the everyday working and living conditions of the people and in their collective forms of living; that is, in their working teams, learning groups, and residential areas, in matrimony and family, and in leisure groups and friendship relations.

7. To reduce the latency of criminal acts and other violations of law and discipline with a view to throwing them open to state and social reactions.

8. To develop consistent, quick, and differentiated responses to modes of conduct that are subject to criticism or contrary to discipline and law in order to prevent their being escalated to punishable acts and to prevent their negative influence as well as to develop activities directed at abolishing and preventing criminal endangering of society.

9. To strengthen the preventive educational effect of measures of criminal responsibility and of their implementation, and of the reintegration of released prisoners into society.

10. To develop comprehensively socialist legal consciousness; that is, to develop socialist attitudes toward law and legality by means of a purposive propaganda and educational effort within the framework of the politico-ideological work for educating socialist personalities.

The progress reached so far is marked predominantly by the fact that crime prevention, as the concern of the whole state and society, has been extended and the democratic foundations broadened considerably. Particularly on the general social level of crime prevention, two new factors, which condition each other, have gained in strength and have influenced the overall level of crime prevention.

First, local popular representative bodies on the district level have stipulated long-term tasks, for a prescribed plan period, that will further consolidate legality and more effectively prevent criminality and other violations of law. The working people participate directly in the elaboration of these tasks which are discussed in working teams and residential areas.

Second, a social mass movement has already developed, as a large number of working teams and residential areas, within the framework of the socialist emulation movement, strive for recognition as "Spheres of Exemplary Order and Safety." Such recognition also preconditions verifiable results in the field of crime prevention.

In the German Democratic Republic, the local popular representative bodies are responsible, to a considerable degree, for safeguarding legality and preventing criminality (Sections 2 paragraph 6; 34, 48, 68 of the Law of July 12, 1973, on the Local Popular Representation Bodies). The district assemblies have a qualitatively new legal responsibility by setting of long-term tasks. Decisions on long-term tasks are aimed mainly at integrating crime prevention, to a greater extent and in a binding way, into the prospective planning and management of economic and social development in the districts and at linking crime prevention more effectively with the politico-ideological process (controlled by the working-class party) of educating socialist personalities. The elaboration of long-term tasks for further consolidating legality and more effectively preventing criminality calls for a new approach, and for criminologists, too, it raises a number of theoretical and practical questions. These questions cannot be regarded as being answered at the moment initial decisions are made. The most difficult problems consist in determining what should be understood by long-term tasks, formulating the tasks to make them suitable for control and accounting, and obtaining the right concept from which to start.

On no account can these tasks proceed only or mainly from the extent, structure, and movement of violations of law, although a knowledge of them is an important prerequisite. What matters is to go more deeply into the systematically managed social processes and the material and intellectual-cultural changes in the working and living conditions of the working people. It is necessary to consider these processes and changes, which occur in the course of implementing the prospective plans, within the area that each task aims at, to display the actual and possible influence of these processes and changes on the social and legal conduct of men, and to derive from this influence the appropriate tasks and requirements for further strengthening legality and preventing criminality more effectively. These prospective starting points call for an improvement of the methodological instruments of criminological research. From the criminological aspect, this means deliberately intensifying the progressive anticriminogenic effects inherent in all socialist development processes, and minimizing and excluding the criminogenic by-effects connected with their uncertain outcomes and with the objectively and subjectively conditioned extent of their control. From state management and administration this requires an improvement in uniform economic and social planning so that the crime-preventive effect is considered, as far as possible, when the social consequences of economic or sociopolitical decisions are examined already before such decisions are taken.

Within the system of crime prevention, the objective collective forms of human life play an outstanding role. It is an established fact that the efficiency of crime prevention depends essentially on the socialist living standard obtained in working teams and learning groups, in families and communities, in leisure groups, and in friendship relations.

That is why the social initiatives and activities of the working people in their working and living environment are of extraordinary significance; their social initiatives and activities become manifest particularly in the mass movement for being recognized as "Spheres of Exemplary Order and Safety." Thousands of working teams strive to be awarded this title. This social mass initiative results from the need of adult working people for a legal, safe, orderly, and clean atmosphere in their working and living environment. They consider this environment to be part of the socialist way of life. This movement is, at the same time, proof of the citizens' increasing capability and readiness to contribute actively, through conscious, voluntary actions, to cultivating a general environment of social security of which legal safety is an element. Simultaneously, it shows the deep understanding of the relationship between effective crime prevention, on one hand, and a further increase in economic efficiency, an improvement in working and living conditions and in the psychological climate within the working team, and the unfolding of socialist democracy, on the other.

What is new with this social initiative is, first of all, that the citizens, in their working teams and residential areas, integrate the tasks they are to accomplish in consolidating legality and preventing criminal acts, as measures and obligations, into their socialist emulation movement. These measures and obligations, when integrated into the enterprise's programs for the socialist emulation, include the fulfilling of the plan terms and maintaining its quality, by taking care that the production processes proceed more smoothly, preventing disturbances of production, and safeguarding labor and health safety. These obligations also concern the prevention of fire and fire risks, safety within the enterprise, the protection of social property, and the disclosure and elimination of attitudes contradictory to the provisions of law and discipline, as well as the exercise of a more effective influence on those who have infringed law and discipline, the improvement of the working and living conditions, and active participation in the honorary working organizations that watch over the observance of socialist legality in various fields. The programs for socialist emulation in residential areas contain measures and obligations aiming at the consistent implementation of town or community statutes, securing fire protection, raising traffic safety, safeguarding public safety and order, assisting citizens who have been sentenced on probation or released from prison, and protecting social and personal property. Moreover, the programs cover measures and obligations in the field of legal education and propaganda and the acquisition of legal knowledge.

The activities always aim at concrete conditions, tangible behaviors, and attitudes, the promotion or liquidation of which corresponds to the direct interests and needs of the working people in the respective field. They thus yield directly noticeable benefit and advantage. This practice makes it possible to unite politico-ideological, economic, technical and technological, social, legal, and organizational measures serving crime prevention, to make these comprehensive measures understandable and clear to all the working people so as to enable the people to implement the measures in their working and living environment with expert knowledge.

The effectiveness of this mass movement is differentiated. Where it has been fully developed, concrete improvements have been achieved or initiated, and these improvements have been acknowledged as exemplary ones.

More favorable conditions are developing for joint work based on the division of labor among the deputies, members of the social courts (dispute commissions and arbitration commissions), lay judges and collectives of law judges, voluntary assistants of the People's Police, honorary working members of the Workers' and Farmers' Supervising Body, those responsible for labor safety and fire protection, the control guards of the Free German Youth, traffic safety groups, groups responsible for order and safety within the residential area committees of the National Front, and other honorary working organizational forms of socialist democracy which are increasingly coming to rely on and be closely linked with the judicial and security organs.

The county councils, together with the county organs of the Confederation of Free German Trade Unions and the National Front of the German Democratic Republic, have worked out uniform minimum criteria for the recognition of exemplary spheres so as to make the tasks more concrete and their fulfillment measurable. Greater importance is attached to the appropriate ideal and material acknowledgment of working people's performances in the consolidation of legality and crime prevention. Thus, the social mass initiative represents a qualitatively new stage in the conscious appropriation and utilization of socialist law by the working people, in their education and self-education to strictly observe laws, safety, order, and discipline. This mass initiative is another proof of the vitality of socialist democracy in everyday work and life, of its immediate effect on all working people. It is ample proof of the dialectic unity of socialist legality and socialist democracy. The connection between long-term tasks, prospective management, and social mass initiative gives fresh impetus to the efficiency of the system of crime prevention and also fecundates the specialized criminological prevention. One of the most important tasks of criminologists continues to be the analysis of the extensive effects of this development.

MANAGING AND PLANNING RESEARCH

The comprehensive character of the objects and tasks of socialist criminology makes great demands on the scientific qualification of criminologists. No criminologist, however, can be expected to master all scientific disciplines and complexes of problems contiguous to criminology. Experience shows that a criminologist can develop as a scientist only if he is also an expert in one of the basic sciences. Thus, criminologists are products of the specialization of interested and capable lawyers from various branches of law; that is, they are criminalists, sociologists, psychologists, or pedagogues, all of them having completed corresponding university studies. It is to their advantage if they already have practical experiences in their professions and fields of specialization. Thanks to this composition of criminologists, the necessary scientific comprehensiveness and collectivity resulting from the object and tasks of criminology are being taken into account. Thus, the theoretical and practical efficiency of criminology is being influenced in a positive manner.

These statements reveal that criminology, as a subject of teaching, can be drafted only in the form of specialized studies that continue and supplement the basic studies of a special branch of science. At present, specialization within the framework of training in the field of state and law is still dominant. However, the emphasis is shifting to corresponding fields of study. Great attention is being given to the dissemination of basic criminological knowledge to today's and tomorrow's practitioners, who perform various functions in all spheres of social life and bear specific responsibility in the area of crime prevention. For that reason, selected criminological topics have been included in the curriculum of political studies at the Academy of State and Law. Criminological aspects have also become more important in the postgraduate training of state and economic functionaries and of judicial and security personnel. This development enhances the unity of theory and practice that is the fundamental principle of socialist criminology and that also determines the management and planning of criminological research.

In charge of criminological research is the Council of Research in the field of state and law of the German Democratic Republic's Academy of Sciences. In addition to other groups, a Crime Prevention and Combating Crime Working Group belongs to this council. This group is made up of university teachers from the corresponding disciplines who work at scientific institutions engaged in problems connected with criminality, as well as leading representatives of organs with a special responsibility for preventing and combating criminality. The group discusses the most important research findings, debates basic theoretical and practical questions regarding the more effective prevention and combating of criminality, exchanges information about international development tendencies, discusses key issues of future research, and coordinates the main complex projects of research in the interest of concentrating scientific ability. Thus, the Working Group performs a special coordinating function. Its composition favors interdisciplinary research and ensures the close affiliation of theory and practice. It also facilitates a survey of the points of contact with research complexes of other branches of science and, theoretically, an integration of the specific research projects into a more general interrelationship.

Influencing the efficiency of criminological research in an outstanding way is the general procurator of the German Democratic Republic, who, according to Article 97 of the constitution, directs the struggle against criminal acts. A department within his office carries out criminological investigations. The criminal statistics kept at the General Procurator's Office form an indispensable basis for criminological research. At the same time, the General Procurator's Office provides criminologists with comprehensive empirical sources for theoretical generalization and good conditions for practical investigations. Because of his specific responsibility, the general procurator gives extraordinarily valuable suggestions and provides an orientation for research planning in the field of criminology.

The Working Group elaborates proposals on long-term research tasks and submits them to the council. When they are confirmed, these long-term research tasks become part of the prospective plans of social sciences; these plans cover a period of five years each. They form the binding basis for the annual research plans of the scientific institutions concerned. Hence, criminological research is directed on the principle of democratic centralism. In this way, scientific integration is linked with deepening specialization, rational concentration with the necessary division of labor, and theoretical progress with practical efficiency. At the same time, the continuity of the development of socialist criminology is being secured.

NOTES

1. E. Buchholz, R. Hartmann, J. Lekschas, and G. Stiller, *Sozialistische Kriminologie, ihre theoretische und methodologische Grundlegung* [Socialist Criminology, Its Theoretical and Methodological Foundation], 2d enlarged ed. (Berlin: Staatsverlag der Deutschen Demokratischen Republik, 1971), pp. 52-66.

2. J. Lekschas, J. Renneberg, et al., *Lehrbuck Strafrecht—Allgemeiner Teil* [Compendium Criminal Law—General Part] 2d revised ed. (Berlin: Staatsverlag der Deutschen Demokratischen Republik, 1976), pp. 31-35.

3. *Statistisches Jahrbuch der DDR* [Statistical Yearbook of the GDR] (Berlin: Staatliche Zentralverwaltung für Statistik, Staatsverlag der Deutschen Demokratischen Republik, 1979), p. 379.

4. W. Hennig and J. Lekschas, "Das historisch bedingte Wesen der Kriminalität und Grundlinien kriminologischer Forschung in der DDR" [The Historically Conditioned Character of Criminality and Basic Lines of Criminological Research in the GDR], *Staat und Recht* 26, no. 11 (1977):1147-1156.

BIBLIOGRAPHY

Bley, G., and G. Lehmann. "Zum Wesen, Inhalt und Begriff der Rechtserziehung" [On the Character, Content and Concept of Legal Education]. *Staat und Recht* 23, no. 1 (1974):68-80.
The authors analyze the state of legal education that has been achieved in theory and practice. They discuss a definition of legal education and outline its aim and content.

Buchholz, E., R. Hartmann, J. Lekschas, et al. *Sozialistische Demokratie, ihre theoretische und methodologische Grundlegung* [Socialist Criminology, Its Theoretical and Methodological Foundation]. 2d enlarged ed. Berlin: Staatsverlag der Deutschen Demokratischen Republik, 1971.
This book is a collective work by leading GDR experts in the fields of criminal law theory and criminology. It is the first summary of the theoretical foundations of perspectives on the social nature and grounding in historical conditions of criminality in socialism.

Buchholz, E., and H. Harrland. "Gedanken zur Kriminalitätsvorbeugung" [Thoughts on Crime Prevention]. *Neue Justiz* 31, no. 11 (1977):321-325.
The authors explain the major tasks of crime prevention, emphasizing the integration of these tasks into the comprehensive social development process.

Buchholz, E. "Die Bedeutung der Durchsetzung der sozialistischen Gesetzlichkeit (insbesondere durch die Tätigkeit der Justizorgane) für die Entwicklung der sozialistischen Rechtsbewusstseins und für die Borbeungung und Bekämpfung der

Kriminalität" [The Importance of the Enforcement of Socialist Legality—Particularly Through the Activities of the Judicial Organs—for the Development of Socialist Legal Consciousness and for Preventing and Combating Criminality]. *Wissenschaftliche Zeitschrift der Humboldt-Universität zu Berlin*, no. 1 (1978):57-60.
The actual enforcement of socialist legality pivots on the development of socialist legal consciousness. What matters here is first and foremost the development of legal convictions, of the ability and readiness to abide by the laws in a more responsible manner. In addition to order and safety, an important prerequisite is the consistent realization of the individual's legal responsibility.

Daehn, U., and J. Renneberg. "Sozialistische Strafpolitik und Aufgaben der Forschung" [Socialist Penal Policy and Research Tasks]. *Staat und Recht* 25, no. 4 (1976):398-407.
The authors elaborate on the tasks of science and research in shaping and implementing socialist penal policy in its struggle against criminality. They assess the GDR's penal policy and its principles that are generally binding.

Daehn, U., J. Renneberg, and H. Weber. "Kriminalitätsbekämpfung und die Rechte der Bürger im Sozialismus" [Crime Combating and the Rights of the Citizens in Socialism]. *Staat und Recht* 26, no. 2 (1977):117-125.
This contribution focuses on the relationship between an effective crime prevention and the safeguarding of the citizens' rights and interests that are protected by law.

Dettenborn, H., and H. J. Föhlich. *Psychologische Probleme der Täterpersönlichkeit* [Psychological Problems of the Offender's Personality]. Berlin: Staatsverlag der DDR, 1971.
The authors examine the psychological aspects of the offender's personality from the angle of the sources of criminality and its effective prevention.

Dettenborn, H., and K. A. Mollnau. *Rechtsbewusstsein und Rechtserzierhung* [Legal Consciousness and Legal Education]. Berlin: Staatsverlag der DDR, 1976.
This work is the first in the GDR to offer a comprehensive presentation of the conclusions of empirical investigations into the problems of legal consciousness and legal education.

Friebel, W., K. Manecke, and W. Orschekowski. *Gewalt- und Sexualkriminalität* [Violent and Sexual Criminality]. Berlin: Staatsverlag der DDR, 1970.
The sources of these two categories of offenses are summarized, along with the problems of prevention and control.

Harrland, H. *Imperialismus als Quelle des Verbrechens* [Imperialism as a Source of Crime]. Berlin: Staatsverlag der DDR, 1972.
The author reveals the sources, structure, and movement of criminality under imperialism; he treats the effects on socialist society.

Harrland, H., and W. W. Klotschkow. "Sozialistische Integration und wissenschaftliche Forschung zu Problemen der Kriminalitätsbekämpfung" [Socialist Integration and Scientific Investigations in the Problems of Crime Combating]. *Neue Justiz* 29, no. 15 (1975):439-443.
Here attention is focused on the development and bases of international scientific coopera-

tion of socialist countries in crime research. The authors particularly consider the key tasks of joint research into criminality.

Harrland, H. "Zu einigen Aspekten der Kriminalität und ihren Ursachen" [On Some Aspects of Criminality and Its Sources]. *Neue Justiz* 31, no. 6 (1977):159-165.
In elucidating certain theoretical aspects of the sources of criminality in capitalism and in socialism, the author underlines the basically different structures of criminality in these two social systems.

Hartmann, R., and J. Keschas. "Kriminalitätsursachen und Probleme der Kriminalitäts-bekämpfung in der DDR" [Sources and Problems of Crime Combating in the GDR]. *Abhandlungen der Akademie der Wissenschaften der DDR*. Berlin: Akademie-Verlag, 1976.
The authors define the Marxist-Leninist positions vis-à-vis the sources of criminality in socialism in conflict with the views of bourgeois ideologists. Statements are made concerning methods of research into the sources of criminality.

Henning, W. "Zu einigen Grundfragen jugendkriminologischer Forschung in der DDR" [On Some Basic Questions of Research in the Field of Juvenile Delinquency in the GDR]. *Staat und Recht* 23, no. 2 (1974):290-305.
A critique is offered of theoretical positions in research into the sources of juvenile delinquency. Possibilities of future such research in the GDR are also considered.

Henning, W., and J. Lekschas. "Das historisch bedingte Wesen der Kriminalität und Grundlinien kriminologischer Forschung in der DDR" [The Historically Conditioned Nature of Criminality and Basic Lines of Criminological Research in the GDR]. *Staat und Recht* 26, no. 1 (1977):1147-1156.
Beginning with a discussion of the nature and sources of criminality in the advanced socialist society, the authors present a number of new findings and methodological suggestions.

Kraeupl, G., et al. "Rückfallkriminalität" [Recidivist Criminality]. *Wissenschaftliche Beiträge der Friedrich-Schiller-Universität*. Jena: Fischer-Verlag, 1978.
This contribution contains the results of representative investigations carried out by criminologists, criminal experts, and criminal lawyers of the GDR and the People's Republic of Poland on the problems of recidivist criminality.

Lehmann, G., and J. Renneberg, et al. "Gesellschaftliche Grundlagen und Wesen der Kriminalitätsbekämpfung und -vorbeungung und das System ihrer Leitung in der entwickelten sozialischen Gesellschaft" [Social Foundations and Nature of Crime Combating and Prevention and the System of Their Control in the Advanced Socialist Society]. *Aktuelle Beiträge der Staats- und Rechtswissenschaft*. Potsdam-Babelsberg: Akademie für Staats- und Rechtswissenschaft der DDR, 1971.
Findings arrived at so far are summarized in regard to the nature of criminality, as well as in regard to the sociopolitical bases, organizational principles, and forms of crime prevention in the socialist society.

Lehmann, G. "Zu einigen theoretischen und praktischen Problemen der Kriminalitätsvor-beungung" [On Some Theoretical and Practical Problems of Crime Prevention]. *Staat und Recht* 27, no. 10 (1977):922-935.

The author expresses ideas on the possibilities of planning and management for crime prevention in residential areas.

Lehmann, G., and J. Renneberg. "The Development of a Complex System of Crime Control and Prevention in the German Democratic Republic." *Law and Legislation*. Berlin: Association of German Democratic Lawyers, 1970. Pp. 16-34.
With a view toward accomplishing crime prevention in the overall state and social form, the authors elaborate on the tasks, working mode, and cooperation of the various state and social bodies.

Lehmann, G. "Grundlagen der Leitung und Planung des vorbeugenden Kampfes gegen die Kriminalität" [Foundations of Directing and Planning the Struggle to Prevent Criminality]. *Staat und Recht* 20, no. 3 (1971):447-461.
The article deals with the vital elements of central planning and management in crime prevention as they relate to public participation.

Lehmann, G., and H. -J. Schultz. *Ordnung und Sicherheit im sozialistischen Wettbewerb* [Order and Safety in the Socialist Emulation]. Berlin: Staatsverlag der DDR, 1975.
The character, content, and efficiency of the social mass movement are summarized. The movement is directed at consolidating legality, safety, and order as part and parcel of socialist emulation within work teams and in residential areas.

Lehmann, G., and H. -J. Schulz. "Zur Rolle der Arbeitskollektive bei der weiteren Festigung der Gesetzlichkeit, Ordnung, Sicherheit und Disziplin" [On the Role of Work Teams in Further Consolidating Legality, Order, Safety and Discipline]. *Staat und Recht* 25, no. 2 (1976):154-162.
The authors define the qualitative characteristics of socialist work teams and point to the outstanding role that is being played by these teams in preventing punishable acts and educating offenders.

Lehmann, G., et al. "Zum Entwicklungsstand der marxistisch-leninistischen Theorie der Vorbeungung der Kriminalität im Sozialismus" [On the State of Development of the Marxist-Leninist Theory of Crime Prevention in Socialism]. *Aktuelle Beiträge der Staats- und Rechtswissenschaft*. Potsdam-Babelsberg: Akademie für Staats- und Rechtswissenschaft der DDR, 1971.
The paper systematically presents views on the theory and system of crime prevention in socialism.

Lekschas, J., and J. Renneberg. *Lehrbuch Strafrecht, Allgemeiner Teil* [Compendium Criminal Law, General Part]. 2d ed. Berlin: Staatsverlag der DDR, 1976.
This compendium is the first systematic presentation of the GDR's criminal law theory. In this context, the sources of criminality are characterized from the perspective of the principles of socialism.

Lekschas, J. "Einige theoretische Fragen der sozialistischen Rechtserziehung in ihrer Bedeutung für die Vorbeugung und Bekämpfung der Jugenkriminalität [Some Theoretical Questions of Socialist Legal Education and Its Significance for Combating Juvenile Delinquency]. *Staat und Recht* 25, no. 3 (1976):267-275.

The author probes the essence, sources, and typical phenomena of the distorted legal consciousness of young offenders, as well as some specific measures to shape socialist legal consciousness.

Lekschas, J. "Entfaltung der sozialistischen Lebensweise und Vorbeugung der Kriminalität in der DDR" [Development of the Socialist Way of Life and Crime Prevention in the GDR). *Sitzungsberichte der Akademie der Wissenschaften der DDR, Gesellschaftswissenschaften.* Berlin: Akademie-Verlag, 1977.
The development of the socialist way of life is related to the reduction of criminality.

Orschekowski, W., et al. *Kriminalitätsvorbeugung und -bekämpfung im Betrieb* [Preventing and Combating Criminality in Enterprises]. Berlin: Staatsverlag der DDR, 1974.
This paper is the first integrated presentation of crime prevention in socialist enterprises. In regard to special offenses, the responsibility for crime prevention is placed clearly with enterprise managers and work teams.

Schlegel, J., et al. "Wirksamere Bekämpfung und Verhutung der Jugendkriminalität" [More Effectively Combating and Preventing Juvenile Delinquency]. *Neue Justiz* 30, no. 2 (1976):33-64.
The author particularly elaborates the role of penal law and penal legislation in the prevention of juvenile delinquency.

Streit, J. "Aktuelle Fragen der Leitung und Planung des vorbeugenden Kampfes gegen die Kriminalität [Topical Questions of Directing and Planning the Struggle to Prevent Criminality]. *Staat und Recht* 20, no. 3 (1971):438-446.
The general procurator of the GDR emphasizes the increased responsibility of the public prosecutor's office in the sphere of crime prevention. He particularly points to the need for close cooperation between that office and the local popular assemblies and the working people. He calls for further work on the basic theoretical problems of crime prevention.

Streit, J. "Zu einigen theoretischen und praktischen Fragen des Kampfes gegen die Kriminalität" [On Some Theoretical and Practical Questions of the Struggle against Criminality]. *Neue Justiz* 27, no. 5 (1973):129-134.
The author investigates the sources of criminality and the development of criminality at the socialist stage of development of the communist society. He presents conclusions on more effective prevention and management of criminality.

Szewczyk, H. *Kriminalität und Persönlichkeit, Psychiatrisch-psychologische und strafrechtliche Aspekte* [Criminality and Personality. Psychiatric-Psychological and Criminal Aspects]. 2d ed. Jena: Fischer-Verlag, 1974.
From the psychiatric-psychological point of view, the author deals with some problems of the sources of criminal behavior that are related to the offender's personality and to the criminal personality.

12

FEDERAL REPUBLIC OF GERMANY

Günther Kaiser

Although the Federal Republic of Germany, like other countries, has no uniform definition of criminology, it at least has reached the consensus that criminology is an empirical science dealing with crime, the criminal, and crime control, at least insofar as criminal sanctions and the prognosis and treatment of the law-breaker are concerned. There is also agreement that criminology encompasses alcoholism, asociality, public nuisance, prostitution, and suicide, as long as these concerns are not taken to claim the entire sociological field of deviant behavior—a field often criticized as too large and vague.

Disparate views on criminology exist mostly in regard to the function and efficiency of criminological theories, interdisciplinary orientation, and the scope and definition of deviant behavior outside the criminal law. Furthermore, there are disagreements as to whether criminology should emphasize studies into the criminal personality; into the "dark field" of crimes outside the scope of official statistics; and into practical crime control issues such as personnel selection in police departments and criminalistics. Criminological research itself raises disputes about the value of empirical experience, about the tasks the researcher may properly undertake, and about the functions criminological research can reasonably be expected to serve in criminal justice administration and/or society at large.

New sources of controversy have arisen over the introduction of the "labeling" or "social reaction" approach of criminal sociology which has focused new attention on the definition of crime, the patterning of behavior, and the efficiency of social control through use of the criminal law. As a result of these discussions, the subject matter of criminology has been extended beyond research into crime, the criminal personality, and the relationship between the criminal and the victim of crime. Now the subject matter also encompasses the overall social control system in analyses of changes in the conceptions of crime (criminalization), the far-ranging environment within which efforts toward crime reduction must operate, and the mechanisms outside the scope of criminal law employed to control other antisocial behavior. Today only psychiatrists and sociologists challenge the idea of criminology as a separate field. In earlier years, criminologists took a more restricted view of the proper boundaries for their research. Even then, however, the research interests of Exner[1] exceeded the boundaries implied by his definition of criminology.

The main object of criminological research is to gain a firm base of reliable knowledge about problems related to crime, criminals, and crime control. Through research into a variety of topics, criminology explores the relationships among the scientific concepts and organizations, respectively, that characterize its particular field of endeavor. As is true of all scientific fields, the availability and relevance of data are crucial to criminology as a science, but the purposes of criminology go beyond capitalizing on the central registration of basic information, an advantage the Federal Republic shares with other European jurisdictions. Moreover, in addition to pure basic research, the criminologists of the Republic pursue applied criminological work on the problems related to the prognosis of the offender's probable future behavior, the relative value of various criminal sanctions, the efficiency of the sanctions, and strategies for organization. Because of the difficulties of concurrently following basic and applied research, practice and science have to a large extent gone their separate ways in West Germany. The definition of purposes for criminological research must include goals for its future development, but the definition does not necessarily accurately describe the present nature of criminological work in the Federal Republic of Germany.

LEGAL AND SOCIAL FRAMEWORK OF RESEARCH

By understanding the legal and social framework of the given country, we are in a better position to evaluate its progress in criminological research and the significance of its research contributions. The penal reaction to deviating behavior is determined by the basic principles of the liberal state's rule of law because criminal law constitutes the strongest degree of state intervention and because the rule of law also sets limits on this form of intervention.

The German Penal Code of the Reich of 1871 was conceived in terms of offense-related and retaliation-oriented substantive law. In any discussions of reforms of the code, the principle of guilt as a statutory rule for the legal protection of the citizen's sphere of freedom and as a means of curbing the state's authority has never been seriously called into question.[2] In fact, the revision of the penal code, which probably put the most emphasis on rehabilitating the offender, stipulated that the lawbreaker "is subject to the state power of sentence only to that measure as is appropriate to his individual degree of guilt."[3] Consequently, one can understand that the indeterminate prison sentence did not find acceptance in German criminal law (with the exception of the juvenile penal law; see Section 19 JGG). It should be noted here that in the Federal Republic of

Germany, in contrast to several other states, the prosecution and the police are expected to prosecute all criminal acts as a general principle.

More recently, the Marburg Program set up by von Liszt[4] has influenced the criminal law of the Federal Republic in the direction of utilitarianism as a rationale for rehabilitating offenders. The acceptance of this approach toward penal reform has been revealed by changes in the administration of sanctions: the reduction of prison sentences generally, and, in particular, greater use of fines in lieu of short-term imprisonment; greater use of sentence remission and probation; and the establishment of social-therapeutic units in correctional institutions.

In the Federal Republic of Germany, the basic socioeconomic structure is that of a highly industrialized society characterized by large population concentrations, weakened family ties, and vulnerability to economic crises. The stock of motor cars has increased by leaps and bounds in the Federal Republic as evidence of prosperity; perhaps even more significantly, the remarkable dependence on motor cars is associated with other developments that have criminological importance. Fatal traffic accidents are high compared to those of other nations. Increased sensitivity to pollution of the environment has brought demands for controls. Rapid mass transportation has given greater opportunities for economic criminality, traffic in drugs, and terrorism.

INSTITUTIONALIZATION OF CRIMINOLOGICAL RESEARCH

Conflicts and competing claims between the empirical sciences and the legal scholars have retarded the development of criminological research in the Federal Republic of Germany. Of equal importance have been the qualitative changes since 1945 in the relative emphasis placed on differing bodies of theory and in the organizational structuring of research.

Until World War II, two patterns were dominant. Most of the research was represented by clinical, forensic-psychiatric, and prison-psychiatric contributions that were based largely on case studies or on small samples. The second pattern involved criminal-statistical studies conducted by lawyers. Then, most criminological research followed the genetic, bioconstitutional, and psychopathological approaches and employed multifactorial analyses.

The redirection of research after World War II can be examined in terms of two phases. During the 1950s, the first impulse was implemented chiefly by dissertations in law schools dealing for the most part with juvenile delinquency. Now that this first postwar trend can be evaluated as a whole and from a long-run perspective, this "pace-making" research in juvenile delinquency appears to lack sufficient impact. Only later were the information and concepts of Anglo-American criminal-sociology to be imported and to effect their stimulation of criminology here. The impact of a number of empirical analyses on criminal procedures also came at a later date. In this preliminary stage, criminologists had to practice

"with their hands tied"[5] because the institutionalization of criminological research had not yet received real recognition.

Not until the early 1960s were professorships in criminology established and
research centers either set up or given sufficient resources. Only then was it
possible to employ library resources and research assistants in long-term criminological investigations, and only then could empirical investigations be done on a
team basis beyond the capacity of one individual researcher. In the 1970s, more
criminological research centers and additional directions for research were created. The German Research Association (Deutsche Forschungsgemeinschaft) set
up the key program "Empirical Criminology" (later broadened toward more
inclusive criminal sociology) within the scope of its supported research projects;
from this program a new and widely effective impulse sprang. Only in the later
1970s did independent research staffs and a certain degree of research pluralism
appear as the prerequisites for organized criminological investigations. In other
words, a number of research centers and research groups had been created, and a
number of publications organs had come into existence. Very different disciplines had established means of cooperation, and receptivity to modern techniques of empirical social research had been shown.

In West Germany, criminological research centers and institutional concentrations are located largely within the university system. After the first specifically
criminological professorship was established at the University of Heidelberg in
1959 and after a subsequent period of stagnation, the number of criminological
professorships increased considerably in the early 1970s. The subject matter of
criminology—together with juvenile penal law and corrections—was made an
optional subject for the law student's first examination administered by the state.
Since then, all universities have offered special courses in criminology in greater
numbers. In the winter term of 1964-1965, courses in criminology covering
forty-four lessons a week were offered at twenty German universities; one decade later, the corresponding statistics were thirty-three German universities and
343 lessons a week, including courses in juvenile penal law and corrections.
Today universities that offer criminology courses average fourteen lessons per
week in a term. Twenty years ago, Anglo-American literature was scarce in the
Federal Republic; now various technical libraries offer a considerable number of
volumes. The concentration of criminological holdings in the Tübingen library is
especially remarkable.

In the nonuniversity area, criminological research has encountered comparatively greater difficulties in establishing an institutionalized form. The Max
Planck Institute for Foreign and International Criminal Law in Freiburg now
includes a criminological research unit dedicated to investigating area by area the
entire system of crime control, the constituent elements of crime, and the individuals affected by its decision-making processes. Along this line, the research
unit has adopted an interdisciplinary orientation and a commitment to searching
critiques.

Among research projects in police agencies, special notice should be given to the Academy for Leading Police Staff (Polizeiführungsakademie) in Hiltrup and, most of all, the Federal Criminal Investigation Office (Bundeskriminalamt). The Bundeskriminalamt has an interdisciplinary group of about twenty researchers who carry out studies in criminalistics; the extent, structure, and development of crime; criminal-phenomenological problems; the criminal; the victim of crime; and societal reactions following breaches of law.

The institutionalization of criminological research within the judicial system has been planned for a long time and has had its first tangible result in the creation of the Planning and Research Section within the Ministry of Justice of Land of Lower Saxony. This group will eventually have a staff of twelve members focusing on research into crime that will overlap the field of corrections (especially investigations into the behavior of justice officials) and the field of correctional planning which lends substance to and complements the measures taken by the courts.

For a considerable time proposals have been offered for the establishment of a criminological center that would be supported by two levels of government, the Bund and the Laender. The task of the institute will be to "promote criminological research, to elaborate criminological data, and to make available to research the legislature, the administration of justice and other administration authorities."[6]

The above report on the development of research institutions appears to be encouraging, but we must recognize that much of the resources and staff are involved in teaching and administrative support and, thereby, are diverted from research per se. With this personnel removed the situation is less promising. Only some fifty graduate research scientists work exclusively within the criminological research area, whereas a total of 100,000 scientists work in the research and development areas in the Federal Republic of Germany. We can take some comfort, however, in Szabo's estimate[7] that about 1,500 full-time workers are active in criminological research in the whole world.

The annual cost of all criminological research in the Federal Republic comes to about 5 million German marks, most of which is for salaries. The German Research Association probably contributes less than half of this amount. The budgets of the different Laender finance most of the remainder. The Max Planck Society, the Volkswagen Foundation, the ministries of several Laender, and the Federal Ministries of the Republic furnish minor amounts.

The major part of institutionalized criminology is found within the faculties of law and medicine because traditionally they have had prime influence on German criminology. This pattern is being broken to some extent by the presence of more psychologists and sociologists than medical men and lawyers in the key programs of the German Research Association. The research projects reported in "Research into Law Relevant Facts and Criminology" (Rechtstatsachenforschung und Kriminologie)[8] convey an idea of the wide spectrum of disciplines participating in criminological research. In contrast to other disciplines, *the* profession of a criminologist does not exist; there is no agreement on the basic features of a criminologist's job description in the Federal Republic, as perhaps in most other countries. In criminal justice practice situations call for more criminological knowledge than personnel are likely to have, but the delineation of special work positions for criminologists per se has not been accomplished. This lack of market demand explains the absence of any special criminological study program culminating in the awarding of a university degree or diploma.

The development of criminology curricula has proceeded to the greatest degree for lawyers within the scope of university education. Within the basic disciplines associated with criminology (in particular sociology and psychology), only specific aspects are taken from overall criminological research, formulated into topics, and then taught to students. Of considerable importance to strengthening instruction are those research institutions that involve scientists drawn from various disciplines who encourage and criticize one another and that involve a considerable number of students in differing curricula in the examination of criminological problems and research strategies. It is difficult, however, to recruit scientists who are prepared to undertake long-term activity within these institutions in spite of the raising of the professional status of criminologists in the last ten years. Because of the shortage of skilled researchers, recruitment from other disciplines is essential to criminological research institutions. The scientist qualified for effective teaching and research continues to have favorable opportunities in his own disciplinary field and therefore has less incentive to specialize in criminology.

CRIMINOLOGICAL ASSOCIATIONS
AND PUBLICATIONS

A survey of criminological research in the Federal Republic of Germany must include at least the most important associations and institutions that deal with criminological problems.

In 1977, the Society for Comprehensive Criminology (Gesellschaft für die Gesamte Kriminologie)—formerly the Criminal-Biological Society (Kriminal-biologische Gesellschaft)—observed its fiftieth anniversary at its nineteenth congress in Bern. The primary objective of this association is to hold workshops for interested scientists, especially practitioners, on acute criminological problems, including possible solutions.

The German Criminological Association (Deutsche Kriminologische Gesellschaft) regularly organizes workshops, and since 1964 has awarded a Beccaria Medal for distinguished service in the field of criminology.

The Study Group of Young Criminologists (Arbeitskreis Junger Kriminologen) was founded at the end of the 1960s in order to improve the exchange of information among criminologists, integrate criminological research into different disciplines, and avoid excessive restrictions on the boundaries of criminology. This group followed a trend which is also evident among the criminologists of Anglo-America and Northwestern Europe. In the early 1960s, the group reformulated its program to be a critique of society in the fashion of critical criminology in seeking an ideology opposing "old" or "traditional" criminology.

In the Federal Republic of Germany, other associations and societies dealing with criminological problems are the German Association for Juvenile Courts and Juvenile Court Aid (Deutsche Vereinigung für Jugendgerichte und Jugengerichtshilfen), the German Association for Preventive Crime Control (Gesellschaft für Vorbeugende Verbrechensbekämpfung), the German Society for Forensic and Social Medicine (Deutsche Gesellschaft für gerichtliche und soziale Medizin), and the German Society for Sexual Research (Deutsche Gesellschaft für Sexualforschung). In addition, criminological research and theories are discussed at most meetings of sociologists and psychologists.

That criminological research has become more firmly institutionalized during the last ten years is demonstrated by the increase in criminological publications. Available censuses of criminological research projects and documentation by the Federal Ministry of Justice of criminological and legal research list three hundred projects previous to the 1970s. According to the Council of Europe, since 1970 about nine hundred research projects have been registered and 10 percent of these projects have been in the Federal Republic of Germany. If research productivity is compared with the total population, the rate for the Federal Republic is double that for all countries in the Council of Europe. If the rate is based on the total gross national product, the Federal Republic has a threefold advantage. However, a more meaningful comparison would be based on projects brought to completion; there is probably a 50-percent mortality in this regard. It is not clear which completed projects have had real impact in advancing the purposes of science or in increasing public knowledge. The findings of many projects are disseminated only among a limited number of scholars. However, the range of dissemination has been extended in the last ten years by the publication of ten German education manuals of criminology and a considerable number of monographs and handbooks.[9]

TRENDS INDICATED BY CRIME REGISTERS

Crime statistics do not present a complete and reliable picture of criminality, but the registration of offenders is an indispensable resource for research in West Germany. These official statistics are used to outline the scope, structure, and changes of criminal behavior.

Since the early 1970s, between 2 and 4 million crimes have been committed annually, or approximately 5,400 cases per 100,000 inhabitants (5,355 in 1977). If traffic offenses are also taken into account (these are not registered in the above statistics), the annual figure is about 4 million. As is true for all of Middle and Western Europe, only half of all criminal offenses result in police action. The police identify only about 1.2 million suspects of crime annually, about 380,000 of whom are ultimately convicted in the courts.

Through the crime registers, we can trace the number of persons convicted of a felony for the first time by age. By the age of twenty-four years, one-third of the total male population has been punished by a court at least once. Among women of the same age, the corresponding figure is only 4.1 percent. In the population as a whole, it is estimated that between 18 and 25 percent have been convicted of a felony.

Many kinds of deviant behavior are reported to the police and result in some type of disposition. What is the relative importance of the various kinds of offenses? In recent years, about half of the dispositions have been traffic offenses because of the growing number of automobiles, the large number of fatal accidents and injured persons, and the substantial material damage caused by traffic accidents. In spite of general prosperity since 1945, property offenses have increased, reaching more than 2.3 million infringements in 1977. Property offenses make up 80 percent of all offenses reported to the police, if traffic offenses are not considered. As in most industrial countries, the Federal Republic has suffered increasingly serious problems of automobile theft and larceny. These delinquencies are examples of prosperity-related criminality in contrast to crime produced by economic distress. They have registered the highest increases, namely a 565-percent increase since 1955. Whether the worldwide economic crisis of the 1970s, including increased unemployment, affected crime trends is the subject of future research.

The anonymity of urban life appears to be reflected in crimes against property, particularly shoplifting, traffic offenses, and willful damage to public property by juveniles. The damages inflicted in all conventional property crimes are estimated to be between 10 and 60 thousand million German marks per annum in the Federal Republic of Germany. In contrast, it is estimated that in 1977 a total of 4.5 thousand million German marks of damage was inflicted by offenders of high social status. The financial cost of their transgressions was approximately one-third of the total damage caused by conventional property crimes.

Drug abuse in the Federal Republic of Germany has also increased considerably since the end of the 1960s, although the absolute number of registered suspects is relatively small. In 1977, a total of 35,876 drug offenses were registered in the Federal territory; in 1967, the total was 1,226 cases. Nevertheless, empirical investigations on drug abuse among juveniles indicate that fewer than 10 percent of all drug addicts and barely 2 percent of all drug consumers are likely to be registered.[10] The most striking change in drug criminality has been the proportion of all drug offenses perpetrated by minors. In earlier years, this share was small, but in the 1970s it rose to two-thirds of all such offenses.

Crimes of violence have great influence on the feeling of safety among a people. Whether or not crimes of violence as a whole have become more serious cannot be assessed because, within this general category, opposing trends are found for the offenses that fall under "crimes of violence." For instance, the number of robberies and the "inflictions of grievous bodily harm" increased in recent decades, whereas during the last five years the cases of criminal homicide and rape have declined perceptibly.

How do crime trends in the Federal Republic since World War II compare with trends in other industrial nations? The number of property offenses and crimes of violence has increased, and the number of sexual offenses and other offenses against personal reputation has decreased in the Federal Republic, Great Britain and Wales, France, Italy, and Switzerland. Compared with fifteen other countries in Western Europe, the Federal Republic of Germany stands in the lower middle range of increase in general crime rates. The nations exhibit a considerable and similar increase in registered crimes perpetrated by youthful offenders and by juvenile gangs. All countries have experienced significant increases in shoplifting, larceny of objects of art, terrorism and political violence, economic criminality, and traffic offenses. However, it can be assumed that in Europe, unlike North America, organized criminality is still of little importance. The rate of female criminality has remained relatively constant, an astonishing finding in light of the considerable social changes of the last decade.

FUTURE COURSE OF CRIMINOLOGY

The setting up of several research centers and research groups and the availability of various publication organs simplify the description of criminological research in the Federal Republic. A survey of criminology in the Federal Republic is complicated by the range of traditional disciplines, such as legal science, medicine, and psychiatry, that are involved. Difficulties are to be expected in interdisciplinary research, and these difficulties have not yet been overcome. Energetic efforts have been made to accommodate social-pathological and social-medical viewpoints, but even greater difficulties are ahead if multiple-factor analyses are to incorporate juridical-medical and sociological concepts. It is especially important that progress be made in criminology which confronts a growing hegemony of claims made by several sciences and a rejection of the interdisciplinary approach by many sociologists. Furthermore, analysis of the contemporary state of criminology in the Federal Republic of Germany must await the results of several research projects.

Nevertheless, when we consider the poor status of research in the 1960s and the handicaps that had to be overcome in initiating viable research, a positive assessment must be made of the accomplishments of the last ten years. In the early 1960s, the general concern was "that German criminological research not only might have lost its former leading position but also might run the danger in missing its connection to international criminological research."[11] This pessimism can be countered by progress made in institutionalizing criminology and opening up new horizons by adopting research perspectives suggested by Anglo-American criminology. Before further documentation of these favorable signs for criminology in the Federal Republic of Germany, some cautions against excessive optimism must be raised.

In spite of the quality of several research works, overall the results have been rather poor and meager, being related to narrow and restricted areas of criminology. We cannot expect epoch-making, or even outstanding, findings.

Rapid advancement in criminological research is particularly difficult in light of the social and political implications of crime analysis and the rapid change in scientific methodologies in the humanities, social sciences, and behavioral sciences when compared with medicine and the natural sciences. There are deficiencies in the formulation of theories, and there is hesitation about undertaking applied research for fear of being suspected of "excluding theory." Paradoxically, in an era when the merger of theory and practice is popular, the gap between practice and science has become even wider.

Traditional concepts and research methods have come under unprecedented scrutiny. As has become increasingly clear, mere refinement of statistical analysis is not the antidote for methodological weaknesses. Phenomenological and participant-observer approaches have challenged the research methods which "traditional" criminologists have accepted without question. The criticisms have been constructive, but they have sometimes been expressed as if *all* previously established conclusions should be rejected. Of particular importance to criminology has been the sweeping rejection of all elements in the criminal law by some critics. Skepticism is a characteristic of science but—along with the ideals of humanism, equality, freedom, and justice—the values implied by efforts to control crime are elements of the human condition.

In expressing their reservations about the technocratic model of science, some younger scientists pursue their sociological examination of power and authority as elements in the study of crime through critiques of crime control administrations that sometimes express disillusionment without the benefit of intimate knowledge of the conditions of such administration. Gaps and tensions exist between practice and science with the structures of each because these respective fields have their own problems to solve. Yet, the potential for conflict also holds the possibility for cooperation that will be fruitful for both because a willingness to challenge previously accepted ideas has become increasingly prevalent.

These developments among criminologists in West Germany have been matched by developments in human activities that are appropriate topics for investigation. Persons who were previously viewed as socially integrated individuals are being recognized as potential lawbreakers. The boundaries of investigation proper for criminology are being extended by such phenomena as new consciousness of the implications of Auschwitz as the so-called final solution of the Jewish question, of white-collar crimes, of the association between rising traffic delinquency and motorization, of the rapid increase in juvenile criminality, and, finally, of the growing problems of unreported crimes.

Criminological thinking appears to be undergoing what Kuhn[12] has described as a paradigm revolution. In the late 1960s, criminological discussions in the Federal Republic, as elsewhere, produced fundamental and vehement disagreements that mirrored issues raised by the labeling approach and by "new," "critical," or "radical" criminology. In one view, we should speak of "disconcerted criminology" tossed to and fro by its critics, but, beneath this turmoil, criminology in the Federal Republic has shifted its focus of research from the biocriminal approach to criminal-psychological, social-psychiatric, and criminal-sociological viewpoints. Beyond that, in criminology, as in numerous social sciences and humanities, the comparative analysis is of growing importance, although a concerted plan of research is still very rare. One of the few examples of well-planned comparative research is the investigation conducted in Stuttgart and Zurich through interviews of crime victims based on a questionnaire already used in North American research.[13] Comparative data were furnished as to victimization, willingness to report crimes to the police, fear of crime, and estimates of the amount of crime in large cities of the Federal Republic, Switzerland, and the United States. Furthermore, the Council of Europe has pressed for the integration of European criminological research activities.

Criminological thinking has become more dynamic and more "interactionist" in its basic terms, approaches, and empirical research. This trend has focused attention on questions regarding the relationships between the criminal and the victim, relationships between unreported crimes (the "dark field") and reported crimes, patterns of police behavior, patterns of prosecutorial discretion, private crime control, and terrorism. Criminologists in the Federal Republic have become more aware of the need for investigations into minorities in the broad sense of homeless persons, mental patients, "public nuisance" offenders, juvenile delinquents, and offenses of foreign workers. The phenomenological approach has been applied to drug criminality, violence, sexual and traffic offenses, and economic crimes.

A wider collection of sociological concepts, such as social control and socialization, is being applied in investigations of types of offenders who have been studied by criminologists for many decades. Longitudinal investigations are still being made into the personality of lawbreakers and into prognoses of their probable future behavior. Research in the field of corrections is not new, but it has taken a new direction recently by testing various modes of correctional treatment and their effectiveness. The later effort has been dampened by recognition of the methodological difficulties—also observed in other countries—raised by the self-fulfilling nature of rehabilitative purposes, and the inefficiency of penal treatment in general. The methodological difficulties, however, give more incentive to designing investigations that would provide reliable empirical foundations for criminal policy. This incentive manifests itself in the key program, Empirical Research into Criminal Sanctions—Procedure, Execution of Sentence, Effects, and Alternatives, set up by the German Research Association, which contributes financially to independent and continuous criminological research.[14]

Ideally, empirical research in the Federal Republic will be initiated at crucial decision-making points in framing criminal policy and in implementing the policies. Perhaps, the decision-makers will recognize the need for this research and will initiate demands that it be conducted. Legislators establish legal norms and sanction systems; judges fix sentences and have key functions in the administration of procedures. Their participation is vital if various reforms are to be inaugurated: decriminalization of minor offenses, provisional detention subject to early release when appropriate, greater use of noninstitutional corrections and monetary fines, greater services for offenders placed on probation, and so on. There is a place for research into the cost-benefits of various sanctions and procedures, already used or now proposed. Empirical studies into the many aspects of general crime prevention have not been sufficiently pursued in the Federal Republic of Germany.

SUMMARY: RESEARCH AND CRIMINOLOGY

It is no longer possible to restrict attention to criminal-oriented analysis. Criminology has now become a larger "science of actualities" shaping the criminal law, with the integration within criminology of legal sociological questions. The so-called labeling, or social reaction, approach has been very influential in extending the field of vision.

The previous dominance of personality-oriented criminology has been reduced in West Germany, but this form of investigation does have a place for cultivating official regard for social equality and rational but humane treatment by recognizing the uniqueness of each personality, including that of the criminal.

Finally, current trends are toward polarization, politicization, and social criticism in society generally and in criminology particularly. Examination of the problems of crime and crime control makes political implications evident in a world that has experienced a high rate of social change since 1945. A practice-oriented and politically aware criminology has much to offer in the Federal Republic of Germany, as elsewhere, if the critiques of contemporary criminology are to avoid sterile polarization.

NOTES

1. F. Exner, *Studium über die Strafzumessungspraxis der deutschen Gerichte* [Study on the Practice of German Courts as to the Fixing of Penalties] (Leipzig: Wiegand, 1931); Exner,"Kriminalistischer Bericht über eine Reise nach Amerika" [Criminological Report on a Journey to America], *Zeitschrift für die gesamte Strafrechtswissenschaft* 54 (1935):345 ff., 512 ff.; Exner, *Kriminologie* [Criminology] (Berlin: Springer, 1949).

2. See H.-H. Jescheck, *Lehrbuch des Strafrechts* [Textbook on Criminal Law], 3d ed. (Berlin: Duncker und Humbolt, 1978).

3. C. Roxin, "Strafrecht und Strafrechtsreform" [Criminal Law and Criminal Law Reform], in J. Baumann (ed.), *Programm für ein neues Strafgesetzbuch* (Frankfurt-Munchen: Fischer, 1968), pp. 75-92.

4. F.v. Liszt, "Der Zweckgedanke im Strafrecht" [Utilitarian Thinking in Criminal Law], in V. Liszt (ed.), *Strafrechtliche Aufsätze und Vorträge*, Vol. 1 (Berlin: Guttentag, 1905), pp. 126-179.

5. K. S. Bader, "Stand und Aufgaben der Kriminologie" [State and Tasks of Criminology], *Juristenzeitung* 7 (1952):17; H.-E. Brauneck, "Der junge Jurist und die Kriminologie" [The Young Lawyer and Criminology], *Juristische Schulung* (1966):222.

6. G.-R. Oberthur, *Kriminologie in der Strafrechtspraxis* [Criminology in the Practice of Criminal Law] (Stuttgart: Enke, 1976), p. 83.

7. D. Szabo, *Criminologie et politique criminelle* [Criminology and Criminal Policy] (Paris-Montréal: Vrin, et al., 1978), p. 151.

8. O. Hartwig, Bundesministerium der Justiz (ed.), *Rechtstatsachenforschung und Kriminologie* [Research into Law Relevant Facts and Criminology], 2d ed. (Bonn: Bundesanzeiger Verlagsgesellschaft, 1978).

9. In this respect, see the bibliography that follows.

10. Among others, see H. Gulzow, *Drogenmissbrauch und Betäubungsmittelgesetz* [Drug Abuse and Law Relating to Narcotics] (Heidelberg: Kriminalistik, 1978).

11. W. Roth, "Das Projekt einer Kriminologischen Zentralstelle von Bund und Ländern" [The Project on a Criminological Center of the Bund and Laender], *Kriminologische Gegenwartsfragen* 11 (1974):201-204.

12. Th. Kuhn, *Die Struktur wissenschaftlicher Revolutionen* [The Structure of Revolutions Within the Sciences] (Frankfurt-München: Suhrkamp, 1973).

13. E. Stephan, *Die Stuttgarter Opferbefragung: Eine kriminologisch-viktimologische Analyse zur Erforschung des Dunkelfeldes unter besonderer Berücksichtigung der Einstellung der Bevölkerung zur Kriminalität* [Inquiry into Victims of Crime in Stuttgart: A Criminological-Victimological Analysis for Research into the "Dark Field" Under Special Consideration of the Population's Attitude Towards Crime] (Wiesbaden: Bundeskriminalamt, 1976).

14. G. Kaiser, et al., "Antrag auf Einrichtung eines DFG-Schwerpunktes: 'Empirische Sanktionsforschung—Verfahren, Vollzug, Wirkungen und Alternativen' " [Application for Setting Up a Key Program of the German Research Association: "Empirical Research into Criminal Sanctions—Procedure, Corrections, Effects and Alternatives"], *Monatsschrift für Kriminologie und Strafrechtsreform* 60 (1977):41-50.

BIBLIOGRAPHY

Since an exhaustive listing is not possible in this limited space, the following works were selected to suggest the flavor of criminological literature in the Federal Republic of Germany. The items are grouped according to some of the major functions served in the literature as a whole.

Textbooks in Criminology

Brauneck, A. -E. *Allgemeine Kriminologie* [General Criminology]. Reinbek: Rowohlt, 1974.

Eisenberg, U. *Einführung in die Probleme der Kriminologie* [An Introduction to the Problems of Criminology]. München: Goldmann, 1972.

Göppinger, H. *Kriminologie* [Criminology]. 3d ed. München: Beck, 1976.

Herren, R. *Lehrbuch der Kriminologie* [Textbook on Criminology]. Vol. 1. Freiburg: Rombach, 1979.

Kaiser, G. *Kriminologie. Eine Einführung in die Grundlagen* [Criminology. An Introduction to the Foundations]. 4th ed. Heidelberg-Karlsruhe: Müller, 1979.

Kaufmann, H. *Kriminologie I, Entstehungszusammenhänge des Verbrechens* [Criminology I, Coherences of the Beginning of Crime]. Stuttgart: Kohlhammer, 1971.

Mergen, A. *Die Kriminologie. Eine systematische Darstellung* [Criminology. A Systematic Presentation]. 2d ed. (München: Vahlen, 1978.

Schneider, H. -J. *Kriminologie: Standpunkte und Probleme* [Criminology: Points of View and Problems]. 2d ed. Berlin: de Gruyter, 1977.

Reference Works

Kaiser, G., F. Sack, and H. Schellhoss (eds.). *Kleines Kriminologisches Wörterbuch* [Small Criminological Dictionary]. Freiburg: Herder, 1974.

Sieverts, R., and H. -J. Schneider. *Handwörterbuch der Kriminologie* [Manual Dictionary on Criminology]. 2d ed. Berlin: de Gruyter, 1966.

University Education

Berckhauer, F. "La situation de la criminologie dans l'enseignement universitaire de la République Fédérale d'Allemagne" [The Situation of Criminology in University Education in the Federal Republic of Germany]. *Revue internationale de criminologie et de police technique* 28 (1975):281-287.

Kreuzer, A. "Zur Lage des Wahlfachs 'Kriminologie, Jugendstrafrecht, Strafvollzug' im juristischen Studium und Referendarexamen" [As to the Situation of the Optional Subject "Criminology, Juvenile Penal Law, Corrections" Within the Law Study and the First State Examination]. *Juristische Schulung* 19 (1979):526-532.

Contributions of the Disciplines

Dechêne, H. Ch. *Verwarhlosung und Delinquenz. Profil einer Kriminalpsychologie* [Demoralization and Delinquency. Profile of a Criminal-Psychology]. München: Fink, 1975.

Opp, K. -D. *Abweichendes Verhalten und Gesellschaftsstruktur* [Deviant Behavior and Social Structure]. Darmstadt-Neuwied: Luchterhand, 1974.

Sack, F. "Probleme der Kriminalsoziologie" [Problems of Criminal-Sociology]. In R. König (ed.). *Handbuch der empirischen Sozialforschung*. Vol. 12: *Wahlverhalten, Vorurteile, Kriminalität*. 2d ed. Stuttgart: Enke, 1978. Pp. 192-492.

Wiswede, G. *Soziologie abweichenden Verhaltens* [Sociology of Deviant Behavior]. Stuttgart: Kohlhammer, 1973.

Criminological Research

Hartwig, O., Bundesministerium der Justiz (ed.). *Rechtstatsachenforschung und Kriminologie. Empirische Forschung in Zivil- und Strafrecht* [Research into Law Relevant Facts and Criminology. Empirical Research into Civil Law and Criminal Law]. 2d ed. Bonn: Bundesanzeiger Verlagsgesellschaft, 1978.

Johnson, E. H. "Comparative and Applied Criminology at the Max Planck Institute in Freiburg." *International Journal of Comparative and Applied Criminal Justice* 3 (Fall 1979):131-141.

Kaiser, G. *Stand und Entwicklung der kriminologischen Forschung in Deutschland* [State and Development of Criminological Research in Western Germany]. Berlin-New York: de Gruyter, 1975.

Kaiser, G., and Th. Würtenberger (eds.). *Criminological Research Trends in Western Germany*. Berlin: Springer, 1972.

Kerner, H. -J. "Fear of Crime and Attitudes Towards Crime: Comparative Criminological Reflections." *International Annals of Criminology* 17, nos. 1 and 2 (1978):83-99.

Tiedmann, K. "The International Situation of Research and Legal Reform Work in the Field of Economic and Business Crime." *International Annals of Criminology* 17, nos. 1 and 2 (1978):51-67.

Issues of Practice

Kaiser, G., H. -J. Kerner, and H. Schöch (eds.). *Strafvollzug, Eine Einführung in die Grundlagen* [Corrections. An Introduction to the Foundations]. 2d ed. Heidelberg-Karlsruhe: Müller, 1977.

Kaufmann, H. *Kriminologie III, Stravollzug und Sozialtherapie* [Criminology III, Corrections and Social Therapy]. Stuttgart: Kohlhammer , 1977.

Kube, E., and G. Steinhilper. "Police Research in the Federal Republic of Germany." *Police Studies* 1, no. 3 (New York: Jay Press, 1978). Pp. 11-16.

13

GHANA

D.N.A. Nortey

Since attaining political independence in 1957, the Republic of Ghana has not had sufficient time to merge the traditional and the modern into a distinctive culture. The national identity has encouraged the convergence of various subcultures toward the building of new political, educational, economic, and religious institutions.

Because Ghana is a nation in the process of "becoming," its criminology is expected to be marginal as a discipline and as an occupational field. The closest approximations of full-fledged criminologists are those sociologists who instruct courses in related topics but who identify with sociology. Very little criminological research has been accomplished. Criminal justice practitioners usually regard criminology as having little relevance to their work.

As discussed below, the low priority given criminology may be explained as the result of allocating scarce resources to the gigantic problems of nation-building. Nevertheless, the social-economic-political conditions of an emergent nation, the social history, the combination of divergent ethnic groups, and the appearance of crimes previously unknown—all of these elements of nation-building make contemporary Ghana a fascinating site for criminological investigations. These opportunities for investigations in themselves justify the inclusion of Ghana in this volume.

THE LAND, THE PEOPLE, AND HISTORY

The Republic of Ghana is located on the west coast of Africa. It covers an area of 239,460 square kilometers with a tropical equatorial climate. The mean monthly temperature ranges between 86°F and 79°F. The vegetation is tropical forest stretching from the west coast up to the midlands. Part of the eastern belt is covered with Guinea savanna and woodland. The vegetation of the northern belt is open savanna, fire-swept grassland. Along the coast the vegetation is scrub, grass, and mangroves. The major rivers are the Volta, Ankobra, Densu, and

Afram. The Volta Hydroelectric Project with an ultimate output of 768 kilowatts provides power for domestic and industrial use throughout the country. The project provided the largest manmade lake in the world, 250 miles long and occupying 3,275 square miles. The main harbors are at Tema and Takoradi.[1]

Almost all Ghanaians are Sudanese Africans, although Hamitic strains are common in North Ghana. The area has been peopled for seven hundred to one thousand years.[2] Most ethnic groups moved in from the north; a few probably came from the east. Among the ethnic groups from the north are the Guans, Rantis, Ashantis, Akims, Kwahus, and Twis. The Ewe and Ga-adangbe came from the east.

The 9.6 million Ghanaians today are divided into five principal ethnic groups, distinguished by linguistic affinities, the "possession of common cultural attributes, and, to some extent, by one myth of origin."[3] These groups are also distinguishable by their social organizations. The main groups are the Akan, Ga-adangbe, Ewe, Guan, and Gur-speaking people. The Akan, who form about 43 percent of the total population, consist of the Ashanti, Fanti, Kwahu, Akim, Nzima, Ahanta, and Akwapim. The Ga-adangbe (9.4 percent) are made up of the Ga, Krobo, Shai, Ada, and Adangbe. The Ewe (14.5 percent) exhibit a large measure of cultural and linguistic homogeneity. The Guan people (2.2 percent) were the earliest migrants. The Gurma and Togo tribes form 1.1 percent; the Mole 12.8 percent; and the Grusi 4.8 percent.[4]

Most contemporary inhabitants claim to have migrated from the ancient Ghana Empire when it was conquered by Mali. The defeated people moved south in the forest belt; later, some settled on the coast.

The Portuguese were the first Europeans to reach the gold-producing areas in the south between the Ankobra and Volta rivers. They named the country Mino, meaning "mine," and the French who came later called it Côte de l'Or, or the Gold Coast, a name the English were to adopt for the whole country. The Gold Coast was first discovered by Europeans in 1471. The lucrative trade in gold and slaves attracted other European nations, notably the Dutch, English, French, Danes, Swedes, and Germans. By the middle of the eighteenth century, strong rivalry for trade developed among the Europeans. By the beginning of the nineteenth century, only the British, Danes, and Dutch were operating on the Gold Coast, with the British controlling about half the trade. Later, the Dutch and Danes sold out to the British and withdrew in 1850 and 1872, respectively. Foreign traders were followed by missionaries who sought to convert and educate the people.

The abolition of the slave trade and increased missionary activities brought revolutionary changes in the nature and scope of European activities on the Gold Coast in the nineteenth century. The British pushed inland and started trading in gold, palm oil, rubber, and cocoa. Some Africans became educated Christians and even ministers of religion, school teachers, lawyers, journalists, and politicians. The British government took direct control from the trading companies to forestall the revival of the slave trade. On March 6, 1844, the government concluded a treaty with coastal chiefs that made the coastal zone the British colony of the Gold Coast. The British waged a series of wars against tribes to the north of the colony and finally defeated the warlike Ashanti in 1901. In 1902, three Orders-in-Council linked the conquered territory of Ashanti and the Protectorate of the Northern Territories. After World War I, in 1919, part of Togoland which had been a German colony was annexed to the Gold Coast under the mandate of the League of Nations.

Because of the economic, social, and political developments, classes of educated Africans emerged. Their awareness of the oppressiveness and limitations of the colonial regime marked the rise of African nationalism. Evolutionary processes culminated in the political independence on March 6, 1957, of the Gold Coast which was the first British colony in Africa to become sovereign. Under the new name of Ghana, it became a republic within the British Commonwealth on July 1, 1960.

Since 1957, Ghana has had three constitutions. The Independence Constitution of 1957 was based on the Westminster parliamentary form of democracy. A Republican Constitution replaced the British monarch as head of state with an elected president when promulgated in July 1961. Following a coup d'etat, the country was ruled by an army junta from 1966 to 1969. Another short-lived attempt at parliamentary democracy in 1969 was overthrown by another coup d'etat on February 24, 1972. A new army junta, the National Redemption Council (NCR)—which later became the Supreme Military Council (SMC)—took over the government to rule by decrees for seven years. The present constitution is based on the executive presidential system.

SOCIAL STRUCTURE OF GHANA

Ghana's social structure consists of two closely interwoven sectors, namely, the traditional and the modern. The dividing line between the two sectors is literacy. No one lives solely in one sector because each sector impinges on the other.

The traditional Akan culture and social organization are very influential. The Akan constitute the largest ethnic group and have played an important role in the development of modern Ghana. Their complex political organization was adopted, mostly through conquest, by the other ethnic groups.

The social structure was woven around intricate systems of kinship ties. In practice, the Akan social and political organization was based on the principles of the unilateral matrilineage and the territorial unit of the nucleated village. The society had a tripartite system of stratification: the royal lineage (the founding lineage of the village), commoner lineage or lineages (those who arrived later), and slave lineages (descendants of slaves captured in war). Important political and social roles were open to only limited numbers of individuals on the basis of sex, age, and lineage membership.

The traditions produced a variety of ethnic groups that refutes any claim of one

Ghanian culture, but the colonial history and more recent processes of modernization suggest an incipient common culture. The most significant sector of influence is political in the efforts to minimize ethnic differences.

Ghana has a central government headed by an executive president and a national assembly of 140 parliamentarians. Election is by universal adult suffrage. The country is divided into nine administrative regions. Regional, district, and local councils handle parochial administration.

Ghana is predominantly an agricultural country; about two-thirds of its people live in rural areas. Its main exports are cocoa, logs and sawn timber, gold, diamonds, bauxite, and manganese. Certain sectors of the economy are controlled exclusively by the state; some are joint state-private enterprises; and others are private enterprises. The country has many untapped natural resources. With the aid of foreign capital, light industries have been established. Industrialization has spurred rapid growth of towns. In the urban centers, kinship ties—the kingpin of the traditional social structure—are yielding to other types of associational ties. Modern occupations have given rise to marked differences in styles of life among people, and a class structure based on achievement is emerging.

The most important basis of stratification is education, creating an elite class of bureaucrats, business executives, professionals, and technicians. Ghana has many educational institutions. It has three universities: the University of Ghana at Legon-Accra, the University of Science and Technology at Kumasi, and the University of Cape Coast at Cape Coast. There are 6,684 primary schools, 3,607 middle schools, 149 secondary schools, 15 technical schools, 3 polytechnical colleges, and 59 teachers' training colleges.[5] The state subsidizes these institutions. In addition, there are a number of private educational institutions. The literacy rate in 1971 was estimated at 53 percent for males and 34 percent for females.[6] English is the official language, but certain indigenous languages—Twi, Ga, Fante, Ewe, Nzima, and Dagbani—are written and spoken.

Religion has also had a significant role in the social evolution. Traditional religion—ancestral worship and cults—is losing ground to Christianity and Islam. The 1970 census reported the following distribution: Christians 50 percent, Muslims 20 percent, and other faiths 30 percent.

CRIME: EFFECTS OF SOCIAL TRANSITION

Sweeping political and economic changes have upset the social structure. Traditional social controls have been more or less replaced by modern statutes and regulations. Secular government has supplanted the authority of traditional rulers. Formal education which was designed to turn out white-collar workers has led to mass unemployment among school dropouts and frustration among unemployable youth. Socioeconomic conditions place a high premium on material acquisition. Aspirations exceed the ability of many to achieve.

General Crime Trends

The impact of far-reaching social and cultural changes is expressed in a greater volume of crime.[7] In 1960, the total number of recorded crimes was 58,381.[8] The number rose to 99,649 in 1970, an increase of 70.7 percent. The 1960 rate was 862 cases per 100,000 in the general population, and the 1970 rate showed an increase to 1,157 cases per 100,000. A disproportionate "share of the increase in crime is attributable to young adult males in urban centers," according to Robert Seidman and J.D. Abaka Eyison.[9]

The rate of population growth was between 2.6 and 3.0 percent,[10] while the mean growth rate in the volume of crime was about 6 percent a year. Population growth alone probably does not account for the greater incidence of crime. It is more promising to look at greater police activity and to the effects of urbanization. During the period under consideration, the rate of urbanization was 5 percent a year.

The strength of the police force increased from 6,212 in 1960 to 16,358 in 1970, an increase of 163 percent. In 1960, there were ninety-two officers per 100,000 in the general population and 190 officers per 100,000 in 1970, an increase of 107 percent. Similarly, the number of police stations and posts rose from 267 to 449, an increase of 68 percent.

As elsewhere, the majority of recorded crimes in Ghana are offenses against property, especially stealing and related offenses. The average annual shares of the three main categories were crimes against property, 46 percent; crimes against persons, 40 percent; and crimes against the public order, 14 percent. The average rates of annual growth for these categories, respectively, were 7.9 percent, 8.3 percent, and 7.0 percent.

Crimes against Property

Petty thefts and stealing as a means of livelihood accounted for the largest share of crimes against property and 36.5 percent of all recorded crimes in 1970. The average value of property stolen was less than $50. About two-thirds of offenders who appeared before juvenile courts were charged with stealing.

Receiving stolen goods, being on premises for unlawful purposes, and possessing housebreaking tools collectively accounted for 7.1 percent of recorded crime and 15.3 percent of offenses against property. Arson and damage to property were only 4.2 percent of offenses against property.

There was a low incidence of the most serious property crimes—robbery, burglary, and house- and storebreaking—less than 1 percent of offenses against property. (More will be said about robbery later.) Fraud, falsification of accounts, and forgery were involved in only 503 recorded cases for the entire decade.

Crimes against Persons

Criminal harm, assault, and rape were involved in 33.2 percent of recorded crimes, second only to petty thefts in 1970. These three offenses accounted for 82.4 percent of all crimes against persons.

Another category of crimes against persons included attempted suicide, abortion, threats, insults, and intentional libel; they represented 16.3 percent of offenses against persons.

Murder, attempted murder, and manslaughter (unintentional homicide) accounted for less than 1 percent of crimes against persons. The annual rate was about three per 100,000. On the whole, homicide is a minor problem in Ghana, probably because among most ethnic groups spilling of blood upon the "sacred earth" is abhorred.

Abduction, child stealing, and slave dealing account for less than 1 percent of crimes against persons—a rate of about two per 100,000 population. Throughout the decade, only eleven cases of slave dealing were recorded.

Offenses against the Public Order

Riots in Ghana occur mainly during disputes over tribal leadership and occasionally during labor unrest. Ethnic confrontations are rare because of patterns of accommodation and cooperation among groups. Interethnic marriages also reduce tensions. Student riots are rare but have increased recently; they do not usually create serious public disturbances.

Offenses against the public order accounted for only 14 percent of recorded crimes, at a rate of 140 per 100,000 in 1970. Riot and unlawful assembly accounted for less than 1 percent of recorded crimes.

Counterfeiting is even less significant because of limited access to the means to commit this crime. Publication of obscene literature is also rare.

Prostitution and kindred offenses occupy a small share of official statistics, but these data give an especially distorted picture. Prostitution by itself is not a crime in Ghana; it is the supporting services like keeping brothels, soliciting, and pimping which constitute crimes. Between 1962 and 1966, the recorded cases increased by 50 percent when Ghana had a female minister of social welfare who instructed the police to conduct a strong campaign against vice. The police rounded up prostitutes in raids on places of entertainment, brothels, and drinking bars.

Corruption, extortion, and unlawful gambling represented 5.6 percent of crimes against the public order. Of the three offenses in this category, unlawful gambling accounted for 41 percent of such crimes.

NEW KINDS OF CRIME

As for the emergent nations of Africa generally, Ghana is an apt case study of the effects of the erosion of the traditions of rural-oriented tribal cultures, of very rapid urbanization, and of the rise of indigenous power elites. Here are opportunities to look into the etiology and nature of political corruption and white-collar offenses as they appear in an emerging modern society and where such offenses have been at least unusual. Armed robbery in Ghana also affords a case study of conditions favoring the greater prevalence of violent crime.

White-Collar Crimes

Formerly unknown in Ghana, white-collar crimes have now become common. During the colonial era, foreigners held the top positions in government, trade, commerce, and industry. They have been replaced because of the government's policy of Ghanaianization and the departure of many foreigners.

In trying to follow the life-style of foreigners, the new bureaucrats soon discovered that legitimate means and traditional kinship obligations barred them from the life-style they desired. Kinship obligations require that they support members of the extended family. Since their regular salaries are insufficient to meet the heavy costs, they have been pressed to find other avenues for augmenting their incomes, including exploitation of their official positions through political corruption.

Politicians, bureaucrats, business executives, and the top echelon of industry and commerce became rich in a short time. The gap between the new elite and ordinary persons widened. From time to time, the government set up committees and commissions to investigate malpractices and to examine the assets of politicians and individuals holding high public office.[11] These investigations revealed that most of the wealth acquired by the new elite class was accumulated through fraudulent means. Monies were extorted from government contractors; civil servants took bribes for performing duties; individuals and business firms made false financial declarations to evade taxes; firms underinvoiced imports to reduce the duties or overinvoiced to allow them to transfer monies out of Ghana illegally.

White-collar crimes were not limited to men at the top. In keeping with the process of differential association, junior officials follow the example of their bosses. Some act as agents of their bosses in collecting bribes and receive commissions from the illicit gains. To curb these offenses, the government has passed laws authorizing confiscation of illegally acquired assets, compulsory refund of embezzled monies, and imposition of prison sentences.

Currency Trafficking

Another emergent crime is currency trafficking which was unknown under the British administration because, then, individuals and companies were free to take money out of the colony.

In the early 1960s, the new government realized that the country was not earning enough foreign exchange to meet developmental needs. It imposed restrictions on the amount of money individuals could take out of the country.[12]

Importation of foreign goods also was restricted to conserve foreign exchange earnings, but individuals and firms were allowed to bring in goods without import licenses under Special Unnumbered License (SUL).

An illegal market in foreign currencies arose to meet the needs of persons who wished to travel abroad and to serve firms and individuals wanting to import goods under SUL. Foreign travelers and Ghanaians who go abroad take advantage of the situation in spite of stringent regulations. Illegal currency trafficking is an important cause of the high rate of inflation in Ghana because individuals bring scarce goods in for sale at exorbitant prices.

Smuggling

Smuggling in and out of Ghana has increased to such an extent that it is a major organized crime and the government has declared it to be a treasonable offense.[13] Crime syndicates are based in Ghana and in the neighboring countries of Togoland, Ivory Coast, and Upper Volta.

The many bush paths into neighboring countries cannot be patrolled effectively, and some border guards are bribed. Large trucks carry Ghana's cocoa, timber, and rice across the borders almost daily without hindrance.

Apart from the smugglers' desire to obtain foreign currency, the official prices paid for these goods in neighboring countries are comparatively higher than those in Ghana. Smugglers also make huge profits in Ghana from the sale of scarce or contraband goods. Even fishermen prefer to sell their catches in the Ivory Coast and Togoland.

Armed Robbery

In the mid-1960s, armed robbery emerged as a result of the unstable political and socioeconomic conditions following the first coup d'etat after independence.[14] Some measures taken by the junta to resuscitate the economy led to mass unemployment. Furthermore, the junta granted amnesty to political and criminal detainees who had been imprisoned without trial. On their release, the criminals found that they risked a small chance of apprehension because the police and army were concentrating then on political security. Predatory crime, especially armed robbery, became flagrant.

When the crimes reached alarming proportions, the government created a special strike force of armed army and police personnel. The arming of the strike force led robbers to arm themselves. They became more violent and vicious and began to operate in organized gangs recruited from the large number of unemployed persons in desperate need of money.

In the years 1966 to 1972, armed robbers raided banks and trucks conveying goods. At times, whole neighborhoods or villages were attacked and looted. Robbers used firearms to frighten victims and to defend themselves. Their operations were carefully planned. Unlike armed robbers in developed countries, they used firearms indiscriminately; many victims were shot dead.

From a peak in 1972, armed robbery has declined because known, hardened criminals, believed to be gang leaders, were rounded up and detained in prison. It is difficult to predict what will follow their future release, but improved internal security and social stability work against a serious resurgence of armed robbery.

CRIMINOLOGY IN CONTEMPORARY GHANA

Criminology may be perceived as a body of scientific knowledge about the "causes" and prevention of crime. The criminologist is an individual who pursues such knowledge or applies it in his work. In this vein, there appear to be two distinct categories of criminologists in Ghana. The first category consists of persons who practice criminology as a full-time occupation. They are the few academic criminologists who teach the subject in educational institutions. The second category includes persons who handle offenders and are among the minority who possess criminological knowledge. They include probation officers, prison officers, and police officers, and members of the judiciary. For the majority of persons handling offenders, criminology has little, if any, relevance to their occupation.

Academic Studies

Criminology as an academic subject was introduced in the undergraduate curriculum in sociology as one of the core subjects in 1952. It was taught by lecturers who did not consider themselves to be criminologists. Every student in the Department of Sociology at the then University College of Gold Coast, now the University of Ghana, read the subject for two years. In 1960, it became an elective subject in the department and has been popular among undergraduate students. The Department of Sociology has postgraduate courses in criminology. Initially, there was a one-year postgraduate diploma program; later, a two-year master's of art curriculum was added. Although criminal law is taught by the Faculty of Law at the university, proposals to offer criminology to law students have not been implemented.

Criminology is also taught by the Social Administration Unit and by the Prison Administration Unit of the Department of Sociology. Social administration students are sponsored by the Ministry of Social Welfare and the Ministry of Education. A few private and foreign students also take this course. At present, three qualified criminologists teach the subjects. Two of them had their initial education at the University of Ghana and then pursued further academic studies in Great Britain. The third academic criminologist received all his education in the United States of America.

For the sociology and social administration students, the one-year programs in criminology cover the conceptions of crime; functions of criminology; methods of criminological research; etiology of crime, criminal careers, and criminal activities; special problems in relation to age, sex, class, and ethnicity, especially in regard to juvenile and female delinquency, white-collar crime, and other classes of offenses; history of penological theory and practice; some aspects of criminal court procedures including sentencing practices; institutional and noninstitutional methods of dealing with offenders; and comparative study of penal systems in other countries. In 1970, the orientation expanded beyond the narrow topics of crime to embrace the perspectives of social deviance and control. The approach continues to be predominantly sociological.

The Prison Administration Unit, established in 1975, teaches a two-year program in criminology. One year is devoted to a more detailed study of the etiology of crime from anthro-biophysical, psychogenic, and sociological perspectives. In the second year, students receive a full course in penology. All students are in the prison service, and their studies are sponsored by the Prison Department.

Students sponsored by the Ministry of Social Welfare are usually junior social workers; those from the Ministry of Education are trained teachers. The content of the criminology syllabus taught to the diploma students is oriented more toward social deviance in general, with particular emphasis on juvenile delinquency. In a sense, knowledge of criminology is considered occupationally useful, but no particular status is conferred. Those completing the course go back to their ministries to be employed as social workers, not as criminologists. School welfare officers handle difficult juveniles and/or their families. The Ministry of Social Welfare runs the probation service and the institutions for juvenile offenders.

Vocational Significance of Criminological Studies

So far, none of the undergraduate or graduate students in sociology, who take courses in criminology, has been employed after graduation as a criminologist in any professional field in Ghana. Apart from the three academic criminologists mentioned above, all other graduates regard themselves, and are regarded by others, primarily as sociologists. There is ignorance about what contributions criminologists can make to the development of Ghana. This general ignorance has opposed the granting of unique occupational opportunities in police or prison work to those graduates with criminological knowledge. When employees realize the contribution criminology can make to efficient performance of their duties, they find that prejudices against college graduates among their peers oppose their educational aspirations. Officers generally fear that persons with superior "paper" qualifications will monopolize opportunities for promotion. College graduates who do gain jobs tend to leave the service out of frustration; their adverse personal experiences put off other prospective graduates. Until quite recently, sociologists have had many opportunities in the civil service and in industries as administrators, but the control of crime has a low priority in the developmental plans of Ghana.

Lack of Organization among Criminologists

Until Ghana comes to grips with fundamental economic and social problems and achieves a reasonable degree of stability, criminology per se will receive relatively little attention.

There is no organization bringing together persons who deal with crime and criminals. Both the police force and the prison service are run by the Ministry of Internal Affairs, but communication between the two departments is minimal. Lectures are given to the senior officers of the two services separately, but attempts to organize joint seminars and symposia have failed.

In 1972, just before the overthrow of the second civilian administration, prosecuting attorneys in the Attorney General's Department, senior police and prison officers, lecturers in the Faculty of Law, and two psychiatrists at the main hospital in Accra were approached about establishing an association made up of persons dealing with crime and criminals. A tentative constitution was drafted, but traumatic political events that year ended the attempt.

Criminological Research

Very little criminological research has been done in Ghana. Academic criminologists have heavy teaching loads and so have no time for research. What research has been accomplished has been chiefly in the field of juvenile delinquency. The major work on the subject was prepared by Professor S. Weinberg when he taught briefly at the University of Ghana.[15] I have published an article on the treatment of juvenile delinquency in Ghana[16] and crime trends in Ghana.[17] A third article on armed robbery is being published. Seidman and Eyison have written about the Ghana penal system.[18]

Facilities for data collection are inadequate. Police statistics have not been published for a number of years, and those published contain little information useful to researchers. The Central Bureau of Statistics in the Police Department is poorly staffed, organized, and operated. Computers ordered for data compilation were idle for years until transferred to the University of Science and Technology, Kumasi. Now officers at the bureau do their work manually.

Officials are reluctant to release current and unpublished statistics to researchers on the grounds that the information is classified and cannot be released without permission of the inspector general of police. Applications for permission are unsuccessful.

Court statistics suffer similar inadequacies. Perhaps the most reliable statistics in Ghana are those of the prison service, but they, too, are of limited value. Of course, the prison population is not a representative sample of criminals.

Proposals for a Firmer Base for Criminology

The Department of Sociology at the University of Ghana has approached the Central Bureau of Statistics with a view to establishing a unified system of collecting crime statistics. After meetings between representatives of the Attorney General's Department, police, prisons, the Department of Social Welfare, and the Department of Sociology, a schedule has been drawn up to incorporate the important data on crime and criminals. The agencies have agreed to forward the completed forms to the Central Bureau of Statistics.

The Prison Administration Unit at the University of Ghana intends to expand gradually, hopefully into an Institute of Criminology someday. Finances are an obvious difficulty. Grants from the Ministry of the Interior for training prison officers are the present resource. The ministry has approved the appointment of two additional lecturers as a means of reducing the teaching load. Time will become available for research.

A former lecturer at the Department of Sociology has completed a postgraduate course in criminology at the London School of Economics. He has been appointed to head the research unit at the headquarters of the Ghana police force. He plans collaboration with the criminologists at the university in expanding the number of researchers trained in criminology. The Prison Department is also negotiating with the university for establishment of a research unit; four graduates will be employed. The Department of Social Welfare already has a small research unit.

A Law Reform Commission is reviewing the laws of Ghana. It is now preoccupied with civil and customary laws but expects to take up criminal laws and criminal policy.

SUMMARY AND FINAL COMMENT

The social structure of the Republic of Ghana is a mixture of the traditional and the modern. Since attaining political independence in 1957, it has been deeply involved in building new political, educational, economic, and religious institutions. Fundamental social, political, and cultural changes have been conducive to social deviance, including the appearance of varieties of crime absent in the traditional and colonial eras. The limited resources of the government and the necessities of cultural development have not encouraged the development of appropriate criminal policies to manage the criminological problems.

Criminology as a profession is now limited to the University of Ghana, Legon, but there are prospects that a more effective foundation for criminology in Ghana will be built in the future. As summarized above, the history and sociocultural environment of Ghana provide a remarkable setting for comparative studies and for a partnership between the theoretical and practical sectors of criminology. Perhaps these potentialities and a viable indigenous criminology will be merged in the future.

NOTES

1. K. B. Dickson and G. Benneh, *A New Geography of Ghana* (London: Longmans, 1970).

2. W. T. Balmer, *History of the Akan Peoples* (London: Atlantis Press, 1929).

3. Philip Foster, *Education and Social Change* (London: Routledge and Kegan Paul, 1971).

4. S. K. Gaisie and K. T. Graft-Johnson, *The Population of Ghana* (Accra: CICRED series, 1976).

5. See *Education in Ghana 1930-75* (Accra: Information Services Department) and *Ghana 1977* (Accra: Information Services Department, n.d.).

6. Gaisie and Graft-Johnson, *Population of Ghana*.

7. The following analysis is derived from D.N.A. Nortey, "Crime Trends in Ghana," *Ghana Social Science Journal* 4 (May 1977):102-116.

8. The data are from police statistics for the period 1960-1970; they should be regarded with caution because of the usual limitations of this kind of officially collected data.

9. Alan Milner, *African Penal Systems* (London: Routledge and Kegan Paul, 1969), p. 36.

10. S. K. Gaisie, "Determinants of Population Growth in Ghana," Ph.D. dissertation, Australian National University at Canberra, 1973.

11. A number of commissions or committees were appointed by governments in Ghana to investigate white-collar criminality, trade and business malpractices, and irregularities by public corporations and individuals. The investigations and their reports include:

(a) *Commission of Enquiry into Trade Malpractice in Ghana* (Accra: State Publishing Corporation, 1965).

(b) *Commission of Enquiry into the Commercial Activities of the Publicity Secretariat* (Accra: Information Service Department, 1967).

(c) *Commission of Enquiry into the Affairs of the Ghana Timber Marketing Board and the Ghana Cooperative Union* (Accra: State Publishing Corporation, 1968).

(d) *Commission of Enquiry into Matters of the State Housing Corporation* (Accra: State Publishing Corporation, 1968).

(e) *Commission of Enquiry into the State Fishing Corporation* (Accra: Ghana Publishing Corporation, 1967).

(f) *Commission of Enquiry into Alleged Irregularities and Malpractices in Connection with the Issue of Licenses* (Accra: Ministry of Information, 1963).

(g) *Commission of Enquiry into Irregularities in the Grant of Import Licenses* (Accra: State Publishing Corporation, 1967).

(h) *Committee of Enquiry into the Operation of State Distilleries Corporation* (Accra: State Publishing Corporation, 1968).

(i) *Committee of Enquiry into Alleged Irregularities and Malpractices in the Affairs of the Tema Development Corporation* (Accra: Ghana Publishing Corporation, 1972).

(j) *Commission of Enquiry into Bribery and Corruption* (Accra-Tema: Ghana Publishing Corporation, 1972-1975), 4 vols.

(k) Jiagge Assets Committee (Accra: Ghana Publishing Corporation, 1968-1969).

(l) *Mayo-Plange Assets Committee* (Accra: Ghana Publishing Corporation, 1969-1970).

(m) *Sowah Assets Committee* (Accra: State Publishing Corporation, 1968-1970).

12. Successive governments have enacted various laws and decrees aimed at conserving Ghana's foreign exchange earnings by limiting the amount of money individuals and firms can export. The major examples are: Currency Act, 1964 (Act 242); Currency (Amendment) Decree, 1967 (NLCD 147); Currency Act, 1964 (Amendment) Decree, 1973 (NRCD 183); Currency (Amendment) Decree, 1974 (NRCD 295).

13. Smuggling is subject to the penalty of death by firing squad or imprisonment for fifteen to thirty years, under the Subversion (Amendment) Decree, 1972 (NRCD 90).

14. This discussion was extracted from my unpublished paper, "Armed Robbery in Developing Countries—A Case Study of Ghana."

15. S. K. Weinberg, "Juvenile Delinquency in Ghana: A Comparative Analysis of Delinquents and Nondelinquents," *Journal of Criminal Law, Criminology and Police Science* 55 (December 1964):471-481.

16. D.N.A. Nortey, "Treatment of Juvenile Deliquency in Ghana," *Ghana Journal of Child Development* 2, no. 1 (1962):30-46.

17. D.N.A. Nortey, "Crime Trends in Ghana," *Ghana Social Science Journal* 4, no. 1 (1977):102-116.

18. Robert B. Seidman and J. D. Abaka Eyison, "Ghana Penal System," in Milner (ed.), *African Penal Systems*.

BIBLIOGRAPHY

Apter, David E. *Ghana in Transition*. 2d ed. Princeton, N.J.: Princeton University Press, 1972.
"In the vast subcontinent today," Apter writes, "we witness a clash of cultures and ideas as the tribal peoples of many colonial territories move toward Western forms of social organization." In this context, he concentrates on the history and development of Ghana in analyzing the obstacles to self-government, although it proceeds "with not only the consent but also the demand of the governed." His study has the central theme of "political institutional transfer" whereby political structures are modeled after those of Great Britain.

Austin, Dennis. *Politics in Ghana 1946-1960*. London: Oxford University Press, 1964.
Major political events are traced from the period of colonial reform through three major elections (1951, 1954, and 1956) to the early years of independence. Austin explains the appearance of major issues and their expression in political struggles.

Boahen, Adu. *Ghana: Evolution and Change in the Nineteenth and Twentieth Centuries*. London: Longman, 1975.
A professor of history at the University of Ghana presents the history of the peoples of Ghana as influenced by geographical factors, the Asante Empire, British colonial administration, the Christian missionaries, socioeconomic developments, the impact of World War II, and the political events following the attainment of independence.

Caldwell, John C. *African Rural-Urban Migration: The Movement to Ghana's Towns*. New York: Columbia University Press, 1969.
Data from the 1960 Ghanaian census, supplemented by field interviews, are used by this demographer to demonstrate the impact of migration to towns and to document the complex variety of population flows that undermine the usefulness of highly generalized statements about the effects of urbanization.

Caldwell, John C. *Population Growth and Family Change in Africa: The New Urban Elite in Ghana*. Canberra: Australian National University Press, 1968.
While at the University of Ghana, Dr. Caldwell set out to determine the attitudes and practices of Ghanaians concerning fertility and family size by field investigation. Among his findings were that extended education in Ghana tends to delay marriage, that the more educated are twice as likely to employ contraception, and that the smaller incidence of family planning among the less educated and rural-born is a reflection of the broad problems of coping with social and technological innovation.

Church, R. J. Harrison. *West Africa: A Study of the Environment and of Man's Use of It*. 7th ed. London: Longman, 1974.
Ghana is among the nations of West Africa considered in this analysis of climate, geographical regions, economic resources, and population.

Clignet, R. P., and P. Foster. "Potential Elites in Ghana and the Ivory Coast: A Preliminary Comparison." *American Journal of Sociology* 70 (November 1964): 349-362.
Two samples of secondary students in Ghana and the Ivory Coast are studied to determine variations in the relationship between school systems (the schools are assumed to have similar roles) and elite recruitment. Respondents shared aspirations in spite of important differences in background items.

Hance, William A. *Population, Migration, and Urbanization in Africa*. New York: Columbia University Press, 1970.
Ghana is considered in the course of this examination of a series of topics related to the population in Africa. The major demographic features of the continent are outlined, including the role of population movements, problems related to urbanization, and the insufficiently recognized impact of population pressure.

Heidenheimer, Arnold J. (ed.). *Political Corruption: Readings in Comparative Analysis*. New York: Holt, Rinehart and Winston, 1970.
Selected articles are employed to analyze administrative corruption, electoral and legislative corruption, and the linkages between modernization and corruption. The emerging nations of Africa are included in the analysis of the settings within which corruption emerges and exhibits special patterns.

Jahoda, Gustav. "'Money-Doubling' in the Gold Coast: With Some Cross-Cultural Comparisons." *British Journal of Delinquency* 8 (April 1958):266-276.
Some observations on confidence games in a British city are compared with twelve cases of "money-doubling" reported to the police during 1951-1955 at headquarters of the criminal investigation department in Accra.

Metcalfe, G. E. *Great Britain and Ghana: Documents of Ghana History 1807-1957.*
    London: Thomas Nelson and Sons Ltd., 1964.
Official British policy toward Ghana is elaborately documented from the first direct
dealings in 1807 to the Ghana (Constitutional) Order in Council at Buckingham Palace on
February 22, 1957, which specified the political independence of Ghana. Metcalfe groups
the stages of political history as follows: The Age of Experiment, 1807-1852; The Age of
Laissez-Faire, 1852-1886; The Age of Expansion, 1887-1918; and The Age of Fulfillment, 1919-1957.

14

GREECE

C. D. Spinellis

Aristotle says that he who cannot live in a society should be either a monster or a god.[1] Today the crime rates in some societies raise fears that there are too many "monsters." Is contemporary Greek society moving in this direction?

The following pages review the conditions of criminality in Greece and the status of criminology. An understanding of these topics requires familiarity with Greece's social structure and sociocultural milieu. To provide this background and the analyses that are built upon it, this chapter utilizes statistics on crimes, demographic characteristics, and the Greek economy. The National Statistical Service of Greece provided documents, publications, and personal counsel. Additional information was collected through library research and personal interviews with most of the leading Greek criminologists.

GREEK SOCIETY IN TRANSITION

Greece has undergone tremendous changes since Homer's time (ninth century B.C.), the building of the Parthenon (fifth century B.C.), the Roman conquest (second century A.D.), the Byzantine Empire (fourth to fifteenth century), the Ottoman occupation (1453-1821), and the war of independence (1821) down to the emergence of the Greek state (1828).[2]

From 1828 to 1978, the population of Greece increased more than twelve times (from 753,400 inhabitants to 9,360,000) while its area almost tripled (from 47,616 to 131,900 square kilometers).[3] According to 1976 data, Greece has 16 births and 8.9 deaths per 1,000 population,[4] but the most criminogenic age category—the ten to twenty-nine-year old group—declined between the 1951 and 1971 censuses.[5] The decline is attributed largely to the massive emigration to Germany and overseas, an outflow that has been almost reversed.

Greece is undergoing urbanization and industrialization. In the 1920s, almost 62 percent of the population was rural, whereas in 1971 it was only 35.2 percent.[6] Industrial employment was gaining ground (19 percent of all employment in 1961, the unemployed included, versus 25 percent in 1971) at the expense of the primary sector (53.9 percent in 1961, unemployed included, versus 41.7 percent in 1971). At the same time, the sector of services increased from 27.1 percent to 33.3 percent[7] mostly because of internal migration. Development is proceeding rapidly along Western patterns. The total gross domestic product (in billions of U.S. dollars) in 1971 was 10.97 and by 1974 had become 19.17. Moreover, the per capita domestic product (in U.S. dollars) surpassed 2,100 in 1974.[8]

Greek society may still be considered a Gemeinschaft type. There is a lot of cultural homogeneity; informal controls are effective in certain areas. Primary relations—or to be more accurate, in-group relations which include friends and relatives[9]—are still functioning; thus, competition often yields to cooperation. Finally, sociologists and anthropologists, both foreign and Greek, describe the *philotimo*, the strong sense of honor, that key value which Greeks share with other traditional Mediterranean cultures.[10] The sense of community, of cooperation, and of honor might be considered deterrents to crime. However, *philotimo* also stimulates "crimes of honor."[11]

Unquestionably, Greece is a traditional society in some respects, but it is in a stage of transition.[12] In the 1980s, Greeks are experiencing some of the stress, aggressions, and even annihilating competition and violence of the highly developed Western societies. Rapid social change disrupts traditional family relations.[13] Often a serious generation gap[14] prohibits adequate socialization of the young, with old values and behavioral patterns losing their effectiveness and new ones not sufficiently tested and institutionalized. Traditional socialization is also impeded by the increasing influence on Greek adolescents of their peer groups and the mass media to the detriment of parental influence. A considerable number of youngsters[15] attend higher institutions of learning, and the majority of those youngsters are politicized in the course of their education. An increasing number of tourists and immigrants—most immigrants come from African and Asiatic countries—is further disrupting Greece's cultural and ethnic homogeneity.[16]

CRIME DATA: DEFINITIONS AND SOURCES

A nonlegal definition of crime, whether Garofalian, phenomenological, or criminological, would seem to be more appropriate for criminological analyses than a legal definition. However, a nonlegal definition is not advisable for at least two reasons: First, there is no consensus among criminologists in Greece or the world regarding a nonlegal definition. Second, in Greece only police and criminal court statistics are sources of information; obviously, these statistics are based on Penal Code definitions. Therefore "crime" is used here in its technical legal sense.

Article 14, paragraph 1, of the Greek Penal Code defines crime in general as an illegal act "imputable to the perpetrator and punishable by law."[17] All crimes, as well as their respective penal sanctions, are described either in the Penal Code or in various special statutes in conformity with the principle of *nullum crimen, nulla poena sine lege* (there exists neither crime nor punishment without law). The Penal Code provides several crime classifications of special interest to criminologists.

First, crimes are distinguished according to their seriousness. Following the Franco-German tradition of the tripartite classification of crimes, the code specifies that "any act punishable by death or by confinement in a penitentiary (5-20 years or life) is a felony. Any act punishable by imprisonment (10 days to 5 years) or by pecuniary penalty, or by confinement in a reformative institution is a misdemeanor. Any act punishable by jailing (1 day—1 month) or by fine is a violation."[18]

Greek crime statistics cover only the most serious offenses—felonies and misdemeanors according to the above definitions—and omit the minor offenses, that is, the "violations."[19] More specifically, in compiling crime statistics, the National Statistical Service of Greece takes into consideration felonies and misdemeanors, as defined above, and as they appear (1) in police records of committed offenses, and (2) in irrevocable decisions of criminal courts regarding convicted offenders.

Second, crimes are distinguished according to the object or good that is violated or is in danger. The Penal Code in its Special Part includes twenty-four chapters dealing with offenses directed basically against the interests of the community at large, on one hand (for example, crimes against the internal order of the state, the external safety of the state, the public order, the fair and impartial administration of justice, the safeguarding of the population from various common dangers); and, on the other hand, against interests of the individual (for example, against life, personal liberty, personal honor and reputation, property).

On the basis of this classification, for statistical purposes, the National Statistical Service of Greece lists the following broad categories:

1. Crimes against persons (for example, homicide, abortion, bodily harm).
2. Crimes against honor (for example, libel, slander, defamation).
3. Crimes against property (for example, theft, embezzlement).
4. Crimes against the community (for example, arson, production or possession of explosives).
5. All other crimes of the Penal Code.
6. Violations of market laws.
7. Violations of labor protection laws.
8. Violations of laws relating to automobiles.
9. Violations of all other special penal laws and statutes.
10. Crimes of the Martial Penal Code.

Because there have been no self-report crime studies in Greece,[20] the available official crime statistics should be used with extreme caution. Crime statistics used here are "considered only as an 'index' of the crimes committed"[21] because arrests might be selective and the laws whose infraction constitutes a crime might reflect the interests of powerful groups.[22] Furthermore, existing Greek criminal statistics lack continuity and comparability.

As early as 1833, the Government Gazette of the Kingdom of Greece published some figures on crime; the first volume of criminal statistics, however, did not appear until 1912.[23] The disruption caused by two world wars and the enactment of a new Penal Code in 1950,[24] as well as methodological changes in gathering and classifying crime statistics, delayed the appearance of systematic and comparable data until the late 1950s. (Some statistics are available for the periods 1911-1913 and 1926-1940.) Since 1957, the National Statistical Service of Greece has annually published a volume entitled *Judiciary Statistics: Civil Justice Statistics, Criminal and Correctional Statistics*. It is written in the Greek language and is divided into three parts. The first part refers to statistics of civil courts, from magistrates' and first instance courts to the supreme court and the Council of State. The second part includes police statistics and criminal and juvenile court statistics. The final part relates to prison statistics.

Police statistics on offenses committed are compiled, not by the National Statistical Service, but by city police for the urban areas, and the *Gendarmerie* for the Athenian suburbs and rural areas. Police statistics contain information on the sex and age of the alleged offender, the type of offense, and the area in which the offense was committed. Data on crimes known to the police have been published regularly since 1971.

The National Statistical Service uses a more elaborate method for the collection of judiciary statistics. The same procedure is used for the juvenile courts. *Judiciary Statistics* has been published since 1958, and since 1973 it has contained data on convicted offenders of foreign nationality.

The secretary of each criminal (or martial) court fills in a special form provided by the National Statistical Service. One form is completed for each offender convicted of a felony or misdemeanor after an irrevocable court decision. Thus, information on three basic areas is collected: (1) the convicted offender (place of birth and residence, sex, age, education, occupation, and marital status), (2) the offense (type, place, and time of commission) and the penal reaction to it (sentence, security measures, suspension of sentence, conversion of imprisonment to financial penalty), and (3) previous criminal record of the offender (kind of recidivism, previous offenses, and so on).

Prison or correctional statistics are collected on each convict released from a correctional institution. The reporting form contains identity card number, age, sex, marital status, education, occupation, type of sentence served, type of crime resulting in this sentence, and date of and reason for release from the institution. Moreover, each January the institutions are required to send to the National Statistical Service the forms of all convicts in their populations on the previous December 31.

For each minor entering, or being released from, a training school a form is completed. The form contains, in addition to the usual information, an indication of the type of environment the child lives in, the type of delinquent behavior, the minor's occupation, if any, the previous record, and the duration of commitment.

Finally, *Judiciary Statistics* includes data on (1) detained accused persons, (2) people imprisoned for private or public debts, and (3) offenders committed to a state psychiatric institution (mentally ill criminals, alcoholics, drug addicts, and so forth).

In addition to the publication described above, information relevant to crime and criminals is found in the *Statistical Yearbook of Greece* which has entries in Greek and English.

INCIDENCE OF AND REACTIONS TO CRIME

As Greek society experiences urbanization and economic development, we may anticipate the loss of the relationships between Gemeinschaft Greek society[25] and low crime rates, which have been expressed in sporadic old-type burglaries and robberies or "honor" crimes. As shown in Table 14-1,[26] the crime rate, with the exception of the years immediately after the 1967 coup d'etat, is increasing but is still short of the level that would make the streets unsafe. Moreover, the official statistics indicate the crime rate for females is rather stable.[27]

Now we focus on ten broad crime categories.[28] More than 25 percent of all convicted crimes in Greece relate to violations of traffic laws.[29] The next largest category is that of market law violations (16.6 percent). Crimes against persons are quite prevalent in Greece (13.9 percent), while crimes against property entail 4.0 percent of total convictions. During the past decade, crime in general has been increasing (see Table 14-1) whereas crimes against property have remained stable and crimes against persons have slightly decreased.[30]

Crimes against the community (for example, violations of city planning regulations, violations of health laws, and arson) have fluctuated during the last seven years.[31] Violations of laws regarding the protection of labor were responsible for 4 percent of total convictions in 1977 and crimes against honor (defamation, libel, and so on) involve 3 percent. The remaining 18.2 percent and 1.9 percent refer to miscellaneous crimes of the Penal Code and of the special penal statutes, respectively, while 0.3 percent concern crimes of the Martial Penal Code.

The nonviolent nature of crime described by judiciary statistics is also found in police statistics. Thus, in 1979 of a total of 294,056 committed offenses known to the police, 246,157 involved various violations of special penal statutes (115,978 concerned traffic law violations).[32] The next most frequently committed offense, according to police data, was bodily injury.[33] Another significant figure was that concerning thefts: 14,871.

For the time being, the Greek public is alarmed neither by intentional homicide[34] nor by bodily injury,[35] although data suggest an increase in those crimes. There exist, however, feelings of insecurity, especially among bank employees, owners and employees of luxury shops, and pharmacists.[36] Moreover, parents

TABLE 14-1
CRIME AND PENAL RESPONSE TO CRIME, 1957-1979

Year	Crimes Known to Police		Court Statistics Re Adults and Minors		Court Statistics Re Minors Only[a]		Suspension of (Adult) Sentence[b]	Imprisonment Below 3 Months and Pecuniary Sentence[c]	Imprisonment 3 Months and All Other Sentences[c]
	Number Arrested	Per 100,000	Number Convicted	Per 100,000	Total Disposed	Reprimand	Absolute Numbers		
1957	NA	NA	71,267	1,006	NA	NA	NA	NA	NA
1958	NA	NA	81,049	1,031	NA	NA	NA	NA	NA
1959	NA	NA	75,589	1,044	NA	NA	NA	NA	NA
1960	NA	NA	82,649	1,134	2,082	NA	11,355	73,437	9,212
1961	NA	NA	79,955	1,081	2,432	NA	11,018	70,507	7,016
1962	NA	NA	83,084	1,121	2,623	NA	11,225	73,409	7,049
1963	NA	NA	83,776	1,125	2,821	NA	10,132	73,732	7,221
1964	NA	NA	70,936	949	2,731	NA	8,721	60,183	8,022
1965	NA	NA	73,059	972	2,654	NA	10,983	62,099	8,306
1966	NA	NA	93,405	1,232	2,885	NA	12,473	81,322	9,196
1967	NA	NA	92,644	1,207	2,793	NA	12,113	79,371	10,480
1968	NA	NA	66,685	859	2,173	NA	11,480	56,277	8,232
1969	NA	NA	78,866	1,013	2,092	NA	15,001	67,975	8,795

Year									
1970	179,331	2,300	72,393	928	2,248	NA	14,978	63,099	7,040
1971	198,315	2,535	74,789	956	2,797	NA	15,697	65,133	6,856
1972	230,296	2,931	102,278	1,031	4,727	NA	20,842	90,112	7,427
1973	196,119	2,481	114,248	1,441	4,857	2,477	19,967	100,693	8,688
1974	199,520	2,507	107,010	1,344	3,959	2,054	18,823	95,566	7,480
1975	184,865	2,298	114,063	1,418	5,481	2,847	20,603	101,418	7,161
1976	248,941	3,041	112,510	1,374	5,873	3,397	21,593	99,134	7,495
1977	254,567	3,071	116,736	1,408	5,554	3,052	20,940	103,597	7,585
1978	261,111	3,115	115,734	1,380	5,110	2,578	21,791	102,210	8,414
1979	294,056	NA	120,281	NA	4,497	2,275	22,470	107,477	8,307

Source: National Statistical Service of Greece: *Judiciary Statistics*, 1957, 1958, 1959, and so on.

NA = No data available.

[a]Minors seven to twenty years of age adjudicated by juvenile courts or convicted by criminal courts. In the "total disposed," the cases disposed of "reprimand" are included.

[b]Cases of suspension of sentence are not included in column of court statistics as court statistics refer to convicted offenders and "suspension" is not considered "conviction."

[c]Cases of minors excluded.

seem to worry about crimes concerning the consumption, possession, or selling of drugs. Police statistics on drugs do not reveal any considerable increase during the last few years.[37] Yet, police reports published in the daily newspapers at the beginning of 1979 underline the threat of the drug problem.[38] Finally, the crime of rape does not seem to threaten Greek society,[39] as it does other societies.

Information on sentencing practices in Greece suggests, first, that Greek criminality is not considered to be grave and, second, that judges typically impose rather mild punishments (Table 14-1). The Penal Code gives some discretionary power to the criminal judge to consider the offender's individual circumstances through provisions for alternative sentences,[40] for minimum sentences,[41] for conversion of prison sentences,[42] for mitigation of punishment,[43] and for suspension of sentence.[44]

Statistics show that imprisonment for less than one month is the most frequent sentence.[45] The second most frequent sentence is the suspended sentence. Statistics indicate that as the length of sentence increases the frequency of imposition decreases.[46] Greek juvenile courts also prefer lenient dispositions; these judges seem to use "reprimand" more frequently and a training school disposition less frequently[47] (Table 14-1).

CRIMINOLOGY IN GREECE

Here criminology is defined as the systematic study of crime, its genesis and its control. The definition includes the phenomenology or symptomatology of crime,[48] the etiology of crime, and the state's reaction to crime. In Greece, criminology is usually placed with the broader field of "penal sciences" which include:

A. The primary fields:
   1. Criminology in the narrow sense.
   2. Penology or corrections.
   3. Police science or criminalistics and the auxiliary disciplines.
   4. Forensic medicine.
   5. Forensic psychology and psychiatry.
   6. Investigation techniques which the Germans call *Untersuchungsschaft, Kriminaltaktik* und *Kriminaltechnik*.
   7. Sociology of (penal) law.
B. Aspects of the law:
   1. Penal law.
   2. Penal procedures.[49]

Following the continental European tradition, Gardikas distinguishes between criminology, on one hand, and criminological sociology (not sociological criminology), criminal biology, criminological psychology, and criminological psychiatry or psychopathology, on the other. He further argues that criminological policy (what the French and Germans call *politique criminelle* and *kriminal politik*, respectively) and criminal statistics do not constitute parts of criminology. Criminal policy simply utilizes postulates of criminology, evaluates the effectiveness of criminal law, and makes suggestions for criminal reform. Criminal statistics is only a method used by criminology.[50]

Daskalopoulos advances the distinction between general criminology which studies the nature of crime, the personality, and the environment and their interrelationships, and special criminology which focuses on the cause and the phenomenology of crime. According to him, criminological biology, criminological psychology and psychopathology as well as criminological sociology constitute parts of special criminology.[51] However, several Greek authors of criminology textbooks, including Alice Marangopoulos-Yotopoulos, believe that criminology in its broader sense includes criminology in its narrow sense, criminal policy, penology, and inquisitive techniques.[52]

Obviously, one could continue this epistemological discussion to argue that neither anthropological criminology nor sociological criminology is a separate discipline; they are simply various approaches to the study of crime.

This section follows more or less the Anglo-American thinking in this matter; it focuses on criminology primarily and, to some extent, on penology. Criminalistics, forensic medicine, forensic psychiatry, and so forth will only be touched upon. This chapter deals, not only with criminology in Greece, but also with the criminology of Greece.

Continental versus Anglo-American Orientations

Criminology in Greece basically follows the old European tradition: it is legally and medically oriented. Before 1970, the Anglo-American sociological tradition was hardly represented.

The legal orientation is reflected in the following events. Criminology is taught in law schools by graduates of those schools who have had graduate and/or postgraduate training in criminology abroad. Most Greek criminologists have been trained in Germany, and others in France, Switzerland, or Italy where the penal codes and legal educational systems resemble those of Greece. Those holding a master's or doctoral degree from England or the United States are a minority at this time, but the modern trend is toward the Anglo-American approach.

Of those psychiatrists or physicians—mostly residents of urban areas—who are involved in criminology, most prefer the medical orientation. They are working in the field of corrections as physicians or psychiatrists, in coroner departments, or in programs treating drug abusers or youths with antisocial behavior patterns. Some are in the teaching profession and spread their knowledge and perspectives through lectures and textbooks.

Promising Beginnings

The discipline born in 1879 when the French anthropologist Topinard coined the term "criminology" was introduced in Greece almost simultaneously. As early as 1883 a book entitled *The Causes of Dueling and Suicide* was written by M. Froudakis, and in 1892 *A Criminological Study of Eighteen Criminal Physiognomies* was written by L. Nakos.[53]

In 1902, Beccaria's *Del delitti e delle pene* was translated into Greek; within the first quarter of the twentieth century, the works of V. Liszt, Lombroso, and Ferri were translated.[54] During the same period, both at home and abroad, Greeks produced more than twenty books, some in French, on certain criminological issues; a double number of articles appeared.

Publications in penology began earlier than those in criminology. A brief study of the penitentiary system[55] was published in 1847 in Italian by G. Granguli, a Greek living on the island of Corfu. Before 1900 more than a dozen books and even more articles appeared.

Nevertheless, the emergence of institutionalized and professionalized criminology was retarded. A course in criminology was first taught in 1930 at the Law School of the University of Athens—the first university in Greece—but a chair of criminology was not established until 1938.[56] Forty years later, there were only three professors of criminology at the university level and three assistant professors: two of criminology and one of penology.

Etiology of Arrested Development

"Criminology without sociology" has emerged in the United States where sociologists have dominated criminology, but the absence of sociology has stagnated criminology in Greece. In the Greek universities there still are no departments of sociology.[57] Sociology is a one-year introductory course in most Greek universities.[58] But none of the universities, institutes, or centers officially entrusted with educating students offers courses in criminological theory and research methodology to stimulate the development of criminology.

The absence of substantial development of criminology in Greece can also be attributed to the belief among government officials that Greek society can survive without criminology. The crime rate has been relatively low for a number of years. Progovernment and antigovernment mass media agree that the crime problem is less serious than inflation, the energy crisis, the avoidance of negative consequences of joining the European Economic Community, Greek-Turkish relations, pollution, and urban traffic.

Greek criminologists are, therefore, denied opportunities to prove themselves and to enhance their status and that of their discipline. Funds for criminological inquiry are limited; officials are either unprepared or unwilling to cooperate with researchers. It is difficult at best to gain access to official archives and permission to interview criminal justice personnel or prisoners. Criminologists have limited employment opportunities and low salaries; new and capable scientists, particularly males, are reluctant to enter the field.

Accomplishments of Greek Criminology

In spite of these difficulties, Greek criminology can claim certain accomplishments. The establishment of the chair of criminology at the Law School of the University of Athens stimulated a distinctively Greek textbook in criminology. Gardikas, the first to occupy the chair and now a retired professor emeritus, wrote a textbook in the European style, especially following Aschaffenburg. His textbook was "Greek" in that it was written in Greek and in that the knowledge and theories were documented, when possible, with Greek facts and figures.

First published in 1932, the textbook was strengthened and enlarged in several editions. It is often used for reference and is one of the assignments for fourth-year law students. It has three volumes and 2,600 pages: Volume 1, *Criminology: The General and Individual Causes of Crime* (Athens: Tjakas Brothers, 1968), 6th ed.; Volume 2, *Police Science* (Athens: Tjakas Brothers, 1968), 6th ed.; and Volume 3, *Penology* (Athens: Tjakas Brothers, 1967), 3d ed.

The Office of Criminological Services was established in 1929 with features paralleling the Federal Bureau of Investigation of the United States. It was first directed by Gardikas who made the arrangements to establish laboratories, card files for dactyloscopy, photographic equipment in the Bertillon style, and so on. These services have stimulated the training of a number of police officers in criminalistics.

The data of the Office of Criminological Services and of the National Statistical Service lend impetus to small-scale, descriptive research. The research has been social-problem oriented and often has used as research subjects the clients of the Office of Criminological Services: hashish addicts, alcoholics, prostitutes, robbers, beggars, vagrants, and the like. Prison files have also served as data sources for applied research. Systematic criminological research was legitimized by the establishment of the Social Sciences Research Center in Greece.

Gradually, various governmental committees have included criminologists together with other professionals—criminal law professors, judges, lawyers, and others. The committee tasks have included, first, the drafting of penal and correctional statutes; and, second, examination of certain social problems and investigation of alternative solutions through collective action. Because criminologists have been useful amending the laws and proposing solutions to Greek realities, they have given their new profession substance and prestige.

Criminology also gained respect when the course on criminology at the Law School of the University of Athens was changed from an elective to a required course. This action was a coup according to the educational values of Greece in the 1940s. Gradually, criminology courses have been introduced by other institutions: the Schools of Policemen and Police Officers, the Panteios School of

Political Sciences, the schools of social work, and the Ministry of Justice's seminars for in-service training of correctional officers and other personnel.

Contemporary Dilemmas

Criminology in Greece is at a crossroads. The struggle for mere existence is over, but excellence is not in sight. The paucity of people involved in applied and, especially, theoretical criminology is symptomatic of the question: Criminology by whom and for whom?

If criminology continues to recruit its members from the law profession—most criminologists also practice law, according to our interview data—criminology will continue to be subservient to the law. Thus, the emphasis will be on criminological praxis rather than on deviant behavior theory.

If, however, criminology attempts to change its identity, the existing criminologists with a sociological background will be neither qualitatively nor quantitatively strong enough to give real impetus to the development of criminology. The field will lose the adherents previously enlisted from the Greek medical profession.[59] A monolithic development would oppose the favorable aspects of a movement toward being an interdisciplinary field.

Related to this issue is the common controversy as to whether or not practitioners should be considered criminologists: directors of various penal and training institutions, supervisors of minors (probation officers), psychologists working with criminals referred to state mental hospitals or with drug users, and so on. Should such personnel be considered criminologists only if they have had training in that area? Is an in-service training course organized by the Ministry of Justice and covering some twenty hours of psychology and twenty hours of sociology and criminology, among other subjects, sufficient to grant the professional status of criminologist? Should a master's degree or a diploma in criminology be minimal requirements? How many more institutions all over the world would offer a degree in criminology?

The question "criminology for whom?" has ontological and normative overtones. The basic issue seems to be: Criminology for conventional liberals or criminology for radicals? Certainly, the new criminology as defined by Taylor, Walton, and Young and as reflected in the writings of Foucault[60] and Robert[61] has its adherents in Greece. However, the majority of Greek criminologists and much of the criminological literature appear to be conventional, and some of the literature is reactionary. Despite their usefulness in the present theoretical desert of Greek criminology, ideological polarization and pro-radical research impede the scientific development of criminology.

In a country with limited human and material resources, other dilemmas are suggested by further questions: Criminology for the use of penal law? Criminology for criminal policy? Criminology to facilitate the work of criminal courts, defense counsels, police, and intra- and extramural institutions?

CRIMINOLOGICAL RESEARCH

The existence of a few, scattered, small-scale research projects suggests that criminological research in Greece continues to oscillate between the semiscientific and prescientific stages.[62] The reasons for this limited accomplishment are indicated above.

The National Center of Social Research was established in 1961 under the name Center of Social Sciences through the cooperation of the Greek government with UNESCO. Some hopes for the development of criminological research were raised, but criminology was neglected in the course of the center's efforts to cover all areas of sociology from religious and rural life to educational and political institutions. A criminological research project materialized only recently, and only two criminological publications have been produced: a doctoral dissertation on criminal areas and delinquent gangs[63] and a survey of the "criminality" (*sic*) of minors in urban Athens.[64] These studies are based chiefly on library research, official statistics, and court files. The recent project is based on a nationwide sample of two thousand respondents by a team headed by a French-trained criminologist (Dr. E. Daskalakis, assistant professor of criminology at Panteios) and aided by a British-trained statistician (Dr. P. Pappas). From a radical perspective, the investigation is considering, first, the functions and effects of the criminal justice system on its clients and, second, the public image of criminal justice.

The Criminological Research Center was founded in 1959 as a nonprofit organization. Since it does not engage in empirical studies, its major contribution has been a two-volume bibliography on materials about criminal issues and the penal sciences published in the 1830-1970 period. The third volume, now in print, covers the years 1971-1978.

In the Aiginiteio Psychiatric Clinic of the Medical School of the University of Athens, a team of psychiatrists has been working for years on a series of projects concerning hashish users treated at the clinic. The most representative publication is a book edited by Stefanis, Fink, and Dornbush.[65]

Recently, the Institute of Penal Studies of the Law School of the University of Athens received a minor grant for research on the criminality of non-Greeks, especially unskilled workers in Greece. (The project directors are Professor of Penal Law N. Androulakis and the author of this chapter.)

Opportunities for criminological research are gradually increasing. At the University of Thrace, Komotini, a laboratory of criminology and forensic psychiatry has been proposed, with a staff of three scientists and two technicians. (The director is Professor N. Fotakis.) For the first time, the Ministry of Coordination included crime causation and control in planning research priorities for 1980.

CRIMINOLOGY AND HIGHER EDUCATION

Greek universities do not prepare criminologists, sociologists, or psychologists. Criminological instruction does not go beyond the general introductory level. An introductory course is offered in the three law schools of Greece and in the Panteios School of Political Sciences.

The four-year program of the Law School at the University of Athens is divided into a Legal Section, a Section of Public Law and Political Sciences, and a Section of Economics. The Legal Section has a three hour per week, required course in criminology and penology for fourth-year students.[66] (The professor of criminology and penology is Dr. M. I. Daskalopoulos, and the assistant delegated for teaching and lecturer is Dr. C. D. Spinellis.)

The Law School of the University of Salonika has no chair of criminology and, at the time of this writing, has an associate professor of criminology and penology. Criminology is also taught by professors of penal law.[67] (The associate professor of criminology and penology is Dr. S. Anagnostakis; professors of penal law are Dr. T. Philippides, Dr. C. Vouyoukas, and Dr. J. E. Manoledakis.)

The Law School of the University of Thrace in Komotini has been operating since the 1974-1975 academic year. A three-year course in criminology and investigative techniques and a three-hour course in forensic psychology and psychiatry are offered to fourth-year students.[68] (The professor of penal law, criminology, penology and investigative techniques is Dr. S. Alexiades; the professor of forensic psychology and psychiatry is Dr. N. Fotakis.)

The Panteios Higher School of Political Sciences focuses on political sciences and public administration. Fourth-year students may take a five hour per week course in criminology (crime causation and treatment of criminals) and investigative techniques.[69] (The professor of criminology is Dr. Alice Marangopoulos-Yotopoulos, and the assistant professor is Dr. E. Daskalakis.)

Criminology and, sometimes, juvenile delinquency are taught in various schools of social work, in the School of City Policemen and Policewomen, in the School of the Gendarmerie, and in the American-sponsored, three-year, liberal arts college, Deree-Pierce.

In Greece, for criminology it is only possible to take a doctoral degree program by thesis and not by course work. The absence of graduate courses necessitates studies abroad. A few criminologists have earned a doctoral degree by writing a thesis, usually based on library research. Otherwise, academic criminologists have been educated in Germany, Switzerland, Italy, France, Denmark, England, or the United States.

CAREERS IN CRIMINOLOGY

In Greece, crime studies and crime control functions are within the state's jurisdiction. If there are to be challenging career opportunities for criminologists, they would have to be in the form of government positions designated specifically for criminologists. Because the government does not do this, employment opportunities are limited.

Except for teaching and university assistant positions, criminologists have access to such career avenues as administrators of crime control and prevention, departments of the Ministry of Justice, the Ministry of Public Order, and police headquarters, staff positions in correctional institutions, supervision of minors, and judges. These positions, however, may be occupied by persons with varied educational and professional backgrounds: law school graduates, graduates of schools of theology, social work students, and those majoring in political science.

If a career system for criminologists is to emerge, the government and its agencies must become sensitive to the benefits of recruiting and relying upon personnel expert in criminological knowledge.[70] Special regulations would probably be necessary to specify that those competent in criminological knowledge would be preferred for particular positions.

International Contacts

The difficulties Greek criminologists face at the national level are not found at the international level. Greek criminologists are employed by international organizations[71] and by foreign countries.[72] Most of them are active in professional associations such as the Société Internationale de Criminologie, the Gesellschaft für de gesamte Kriminologie, the Association Internationale de Droit Pénal, the Research Committee for the Sociology of Deviance and Social Control, and the International Sociological Association. International contacts have been maintained by a number of veteran Greek criminologists through international symposia in Greece. Foreign experts visiting Greece in the past fifteen years include M. Ancel, T.N. Attila, G. Canepa, N. Christie, I. Drapkin, the late professor B. Di Tullio, P. Friday, T. Grygier, Göppinger, W. Middendorf, J. Pinatel, L. Radzinowicz, H. Schüller-Springorum, J. Short, and D. Szabo.

At the national level, most Greek criminologists are members of the Greek Association of Penal Law, the Society for the Protection of Minors, the After-Care Society, and, especially, the newly founded Hellenic Society for Criminology.

PROSPECTS FOR CRIMINOLOGY IN GREECE

Can criminology in Greece surpass the mere survival stage? A positive answer depends on the continuation of trends identified earlier in this paper.

The founding of new universities has created new teaching and tutoring opportunities that open the way to experimentation with new fields such as forensic psychology and psychiatry. We may hope that criminological research will be stimulated.

The slow but constant growth of sociology in Greece should enrich the sociology of deviance which has been neglected.

The increased contacts of Greek criminologists with colleagues abroad should expand the opportunities of Greeks to conduct research on doctoral dissertations to be submitted to Greek universities; should familiarize Greeks with recent world developments in criminological theory and research; and should permit avoidance of errors made elsewhere in the earlier development of criminology.

The merits of well-directed team research are being recognized in Greece and possibly may replace small-scale, individual, monolithic, or reformist research.

Finally, increased criminality and new forms of criminality already have been forecast for Greece; Androulakis talks about "imported criminality." Although such trends are regrettable, they are likely to press government officials and the general public toward firmer support of criminology as a field for education, research, and practice.

NOTES

1. Aristotle, *Politika* A, 1, 12.
2. C. D. Spinellis, V. Vassiliou, and G. Vassiliou, "Milieu Development and Male-Female Roles in Contemporary Greece," in Georgene H. Seward and Robert C. Williamson (eds.), *Sex Roles in Changing Society* (New York: Random House, 1970), p. 309.
3. National Statistical Service of Greece, *Monthly Statistical Bulletin*, January 1979 (information on population), *Statistical Yearbook 1977* (Athens: 1979), p. 15 (information on surface).
4. *Statistical Yearbook*, p. 39.
5. Ibid., p. 29.
6. Ibid., p. 17.
7. A. Gana, *Comparative Study on Social Protection in Greece and in the E.E.C. Countries* (Athens: Center of Planning and Economic Research, n.d.), p. 67 (mimeo in Greek).
8. *Statistical Yearbook*, p. 487.
9. Vasso G. Vassiliou and George Vassiliou, "The Implicative Meaning of the Greek Concept of 'Philotimo'," *Journal of Cross-Cultural Psychology* 4 (September 1973):326-341.
10. J. G. Peristiani (ed.), *Honour and Shame: The Values of Mediterranean Society* (London: Weidenfeld and Nicolson, 1965).
11. C. Safilios-Rothchild, " 'Honor' Crimes in Contemporary Greece," in C. Safilios-Rothchild (ed.), *Toward a Sociology of Women* (Lexington, Mass., Toronto: Xerox College Publishing, 1972), pp. 84-95.
12. I. Lambiri [Dimaki], *Social Change in a Greek Country Town* (Athens: Center of Planning and Economic Research, 1965), pp. 111-114.
13. Ch. Katakis, "On the Transaction of Social Change and the Perception of Self in Relation to Others: A Study of Greek Pre-adolescents," *Mental Health and Society* 6 (in press).
14. I. Lambiri-Dimaki, "The Generation Gap in Greece: Unchanging Elements and Modern Characteristics," in John Koumoulides (ed.), *Greece: Past and Present* (to be published shortly in Great Britain).
15. In the academic year 1974-1975, there were 97,759 students studying in universities and colleges. *Statistical Yearbook*, p. 152.
16. While 1,105, 293 foreigners arrived in Greece in 1966, ten years later 4,247,233 arrived. *Statistical Yearbook*, p. 380.
17. The American Series of Foreign Penal Codes, *The Greek Penal Code*, translated by Nicholas B. Lolis (South Hackensack, N.J.: Fred B. Rothman and Company; London: Sweet and Maxwell, 1973), p. 42.
18. Ibid., art. 18, p. 43.

19. C. D. Spinellis, "Crime in the Changing Greek Society; Reflections on Statistical Data," *Mental Health and Society* 2 (1975):190.

20. Cf. for example, Martin Gold, *Delinquent Behavior in an American City* (Belmont, Calif.: Wadsworth Publishing Company, 1970).

21. Edwin H. Sutherland and Donald R. Cressey, *Principles of Criminology*, 7th ed. (Philadelphia: J. B. Lippincott, 1966), p. 27.

22. Ian Taylor, Paul Walton, and Jock Young, *The New Criminology: For a Social Theory of Deviance* (London: Routledge and Kegan Paul, 1977), p. 11.

23. C. D. Spinellis, *Crime in Contemporary Greece*, Technical Report XIII (Athens: Athenian Institute of Anthropos, n.d.), p. 8 (mimeo).

24. See the excellent introduction written by Professor G. A. Mangakis, in the American Series of Penal Codes, *The Greek Penal Code*, pp. 1-33, especially p. 4.

25. N. Gage, "Greek Crime Rate Is Lowest in Europe," *New York Times*, August 19, 1979. C. D. Spinellis, "Surveying the Fluctuations of Criminality in Greece, During the Decade 1960-1970," *Penal Chronicles* 12 (1972):658 (in Greek).

26. Under the provision of art. 122 of the Greek Penal Code, minors are youngsters seven to seventeen years of age. Nevertheless, there are cases of youthful offenders seventeen to twenty years of age who are treated as minors. The latter cases are also included in the crime rate figures of Table 14.1.

27. In 1960, for every one hundred offenders, twelve were females. In 1970, approximately ten were females, and in 1976 the percentage decreased to 9.5. National Statistical Service of Greece, *Judiciary Statistics*, 1961, 1970, and 1976 (hereafter cited simply as *Judiciary Statistics*.) (The year refers to the year of the data, and not to the year of publication.)

28. See above "Crime Data: Definitions and Sources."

29. With almost complete consistency, traffic cases have taken a progressively greater share of total convictions in recent years. Violations of automobile laws were 24.8 percent in 1976, 27.4 percent in 1977, 27.8 percent in 1978, and 26.6 percent in 1979. *Judiciary Statistics*, 1976, 1977, 1978, and 1979.

30. For example, crimes against persons accounted for 17.3 percent of total convictions in 1967, 17.9 percent in 1970, 16.3 percent in 1973, 12.9 percent in 1977, 13.7 percent in 1978, and 13.2 percent in 1979. *Judiciary Statistics*, 1967, 1970, 1973, 1977, 1978, and 1979.

31. For example, the figure was 4.7 percent in 1973, 11.8 percent in 1975, 9.4 percent in 1977, 6 percent in 1978, and 8.3 percent in 1979. *Judiciary Statistics*, 1973, 1975, 1977, 1978, and 1979.

32. Consult especially *Judiciary Statistics*, 1979, pp. 50-53.

33. The figure is 23,207, and 18,807 refers to the so-called negligent bodily injury by automobile, ibid.

34. There were 79 arrests in 1973, 118 in 1976, 111 in 1977, 117 in 1978, and 108 in 1979. *Judiciary Statistics*, 1973, 1976, 1977, 1978, and 1979.

35. In 1973, there were 2,967 cases, excluding the cases of negligence; in 1976 there were 4,265, in 1977 4,323, in 1978 4,457, and in 1979 4,048. *Judiciary Statistics*, 1973, 1976, 1977, 1978, and 1979.

36. Pharmacists, especially during their nightshifts, are afraid of drug addicts. The data suggest an increase in burglaries and robberies. There were forty-eight arrests in 1973, ninety-one in 1976, seventy-seven in 1977, sixty-two in 1978, and eighty-one in 1979. *Judiciary Statistics*, 1973, 1976, 1977, 1978, and 1979.

37. There were 166 arrests concerning use and/or selling and/or the possession of drugs in 1973, 212 arrests in 1976, 189 arrests in 1977; in 1978, there were 267 arrests, and in 1979 there were 307. *Judiciary Statistics*, 1973, 1976, 1977, 1978, and 1979.

38. Newspaper: VIMA April 14, 1979 (in Greek). The police reported 182 cases, a figure consistent with data from the previous years.

39. There were twenty-six convictions for rape in 1973 versus fifteen convictions in 1976, eighteen in 1978, and fourteen in 1979. *Judiciary Statistics*, 1973, 1976, 1977, 1978, and 1979.

40. For example, art. 299 of the Greek Penal Code provides: "One who intentionally kills another shall be punished *by death or by confinement* in a penitentiary for life." Further, art. 428 states: "one who throws litter...shall be punished *by fine or criminal detention*" (emphasis mine).

41. For example, art. 336 of the Greek Penal Code says: "One who by bodily duress or threat of serious and immediate danger forces a female into extra-marital intercourse shall be punished by confinement in a penitentiary *for not* more than ten years" (emphasis mine).

42. For example, art. 82 of the Greek Penal Code, as amended, provides: "a court imposing punishment deprivative of liberty not in excess of one year may provide...for conversion of punishment to a fine or pecuniary penalty, if on investigating the offender's character and other circumstances the court finds that the fine or pecuniary penalty suffice to deter him."

43. Art. 83 of the Greek Penal Code provides for five possibilities of mitigated punishment.

44. Arts. 92-102 deal with the institution of conditional suspension of sentence.

45. This is illustrated by the following data referring to 1979. Total of convicted offenders: 115,784. Imprisonment up to one month: 88,817. Suspension of sentence (not included in total because defendants were not finally convicted): 28,470. Imprisonment 1 to 3 months: 10,316. Pecuniary penalty: 8,344. Imprisonment 3 to 6 months: 4,800. Imprisonment 6 to 12 months: 2,344. Imprisonment 1 year and above 1,085. Temporary confinement: 65. Confinement for life: 0. Not declared sentence: 13. *Judiciary Statistics*, 1979, p. 54. The above figures do not present appreciable differences for the last five years.

46. See note 45.

47. This is illustrated by the following data referring to 1979. Total of juvenile court cases involving minors seven to twenty years of age: 14,708. Reprimand: 2,275. Responsible supervision by parents: 1,419. Supervision by supervisors of minors (probation officers): 750. Convicted thirteen to seventeen years of age: 915. Training school: 28. Reformatory school: 14. Not declared punishment: 1. To the above figures 9,303 convictions of minors eighteen to twenty years of age should be added. *Judiciary Statistics*, 1979, pp. 62-63.

48. Hermann Mannheim, *Comparative Criminology*, Vol. 1 (London: Routledge and Kegan Paul, 1970), p. 3.

49. For a somewhat similar classification of "penal sciences," see J. E. Manoledakis, *General Theory of Penal Law*, Vol. A (Thessaloniki-Athens: Sakkoula Bros., 1976), p. 81 (in Greek).

50. C. G. Gardikas, *Criminology*, Vol. A, 5th ed. (Athens: Tjaka Bros., 1966), pp. 83-91 (in Greek). For excellent definitions and delineations of the various auxiliary disciplines and/or approaches to the study of crime, see Günther Kaiser, *Kriminologie*, 3. überarbeitete und ergänzte Auflage (Heidelberg-Karlsruhe: C. F. Müller Juristischer Verlag, 1976), especially pp. 22-28 and 54-73.

51. I. M. Daskalopoulos, *Elements of Criminology*, Vol. 1: *General Criminology*, Part I, *The Nature of Crime* (Athens: Tjakas Bros, 1972), pp. 1-2 (in Greek).

52. A. Marangopoulos-Yotopoulos, *Lectures on Criminology*, Vol. A (Athens: A Sakkoulas), 1979, p. 32 (in Greek).

53. Those books are mentioned in Series of Criminological Research Center, *Bibliography of Criminological and Penal Studies in Greece* (1830-1964) by S. C. Anagnostakis (Athens: Papadimitriou), 1964, pp. 46 and 48 (in Greek).

54. Ibid., pp. 45, 48, and 70.

55. Ibid., p. 71.

56. Spinellis, *Crime in Contemporary Greece*, p. 1.

57. L. Nikolaou, *The Growth and Development of Sociology in Greece* (Boston: n.p., 1974).

58. An exception to the rule is Deree-Pierce College, an American-sponsored institution in Greece which has a Sociology Department. For some exceptions, see ibid., p. 14.

59. Mostly psychiatrists have been active in the area of crime causation and control. Among those of the previous generation, Dr. M. Strigaris should be mentioned. Cf. M. G. Strigaris, *The Hashish. Psychopathological, Clinical and Sociological Study on the Consequences of Cannabis* (Athens: M. Saliveros, 1937) (in Greek). The tradition is followed by Dr. C. Stefanis, professor of psychiatry of the Medical School of the University of Athens and his team. Cf. C. Stefanis, M. Fink, and R. Dornbush (eds.), *Studies of Chronic Hashish Use* (New York: Raven Press, 1977). Dr. N. Fotakis, another psychiatrist, is also involved in criminological work; he is professor of forensic psychology and psychiatry at the Law School of the University of Thrace, Komotini.

60. The provocative books of Michel Foucault have already been translated into English. See the excellent review essay of Stanley Cohen, "The Archaeology of Power," *Contemporary Sociology* 7 (September 1978):566-568.

61. See, for example, Philippe Robert and Claude Faugeron, *La Justice et son Publique: Les Représentations sociales du système pénal: Collection Déviance et Société* (Genève: Médicine et Hygiène, 1978).

62. Mannheim, *Comparative Criminology*, pp. 84-85.

63. M. Pothos, *Criminal Areas and Gangs of Minors* (Athens: National Center of Social Research, 1971) (in Greek).

64. D. G. Tsaoussis and E. Korre-Grueger, *The Criminality of Minors in the Capital's Area* (Athens: National Center of Social Research), 1974 (in Greek).

65. See above, note 59.

66. National and Kapodistrian University of Athens, *Catalogue of the Academic Year 1977-78. Provisions Relating to Students and Program of Courses* (Athens: Eptalofos, 1978), pp. 55-56 (in Greek).

67. Aristotelian University of Salonika, *Catalogue of the Academic Year 1978-79* (Salonika: Georgiades, 1978), pp. 147-148 (in Greek).

68. Dimokritian University of Thrace, *Catalogue of the Academic Year 1977-78* (Komotini: no publisher, 1978), pp. 48, 68-69.

69. Panteios Highest School of Political Sciences, *Catalogue of the Academic Year 1976-77* (Athens: Tsironis, 1978), p. 120.

70. See earlier discussion, "Etiology of Arrested Development," pp. 298-299.

71. For example, Dr. A. Tsitsouras is associated with the Division of Criminal Affairs of the Council of Europe.

72. For example, Dr. D. Kalogeropoulos is research director of the French National Center for Scientific Research (CNRS) in Paris.

BIBLIOGRAPHY

In writing this chapter, an effort was made to refer to the essential Greek criminological literature. Therefore, the previous references are quite indicative of the existing bibliography in Greek. The section that follows should be read in conjunction with the bibliographical references that preceded. Emphasis is given to English, French, and German materials because the number of books written in Greek is limited.

Major Books in the Greek Language Published after 1945*

Textbooks of criminology written by Gardikas, Daskalopoulos and Marangopoulos-Yotopoulos are mentioned in the notes above. The following books on general criminology are in addition.

Alexiadis, S. *Inquisitive Techniques*. Salonika: 1978.

Anagnostakis, S. C. *A System of Penological Science. Correctional Law*. Part I. Salonika: 1978.

Bakatsoulas, M. *General Principles of Penology*. Athens: 1972.

Caranikas, D. *Penology*. Vol. A. Salonika: 1948. Vol. B. Salonika: 1950.

Caranikas, D. *Criminology: According to University Lectures*. Salonika: 1956.

Caranikas, D. *Textbook of Penology*. Salonika: 1963.

Papadatos, P. A. *General Principles of Contemporary Rational and Humanistic Criminal Policy*. Vol. 1. Athens: 1973. Vol. 2. Athens: 1977.

Papazachariou, J. *General Criminology*. Vol. 1. *Introduction: On the Meaning and Methods of the Science of General Criminology*. Athens: 1950.

Papazachariou, J. *Studies from the Cultural and Biosocial Pathology*, Part I. Athens: 1965.

The following two volumes with an index of authors, a detailed index of subjects, and a chronological index cover (1) most of the books published in Greece or by Greeks abroad during the years 1830-1970, and (2) a considerable number of articles included in periodicals between the years 1830 and 1900. (The third volume is in print.) This bibliography, while not inclusive, is of interest because it refers to publications on criminology, penology, interrogation techniques, police science, criminalistics, forensic medicine, psychiatry and psychology, and penal law and penal procedure.

Series of Criminological Research Center. *Bibliography of Criminological and Penal Sciences in Greece 1830-1970*, by S. C. Anagnostakis. Vol. 1. Athens: 1964, Vol. 2. Athens: 1970.

Among the most important monographs and articles in the area of crime and corrections are the following:

Alexiadis, S., et al. *The Criminality of Minors in Salonika, 1959-1966*. Salonika: 1966.

Anagnostakis, S. C. *The Open Prisons in Greece: A Recent Experiment*. Salonika: 1966.

Anagnostakis, S. C. *The Correctional Possibilities of the Criminal*. Salonika: 1968.

Andrianakis, E."Criminality in Crete." Ph.D. Dissertation, Athens: 1968.

Bakatsoulas, M. *The Habitual and Professional Offenders: Criminological, Comparative and Penological Study*. Athens: 1945.

---

*The publishing company is omitted because in most of the books it is not mentioned.

Bakatsoulas, M. *The Causes of Suicide*. Athens: 1968.

Christodoulou, A. *The Crime of Homicide in Greece During the Years 1960-1964 as a Social Phenomenon*. Salonika: 1966.

Daskalakis, E. *The Functions of Punishment Under the Light of Criminological Data*. Athens: 1973.

Daskalopoulos, J. M. *The Psychological Causes of the Erroneous Judicial Judgment*. Athens: 1965.

Daskalopoulos, J. M. *On the Deeper Nature of Crime*. Athens: 1968.

Fotakis, N. *Topics of Judicial Psychology and Judicial Psychiatry: The Imputability: [Mens Rea Aspects]*. Salonika: 1978.

Fouta, B. *The Problem of Antisocial Behavior of Minors and the Court*. Athens: 1964.

Ierodiakonou, Ch. *Psychiatric Research on the Antisocial Behavior of Children and Adolescents: One Hundred and Twenty Cases of the Child Guidance Clinic*. Salonika: 1968.

Kanellos, Ch. *The Upbringing as a Preventive Factor of Criminality of Minors*. Athens: 1973.

Kazakopoulou, M. *Social Workers and Supervisors of Minors*. Athens: 1972.

Lachanos, A. "Schizophrenia and Criminality." Ph.D. dissertation, Athens: 1966.

Marangopoulos-Yotopoulos, A. *The Witness in Criminal Trial*. Athens: 1966.

Marangopoulos-Yotopoulos, A. *The Treatment of Abnormal Offenders*. Vol. A. Athens: 1975.

Mavrommati, M. *Means Used Towards the Welfare and Successes in the Welfare of the Deviant Minor*. Athens: 1955.

Pipinelli-Potamianou, A. "The Causes of Antisocial Behavior," Ph.D. dissertation, Athens: 1958.

Protopapadaki, E. *The Institution of Conditional Release*. Athens: 1954.

Stamatiadis, P. *Prostitution*. Salonika: 1954.

Trojanou-Loula, A. *The Service of Supervisor of Minors in the Juvenile Court in Greece*. Athens: 1977.

Tsitoura, A. "The Examination of the Personality of the Offender." Ph.D. dissertation, Salonika: 1959.

Tzortzis, P. G. *The Psychology of Witness*. Athens: 1966.

Vallindras, D. *The Criminological Importance of the Motives*. Athens: 1971.

Vouyoukas, C. *The Substantial and Procedural Law on Minors Presently in Force in Greece*. Salonika: 1969.

Xeroteres, J. *The Causes of Antisocial Behavior in Children and Adolescents*. Salonika: 1958.

Selected Works Written in Foreign Languages

Anagnostakis, S. C. "Il primo Codice Penitenziario Greco." [The First Greek Penitentiary Code]. *Rassegna di Studi Penitenziari* 5 (1968).

Anagnostakis, S. C. "The Contemporary Outlook of Criminology." *Cyprus Legal Tribune* 1 (1975):15-24.

Caranikas, D. "Sur quelles bases faut-il établir une classification des condamnés?" [On What Basis Must One Establish a Classification of Convicted Persons?] *Travaux Préparatoires du 12me Congrès Pénal et Pénitentiaire* (1950), pp. 1-10.

Cotsianos, S. "Les Pénitentiaires Agricoles" [Agricultural Prisoners] (Thesis.) Paris: 1948.

Daskalakis, E. *Unité et Pluralité d'Infractions* [Unity and Plurality of Infractions]. Paris: 1969.

Deliyanni, H. "Blood Vengeance Attitudes in Mani and Corsica." Ph.D. dissertation, University of Exeter, England, 1978.

Kourakis, N. C. "Introduction à l'étude de la criminalité en col blanc" [Introduction to the Study of White-Collar Crime]. *Revue de Science Criminelle et de Droit Pénal Comparé* (1974):765-781.

Kourakis, N. C. "Réflexions sur la problématique de la criminalité en col blanc" [Reflections on the Problem of White-Collar Crime]. *Revue Pénitentiaire et de Droit Pénal* 100 (1976):263-278.

Kourakis, N. C. "Contribution à une analyse pluridisciplinaire de l'infanticide" [Contribution to a Multidisciplinary Analysis of Infanticide]. *Revue Pénitentiaire et de Droit Pénal* 102 (1978):345-362.

Lianandonakis, E. "Parental Attitude of an Educative-Learning Character, as a Factor of Psychological-Physical Disturbances in Pre-School Age." *Athenian International Symposium on the Child in the World of Tomorrow*, July 2-8, 1978.

Marangopoulou-Yotopoulou, A. *Les Mobiles du Délit: Etude de Criminologie et de Droit Pénal Suisse et Comparé* [The Motives of the Crime: Study of Criminology and Swiss and Comparative Criminal Law]. Paris: Librairie Générale de Droit et de Jurisprudence, 1974.

Mitsakis, A. "Le Délinquant Mineur en Grèce" [The Juvenile Delinquent in Greece]. Thesis. Paris: Lavergne, 1947.

Papadakis, J. "Games and Gaming in Greece." *Harmossyno Karanika* (1966):257-273.

Papadatos, P. *Le Délit Politique: Contribution à l'Etude contre l'Etat* [The Political Crime: Contribution to the Study Against the State]. Geneva: Droz, 1954.

Papadatos, P. *Le Procès Eichmann* [The Eichmann Trial]. Geneva: Droz, 1964.

Spinellis-Nomicou, C. "Problems and Peculiarities of the American Juvenile Court: Some Lessons for Greece." Ph.D. dissertation, University of Chicago Law School, 1964.

Spinellis-Nomicou, C. "Children of Female Inmates." *Athenian International Symposium on the Child in the World of Tomorrow*, July 2-8, 1978.

Spinellis-Nomicou, C. "Crime in the Changing Greek Society: Reflections on Statistical Data." *Mental Health and Society* 2 (1975):189-195.

Yamarellos, E. *Introduction à la Criminologie* [Introduction to Criminology]. Paris: Poitiers, 1965.

15

HUNGARY

Katalin Gönczöl

Modern Hungarian criminology began around the turn of the century. After the first written criminal code took effect in 1878, a growing interest in the study of the causes of crime surfaced. As a result of the rapid economic development and social transformation of this period, the number of adult and juvenile offenders increased and recidivistic crimes took new forms. The adjustments of criminal policy to new forms of crime relied heavily on contemporary works in criminology. In view of all the social developments, Hungarian criminology caught up rather quickly with the contemporary and highly developed criminologies of Western Europe. This "intermediary tendency" was especially assisted by the works of F. von Liszt, G. A. van Hamel, and A. Prins.

RISE OF MODERN CRIMINOLOGY IN HUNGARY

The period after World War II was characterized by a gradual retrogression of Hungarian criminology. The state power that settled in after the war preserved its rule primarily by dictatorial methods. Criminology could not flourish under political circumstances that opposed the disclosure of grave social contradictions in the course of analyzing crime. Dogmatic legal theories, slavishly serving the regime, came into prominence.

In the post-World War II period, as a result of a dogmatic interpretation of Marxism, criminology could not reveal the realistic features of crimes. Under the political circumstances prevailing at the beginning of the 1950s, crime as a social phenomenon was considered to be utterly alien to the socialist order: ". . . and the objective reasons for crimes appearing under the developing socialist conditions are searched for in the social-economic relations of capitalism, whilst the subjective ones are to be found in the remnant awareness of capitalism."[1]

If crime is not the function of the prevailing development of socialist society but exists, regardless of circumstances, as the effect of external capitalist environment, then science can do nothing else but wait until the change of political conditions automatically stops this harmful phenomenon. It would be unnecessary to disclose the criminological nature of crimes in other respects as well, when the situation of the time, as characterized by András Szabó, is: "What need is there for the criminological research of crimes when we are aware of the lag of social consciousness compared to social existence as a matter of course and therefore, all attitudes offending the norm may be put to the account of the remnant awareness of the past?"[2] Without doubt, social consciousness usually lags behind the development of the reality of life experiences and only in the long range will it be equal to the circumstances determined by that reality. The mere recognition of this fact, however, does not create social conditions adequate for bringing scientifically based methods in support of crime-fighting.

The development of sociology and psychology, as well as of criminology, was hindered by the dogmatic political circumstances of those years. All three sciences were degraded as "bourgeois pseudosciences." From the primary period of eliminating contemplation of society from the view of voluntarism, that is, from 1957 on, the three branches of science began a revival at about the same time.[3]

The change in attitude in criminal jurisprudence had the most direct impression on postwar criminology. The new perspective in criminal policy was expressed primarily in the restoration of legality. Inquiries were begun in criminal jurisprudence with the aim of strengthening the guaranteed rules of socialist criminal law and placing them on scientific grounds. The monographs by Laszlo Viski and Tibor Király on legal dogmatism are good examples.[4] Simultaneously with the publication of these works, interest arose in the factual social problems connected with crimes. Ready-made answers, routinely offered through contemplation of society, were not accepted for the questions that should be the prerogative of criminology.

The first criminological works of theoretical significance were aimed at establishing the necessity of this functional science, its character as a self-reliant branch of science, and the methodological particularities of its subject.[5] Several studies evaluated the modern bourgeois trends of criminology.[6]

The most comprehensive inquiries in criminology were directed at the disclosure and empirical analysis of juvenile delinquency. The authors attempted to answer some general theoretical questions of criminology. They propounded the scientific conditions for perceiving crimes, the theoretical and methodological questions of motive research, and the possibilities of science-based prevention.[7] From the viewpoint of sociology, the most valuable statements may be found in the work of József Vigh. The investigation of the criminological particularities of juvenile delinquency is completed by revealing the singularities of psychology.[8]

In the early 1970s, Hungarian criminologists also dealt with empirical analysis of recidivist crimes and of crimes against property. Various journals for several years carried debates on the evaluation of habitual offenses under the criminal law and by criminology, the dangers they held for society, and the effectiveness of the means criminal law used against them.[9] The first reference book published about investigations of habitual criminals contained useful empirical knowledge that turned the arguments towards more concrete suggestions for drafting criminal policy.[10] To expand knowledge of the criminological nature of crimes against property, fact-revealing works were begun.[11]

An important impetus to the development of criminology into a science was the appearance of the first university lecture notes.[12] In several respects, these notes extended beyond the accomplishments of contemporary criminological inquiries in Hungary. They provided sound theoretical foundations and methodological guidance for further research on the social nature of crimes. The notes took the standpoint that under existing circumstances crimes are inevitable as a mass phenomenon of society and their causes must be sought in the social conditions.[13] They took stock of macro- and micro-structural relations, emphasizing the stochastic relation of social determinants that are encouraging crimes. They dealt with the problem of personal causality, that is, the environmental and psychic factors instrumental in committing individual crimes. They introduced the most up-to-date results of research on the specific outward forms of crimes; thus, they dwelled on causal, habitual, and juvenile crimes. They outlined an extensive range of practical crime prevention activities, relying on criminological research. To establish the historical basis for the new scientific view, the lecture notes summarized the development of criminological thought and analyzed the new tendencies and findings of post-World War II bourgeois criminology.

Postwar criminology in Hungary rather rapidly overcame the disadvantageous conditions produced by the given historical circumstances. Hungarian jurisprudence helped set this pace through its animated discussions of the problems of legal responsibility, determinism, and free will, which had been controversial subjects for almost a century.[14] By denial of free will, a new conception of responsibility has come into being and has advanced the recognition of criminological research related to the social determination of human attitudes.

The revival of Soviet criminology nearly coincided with endeavors to establish criminology in Hungary.[15] Hungarian criminologists could find support in several questions of a theoretical and methodological nature; they could rely on the results of Soviet criminology too.[16] They also used the results of research in Soviet philosophy and psychology.[17]

The precondition of creating an up-to-date criminology is the development of statistical data on the morphology of crime, which is a complex and time-consuming process. Data appropriate for scientific criminology did not become available until 1964. Now the Chief Prosecutor's Office, cooperating with the Ministry of the Interior, annually releases information on the dynamics and structural changes of crimes.

On the basis of its initial scientific results, modern Hungarian criminology was recognized in the mid-1960s as an independent branch of science. "In the meanwhile," András Szabó says, "the practice of guiding society takes a fundamental change in its entirety; it does not create ideological restrictions in respect of scientific research but expects concrete assistance to solve the particular problems attached to specific periods."[18] The self-reliance of criminology, of course, is relative; it does not mean total independence of other social sciences. It has its closest connection with the rest of the criminal sciences, all of which are interconnected by their common interests in the criminal act, the criminal person, crimes, and the questions of how to fight crimes. They have the common task of promoting the most effective means of overcoming crime. Criminology differs from criminal law and procedure in terms of divergent investigative means, depths of analysis, and theoretical perspectives.

The organizational prerequisites for an up-to-date Hungarian criminology were established at the beginning of the 1960s. The Research Institute of Criminology and Criminalistics was created in 1960. This institute has moved beyond its initial empirical examination of the specific forms of committing crimes to take up significant, all-embracing theoretical works. Nearly at the same time, the Department of Criminology was set up in the Institute of Political Science and Jurisprudence of the Hungarian Academy of Sciences; it has become one of the most successful facilities for Hungarian criminological research. Other criminological research units have evolved in the secretariat of the Chief Prosecutor's Office, the Ministry of Interior, and the National Headquarters of Law Enforcement for selective analyses into the forms and causes of crimes and the specific means of prevention.

Organized instruction of criminology on the university level was started in 1961. General criminology has been a compulsory subject for one semester in law school since 1964. Those law students aspiring to the judiciary have been required since 1971 to take a one-semester course of lectures, under the title "Special Chapter of Criminology," which analyze certain concrete outward forms of crime. Special university summary notes also help the students for examinations on this topic. Departments of criminology in law schools conduct criminological inquiries which further develop this education.

The College of Police Officers offers instruction in criminology for four semesters. Criminology is a required subject in the college training of educators employed in law enforcement. Since 1974 special problems, primarily of a criminal-social nature, have also been included in the university instruction of sociologists.

In addition to their scientific work, professional criminologists in Hungary help criminological practitioners, persons engaged in crime prevention, and lay persons such as voluntary policemen, lay assessors, and voluntary social workers involved in after-care. The exchange of up-to-date scientific findings is promoted by various forums, including those sponsored by the Criminological Panel of the Eötvös Loránd University, the Research Institute of Criminology and Criminalistics, and the programs of the Hungarian Academy of Sciences. The merger of scientific and practical aspects of criminology is especially cultivated in the sessions of the Hungarian Federation of Legal Profession. The popularization of scientific results which should be put to use rapidly is the task of the Legal Department of the Scientific Educational Society within the framework of extension programs of the profession.

CRIME AS A SOCIAL PHENOMENON

By the 1960s, crime in Hungary had fallen 40 percent below the level in 1938, which is considered the last year of peace in Hungary. The number of criminal acts committed since 1965—after a downtrend—became stagnant (see Table 15-1). The rate of criminal acts per 10,000 persons, however, has decreased. The number of known perpetrators of crimes and their rate per 10,000 persons also declined.

TABLE 15-1
NUMBER OF CRIMES AND CRIMINALS SUBJECT TO
PUBLIC PROSECUTION, 1965-1977

Year	Number of Known Crimes Falling Under Public Prosecution	Base Rate (1965 Equals 100 percent)[a]	Rate of Known Crimes Falling Under Public Prosecution per 10,000 Persons	Number of Known Perpetrators Falling Under Public Prosecution	Base Rate (1965 Equals 100 percent)[a]	Rate of Known Perpetrators Falling Under Public Prosecution per 10,000 Persons
1965	121,961	100.0	120.3	90,713	100.0	89.5
1966	121,020	99.2	119.1	90,674	99.9	89.2
1967	119,872	98.3	117.6	87,894	96.9	86.2
1968	118,254	97.0	115.5	82,340	90.8	80.4
1969	110,622	90.7	107.7	81,785	90.2	79.6
1970	122,289	100.3	118.5	84,863	93.6	82.2
1971	123,147	101.0	119.3	88,126	97.1	85.1
1972	116,073	95.2	112.1	90,520	99.8	87.2
1973	119,061	97.6	114.6	83,531	92.1	80.2
1974	111,825	91.7	107.3	76,308	84.1	73.0
1975	120,889	99.1	115.0	81,045	89.3	77.1
1976	129,424	106.1	112.4	83,655	92.2	79.1
1977	123,623	101.4	116.3	82,608	91.1	77.7

Source: *Information About Crimes—1977* (Budapest: Ministry of Interior and Secretariat of Chief Public Prosecutor, 1978).

[a]Statistic for the given year is divided by the 1965 statistic.

In keeping with the pattern of previous years, more than half the criminal acts in 1977—55 percent to be exact—were crimes against property, 17 percent traffic violations, and 11 percent acts of violence. Among the above-mentioned kinds of criminal acts, those of a fairly serious nature—the so-called "real crime" —represented 56.2 percent; the rest were regarded as only minor threats to society, the so-called delict. Of all crimes, only a small proportion were very serious violent crimes; willful homicide 0.2 percent, robbery 0.6 percent, rape 0.6 percent, and malicious injury causing serious bodily harm 3.5 percent. From another perspective, willful criminal acts made up 94.3 percent of total offenses; the rest were negligent ones.

The ratio of previously convicted criminals increased by 12 percent from 1974 to 1977. In 1977, almost one out of three offenders in Hungary had been convicted previously. The proportion of women among offenders is rather modest; only 11 to 13 percent of the perpetrators have been women in recent years. Juveniles—fourteen to eighteen years of age—account for only 8.5 percent of all offenders, but the criminal activity of juveniles has increased in the past few years. The rate of juvenile offenders per 10,000 persons was 107.7 in 1967 and 123.8 in 1977. Juveniles tended to concentrate on certain offenses. In 1977, juveniles perpetrated one out of every four breaking-and-entering incidents, one out of every six rapes, and one out of ten incidents of rowdyism.

SOCIOECONOMIC DEVELOPMENT AND CRIME

In 1890, Lacassagne said that "societies have exactly the kind of criminals they deserve." Accordingly, we should examine the most typical criteria regarding the present state of Hungarian society.[19] Only thus may we explain how crimes briefly described above emerged from particular social circumstances.

Hungary has been a socialist country since 1948. Her population numbered 10,625,000 in 1976; her area is 93,000 square kilometers, only 1 percent of Europe's land area. The population has increased 14.3 percent since 1950. Change of the country's political and power relations has transformed the economic and social structure. Employment in the industrial and service sectors has doubled since 1950, and simultaneously agricultural employment has declined by almost one-third. Of all women, 77.6 percent are salary or wage-earners. The proportion of the population earning income has increased by 5 percent since 1950. The standard of living has improved significantly since 1959. Between 1960 and 1976, the average real income per person doubled. In 1960, only 47 percent of the population was eligible for social security allowances; in 1975, every single inhabitant was covered.[20]

In light of a rather favorable social transformation in Hungary in nearly thirty years, why have the number of crimes remained stable instead of decreasing? Hungarian criminologists agree that crimes today are reproduced by the social processes that take place in the macro-structure as a regular social mass phenomenon.[21] József Vigh writes: "The structural transformation of society in a favorable way may bring along some negative phenomenon with it, particularly when this change comes about not conforming to the rules of proportionate evolution, if the realization of the proper theories and aims is done wrongly."[22] The proportionate evolution may suffer if the establishing of human conditions—helping one to adapt to society while also assisting in social integration—does not keep pace with the development of economic factors. The simultaneous adaptation to the new social-economic circumstances taxes the individual's abilities in an extraordinary way. The negative functional effects of the positive economic progress may therefore be systematically minimized by society but in such a way as to bring about both the subjective and objective conditions for adapting to new circumstances.

From 1950 until 1976, the ratio of population employed in industry increased by 20 percent, while those working in agriculture dropped by more than 30 percent. The alteration of work status usually means a change in life-style and, frequently, a change of residence. In 1949, 38 percent of the total population lived in cities; by 1976, the percentage was 50.7. Almost a million and a half—nearly 15 percent of the population—have become city dwellers in the past twenty-eight years.[23] The vital conditions of city life-style had to be created for the strata entering different circumstances of life; dwellings—as well as various institutions of a social, supplier, and cultural type—had to be provided. Their training had to be coordinated with the labor market.

This process has not been entirely without jolts, particularly in the initial period of building socialism—in the 1950s—when the coordination of economic development suffered heavily. Several criminological research studies in Hungary have established the stochastic interconnections—of society undergoing a structural change as well as that of migration—with various forms of crime.[24]

Social mobility in Hungary has gone hand in hand with economic development; therefore, structural change has meant economic improvements for the masses. Economic progress has had favorable social consequences, but it has also influenced crime patterns. Empirical research has demonstrated the stochastic connection only in relation to crimes against property. Using factor analysis, András Szabó investigated the interrelation of juvenile delinquency with the progress of economy; he reached the following conclusions:

1. Socioeconomic development eradicates crimes stemming from poverty and want.

2. Although crimes of want have vanished, improved circumstances in respect of affluence and earnings have brought an increase in the standard of needs; hence, crimes against property do not seem to be unmotivated.

3. The most dynamic factor of economic development is industrialization which increases the mobility of the populace. This change has resulted in a higher ratio of crimes committed by people living in the industrialized areas, since the effect of the attraction of crime in the richer areas providing more opportunities is extended for the *de facto* population too.

4. Industrialization also influences population mobility by way of the agricultural workers' migration. Since the capacity of the cities is not parallel to the transformation of the occupational structure, huge agglomerates have come into existence around the large industrial centers. These agglomerates in turn provide favorable opportunity for crime increases by reason of the disorganized and temporary circumstances.

5. The occupational structure of the active population is being changed rapidly by the extensive period of industrial development. However, the alteration of the structure of settlements does not proceed simultaneously with it. Since there is a discrepancy between the factors, the daily mobility of the most active population between work and residence also affects the growing crime rate from the point of view of the active population and crime.[25]

There is also a possible relationship between criminal careers and increased daily movement from work and residence. The pendulum-like life-style evolved prior to eighteen years of age definitely promotes the development of a long-lasting criminal career.[26]

Of all the categories of relations within the social structure, the division of labor within the economy is of decisive importance because the position of the individual or of a group in the social structure increasingly may be defined in these terms. Under socialism, the status according to the division of labor is more informative than social-class position in the economy based on private ownership. Class relations lost their formerly determinant significance after the development and stabilization of the socialist structure of ownership. The most important means of production ceased to be privately owned, and thus the capitalist class, along with the possibility of exploitation, disappeared. The theory of socialist distribution—in accordance with the quantity and quality of work—conforms to the systematic arrangement of the division of labor on the social level. Therefore, the economic and social standing of individuals or groups may be defined on the basis of the given social layer's position. The place taken in the systematic arrangement of the division of labor signifies the particularities of life-style as well as the cultural and educational standard.

Under socialism, many crimes are a product of society in the sense that they are produced by a relationship between position in the division of labor and a well-defined life-style. The tendency of criminological research is sociological, as András Szabó explains:

On the level of sociology we are interested not so much in the causal relation between the criminal acts and the social processes or facts as in those social conditions which make the committing of these acts possible with a stochastic probability. Therefore, we are interested not in the effect of social conditions impressed upon the individual but in the likely connection of the social arrangement— devoid of the motive of individuality—with crimes. This connection of probability may be measured with statistical frequency; however, its essence is, not in the possibility of being measured, but the sociological stir that comes about in accordance with statistical regularity.[27]

Sociological analyses have helped define the relation between position in the economic strata and life-style, and have given some understanding of crime in the course of the survey of the whole of Hungarian society.[28] However, comprehensive investigations have not focused on the sociological significance of the three phenomena (economic status, life-style, and crime), although attempts have been made in that direction incidental to studying specific forms of crime, such as violent and parasitic crimes, crimes against property, juvenile delinquency, and dangerous recidivism.[29]

Positive social development has also changed women's social position. Since more than three-quarters of Hungarian women have active occupations earning income, a change has taken place in the traditional functions of the family. Society has had to accept more and more of those tasks that formerly belonged within the family as a community—for instance, the placing of children in nurseries and kindergartens, the facilitating of household tasks by state benefits, and the caring of elderly, ill members of the family. Meeting these demands on a social level leaves much to be done as well. The necessity of women going to work came before society found it economically feasible to take over the former functions of the family. The growing number of women earning wages is therefore a social phenomenon for the time being in stochastic relation to crimes. (The correlation is $+ 0.37$ nationwide.)[30] The increased employment of women has a bearing on both juvenile and adult crime.

In addition to increased female employment, the weakened functioning of the family may be traced to industrialization, the socialist reorganization of agriculture, and rapid socioeconomic progress. Previously, half of all Hungarian families worked in agriculture in a communal way. Today the communal aspect is nonexistent, and the economic functions of farming have gained prominence instead. Women's financial independence, increasing democracy within the family, and newly surfacing emotional factors made the family in Hungary rather vulnerable.[31] This vulnerability is expressed by the growing number of divorces. In 1960, the divorce rate was 6.5 per 1,000 existing marriages; by 1976, the rate was 8.7.[32] Research has indicated that the number of divorces and the number of crimes are interrelated (correlation coefficient of $+ 0.66$).[33] Every empirical investigation of crime in Hungary has referred to the influence of divorce on juvenile and adult crime.

The contradictions in the social structure have a multiplying effect in the school system which is the institutionalized instrument of social advance. In the theoretically perfect school system, pupils of the most varying social positions are given equal chances, but schools everywhere, and in Hungary too, have not leveled social inequities.[34] Those persons with inadequate education are at a disadvantage. Perpetrators of crime, especially habitual offenders, have below-average educational attainment. Eight years of school in Hungary is obligatory and free for everybody; yet, 18.1 percent of the inhabitants over fifteen years of age had not achieved this level of schooling in 1975.[35] Of habitual criminals prone to violent crimes, 69.6 percent had less than eight years of schooling; the similar figure was 43.6 percent of habitual property offenders.[36]

The association between alcoholism and crime has been widely discussed. Consumption of alcohol in Hungary has increased at a greater rate than the standard of living. Between 1960 and 1976, the number of liters consumed per person increased for wine from 29.9 to 34.0, for beer from 36.8 to 77.0, and for liquor from 2.8 to 8.2.[37] In 1977, nearly one out of four offenders committed a crime either while in a drunken condition or in connection with a drinking life-style.[38] One of two violent crimes against a person was perpetrated by an offender carrying on a drunken life-style, but a drunken condition was even more common in traffic offenses.

Criminology investigates not only the effects of social and environmental factors, taken in the broadest meaning, on crimes, but it also attaches great importance to microenvironmental elements directly shaping personality. József Vigh explains:

The fundamental conditions of people's existence are determined by macrostructures which are the basic processes of society, and the personalities of people are formed and shaped by these very same conditions. As the development of one's personality is affected by the macroenvironment through the medium of the microenvironment, in the same way one's views about the macroenvironment, as well as one's frame of mind are being shaped by means of the microenvironment.[39]

Microenvironmental factors are involved in the face-to-face system of human relations, and, as such, they do not avail themselves of relative self-determination. They do not reflect mechanically the social effects taken in the broadest sense but may distort them in either positive or negative directions.[40]

Most criminological works in Hungary have considered the effect of the concrete factors of microenvironment upon perpetrators. The search for patterning of individual behaviors has been found to take researchers to regularities existing on a level of mass phenomenon.[41] The questions of free time and juvenile delinquency are treated, for instance, by Miklós Vermes in one of his latest studies.[42]

Results of research into the social causes of crime are being used primarily in the deliberate and methodological shaping of criminal policy. Poorly coordinated policy in itself may contribute to the incidence of crime. Planned guidance of society cannot be effective solely through uses of the law or limitation of the social functions of criminology to the sphere of criminal policy. Scholars of socialist criminology are encouraged to step out of the "ivory tower" of science and to fulfill their social mission. Of course, the implementation of scientific conceptions through policy must be within financial possibilities.

As an example of careful channeling of change of the social structure, new industrial enterprises requiring less raw material are located to coincide with available labor. Migration or lengthy travel between residences and work are minimized, undesirable expansion of large industrial cities is avoided, differences among various forms of housing are lessened, and social mobility is cultivated under humane conditions. As another example, the establishment of the subjective conditions of intergenerational mobility can be realized today solely in the school system. Education is the unequivocal prerequisite of social advancement. Through centralization of schools and the extension of a boarding school system, the state deliberately endeavors to eliminate inequities in schools. Free adult instruction at the public high school and college levels enables persons to obtain a university degree while continuing full employment. Previously, social and financial considerations made this impossible.

The direct purpose of eliminating social contradictions is obviously not to reduce the crime rate but rather to prevent crimes. More direct effect may be attained by expressly sociopolitical measures. The state's planned sociocultural policy has been directed toward social integration of the underprivileged strata. The construction of flats, supported by extensive state subsidies, is, for example, one of the most important means of social adjustment. Contrary to the principle of distributing rewards according to work performance, the allocation of flats, financed by central expenditures, is in accordance with social necessities and the support of large families. To somewhat slow the rapid transformation of family functions, certain steps have been taken. Mothers are allowed to be absent from their work until their infants are three years of age; during this time, they receive one-third of the average wage of a skilled worker. As a result of the expansion of social security benefits, medical care is free, ending an important source of uncertainty. The fight against alcoholism and the curing of alcoholics are also state tasks.

SUBJECT AND METHOD OF CRIMINOLOGY

Hungarian criminology examines crimes, first, as a historically changing mass phenomenon and, second, as an attitude of individually offending the legal norms.

There is an agreement that there is no need for a separate notion of the criminal act as an individual phenomenon when the main point of criminology is the prohibitive nature of the criminal law. All other criteria are given expression in this or originate from it. Criminology revolves around the question of the act regulated by criminal law. Whatever else is being examined is done not as a subject of its own but in order to understand it better. This examination is done without restriction.[43]

Hungarian literature includes digressions from the concept of crimes being the central subject of criminology. According to József Vigh, "Crimes are such historically changing social mass phenomena of the criminal law which consist of the totality of criminal acts and their perpetrators in a defined area and period."[44] József Gödöny emphasizes that here we are dealing with the complexity of an individual phenomenon which, on the one hand, has a particular structure, regularities, and form of motion at its disposal, and a reaction on its own formation. On the other hand, its close connection and interrelationship with other social phenomena has an effect on its own situation, changes, and motion.[45]

Paraphrasing the concept, András Szabó sums up the social definition of crime. The social relation of crimes lies first of all in that they are forbidden, and this relation keeps forming in accordance with the historically changing order of the system of criminal law.[46] Furthermore, crime is the totality of behavioral forms directed to solve problems and satisfy demands, and as such it is defined socially too.

Crime is such a forbidden type of behavior which connects normally with the given conditions of existence, is meaningful and rational because it solves problems and satisfies demands...an act of instrument, in other words. These acts of instrument become discriminated against precisely because of their sociality being obvious and not on account of primarily being aberrant, pathological or immoral....In its relation to the conditions of existence, criminal attitude is socially possible, and therefore it is a normal, intelligent and rational type of behavior.[47]

According to Szabó, crime is a social product in its orientation of value too. Values set upon or endangered are personified, that is, defended by the existing social institutions. Denial of value is just as much an objective quality of criminal behavior as the social definition of values is objective.[48] Szabó states that in its consequences, crime is a phenomenon corresponding to the denial of value; crime is identified and revealed by social routine; it is reproduced in a reciprocal effect of social relations; and the methods of struggling against it are developed as historical effects.[49]

These differences in theoretical perspective do not mean divergent opinions on fundamental questions. The theoretical difference, however, promotes the investigations of crime from a multitude of approaches and a recognition of their ample social nature.

Criminological research is being conducted on two levels: the level of social mass phenomena mainly through sociological methods, and the level of individual phenomena mainly by sociopsychological methods. Szabó sees these two levels as bodies of substantive knowledge entirely separate from one another: "The two materials of knowledge may not even be homogenized as a matter of course; sociology may not be made into psychology, and psychology may not be substituted by sociology; there is no possibility for their synthesis, and thus there is no possibility for criminology synthesizing them either."[50]

His view stands almost unparalleled in Hungarian criminology. Since crime and the criminal act are social phenomena consisting of the relation between the whole and the part, breeding on identical social roots, they may not be disconnected from each other just because their recognition necessitates different kinds of methods. Miklós Vermes writes: "Such type of separation of the process being on both general and individual levels may hardly be endorsed when their close interrelation is obvious and, in the course of the activity aimed at disclosing and explaining crimes, the results of the two levels of investigation necessarily complete each other."[51]

Even Szabó provides an excellent example of how the process of social definition of crime may be followed on the levels of both individual and mass phenomena.[52] We do not intend to wash away the clear differences between the two levels. The diverse mechanism effect prevailing in the processes on various levels may not be denied either,[53] but the summarizing of information gathered by different methods must be acknowledged.

The mechanism effect of the factors appearing on various levels are endeavored to be explained not by setting the various phenomena side by side, that is, by mechanical comparison, but by applying dynamic synthesis; in other words, after analyzing the motion and reciprocal effect of the diverse phenomena, the entire dialectic movement of these appearing in crimes have to be taken into consideration.[54]

The summary of information related to crime and individual criminal acts is aided by criminological investigation of the differences between the general and specific phenomena and by analyzing each outward form or different type of crime. Crime, being a phenomenon of reality, does not constitute a homogeneous social category. As for all mass phenomena, crime also possesses a natural structure. On the basis of the realistic character of social circumstances, we may distinguish, for instance, criminal acts directly attacking the ruling political circumstances, those acts offending the property structure, and those damaging general human intercourse. The individual phenomena of crime may also be classified, for instance, by the legal category injured, the method of committing the act, and the perpetrator's form and degree of culpability from the victim's standpoint.

As asserted by József Gödöny, "the categories and groups have two sides; partly they reflect the particularities of the individual phenomena and partly they are drawing nearer to crimes as a mass phenomenon."[55]

In the interest of reaching a determined goal, the classification may be used on the basis of those qualities to form wholly or relatively homogeneous groups in the heterogeneous composition of crimes. Criteria summarized on the level of the homogeneous groups may be compared with one another, and their relation may be clarified in respect to the totality of crimes. The disclosure of homogeneous groups, evolved within crimes and in relation to other general and special social phenomena, will also be possible. In the scheme thus developed, it is possible to get closer to the recognition of the social nature of crime and to change the method of studying individual criminal acts. A new chance will come about for comparison; the relation of the specific to the particular will get into the center of inquiry that helps recognize the typical qualities of the specific. Should causal research of criminology take such a turn, the struggle against crime may be more effective because of knowledge disclosed. Because the social causes of crime may be pointed out more amply and comprehensively, the instruments of crime prevention and the struggle against crime may be better differentiated.[56]

Crimes against property, violent, parasitic, and traffic crimes, as well as crimes against the people's economy have become subjects of criminological analysis by reason of the similarities manifested in criminal attitudes.[57] With regard to female, habitual, juvenile, and gypsy criminals, recent research has dealt with specific attitudes—that is, similar factors—existing in their personality, personal circumstances, and life-style.[58]

CRIMINOLOGY AND CRIMINAL POLICY

The role of criminology in shaping criminal policy is determined largely by the prevailing theory of responsibility in criminal law, by how open this theory is to acceptance, and by the use made of the results of criminological research. Szabó writes:

If, namely, the human attitude is indeterminate, then the institution of responsibility has to be accepted by us merely as a judgment of value dealing with the main part of moral attitude that is an ethical disapproval, which has no influence upon the further development of the human attitude. If, on the other hand, the human attitude and action are considered as determined ones, then the institution of responsibility is acknowledged as the attitude's further determinant. Therefore, set upon the viewpoint of the attitude being determined, we should not look for metaphysical or moral categories in responsibility but regard it as the means of changing reality.[59]

Szabó points out an important connection between criminology and criminal policy. True enough, solely by accepting the determinate human action, criminal policy might adequately utilize the results of criminological research. Criminal responsibility based on the determined nature of the human act and the prevention of it are legal institutions inseparable from one another. Prevention, in both the general and special sense, is made possible by the determined nature of future attitude. This may be realized solely by the knowledge of the causes of crime and concrete criminal acts. The prerequisite of adequate education is to know the causes of criminal behavior.

The establishment of criminal law's determinist responsibility offers an explanation of how criminology sets about performing its task and by what means. "Regarding the establishment of criminal law's responsibility," Szabó says, "we may state that the prevention of criminal acts is its social purpose and in the interest of this goal the application of criminal law's compelling measures will be permitted—with regard to antisocial attitudes and their perpetrators as well—against those only which or who may be determined by these particular means."[60]

According to this viewpoint, the rationality of the historic development of criminal law is to be found in the conviction that only those attitudes should be punished that may be influenced in this way, and only those persons should be dealt with by law whose future behavior may be moved in a positive direction by the instruments of criminal law. (The death penalty is an exception here, of course, because by applying it we may speak merely of a general preventive effect.) All of these arguments mean for criminology that the subject of its research consists of dangerous acts toward society, to a large degree acts of those persons having normal will-power in a medical sense. In dealing with this subject matter, criminology must disclose the social causes of critical behavior and work out the social means for their prevention and, within this, the instruments of criminal law.

Criminal sanctions express social disapproval necessarily when they react to extensively dangerous attitudes towards society; the mission of criminal law is the punishment of these perpetrators. The nature of such punishment asserts itself in the compelling character of the criminal sanction. The constraints it imposes not only are declarations of disapproval by society but also must mean encouragement for showing adequate attitudes.

In the course of applying criminal sanctions, the fundamental rights of a small number of citizens—the perpetrators of crimes—are restricted. Therefore, in a constitutional state guaranteed rules are attached to these restrictions. Criminal sanctions may not interfere with the life of even a criminal citizen to a greater degree than warranted by the interest of protecting society and preventing a new crime. Punishment may be applied solely on the basis of a criminal attitude dangerous to society. Even punishment must primarily adhere to the two previously mentioned factors: guilt and the act's danger to society. In the interest of resocialization serving a special preventive objective, the perpetrator's personality and his intensity of danger to society must also be given due consideration.

As long as the person's danger to society reflects unequivocally in the act being the subject of criminal responsibility, the three aspects mentioned above may be harmonized in the sentence. Up to now the criminal attitude may have been entirely alien to the perpetrator of the crime; the criminal act may be an unexpected phenomenon, or it may reflect an habitual antisocial life-style. This distinction must be pointed out beyond the shadow of a doubt, regardless of the seriousness of the act. Following the three viewpoints in meting out punishment results in a contradictory situation. Recognition of this contradiction helps explain the conflict between the traditional conception of criminal law, adhering to the theory of responsibility proportionate to the act, and the view of criminology observing the possibility of reforming the perpetrator.

Recent analyses by Hungarian criminologists reveal that sentences based on traditional criminal law did not adequately serve the purpose of special prevention. In sentencing, the assessment of the criminal act's objective danger to society was emphasized. Beyond the question of intentional or negligent guilt, the decisive factor in the court's fixing of a punishment was the act itself and the degree of damage caused:

When meting out punishment, the nature of the act naturally may never be ignored; when calling someone to account originates out of it, that is the reason we apply some measure of punishment with respect to the person committing the act. On the other hand, the nature of punishment may not be solely the consequence of the seriousness of the act. The perpetrator's personality, the chances of socializing and the conditions of resocializing him must be taken into consideration the same way or even more so. If it pleases, let the punishment be proportionate not only with the happenings of the past but also with the consequence of the favorably directed determination in the future.[61]

Sentencing practices were not affected solely by theoretical criticisms; concrete suggestions were based on empirical knowledge. Arguments ensued about the effectiveness of short-term imprisonment and its role in preventing recidivism.[62] Sentencing policy in regard to habitual criminals and the disparity among sentences for various crime categories were also questioned.[63] Efforts to impose uniform sentences for crimes against property were criticized for resulting in unjustified severity, particularly when compared to violent crimes.[64] Ultimately, the idea of reforming the entire penal system also came under consideration. A series of studies by both criminal lawyers and criminologists called for a new, more progressive Criminal Code more suitable to the requirements of the period.[65]

The first Criminal Code (the law of IV, 1978), reflecting up-to-date research in Hungarian criminology, has been recently embodied.[66] For the sake of brevity, only the most important modifications reflecting criminological research are considered here.

The new Criminal Code assigns only prevention as the purpose of punishment in lieu of retribution. Expansion of the range of punishment increases the chances for a penal policy based on individualization of punishment. In certain cases and under well-defined conditions, the secondary penalties may nowadays be applied as primary ones. By introducing the new method of imposing fines in the so-called daily lots, more favorable conditions have developed for individualization. Instead of categorical punishments, provisions and their forms have also been augmented. Thus, the frequency of short-term incarceration should diminish; the lower limit of incarceration has been raised from thirty days to three months. The death penalty has been made markedly exceptional, never obligatory, and is imposed only as a last resort.

Reform of the criminal law has transformed the regulation of repeaters in keeping with research findings. Instead of the previous two categories, the new law establishes four categories of recidivists. Punishments are differentiated according to the simple repeater, the "homogeneous" criminal committing the same type of criminal act, habitual criminals, and the recidivist especially dangerous to society. Research was considered in decriminalizing certain offenses— traffic violations and crimes against the people's economy. Another contribution of research has been the procedural requirement that authorities reveal those causes and circumstances that made the criminal act possible or contributed toward it.[67]

Perhaps the greatest change in the past decade and a half may be seen in the system and practice of criminal execution. Criminological research had an important part in this too. In the 1950s, the political perspective and the dogma of criminal law were not prepared to develop a new penal system in accord with the new social requirements. Only criminological research could develop the factual basis for a humanely centered penal system serving the aims of special prevention. The first socialist provision of law for the penal system (the law decree of 1966, paragraph 21) exhibited the first results of the then young criminology. From this decree came the organization of education as the pivot of the penal system and the payment of regular wages for inmate labor. Education in a stricter sense—schooling and the instruction of skilled workers—is carried out individually and collectively to prepare prisoners for a free life. The techniques of psychology and psychotherapy take second place. These policies were suggested by research indicating that antisocial attitudes are derived from social factors and therefore are more likely to be influenced by the methods of adult pedagogy than by psychology.[68] The theory of differentiated education expressed in the penal code strongly supports the idea of resocialization and provides for isolation from the outside world only in the most justified instances.

Criminology also had the initiative role in creating the system of after-care activity and sponsorship established since 1965. The first statutory provision emphasized putting the released prisoners to work. The new provision (the law decree of 1975, paragraph 20) expanded authority to assure living accommodations, in addition to employment, among the tasks of after-care.

The number of released prisoners receiving after-care service was increased, and the system improved by adding professional and voluntary social workers. The new Criminal Code expanded the clientele to cover those convicted offenders who were placed on probation or received a suspended sentence. These provisions also reflect the depenalizing efforts evolved from criminological research.[69]

PROSPECTS FOR INFLUENCE OF CRIMINOLOGY

The further development of criminology is therefore even more completely determined by the demands of systematic criminal policy. In criminal justice planning, research works dealing with the prognosis of crime[70] have very important roles. The framing of the new Criminal Code and the provisions of the penal system followed the results of criminological research on the effectiveness of imprisonment.[71] The importance of such research will increase. We may also count on the further development of research having typological character for penal policy based on the viewpoint of resocialization. Since the significant majority of criminological research is carried on in self-sufficient scientific institutions, there is no danger in their serving the daily requirements of penal policy.

Up-to-date research in criminology has had an effect on practice through its transmission in educational programs. In the past fifteen years, every policeman, prosecutor, judge, defense attorney, professional social worker, and so on, finding employment in the criminal justice field has obtained a diploma in a program that included instruction in criminology. Thus, the rising generation does not have particular difficulties in practical application of the new scientific results of criminology. The gap between criminology and criminal law is slowly disappearing.

Criminology has had less effect on public attitudes. The new ideas based on the determinist theory of responsibility and on the causes of criminal behavior clash almost daily with the traditional view of punishment. Public views must be considered in the communication of criminological research findings. An informed public opinion is crucial to the development of the instruments of criminal justice jurisdiction.

NOTES

1. Contemporary viewpoints are quoted in the first of the university summaries of criminology: J. Földvári and J. Vigh, *Criminology* (Budapest: 1965), p. 93. The source of the viewpoints quoted is M. Kádár, *Criminal Law* (Budapest: 1961, General Section, I. Unified University Summary Notes), pp. 105-110.

2. A. Szabó, "Crimes, People and the Society," Ph.D. dissertation (Budapest: 1977), p. 9.

3. The bibliography at the end of this chapter includes works that contributed to the revival of the social sciences at that time.

4. L. Viski, *Wilfulness and Danger to Society* (Budapest: Publisher of Economics and Law, 1959); T. Király, *The Defense and the Counsel for Defense in Criminal Cases* (Budapest: Publisher of Economics and Law, 1962).

5. K. Kulcsár, "Demographic Factors in Crimes," *Demography*, Issues 2 and 3 (1959); M. Vermes, "The Methodological Questions of Criminological Research," *Gazette of the Institute of Political and Judicial Science*, Issues 1 and 2 (1961); M. Vermes, "The State and Formation of Crimes," *Reality*, Issue 1 (1962); P. Barna, "The Causes and Outward Forms of Crimes," *Police Gazette*, Issue 5 (1961).

6. For instance, L. Viski and A. Szabó, "The Theory of Criminal Policy in Defense of Society," *Judicial Gazette*, Issue 3 (1960).

7. A. Szabó, *Juveniles and Criminal Law* (Budapest: Publishers of Economics and Law, 1964); J. Molnár, *The Investigations about the Personality of Juvenile Criminals; Criminological Studies*, Vol. 1 (Budapest: Publishers of Economics and Law, 1962); T. Huszár, *Juvenile Criminals* (Budapest: Publishers of Textbooks, 1964).

8. P. Popper, *Emotional Catastrophes: A Possible Determinant of Juvenile Criminality* (Budapest: 1960); Gy. Majláth, "The Criminality of Childhood," *Hungarian Psychological Review*, Issue 4 (1960); J. György, *The Anti-Social Personality* (Budapest: Medicina Publisher, 1967); P. Popper, *The Development of Criminal Disorder in Personality* (Budapest: Academic Publisher, 1970).

9. The initial discussion was by M. Vermes, "Some Questions about Recidivists' Crimes," *Internal Review*, Issue 11 (1963). In two years, nine comments appeared in this periodical.

10. "The Investigation of Recidivist Crimes," *Information Bulletin*, no. 10, the Research Institute of Criminology (1965). Certain conclusions drawn from the report are contained in T. Tavassy, *The Recidivist Crimes of Young Adults: Criminological Studies*, Vol. 5 (Budapest: Publishers of Economics and Law, 1966).

11. Such results are offered, for instance, in "The Criminological Investigation of Intellectual Criminal Acts Against Public Property," *Information Bulletin*, no. 2, Research Institute of Criminology (1963).

12. See Földvári and Vigh, *Criminology*.

13. Ibid.

14. Of studies published around this time, see especially T. Földesi, *The Problem of Will Power* (Budapest: Gondolat Publisher, 1960) and Gy. Eörsi, *The Fundamental*

Problem of Legal Responsibility: The Legal Responsibility of the Civil Law (Budapest: Academic Publishers, 1961).

15. Until 1933, the Soviet Union made a serious effort to study the causes of crime. In 1925, by resolution of the Commissarial Council of the Russian Republic, an institute was established, in connection with the Internal People's Commissariat of Moscow, which had among its tasks the study of criminals and crimes. The institute was directed by Professor Gernet. Numerous publications prove that the first Soviet criminologists achieved important results in studying subjective and objective causes of crime. For further evaluation, see M. Vermes, "The Valuation of the System and Method of Criminology," *Gazette of the Institute of Political and Judicial Science*, Issues 1 and 2 (1961).

16. A. A. Gercenzon, "The Mission of Soviet Jurisprudence and the Prevention of Crimes," *Szovjetszkoje Goszudarstvo i Pravo* (Moscow), Issue 1 (1962); A. B. Szacharov, *The Personality of Criminals and the Cause of Crimes in the Soviet Union* (Moscow: 1961); V. N. Kudrajavcev, *What Is Crime?* (Moscow: 1959).

17. A. Szoboljev, "The Contradictions of Society and Means of Solving Them," *Hungarian Philosophical Review*, Issues 3 and 4 (1958); A. N. Leontyev, "The Historical Method of the Examination of the Human Psyche," *Hungarian Philosophical Review*, Issues 3 and 4 (1959); Sz. L. Rubinstein, *Existence and Consciousness* (Budapest: Kossuth Publishers, 1962).

18. Szabó, "Crimes, People and Society," pp. 11-12.

19. Quoted by A. Irk, *Criminology* (Budapest: 1912), p. 192.

20. *Hungarian Statistical Manual, 1977* (Budapest: Publishers of Statistics, 1978).

21. See M. Vermes, *The Fundamental Questions of Criminology* (Budapest: Academic Publishers, 1971), p. 83.

22. J. Vigh, "Causality, Determination and Prognosis in Criminology," Ph.D. dissertation (Budapest: 1975), p. 234.

23. *Hungarian Statistical Manual, 1977*, p. 36.

24. For example, see *Crimes, the State of Crime-Fighting and the Causes of Crimes in the County of Bács-Kiskun* (Budapest: Secretariat of the Chief Prosecutor, 1968); A. Szabó, "Socioeconomic Development and the Crimes of the Younger Age-Group," *Society and Law* (Hungarian Academy of Sciences), Issue 3 (1972); J. Gödöny, *Social-Economic Progress and Crimes* (Budapest: 1976); K. Gönczöl, "The Typology of Recidivists," manuscript (Budapest: 1978), Part III.

25. Szabó, "Socioeconomic Development and the Crimes of the Younger Age-Group," p. 73.

26. Gönczöl, "The Typology of Recidivists," pp. 172-175.

27. Szabó, "Crimes, People and Society," p. 187.

28. See "Crime and Society" in the bibliography at the end of this chapter.

29. See "Specific Forms of Crime" in the bibliography at the end of this chapter.

30. *Crimes, the State of Crime-Fighting*, p. 18.

31. The sociological characteristics of Hungarian families are discussed in *Family and Marriage in Today's Hungarian Society* (Budapest: Publishers of Economics and Law, 1971).

32. *Hungarian Statistical Manual, 1977*, p. 40.

33. *Crimes, the State of Crime-Fighting*, p. 19.

34. See Zs. Ferge, *The Social Determination of the School System and the Knowledge Acquired at School* (Budapest: Academy Publishers, 1976).

35. *Hungarian Statistical Manual, 1977*, p. 37.

36. Gönczöl, "The Typology of Recidivists," pp. 158-162.

37. *Hungarian Statistical Manual, 1977*, p. 152.

38. *Information about Crimes, 1977*, pp. 79-80.

39. Vigh, "Causality, Determination and Prognosis in Criminology," p. 234.

40. Gönczöl, "The Typology of Recidivists," Part III.

41. In the bibliography at the end of this chapter, the category "Specific Forms of Crime" includes references on violence and parasitic offenses as examples of these regularities.

42. M. Vermes, *Leisure Time and Juvenile Delinquency: Studies on Criminology and Criminalistics*, Vol. 15 (Budapest: Publishers of Economics and Law, 1978).

43. A similar position is taken by L. Viski in his doctoral dissertation, "Criminal Law in Traffic" (Budapest: 1972), pp. 645-655.

44. J. Vigh, "Causality, Determination and Prognosis in Criminology," p. 22.

45. Gödöny, *Socioeconomic Development and Crime* (Budapest: 1976), p. 22.

46. Szabó, "Crimes, People and Society," p. 135.

47. Ibid., p. 142.

48. Ibid., p. 152.

49. Ibid., pp. 153-172.

50. Ibid., p. 22.

51. Vermes, *Fundamental Questions of Criminology*, p. 148.

52. Szabó, "Crimes, People and Society," p. 148.

53. On differences that can be detected in the causality mechanism, see in particular Vigh, "Causality, Determination and Prognosis in Criminology," Chapter 3.

54. See A. Szabó's previous position in Vermes, *Fundamental Questions of Criminology*, p. 150; A. Szabó, "The Fundamental Questions of Basic Criminological Research," *Political Science and Law* 6, no. 3 (1964):328.

55. J. Gödöny, *On Some Questions of Committing Crimes: Studies on Criminology and Criminalistics*, Vol. 10 (Budapest: Publishers of Economics and Law, 1973), p. 28.

56. Similar conclusions can be drawn from T. Horváth, "Thoughts of Our Problems of Punishment," *Hungarian Law*, Issue 5 (1971):259.

57. For example, see *Information Bulletin*, nos. 3, 11, and 12 of Research Institute of Criminology, 1963, 1966, and 1968; Vigh, et al., *Violent Criminal Acts and Their Perpetrators*; F. Irk, "The Criminological Aspects of Road Accidents," Ph.D. dissertation (Budapest: 1976); I. Tauber and J. Kovács, "The Criminological Problems of Criminal Acts Committed against the National Economy," *Review of Ministry of Interior*, Issue 10 (1977); M. Vermes and A. Egressy, *Current Questions of Criminal Acts Committed in Course of Economic Management: Studies of Criminology and Criminalistics*, Vol. 15 (Budapest: Publishers of Economics and Law, 1978).

58. See items included under "Specific Forms of Crime" in the bibliography at the end of the chapter.

59. Szabó, *Juveniles and Criminal Law*, p. 240.

60. Ibid., p. 251.

61. Vigh, "Causality, Determination and Prognosis in Criminology," p. 364.

62. See "Law and Execution of Sanctions" in the bibliography at the end of the chapter.

63. See in particular J. Vigh, et al., *Violent Criminal Acts and Their Perpetrators*, Chapter 11.

64. Ibid.

65. See "Law and Execution of Sanctions" in the bibliography at the end of the chapter.

66. Hungary had had a Criminal Code since 1878. The law (Act No. 5) passed in 1878 has been amended several times, but it remained in force until after World War II. The amendment changing the general part of Act No. 5 dates back to 1950. The first comprehensive Criminal Code of the socialist society (Act No. 5, 1961) could hardly reflect the results of criminology which was then in the process of attaining scientific status. The updating of criminal provisions began in the early 1970s. Before Act No. 4, 1978, was passed, Act No. 5 of 1961 had been partially amended on three occasions:

1. In 1971, a classification was made according to the seriousness of the acts and, as a result, two categories were established: one of real criminal acts and one of delicts. The range of applicability of capital punishment was narrowed, and provisions were modified in regard to criminal acts committed in traffic, against the national economy, and against property.

2. In 1973, legal conditions were created for a broader use of fines.

3. The legal provisions dating from 1974 and referring to preventive detention and subjecting alcoholics to treatment in special institutions based on labor therapy were designed for society's protection against especially dangerous recidivists and the crimes of alcoholics.

67. Paragraph 13 of Government Decree No. 8, 1962, and paragraph 5 of Act No. 1, 1973, which modified it.

68. See "Law and Execution of Sanctions" in the bibliography at the end of this chapter.

69. Of works on after-care, see in particular J. Vigh, "Some Experiences of Aftercare Extended to Juveniles Released from Prison," *Acta Juridica* (1969); M. Ficsor, "Current Questions of Resocialization of Especially Dangerous Recidivists," *Hungarian Law*, Issue 6 (1972); K. Gönczöl, *Aftercare: Chapters from the Domain of Special Criminology* (Budapest: 1973), Chapter 8.

70. A. Szabó, "Forecasting of Crime Figures," *Economics and Law* 6, nos. 2 and 4 (1971); "Prognosis of Criminals," a manuscript by a team of authors (Budapest: 1975).

71. J. Vigh and I. Tauber, "The Major Characteristics of the Effectiveness of Imprisonment," *Judicial Gazette*, Issue 11 (1976); J. Vigh and I. Tauber, "The General Preventive Influence of Imprisonment as a Punishment," *Acta Facultatis* (1977).

BIBLIOGRAPHY

The chapter proper presents comprehensive and representative coverage of the Hungarian literature on criminology. In addition to those resources, the following references are offered for the reader interested in further study of specified topics.

Crime and Society

Ferge, Zs. *The Differentiation of Our Society*. Budapest: Gondolat Publishers, 1969.
Hegedüs, A. *The Changing World*. Budapest: Academy Publishers, 1970.

Kulcsár, K. *The Human Being and His Social Environment*. Budapest: Gondolat Publishers, 1969.
Losonczi, A. *The Way of Life in Time, Subject and Value*. Budapest: Gondolat Publishers,
1977.

Treatises on Criminology

Földvári, J., and J. Vigh. *Criminology*. Budapest: 1965.
Geréb, Gy., and J. Berencz. *General Psychology*. Budapest: 1959.
Kardos, J. *The Basic Problems of Psychology and the Pavlov Type Research*. Budapest:
1957.
Kulcsár, K. *The Problems of Legal Sociology*. Budapest: 1960.
Szabó, A. "Modern Bourgeois Theories of Juvenile Delinquency." *Gazette of the Institute
of Political and Judicial Science*, Issue 1 (1961).
Szabó, A. "The Theoretical Question of the Basic Research of Criminology." *Political
and Judicial Science* 6 (1963).
Vermes, M. "Certain Questions of the System and Method of Criminology." *Judicial
Gazette*, Issues 1 and 2 (1960).

Law and Execution of Sanctions

Földvári, J. "Thoughts on the Execution of Prison Sentences." *Hungarian Law*, Issues
1 and 2 (1966).
Fonyo, A. "Questions of Principles for Further Development of Our System of Punish-
ment," *Judicial Gazette*, Issue 9 (1974).
Hamori, E. "The Objectives, Tasks and Content of Socialist Execution of Punishment."
Judicial Gazette, Issues 1 and 2 (1966).
Hazai, T. (ed.). *Law Governing the Execution of Punishment*. Vol. 2. Budapest: 1978.
Horváth, T. "The Creative Factors of Criminal Policy of the Socialist State." *Bulletin of
the Institute of Law and Political Science* (1960).
Horváth, T. *Law Governing the Execution of Punishment*. Vol. 1. Budapest: Textbook for
College of Police Officers, 1975.
László, J., and M. Ficsór. "Ideas About the Further Development of the System of
Punishment." *Hungarian Law*, Issue 9 (1976).
Szabó, A. "Education Given During Imprisonment." *Judicial Gazette*, Issue 5 (1966).
Vavro, I. "Differences Between System of Law and System of Judges." *Review of
Ministry of Interior*, Issue 9 (1970).

Specific Forms of Crime

Diczig, I. *Protection of Social Property*. Budapest: Publishers of Economics and Law,
1978.
Molnar, J. *Crimes Committed by Groups*. Budapest: Publishers of Economics and Law,
1971.
Patera, A. "Judging Recidivists and Crimes Committed by Recidivists." *Prosecutors'
Library*, Issue 21 (1968).
Patera, A. *The Criminological Examination of the Intensity of Recidivist Crimes: Studies*

on Criminology and Criminalistics. Vol. 12. Budapest: Publishers of Economics and Law, 1975.

Patera, A. "Questions of Principle of Criminological Research on Criminal Acts Committed by Gypsies." *Acta Facultatis* (1979).

Tauber, I. "The Criminology of Parasitic Criminal Acts." *Acta Facultatis* (1974).

Vavro, I. "Some Questions Relating to Recidivists." *Judicial Gazette*, Issue 1 (1973).

Vigh, J., K. Gönczöl, Gy. Kiss, and A. Szabó. *Violent Criminal Acts and Their Perpetrators*. Budapest: Publishers of Economics and Law, 1979.

16

INDIA

Harjit S. Sandhu

India presents a number of peculiar patterns of special interest to comparative criminology. In spite of serious socioeconomic problems, India's traditionally low crime rate is undergoing only a modest increase. The continued dominance of the family among social institutions and of the rural people as a share of the population must be considered in seeking an explanation. India's remarkable geographical expanse and large population are matched by a cultural heterogeneity that mirrors centuries of history and by major distinctions among regions that contribute to major differences in official crime rates.

HISTORICAL AND CULTURAL SETTING

By the high Himalayas in the north and the Indian Ocean on the south, India is separated geographically from the rest of the Asian continent. Its seclusion was interrupted for the first time by the Aryans who hailed from Central Asia around 1500 B.C. They destroyed the well-developed urban culture of Harappa and established their own in the plains of Punjab and the upper Ganges. The following two thousand years in India saw the fusion of diverse cultures out of which evolved Hinduism, the caste system, patterns of village life, and some of the distinguished literature known as *Rg. Veda*. Once the Aryans entered India through the Kyber Pass, they showed the way to several other invaders, such as the Greeks, the Afghans, and the Mongols, who also left their imprint on Indian culture.

After the invasion and return of Alexander the Great around 326 B.C., India saw stability under the efficient administration of Chandragupta Maurya. His adviser, Kautilya, authored the first treatise on administration of justice, the *Arthasastra*.[1] The historians of criminology and penology have a lot to learn from the writings of Kautilya. Another notable member of the Maurya Dynasty was Asoka (273-236 B.C.) who is remembered fondly by Indians for his pacificism. (Twenty-two hundred years later, Asoka's traditions were reinforced by

Mahatma Gandhi.) Invaders kept coming from the west, and, in 1526, Babur founded the Mughal Dynasty, which attempted to rule India according to Muslim law. Toward the mid-1800s, the British took over from the Mughals and introduced the English Common Law. The Indian Penal Code was designed by Lord Macaulay in 1860.

After a century's struggle for freedom, India achieved independence in 1947. Now India is a sovereign democratic republic with a parliamentary system of government. The judiciary is completely independent and has been separated from the executive at all levels. Since independence, India has experienced a large variety of socioeconomic problems, all with some bearing on crime and criminology in India. On the political front, there have been an unending reorganization of states, riots, three expensive wars with Pakistan, one humiliating skirmish with China, and a growth in political parties all fiercely struggling for power. On the socioeconomic front, the country has suffered population explosion, food shortages, unemployment, poverty, a sluggish economy, high inflation, and widespread discontent.

India's land area is 1,265,018 square miles, and its estimated population in 1977 was 625.8 million. Next to China, it is the most populated country in the world, with a birth rate of 41.1 per 1,000, and a density of 177 per square kilometer. The population is largely rural (80 percent) rather than urban (20 percent). For every 1,000 males there are 930 females at present—the number declining from 950 in 1931 and 972 in 1901. The major religious communities are Hindus (82.72 percent), Muslims (11.20 percent), Christians (2.60 percent), and others (0.88 percent). Indians speak fifteen languages and a large number of dialects. With all of their diversity, Indians share one thing—their culture of poverty.

The Indian economy is still predominantly agricultural; about half of the national income is derived from agriculture and allied activities which absorb nearly three-fourths of the working force. The per capita income for the year 1975-1976 was Rs. 1,005 (U.S. $125), and over a period of fifteen years it has increased by only $7.50 when one compensates for inflation.[2]

CRIME IN INDIA:
INCIDENCE, TRENDS, AND PATTERNS

Not only is India's crime volume low, but also its rate of increase is very slow. In comparing *Crime in Developing Countries*, Clinard and Abbott found India to have a slow increase in crime. They further remarked that as the developing countries grow in productivity and undergo structural changes, property crime is much more vulnerable to increase, but personal crime shows only a small increase.[3]

On the whole, development appears to be more directly related to property crime and not to crimes against the person. Homicide, assault, and forcible rape, for example, tend to emanate from an established subculture of violence evident in both developed and developing countries, but this subcultural formation does not appear to be directly linked to the type of social change presently occurring in the less developed countries.[4]

Cross-national comparisons are always suspect, but if we allow some differences for various factors at play, such comparisons are justifiable, at least in broad terms. One such comparison is presented here between crime in India and crime in the United States. (See Table 16-1.) The two countries are extreme examples in economy, and they also make a similarly striking comparison in crime incidence and rate.

TABLE 16-1
CRIME IN INDIA AND THE UNITED STATES: A COMPARISON FOR 1973

Category	Crime in India (Estimated Population 573,400,000)			Crime in the United States (Estimated Population 209,851,000)		
	Incidence	Rate per 100,000	Pct. Change in Rate 1963-1973	Incidence	Rate per 100,000	Pct. Change in Rate 1963-1973
Murder	17,072	3.0	30.4	19,510	9.3	106.6
Rape	2,861	0.4	NA	51,000	24.3	161.3
Robbery	18,857	3.3 } 5.2	94.1	382,680	182.4	196.6
Dacoity*	10,627	1.9	72.7			
Burglary	181,433	31.6	5.3	2,540,900	1,210.8	112.2
Theft	379,412	66.2	29.3	4,304,400	2,051.2	70.0
Auto theft	NA	NA	NA	923,600	440.1	109.1
Riots	73,388	12.8	109.8	NA	NA	NA
Total	1,077,181	187.9	30.9	8,638,400	4,116.4	90.6

Sources: Bureau of Police Research and Development, *Crime in India—1973* (New Delhi: Ministry of Home Affairs, Government of India, 1974), pp. 2-3; Federal Bureau of Investigation, *Crime in the United States—1973* (Washington, D.C.: U.S. Department of Justice, 1974), p. 59.

*"Dacoity" refers to the robberies of the so-called "criminal tribes" of India.
NA = not available.

To what do we attribute this relatively low rate of crime in India? There are no cross-national studies aimed at this question, although such comparative studies could be very productive for criminology. One could hazard an explanation that, if social institutions like family, school, church, work world, and state enforce behavioral norms, the family seems to be the only effective source of socialization and social control in India. Indian schools with many strikes and malpractices, the work world with its high rate of unemployment, underemployment, and attending frustrations, and the state with its endless turmoil—these social institutions are all crime-generating rather than crime-controlling agencies. Whatever influence the religions of India have seems to be permeated in everyday life and comes through the family.

Now that the family is losing some of its control under the impact of social change, delinquency and crime are registering a slow increase. The rate of increase is slow because social control of the Indian family is still somewhat intact. Several family researchers suggest that the splitting away of nuclear units from joint families has not necessarily led to family disintegration; the nuclear family cannot live in isolation without cooperation and contacts with extended kin. Chekki, in his Karnataka study, observes that "there appears to be no manifest conflict between the young and the old, who stand for change and continuity, respectively. This empirical research suggests that in an Indian city, kinship in the main, far from being atrophied, has been resilient."[5]

Arrests under Special Laws

In India, a large number of persons are arrested under local and special acts, besides arrests under the Indian Penal Code. In 1973, the number of arrests under local and special acts was 2,687,183 compared to 1,242,502 under the Indian Penal Code. The special acts are enacted both by the central parliament and the state legislatures; some of these laws are intended to be crime-preventive in nature. These acts are the Arms Acts, Opium Act, Gambling Act, Excise Act, Prohibition Act, Explosives Act, Suppression of Immoral Traffic in Women and Girls Act, Motor Vehicles Act, Prevention of Corruption Act, Customs Acts, Indian Railways Acts, and Miscellaneous Acts.

Under the Miscellaneous Acts alone, there were 1,352,843 arrests in 1973. Some of these arrests are for very frivolous reasons; the offenders are fined a few rupees, or, in default of payment of fine, they are required to undergo two days' imprisonment in a jail. It is unnecessary work for the administration with very dubious advantages. There are wide variations in the number of arrests under special acts in different states.

Of all the cases reported in India in 1973 under the Suppression of Immoral Traffic in Women and Girls Act, more than 50 percent were reported in the state of Tamil Nadu alone.[6] A plausible explanation is that this special act is enforced differentially rather than uniformly in the country. Another, somewhat controversial explanation, may be found in the imbalance of the sex ratio in Tamil Nadu: there are more women.

Again, the enforcement of the Arms Act is vigorous in the northern states of Punjab, Haryana, Uttar Pradesh, and Nagaland, and almost negligible in the southern states of Tamil Nadu, Kerala, and Karnataka. This differential enforcement of the Arms Act may be a response to a higher murder rate in these northern states. Similarly, arrests under the Opium Act are higher in Punjab and Haryana than in the rest of the nation. These variations warrant further studies.

Persistence in Crime Pattern in Indian States

The incidence of a crime category in different states falls in a certain rank order, and the states tend to retain their rank from year to year with minor fluctuations.

There is a high level of persistence in the ranking of states on a given crime, especially at the upper and lower ends of the scale. In other words, although there may be general increase or decrease in crime, the states tend to maintain, to a considerable degree, their position in the ranking order. The past level of conflict and crime thus serves as a predictor of the future level of conflict and crime. To a certain extent, the incidence of violence and crime in a given state may therefore be described as an attribute of the culture of a state or, in the case of political violence such as rioting, an element in the political culture of the state.[7]

Nayyar divided the twenty states into five blocks—very high, high, medium, low, very low—with respect to three crime groups: (1) offenses against public tranquility (or riots), (2) offenses against persons, and (3) all property offenses. For riots from the year 1959 to 1968, Tripura ranked number one for seven years; number two for one year; number three for one year; and number six for one year. Having the lowest rate of riots, Punjab ranked number twenty for eight years and number nineteen for two years. The same pattern of ranking holds good for the other eighteen states falling between the highest and the lowest states. State ranking for offenses against persons was still more impressive: Manipur was number one every year for ten years, and Kerala ranked number twenty for the same years.[8]

If the individual states maintained a persistent ranking for specific categories of crime, a group of states also tended to retain ranking for total cognizable crime for the years 1971 to 1973 (Table 16.2). This ranking also has greater persistence at the upper and lower ends.

REGIONAL CHARACTER OF CRIME

Similar to the persistent ranking of states in crime, there is a regional character to the incidence of violence and crime in India. Based on the incidence of riot cases, Nayyar found that the contiguous states of the eastern region (Tripura, Manipur, Assam, and West Bengal) emerged as the most turbulent, and the neighboring northern states of Punjab, Haryana, and Himachal Pradesh as domestically secure states.[9] This pattern stood the test of time over a ten-year period from 1959 to 1968.

By pooling Indian Penal Code crimes for the years 1971 to 1973 (Table 16-2), the average crime rates for the states can be divided into highest, high, low, and lowest groups. The mapping of these four groups gives a pattern of belts running

TABLE 16-2
CRIME RATES PER 100,000 POPULATION
FOR STATES OF INDIA, 1971-1973

State	1971	1972	1973	Average (1971-1973)
States with Highest Rates				
Uttar Pradesh	266.3	241.3	240.5	249.3
Maharashtra	195.9	202.2	255.9	218.0
Madhya Pradesh	211.3	222.4	215.8	216.5
Assam	175.6	199.6	204.8	193.0
States with High Rates				
Manipur	179.6	174.2	195.5	183.0
Nagaland	194.2	174.1	172.2	180.1
West Bengal	175.8	170.9	176.7	174.4
Kerala	138.8	161.3	186.2	162.1
Tamil Nadu	144.3	168.3	168.3	160.3
States with Low Rates				
Rajasthan	142.0	147.8	162.9	150.9
Bihar	147.2	143.5	156.9	149.2
Tripura	114.1	149.1	184.5	149.2
Orissa	138.3	142.0	136.0	138.7
Karnataka	124.3	125.8	144.9	131.7
Gujarat	121.9	131.3	161.0	131.7
Jammo & Kashmir	119.0	127.2	137.0	127.8
Andhra Pradesh	106.4	112.0	112.9	110.4
States with Lowest Rates				
Punjab	84.5	87.3	88.5	86.8
Haryana	82.2	88.2	89.0	86.5
Himachal Pradesh	72.7	87.6	94.2	60.6

Source: Crime in India, 1971, 1972, 1973.

vertically. The central states make a belt of highest crime, surrounded by belts of low-crime states.

SPECIAL FEATURES OF CRIME IN INDIA

The regional diversity in crime can be explained only by comprehensive analyses of social, cultural, political, and economic factors.

INDIA

Category	Crime Rate for 100,000
Lowest	50 to 100
Low	110 to 150
High	151 to 200
Highest	201 to 250

°figures based on average crime rate from 1971 to 1973
Mean: 153.0

JAMMU & KASHMIR 127.8

HIMACHAL PRADESH 60.6

PAKISTAN

PUNJAB 86.8

CHINA

HARYANA 86.5

DELHI

NEPAL

RAJASTHAN 150.9

UTTAR PRADESH 249.3

ASSAM 193.0   NAGALAND 180.1

MANIPUR 183.0

BIHAR 149.2

BANGLADESH

GUJARAT 131.7

MADHYA PRADESH 216.5

WEST
BENGAL
174.4

TRIPURA 149.2   MIZORAM

BURMA

ORISSA 138.7

MAHARASHTRA 218.0

BAY OF BENGAL

ARABIAN SEA

ANDHRA PRADESH 110.4

KARNATAKA 131.7

TAMIL NADU 160.3

KERALA 162.1

INDIAN OCEAN

Source: Crime in India, 1971, 1972, 1973.

Female Criminality

Females are greatly underrepresented in the crime scene, both at the juvenile and adult levels. This is another cultural feature of crime in India: women in an agrarian society are in a protected status, with little exposure to crime-provoking situations. The arrest rate for women in India is much smaller than that of the United States (Table 16-3); many of these arrested women play a secondary role in the commission of the offense. Obviously, women arrested for rape could not have played a primary role; they may have abetted the rapists.

In his study of forty-nine female prisoners in the Rajasthan Reformatory and thirty-one probationers, Ahuja found that a "high proportion of female crime is due to faulty interpersonal relationships within the conjugal family."[10] About two-thirds of the incarcerated women were involved in offenses against persons. Of the women convicted for murder, about 90 percent killed someone in the family.[11] Since most of these women were married, their victim was generally either the husband or someone in the husband's family—the husband's oppressive mother or sister. There was a lot of conflict in the married life of these women which centered around the infidelity of the spouse or mistreatment by the husband. In many cases there was a long history of mistreatment, and about half of the murder cases were victim-precipitated.[12] In Ahuja's words, these women "had indulged in criminal acts, but did not have the criminal character."[13]

Prostitutes are generally sent to women's rescue homes, but occasionally they are also sent to a jail or a prison. Many criminologists in India favor the decriminalization of prostitution. According to Rao, prostitution existed in India from time immemorial and has its roots in social customs and tradition. During the time of Mauryas, the position of prostitutes as accomplished courtesans had improved to such an extent that they came to be looked upon as important members of the royal household. Many families dedicated their girls to live at the temples and dance before the images of deities. These girls were called *Devadasis*.[14] The temple dancers became "brides" of God and were therefore barred from marrying. This role was so meaningful to girls that its impression still lingers on. In a study of 425 Bombay prostitutes in 1962, a third of the women interviewed stated that they were *Devadasis* in the service of the goddess *Yellamma*.[15] By 1925, a reformative and puritanical zeal set in, which led to the passage of Acts for Suppression of Immoral Traffic in Women in different states.

Companionate Crime

Most offenses against persons in India are committed in the company of one or two accomplices. The companionate nature of crime is evident from the number of persons arrested per case. The multiple arrests in cases of riots and dacoity are understandable, because these offenses are committed by groups rather than by an individual, but multiple arrests in murder make it a case of special interest. The average numbers of persons arrested per case in different crime categories

TABLE 16-3

TOTAL ARRESTS AND FOR SELECTED OFFENSES, DISTRIBUTION BY SEX, 1973, INDIA AND THE UNITED STATES: A COMPARISON

	India					United States of America				
	Total	Male	Female	Pct. Male	Pct. Female	Total	Male	Female	Pct. Male	Pct. Female
Total	1,242,502	1,211,825	30,677	97.5	2.5	6,499,864	5,502,284	997,580	84.7	15.3
Murder	40,580	39,808	772	98.1	1.9	14,399	12,223	2,176	84.9	15.1
Manslaughter	4,759	4,686	73	98.5	1.5	2,996	2,654	342	88.6	11.4
Rape	3,740	3,719	21	99.4	0.6	19,198	19,198	—	100.0	—
Kidnapping and abduction	12,664	12,204	460	96.4	3.6					
Dacoity	43,499	43,288	211	99.5	0.5					
Robbery	18,490	18,313	177	99.0	1.0	101,894	94,998	6,896	93.2	6.8
Burglary	104,733	102,986	1,747	98.3	1.7	316,272	299,286	16,986	94.6	5.4
Theft	211,967	206,954	5,013	97.6	2.4	644,190	441,073	203,115	68.5	31.5
Riot	397,926	390,671	7,255	98.2	1.8					
Criminal breach of trust	13,088	12,988	100	99.2	0.8					
Cheating	10,745	10,577	168	98.4	1.6					
Counterfeiting	309	306	3	99.0	1.0					
Aggravated assault	NA									

Sources: *Crime in India,* 1973, pp. 76-79; *Crime in the United States,* 1973, p. 131.

NA = not available.

are as follows: riot, 5.61; dacoity, 4.27; murder, 2.41; criminal homicide short of murder, 2.08; rape, 1.3; and robbery, 1.01. It could be that in Indian culture, offenses against persons are companionate in nature (for example, a group of farmers fighting for land), or perhaps the police spreads its dragnet a little wider and drags in more persons as accomplices. In property offenses, arrests per case are lower: burglary, 0.59; theft, 0.59; the statistic means that in two theft cases, only one person is arrested, or the offender is not arrested in half of the property offenses.[16] An average rate of arrest per cognizable crime is 1.28. Indian police have a fairly high rate of detection (53 percent) and are able to obtain convictions in 62 percent of the cases prosecuted in the courts.

Recidivism

The rate of recidivism in India is low. 1973 statistics show that for murder, 95.8 percent had never been arrested previously; 3.3 percent had been arrested once; 0.48 percent had been arrested twice; and 0.4 percent had been arrested three times or more. The rate of recidivism for aggravated assault, rape, and abduction is similar to that of murder. In robbery (and also dacoity), 89.3 percent had no previous arrest; 7.4 percent had one previous arrest; 2.4 percent had two previous arrests; and 0.9 percent had three or more previous arrests. As expected, in burglary the recidivism rate was a little higher but still much lower than that in Western countries. In burglary, 85.1 percent of the offenders had never been arrested previously; 9.5 percent had been arrested once; 3.3 percent twice; and 2.1 percent three times or more. Recidivism for theft is about the same.[17]

Dacoity and Dacoits

When five or more persons conjointly commit or attempt to commit a robbery, it is called a "dacoity" in India (Section 391 of the Indian Penal Code). Although we hear of bands of dacoits from early Indian history, they gained greater notoriety in central India after the middle of the 1800s. They hide in the labyrinthal ravines of Chambal Valley, Madhya Pradesh, and the desert wastes of Rajasthan. They come out of hiding in large groups—fifteen to thirty strong—to rob their chosen victims and carry with them large booty.

Katare, in his incisive study, found these dacoits to be part and parcel of society.[18] They are created by the surrounding communities, harbored and supported by their families and friends living in these communities. They command the admiration of a large number of people, and their ranks keep swelling by the new recruitment of fugitives from the law and also by those who desire to take revenge on society. Since these dacoit gangs are creatures of society, they could not be eliminated over the centuries by any government—the Pathans, Mughals, Marathas, British, or the post-independence administration. When some dacoits were killed by the police, new ones took their places. Recently, some influential leaders exhorted them to come out and surrender themselves to the government. A few did, but most ignored the call.

Dacoity gangs have a lot in common with the society from which they draw their members—the same castes and the same customs. They worship their deities (generally the goddess Kali), donate freely to temples, visit sacred cities, perform religious services, and even make secret contributions. Living in seclusion, their women cannot live with them, which leads to sexual crime and prostitution in the area.

Criminal Tribes

Another remarkable feature of Indian criminality has been that of wandering tribes comprised of about six million persons, whose main occupation in life was crime.[19] They wandered in groups of ten to twenty families under the leadership of a strong patriarch whose enterprise held the families together. Their crimes ranged from cattle lifting to crop stealing, from train thefts to robbery, and from picking pockets to counterfeiting. Their women worked as spies for the men who learned stealing from early childhood under the tutelage of an experienced person. The youth who did well in theft were applauded by the leaders, rewarded liberally, and were bestowed prettier brides in the tribes. The children were trained to stay loyal to the group and were expected to keep any secret from the police if arrested. They had no guilt feelings—their gods approved of the crimes— and they were very proud of their successful capers.

The tribe had a strict code of conduct, and the members were responsible for the mutual safety. They all spoke the same dialect and used an elaborate system of signs to communicate with each other in the presence of the police and strangers. They settled their internal disputes through their own eldermen's assembly and never approached the official criminal justice system for any of their complaints because they had a punishment code of their own.

These tribes originated when India was invaded by a series of foreign raiders from Central Asia and the dislodged tribes became the wandering criminal tribes. Their economy was based on hunting, but they took to pastoral living. The British rulers labeled them criminal tribes, registered them, arrested them, and put them in reservations. Some tribes were restricted to their villages which they could not leave without a pass. Criminal Tribes Acts (1879, 1911, and 1924) were passed to regularize these restraints on the tribes. After independence in 1947, these tribes were decriminalized and absorbed in the rest of society. Settled on agricultural lands, they tended to give up their criminal activities in an exceptional example of the mass reintegration of offenders into society.

Juvenile Delinquency

The Children Act of 1960 defines a juvenile delinquent as a child—a boy less than sixteen years of age and a girl under eighteen—who has been found to have committed an offense.[20] The word "offense" means any act or omission made punishable under any law in force at a given time. A progressive feature of this act is that neglected and uncontrollable children are dealt with by the child welfare boards and not by the juvenile courts.[21]

Delinquency is of such small magnitude that it is hardly a problem from the standards of more industrialized societies. There is hardly any delinquency in rural areas, but the national rate of delinquency is rising, though slowly. In 1973, 71,134 juveniles under the age of eighteen were arrested under both the Indian Penal Code and the Special Acts, compared to 1,717,366 in the United States. The estimated population of India in 1973 was 573.4 million compared to the estimated population of 209.8 million in the United States. Other noteworthy features of delinquency in India are given below:

1. Juveniles in India make a relatively much smaller contribution to the total crime picture. They committed only 3.4 percent of the total crime in 1973, whereas American juveniles were responsible for 50.8 percent of property crimes and 22.7 percent of violent crimes.

2. In 1973, more children under age eighteen were arrested under special and local acts (50,384) than under the Indian Penal Code (20,750). The catch-all category of Miscellaneous Acts accounted for 16,913 juvenile arrests, followed by the Gambling Act (6,005), the Prohibition Act (2,678), and the Excise Act (1,922), respectively.[22] Many juveniles were not acting on their own; for example, they were exploited by adult criminals, especially in the manufacture and delivery of illicit brew and for prostitution and immoral traffic in females.

3. Juvenile delinquency in India is typically a male activity; females contribute only about 5 percent to juvenile arrests, in contrast with 22 percent in the United States. Not a single female juvenile was arrested in two states— Tripura and Manipura—and Bihar, Haryana, Kerala, Meghalaya, Nagaland, Punjab, and Uttar Pradesh had less than ten arrests each in 1973.

4. Juvenile delinquency is not a nationwide phenomenon; two central states, Madhya Pradesh and Maharashtra, account for 45 percent of the delinquency in the entire country.[23] Although they, too, suffer the multiple problems of an underdeveloped economy, low literacy rates, unemployment, and political unrest, several states make only a negligible contribution to the total incidence of delinquency: Jammu and Kashmir, 0.4 percent; Himachal Pradesh, 1.2 percent; Punjab, 0.6 percent; Haryana, 1.6 percent; Uttar Pradesh, 1.1 percent; Andhra Pradesh, 2.1 percent; and West Bengal, 3.1 percent. The small amounts of official delinquency may reflect the accommodating attitude of these millions of people toward their juvenile population. Uttar Pradesh is the second highest among the states in adult crime rates; yet, it contributes only 1.1 percent to delinquency. Apparently, juvenile delinquency does not correspond with adult crime in

this state, and the people do not seem to take cognizance of delinquency of their juveniles and youth.

5. There is little evidence of delinquent gangs in India.[24] Indian society does not seem to generate conditions which repel the youth from the home to the street. The youths do not seem to seek what the gang has to offer. Recognizing the importance of the family in exerting social control, Indian criminologists strongly advocate actions to maintain the strength of its bonds.[25]

OTHER CULTURAL ASPECTS OF CRIME

Contemporary India combines the traditions of the past, new opportunities for occupational crimes, and political dissension.

Superstitions in Crime

Illiterate, suggestible persons may be persuaded by mendicants and fakirs to commit senseless criminal acts. Children sometimes have been sacrificed to propitiate a certain god or to placate an angry deity. Ignorant people are susceptible to being robbed, exploited (sexually or otherwise), and victimized by the wandering mendicants.

Some well-meaning people believe there is religious approval for some acts which are a coded crime. Accompanying the morning prayers, a Hindu sect may offer marijuana to the image of Lord Siva and consume the rest of it as a rite. Many of these acts acquire a special religious significance if a deity is believed to be present.

It is interesting to note how the source of and the use of some of these intoxicants find a place among the rituals of the Hindu. The date palm from which he received his favorite beverage is sacred to the goddess "Chandi"—a form of Durga, Siva's consort, who is supposed to reside within this palm.[26]

White-Collar Crime

With all of the developmental plans in post-independent India, corrupt officials, political leaders, businessmen, and contractors found a great opportunity for white-collar crime. With chronic shortages of essential commodities, businesses began selling everything secretly on the black market at much higher prices. The Vivian Bose Commission (1963) and Sanathanam Committee (1964) exposed many scandals. White-collar crime hurts even affluent societies, but poor societies do not have the resilience to repair easily the damages inflicted by corrupt officials, profiteers, hoarders, black marketeers, and white-collar criminals.

Protests, Riots, and Political Prisoners

Since independence in 1947, India has never been free of protest rallies, communal disturbances, political agitation, riots, violent manifestations of student indiscipline, industrial disputes, and strikes. Although the stewardship of Mahatma Gandhi made the liberation movement essentially nonviolent, the struggle against British colonial rule set a precedent for the various forms of political protest. With independence gained, the peace was marred by large-scale killing, robbing, raping, and forced migrations on both sides of the India-Pakistan borders. During the post-independence era, India created domestic conditions favorable for a series of riots: reorganization of states on a linguistic basis, new political parties, agrarian unrest, some emotional issues such as cow slaughter, and, more recently, police strikes. The political regime in power arrests a large number of political opponents every year which increases the expenditures and clogs the facilities of the police, courts, and corrections.

Although every state in India has riots, Nayyar found the highest incidence of rioting in the eastern region, followed by the central and southern regions, and the lowest in the western and northern regions. The regional concentration was explained as a product of the history and political culture of the region. Nayyar went on to say:

Riots tend to have a higher incidence in states with a lower level of urbanization and/or lower foodgrain production per capita in rural areas. On the other hand, offenses against the person and fraudulent practices are largely a function of the rate of growth of urbanization, while property offenses are somewhat related to the proportion of scheduled castes and tribes in the population.[27]

CRIMINAL JUSTICE AGENCIES

Let us now review briefly the apparatus for managing offenders.

Police and Courts

There are two kinds of police—armed (74 percent) and unarmed (26 percent). The unarmed police conduct most patrolling, prevention duties, and investigation of crime; the armed branch deals with riots and other violent situations. The top officials of the Indian Police Service are a well-educated elite selected through competitive examination. The lower ranking constable is poorly paid and educated but enjoys substantial powers under the criminal procedure code.[28] In 1973, India had 1.33 policemen per 1,000 population compared to 2.4 in the United States. On an average, there were twenty-four policemen for every 100 square kilometers, but these figures varied substantially from state to state.[29] The average jurisdiction of a police station is about 200 square miles with about 75,000 inhabitants.[30]

The courts endeavor to stay free of politics and the influence of the executive branch of government. The supreme court of India has a good record of acting independently. The state high courts appoint district and sessions judges, and the state governments may appoint any number of judicial magistrates after consultation with the high court.

Prisons

The prisons of India have a long history of reforms: there have been as many as six All-India jail reforms committees since the mid-1800s. Each state has a few central jails to keep long-termers and district jails for short-termers. The district jails also have a judicial lockup for untried prisoners. (Prisons are generally referred to as "jails" in India.) Prisoners are not sent far away from their homes; they are normally kept in the nearest district jail. These district and subsidiary jails are small units, not large fortress-type prisons. There is nothing to recommend the jails so far as physical amenities are concerned, but these units are somewhat convenient for the families to visit, being close to home. Indian jails do very little by way of correction; community influence and benign family contacts are the only hope of corrections, if any.

After India's independence, many states opened camps, mostly agricultural camps for the reclamation of wastelands that were needed to produce more food. Prisoners preferred to stay and work in open camps where they earned normal wages and a higher rate of remission in their sentences. The state of Uttar Pradesh started a Model Prison at Lucknow, where prisoners could grow their vegetables and sell their products on the open market.

New prison units are comfortable, equipped with ceiling fans and other amenities. Prison manuals are being revised, and living conditions have been somewhat humanized.

ORGANIZED REACTION TO CRIME AND CRIMINALS

Judging from Western standards, Indian societal reactions to crime and criminals are relatively moderate. Although India still has the death sentence, it was used only sparingly in the 1960s and 1970s. Under Section 365(5) of the Criminal Procedure Code, as amended in 1955, the courts are required to record their justifications for a death sentence. Bills for abolition of the capital sentence, introduced in the Indian Parliament in 1956, 1958, and 1962, were either rejected or withdrawn.[31] The Whipping Act of 1864 (replaced by the Whipping Act of 1909) was abolished in 1955. Banishment was introduced by the British, with life prisoners transported to the Andaman and Nicobar Islands. This practice was repugnant to Indians, who never liked being exiled far from their community and family. Transportation of prisoners was suspended in the 1940s and abolished by law in 1955.

Inspired by the Benthamites, the Indian Penal Code grades various offenses according to the perceived gravity of the offense, and gravity is assessed in terms of social danger, public alarm, social disapproval, harm, and wickedness in the act. Sentences are generally short, 87 percent of the sentences being less than six months.[32] Sentences are fixed, and a prisoner can earn remission from one-fourth to one-third of his or her sentence. Appeals to superior courts, high courts, and even supreme courts are very common. Poor prisoners can file their appeal without cost through the prison administration. There are no jury trials. Presentencing investigation reports are made only in the case of juveniles. There are not enough probation officers to make social investigations. Fine sanctions are used quite frequently.

The courts and correctional agencies rely greatly on the offender's family, to stand surety for the offender's behavior and for monitoring his conduct. There are no professional bondsmen, and the courts are willing to accept the bail bonds furnished by family members and friends. Similarly, there are no parole agents, and the correctional officials release the prisoner to the custody and supervision of family members and friends. An outstanding example is that of a life prisoner who, upon completion of eight or nine years of a life sentence, was released to the custody of his young wife for the unexpired portion of his life imprisonment.

To maintain the prisoner's links with his family and community, he is sent home on furlough for a maximum period of six weeks. To be eligible for such a home visit, the prisoner must be well behaved, and there should be a valid reason for furlough: illness of a close family member, the need to bring harvest home, or to attend any other exigency at home. As a society with a strong family orientation, India takes advantage of the family as a correctional tool.

The community is willing to play its role. Most petty disputes in rural areas are settled by an assembly of village elders called *Panchyat*. Every district has a prisoners' aid society willing to help both incarcerated and discharged prisoners.

CRIMINOLOGY IN INDIA AND ITS CHARACTERISTICS

Criminology in India is an infant but growing branch of learning. Multidisciplinary in nature, it borrows largely from sociology, psychology, law, social sciences, and anthropology. In Chandra's opinion, research in criminology preceded and influenced the direction of instruction in criminology. The earliest research projects date back to the 1930s, but its instruction did not start in universities until the late 1940s and early 1950s. In those days, the problem of criminal tribes received the special attention of social scientists. With a number of social science courses dealing with criminology, the University of Lucknow started a post-bachelor diploma which later developed into a master's program.[33] Criminology programs developed around the special interests of certain professionals in the more traditional disciplines. At least this is the way criminology started at the University of Lucknow in the Department of Sociology and Social Work and at the University of Karnatak at Dharwar in the Department of Sociology. Saugar University developed a separate Department of Criminology and Forensic Science, awarding a master's degree. At this writing, Madras University has been approved by the University Grants Commission to establish a separate graduate program.[34]

In 1951-1952, Indian criminology received impetus when the United Nations (UN) deputed two criminologists—Walter C. Reckless, a professor at Ohio State University, and Edward Galway, a UN official—to study the Indian situation and also to teach a class of fifty selected correctional officials for six months at the Tata Institute of Social Sciences in Bombay. Subsequently, this institute developed a department of postgraduate studies and research with major emphasis on correctional administration.

Another significant step in the early 1970s was the establishment of the Government of India's Institute of Criminology and Forensic Science at New Delhi. This institute imparts in-service training to officers from various branches of criminal justice administration, namely, the police, judiciary, magistracy, prosecution agency, and correctional services. To meet the diverse needs of the variegated clientele, the faculty represents several disciplines: criminology, sociology, psychology, law, chemistry, biology, serology, ballistics, photography, analysis of documents, and so on. The institute has received students from Malaysia, the Philippines, Singapore, Thailand, Iran, Iraq, and Nepal.[35] While India attracts trainees from neighboring countries, it sends many of its own workers to the United Nations Institute for Treatment of Offenders and Prevention of Crime in Fuchu, Japan.

Criminology is not confined to these major university and institute programs. Kashi Vidyapith in Varanasi and the Institute of Social Sciences at Agra University provide courses in criminology with specialization in correctional administration.[36] The states of Uttar Pradesh and Madhya Pradesh, with the highest crime rates, were the first to start these academic programs. Criminology is also taught in some law colleges, but, with no specialized faculty, the courses are mere orientations. Police academies and other in-service training centers teaching criminology are the following: jail training schools at Lucknow, Poona, and Hazaribagh; the Regional Institute for Correctional Administration, Vellore, Tamil Nadu; police training colleges in the states and the National Police Academy; and the National Institute of Social Defense, New Delhi.

The regular flow of new criminologists depends on the universities and the actual field of experience. The training facilities are meeting part of the need for in-service training of personnel, and the colleges are introducing a limited number of new professionals to the field. A majority of the new professionals are likely to be behavioral and social scientists. However, to increase the level of competence of personnel in the work of the police, courts, and corrections, chief reliance is likely to be placed on institutes, workshops, and short and long courses both in India and abroad. Only a few criminologists are trained in foreign universities, and a few others have made observational tours to other countries.

CRIMINOLOGY AS AN OCCUPATION

As is true of many other countries, India provides no clear demarcation of special boundaries for the profession of criminologist. The interests of persons who see themselves as criminologists are too diverse for precise identification. The International Society for Criminology welcomes specialists from all fields who have an active interest in criminology and in the solution of the problems of crime and delinquency.[37]

The Indian Society of Criminology has a widely ranging membership of criminologists, criminal psychologists, sociologists, criminal biologists, criminal lawyers, police officers, forensic scientists, correctional administrators, social workers, and others interested in the problem of crime prevention and treatment of offenders. Most of these people are making their living as university teachers, administrators of state and federal agencies, statisticians, laboratory technicians, lawyers, judges, psychiatrists, social workers, prison psychologists, and prison doctors. They draw their salaries for the job they are doing, regardless of their orientation to criminology.

Only rarely does anyone have private practice as a criminologist. It is almost impossible for a criminologist in India to make his living as a consultant or a private detective.

At the national level, the Indian Society of Criminology provides a forum to criminologists from different disciplines. Founded in 1970 and based at Madras, the society has about 350 members and publishes the biannual *Indian Journal of Criminology* and a quarterly news bulletin. Held annually in one of the cities, its conferences are attended by delegates from all parts of the country. Periodic symposia and meetings also are held at the headquarters of the society at Madras. Local chapters are being organized. The society is affiliated with the International Society for Criminology.

LEVEL AND DIRECTION OF RESEARCH

Research in the 1940s concentrated especially on the criminal tribes; anthropology preceded sociology in India, and tribes were the appropriate subject of study for anthropologists. After India gained independence and the Criminal Tribes Act was repealed, research interests were diversified because the new administration had to face complex problems and assume new responsibilities.

The government of India started to compile national crime statistics and to publish them in an annual report entitled *Crime in India*. These statistics stimulated research into trends of specific crimes, regional characteristics of crime, and correlations between crime incidence and socioeconomic indicators such as population density, urbanization rate, unemployment, and productivity.

Juvenile delinquency in large cities elicited some analytical and descriptive research. Theses and dissertations probed into the history of punishments and the history of the police in India. Special categories of offenders like bandits of Madhya Pradesh, murderers, women offenders, and prostitutes were also studied.

A few criminology texts were prepared, drawing heavily from the literature of Western countries. The theories of crime causation developed by industrialized societies have not been adapted to the context of India. Very few evaluation studies have been implemented to test the effectiveness of different practices and programs. University research in criminology is dependent on funding by the University Grants Commission, Indian Council of Social Sciences Research, New Delhi, and the Ministry of Home Affairs. Diaz points out the great need for both fundamental and applied research in spite of the contributions made by the Tata Institute of Social Sciences, Bombay; the National Institute of Social Defense, New Delhi; and various universities.[38]

Among the journals publishing articles of criminological interest are the *Indian Journal of Criminology, Social Defense, The Journal of Correctional Work, Indian Journal of Social Work, Sociological Bulletin*, and *Police Research and Development*. The *Indian Journal of Criminology and Criminalistics* was at the planning stage when this chapter was prepared.

FINAL COMMENT

It is most appropriate to examine criminological developments since 1945—the integrating theme of this volume—because India emerged as an independent nation in 1947, although its cultural roots stretch back many centuries. It has characteristics that qualify it as a remarkable criminological laboratory. Cultural heterogeneity, basic differences among its regions, the concurrent existence of crimes grounded in cultural traditions and of crimes that reflect the contingencies of socioeconomic development, the conformity that is cultivated by the continued influence of the family that stands in contrast to the violence that expresses political unrest, and, nevertheless, continued low crime rates—these characteristics of contemporary India invite criminological attention.

In India, criminology has not institutionalized the role and status of the criminologist as a distinct occupation; rather, it exists as a meeting place for scholars of established disciplines who have an interest in criminological questions. Academic programs have been established relatively recently in this multidisciplinary mold. The training of action personnel has also been initiated. Therefore, it may be concluded that criminology in India is at an early stage of development.

NOTES

1. A. L. Basham, *The Wonder That Was India* (New York: Grove Press, 1954), p. 50.

2. Government of India, Ministry of Information and Broadcasting, *India: A Reference Annual 1977 & 78* (New Delhi: Publications Division, 1978), p. 161.

3. Marshall B. Clinard and Daniel J. Abbott, *Crime in Developing Countries: A Comparative Prospective* (New York: John Wiley and Sons, 1973), pp. 16-17.

4. Marvin E. Wolfgang and Franco Ferracuti, *The Subculture of Violence* (London: Tavistock, 1967), p. 150; Clinard and Abbott, *Crime in Developing Countries,* pp. 17-18.

5. K. Acharya, "Some Possible Variations in Family Types in Gujrat"; D. A. Chekki, "Modernization and Social Change—The Family and Kin Network in Urban India"; and K. Ishwaran, "The Interdependence of Elementary and Extended Family," in George Kurian (ed.), *Family in India—A Regional View* (The Hague: Mouton, 1974), pp. 179-190, 202-232, 163-178.

6. Government of India, Ministry of Home Affairs, *Crime in India—1973* (New Delhi: Bureau of Police Research and Development, 1974), p. 62.

7. Balder Raj Nayyar, *Violence and Crime in India: A Quantitative Study* (Delhi: MacMillan Company of India, 1973), pp. 131-132.

8. Ibid., pp. 77 and 85.

9. Ibid., p. 132.

10. Ram Ahuja, *Female Offenders in India* (Meerut: Meenakshi Prakashan, 1969), p. 109.

11. Ibid., p. 32.

12. Ibid., p. 125.

13. Ibid., p. 104.

14. S. Venugopal Rao, *Facets of Crime in India*, 2d rev. ed. (Bombay: Allied Publishers Pvt. Ltd., 1967), pp. 174-175.

15. S. D. Punekar and Kamla Rao, *A Study of Prostitutes in Bombay* (Bombay: Lalvani, 1967), pp. 1-4 and 179.

16. Government of India, Ministry of Home Affairs, *Crime in India—1973*, p. 84.

17. Ibid., p. 130.

18. Shyam Sunder Katare, *Patterns of Dacoity in India* (New Delhi: S. Chand, 1972), p. 58.

19. Bhawani Shankar Bhargava, *The Criminal Tribes* (Lucknow: Ethnographic and Folk Culture Society, 1949), 141 pp.

20. *The Children Act*, 1960, Sec. 2(f).

21. *The Children Act*, 1960, Sec. 4.

22. Ministry of Home Affairs, *Crime in India—1973*, p. 100.

23. Ibid., p. 91.

24. S. Venugopal Rao, *Facets of Crime*, p. 157.

25. Ibid., pp. 161-162.

26. Augustus Somerville, *Crime and Religious Beliefs in India* (Calcutta: Thacker, Spink and Company, 1966), p. 65.

27. Balder Raj Nayyar, *Violence and Crime in India* (Calcutta: Thacker, Spink and Company, 1966), pp. 132-133.

28. Ahmad Siddique, *Criminology: Problems and Perspectives* (Lucknow: Eastern Book Company, 1977), pp. 160-194.

29. Ministry of Home Affairs, *Crime in India—1973*, p. 134.

30. A. R. Nizamuddin, *Unarmed Police in India*, p. 12, in Siddique, *Criminology*, p. 172.

31. Siddique, *Criminology*, pp. 61-62.

32. Ibid., p. 219.

33. Sushil Chandra, *Sociology of Deviation in India* (Bombay: Allied Publishers, 1967), p. 254.

34. Courtesy of N. Pitchandi, Indian Society of Criminology, and S. M. Diaz, Professor of Criminology, University of Madras.

35. Courtesy of Director of the Institute of Criminology and Forensic Science, Ministry of Home Affairs, New Delhi.

36. Courtesy of M. Choudhari, Assistant Inspector General of Prisons, Bihar (now retired).

37. Walter C. Reckless, *The Crime Problem*, 4th ed. (New York: Appleton-Century-Crofts, 1967), p. 1.

38. S. M. Diaz, "The Future of Criminological Research in India," *Indian Journal of Criminology* 7 (January 1979):172.

BIBLIOGRAPHY

Ahuja, Ram. *Female Offenders in India*. Meerut: Meenakshi Prakashan, 1969.
Interviews with eighty women offenders reveal that the large number of crimes committed by women can be traced to difficulties within their families.

Aiyar, R. P. *In the Crimelight*. Bombay: India Book House, 1967.
A reporter compiled his news stories of crimes and the court trials earlier in Blitz. The chief actors in the sensational murders are princes and their prostitutes and the playboys and their women friends. Limited insights are provided on violence in the middle and upper socioeconomic strata of Indian society.

Chandra, Sushil. *Sociology of Deviation in India*. Bombay: Allied Publishers, 1967.
Chandra deals with juvenile destitution, adult crime, and trends in the teaching of criminology in India.

Clinard, Marshall B. and Daniel J. Abbott. *Crime in Developing Countries: A Comparative Perspective*. New York: John Wiley, 1973.
In comparative context, India is described as a country with a slow growth in crime. The rate of juvenile delinquency and vandalism is almost negligible. The authors believe that well-respected loyalties and traditional values associated with family life can be brought forcefully into the struggle against juvenile crime.

The Criminal Court Manual (Central Acts). Vol. 1, 8th ed. Madras: Madras Law Journal Office, 1971.
This is India's Criminal Procedure Code (Act V of 1893) dealing with the constitution, the powers of criminal courts, and procedures of arrest, prosecution, framing of charges, different kinds of trials, delivering of judgments, appeals, bails, bonds, and prevention of offenses.

Katare, Shyam Sunder. *Patterns of Dacoity in India: A Case Study of Madhya Pradesh*. New Delhi: S. Chand, 1972.
This detailed sociological study focuses on banditry in Madhya Pradesh.

Nayyar, Baldev Raj. *Violence and Crime in India: A Quantitative Study*. Delhi: MacMillan Company of India, 1975.

Analyzing crime statistics for the period 1953 to 1970, Nayyar identifies the year 1960 as a watershed, after which every crime group increased, thereby demonstrating economic and political deterioration.

Rao, S. Venugopal. *Facets of Crime in India*. 2d rev. ed. Bombay: Allied Publishers Pvt., Ltd., 1967.
Rao deals with both traditional and modern crime in India: dacoity (traditional brigandage); white-collar crime; confidence trickery; juvenile delinquency; and illicit traffic in women.

Sandhu, Harjit S. *A Study of Prison Impact*. Chandigarh: Panjab University Publications Bureau, 1968.
Two hundred prisoners, admitted consecutively in District Prison Faridkot, were administered a number of scales and questionnaires shortly after admission. The tests were repeated after three months of incarceration. In the interim, the socialization index declined and the hostility index rose.

Sethna, M. J. *Society and the Criminal*. 3d ed. Bombay: N. M. Tripathi Private, Ltd., 1971.
This book treats comprehensively the theories of crime causation and methods of controlling criminals.

Siddique, Ahmad. *Criminology: Problems and Perspectives*. Lucknow: Eastern Book Company, 1977.
This introductory text on Indian criminology discusses individualistic and environmental approaches to crime causation and also Indian reactions to crime and criminals. The author examines the criminal justice system.

IRAN

Parviz Saney

In this chapter, the word "criminology" is used in two separate but related senses. First, we shall examine the Iranian concept, either explicitly or implicitly, of criminal behavior and their approach to punishments of the "criminal" in practice. Second, we shall review the attempts made to study, on a scientific basis, the social nature of deviance, its causes or correlations with other phenomena, as well as the various measures adopted for its prevention or modification. The second application of criminology, as will be seen later, has relevance only to the recent past when the social sciences were introduced in Iranian universities as legitimate fields of study.

CONCEPTS IN ANCIENT IRAN

As in other ancient civilizations, the concept of "crime" in ancient Iran was closely related to the idea of "sin."

Zoroastrian theology, which was the prevailing religion in Iran before the advent of Islam, maintains that the whole universe is a battleground for the basic opposing forces of "good" and "evil." All creatures, large or small, take part in daily activities in this ongoing struggle which eventually ends in the final victory of the "good" and the establishment of the "good life" on earth. As a conscious agent in the struggle, man knowingly and voluntarily sides with one of these two forces. Human beings either act in accordance with moral principles—fighting poverty, sickness, ignorance, greed, rage, and so on, supporting the good forces, and facilitating the final conquest— or they may commit wrongful and forbidden acts, thus siding with the evil forces and impeding the eventual victory. "Redemption lies in cooperation with good and conflict with evil.... Helping the wicked was tantamount to being wicked."[1] Therefore, a person who commits a crime is willfully spreading evil on earth and, being a free agent, is held responsible and punished for such an act.

Noteworthy in this doctrine is the "freedom of will" attributed to every human being. The concept, a very late arrival in the Western history of criminal law and punishment, was instrumental in delimiting the individual wrongdoer's responsibility, thus sparing kinsmen from arbitrary and vicious punishments. The concept also implies that the criminal's responsibility should be measured and used as the basic criterion in determining the type and severity of his punishment. This concept again was a definite improvement in a time when even a minor offense, depending on the circumstances, could bring the cruel and unlimited wrath of the whole community on the wrongdoer.

Certain other penal practices in ancient Iran presaged some of the latest developments in criminal law and criminology. For example, an offender was always judged, not on the basis of a single, isolated act that could very well be a chance accident, but in the context of his whole life history, with due regard for all his positive deeds and services rendered to the community. His commendable acts, such as helping in the struggle against evil forces, could be balanced against at least part of the wrong inflicted on society. Herodotus describes the practice:

I admire...the custom which forbids even the king himself to put a man to death for a single offence, and any Persian under similar circumstances to punish a servant by an irreparable injury. Their way is to balance faults against services, and then, if the faults are greater and more numerous, anger may take its course.[2]

We also read that on another occasion:

Sandoces, who was one of the royal judges, had been arrested by Darius some time before and crucified, on charge of perverting justice for money. But while he was actually on the cross, Darius came to the conclusion that his services to the royal house outweighed his offences, and realizing in consequence that he had acted with more promptitude than wisdom, caused him to be taken down.[3]

Another practice, though used mostly against religious "heretics," measures up to some of the most progressive concepts in criminology today, namely, that the rehabilitation of the offender and the protection of society should be considered the most important objectives of the criminal justice system. We are told that:

In the time of Chosroes I the penalties were modified. Before heretics were put to death, they were kept in prison and catechized for a whole year. If they repented, they were set at liberty. This law applied chiefly to the Manichees and Mazdakites who were guilty of making innovations affecting the state religion.[4]

No matter how interesting these examples may seem—and they clearly indicate that some "modern" ideas in criminology existed long ago—they are not meant to imply that ancient Iran had a systematic, progressive, and humanitarian model of criminal justice administration. In fact, the Iranian criminal justice system was on the whole about as cruel and arbitrary as any other that prevailed in the ancient world. Since crime was simply considered a manifestation of the alignment between the offender and the evil forces, there was no reason or incentive to study the forces presumably responsible for the formation of the criminal personality or to examine how the incidence of crime can be prevented or reduced.

APPROACH OF IRAN UNDER ISLAM

For all practical purposes, the fate of the Sassanian Empire was sealed in 642 A.D. when the Arab invaders soundly defeated the Persian army at Nahavand. Even though the last monarch, Yezdigird III, lived as a fugitive until 652 A.D., the country was actually subjugated from that decisive battle on.[5] The new religion, Islam, gradually spread to all corners of the realm. Very soon, however, the Iranian nationalists started to resist the foreign domination and established semi-independent local dynasties in the Caspian Sea areas and in Khorasan. These little states eventually paved the way for the reemergence of a strong central power in Iran and a complete break from the Arab domination. Nevertheless, the religion of the invaders endured in Iran, even though it was modified to fit the former customs and beliefs of the Iranian people.

Like Zoroastrianism, Islam is an all-embracing religion that attempts to regulate not only the spiritual life of man but his social activities as well. A large body of law was developed to encompass every aspect of behavior in society. "Law in the eyes of the Muslim scholars was not in fact an independent or empirical study. It was the practical aspect of the religious doctrine preached by Mohammed."[6] This tradition has persisted, making the study of law an indispensable part of all religious learning.

To get a better grasp of penal regulations and practices in Islam, it should be noted that there are four sources of Islamic law. In order of significance, they are as follows:

1. The Koran or the Holy Book of Islam.
2. Traditions of the Prophet, that is, what he did or said when faced with everyday problems.
3. Consensus of the clergy, called *ijma*, when no decision can be reached according to the two preceding sources.
4. "Reason" or logic which should be employed when no solution is found in the other sources.

Only four specific offenses are provided for in the Koran, with specific punishments called *Hodood* which include:

1. Theft, which is punished, in both male and female, by cutting off the hand.[7]
2. Adultery, punished with a hundred stripes.[8]
3. Accusing someone, without proof, of adultery, punished by eighty stripes.[9]

4. Making war upon Allah and His messenger, "striving for corruption in the land." Such offenders "will be killed or crucified, or have their hands and feet on alternate sides cut off, or will be expelled out of the land."[10]

In addition to the preceding four offenses, three others are frowned upon in the Holy Book, but no specific punishments are provided for them. They are punished, however, on the basis of these other sources:

1. Sodomy, punishable by death inflicted by use of a sword, burning, throwing stones, demolishing a building over, or throwing down from high places.
2. Drinking of alcohol, punished by eighty stripes; but if repeated three or four times, then punishable by death.
3. For forceful robbery—if only a weapon is used, nobody molested, and no property taken—the punishment would be cutting off the hands and feet on alternate sides. However, if property is also stolen and/or a person killed, the punishment would be death by execution.

In addition to the foregoing seven offenses provided for specifically in the Koran or in other sources of Islamic law, the punishment of other crimes is entrusted to the religious judges who determine the extent and severity of the penalty in accordance with the seriousness of the offense. Punishments meted out for such crimes—called *tazirat* or minor offenses—include imprisonment, banishment, confiscation of property, and punishments bringing social disgrace upon the offender. In no case, however, should an offender be put to death because of a *tazir*, that is, a minor offense.[11]

On the basis of the various pronouncements, and the age-old practices of Moslem judges, the following principles can be deduced as governing the criminal law system.

Individual Responsibility

There are numerous instances in the Koran where individual responsibility is stressed, for example, "Say: Ye will not be asked of what we committed, nor shall we be asked of what ye do."[12] And again, "No laden soul will bear another's load."[13]

Before the advent of Islam, collective responsibility of the offender's tribe was the rule among Arabs, and his wrongdoing would bring retaliation. A famous example showing that the practice was abandoned is the case of Imam Ali's martyrdom; he requested at his deathbed that if he died because of the wound inflicted on him by his assailant, the latter be held solely responsible and punished with a single stroke of the sword.

There is one exception to the rule; if the punishment imposed involves payment of "blood money" (or compensation) to the relatives of the deceased, then the offender's next of kin on his father's side would be jointly responsible for such payment.

The Talio Principle *(Lex Talionis)*

The Talio principle (eye for an eye and tooth for a tooth) existed in the Arab community before the Prophet who retained the principle but regularized its application.[14] He also recommended to his followers to forgive the murderer:

And we prescribed for them therein: The life for the life, and the eye for the eye, and the nose for the nose, and the ear for the ear, and the tooth for the tooth, and for wounds retaliation. But who so forgoeth it (in the way of charity) it shall be expiation for him.[15]

If the next of kin or the injured party, as the case may be, cannot forgive, then it is advised that they should choose compensation instead of revenge:[16]

O ye who believe! Retaliation is prescribed for you in the matter of the murdered; the freeman for the freeman, and the slave for the slave, and the female for the female. And for him who is forgiven somewhat by his (injured) brother, prosecution according to usage and payment unto him in kindness.

Nonretroactive Application of Penal Laws

The prohibition of *ex post facto* laws is not incorporated in the Koran, but on the basis of numerous pronouncements which make one's responsibility conditional on the fact of his possibilities (for example, "Allah tasketh not a soul beyond its scope"),[17] the principle has become part of Islamic criminal law and is reflected in the adage: "It is unjustified to punish without pronouncement."

Gradation of Punishments

Like other great religions, Islam preaches that the door to salvation is always open for the deviating souls who return to the right path. "Forgiveness is only incumbent on Allah toward those who do evil in ignorance (and) then turn quickly (in repentance) to Allah. These are they toward whom Allah relenteth."[18] In the same spirit which is reflected throughout the Koran, Islamic law is also anxious to leave the doors open for wayward Moslems who see the light in the middle of a wrongful act. It also provides that if an offender refrains in the middle of an offense, from completing it, then he will suffer a more lenient punishment. As already mentioned for attempted armed robbery, if no property is taken or no person injured, the punishment is considerably milder.

It should be stressed here that, even though Iran became a Moslem country more than thirteen centuries ago and the precepts of Islamic law have been studied and discussed ever since in all religious schools, the government in all periods has remained beyond the reach of this law and has not felt bound by any rule or regulation. In civil law matters, there is a well-developed body of law in Islam according to which religious judges usually ruled. However, the criminal law of Islam, while adequately serving the limited needs of the small consensual society of Arabia thirteen centuries ago, remained somehow sketchy and inoperative in the face of the then existing criminal law system of the Sassanian Empire. With few alterations, the latter system has remained active until modern times. During all this time, only the wishes of the monarch and other influential functionaries were carried out in the name of the criminal justice system. Punishments were determined arbitrarily and in accordance only with the offender's social standing and wealth. In fact, many of the acts, which if committed by a commoner would have been punished severely, were perpetrated by powerful and rich persons as routine behavior.

Although arbitrary, cruel, and discriminatory punishments are common in Iranian history, it suffices for our purposes to give only a few examples from the Qajar period, which immediately preceded the adoption of a constitution and modern legal codes in Iran.

Dr. Feuvrier was Nasiru'd-Din Shah's special physician and published his memoirs under the title *Trois Ans à la Cour de Perse*. In his entries for November 16 and 20, 1891, he reports that a new servant, a lad of fifteen years, had stolen a few jewels from the Peacock Throne and was hanged immediately from one of the gates to the capital city of Tehran.[19] Another narrator of recent Persian history summarizes the criminal law practices:

In case of a rebellion or of a conspiracy against the throne, the monarch could put to death hundreds of his subjects and confiscate their property. Again, members of the royal family, ministers of State and all public officers and dependents were entirely in the power of the Shah, who could sentence them to punishment, which was as a rule carried out immediately. In other cases where the death penalty could be inflicted, law and custom had to be observed.[20]

As already indicated, punishments were arbitrary, cruel, and inhuman. The offender was still considered a wicked soul who intentionally committed an act that was against the will of God and should be punished for it. Otherwise the transgression was considered harmful to the state and was punished severely in order to intimidate others from committing the same. The prevailing doctrine for punishing people, which was enunciated only indirectly and informally, was that of deterrence.

Punishments are still very cruel, every torture imaginable being practiced. A new ruler frequently tortures the first gang of brigands that he captures, not from cruelty but in order to inspire terror. Gradually, however, European influence is humanizing Persian justice, and fewer cases of burying alive in mortar, shoeing with horse-shoes and similar punishments are now heard of.[21]

During this period, no need was felt to study the problem of criminal activity, the causes of crime, or the personality of the criminal on a scientific basis. The religious outlook regards any deviant act as the manifestation of an intentional "sinful" proclivity. Furthermore, the sociopolitical premises and practices of the times made such a study appear to be superfluous.

The average individual, even if living within the boundaries of the legal system, was not considered worthy of serious attention. Developments in psychology and sociology have revolutionized the concepts of "crime" and "the criminal" in the West, but they were not relevant or even feasible within the context of the Persian society of the late nineteenth century.

IRANIAN CRIMINOLOGY IN THE MODERN ERA

At the beginning of the twentieth century and following the constitutional revolution, Iran adopted a series of laws modeled after Western codes. On December 30, 1906, for the first time in its history, Iran adopted a constitution based on Western, especially Belgian, documents. Herein, and in the Supplementary Constitutional Law of October 8, 1907, the foundations of a modern state were laid down, at least theoretically. In the latter document, eighteen articles are devoted to the "Rights of the Iranian People." Article 12 specifically provides for one of the basic principles in Western criminal law: "No penalty may be decreed or carried out except in accordance with the law." The same principle is reiterated in the Penal Code of January 13, 1926, which in structure and content is based on the French Penal Code of 1810. The French Penal Code closely followed the concepts propounded by the classical school of criminology, considering the principal aim of punishment to be the security and safeguarding of public interests, trying at the same time to match this aim with the requirements of criminal justice. The main objective of the Iranian model is, therefore, to deter potential offenders from committing crimes by punishing the criminal within a strictly defined frame of reference.

With the introduction of modern concepts, the Iranian penal system has also been influenced by the positivist school of criminology. Through various enactments, other considerations than that of deterrence became embedded in the criminal justice system. Articles 47 to 50 of the code provide for "suspended sentences." Besides, the following enactments have been added to the main core of the law: conditional release of prisoners (1959), juvenile courts (1959), security measures (1960), and probation (1977).

With the introduction of the social sciences in Iran and more frequent contacts with the West, keener interest has been gradually aroused concerning the basic objectives of the criminal justice system, the social-psychological qualities of the criminal, the influences of the social environment in generating criminal behavior, and the purposes and programs of the penal system.

Scientific Study of Crime

Criminology specifically defined is only a recent happening in Iran. During the reign of Reza Shah, the founder of the Pahlavi Dynasty, groups of students were sent to European countries to study modern sciences. Iranian students had been sent abroad earlier, but for the first time they were sent on a regular and extensive basis. Some of these students took up the study of law in France and became acquainted indirectly with criminology. Upon their return, they influenced the course of criminal law development, either through their writings or actual participation in the legislature or the judiciary.

In a book called *The Capital Punishment* (1951), Dr. Amir Alai presents his arguments for and against the said punishment, along with a cursory review of prevailing penalties in Iran and visual representations of executions.

Dr. Ahmad Hooman, a professor at Tehran University and president of the Iranian Bar Association for several years, published a book in 1960 entitled *Prison and the Prisoner, or the Penitentiary System.* Using a comparative approach, the book discusses in detail the penitentiary system and its philosophy, as it exists in the United States and several European countries. Only seven of 365 pages are devoted to the Islamic rules governing crimes and criminals, and forty pages to the Iranian penal system! Still, the book is more concerned with Iranian issues than many other published materials in Iran that bear the title "Criminology."

Dr. Said Hekmat has also published books on criminology and related subjects. His *Forensic Medicine* is a textbook based to a large extent on his many years of first-hand experience as chief coroner for the Ministry of Justice.

In recent years, Dr. Reza Mazlooman has published extensively on the subject. His works include a two-volume book on criminology, another two volumes on the sociology of crime, and numerous articles in the Iranian law reviews. The weakness of his work is that of all other publications in the field. They are mostly translations of foreign material and research. As shall be seen, they have little bearing on the Iranian scene. They may give a distorted view of what may be relevant in the particular setting of Iranian society to the problems of criminal behavior and its modification.

Finally, I also have prepared materials in the fields of criminal sociology and criminal psychology. These books and articles have been used in Tehran and National University Schools of Law. Having been impressed by new theoretical developments in sociology, I have tried to discredit the single-factor explanations so conveniently presented in most European and many American textbooks on the subject. I have reiterated the view that criminal behavior is mostly learned behavior and that it should been studied in the sociocultural contexts that foster this type of behavior. I use the same approach in numerous articles written for various law reviews in Iran, especially "Criminal Responsibility," "Social Interaction and Criminal Behavior," and "The Positive Functions of Criminality."

Regardless of the merits of my endeavors to clarify the theoretical issues, my work also suffers from lack of factual information about the question of crime and criminality in Iran. Except for a research project done under my supervision for the United Nations Social Defense Research Institute on the "Changing Conceptions of Deviance," like my Iranian colleagues, I have done nothing directly related to the particular issues pertaining to this country.

Irrelevance to the Iranian Situation

As already pointed out, the main problem with published materials on criminology in Iran is that they are largely irrelevant. The main bulk of the published work consists of translated accounts of what European and American writers have produced in the field. Besides the history of criminology, which of course has some use for the Iranian reader, the theories of causality and the accounts of researches done in the different countries are presented in a faulty way. First, the foreign literature is presented uncritically as though the books and articles present the undeniable truth. Second, it is taken for granted that the reported conclusions are directly applicable to Iranian conditions. We know that these conditions are quite different from those prevailing in Western (including American) cultures.

The outcome is a futile and probably dangerous misunderstanding. For example, on the basis of theoretical explorations and research findings, it is argued that poverty is largely responsible for criminal behavior, but in Iran the lower classes are earnest believers in fatalistic predetermination. There is no doubt in the minds of the poor that their poverty is a result of God wanting them to be poor. They also believe that, in compensation for their suffering in this world, they are to be provided with eternal bliss in the next. These people are quite submissive in the face of hardship. Incidentally, this trait is one of the reasons they have put up with authoritarian regimes and relationships for such a long time. Criminal activities are much less prevalent among the poor in Iran than in most other nations. The notion that the poor, even in Iran, are particularly prone to criminality is more of an impression than an established fact. The visibility of whatever crimes the Iranian lower classes commit is heightened by the illusion that the middle and upper classes are crime-free. Of course, the white-collar and other offenses of the rich and influential are seldom reported to the courts.

As another example, consumption of alcohol is supposed to be correlated with violent crime, according to studies conducted in certain countries. This relationship may hold in the West where drinking takes place openly and in public. Iran has a religious ban on alcoholic beverages. Although the middle-class Iranian does not really abstain from drinking, his indulgence usually takes place in the privacy of the home and in the company of close friends or relatives. Traditionally, alcohol loosens the ego-control mechanisms. Realizing his living conditions, the Iranian drinker is apt to be quite sorrowful and subdued rather than violent. Any relationship between consumption of alcohol and violent crime is almost indiscernible. Nevertheless, Iranian books on criminology describe the available information from Western sources as if it is true for Iranians and as if the correlation is not affected by cultural differences.

Obstacles to Scientific Investigation

These failures of Iranian authors may be attributed in part to the absence in Iran of an attitudinal climate favorable to unbiased scientific studies. The scarcity of indigenous research in Iranian criminology is a reflection of a refusal to acknowledge that social problems exist. This attitude is prevalent in many countries. If one does not admit the existence of a problem or forces oneself to forget it, the burden of the given difficulty will be eased and its contours delimited. Somehow, the self-respect of the individual and of the community with problems will be preserved. Thus, in Iran and many other countries, it is almost taboo to admit, let alone scientifically investigate, the prevalence of addiction, prostitution, embezzlement, the adverse conditions of prison life, and so on. Any research project pertaining to such subjects has been considered subversive and faced with various obstacles.

Blocked perceptions that the crime problem exists partially explain the inadequacies of crime statistics which, in themselves, are a major handicap for the researcher. Why spend time and energy in collecting information and assessing their implications, it is argued, when the conclusions are already obvious? It is known that all sorts of criminal activity take place in the country. With some justification, it is contended that any study of prison life in Iran supported by reliable statistics, for example, will be worthless unless the government is willing and able to ameliorate the situation.

Research is also inhibited by the nonavailability of necessary funds. In recent years, the Ministry of Higher Education provided limited funds on the basis of the ministry's priorities set according to official views on what fields of investigation should receive support on a competitive basis. The number of applicants greatly exceeds the opportunities provided by available grants.

MORE PRACTICAL ACHIEVEMENTS

When the International Congress of Criminology convened in 1951, Iran had its first representative at that convention. Since then, Iran has been represented in most international conferences. At about the same time, a group of experts and interested people formed the so-called Society for the Protection of Prisoners in association with the Ministry of Justice. Cognizant of the urgent need of the prisoners' families for financial support and assistance, the society changed its name to the Society for Guidance of Prisoners and Protection of Families to include this latter concern as one of its main objectives.

Another worthwhile project has been the establishment of the Center for the Education of Juvenile Delinquents, which is also associated with the Ministry of Justice. The center's staff is composed of judges, educators, psychologists, and social workers. It has been instrumental in introducing important innovations in the field of criminal justice administration. The most significant was the establishment of juvenile courts and the Center for the Rehabilitation of Children. Even though the juvenile courts are headed by trained judges for sound legal reasons, the courts are not bound by formal procedures applicable to regular courts of law. They also receive much needed counsel and help from social workers and psychologists on the staff of the center.The juvenile court meets at the center, has regular contact with the children, and can alter its previous decisions to take advantage of the progress made with each juvenile delinquent.

The Center for the Rehabilitation of Children does not resemble a detention house. The children are free to move around the place and become interested in the several educational workshops, recreational activities, and regular school classes, including courses in English. They can leave the place once a week to visit their parents. When the children are orphaned, they can visit one of the many volunteer families who offer patient understanding and warm hospitality.

The Police Department has a small museum of criminology as a showplace for different weapons and other paraphernalia used in committing various crimes. Its fingerprinting and "scientific police" sections are an educational resource for law students and the Police Cadets School.

The Institute of Criminology includes a sizable library of special books and articles on the subject. The institute seemed to be a good incentive for more extensive studies in criminology and related fields. However, because of certain differences of opinion as to its real worth, the institute was dissolved before its development became significant.

THE ISLAMIC REVOLUTION AND AFTER

A few words are in order here concerning the future of criminology in Iran following the Islamic Revolution in 1980 and the establishment of the Islamic Republic. Since the beginning of the Revolution, hundreds of people have been tried and executed for allegedly committing crimes punishable under the general heading of "making war upon Allah and His messenger" and "striving after corruption in the land" as specified in the Koran. The punishments for these very general and broad categories are specified in the following verse:

The only reward of those who make war upon Allah and His messenger and strive after corruption in the land will be that they will be killed or crucified, or have their hands and feet on alternate sides cut off, or will be expelled out of the land. Such will be their degradation in the world, and in the Hereafter theirs will be an awful doom.[22]

There is difference of opinion as to whether the cited verse was a commandment made for particular occasions or whether it was a general enactment applicable to all similar circumstances. There is also disagreement over the limits and borderlines of the concepts and what they may include. Certain

of the Ayattollahs believe that many of the alleged offenses of persons executed did not fall within the intended meaning of those broad phrases. Certain
other Ayattollahs, however, have tried to justify the executions and the way
decisions were reached in the Revolutionary Courts. They have referred to
this verse and to the revolutionary realities and exigencies.

What will be the future of criminology in Iran? We do not yet know.
Contrary to the basic premises of criminology, prostitutes and drug addicts
have been executed, and persons consuming alcohol have been whipped
eighty times in public. Both the common man in the street and certain religious leaders have registered objections. Moslem apologists, meanwhile,
consider these incidents to be aberrations. Nevertheless, if the political atmosphere is not modified and the government insists on implementing the "true
spirit" of Islam as understood by certain extremist groups, criminology will
be relegated to the background as just another concept belonging to the
"decadent" West, and without relevance to the true "Islamic" society. In that
event, more reliance will be placed on morality and religious education as
sure solutions to all social problems.

NOTES

1. Rustom Masani, *Zoroastrianism: The Religion of the Good Life* (New York:
Macmillan Company, 1971), p. 68.

2. Herodotus, *The Histories*, Book I, trans. Aubrey de Selincourt (Hammondsworth,
England: Penguin, 1954, 1965). p. 70.

3. Ibid., Book VII, p. 483.

4. Clement Huart, *Ancient Persia and Iranian Civilization* (London: Routledge and
Kegan Paul, 1972), p. 159.

5. Sir Percy Sykes, *A History of Persia*, Vol. 1 (London: Macmillan and Company,
Ltd., 1958), pp. 500-502.

6. H.A.R. Gibb, *Mohammedanism: An Historical Survey* (New York: Mentor Books,
1955), p.73.

7. *Koran*, Surah V, Verse 38.

8. *Koran*, Surah XXIV, Verse 2.

9. *Koran*, Surah XXIV, Verse 4.

10. *Koran*, Surah V, Verse 33.

11. G. H. Bousquet, *Précis de Droit Musulman*, Tome I (Alger: La Maison des Livres,
1950), p.86.

12. *Koran*, Surah XXXIV, Verse 25, quoted from *The Meaning of the Glorious Koran*
(New York: Mentor Books, 1959), p. 309.

13. Ibid., *Koran*, Surah XXXIX, Verse 7, ibid., p. 329.

14. Louis Milliot, *Introduction à l'Etude de Droit Musulman* (Introduction to the
Study of Muslim Law) (Paris: Recueil Sirey, 1953), p. 757.

15. Koran, Surah V, Verse 45, quoted from *The Meaning of the Glorious Koran*, p.
100.

16. *Koran*, Surah II, Verse 178, ibid., p. 48.

17. *Koran*, Surah II, Verse 286, ibid., p. 60.

18. *Koran*, Surah IV, Verse 17, ibid., p. 81.
19. From the Persian translation by Abbas Iqbal (Tehran: 1947), pp. 228 and 230.
20. Sykes, *History of Persia*, Vol. 2, p. 382.
21. Ibid., p. 386.
22. *Koran*, Surah V, Verse 33.

BIBLIOGRAPHY

From a large volume of articles and reviews on criminology, a selected number are presented below. All are published in Persian, but the titles are given in English. If the reader seeks the original in Persian, the author's name should provide the necessary guidance. When the publication date is not given in the work, this is noted in the listing below. The reader also will find useful works in the following journals: *Tehran University Law Review*, *National University Law Journal*, *Iranian Bar Association Law Journal*, *Law Today*, *People's Law*, *Ministry of Justice Law Review*, *Army Monthly Review*, and *Police Review*.

Ali Abadi, Hossein Abdol. *Criminal Law*. Tehran: Tehran University Publications, 1958.
Amir Alai, Shamseddin. *The Capital Punishment*. Tehran: n.d.
Danesh, Taj Zaman. *Penology and Prisoners' Rights*. Tehran: Prison's Printing House, 1976.
Eiman, Hafiz. *Social Defense Against Crime and the Criminal*. Tehran: Chehr Publications, 1964.
Hamidi, Manouchehr. *Partnership in Crime*. Tehran: n.d.
Haydarian, Mahmood. *Criminal Psychology and Criminology*.Tehran: Dehkhoda, 1967.
Hekmat, Said. *Forensic Medicine*. Tehran: National University Publications, 1977.
Hooman,Ahmad. *Prison and Prisoners or the Penitentiary System*. Tehran: 1960.
Kaynia, Mehdi. *Criminal Sciences*. 3 vols. Tehran: Tehran University, 1966-1967.
Kaynia, Mehdi. *Principles of Criminology*. Tehran: 1978.
Kayvan, Sadri. *Iran's Penal Policies During the Shah and People's Revolution*. Tehran: 1975.
Khakpour, Mohammad Mehdi. *Criminology of Delinquent Women*. Tehran: Atai, 1975.
Massoud Ansari, M. A. *Crimes and Sexual Aberrations*. Tehran: Amir-Kabir, 1961.
Mazlooman, Reza. *Criminal Law and Criminology*. Tehran: 1972.
Mazlooman, Reza. *Criminal Sociology*. Tehran: 1972.
Mazlooman, Reza. *Criminology*. 2 vols. Tehran: 1974, 1976.
Mazlooman, Reza. *Television, Radio and Criminality*. Tehran: Agah, 1976.
Oloomi, Reza. *Juvenile Delinquents*. Tehran: Amir Kabir, 1969.
Oloomi, Reza. *Criminology*. Tehran: Igbal, 1970.
Salahi, Javid. *Penology*. Tehran: Arash, 1973.
Saney, Parviz. *Psychology of Crime*. Tehran: National University, 1977.
Saney, Parviz. *Criminal Law*. 2 vols. Tehran: National University Publications, 1977-1978. 3d printing.
Sedarat, Ali. *Criminal Law and Criminology*. Tehran: Marefat, 1961.
Siassi, Ali Akbar. *Criminal Psychology*. Tehran: Tehran University, 1963.
Zahedi, Latif. *Provocation*. Tehran: n.d.

18

ISRAEL

Israel L. Barak-Glantz

Established in 1948, the State of Israel has scored developmental gains in its relatively brief history that few nations can claim. Development has been most pronounced in the economic-technological sphere, but very significant concomitant advances have been made in the sociopolitical sphere as well. This chapter reviews the developments in criminology, as one of the aspects of the birth and subsequent growth of science in a particularly young society.

SOCIAL MILIEU OF CRIMINOLOGY

For a more complete understanding of contemporary developments in criminology in Israel, it is fruitful to outline the history and characteristics of Israeli society.

Demography

First and foremost among three major sociological realities, Israel is quite unique from the demographic point of view. After two millennia, the Jews established an independent and democratic state. Prior to 1948, the Jewish people were spread all over the world in large and sometimes very small and segregated communities. The situation began to change in 1882 with the onset of the First Aliyah[1] when Jews started a series of at least five migration waves to Israel, which was then called Palestine.[2] By 1948, the population in the country numbered approximately 650,000. From 1948 to 1952—the peak period of mass immigration to Israel—the population grew to about 1.5 million, an increase of 131 percent in only four years. Many of the Jews arriving then and thereafter were survivors of the Nazi concentration camps. The influx of "New Olim"[3] continued, to reach 1,981,000 by 1961, 2,384,000 by 1967, and peaking at 2,561,000 by 1970 according to official census figures (*Israel Statistical Ab-*

stract, 1971). It is estimated that in 1979 the population approached, if not exceeded, 3.5 million.

Ethnic Diversity

As the second major sociological reality, the ethnic composition of this small society is perhaps even more significant than the absolute increase in population numbers and the capacity of a very small society to absorb more than twice the population it had only some thirty years earlier. Jewish people came from Germany, Poland, Romania, France, Hungary, England, and other European countries, leaving large Jewish communities in only a few places—England, France, North and South America, and Soviet Russia. Immigrants also flocked from the Middle East: Egypt, Syria, Yemen, Morocco, Iraq, Persia (Iran), Turkey, and other countries. Unlike earlier immigrants, those from the Middle East frequently settled in Israel as total communities. For example, one whole Syrian community was "removed" virtually intact and settled in Beer-Sheba, later to become the capital of the Negev, the southern region of the country.[4]

Heavy immigration after 1948 brought marked changes in the ethnic composition over time. Between 1919 and 1948, of the 452,158 immigrants, 89.6 percent came from Europe and America and only 10.4 percent from Asia and Africa. In the subsequent fourteen years—1948 to 1962—only 45.4 percent of the 1,074,792 immigrants came from the United States and Europe, and 54.6 percent from Asia and Africa (*Israel Statistical Abstract*, 1965). Taking a shorter time period, immigrants from America and Europe constituted 54.8 percent of all immigrants in 1948 and 31.9 percent in 1964, or a decline of 22.9 percent. In comparison, there was an 18.9-percent growth in the share represented by the Sephardic Jews.[5] These fluctuations clearly changed the distribution of ethnic groups in the Israeli Jewish population. In 1964, the Sephardic Jews reached 28.7 percent of the population as compared with only 9.8 percent at the birth of the nation (1948). When one adds to these figures those who were native-born to parents of Asian or African extraction, 17.0 percent of the population at the end of 1964, the picture changes radically, as Shmuel Eisenstadt has observed: "More than 45 percent of the Jewish population in Israel are of Asian and African origin, 6 percent are native-born to native-born parents and the rest (49 percent) are of European or American descent."[6]

The pluralistic nature of Israeli society is even more evident when the country of origin is considered. Of all the newcomers between 1948 and May of 1961—the period of the most massive immigration—14.6 percent came from Romania, 13 percent from Poland, 13.3 percent from Iraq, 12.8 percent from Morocco and Tangier, 5.2 percent from Yemen and Aden, 4.5 percent from Algeria and Tunisia, and less than 1.1 percent from the United States. The remaining 34.5 percent of the immigrants came from numerous other countries; their respective percentages were equal to or smaller than 1.1 percent.[7]

Israel not only has the characteristics of other rapidly developing countries (such as industrialization and urbanization), but the nation also is remarkable in being a melting pot of more than seventy different and often highly divergent cultural and subcultural groups, as Israel Drapkin, one of the founders of Israeli criminology, has stated:

A large proportion of the population originates from countries where the democratic way of life is practically unknown. The country is undergoing profound and most rapid growth and changes in size, demographic composition and ecological distribution of its population. In the new environment many frustrating situations arise, and in many parents an increasing amount of resentment is observable if, for instance, their children are brought to courts.[8]

Threat to Nation's Survival

A third very important sociological reality is that Israel is a developing society under constant threat to its physical survival. Within less than twenty years, it has undergone three major wars with its Arab neighboring countries: the Sinai Campaign in 1956, the Six-Day War in 1967, and the Yom Kippur War in 1973. Amir speaks of a psychology of being in a state of siege.[9] The cycles of war have led many Israelis to develop "an inclination to take life in stride and not to postpone pleasures for a better time to come. There is a desire for immediate gratification, which is foreign to the patterns that once prevailed here."[10] It is not only possible but highly probable that the ongoing Arab-Israeli conflict has had impact on the genesis, scope, and nature of crime in Israel and on the societal reaction to lawbreakers.

Furthermore, the Israeli criminal justice system has faced quite another serious problem, that is, criminality among Arabs who decided to remain in the country after 1948 and assumed Israeli citizenship. While most citizens were exposed to rapid urbanization and industrialization, the Israeli-Arabs insulated themselves to maintain many of their traditional values, customs, and rituals by settling in small villages remote from large cities. A very special crime problem[11] emerged later among young Israeli-Arabs. By the late 1960s, it appeared that, although only 15 percent of the seventeen to nineteen year olds in Israel were Arabs, they accounted for 31 percent of all juvenile delinquents in this age group. Researchers[12] attributed this situation to cultural conflict, the byproduct of the Israeli-Arab youth experiencing the shock of urban society, the changes in the Arab village life, the weakening of the patriarchal Arab family, and many other factors. Within the Middle East context, the political overtones of this reality render it unique.[13]

POLITICAL SYSTEM AND CRIMINAL LAW

Let us turn to the nature of the Israeli political system and the style of its government.

Absence of a Constitution

One salient political characteristic of Israel is the absence of a constitution in the formal legal sense; that is, there is no document (or even a series of documents) which in principle transcends all others, including the legislative arm(s) of the government. In Israel, as in Great Britain but quite different than in other Western countries, all laws assume equal validity; all are legislated by following the same procedures. When two laws conflict, the most recent one possesses obligatory power. However, when the Knesset—the Israeli legislative body—decides to label some laws as "foundation laws" or "ground laws," they are considered as potential chapters in a future constitution, for example, the "law of return." Nevertheless, at the present time even these do not possess any preference over others.

It is believed that the absence of a written constitution grants Israeli society and its government a great deal of legal flexibility. This "built-in" feature of the sociolegal environment allows the Knesset, without much difficulty, to change the nature of the government, its various institutions, and their respective functioning. Consequently, the Israeli Parliament is considered the supreme legislative power center which is not restricted by any body or any rules or regulations. The Knesset itself is not even bound by those rules it had previously enacted.

The government is a republican and a democratic parliamentary government. It relies on a majority consensus of the population, which enjoys the freedom to choose its candidates for public office. Indirectly, Israelis also provide input into the determination of the principles of its governance. Such democratic rights as free speech, freedom of the press, and freedom of political association are basic and fundamental. Rather than a direct democracy, it is a democracy by proxy. With the exception of a few local governmental units, there is no political body such as the people's assembly. Nor does the government rely on such practices as national referenda. The average Israeli ordinarily provides his input once every four years in national elections.

An interesting *modus vivendi* emerged from this situation in Israel. The protection of civil liberties is based upon the British paradigm of no bill of rights. However, members of this society are entitled to engage in any activity or behavior that is not prohibited by law. On the other hand, public governing agencies are entitled to operate only within the confines of the tasks and authority given them by the law or legal precedence. An individual in the Israeli society is granted the right to argue against any governing body or agency before the supreme court of Israel in its capacity of "the highest court of justice." When it acts in this capacity, the supreme court usually hands down a conditional decree, which becomes binding if the government or any of its organs fail to demonstrate to the court's satisfaction that the plaintiff has no case. This extremely important mechanism compels the government, among other things, to abide by the rule of law. The implication for criminology is that no agency of the government, including the police, the prosecution, and even more so the correctional system, is immune to public scrutiny via the supreme court.

History of Criminal Law

The second sociolegal factor has to do with both the history of Israeli criminal law and the structure of the court system. It is necessary to deal with these aspects separately since they are central to understanding the Israeli criminal justice system.

The very first law enacted in 1948 by the State of Israel provided that the then existing law in Palestine remain in force subject to such modification necessitated by the establishment of the state. This situation was to remain unless or until varied or repealed by the Israeli legislature. Thus, all Israeli laws were inherited in 1948 from the British Mandatory Administration of Palestine. As a result, they are not homogeneous in nature; rather, they draw legal principles from a number of major legal sources. The three most identifiable sources are: (1) the 1859 Criminal Code of the Ottoman Empire which was French in origin; (2) laws and ordinances legislated by the British Mandatory Government when it ruled Palestine; and (3) the British Common Law and England's principles of equity.

The present Israeli criminal law is no exception, and it, too, represents in its principles the Anglo-Saxon legal tradition. The Israeli Criminal Code Ordinance was first introduced as a bill in 1933, and it became a law in 1936. This law clearly provides for linkages with English Common Law in one of its introductory sections where it states:

This Code shall be interpreted in accordance with the principles of England, and expressions used in it shall be presumed, so far as is consistent with their context and except as may be otherwise expressly provided, to be used with the meaning attached to them in English law and shall be construed in accordance therewith.

This open door to English precedents has been and still is being used by Israeli courts in criminal cases, but it is now generally agreed that legal interpretations obtained in England are no longer binding to Israeli courts.

After 1948, the Israeli legislature introduced a number of significant changes in the Criminal Code Ordinance of 1936, in an attempt to adapt it to the emerging needs of Israeli society. The most important changes deal with the abolition of the death penalty in 1950. In addition, the chapter dealing with modes of punishment was replaced *in toto* by the Israeli legislature in 1954.[14]

Nature of Criminal Code

The Israeli Criminal Code Ordinance is generally divided into two main parts. The first part contains a series of axioms or general provisions. These include what Justice Cohen identified as "rules of interpretation, territorial applications, general rules as to criminal responsibility, parties to offenses such as attempts, incitements and conspiracies, and modes of punishments."[15] The second part includes specific offenses subdivided into seven legal categories: offenses against the public order, offenses against the adminstration of justice and lawful authority, offenses injurious to the public, offenses against persons, offenses against property, forgery and counterfeiting offenses, and minor offenses.

The law further distinguishes between three classes of crimes based on the severity of the sanction that it entails. A felony carries a minimum of a three-year prison term. A misdemeanor is punishable by imprisonment up to five years or any fine. Contraventions, the third class, are the least serious crimes and carry a sanction of up to a seven-day jail sentence.[16]

The Israeli Criminal Code Ordinance provides for the following sanctions: (1) death penalty for crimes of treason, (2) imprisonment which can be suspended pending various conditions, (3) fine, (4) restitution, (5) payment of court costs, (6) probation, and (7) binding security to keep the peace and a commitment to be of good behavior. All these penalties can be imposed singularly or in combination, as stated in the law.

The Court System

The jurisdiction of the courts in Israel is basically dictated by territorial principles, as well as by the seriousness of the crime. The courts have jurisdiction, both civil and criminal, over anything that occurs within the state itself and over all individuals found within its internationally defined boundaries.[17] The courts are bound by state laws and the principles of international law.

The courts in Israel are divided into three levels. The lowest level is occupied by all magistrate courts found practically in every district and/or region. In criminal matters, offenses classified as contraventions and misdemeanors fall within their jurisdictions. In special felony cases, this court can have jurisdiction upon the special request of the prosecution and the consent of the defendant. A judge of this court could impose a jail term of no longer than one year and a limited low fine penalty. Magistrate court decisions are appealed to the next higher level, the district courts.

As of the early 1970s, there were five district courts, located in the four largest cities (Jerusalem, Tel Aviv, Haifa, and Ber-Sheva) and in Nazareth serving northern Israel. These district courts have a dual function: original jurisdiction and appellate jurisdiction. In original jurisdiction capacities, they deal with all matters, civil and criminal, which transcend the magistrate courts' jurisdiction. In the appellate function, the district courts review the decisions of magistrate courts and the decisions of many other administrative-municipal tribunals located in the court's respective region or district. The district courts' rulings are appealed to the supreme court.

The supreme court, located in the capital, Jerusalem, has both appellate and original jurisdiction for the whole country. In its appellate function, it reviews the rulings of both lower level courts. The supreme court enjoys final and exclusive jurisdiction, not subject to appeal, in matters when it acts as a high court of justice. It issues various writs and decrees that would enable the court to examine the legality of arrests and/or various other actions or inactions of the government, its agencies and/or officials.

At all levels of the court system, jurisdiction is exercised exclusively by professional judges, who are appointed, not elected. The president, following a recommendation of an appointments committee chaired by the minister of justice, appoints judges. The Appointments Committee represents all branches of government: the judiciary (by three supreme court justices), the executive (by two members of the cabinet), and the legislative (by two members of the Knesset). Two additional members represent the Israeli Bar Association.

Place of "Jewish Law"

Perhaps the most unique characteristic of Israeli society—especially from the standpoint of jurisprudence and the sociology of law—is its partial reliance on "Jewish law." Even though the principles of traditional Jewish law date back centuries and even millennia, some laws have been carefully blended into the state's secular legal system.[18]

Israel is a Jewish state in which there is a *de facto* separation of religion and state with some exceptions. Specifically, according to Jewish law, Israel should have been a religious state much like some of its Moslem neighbors. However, because of social and political realities existing at the time a *status quo* was struck between various factions in society, it was agreed that Jewish law would prevail only in certain very fundamental areas. Most notably, these areas are the "law of return," marriage and divorce, the recognition of all religious holidays as national holidays (the observance of the Sabbath and other Jewish holidays by the state), and the two very controversial areas of abortion and the conduct of postmortems. Intense conflicts in all of these areas often led to very sharp political divisions, even during times of serious crises.

According to one outlook, Israel is a unique Jewish state and a leading model of successful nation-building. The other view portrays Israel as a neo-colonial, partially theocratic state dominated by secular Jews. It is a pluralistic state that still strives, unsuccessfully according to some,[19] to create an optimal social mix and group harmony. Despite many preventive efforts to the contrary, the potentials for conflicts between Oriental (non-European) and Ashkenazi (European) Jews, between religious and nonreligious, and between Israeli-Arabs and Jews cannot be easily eradicated. It is against this backdrop that one must view the emergence and evolution of criminology in Israel.

PATTERN OF CRIME IN ISRAEL

As previously noted, Israeli society can be characterized as a developing Western society in constant flux. Since World War II, there has been an almost steady rise all over the world in the volume and seriousness of crime and delinquency, a proliferation of criminal organizations, and a marked increase in the sophistication of criminal methods and techniques. Israel is no exception; there one observes drastic changes in the patterns of crime, especially in the last decade.

A number of remarks are in order before undertaking an outline of the complex crime situation in Israel. First, the following discussion focuses on population and trends for major crimes for the years 1949, 1967, 1972, and 1976.[20]

Second, comparisons over time between cultures present serious methodological difficulties, especially for rapidly developing countries. To be sure, each country has its own way of defining crime and criminality and its own methods of recording crime for statistical and/or applied purposes. Each country is unique in many respects that bear upon its crime problem. For example, to compare crime in Tel Aviv with another city, ideally, one would have to find a city that matches Tel Aviv in population characteristics, economic base, standard of living, and the like. Although this ideal eludes us, available statistics afford a general idea of how crime in Israel compares with that of other countries.

Third, to facilitate comparability, only conventional street crimes are dealt with here. Compiled by the Israeli Police Force, these data are similar in principle to the *Uniform Crime Reports* of the American Federal Bureau of Investigation in that they represent crimes known to the police as a result of a filed complaint. In all cases, the police decided to pursue actively a criminal investigation. Special attention is given to certain Type I felonies that are, at least behaviorally, comparable to similar crimes in other countries.

TABLE 18-1
SUMMARY TABLE OF POPULATION SIZE AND
CRIME TRENDS IN ISRAEL, 1949-1976

Year	Population Size	Crimes Known to Police	Crimes per 100,000 Population
1949	1,174,000	26,982	2,298.2
1967	2,775,000	106,110	3,824.5
1972	3,199,000	146,448	4,577.9
1976	3,556,800	189,552	5,329.3
Percent change 1949-1976	+ 203.0	+ 602.5	+ 56.8

Source: Compiled from *Report of the Shimron Committee for Study of Criminality in Israel* (Jerusalem: February 1978), p. 8 (in Hebrew).

Upsurge in Crime Rates

The data in Table 18-1 yield the following general findings. During the twenty-seven years from 1949 to 1976, the Israeli population more than tripled from 1,174,000 to 3,556,000 marking an increase by 203 percent. In 1949, 26,982 crimes were reported to the police, as compared with 189,552 in 1976, yielding a 602.5-percent growth. The rates per 100,000 population cancel out the distorting effects of absolute population increases to pinpoint the remarkable increase in crimes reported to the police.

Table 18-2 shows that Israel has experienced a tremendous increase in various types of major crimes.[21] As in many Western countries, the most common crimes in Israel are burglary and larceny for all the years studied here, 1949, 1967, 1972, and 1976. Over time, the largest increases were in burglary (1,353 percent). Narcotic drug-related crimes increased by 978.7 percent, assaults by 783.9 percent, and larcenies by 392.5 percent. Although robberies increased by only 76 percent from 1949 to 1976, they rose by 414.9 percent between 1967 and 1976, while the total population gained by 28 percent. This upsurge is remarkable when compared with the 1967-1976 increase for burglary of 112.7 percent, drugs 109.9 percent, assaults 64.2 percent, and larcenies only 6.1 percent. All other crimes not mentioned above rose considerably by 522.3 percent between 1949 and 1976, and by 11.4 percent for the 1967-1976 period.

Effects of Wars

Much of the increase in crime rates, particularly during the last decade, may be explained as a part of the postwar phenomena characterized by "urbanization, inflation, a general economic boom that has increased the appetite for luxuries that were unavailable before the war."[22] Some claim that at present there are an unprecedented number of guns in private hands of persons very experienced in using them.

The appearance of Israel's narcotic drug crime problem is also attributed to recent wars. Since the Six Day War in 1967, narcotic drug crimes reported to the police have risen by 109.9 percent (see Table 18-2). The smuggling, selling, buying, and using of drugs were first introduced into Israel on a large scale after 1967, when this society found itself squarely in the old Arab smuggling routes. In 1973 alone, it was reported that there was an increase of 60 percent over the previous year of cases involving drugs, with the police capturing more than 500 pounds of hashish and opium. Some 80 percent of the younger prison inmates in 1974 reported having a drug dependency problem.[23]

Organized Crime

In the late 1960s and early 1970s, a debate raged over whether organized crime exists in Israel. In the spring of 1971, *Ha'aretz*, one of Israel's morning

TABLE 18-2

FREQUENCY DISTRIBUTIONS OF ASSAULT, ROBBERY, BURGLARY, LARCENY, NARCOTIC DRUGS, AND OTHER CRIMES IN ISRAEL, 1949-1976

Year	Assault	Robbery	Burglary	Larceny (except auto)	Narcotic Drugs	All Other Crimes
1949	1,134	196	3,330	6,633	108	15,581
1967	6,104	67	22,746	30,782	555	45,856
1972	6,656	190	34,983	49,339	837	54,443
1976	10,023	345	48,385	32,667	1,165	96,967
Percent change 1949-1976	+783.9	+76.0	+1,353.0	+392.5	+978.7	+522.3

Source: *Report of the Shimron Committee for the Study of Criminality in Israel* (Jerusalem: February 1978), p. 9 (in Hebrew).

newspapers, published a series on organized crime by reporter Ran Kislev, claiming that it did exist and was led by a man whose "family" was involved in protection, vice, gambling, and debt collection. Some argued that this individual was connected with Mayer Lansky, an American Mafia leader of the "Miami family" who had been denied entry into Israel in 1972. Kislev argued that the "Israeli family" used contacts in high places to close police files, grant municipal licenses to restaurants, and protect vendors in various markets (for example, the carmel market) who operated without licenses. The then attorney general, Meir Shamgar, denied the existence of a criminal organization patterned after the American Mafia.

It is clear that there was no Mafia at the time, similar in structure and *modus operandi* to American organized crime, but there were and certainly at the present there are indications of organized crime operating in Israel. One of Israel's experts on organized crime, Menachem Amir, estimates that:

half of the "full time" criminals are involved in organized crime, with the other half working on their own or in pairs. . . . It really began to expand in the wave of affluence that followed the 1967 Six-Day War. With high custom duties and tariffs, together with an internal tax structure which creates a rash of tax evasion, the ground was ripe for the supply by illegal means of components of the good life, particularly to those anxious to obtain the goods without attracting the attention of the tax inspectors. It became very profitable for criminals to attempt to meet the demand. As it increased the nature of the organization to meet it became more sophisticated and complex.[24]

The *Report of the Shimron Committee for the Study of Criminality in Israel* (1978) devoted a special section to the problem of organized crime and its related protection racket in Israel in the 1970s. The committee that investigated all forms of criminality establishes unequivocally that there is organized crime in Israel, albeit somewhat different from its American counterpart.

CRIMINOLOGICAL THEORY AND RESEARCH

Criminology is generally perceived as an interdisciplinary subject, receiving contributions from sociology, psychology, law, public administration, psychiatry, and other academic fields.

Background

In the United States, the evolution of criminology was marked by a strong sociological emphasis on theory and research. Some claim that social conditions in America, coupled with the personal backgrounds of early American sociologists, led them to cast their preoccupation with deviance and crime in sociological terms. This tradition began with a social reform concern such as Lester Ward's, culminating during the early years of the twentieth century in the works of sociologists from the Department of Sociology at the University of Chicago. The major thrust of this preeminent department was the study of social problems as a means for social reform. Eager students combed slums, ghettos, and other poverty and disease pockets of the city, studying the deviant, the poor, the sick, the mad, the bad, and other "problem people." The impact of this tradition is suggested by the concentration of most criminological theorizing and research in American departments of sociology.[25]

The Europeans, on the other hand, built their criminological tradition on the works of both the classical school of the late eighteenth century and the positive school that evolved subsequently. The classical school represented a critique of law and the legal order; the positive school claimed that man's gravitation toward criminality was caused by biological predispositions, by situational factors, and by psychogenic tendencies. The former advocated the study of crime by legal experts as a violation of a legal statute; the latter relied on studies of human biology and psychology. These emphases resulted in a forensic-psychiatric-medical criminology that mostly followed the positive paradigm. It is not surprising that criminology in Europe is taught in law schools, medical schools, and departments of psychology rather than in departments of sociology.

Concern with Social Problems

These differing traditions abroad were mixed in a special way in the development of criminology and criminological research in Israel. After gaining nation status in 1948, Israel was confronted with social problems that bore some similarity to those of Chicago in the 1930s—mass immigration, disease, especially among Nazi concentration camp survivors, and so on. In Israel, however, research into crime and deviance was first conducted by individuals in the legal profession, because the Law School of Hebrew University was well established by then, unlike the Sociology Department. Thus, professionals trained in law were instrumental in the development of Israeli criminology, particularly during its early stages. Perhaps geographical proximity to Europe may also have influenced the evolution of a law-based criminology.

The situation changed dramatically in 1965 when the Law School Board of Hebrew University agreed to the establishment of an institute of criminology that would conduct interdisciplinary—rather than purely legal—criminological research. This development paved the way for behavioral scientists to become involved. At present, the majority of Israeli criminologists are educated in sociology and/or psychology rather than in law or psychiatry.

Theoretical Orientations

It is impossible to discuss criminological research intelligently without dealing with the difficult question of the prevailing theoretical paradigm in Israeli criminology. Clearly, paradigms in the Kuhnian sense[26] change over time and Israel is no exception. However, some trends remain characteristic of criminological theory and research in Israel. As noted earlier, three issues command central attention in Israel: absorption of immigrants, national defense, and rapid modernization and development. These important processes must also be viewed in light of their influence on the views of Israeli criminologists on the genesis of criminal and deviant behavior and on the nature of societal reaction to crime.

There seems to be agreement that the cultural conflict paradigm, in the broadest sense, dominated criminological theory and research for the two decades after 1948.[27] First developed in the United States by Thorsten Sellin,[28] this paradigm has been widely applied in Israel, most notably by Shlomo Shoham who was one of the founders of Israeli criminology.[29] In research, Shoham and others demonstrate that:

It may be that the clash between the cultural codes, norms and values of these immigrants and those of the receiving community causes a relative increase in the crime rates of such immigrants. The process of integration may also injure the social and economic status of the head of the family, for when he comes to Israel, the different group setup may prevent him from fully exercising his former authority and leave him in a state of confusion in which he cannot retain proper control over his family, so that the children may realize that their father is not the omnipotent patriarch he was supposed to be.[30]

Many students of crime in Israel conclude that further research is needed into this link between criminality and cultural conflict.

While cultural conflict was central for a long time in Israeli criminological research, many later studies concentrated on other ideas. In a report submitted to the Shimron Committee, Amir identifies the most significant variables accounting for criminality in Israel in the 1970s.[31] His statement suggests the theoretical orientations of Israeli criminologists by identifying the following processes in the explanations of criminality: the formation and crystalization of a social class structure based upon economic and life-style disparities, perceived blockage of social and economic mobility leading to a differential opportunity structure, urbanization and internal migration, tremendous economic growth for some, and inflation, economic recession, and unemployment for others. When these factors are coupled with the weakening of both formal and informal social controls, they tend to produce a generic, perhaps eclectic, etiological paradigm. It incorporates primarily the ideas of American criminologists such as Sutherland, Cohen, Miller, Cloward and Ohlin, Merton, Wolfgang, Reckless, Quinney, and Chambliss.

In sum, it seems that during the earlier period of the evolution of Israeli criminology (1948-1965) the cultural conflict hypothesis dominated criminological theory and research. In the later years (1966-1980), there was an effort to test the merits of many other theories of crime. No single dominant approach emerged. On the contrary, Israeli criminology became eclectic, encompassing a variety of theoretical orientations drawn in the main from the sociological and psychological literatures.[32]

Broad Definition of Criminological Research

In Israel, nearly all research that has relevance to crime, criminality, and the criminal process is perceived as criminological research. Many projects, however, concentrate on well-defined, exclusively criminological problems. One finds studies focusing on juvenile delinquency, its characteristics, dynamics, organizational aspects, its prevention and control. Similarly, various offender types—the aging prostitute, the pimp, the addict, the sex offender, the violent offender, the psychopathic offender, the female delinquent or criminal—as well as special categories of crimes—white-collar crime, organized crime, traffic offenses—were subjected to in-depth criminological investigation. Penological research in Israel focused on a wide variety of aspects, such as the law, deterrence, correctional policy, correctional treatment, institutional treatment, group therapy, probation, correctional institutions, rehabilitation, and amnesty.[33]

Reports on research are published primarily in Israeli professional journals, as well as many others in the United States and Europe. In addition, many reports, theses, dissertations, papers, and books clearly testify to the breadth and depth of Israeli criminological research that is conducted under conditions described by Amir:

Criminological research is conducted mainly in universities in the institutes of criminology and the departments of sociology and psychology. Some criminological research is conducted in research institutes where criminologists from the institutes are employed part-time.

Public and governmental agencies conduct almost no criminological research on their own, but they fund much of the research which is conducted at the university. Such funds come from the Ministries of Welfare, Police, Labor, Education or Transport. Naturally these bodies place emphasis on applied and operative orientation of the studies they commission. The university is thus left to support more basic and theoretical research.[34]

Sources of Data

What are the variety and quality of available data on crime in Israel? The *Israeli Police* publishes an annual report on criminal statistics. Collection of this data is not centralized; rather, each police precinct gathers its data on crime and the criminal for submission to the Statistics Division located at the National Police headquarters. The data are similiar to, but in a way more limited than, those of the *Uniform Crime Reports* published by the Federal Bureau of Investigation in America. Both are based on crimes known to the police.

A special section of the Israeli police report is devoted to traffic control and traffic offenses, probably because the rate of traffic offenses and the number of fatalities and injuries are among the highest in the world.

The *Israel Prison Service Annual Report* provides information on the structure, activities, innovations, and statistics on the prison service and the prisoners.

This report also contains a brief description of all Israeli correctional facilities. *Israel Statistical Abstract* is more generic and includes crime-related statistics, along with data on other sociodemographic characteristics of the Israeli society. These volumes are issued annually by the Israeli Central Statistical Bureau and are also used extensively by researchers overseas since an English edition is published.

Many other sources of data are available among governmental offices and ministries, that is, Labor and Welfare, Interior,[35] Justice, and others. One can generate his own research data; generally, officials facilitate data gathering, conditional upon the written approval of a senior official. Gaining approval may be a long process.

PROFESSIONAL AND OCCUPATIONAL ASPECTS

An examination of occupational and professional practices is a useful means of gaining insights into the criminology of a given nation.

Criminology as an Occupation

As in many other developing countries, criminology in Israel is in the main an academic occupation. The criminologist *per se* has been generally equated with university professorialism, although there are individuals outside academia who identify themselves as criminologists.

Criminology has been transformed over the years from an almost exclusively legal profession into a relatively autonomous entity. During the early years of Israel's existence (1948-1959), many academic departments in universities taught courses of criminological relevance, taken by individuals holding positions requiring ongoing contacts with deviants, criminals, and delinquents (lawyers, social workers, psychologists, and so on). With the establishment of the Institute of Criminology at the Hebrew University in 1959, academicians began recognizing criminology as an autonomous interdisciplinary field at the university.[36] The trend toward autonomy culminated in 1978 when the Israeli Higher Education Council granted the Bar-Ilan University's Institute of Criminology the status of an independent academic department within the College of Social and Behavioral Sciences, offering a bachelor of arts degree in criminology.

Education of Criminologists

Of the seven major institutions of higher learning in Israel, only two offer comprehensive and systematic programs in criminology. Courses in criminology and deviance-related courses are more likely to be located in departments of sociology, psychology, social work, education, and so forth.

When the Hebrew University established the first institute of criminology in Israel in 1959, Israel Drapkin, a pioneer in Israeli criminology, was its head.

Established within the Law School to offer a graduate multidisciplinary program in criminology, the institute was directed primarily to teaching and research in an independent capacity and in support of other departments of the university.

During the early 1960s, another institute of criminology was established at the Bar-Ilan University by another of the founding fathers of Israeli criminology, Shlomo Shoham. Initially, it offered a one-year program awarding a diploma in criminology and an additional year of study to gain a specialization degree. Both programs were quite useful to criminal justice practitioners; many high-ranking officials of the Israeli Police Department were among its graduates. By the late 1960s, an undergraduate could declare criminology as a minor at Bar-Ilan, and a decade later it became a major field of undergraduate study. This program evolved into the only comprehensive undergraduate program in Israel, totally independent of any other department from its inception. There was no law school or any similar program at Bar-Ilan that could administratively house the criminology program.

An effort to build a graduate criminology program was launched in 1970 at the Tel Aviv University Law School and again by Shlomo Shoham. This program survived for about half a decade in its teaching capacity, but now the Institute of Criminology and Criminal Law of Tel Aviv University is basically a legal research institute that is headed by David Libai, a graduate of the University of Chicago Law School. Some speculate that the demise of the master's program is linked, *inter alia*, to the persistent conflict in Israeli criminology between the by now well-developed sociological perspective and the legal approach to the study of criminal behavior.

The Department of Sociology and Anthropology of the University of Haifa— one of Israel's newer institutions of higher learning—offers bachelor and master degrees in sociology with a specialization in criminology. These courses were first introduced in 1974-1975 by one of Israel's leading young criminologists, Gideon Fishman, who received his graduate degree in sociology at Ohio State University.

The institutions offering courses related to criminology rely heavily on many part-time faculty, most of whom are not self-professed academic criminologists. Psychiatrists, physicians (coroners), statisticians, attorneys, justices, correctional specialists, therapists, as well as many other professionals, do a good deal of the teaching and provide vital linkages to the fields of practice.

The education of criminological specialists is not limited to Israeli institutions. Most of the younger Israeli academic criminologists, if not all of them, have had some of their education abroad, mostly in the United States, including post-doctoral studies or a sabbatical. Two American institutions stand out in this regard. The Tel Aviv group—Shoham, Leon Shellef, and Fishman—received some of their education at Ohio State University with Simon Dinitz. The University of Pennsylvania has been part of the academic experience of Amir, Landau, Sebba, and Israel Nachshon from the Hebrew University and the Bar-Ilan contingent in studies primarily with Marvin Wolfgang. Cromer and Cohen were at

Queens College and the University of Ottawa, respectively. Thus, with the exception of the Honorable Justice Jacob Bazak and another young Israeli-educated criminologist, Yael Hassin, all Israeli academic criminologists had some academic preparation in North America, returning with new ideas, methods, and research experience.

Formal and Informal Associations

A new spirit of cooperation, rather than conflict, exists at the present time among Israeli criminologists; Amir has observed in another context that:

An atmosphere of "Gemeinshaft" has been developed among criminologists which has led to more informal and formal cooperation in research and study. Thus we see joint projects, while master and Ph.D. students from other centers are supervised by the Jerusalem staff and vice-versa.[37]

This spirit may be explained by the close geographical proximity between universities and the economic conditions in Israel. Sheer economic necessity presses faculty members to assume part-time positions along with their full-time commitments. It is quite common to find an individual holding a full-time position at the Hebrew University, for example, also teaching criminology on a part-time basis at Bar-Ilan and vice-versa. In this way, Israeli criminologists of disparate institutions develop informal interactional networks. Two professional associations—the Israeli Society of Criminology and the Israeli Sociological Society—are crucial structures for formal interaction.

Criminological Publications

Israeli criminologists essentially use two main means to communicate ideas in writing. First are local professional periodicals and journals outside of Israel in English, French, Italian, and other languages. Since all Israeli criminologists communicate relatively well in English, their articles appear frequently in respected American and British refereed journals. A whole array of local Israeli periodicals and journals are published in Hebrew and English. Some Israeli journals devote a section of each issue to abstracts of the articles in the English language.

Among the Israeli periodicals that publish criminological papers are the *Bulletin of the Israeli Society of Criminology, Crime and Social Deviation, Crime and Society in Israel, Criminology, Criminal Law and Police, Megamot, Society and Welfare, Welfare,* and *Israeli Police Quarterly.* In addition, beginning with 1970, the *Israeli Studies in Criminology* has been publishing on an almost annual basis in a model much like the *Scandinavian Studies in Criminology.* The volumes are edited by Shlomo Shoham of the Tel Aviv University Law School and are published in English, presumably to share Israeli criminology with the world criminological community.

Numerous technical and research reports are published annually by the various institutes and by the Department of Criminology at Bar-Ilan. Of special importance are the reports of the proceedings of the many national and international seminars and symposia conducted under the auspices of the Institute of Criminology at the Hebrew University.

SUMMARY

In its evolution, criminology in Israel has been shaped by the unique features of Israeli society along social, sociolegal, and sociopolitical dimensions. The professional and occupational aspects of criminology reflect these dimensions. The volume, nature, and fluctuations of major crimes have provided a remarkable subject matter for research.

Born slightly after the establishment of the nation in 1948, Israeli criminology developed in a highly pluralistic society, at least in the sociodemographic and particularly in the ethnic sense. The multiple sources of the legal system are, in themselves, an example of Israel's development as a promising arena for comparative research into the foundations and implementation of legal systems. The rapidity of nation-building, the ethnic diversity, and the effects of three wars have generated a serious crime problem that has stimulated the establishment of Israeli criminology and that has provided a need for criminological research. Whether prepared by domestic or foreign institutions of higher education, Israeli criminologists have conducted intensive and sophisticated research focusing on a wide variety of topics and using many theoretical orientations. Over the years, the various institutes of criminology in Israel have become more and more involved with applied criminological problems, providing scientific and empirical input for framing criminal and correctional policy. These conditions are favorable for further maturation of the field and credibility of policy recommendations based upon criminological research.

NOTES

1. "First Aliyah" refers to the first wave of mass immigration to Israel.
2. Shmuel Eisenstadt, *The Israeli Society* (Jerusalem: Hebrew University Magnis Press, 1967).
3. In Hebrew, the term designates immigrants as "newcomers."
4. At the time this was the policy of the Jewish Agency, an organization established to promote immigration to Israel and to aid immigrants and their families in becoming absorbed in the country.
5. These are the Jews who came to Israel from predominantly Moslem Middle East countries. They are also known in Israel as "Oriental Jews."
6. Eisenstadt, *Israeli Society*.
7. Ibid.
8. Israel Drapkin, *The Prevention of Crime and the Treatment of Offenders in Israel* (Jerusalem: July 1965).

9. Menachem Amir, "Criminology in Israel," in Israel Drapkin, *The First 15 Years of the Institute of Criminology (1959-1974)* (Jerusalem: Akademon, 1979), pp. 174-180.

10. David Reifen, *The Juvenile Court in a Changing Society* (Philadelphia: University of Pennsylvania Press, 1972).

11. This "special problem" is exclusive of offenses against the Defense (Emergency) Regulations of 1956.

12. Shlomo Shoham, Esther Segal, and Giova Rahav, "Secularization, Deviance and Delinquency Among Israeli Arab Villagers," in Shlomo Shoham (ed.), *Israel Studies in Criminology*, Vol. 3 (Jerusalem: Academic Press, 1976), pp. 72-85.

13. For a more complete discussion, see Reifen, *Juvenile Court in a Changing Society*, pp. 49-62.

14. Capital punishment has been retained in the law for cases of wartime treason. Similarly, it was left in effect under the Act for the Punishment of Nazis and Nazi Collaborators and the Act for the Punishment of the Crime of Genocide. Both acts are retroactive and were the first criminal laws (1950) to be enacted by the State of Israel, apart from the 1949 act proclaiming general amnesty.

15. Haim H. Cohen, "Legislation and Judicial Process in the Field of Criminal Law," in Drapkin, *The Prevention of Crime and the Treatment of Offenders in Israel*, pp.15-32.

16. Although these distinctions have undergone some changes, they still prevail and are most meaningful in determining the jurisdictions of courts at their various levels.

17. In some specific matters, the arm of a court reaches beyond the confines of its geographical territory.

18. The most concise statement of the Jewish Law is found in the Shulhan Aruch written by Joseph Karo of Spain. In his authoritative statement, he draws heavily on Maimonides. The final binding authority is clearly in the Talmud (the oral tradition).

19. Sammy Smooha, *Israel: Pluralism and Conflict* (Los Angeles: University of California Press, 1978).

20. Criminal statistics were first collected in Israel in 1951 in a form consistent with data of later years. Conclusions drawn from the statistics gathered in the years before 1951 should be regarded with caution.

21. Data on homicide were not available.

22. Sheldon Kirsher, "Crime in Israel," *The Chronicle Review* (June 1974):59-64.

23. Ibid.

24. Quoted in Avi Gil, "Organized Crime on the Increase in Israel," *Jewish Observer and Middle-East Review* 25, no. 9 (February 1976):11.

25. This was the case until the early 1970s when many criminal justice programs appeared. Most of these programs concentrate on teaching applied criminal justice, producing little criminological research.

26. Thomas Kuhn, *The Structure of Scientific Revolutions* (Chicago: University of Chicago Press, 1962).

27. For concrete evidence, consult a recently published comprehensive bibliography on crime in Israel: Menachem Amir, *Crime, Delinquency, and Corrections in Israel: A Bibliography (1948-1978)* (Jerusalem: Akademon, 1979), in Hebrew.

28. Thorsten Sellin, *Culture Conflict and Crime* (New York: Social Science Research Council, 1938).

29. Shlomo Shoham, "The Application of the 'Culture-Conflict' Hypothesis to the Criminality of Immigrants in Israel," *Journal of Criminal Law, Criminology and Police Science* 53 (June 1962):207-214.

30. Shlomo Shoham and D. Phillip, "Crime in Israel," in Refael Patai (ed.), *Encyclopedia of Zionism and Israel* (New York: McGraw-Hill, 1971), pp. 221-224.

31. *Report of the Shimron Committee for the Study of Criminality in Israel* (Jerusalem: February 1978).

32. A heavier sociological emphasis in recent years has come primarily from the return to Israel of many American-educated Israeli criminologists.

33. For references, consult Amir, *Criminality, Delinquency, and Corrections in Israel*.

34. Ibid.

35. This ministry at present includes what was the Ministry of Police, prior to the reorganization of ministries by the Begin government.

36. This particular institute follows the model of European institutes rather than those in the United States, primarily because of "historical and academic politics."

37. Amir, "Criminology in Israel."

BIBLIOGRAPHY

Rather than being a representative sample of the most notable works in the Israeli criminological literature, this bibliography draws selectively on sources available to the author while he was in the United States.

Amir, Menachem. "Criminology in Israel." In Israel Drapkin. *The First 15 Years of the Institute of Criminology (1959-1974)*. Jerusalem: Akademon, 1979. Pp. 174-180.
The postscript to this volume traces the history of the first fifteen years of the Institute of Criminology of the Hebrew University, including its involvement in the development of criminology in Israel and the ways in which the institute participated in the process.

Amir, Menachem. *Criminality, Delinquency, and Corrections in Israel: A Bibliography (1948-1978)*. Jerusalem: Akademon, 1979. In Hebrew.
This comprehensive bibliography includes various research reports, papers, journal articles, theses, and so on.

Cohen, Haim H. "Legislation and Judicial Process in the Field of Criminal Law." In Israel Drapkin (ed.). *The Prevention of Crime and the Treatment of Offenders in Israel*. Jerusalem: July 1965. Pp. 15-32.
The Honorable Justice Haim Cohen reviews the Israeli Criminal Code Ordinance, its origins, its principles, structure, and implementation. Cohen also reviews the Juvenile Offenders Ordinance (1937) and some major revisions in the law of criminal procedure.

Drapkin, Israel (ed.). *The Prevention of Crime and the Treatment of Offenders in Israel*. Jerusalem: July 1965.
This report was prepared for the 1965 United Nations Congress on the Prevention of Crime and Treatment of Offenders. Several articles describe the operation of the various Israeli criminal justice agencies, for example, the police, corrections, the law, and the courts.

Drapkin, Israel. *The First 15 Years of the Institute of Criminology (1959-1974)*. Jerusalem: Akademon, 1979.
The founder of the Institute of Criminology of the Hebrew University discusses its

background, objectives, advisory board, facilities, personnel, teaching, research, national and international role, and its future programs. Other sections deal with criminology and selected criminological problems in Israel.

Fishman, Gideon, and Simon Dinitz. "White Collar Crime: A Conceptual Analysis and Assessment." *Social Research Review* 12-19 (1977):273-288. In Hebrew.
In this theoretical-conceptual analysis of the white-collar crime concept, the authors discuss the work of Sutherland, Hartung, Clinard, Becker, Newman, Quinney, Geis, and Herbert Edelhertz, and assess the state of white-collar crime in Israel.

Rahav, Giora. "Family Relations and Delinquency in Israel." *Criminology* 14 (August 1976):259-270.
The traditional conception that harmonious families are insulators against delinquency is questioned by this study that shows family variables are relatively less important from the etiological viewpoint in Israel.

Rahav, Giora. "Ethnic Origins and the Disposition of Delinquents in Israel." *International Journal of Comparative and Applied Criminal Justice* 4 (Spring 1980):63-74.
It is hypothesized that in juvenile dispositions, Oriental Jews will receive harsher reactions than European Jews in Israel and Arab juveniles harsher reactions than either of the two categories of Jews. Official data reflect this tendency, but the authoritarian structure of the Arab community, rather than prejudice, explains the difference for Arabic cases.

Reifen, David. *The Juvenile Court in a Changing Society*. Philadelphia: University of Pennsylvania Press, 1972.
The chief justice of juvenile court reviews the status of juvenile delinquency in Israel and particularly Israel's unique adjudicatory responses to juvenile delinquency.

Report of the Shimron Committee for the Study of Criminality in Israel. Jerusalem: February 1978. In Hebrew.
This task force conducted a study of many facets of Israeli criminality. From data gathered and expert testimonies, it set forth 127 recommendations for social policy and change.

Shoham, Shlomo. "The Application of the 'Culture-Conflict' Hypothesis to the Criminality of Immigrants in Israel." *Journal of Criminal Law, Criminology and Police Science* 53 (June 1962):207-214.
One of the first studies testing the cultural conflict hypothesis in Israel found higher crime rates among new immigrants as opposed to native-born Israelis. A higher crime rate was also evident among Oriental Jews versus European Jews.

Shoham, Shlomo. *The Sentencing Policy of the Criminal Courts in Israel*. Tel Aviv: Am Oved, 1963. In Hebrew.
For the first time in the Hebrew language, a systematic analysis is made of the fundamental principles, justifications, philosophies, ideologies, and rationales of punishment: retribution, deterrence, prevention, and rehabilitation.

Shoham, Shlomo. *Introduction to Criminology*. Tel Aviv: Am Oved, 1964. In Hebrew.
The first introductory textbook in criminology in Hebrew discusses in detail many tradi-

tional etiological frameworks (for example, biophysical, psychological, socioeconomic), with special emphasis on the culture conflict frame of reference. Anomie theory, stigma theory, juvenile gang delinquency, and middle-class delinquency are also considered in the Israeli context.

Shoham, Shlomo, and Meir Hovav. "'Bnei-Tovim'—Middle and Upper Class Delin-
    quency in Israel." *Sociology and Social Research* 48 (July 1964):454-468.
The authors test four hypotheses as factors in an etiological framework of Israeli delinquency among middle- and upper-class juveniles: masculine protest, a faulty process of
adolescence, conspicuous consumption, and family conflict situations during the socialization process.

Shoham, Shlomo, Ruth Erez, and Walter Reckless. "Value Orientation and Awareness of
    Differential Opportunity of Delinquent and Non-Delinquent Boys in Israel."
    Criminologica 2 (November 1964): 11.
The Landis and Scarpitti Value Orientation Scale was replicated in Israel. Also replicated
was a scale measuring the degree of awareness of limited access to the legitimate opportunity structure. Partial support for Cohen's value orientation theory and for Cloward and
Ohlin's differential opportunity theory was demonstrated.

Shoham, Shlomo. "Culture Conflict as a Frame of Reference for Research in Criminol-
    ogy and Social Deviation." In Marvin Wolfgang (ed.). *Crime and Culture: Essays
    in Honor of Thorsten Sellin.* New York: John Wiley and Sons, 1968. Pp. 55-82.
The author examines in detail the feasibility of the application of Sellin's culture conflict
hypothesis to crime and deviance in Israel.

Shoham, Shlomo, and Leon Shaskolsky. "An Analysis of Delinquents and Non-Delinquents
    in Israel: A Cross-Cultural Perspective." *Sociology and Social Research* 53 (April
    1969):333-343.
Eight research schedules developed in the United States were translated into Hebrew,
adjusted to Israeli culture, and administered to two groups of Israeli juveniles, that is,
100 delinquent boys and 100 nondelinquent controls. For the most part the instruments did
not differentiate between delinquents and nondelinquents in Israel.

Shoham, Shlomo, Nahum Shoham, and Adman Abd-El-Razek. "Immigration, Ethnicity,
    and Ecology as Related to Juvenile Delinquency in Israel." *Bar-Ilan Volume in
    Humanities and Social Sciences.* Jerusalem: 1969. Pp. lxi-lxxxi.
Nine culture conflict hypotheses are applied to juvenile delinquency, including urbanization, immigration, the magnitude of the cultural gap between the immigrants and the
receiving community, and being second-generation juveniles of immigrant parentage.

Shoham, Shlomo (ed.). *Israel Studies in Criminology.* Vols. 1, 2, 3, 4, 5. Jerusalem:
    Academic Press, 1970-.
These volumes communicate original scholarly works of Israeli criminologists to the rest
of the world.

Shoham, Shlomo, Esther Segal, and Giova Rahav. "The Classification of Prisoners in
    Israel." In Shlomo Shoham (ed.). *Israel Studies in Criminology.* Vol. 3. Jerusa-
    lem: Academic Press, 1976. Pp. 13-23.

The criminality of rural Arabs in Israel is analyzed in light of the culture conflict and the processes of rapid modernization having impact on traditional social structures.

Weller, Leonard. *Sociology in Israel*. Westport, Conn.: Greenwood Press, 1976.
In this review of sociological theories and research in Israel, one chapter is devoted to criminology.

19

ITALY

Franco Ferracuti and Gilda Scardaccione

In aspiring to revolutionize substantive and procedural law, the founders of the positive school placed Italy in the forefront of criminological history. That this school has also been called the Italian school suggests that key ideas in criminology converged in Italy. The issues raised and the conceptual system developed then to deal with these ideas continue to influence many criminologists in other parts of the world, but, in light of the topic of this chapter, it is especially significant that this heritage continues to have marked influence on Italian criminology.

THE BEGINNING OF CRIMINOLOGY IN ITALY

It is universally acknowledged that the origin and development of the criminological sciences and related research in Italy can be traced to the birth of the positive school at the end of the nineteenth century. The rationale and purposes of this widely known school emerged as an antithesis to those of Francesco Carrara's classical school which until then had dominated the field of criminal justice. The founders of the new positive school aimed at nothing less than a full-fledged revolution in both substantive and procedural law. They opposed the dominant interest of classicists in the criminal act and in finding a proper balance between the perceived seriousness of the crime and the severity of the imposed penalty along a predetermined scale. The positivists had two interrelated goals. First, they intended to ascertain the incidental or root causes of criminal behavior; here, criminogenesis was the subject of investigation. Second, they sought to identify the most effective means of preventing and controlling the criminal phenomena; thus, the damage criminals inflicted on the established order would be held to a minimum.

The tenets of the positive school were perfectly in keeping with the ideological climate of *fin de siècle* Europe. At this point in the history of ideas, European intellectuals were bubbling over with enthusiasm for the analysis of the social facts of reality as experienced by human beings. The "true religion" of the *grand être* would be substituted for metaphysical and doctrinaire considerations of the human condition.

Accordingly, the beginning of criminology was marked with the posture of a science dedicated to studying crime as the expression of a given human and social reality. The administration of criminal sanctions was to be in harmony with that reality, with the objective of employing the penalties simultaneously as instruments of prevention and reeducation. From the onset, a peculiar dualism characterized the efforts to achieve the general objective; two irreconcilable purposes were pursued concurrently. One purpose was to examine the pathological aspects of criminal behavior under the inherent premise that criminality is the direct result of the individual pathology. The other purpose was to relate the criminal phenomena to the social environment as a basis for juridical reactions to criminality.

The initial criminological research was almost exclusively anthropological and oriented toward establishing the inherent pathology of criminals. Eminent scholars— Lombroso the first among them but also Virgilio and Tamassia—were searching for direct contact with the "criminal man" in prisons and hospitals for the criminally insane. In their view, crime was essentially a pathological phenomenon or a sign of underlying pathology. The first typologies of criminals were constructed in keeping with the positivist principle that science would identify the distinctive categories of criminals and that science-trained technicians would administer those corrective measures tailored to deal with the inherent pathologies found in a given type. These early criminologists also endeavored to single out and assess those elements that distinguished "criminal man" from "normal man."

This emergent conception of criminology called itself "criminal anthropology." The first chair bearing this title was conferred *ad personam* upon Cesare Lombroso at the University of Turin where in 1912 he had established the Institute of Criminal Anthropology in the medical school. The location in a medical school was not a chance event; from its beginning, criminology in Italy has assumed the structure of a medicopathological discipline and has acquired associated difficulties of identity and autonomy. It is considered ancillary to, or a part of, other disciplines such a forensic medicine, criminal law, and sociology.

The other path—that of conceiving criminal phenomena from a sociojuridical perspective—was followed in the theoretical tenets of Enrico Ferri who also was one of the eminent founding fathers of criminology at the turn of the century. In attempting this approach, Ferri proposed a major reform of the criminal code, stretching from the criminal code to corrections. He also established the Scuola di Applicazione Giuridico-Criminale, now called Scuola di Specializzazione in Diritto Penale e Criminologia. The school, which will be described in more detail later, has lost its original applied criminology character; it has become primarily technical-juridical and is predominantly concerned with criminal law.

Establishing a clearcut distinction between criminal anthropology and criminal sociology, Canepa says, is one of the achievements of the positive school.[1] His statement is correct, but the distinction has become an unbridgeable gap, and the sociological aspects have been essentially overlooked or only marginally considered in Italian criminological research. Ferri's thinking had a paradoxical effect; it had a greater impact abroad than in his own country. Outside of Italy there was a much greater dissemination of the sociological and more strictly positivist content of his doctrine. Nevertheless, in spite of obstacles and outright opposition from his compatriots, Ferri was undoubtedly the leading figure in Italian criminological research at the beginning of the century. The task of reforming the old Zanardelli criminal code was entrusted to him when it was recognized that it was obsolete in light of the impact of sociocultural change on juridical matters. Although the Ferri project has had great influence on the structure of the new criminal codes in other countries—such as those of many South American countries and the U.S.S.R. Criminal Code of 1927—it did not meet the approval of Italian authorities, then fascist, who commissioned a new, less drastic project to A. Rocco that culminated in the contemporary Italian code.

THE POSITIVISTS LOSE THEIR MOMENTUM

In spite of criticisms directed against the positive school, the early decades of the twentieth century represented a golden era for criminological research in Italy that was not to be equaled in subsequent years. In fact, for the years until the end of World War II, Italian criminological research was at a standstill for two major but separate reasons.

First, the fascist state opposed "socialist" Ferri and had little sympathy for Lombroso's Jewish origins. The fascist state felt a pressing need to overcome crime, but this concern was directed toward maintaining public order rather than following Ferri's social and reeducational philosophies. Consequently, he was not able to carry out the sweeping reform of the criminal code he recommended.

Second, Catholic thinkers conducted a doctrinal attack on the positive school, especially against the principles advanced in Ferri's *Criminal Sociology*. The Catholic Church could not accept a critique of the concept of free will which was implicit in the tenets of the positive school, because free will was vital to Catholic theology. Father Agostino Gemelli, an eminent scholar deeply interested in criminological research, became the most vehement opponent of the positive school.

In this ideological climate, sterile doctrinaire debates monpolized the time of scholars and dissipated scarce resources that could have gone to meaningful operational research. There were worthy efforts by important scholars, such as Niceforo and Ottolenghi who established systematic collection of data on prisoners. Their "biographical file" has at long last been modernized. Nevertheless, during these decades, criminological research in Italy was characterized by a warming over of the old and sterile postulates of early positivism in almost total isolation from the more modern trends shaping criminology in other countries. Originally, the Italian positive school had inspired and given ideological identity to criminologists in other countries, but obstinate adherence to traditions isolated the later Italian researchers from subsequent development of criminology outside the borders of Italy. Positive scholars failed to convince Italy to adopt a criminal code based on the conception that offenders are dangerous. As Radzinowicz points out in a bitter but realistic statement,[2] instead, the positivists made criminology itself appear to be "dangerous."

PERSISTENCE OF TRENDS INTO THE 1960s

The historical trends summarized above persisted through the years immediately following World War II, limiting criminological research in Italy to implementation of the positive school's principles. The constitutional biotypological approach was emphasized to the almost total exclusion of sociojuridical studies. The constitutional and biological parameters of Lombrosian research continued to be focused on the "criminal man" and on analyses of the personality of the deviant as an individual. The approach was strongly reinforced by the endocrinological investigations of Nicola Pende[3] who tried to attribute criminal behavior to endocrinal and hormonal abnormalities.

In this period, the positivistic tradition was followed in the classification of criminal behaviors and the construction of progressively more complex and sophisticated typologies of criminals. Criminology was defined variously as criminal anthropology, clinical criminology, or criminological medicine, developing within the fields of forensic medicine and forensic psychiatry in the course of increased provision of expert opinion to the courts. The "criminological physician" surfaced as an expert status and a domain of specialized knowledge established theoretically by the work of Benigno Di Tullio. He was the recognized leader of a school that for almost fifty years conducted research and teaching in Italy and abroad, particularly in Latin America.

The medical model stimulated research and action in a broad sphere of criminological work in keeping with the implications of positivism that criminal behavior resembles disease in its susceptibility to diagnosis as a distinct entity and as a symptom of physical or intrapsychic abnormalities. Therapy itself was considered to be strictly medical. The clinical-diagnostic approach prevailed over the social-structural approach to the problem of crime. The investigation of the etiology of crime turned toward the abnormalities of the offender's personality and away from the social context of his behavior. Crime was conceived more as a subjective pathology and not as an objective expression of a social pathology. There was limited interest in the relationship between criminality and the social structure in terms of either monofactorial or multifactorial analyses. Social factors were not seen as possible predictors of criminal behavior.

The criminological research of this period presented a number of deficiencies that may be summarized in the following fashion. First, there were no analyses of the social structure as either a predisposing or causal factor in criminality. This absence occurred at a time when other countries, particularly the United States, were the scenes of an impressive expansion of sociologically and statistically oriented research through the work of scholars such as Sutherland, Cohen, the Gluecks, Wolfgang, Cloward, and Ohlin. Second, there was an absence of prediction research that took social context into consideration. Clinical diagnosis continued to be the most frequently employed tool for prediction. Third, there was a lack of sophisticated statistical methodology for probing the etiology of crime and the treatment of offenders.

The overall consequence has been an isolation of Italian criminologists from the development elsewhere of criminology as an autonomous science with a well-defined research domain that is identified with the social context and that enjoys a close interrelationship with criminal policy. Lacking the qualities of a social system with established roles and functions relating investigators and consumers, criminological research in Italy had minimal operational impact and did not benefit from feedback from social reality.

ORIENTATION OF APPLIED RESEARCH

Against this background, the first applied research into corrections and other penal measures was based mostly on the observation and analysis of the offender's personality. This direction for inquiry suffered limitations and uncertainty of results. This style of applied research grew out of the increased diffusion of psychological testing used to analyze the personality of the offender but directed toward more objective and meaningful analysis beyond the reach of the Lombrosian biological and biometric model of traditional positivism. The Observation Institute at Rebibbia[4] still functions in this style of applied research.

There were attempts to establish communication between criminology and the penal system and to make research into the etiology of crime an active force in the legislative and judicial fields. Still, these several constituencies continued to be in conflict. Research tasks are difficult to accomplish under the best of circumstances, but the practical possibilities that the Italian criminologists would influence the criminal justice system were very remote at the legislative, judicial, and correctional levels of public policy. The 1950s were not without progress, however; three developments are worthy of special note. Several research units were established within the structure of criminal justice administration, for example, the Rebibbia Observation Institute and the Center for Correctional Study at the Ministry of Justice. Researchers showed a clearer interest in sanction systems and the correctional agencies, including the analysis of the prison structure and environment. Comparative studies were undertaken in Italy on the legislation and administration of criminal justice in other countries.

In the following years, a large number of research projects were sponsored by the Studies and Research Office of the Directorate of Correctional Affairs in the Ministry of Justice, by the National Center of Social Prevention and Defense in Milan, and by the United Nations Social Defense Research Institute (UNSDRI). Clinical research continues to be the basic trend, and the favorite concepts are anamnestic-biographic, constitutional, endocrinological, functional, or psychiatric-psychological in analyses of offender behavior.[5] This research approach was in line with the thought of Benigno Di Tullio, who was foremost among Italian scholars in the 1950s. In the mode of the earlier work of the positive school, clinical-diagnostic case studies and typological classifications were popular in keeping with the "medical model" interpretation of criminality. Many criminologists have rejected this interpretation as inadequate in providing etiological explanations and a platform for planning treatment modalities. Comparative studies, whether cross-sectional or longitudinal, had been absent even in investigations of criminal personality.

Existing textbooks and treatises that have particular influence are also organized around biotypological and constitutional concepts. It is very difficult to write a comprehensive and multifactorial-oriented treatise, especially when trying to strike a balance between criminology and criminal policy while considering properly the complex sociological variables involved in the perceptions of and reactions against criminality. Mannheim's well-known textbook, *Comparative Criminology*, is an example of such an enterprise, and it has been translated into Italian. No equivalent work has been produced by Italian criminologists. Di Tullio's *Principi di Criminologia Clinica* is the definitive work for Italian clinical criminology, but it falls short in comprehensiveness and balance among alternative theoretical perspectives. More recent texts—such as *Medicina Criminologica e Psichiatria Forense* by Semerari and Citterio—follow a phenomenological and forensic psychiatric approach.

Di Tullio's clinical approach continued to be most prevalent in criminological research from the time of Enrico Ferri's death (1928) to the years immediately after World War II, but another trend must be recognized. The revival and elaboration of Ferri's principle of social defense took a sociojuridical perspective, largely cultivated by the International Society of Social Defense under the leadership of Filippo Gramatica,[6] the president of the society and the leading promoter of social defense principles. The trend has been toward elaborating social defense principles in the reform of the juridical system to integrate that system, or to supplant criminal sanctions, within the contemporary normative structure. Some ongoing research follows this purpose as a reflection of the influence of the International Society of Social Defense and Professor Marc Ancel, a prominant advocate of the approach.

In spite of the limitations and deficiencies we have outlined, there was evidence of incipient change in criminological research in the years immediately following World War II. For example, the First International Meeting of Clinical Criminology, held in Rome in April 1958, constituted an attempt to coordinate clinical research on the international plane, something not previously attempted in Italy. The need for substantial correctional reform became evident in those years because the field had been static since 1931. The debate on reform of correctional institutions and community-based treatment culminated in 1975 with a new penal code that was the vehicle of many changes and amendments.

TEACHING CRIMINOLOGY IN UNIVERSITIES

The development of criminology as a scientific activity has been reviewed in the preceding pages. This history is reflected in the instruction of criminology in the Italian universities. Examination of the patterns of instruction is another method for extracting the implications of this history. For that purpose we now turn to the situation in Italian universities as of 1980.

Medical faculties have a total of twenty chairs devoted to criminological teaching. The subject matter to which the chairs are allocated tells us something about the nature of the contemporary conception of criminology in Italy. The residual effects of criminological traditions are reflected in this distribution: fifteen chairs of criminal anthropology, three of clinical medicine and forensic psychiatry, and one of juvenile delinquency. In faculties of law there are eleven chairs: five of criminal anthropology, five of criminology, and one of criminal sociology. Here the heavy hand of tradition is less evident. Similarly, there are three chairs of criminology among the faculties of political science and one each in the various faculties of economics and of psychology. For all of the faculties, courses related to criminology are elective rather than required of students in a curriculum.

What are the implications of this rather peculiar distribution of prestigious opportunities to instruct criminology in Italy? Since courses universally are elective rather than required, it is clear that instruction in the subject matter of criminology is regarded as only incidental to preparation of university students for professional careers other than that of the criminologist. Obviously, criminal anthropology—with a share of twenty chairs out of a total thirty-six—still holds its traditional dominance among the specializations within criminology. Criminological medicine and forensic psychiatry—a combination that is significant—hold four of the chairs, one of which also involves clinical criminology. Of the remaining twelve chairs, only one is devoted to criminal sociology. More recent trends in criminology outside of Italy might lead us to expect a larger representation than that.

The heavy concentration of criminological teaching in medical faculties—whether as criminal anthropology, criminological medicine, or forensic psychiatry—is a noteworthy pattern not found in any other country. Thus, the teaching of criminology, and consequently criminological research, has gained scarce acceptance in schools of law, whereas law schools in many other countries are the most active of all schools in the field of criminology.

Another striking feature of the Italian scene is the failure of faculties of sociology to participate, but instruction in sociology is meagerly represented in Italy. In general, Italian universities have given scant heed to the complex parameters of the criminal phenomenon, especially in regard to the social aspects permeating even the specialized fields of medicine and the law.

Postgraduate specialization in criminological topics is also an important facet of university instruction where we may also test the commitment of Italian higher education to criminology. Schools of criminology at the graduate level have been established at the medical schools of the universities in Naples, Genoa, and Modena. At the University of Rome there is the School of Criminological Medicine and Forensic Psychiatry in the Faculty of Medicine and the School of Criminal Law and Criminology in the Faculty of Law that offer postgraduate studies. Although its founder, Enrico Ferri, planned a criminological content for its instruction, the contemporary School of Criminal Law and Criminology in Rome specializes in criminal law rather than in criminology. For postgraduate studies as a whole, this ignoring of the social aspects of criminology—and their implications for the administration of the criminal law—is as typical of other programs as that of the University of Rome.

In university teaching, only the medical-psychiatric approach has been adequately represented and developed. The instruction typically concentrates on the traditional topics of psychopathology, criminalistics, and the rather routine administration of criminal law and penal sanctions. Little attention is devoted to the broader sociopolitical context and a host of important issues, such as the concept of social dangerousness, the inherent problems of managing the criminal justice system, and the framing of criminal policy under contemporary conditions. The opportunities for developing an interdisciplinary, unified, and autonomous criminology have been lost in the course of the style of university instruction described above.

CURRENT STATUS OF CRIMINOLOGICAL RESEARCH

Towards the end of the 1960s and into the 1970s, new themes were surfacing in Italian criminological research, and some modest success was achieved in overcoming the narrowness of the biological-constitutional emphasis we have described. These tenuous shifts in criminology are not adequately reflected in existing textbooks which continue to take the traditional approach.

Generally, current research is oriented toward analysis of the personality of the individual offender; conceptual approaches range from medical-psychiatric and clinical-psychological to various uses of psychological tests and psychodiagnoses. Juvenile delinquency has taken on unprecedented importance as an area for criminological research, sustained by demands for more effective preventive actions against crime and by wider recognition of the need for reform of laws directed against juvenile offenders.[7] When personality theory is applied to the criminogenesis and criminodynamics of antisocial behavior, the relationship between delinquency and family dynamics is likely to be seen as a logical and promising starting point for research into the etiology of crime.[8] Another major theme is that diagnostic instruments must deal with more parameters of personality and more effectively manage their interaction within the real world than has been possible within the restrictions of the traditional clinical or juridical model of diagnosis in criminology. Canepa has emphasized the need for reexamination of the premises and utilization of diagnoses in his in-depth discussion of the concept of "social dangerousness."[9]

We have made clear that the sociological orientation has been made conspicuous by its absence in the criminological literature of Italy. In a volume entitled "Criminal Sociology," Ferri argued that a person exists not only as an individual but also as an element of society. Furthermore, the general intellectual movement known as positivism had given birth to sociology under the aegis of Auguste Comte, the person who gave this social science its name. He stimulated a peculiar coupling of the advocacy of the scientific method with organicism, the doctrine that the parts of society can be compared to the organs of a living body. In this vein, Comte directed early sociology toward analysis of the social organization as opposed to analysis limited to persons composing it. The Italian positivists, however, interpreted Social Darwinism of that time in a fashion that directed attention away from analysis of social organization.

More recently in Italy, the sociological orientation has received more research interest through the popularity of deviance theory and the diffusion of the theoretical and methodological foundations created by American criminology which has emphasized sociological principles. A noteworthy example has been the application of subcultural theory in the analysis of violence within the broader topic of the etiology and prediction of criminal behavior.[10] Nevertheless, it would be an exaggeration to conclude that the trend toward subcultural theory constitutes a major development at the operational level in contemporary criminological research in Italy.

Increased interchange with foreign scholars, particularly through the activities of the Council of Europe, has injected a degree of innovation into Italian criminological research. Nevertheless, limitations and incompleteness are characteristic at the theoretical level and especially at the methodological and operational levels. The dualism of "clinical" and "sociological criminologies" has been perpetuated by the cultural history and current nature of Italian criminology. In other words, the dualism has become a chronic characteristic.

Italian criminologists cannot deal with their subject matter in an integrated way because they lack the intellectual foundations of an interdisciplinary conception of the criminal phenomenon. The clinical approach continues to be dominant. A major cost is that the relationship between crime and the social structure is largely ignored in an essentially academic and doctrinaire approach. Even the analysis of deviant behavior follows the psychological model in assessing personality dynamics. Those sociological studies that have been undertaken also suffer from substantial methodological deficiencies. The rather elementary statistical methodology, with a few exceptions, does not take advantage of multivariate analysis and the comparative method. Longitudinal analysis and proper use of control are not provided for generation of reliable conclusions.

BARRIERS AGAINST APPLIED RESEARCH

In light of these deficiencies, it is understandable that from its beginning Italian criminological research has had modest impact on criminal policy and on criminal legislation. The marginal contributions of criminological research to actions against crime can be attributed to the deficiencies in the design and methodology of research, but the substantial and atavistic opposition of political leaders and criminal justice executives to research must also be taken into consideration. They distrust any research that goes beyond technical support of contemporary policy and advancement of narrowly defined juridical functions. The result is a chronic lack of essential funding and the erection of roadblocks, not necessarily intentional, to the accessibility of data.

The uncertain place of criminology among the disciplines and in the social system of higher education has denied criminological researchers the resources for sustained investigation, but the dominant clinical approach deprives operational research the advantages of applied research that would concentrate on the environmental variables of the criminal justice system as a micro-system and the parameters of criminal justice administration as a part of society's macro-system. Thus, applied research is restricted by the resistance of criminal justice policymakers and administrators, the tenuous position of criminology among the disciplines, and the narrowness of the clinical approach.

Criminological research appears to ignore the importance of utilizing concrete data rather than relying on abstract and hypothetical tenets. Research products are unlikely to be relevant to issues of criminal policy and practice without the development of reliable predictive techniques, sound evaluation of treatment programs, penetrating investigation of recidivism, and analysis of cost-benefits.

Operational research must overcome the inherent resistance of governmental authorities and bitter disagreements among scholars. Bureaucracies raise time-consuming barriers against their approval of research proposals and the granting of access to data. Administrators often are unaware of the problems that demand reliable assessment. If they are concerned, they are likely to prefer findings that are favorable to their immediate political interests rather than those that are based on reality. Scholars are apt to disagree on the appropriate choice of methodology and on the precise goal of the research; too often, neither methodology nor goals are clearly defined. Whether scholars or officials, all parties are quick to blame the organizations of which they are members for the failures of research. Organizational deficiencies do exist, but other difficulties are also present: inadequate coordination of action programs, inferior management of research projects, and conflicts between researchers and political authorities in their perspectives and purposes. These difficulties inhibit research as well as the direct involvement of criminologists in criminal justice activities of which research is only a part.

These inhibitions operate even in countries where applied research is more prevalent than in Italy, but here the inhibitions are more marked and have greater effect in minimizing the relevance of applied research. Many scholars and a few "progressive" jurists have exerted pressure to ease those inhibitions. Nevertheless, jurists alone have undertaken projects to reform the codes of substantive and procedural law, seeking only technical modifications, without taking into account the criticisms of criminologists who call for more fundamental reforms. The criminologists have urged fuller consideration of the qualities of the offender, in both psychological and sociological components, within the criminal procedures. Their goals are greater individualization in application of penal sanctions and greater concentration of effort on general and special prevention. The criminologists proposed improved differentiation of accused persons at trials, at the time of sentencing, and in the administration of corrective measures more in keeping with contemporary knowledge.

One bright spot has been the enactment of No. 354 Law, enacted on July 25, 1975, which establishes a metajuridical function, as a science applied to criminal law, to be performed by criminologists. The law sets the stage for sweeping reform of corrections. In spite of the influence of criminologists in this instance, however, the changes were finally enacted because of pressures for penal reform felt by politicians and the necessity to keep pace with other European countries. Factors other than research alone are necessary to explanations of the recent willingness of decision-makers to take action. Since Lombroso's time, researchers have demonstrated the backwardness of the Italian penal system, the deteriorating effects of prison conditions on inmates, and the failure of the system to curb criminality.

The persistent and substantial deficiencies in the organizational structure and functioning of the correctional system raise problems for those criminologists who would provide diagnostic services and carry out treatment. In view of the new approaches and techniques now available, continuous and systematic evaluation of the effects of treatment programs is even more vital, but such efforts have not been undertaken. A factual balance sheet would be essential to testing implementing actions taken after enactment of the correctional reform law. Because this broad assessment has not been undertaken, the chances for further reforms are in jeopardy. At this writing, the Ministry of Justice is planning a rather extensive set of research projects which, it is hoped, will fill this vacuum.

In conclusion, after a promising beginning, criminology in Italy has fallen short in its further development as an interdisciplinary, autonomous field of scientific inquiry. Consequently, its research efforts do not have operational impact on the prevention and control of crime for lack of influence on the decisional and administrative structures. Interaction among scholars is not coordinated, with each researcher primarily oriented to the parochial concerns of his specific research specialization. The political leaders and criminal justice bureaucrats show little interest in taking advantage of the benefits of authentic research at a time when other countries have found criminological research an asset in coping with serious crime problems. In this general sense, Italy is far from achieving the research and development model that fits criminological research into the far-ranging parameters of social planning for a society that, as in other countries, has experienced great changes since 1945.

NOTES

1. G. Canepa, "L'insegnamento universitario della Criminologia e dell'Antropologia Criminale" [The University Teaching of Criminology and of Criminal Anthropology], *Quaderni di Criminologia Clinica* 1 (1965):31-53.

2. L. Radzinowicz, *Alla ricerca della Criminologia* [In Search of Criminology] (Milan: Giuffrè, 1964).

3. An important byproduct of these research activities was one of the few dictionaries of criminology: E. Florian, A. Niceforo, and N. Pende, *Dizionario di Criminologia* [Dictionary of Criminology] (Milan: Vallardi, 1943).

4. The complex diagnostic methodology followed in the institute is described in G. Di Gennaro, F. Ferracuti, and M. Fontanesi, "L'esame della personalità del condannato nell'Istituto di Osservazione di Rebibbia" [The Examination of the Personality of the Inmate at the Rebibbia Observation Institute], *Rassegna di Studi Penitenziari* 1 (1958):371-393.

5. These concepts, for example, dominated the methodology of the Rebibbia Observation Institute. One consequence has been that in-depth analysis of cases is not matched by competent statistical management of data.

6. In his *Principi di Difesa Sociale*, Gramatica has provided the classic, although general, discussion of the principles of social defense.

7. Under the direction of Professor G. Canepa and his associate, Professor Tullio Bandini, the Institute of Criminal Anthropology at the University of Genoa has made important contributions in juvenile delinquency research.

8. The relationship between delinquency and family dynamics is treated by T. Bandini and U. Gatti, *Dinamica familiare e delinquenza giovanile* [Family Dynamics and Juvenile Delinquency] (Milan: Giuffrè, 1972).

9. See G. Canepa, *Personalità e delinquenza* [Personality and Delinquency] (Milan: Giuffrè, 1974).

10. The subculture of violence is treated in F. Ferracuti and M. E. Wolfgang, *Il comportamento violento* [Violent Behavior] (Milan: Giuffrè, 1966).

BIBLIOGRAPHY

To lend further support to the key arguments of our review of Italian criminology, items were selected from the Italian literature without intending full coverage. Accordingly, the items are grouped into three major categories.

Criminological Research

To supplement the analysis of the nature and problems of criminological research, recent trends in Italy are delineated and the necessity for coordination and interdisciplinary research is emphasized.

Di Gennaro, G., and F. Ferracuti. "Il campo di azione della criminologia nel sistema penale italiano. Attuali possibilità e prospettive operative" [The Field of Action of Criminology in the Italian Criminal Justice System, Current Possibilities and Operational Perspectives]. *Quaderni di Criminologia Clinica* 2 (1970):185-204.

Ferracuti, F., and M. C. Giannini. "Tendenze prevalenti della ricerca criminologica in Italia negli ultimi cinque anni" [Criminological Research Trends in Italy in the Last Five Years]. *Quaderni di Criminologia Clinica* 4 (1969):1-83.

Portigliatti, Barbos M. "La coordination des recherches interdisciplinaires en criminologie" [The Coordination of Interdisciplinary Research in Criminology]. *Rassegna di Criminologia* 1 (1971):1-15.

Teaching and Practice of Criminality

The teaching of research is concentrated especially in medical schools, with the heritage of criminal anthropology still influential in both teaching and diagnostic functions.

Canepa, G. "L'insegnamento universitario della Criminologia e dell'Antropologia Criminale" [The University Teaching of Criminology and of Criminal Anthropology]. *Quaderni di Criminologia Clinica* 1 (1965):31-53.

Di Gennaro, G., F. Ferracuti, and M. Fontanesi. "L'esame della personalità del condannato nell'Istituto di Osservazione di Rebibbia" [The Examination of the Personality of the Inmate at the Rebibbia Observation Institute]. *Rassegna di Studi Penitenziari* 1 (1958):371-393.

Di Tullio, B. "L'opera del medico nella lotta contro la criminalita" [The Work of the Physician in the Fight Against Crime]. *Quaderni di Criminologia Clinica* 2 (1964):135-148.

Radzinowicz, L. *Alla ricerca della Criminologia* [In Search of Criminology]. Milan: Giuffrè, 1964.

Treatises in Criminology

Criminal anthropology and forensic psychiatry are the predominant topics of textbooks. Also influential is clinical criminology which has cultivated an interest in juvenile delinquency. No textbook covers what is usually called "general criminology," such as the translated work of Mannheim.

Bandini, T., and U. Gatti. *Dinamica familiare e delinquenza giovanile* [Family Dynamics and Juvenile Delinquency]. Milan: Giuffrè, 1972.

Canepa, G. *Personalità e delinquenza* [Personality and Delinquency]. Milan: Giuffrè, 1974.

Di Tullio, B. *Antropologia Criminale* [Criminal Anthropology]. Rome: Pozzi, 1940.

Di Tullio, B. *Principi di Criminologia Clinica* [Principles of Clinical Criminology]. Rome: Istituto di Medicina Sociale, 1954.

Ferracuti, F., and M. E. Wolfgang. *Il comportamento violento* [Violent Behavior]. Milan: Giuffrè, 1966.

Florian, E., A. Niceforo, and N. Pende. *Dizionario di Criminologia* [Dictionary of Criminology]. Milan: Vallardi, 1943.

Gramatica, F. *Principi di Difesa Sociale* [Principles of Social Defense]. (Milan: Padua, 1961.

Niceforo, A. *Criminologia* [Criminology]. Milan: Bocca, Vol. I, 1941, Vol. II, 1943, Vol. III, 1951.

Semerari, A., and C. Citterio. *Medicina Criminologica e Psichiatria Forense* [Criminological Medicine and Forensic Psychiatry]. Milan: Vallardi, 1975.

20

JAPAN

Kazuhiko Tokoro

Japan enjoys a remarkably low crime rate for a heavily industrialized and urbanized nation, removing a primary incentive for the dedicated development of criminology but also offering a special inducement for considering the conditions under which Japanese criminology has emerged and now operates.

WHAT IS CRIMINOLOGY?

In Japanese *hanzaigaku* is roughly equivalent to "criminology" in English—*hanzai* means "crime" and *gaku* means "ology." *Hanzaigaku* usually has little to do with criminalistics which has had a relatively independent development, although sometimes *hanzaigaku* is used as including criminalistics. This chapter does not include criminalistics within the sphere of criminology.

Although the trend is toward treating *hanzaigaku* as the equivalent of "criminology," some elements continue to have distinctive titles. *Keijiseisaku* (literally, penal policy) is the equivalent of German *kriminal Politik* and is dealt with mostly by criminal law scholars. However, scholars who emphasize the scientific approach prefer that *keijiseisaku* be regarded in the sense of *keijigaku* (literally, penology). Originally, *keijigaku* was a translation of *science pénale* in French and was then regarded as a popular equivalent of "criminology."

By any name, however, criminology in Japan is not an autonomous branch of learning. Basically, it is a conglomeration of practical applications of various disciplines, such as psychiatry, psychology, sociology, and law. No Japanese university has a department, or even a subdepartment, of criminology, although a medical school maintains a research center for criminal psychiatry. Many universities offer classes on subjects related to criminology, but usually the courses are only special adaptations of an established discipline, such as criminal psychology and criminal sociology. Law schools present courses in criminology that are only brief reviews of subject matter and are generally taught by law professors who have only a secondary interest in criminology. Books in *hanzaigaku* or *keijigaku* come in three classes: those written or edited by criminal law professors; those developed by a set of criminologists drawn from various disciplines; and those that are translations of foreign books.[1]

THE SETTING FOR CRIMINOLOGY

One of the wealthy nations, Japan has 120 million people who live on mountainous islands that have a total land area of 140 million square miles. They produce the second largest gross national product (GNP) among the capitalist countries because the scale of industrialization is the greatest in the non-Western world. Industrialization began in the 1850s when the Western powers gained access to Japanese ports for commercial trade through a show of force when Japan was in the stage of mature feudalism. The feudal reign of the Tokugawa Shogunate was replaced by the more nationalistic Meiji Emperor who set out to strengthen the nation by adopting Western civilization. In the early twentieth century, Japan entered the modern industrial period. By 1937, Japan was a leading competitor in the world market when militarists secured control over the government. They were determined to control China as a means of further strengthening Japan's trade position.

For eight years Japan was on a war basis. Surrender in 1945 found its economy in ruins, but it rebounded under the American occupation that lasted until 1952, and then made striking advances to reach today's level of prosperity.

Japanese criminologists have contributed little to world criminology—perhaps because Japan's low crime rate has removed a public issue that stimulates an interest in criminology elsewhere. However, other reasons should be considered, including the social psychology of Japanese intellectuals.

Historically, the Japanese have imported civilization; until 1868, cultural elements came from the Asiatic mainland and then from the West. For the last century or so, the intellectuals have followed the Japanese style of borrowing cultural elements, then exhibiting inventive talent through the processes of adaptation and improvement. This style of cultural transmission has accelerated the absorption of Western ideas by Japanese intellectuals, but it has inhibited their creativity, particularly in the social and behavioral sciences. Moreover, the cultural exchange has been one-sided; few ideas and little information flow from Japan to the West. The reluctance of its people to exchange ideas reciprocally with the rest of the world, the undermining of cultural self-confidence by the rapid influx of foreign ideas, the small proportion of foreigners familiar with the Japanese language and culture, the small number of Japanese intellectuals able to write well in foreign languages, even though most of them read one or more European languages—all of these factors have contributed to Japanese social and behavioral sciences remaining at the borrowing and adaptive stages of innovation and have delayed their movement to the stage of unique and creative developments. Few of the numerous criminological studies made in Japan are known to the world.

Furthermore, the development of professionalism in a fashion congenial to development of criminology as an autonomous discipline has been opposed by the Japanese social structure which tends to be multilineal, status-oriented, and often quasi-kinship in nature. "For whom one works" is more important than "with what one works." Even labor unions are usually organized by affiliation rather than qualification. Employers prefer in-service training after recruitment over the elasticity of preservice education for providing specialized knowledge. These structural tendencies cultivate relationships that keep crime rates low, but professionalism is inhibited by the opposition of bureaucratic patterns to creativity.

Governmental organizations are highly centralized in Japan, especially those involved in crime control. City police, first established after World War II, have been replaced by prefectural police, the management of which is held by the National Police Agency and the National Safety Commission. All prisons are administered by the Ministry of Justice, except for police jails. Training schools and juvenile detention and diagnostic centers are also under the Ministry of Justice; the less coercive institutions for younger delinquents are administered by prefectural governments. The Ministry of Justice also maintains a probation and parole office in each prefecture. Public prosecutors form a bureaucratic hierarchy in the Ministry of Justice. All courts are administered by the supreme court, which appoints all judges except its own members. Investigative officers in family courts, who comprise one of the major sources of criminologists, are under the complete control of judges and the supreme court.

Because of this high degree of centralization, practitioners in criminal and juvenile justice as a rule operate within a nationwide communication network controlled by centralized administration. Interorganizational communications are considerably retarded, and the growth of professionalism is hindered.

There is an interesting exception to the centralization of responses to crime: private persons and neighborhood organizations are given various functions that are governmental in Western countries. In these matters, the government encourages or authorizes private participation. Police are assisted in the prevention of crime, street patrol, and improvement of street lighting. As a rule, probationers and parolees are supervised by unpaid lay officers selected from persons who have neighborhood influence. The number and functions of trained criminologists are minimized.

PATTERNS OF CRIME RATES

From 1959 to 1973, crime rates declined with the exception of traffic offenses. The decrease was halted in 1973, although the rate for crimes of violence has continued to decline. Thefts have been increasing gradually, but more and more of the thefts are minor crimes committed for casual convenience or pleasure rather than for economic reasons.

The decreased crime rate is explained in the following way. Japan experienced very high rates in 1947 and 1948 because of widespread starvation, the collapse of traditional authority, and the deterioration of general morality which stemmed from the country's prolonged involvement in war and from the final defeat. According to this explanation, it has taken Japan twenty-five years to reach its normal level of law and order. It should be noted, however, that the annual crime rates since 1973 have been twice those of 1907-1923 when prewar Japanese society was most stable. Its industrialization and urbanization undoubtedly have influenced patterns of crime. Crime rates are higher in urban areas than in rural areas. Crimes become more prevalent when new industries bring urban influences to villages. Yet, Japan remains one of the safest countries in the world, in stark contrast to most of the other highly developed countries.

Why the low incidence of crime compared with that of other countries?[2] One explanation has to do with the affluence of postwar Japan. Even the lower classes have experienced an ever-increasing material standard of living. Currently, 90 percent of the people see themselves as middle class. Apparently, fewer and fewer persons are economically frustrated in an era comparable to the decades before World War I in Germany, Great Britain, and some other European countries.

The second explanation emphasizes a value system based on group solidarity, mutual dependency, and concord rather than individual liberty, independence, and assertiveness. The children of Japanese immigrants in the prewar United States had low delinquency rates in spite of the low income and the residential handicaps of their families. Similarly, the population homogeneity of the Japanese helps explain the low crime rate; there is no serious racial problem in postwar Japan. Nevertheless, the degree of cultural homogeneity has been questioned. Jiro Kamishima, a political scientist, argues that the Japanese pretend to be homogeneous as a means of lowering the level of conflict.[3] If he is correct, structural pressures, rather than value consensus alone, must be considered.

The last explanation to be considered here refers to the high efficiency of criminal justice administration. Japanese police are proud of their high clearance rates, although they recently began a gradual decline. Highly centralized police administration enjoys the benefits of a well-isolated territory that improves chances for apprehending offenders and controlling traffic in firearms and drugs that stimulate crimes. Furthermore, the police enjoy good relationships with the public. Most criminal cases are cleared without arrest, and almost all of the rest are cleared through confessions. Police campaigns against drugs, vice, and drunken driving gain the support of ordinary citizens. The emphasis on social concordance is basic; in addition, the police encourage police-public intimacy by maintaining small substations with one or a few policemen awaiting visitors on a twenty-four-hour basis.[4]

CRIMINOLOGY AS AN OCCUPATION

Although various occupations are related to criminology, few involve criminologists as distinct specialists. The majority of probation and parole officers, for example, were promoted from clerical positions after years of experience in assisting regular officers. The other officers are civil service specialists qualified as sociologists, social workers, psychologists, educators, or lawyers—but never as criminologists. Both groups of officers receive three months of in-service training when, for the first time in their careers, they are exposed to some criminological principles. Otherwise, work experience is the means of learning which, critics contend, does not provide clinical experience because lay officers as a rule supervise probationers and parolees. Regular officers tend to be expert in administration rather than in treatment. Now the trend is toward assigning the difficult cases to regular officers who are becoming a major cadre within the ranks of criminologists.

In-service training is more intensive for workers in correctional institutions. Civil service specialists enter six-month training courses which also receive promoted workers originally employed on the basis of their general education. The latter group is given six months of in-service training before assignment. After years of practice, selected members of that group who have been promoted enter a three-month advanced course. Having completed this course, they then enter the most advanced course including civil service specialists.

Courses are of two kinds, one for prison workers and the other for workers at training schools and juvenile detention and diagnostic centers. Courses of the second kind are more treatment-oriented. Workers in juvenile institutions generally have a higher level of preservice education than workers in prisons and jails. Psychologists in juvenile detention and diagnostic centers and educators in training schools form an important source of criminologists. Moreover, the Ministry of Justice maintains a research institute where specialists engage in research on a rotating basis for a few years each.

Family court investigation involves direct intervention in delinquency cases and, therefore, requires specialized knowledge in criminology. These officers, however, are not criminologists per se; rather, a psychologist, sociologist, social worker, or educator becomes an investigator by passing a special examination administered by the supreme court. In-service training increases skills in handling either delinquency or domestic cases. Although preservice eligibility and in-service training are not oriented toward a distinctive status of criminologists, family court investigation officers make up a significant proportion of those practitioners who identify themselves as criminologists.

What of the police, the largest group specializing in criminal justice work? Policemen are usually recruited on the basis of a general education received in high schools. After a year of in-service training, they are assigned to substations. Some eventually become detectives who receive a month of additional training. Civil service specialists are channeled into top administrative positions; they are selected from among those qualified as lawyers in the administrative branch, as public administrators, or as economists. They receive three months of in-service training on every aspect of policing. However, those in the police service who qualify as criminologists are most likely to be psychologists or sociologists engaged in research at the National Research Institute of Police Science. The institute also has specialists in criminalistics. Local guidance centers maintained by the police employ psychologists and sociologists who occasionally handle delinquents.

Physicians who work for correctional institutions or courts are also an important source of criminologists. Some are sufficiently specialized in psychiatry to make diagnoses for juvenile courts or institutions. Because they are independent professionals with great income potential, physicians are often employed part-time. Sometimes a physician is completing a doctoral dissertation with the aid of data acquired through a part-time job. Criminal courts frequently summon psychiatrists at universities and medical colleges to testify on the mental competence of defendants. They were especially influential in the early years of the establishment of criminology in Japan.

Lawyers have also influenced criminology. Public prosecutors, who have considerable discretionary authority, were active in promoting the Juvenile Court Act in 1922. After World War II, their authority to divert cases from the criminal justice system was narrowed to cover only adult cases. Nevertheless, since the top administrators of the Ministry of Justice are selected from the public prosecutors, they have particular influence on criminal policy. Judges and practicing lawyers are among those with great interest in research into sentencing, prison administration, and casework. Knowledge of criminology, however, is an optional qualification for lawyers.

Outside the administration of national government, there are also sociologists and psychologists who work in child guidance centers and clinics maintained by local governments. These clinics and centers are prone to employ graduates of master's programs, some of whom have concentrated on courses in criminology.

ASSOCIATIONS AMONG CRIMINOLOGISTS

There is no unified organization embracing all criminologists in Japan. The Japanese Association of Criminology, the oldest of the criminological groups, is composed predominantly of physicians involved in forensic medicine, insanity testing, or the etiology of crime. It publishes *Acta Criminologiae et Medicinae Legalis Japonica*. Psychiatric criminologists also associate within the Japanese Society of Psychiatry and Neurology which publishes *Psychiatria et Neurologia Japonica*.

The psychologists involved in criminology gather in the Japanese Association of Criminal Psychology which publishes the *Japanese Journal of Criminal Psychology*. The Japanese Association of Criminal Sociology, established in 1974, publishes the *Japanese Journal of Sociological Criminology*. The Criminal Law Society of Japan specializes in criminal law and criminal policy and publishes the *Journal of Criminal Law* for lawyers.

These associations have some overlapping memberships. Many criminologists join two or more associations as a means of meeting criminologists in other fields and disciplines. Intraorganizational communication networks promote interdisciplinary interests. A notable example is the efforts of the Japanese Association of Correctional Medicine in gathering the psychologists and physicians working for the Ministry of Justice. Other journals are oriented in intraorganizational communication networks promoting interdisciplinary interests.[5]

For years, a rather informal group of leaders in each of the fields has actively promoted interdisciplinary communication. In the early 1960s, the group published the *Japan Annual of Criminology* containing original papers from various fields. Published in 1969-1970, four volumes of *Japanese Studies in Criminology* presented abstracts of representative criminological works in various disciplines.[6] The group is now editing another set of volumes. For years, a private foundation has published *Crime and Delinquency*, an interdisciplinary and interorganizational journal.

The associations listed above have been criticized for denying membership to lay persons and for lacking political power in influencing criminal policy. The Japanese Conference on Crime and Delinquency was founded in 1976 as a vehicle for merging professionals and volunteers in the same organization and for influencing policy. So far, it has had little influence.

What is the role of universities in associations of criminologists? Academic leadership has been prominent in all the associations except the Japanese Association of Correctional Medicine. Practitioners have major leadership roles in the Japanese Association of Criminal Psychology. Leadership of the Criminal Law Society of Japan is almost exclusively academic. University professors are sometimes summoned to mediate interorganizational disputes. Congresses of the associations are often held at universities, and professors frequently conduct informal discussions among criminologists on the campuses. However, regular classes and seminars for employed criminologists are unlikely.

As is the pattern among scientists in Japan, the interaction among criminologists is predominantly within Japan. Only a few are active members of international associations. Others are sensitive to trends in the West but do not interact with foreign criminologists. A major exception is the United Nations Asia and Far East Institute for the Prevention of Crime and the Treatment of Offenders (UNAFEI) in Tokyo which has cultivated international communication. Its annual reports and resource material series contain many articles written in English by Japanese criminologists. Two international meetings on criminology have been held in Japan in the last decade: the Fourth United Nations Congress on the Prevention of Crime and the Treatment of Offenders in 1970, and the sessions of the Research Committee on the Sociology of Deviance and Social Control of the International Sociological Association in 1976.

EDUCATION OF CRIMINOLOGISTS

Rarely do criminal justice workers qualify as criminologists at the time of their first employment. Japan lacks any semblance of a school of criminology, although some institutions of higher education offer classes related to criminology. Law schools universally offer optional classes on penal policy, penology, and/or criminology. Few of the students taking these courses, however, are admitted to the bar because of the extreme difficulty of the highly competitive tests for admission to the National Training Institute of Justice, the sole gateway to the bar. Because penal policy is among the optional fields for the admission tests, some of those admitted to the bar are knowledgeable in criminology. The police and other agencies in criminal and juvenile justice administration often employ law school graduates. Some of the graduates so employed also have passed civil service examinations to qualify as lawyers in agencies, but the examination does not refer to criminology.

Medical schools offer no classes in criminology. If a physician is knowledgeable in criminology, he has developed it on his own during professional work or has made it the subject of a doctoral dissertation. Departments of psychology or of sociology sometimes offer optional classes on criminal psychology or criminal sociology. The departments usually require a bachelor's thesis which may consider some aspect of the crime problem. Few of these students become criminologists because, again, highly competitive civil service examinations, without content on criminology, are the gateway to the jobs. In one instance, study of criminology is specifically rewarded; completion of a master's degree program, involving criminological study, offers access to positions as counselors in local centers.

Thus, with the few exceptions noted above, preparation for careers in criminological occupations is limited to in-service training. The in-service curricula are mixtures of instruction in relevant laws and regulations, techniques appropriate to the given duties, and ideas selected from various disciplines; criminological knowledge is not systematically developed. In the three-month course for probation and parole officers at the Ministry of Justice, one-third of the hours are devoted to laws and regulations; another third to criminal policy and to techniques drawn from psychiatry, psychology, sociology, pedagogy, and social casework; and a third to development of practical skills in case management, interviewing, research, or other skills. Trainers vary in the special knowledge they bring to their work because only one general course is available.

In summary, many who study criminology will not be criminal justice practitioners, and many of those who become practitioners have not studied criminology. It is not clear, however, whether or not the quality of criminal justice work is seriously impaired. One may speculate that lay knowledge at the time of job entry may favor development of closer contacts between professional and lay persons, especially volunteers.

Many criminologists in Japan have had experience at Western universities, usually acquired after employment. Rarely does graduation from a foreign university qualify a candidate for employment in a criminal justice agency. When such graduates are accepted, they already have had strong ties with the given agency. This situation also applies to Japanese who have spent a portion of their student career abroad, but civil service qualifications specifically rule out foreigners. Competence in the Japanese language is in itself a major limitation for foreigners. Even universities are generally reluctant to accept professors who do not speak Japanese; courses in languages other than Japanese are the primary exception. UNAFEI is the only educational facility that regularly employs foreign criminologists. Paradoxically, the barrier against foreign professors did not exist in the early Meiji period of Westernization.

LEVEL AND DIRECTION OF RESEARCH

Historical Review

Earlier, this chapter noted that Japanese criminologists, following the typical pattern of cultural innovation of Japan, have been generally absorbed in borrowing and modifying theories imported from the West, but more recently they have begun to explore theoretical issues on their own. The theoretical borrowings were first from the French, then from the Germans, and finally from the Americans after World War II. Too often, criminal policy issues were debated on the basis of borrowed theories without careful examination of their relevance to the Japanese conditions.

Characteristically, there was little effort to obtain domestic data to test the relevance of conclusions arbitrarily accepted on the basis of foreign research. This fault is especially noteworthy because the collection of official statistics nationally has existed since the late 1870s, thanks to the influence of the French and the centralization of governmental administration. The statistics included information on the incidence of crime and on related matters and remained the major source of data until the late 1920s. Then Shufu Yoshimasu, a psychiatrist, pioneered the application of research procedures in studies of various groups of Japanese convicts. By 1951, he developed a unique typology of recidivists. The criminal career of a recidivist is traced by a curved line through several categories of recidivism that are differentiated by age at the time of beginning the criminal career, the frequency of criminal involvement, and the particular variety of offenses.[7]

By 1951, serious utilization of official statistics was providing a reliable foundation for developing theories in criminology. Masami Takahashi, a lawyer, disproved the racist views that had permeated Japanese criminology by demonstrating that methodological corrections of data for sex, age, and occupation as demographic variables canceled out what had been taken as evidence of higher crime rates for Korean immigrants in prewar Japan.[8]

During the American occupation, special efforts were made to uproot the sociopolitical remnants of an authoritarian regime. The scientific perspective gained widespread support, including the employment of behavioral scientists, especially psychologists, in handling delinquents and criminals. Various personality tests were administered to delinquents awaiting court disposition and to inmates of prisons and training schools. These tests were of Western origin, but they were more or less adapted for Japanese respondents. In some cases, modifications qualify as inventions. Tetsu Hirezaki, a psychiatrist who directed a juvenile detention and diagnostic center, developed a theory named *shinjo-shitsu* (emotional character), which included a graphed profile of fourteen scales applied to emotional abnormalities as suggested by Schneider's typology of psychopaths.[9] The findings from these tests supported the development of psychological theories regarding the nature and origin of the criminogenic ego.

In the late 1950s, sociologists and social psychologists began to make unique contributions to criminology. A group led by Junkichi Abe examined the life histories of selected convicts in relation to the conditions of their "life space" and to overall sociocultural changes.[10] In 1958, Soji Kashikuma and Kosaku Matsuura tested in Tokyo the validity of Shaw's thesis on the criminogenic function of the neighborhood.[11] Their results suggest a necessary modification of the key concept of neighborhood by showing an extremely high concentration of delinquent *acts* in downtown amusement areas but a low concentration of *residences* of delinquents. Increasing concern about the social sources of criminality involved even some psychiatrists who had previously accepted the biological interpretation learned in the period of German influence. In a 1960 investigation of a group of epileptic criminals, Takemitsu Henmi examined the function of interpersonal relationships in the socialization of the handicapped.[12]

Also in the late 1950s, Taro Ogawa and others began to systematically introduce various counseling techniques into correctional institutions. While most techniques were of Western origin, *naikan* (self-insight) was a purely native technique of counseling developed by a Buddhist denomination. The client of *naikan* is merely requested to recall the details of what *he* did to others. The rehabilitation of released offenders also came under scrutiny. Shunki Ifukube revealed the latent pressures of role expectations on ex-convicts in 1960 by showing that, compared with first-time ex-convicts, second timers ran away earlier from home when they returned from prison in spite of the fewer difficulties they had in relationships with other family members.[13]

In about 1960, Japanese criminology reached maturity in the sense of exhibiting a capacity for making independent contributions. A noteworthy example is the theory of "alienation" formulated by Keiich Mizushima and derived from his comparison of groups of delinquents and nondelinquents. He proposed a multiplex model of criminogenesis, the core of which was "alienation from ties with socialized persons."[14] The contributions that followed such pioneering studies are reviewed below.

Physiological and Psychological Aspects

Searches for relationships between physiological qualities and criminality have taken up phrenological abnormalities, body types, brain waves, and chromosome abnormalities. Brain wave abnormalities are often sought in diagnoses of offenders. Studies of psychopathological conditions have considered schizophrenia, epilepsy, manic-depression, psychopathy, feeble-mindedness, and intoxication by alcohol and drugs. Psychiatric criminologists have also endeavored to measure the effect of heredity on criminality by differentiating rates of criminal behavior among identical and fraternal twins.[15] Studies of identical twins have also shown how hereditary tendencies were modified by environmental conditions.[16] Similarly, psychiatric criminologists have explored sociopsychological elements of pathology such as inferiority complexes and identity crises.[17]

Psychological Aspects

Various psychological tests have been used to identify crime-prone personalities. These tests include the Rorschach, TAT, MMPI, hand test, Krepelin-Uchida, SCT, PF study, and MJPI. The Ministry of Justice recently standardized the MJPI test. One research project using the PF test has revealed distorted perceptions of parental discipline in some delinquents, through finding discrepancies between the delinquents' perceptions of their parents and the parents' perceptions of themselves, and relationships between these discrepancies and the personality inclinations of those delinquents.[18]

Recently, investigations have been extended to include value systems, moral judgments, attitudes toward life, images of self, social maturity, learning ability, and risk-taking. In addition, multiplex patterns of personality inclination relevant to criminality have been examined by combining various personality traits, often utilizing factor analysis and other advanced statistical techniques.[19]

Sociocultural Aspects

Various sociocultural conditions have been related to the etiology of criminality: broken homes, parental discipline, school achievement, social class, neighborhood, gang membership, underworld connections, minority group membership, urbanization and other sources of social change, migration into cities, birth cohorts, sex roles, and so on. Recently, the impact of social changes in regard to criminality has received special attention; the most theoretically suggestive study explores chronological changes in criminogenic factors.[20] Correlation of crime rates with indices of poverty definitely changed from plus to minus around 1960 when the effects of the rapid economic growth of postwar Japan surfaced. Another study utilized official crime rates and statistics on police forces to suggest that the degree of criminalization was related to urbanization.[21] Another investigation used questionnaires for reporting crimes to the police in a comparison of urban and rural populations on attitudes about crime.[22] Much attention has been devoted to new patterns in delinquency and crime: delinquency in middle-class families, delinquency among females and the very young, offenses for recreation, violence in schools, and so on. One of these investigations concluded that a low level of parental concern for children which characterizes lower-class families was also found among middle-class families that included a delinquent member.[23]

Of course, peculiarly Japanese features in criminality would be of particular interest to readers of this handbook. In a pioneer study of Japanese underworld organizations, Hiroaki Iwai revealed that quasi-kinship relationships served as structural bonds in those organizations.[24] Psychological tests suggest that, unlike the situation in the United States, high aggressiveness does not explain delinquent behavior in Japan.[25] Aggressive behavior appears to be stimulated by frustrated desires for dependency (*amae*)—a key concept for understanding Japanese culture.[26] Furthermore, another investigation found that the family's class status seems to affect delinquency rates more than that of the neighborhood, contrary to the situation in the United States.[27] However, similar patterns of problem conduct were found in comparisons of American and Japanese samples of delinquents.[28] The National Science Foundation of Japan allocates special funds to encourage cross-cultural investigations.

Types of offenses and offenders have been subjects of investigation: murder, parricide, infanticide, arson, rape, theft, fraud, traffic violations, negligent manslaughter, drug abuse, prostitution, predelinquency, gang offenses, female offenses, offenses by the aged, recidivism, first offenses, and others. Victimological projects are concerned with relationships with the offender prior to crimes such as murder, rape, and fraud. Investigations of deviance not defined as crimes in Japan have considered suicide, incest, and vagrancy.

Prognosis and Treatment

Yoshimasu initiated prediction studies in prewar Japan, but the introduction of Gluecks' prediction tables brought a wave of these studies. Prediction tables were proposed for decision-making in parole, probation, police diversion, and school counseling. Statistical techniques have been improved.

The effects of various correctional measures have been examined: individual and group therapies, short- and long-term imprisonment, closed and open institutions, imprisonment with or without forced labor, fines, probation with or without supervision, suspended prosecution with or without after-care, parole, professional and lay supervision, supervision by various types of lay officers, and large and small shelters for ex-convicts. The most popular variables used for measurement have been changes in offender conduct, changes in personality traits, and recidivism rates.

Naikan therapy, a Japanese invention, has been examined to determine its effect and its psychological mechanisms.[29] Increasing emphasis has been placed on the adaptability of each measure to the personality type of each offender. Values and group dynamics among inmates have been examined through sociometric tests and behavioral observations. Mental deterioration and physical disease have been investigated as effects of imprisonment. Convicts' accounts of prison life have been collected. Participant observation research, however, has been unsophisticated.

Policing and Prevention

Japanese police remained outside of criminological studies for a long time, with two exceptions. Criminalistics already were at a high level before World War II. After the war, the political functions of the Japanese police were analyzed through historical reviews.[30]

The efficiency of police crime control has come under scientific scrutiny in the last decade. Kanehiro Hoskino, a sociologist at the National Research Institute of Police Science, has correlated various police activities with the level of safety as measured by official crime rates or the residents' perception of safety.[31] The deterrent effects of formal and informal sanctions have been recently studied through interviews of samples of offenders and the general population.[32]

Questionnaire surveys have been conducted on people's attitudes toward crime, criminals, and sanctions. In addition, community projects for crime and delinquency prevention have incorporated evaluations of their circumstances and impact. The structures and functions of voluntary organizations have been scrutinized.[33] Organized campaigns against the establishment of correctional or after-care institutions in a neighborhood have also been analyzed.[34]

Decision Processes

Sentencing practices have been studied in Japan since the late 1930s, when Takeo Fuwa, a judge, found fairly well-standardized penalties for certain types of cases in spite of the most extensive discretionary authority of judges.[35] After the war, a variety of statistical techniques were applied to test the relevance of customary standards used in sentencing. These techniques have been extended to other decision-making areas, such as prosecution, parole, pardon, disciplining of prisoners, juvenile court dispositions, and inmate classification.

The research has increased insights into the influences exerted on decision-making policies by individual and mass ideologies, training and job career of the decision-maker, his role and position, and the patterns of communication among participants. In a pioneering study, Tadashi Uematsu found less severe and less divergent sentencing decisions in mock infanticide cases among judges and public prosecutors than he found in recommendations made by school teachers and college students in prewar Japan.[36] My recent study questioned the general population on the relationship of criminal sanctions to restitution and found the responses to be related to indices of modernization.[37] Cross-national comparison of sentences has also been attempted. Attention has been increasingly centered upon the cultural factors affecting criminal and juvenile justice administration.

FINAL COMMENTS

In spite of the handicaps described above, Japanese criminologists appear to be moving from their earlier heavy dependence on imported ideas and are beginning to develop versions of criminology suited to the sociopolitical environment and crime problems of Japan. Their heritage has benefited from borrowings of theories and techniques from several Western countries. Now their own ideas are being incorporated within this heritage, and theoretical explanations are being fitted to the Japanese situation and the effects of drastic and sweeping social changes since 1945.

Master theories have not been developed in Japan as they have in those nations that have progressed further in building criminology. Nevertheless, the progress already achieved merits a full report to the criminologists of the world. This chapter has provided a preliminary and tentative summary with the hope that this "appetizer" will stimulate a demand from the international community for a more complete report on Japanese studies in criminology. If this should result, the efforts made here will be well rewarded.

NOTES

1. An important exception is Shufu Yoshimasu, *Hanzaigaku Gairon* [An Outline of Criminology] (Tokyo: Yuhikaku, 1958).

2. Convenient to foreign readers is Teruo Matsushita, "Crime in Japan—A Search for the Causes of Low and Decreasing Criminality," *UNAFEI's Resource Material Series*, no. 12 (1976). Also see William Clifford, *Crime Control in Japan* (Lexington, Mass.: Lexington Books, 1976).

3. "Naze 'Nihon Jin to Ho' ka" [Why "the Japanese and Law"?], in Jiro Kamishima et al. (eds.), *Nihon Jin to Ho* [The Japanese and Law] (Tokyo: Gyosei, 1978).

4. David H. Bayley, *Forces of Order: Police Behavior in Japan and the United States* (Berkeley, Calif.: University of California Press, 1976), Chapter 2.

5. *Kosei Hogo to Hanzai Yobo* [Rehabilitation of Offenders and Prevention of Crime] is directed to probation and parole officers in the Department of Rehabilitation of the Ministry of Justice; *Keisei* (Penal Policy) is for prison workers under the Department of Correction, Ministry of Justice; *Case Kenkyu* (Case Study) is for family court investigation officers; and *Keisatsugaku Ronshu* (Journal of Police Science) is for higher police officers in the National Police Agency.

6. Hiroaki Iwai, Tatsuo Endo, Kokichi Higuchi, and Ruichi Hirano (eds.), *Nihon no Hanzaigaku* [Japanese Studies in Criminology] (Tokyo: University of Tokyo Press, 1969-1970). Iwai represented sociology; Endo, psychology; Higuchi, psychiatry; and Hirano, law. The most prominent promoter was Hirano, a distinguished criminal law professor at the University of Tokyo. He actively promoted interdisciplinary communication among Japanese criminologists and international communication for many years.

7. "Hanzai no Keika Keishiki ni kansuru Kenkyu" [A Study of the Patterns of Criminal Career], *Keiho Zasshi* (Journal of Criminal Law) 2, no. 2 (1951): 16 ff; "Ueber die kriminellen Lebenskurven," *Arch. Psychiat. Nervenkr.* 199 (1959):103 ff.

8. "Haisen go no Nihon ni okeru Chosenjin no Hanzai" [Korean Crime in Defeated Japan], *Keiho Zasshi* 1, no. 2 (1950):263 ff.

9. Described as "Joi Chohyo" in Hirezaki's *Gutaiteki Sishin Igaku* [Clinical Psychiatry] (Tokyo: Tohodo, 1952), pp. 172 ff.

10. "Hiko Keisei ni Kansuru Shakai Shinrigaku-teki Kenkyu" [A Social-Psychological

Study of Delinquency Formation], *Tohoku Kyosei Kagaku Kenkyujo Kiyo*, Vol. 2, 1957, pp. 183 ff.

11. "Tokyo-to ni okeru Hiko Shonen no Seitaigaku-teki Kenkyu" [An Ecological Study of Juvenile Delinquency in Tokyo] (Tokyo: Hosokai, 1958).

12. "Tenkan oyobi Rui-tenkan no Hanzai Seishin Igaku-teki Kenkyu" [A Crimino-psychiatric Study of Epileptic Cases], *Japanese Journal of Correctional Medicine* 9, no. 2 (1960) (with English summary).

13. "Karishutsugoku-sha no Saihan Made" [Parolee's Life Up to the Time of Recidivism], *Hanzaigaku Nenpo* [Japan Annual of Criminology] 1 (1960):89 ff.

14. *Hiko Shonen no Kaimei* [Unravelling Juvenile Delinquency] (Tokyo: Shinshokan, 1964).

15. Shufu Yoshimasu, "The Criminological Significance of the Family in the Light of the Studies of Criminal Twins," *Acta Criminologiae et Medicinae Legalis Japonica* 31, no. 4 (1961). The study included a twenty-year followup of forty-six pairs of twins.

16. Shuzo Hayashi, "Shonen Hiko no Soseiji Kenkyu" [A Study of Juvenile Delinquency by Twin Method], *Acta Criminologiae et Medicinae Legalis Japonica*, 29, nos. 5-6 (1963):13 ff. (with English summary).

17. Seiji Urashima, "Hogoshonen no Rettokan ni Tsuite" [On Inferiority Complexes Among Delinquent Juveniles], *Psychiatria et Neurologia Japonica* 55, no. 3 (1953):463 ff.; Akira Fukushima, "Jiga Doitsusei Kiki to Hanzai" [Identity Crisis and Crime], *Acta Criminologiae et Medicinae Legalis Japonica* 38, nos. 5-6 (1972) (with English summary.) A number of delinquency cases are viewed in terms of identity crisis by Hiroshi Wagatsuma (ed.), *Hiko Shonen no Jirei Kenkyu* [Delinquent Juveniles in the Light of Case Study] (Tokyo: Seishin Shobo, 1973).

18. Katsuzo Hayashi, "Hiko Shonen no Oya ni taisuru Ninchizo no Kenkyu" [A Study of Cognitive Images of Parents in Juvenile Delinquents], *Japanese Journal of Criminal Psychology* 1, no. 1 (1963):45 ff. (with English summary).

19. For example, see Hitomi Shindo, et al., "MMPI Profile Bunseki ni kansuru Kiso Chosa" [A Preliminary Study of MMPI Profile Interpretation], *Japanese Journal of Criminal Psychology* 9, no. 2 (1972):95 ff.

20. Munetaka Kurusu, et al., "Shakai Hendo Shihyo ni yoru Chiikibetsu Hanzairitsu no Suitei" [Crime Rate Estimation by Indices of Social Changes], *Homo Sogo Kenkyujo Kiyo* (Bulletin of Criminological Research Department, Research and Training Institute, Ministry of Justice), no. 17 (1974):91 ff.

21. Kazuhiko Tokoro, "Hanzai Mondai no Seiritsu to Kozo" [The Structure of Crime Problem], in Yasuhiko Yuzawa, et al. (eds.), *Kazoku, Fukushi, Kyoiku* [Family, Welfare, and Education] (Tokyo: Yuhikaku, 1972).

22. Shigenobu Yonekawa, et al., "Hanzaika Hihanzaika no Jittai to Hanzai Gensho eno Eikyo" [Criminalization in the People's Mind and Its Impact on Criminality], in Hiroaki Iwai, et al. (eds.), *Hanzaikan no Kenkyu* [The Perception of Crime Surveyed] (Tokyo: Taisei Shuppan, 1979).

23. Kanehiro Hoshino, "Hiko Shonen to Kazoku" [Juvenile Delinquency and the Family], *Kyoiku Shakaigaku Kenkyu* no. 21 (1966):57 ff. (with English summary).

24. *Byori Shudan no Kozo* [The Structure of Pathological Group] (Tokyo: Sheishin Shobo, 1963).

25. For example, see Yasuko Minoura and Yumiko Takeda, "Characteristics on the Hand Test with Japanese Delinquent Boys), *Japanese Journal of Criminal Psychology* 9, no. 2 (1972):38 ff. (with English summary).

26. Akira Fukushima, "Amae to Kogeki" [Dependency and Aggressiveness], in his *Gendaijin no Kogekisei* [Today's Aggressiveness] (Tokyo: Taiyo Shuppan, 1972); Hideo Goko, "Kogekiteki Hanzai no Doki to shiteno 'Urami' no Kosatsu" [A Study of 'Urami' as the Motive of Aggressive Offenses], *Japanese Journal of Criminal Psychology* 12, no. 1 (1976):21 ff. (with English summary).

27. Yoshio Matsumoto, "Shakai Kozo-nai ni okeru Shonen Hiko no Bunpu" [Distribution of Juvenile Delinquency in the Social Class Structure], *Japanese Sociological Review* 20, no. 4 (1970):2 ff. (with English summary).

28. Katsuzo Hayashi, et al., "Hiko Shonen no Kodo Tokusei Bunrui ni kansuru Bunka Kosa-teki Kenkyu" [A Cross-Cultural Study Concerning the Differential Behavioral Classification], *Japanese Journal of Criminal Psychology* 11, no. 2 (1976):21 ff. (with English summary).

29. For example, see Masaru Makino, et al., "Naikan no Shinrigaku-teki Kosatsu" [A Psychological Study on the "Naikan" Method in Prison], *Japanese Journal of Psychology* 5, no. 2 (1968):7 ff.

30. Toshio Hironaka, *Sengo Nihon no Keisatsu* [Police in Post-War Japan] (Tokyo: Iwanami Shoten, 1968).

31. Kanehiro Hoshino, "Kokyo no Anzensei ni Kiyo suru Keisatsu Katsudo no Kenkyu" [Police Activities to Raise the Level of Public Safety from Crime], *Reports of National Research Institute of Police Science, Research on Prevention of Crime and Delinquency* 17, no. 2 (1976):145 ff; 18, no. 1 (1977):1 ff. (with English summaries).

32. Yoshiaki Takahashi and Haruo Nishimura, "Hiko Shonen no Shakaiteki Tosei ni taisuru Nichi" [Delinquents' Risk Perception of Their Transgression], *Japanese Journal of Criminal Psychology* 11, no. 1 (1975):1 ff.; Yoshiaki Takahashi, "Hanzi Yokushiryoku kara mita Shakaiteki Seisai no Shakudo-ka" [Scaling Deterrence of Social Sanctions Against Crime and Delinquency], *Japanese Journal of Criminal Psychology* 12, no. 2 (1977):1 ff. (with English summary).

33. For example, see Tatsumi Makino, et al., "Chiiki Soshikika Katsudo ni kansuru Kenkyu" [A Community Organization Project Surveyed], *Seishonen Mondai Kenkyu Hokokusho* 40, no. 2 (1965):1 ff.

34. Takuji Kawasaki, "Kosei Hogo to Chiiki Shakai" [After-Care of Offenders and the Local Community], *Japanese Journal of Sociological Criminology*, no. 3 (1978):72 ff.

35. "Kei no Ryotei ni kansuru Jisshoteki Kenkyu" [A Survey of Sentencing Practice], in his *Keijihojo no Shomondai* [Problems in Criminal Law] (Tokyo: Kobundo, 1950).

36. "Kei no Ryotei ni okeru Jinteki Joken no Kanyo" [Personal Determinants of Sentencing Policy] in his *Saiban Shinrigaku no Shoso* [Studies in Judicial Psychology] (Tokyo: Yushindo, 1958).

37. Kazuhiko Tokoro, "Keiji Seisai to Songai Baisho" [Criminal Sanction and Restitution], in Takeyoshi Kawashima and Ruichi Hirano (eds.), *Jidosha Jiko o meguru Funso Shori to Ho* [Dispute Resolution and the Law in Traffic Accidents] (Tokyo: Iwanami Shoten, 1978).

BIBLIOGRAPHY

The following publications are the most useful for an overall view of crime, crime control, and criminology in present Japan.

Crime Reports

Hanzai Hakusho [Crime Report]. Issued annually by Homu Sogo Kenkyujo (Research and Training Institute, Ministry of Justice).
Keisatsu Hakusho [Police Report]. Edited annually by Keisataucho (National Police Agency).

Textbooks

Ako, Hiroshi, and Fumio Muguishima (eds.). *Hanzai Shinrigaku* [Criminal Psychology]. Tokyo: Yuhikaku, 1975.
Hoshino, Kanehiro. *Hanzai Shakaigaku* [Criminal Sociology]. Tokyo: Yachibana Shobo, 1981.

Selected Readings

Iwai, Hiroaki, Tatsuo Endo, Kokichi Higuchi, and Ruichi Hirano (eds.). *Nihon no Hanzaigaku* [Japanese Studies in Criminology]. Tokyo: University of Tokyo Press, 1969-1978. Ruichi Hirano was sole editor of volumes 5 and 6, published in 1980. The last section of the chapter above owes much to those volumes.

21

REPUBLIC OF KOREA

Koo Chin Kang

The term "criminology" is more or less foreign to Korean scholarship as well as to administration and professional practice within criminal justice agencies in Korea. Instead, the term "penal policy" is used more frequently in Korea, where the German influence is still strongly visible. It was not until 1957, when part of E. H. Sutherland's *Principles of Criminology* was translated into Korean, that the term "criminology" was imported to Korean soil on a scholarly level.[1]

CRIMINOLOGY AT THE UNIVERSITIES

When utilized, the term "criminology" normally conveys two different notions of a science or branch of learning. The first notion is somewhat narrow in the sense that it is directed to how and why persons engage in crimes, and what are the causes of such crimes. It may be called the "science on crime" or "criminology in a narrow sense." This notion of criminology is generally taken in university departments other than law departments.

Another notion is directed not only to the study of crime and criminals but also to the most appropriate responses of organized society to crime, whether they be informal or official. The law departments at various universities prefer the concept of criminology that is more or less the equivalent of penal policy.

The term "criminologist" is not widely used in Korea, partly because criminology, whether in a broad or narrow sense, is still in its germinal phase and partly because there is no visible meeting place for criminological specialists drawn from various established disciplines. Criminology is not fully institutionalized as a branch of learning to such an extent that the so-called criminologists form an independent society conducting its own academic and research activities. The subject matter of criminology is often dealt with within the framework of various traditional branches of learning. Professors of criminal law are dominant among teachers of criminology at the universities as their secondary interest, but scholars other than jurists—sociologists, psychologists, and psychiatrists—show an increasing concern about crime and criminals.[2]

Those sociologists who have studied in the United States have opened classes in criminology within sociology departments. Because of the growing influence of the United States in every sphere of Korean society since 1945, those law professors who teach "penal policy" usually pay great attention to American criminology. Recently, governmental agencies such as the Ministry of Justice and the Ministry of Internal Affairs have shown great interest in the study of crime and criminals and in expanding the education of convicted criminals.

HISTORY AND DEVELOPMENT OF KOREA

Korea is a peninsular nation with a claimed history of about five thousand years. A land bridge between the Xsian mainland and countries to the east and south, Korea has been a me —ing ground for many influences and rivalries. This small nation has survived many invasions from foreign countries and endured long-term occupation on only two occasions: the Mongolian occupation from 1231 to 1270 and the Japanese from 1910 to 1945. In other periods, Korea has been primarily under the influence of China in the north but maintained its own independent national development. It has been characteristic of Korean history that various dynasties that had existed on the Korean peninsula kept a long history of their own under the same royal court, ranging from five hundred to about one thousand years. Until the Yi Dynasty (the last dynasty on the peninsula) became colonized under the Japan-Korea Annexation Treaty in 1910, it had been in control for 519 years.

Korea is a densely populated area. It is now divided ideologically into a northern and southern part. The demography of North Korea is not well known, but the population of South Korea in June 1979 was nearly 37 million, with a density of 373 persons per square kilometer.

Korea has strong Buddhist traditions. Buddhism was transmitted to the Korean peninsula from 372 A.D. until 450 A.D. During the Koryo Dynasty (918-1392 A.D.), it was the national religion. During the Yi Dynasty (1392-1910 A.D.), Confucianism was relevant in the rules of government and general conduct. Christianity appeared in Korea about two hundred years ago and has continuously spread its sphere of influence since the end of World War II. Today six million Koreans are estimated to believe in Catholicism and Protestantism.

Korea has traditionally been an agricultural country, but since the early 1960s there have been four successive Five-Year Economic Development Plans for rapid industrialization. As a result of these economic plans, the per capita income in a year increased from approximately 100 U.S. dollars in the early 1960s to about 1,000 U.S. dollars at the end of the 1970s. Such dramatic growth in the economy has caused great changes in Korean society.

BRIEF REVIEW OF CRIME PATTERNS

Korean society has experienced great instability since the end of the last world war and especially during the Korean War, which began in 1950. Rapid change has had its effects in adding new varieties of crime and increasing its quantity, but lack of crime statistics for earlier years does not permit verification of this impression. Only in 1964 did the Bureau of Statistics of the Economic Planning Board begin to collect nationwide statistics on important crimes and thus make available to the public officially recognized data on criminality. These data are used in the following brief analysis of criminality in Korea.

TABLE 21-1
TOTAL CRIMES AS SPECIFIED IN THE PENAL CODE, 1965-1975

Year	Amount	Year	Amount
1965	263,554	1971	250,202
1966	234,332	1972	294,476
1967	253,739	1973	260,606
1968	245,342	1974	265,152
1969	238,226	1975	308,760
1970	239,756		

Source: Bureau of Statistics, Economic Planning Board.

Table 21-1 reports the total crimes, as defined by the Penal Code, according to police statistics for the years 1965 through 1970. Violations of other laws are excluded from the table. Because of widely known methodological problems, these data should be seen more as descriptions of the amount and nature of the work performed by the Korean police rather than as a complete census of criminality.

The workload as measured by reported offenses tended to decline in a rather irregular pattern from 1965 through 1969. Then, another irregular pattern appeared in an increased number of offenses. The net effect was that the absolute size of police work was 14.7 percent greater in 1975 than in 1965. In 1975, the estimated official crime rate per 100,000 population was 1,109.

Estimates of seven major crimes, as reported in National Police statistics, are given in Table 21-2 for each year from 1965 through 1975. As those knowledgeable in crime statistics would expect, crimes against property hold a much larger share of these major crimes overall than crimes against persons. Furthermore, larceny is the dominant offense among crimes against property and assault and battery among crimes against persons.

Nevertheless, crimes against persons have become increasingly significant. To measure changes in the relative importance of particular crimes, 1965 is taken as the base year for the following years. Each number of reported offenses for a given year is divided by the number of offenses reported in 1965 for the given crime. Table 21-2 offers the computations.

Crimes against persons recorded the greatest gains in number of offenses reported. In 1976, rapes increased 362 percent over the 1965 figure; this was the greatest proportionate increase among the offense categories. The category of assault and battery (a 283-percent gain) was also remarkable. Robberies declined

TABLE 21-2
COMPARISON BY YEARS OF SEVEN MAJOR CRIMES, 1965-1975

	Crimes against Persons				Crimes against Property		
Year	Murder	Robbery	Rape	Assault-Battery	Larceny	Fraud	Forgery
1965	388	1,198	532	35,094	133,198	17,338	4,946
1966	383	1,163	668	74,766	101,678	19,342	4,873
1967	392	1,116	775	63,875	103,201	20,469	3,414
1968	448	973	938	72,623	84,184	20,059	3,859
1969	451	961	962	72,595	74,353	19,926	3,719
1970	502	1,020	1,139	74,841	69,263	19,290	4,189
1971	493	1,176	1,386	74,312	71,190	19,543	3,729
1972	494	1,295	1,517	79,074	78,558	23,900	4,750
1973	393	956	1,481	71,079	72,715	23,965	4,549
1974	463	1,399	1,414	78,693	76,310	23,021	3,637
1975	509	1,735	1,928	99,021	79,280	24,735	4,192
		Comparisons with 1965 Taken as Base Year					
1965	1.00	1.00	1.00	1.00	1.00	1.00	1.00
1966	0.99	0.97	1.29	2.13	0.76	1.12	0.98
1967	1.01	0.93	1.46	1.82	0.77	1.18	0.69
1968	1.15	0.81	1.76	2.07	0.63	1.16	0.78
1969	1.16	0.80	1.81	2.07	0.56	1.15	0.75
1970	1.29	0.85	2.14	2.13	0.52	1.11	0.85
1971	1.27	0.98	2.61	2.12	0.53	1.13	0.75
1972	1.27	1.08	2.85	2.25	0.59	1.38	0.95
1973	1.02	0.80	2.78	2.03	0.55	1.38	0.91
1974	1.19	1.17	2.66	2.24	0.57	1.33	0.74
1975	1.31	1.45	3.62	2.83	0.59	1.43	0.85

Source: Bureau of Statistics, Economics Planning Board.

proportionately for the years 1966 through 1970, and then they irregularly increased to reach a 145-percent gain in 1975 over 1965. In the sense of this climactic gain, the pattern of increase was less impressive for murders, but, considering the greater consistency of gain over the years, murder had more impact among major crimes than the relatively small number of murders would suggest.

Among crimes against property, only fraud scored important gains with a reasonable degree of consistency. In spite of its numerical dominance, the category of larceny had the greatest loss over the years in its proportionate share of all major crimes. Forgery declined in relative importance.

What about juvenile delinquency? In Korea, only persons over thirteen years of age are counted in offender statistics. In 1975, offenders up to age twenty were involved in the following percentage share of these offenses: 12.9 percent of 59,045 minor offenses, 16.4 percent of 85 murders, 42.2 percent of 1,055 robberies, 34.0 percent of 858 rapes, 35.7 percent of 21,120 larcenies, 17.6 percent of 213 extortions, and 2.1 percent of 553 frauds. These figures suggest that juvenile delinquency in Korea constitutes a serious problem.

Statistics from the Correctional Bureau of the Ministry of Justice indicate that in the Republic of Korea, along with other nations, a high rate of recidivism constitutes one of the most serious dimensions of the crime problem. Statistics of the bureau shown in Table 21-3 report the recidivism among adult prisoners for the years 1968, 1970, and 1972, respectively. The median number of prison terms shows little change in recidivism over the years, although a slight increase is found among the proportion of all prisoners who were serving their first prison term. Nevertheless, the most significant impression is that repetition of offenses is characteristic of about half the prisoners. As in other countries, the Republic of Korea finds the recidivist to be a central aspect of the crime problem.

TABLE 21-3
RECIDIVISM AMONG ADULT PRISONERS, 1968, 1970, AND 1972

Number of Prison Terms	Number of Prisoners by Year					
	1968		1970		1972	
	Number	*Pct.*	*Number*	*Pct.*	*Number*	*Pct.*
One	9,646	48.0	10,754	50.0	13,376	51.1
Two	5,025	24.9	4,666	21.7	4,986	19.1
Three	1,983	9.8	3,024	14.1	2,946	11.3
Four	1,222	6.0	1,024	4.7	1,688	6.5
Five or more	2,275	11.3	2,051	9.5	3,162	12.0
Total	20,151	100.0	21,519	100.0	26,158	100.0
Median prison terms	3.41		3.41		3.37	

Source: Correctional Bureau, Ministry of Justice.

PRACTICAL INTEREST IN THE FIELD

Generally, criminology does not exist in Korea as a distinct occupation. One cannot live on criminology alone. Criminology is subjected to research by a few scholars in established disciplines—in most cases, by professors of criminal law—but also by sociologists who have a secondary interest in criminology. Thus, in Korea no criminologists perform in a specialized activity independent of other roles.

A small number of correctional officials, police officials, and public prosecutors show some interest in the study of the treatment of offenders and of criminal policies. In many cases, however, owing to their official obligations, these investigations are conducted on a piece-meal basis. Thus, at this juncture, probes into criminological questions do not constitute a distinct and independent vocational activity.

The number of those who would like to specialize in criminology is gradually increasing, however. The Korean government has always emphasized economic development as a first national priority; now serious attention is being given to social development. Governmental authorities have a new interest in the scientific study of crime and criminals as an aspect of national welfare programs. Among the issues being considered are the treatment of prisoners and their after-care. With the assistance of the Ministries of Justice and Education, I am conducting research into the relationship between education and vocational training in prisons with the reduction of recidivism. Findings will become available on a comparison of samples of approximately four hundred inmates and approximately four hundred released prisoners.

LIMITED PROGRESS TOWARD INSTITUTIONALIZATION

Korean criminology must be regarded to be in its germinal phase. Criminological problems have yet to receive serious attention from the academe and the general public. Academic seminars on criminology have been infrequent. From time to time, a particularly urgent criminological problem will cause criminal justice administrators to assemble for a seminar or conference. These seminars or conferences are not initiated by and are seldom actively guided by the academic profession. Interaction between the Faculty of Law and criminal justice administrators is rare. Korea presents few criminological research investigations and discussions on a nationwide scale.

This climate is not congenial to the institutionalization of criminology. Korea has no professional organization composed of criminologists alone. Interaction among criminologists is usually incidental to membership in more general organizations, such as the Society of Criminal Law or the Society of Sociology. Otherwise, information is shared on an individual basis.

A generally prevalent idea is that criminology should be the preserve of jurists and lawyers. Law professors who specialize in criminal law usually get interested in criminology as a secondary field of study. In addition, a limited number of sociologists, psychologists, and psychiatrists take part in criminological discussions.

Nevertheless, there are also encouraging sides to Korean criminology. First, criminology is taught in most of the law schools,[3] usually as an elective course, during the fourth year of studies of the law students. Those members of the Law Faculty who instruct criminology are criminologists secondarily. Their interest in criminology is encouraged by the inclusion of the subject as one of the elective subjects for the national bar examination which is held once a year throughout the country.

A limited number of scholars have made an even more significant contribution. Professor Ki Doo Kim at the College of Law, Seoul National University, published a book entitled *Hanguk Sonyon Pomjoe Yonku* [A Study of Korean Juvenile Delinquency] in 1967 which has been a pioneering contribution to Korean criminology. His study was based on field research of juveniles in regard to their family life, school life, and regional community life. He compared the economic backgrounds of one hundred juvenile offenders (inmates of two juvenile reformatories in Korea) with those of one hundred students selected at random in middle and high schools on the outskirts of Seoul.

The Central Committee Regarding Protective Measures for Juveniles is under the administrative control of the Ministry of Internal Affairs. It has conducted research into the prediction of delinquency. An extensive examination was made of three groups of juveniles; namely, a sample of 3,466 conventional juveniles, a control group of 3,340 potential juvenile delinquents, and a control group of 3,508 officially defined juvenile delinquents. The purpose was to construct a prediction table for juvenile delinquency. The study was authored by Chong-Kuk Kim and three colleagues, and it was published in 1973 under the title "Prediction of Juvenile Delinquency." Construction of the prediction table may be called the first governmental attempt in Korea to give the national police a means of predicting delinquency among juveniles coming to police attention.

A KOREAN THEORETICAL PERSPECTIVE

There are several Korean textbooks on criminology, but special attention may be given to the textbook of Professor Jin-Kew Shin at Kyŏngbuk National University. One of his textbooks, unlike other such books, carries the title "Criminology" (*Hyongsahak*). Other texts published in Korea carry the title "Penal Policy." Professor Shin's textbook has made a special contribution to the development of Korean criminology because it carefully explains theories developed in advanced Western countries. More significantly, he advances his own theory of criminology which he calls the Dynamical Theory of Criminal Behavior.[4]

Shin claims that the causes of crime (c) are dependent on the relationship between "tempting power of crime" (t) and "deterring power against criminal action" (d) in terms of this formula:

$$c = \frac{t}{d}$$

Where the relationship $t>d$ is found, a criminal action will occur, but in $t<d$ the crime does not take place, he explains. The intensity of "tempting power" (t) is determined through the interaction of "desires of inner mind" (D)

and those factors associated with temptations to engage in a specific kind of criminal activity (*T*). Then: $t = D \cdot T$. The intensity of "deterring power" (*d*) depends upon the two factors of "moral sentiments" (*M*), which involve restraints against criminal behavior in one's inner mind, and "social sanctions" (*S*), which are found in the external controlling environment of the individual. Then: $d = M + S$. Shin summarizes the relationship between these definitions in the formula:

$$C = \frac{D \cdot T}{M + S}$$

When $D \cdot T < M + S$, crimes are less probable. However, under certain circumstances, one's moral sentiment (*M*) alone exceeds the total tempting power ($D \cdot T$), as in the case of a conscientious objector. Taking these circumstances into consideration, Shin formulates the cases of crimes not occurring as follows:

$$D \cdot T < M \sim M + S$$

Even in the case of $D \cdot T = M \sim M + S$, the crime will not happen. Therefore, to explain the instances of crime not occurring, he proposes the formula:

$$D \cdot T \leqq M \sim M + S$$

PROMISING CLUES TO THE FUTURE

In summary, Korean criminology is undeveloped; there is little demand for the criminological occupation. It cannot be denied that it is still in its germinal stage. Until comparatively recently, it largely echoed criminology in Japan and in the Western hemisphere. Yet, several educational institutions promote the preparation of criminologists. Major schools of law include criminology in instruction. Systematic study of criminology usually figures in the graduate curricula of the leading law faculties.

Some professors in departments of sociology and psychology have great interest in criminological issues, and their students usually see the relevance of criminology to their major fields of study. It may be that these students will end up as criminologists.

Criminology is included in the curricula of various specialized training and educational institutes connected in some fashion with criminal justice administration. For example, in the Ministry of Justice Training Institute, the training of correctional officials includes criminology in the program of instruction. The National Police Academy, established under the Ministry of Internal Affairs to train police officers, also includes the study of criminology. The four-year Police

College which will be established next year is expected to expand the systematic teaching of criminology.

Finally, criminological study and research are often conducted in graduate schools of law and sociology. From time to time, one can find dissertations for the degrees of master of laws or of sociology that deal with criminological problems. A few scholars have studied abroad and have returned to Korea. Occasionally, prosecutors and police and correctional officials are sent to criminological training institutes in foreign countries, most notably to UNAFEI in Tokyo, Japan.

NOTES

1. See *Hyŏngsahakwonri* (Seoul: Minjungsokwan, 1957), translated by Ki Doo Kim, professor of law at Seoul National University.

2. Professors of Sociology Byong Je Jon at Yonsei University, Yong Bok Ko at Seoul National University, Chang Hyon Yi at Ewha Women's University, Yong Mo Kim at Chungang University, Hy Sop Lim at Korea University, and Yong Hi Sim at Chonnam National University are sociologists with considerable interest in crminological problems. Professors Byong Rim Chang at Seoul National University and Kyong Hi Kim at Yonsei University are Professors of Psychology with similar interests. Professor Chu Yŏng Cho at Seoul National University is one of the psychiatrists with this bent.

3. For details on legal education in Korea, see Jay Murphy, *Legal Education in a Developing Nation: The Korea Experience* (Dobbs Ferry, N.Y.: Oceana Publications, Inc., 1967).

4. For the details of this theory, see Jin-Kew Shin, *Hyongsahak* [Criminology] (Seoul: Popmunsa, 1977), pp. 63-75.

BIBLIOGRAPHY

Chong, Yong-Suk. *Hyŏngsajŏngchaek* [Penal Policy]. Seoul: Pakyongsa, 1963.
This standard textbook is written in traditional style for students of penal policy at the university level.

Hahm, Pyong-Choon. *The Korean Political Tradition and Law*. Seoul: Hollym Corporation, 1967.
This book, written in English, deals with a profound problem: how to apply cherished Western ideals of law to the Korean situation, where political values and institutions have been consciously modeled after those of ancient China. Furthermore, the following important issues are taken into consideration: What is the function of law and social justice in "late-developing" Asian countries? In view of Korea's socioeconomic tradition, can these abstract Western principles be applied to such practical problems as abortion, usury, property rights, penitentiaries, and the treatment of the insane?

Kang, Koo Chin. "Functions of Law in Korean Society." *Seoul Law Journal* 15 (1974):135-168.
This article analyzes obstacles to the positive function of law in Korean society and makes

operative proposals that may enhance the role of law for the development of a free and just society where the rule of law prevails.

Kim, Ki-Doo. *Hanguk Sonyŏn Pomjoe Yonku* [A Study of Korean Juvenile Delinquency]. Seoul: Pakyongsa, 1967.
This pioneering work on research on juvenile delinquency in Korea analyzes the present status and causes of juvenile delinquency.

Kwon, Sung-Yong, and Ho Chu-Uk. *Haenghyonghak* [Science of Correction]. Seoul: Ilchokak, 1977.
This standard textbook is written for students and practitioners who are interested in the science of correction. It describes the Korean correctional system as a whole as envisaged by the Korean Correctional Act.

Lim, Hy Sop. "A Study of Legal Values in Korea." *Seoul Law Journal* 15 (1974):56-81.
This work analyzes Korean attitudes toward law, based on a sociological field survey carried out in May 1972.

Nam, Hung-U. *Hyŏnsajongch'aek* [Penal Policy]. Seoul: Pakyongsa, 1963.
This standard textbook is written in conventional style for students of criminal policy at the university level.

Shin, Jin-Kew. *Hyŏngsahak* [Criminology]. Seoul: Popmunsa, 1977.
This book reflects recent criminological developments in the Western world and presents statistics on the general crime trend in Korea.

Yi, Chong-Won. *Kyongjebomjoeron* [A Study on Economic Crimes]. Seoul: Ilsinsa, 1974.
An extensive study on criminal aspects of economic regulation, this book analyzes the present status of economic crimes in Korea. It sets forth their causes and presents measures for their prevention and control.

22

THE NETHERLANDS

Jac Van Weringh

Criminology has been an academic subject in The Netherlands since 1918 when academic statutes were changed, making it possible for criminology and sociology to be taught at Dutch universities. This is not to say that there was no concern for criminology before then.

THREE PERSPECTIVES IN EARLY DECADES

At the beginning of this century, crime and the criminal were studied from three distinct points of view. The first was the criminal-anthropological perspective advocated by A. Alestrino (1858-1916) who was attached as a private teacher for some time to the Municipal University of Amsterdam. He was a Dutch follower of C. Lombroso. In 1902 and 1904, his two-part study on criminal anthropology was published; he presented a general outline of the state of affairs regarding Lombrosian ideas and made criticisms of them. These ideas found a very limited response in The Netherlands.

A second point of view of a more psychological nature was inspired by the psychologist-philosopher G. Heymans (1857-1930) at the University of Groningen. Around three psychic functions—emotionality, activity, and the secondary function— he constructed a typology of eight temperaments: the nervous, the sentimental, the phlegmatic, the sanguine, the choleric, the passionate, the amorphous, and the apathetic. Several of Heymans's pupils attempted to apply this typology in theses that analyzed the arsonist, the murderer, and the vagabond.

Apart from—and opposing—these approaches directed toward the individual criminal, W. A. Bonger (1876-1940) developed a third point of view that drew heavily on Friedrich Engels's book *The Condition of the Working Class in England*. In 1905 he defended his thesis *Criminalité et conditions économiques* at the University of Amsterdam. The American edition, *Criminality and Economic Conditions*, appeared in 1916. The book has become one of the standard works of criminological literature. In Bonger's view, crime is a social phenomenon and not primarily an individual-pathological aberration. After his thesis was published, Bonger took up this theme in several books and many articles, emphasizing the influence of the capitalist system on different kinds of crime.

Bonger was a scientist of great political awareness. As an active member of the Sociaal-Democratische Arbeiderspartij—SDAP (Social Democratic Labor Party), he stood at the firing line in the struggle for political rights and social improvement for depressed groups in society. In the 1920s, he also criticized the negative approach to homosexuality in Dutch society. He believed that the good and the bad, the stupid and the clever were to be found among both heterosexuals and homosexuals. At the beginning of the 1930s, he uttered militant warnings against the dangers of national socialism in Germany and its spreading to The Netherlands. On May 15, 1940, when the Dutch army capitulated shortly after the German invasion, Bonger took his own life.

Dutch criminology owes Bonger a great deal. He advocated an empirical approach at a time when there was much speculation in The Netherlands on both the criminal and criminality. He attacked the idea, then popular in Holland, that the growing neglect of religion was responsible for an increase in crime. In 1939, he wrote *Ras en Misdaad*, a book that appeared in the United States in translation in 1943 as *Race and Crime*, as an antidote to the race-mythology so popular both within and outside Germany. In this book, which was published shortly before he died, Bonger appears as a supporter of the philosophy of social progress, despite the developments around him. Criminality, he states, is one of the products of an uncivilized and unjust society. His last message was that Western society would move slowly toward a higher level of civilization, cultural development, and social equality.

DOMINANCE OF CRIMINAL LAW

Bonger was appointed professor of criminology at the Municipal University of Amsterdam in 1922, becoming the first professor in that subject. The fact that his appointment was to the Faculty of Law is typical of the Dutch situation, which has not changed since 1945. Officially, criminology is still part of the Faculty of Law. Until the 1960s, the professors of criminology (one exception being a moral theologian) had legal backgrounds. Although several social scientists were later appointed as professors of criminology, officially they belonged to the law faculties. Of late, however, there have been links in some cases with social science departments.

These ties with law, especially with criminal law, have not been without their consequences for criminology in The Netherlands. Books on criminal law often tend to state that criminology is an "auxiliary science" of criminal law, such as criminalistics and forensic psychiatry. This claim has meant that the subjects examined by criminologists have been strongly determined by criminal law. Criminology was "imprisoned" within the framework of criminal law, and consequently fundamental questions regarding the very existence of criminal law did not arise.

Only a few criminologists noted that the creation of rules of criminal law is somehow linked with power relations in society. One of these few was Clara Meijer-Wichmann (1885-1922). In a series of publications on criminal law and criminology, she questioned the boundaries of criminal law. Her opinions were very progressive for her time and were not to become common property in radical criminological circles until much later. She emphasized the class character of criminal law.

Bonger also believed that the content of criminal law is determined by the interests of the ruling classes. However, by the time he published his *Inleiding in de Criminologie* in 1932—which appeared in English in London in 1936 as *An Introduction to Criminology*—he had refuted the idea. In the meantime, universal suffrage had been introduced in The Netherlands (for men in 1917 and for women in 1922), and Bonger probably felt that criminal law had therefore become the expression of popular will in a parliamentary democracy.

In the 1930s and immediately after the war, several empirical studies on the nature and development of crime in The Netherlands appeared. These studies could be called "criminographic" because they are relatively descriptive and deal with the existence of crime in a certain area (town or province) or the relation between crime and some other social phenomenon. A well-known example of the latter type is G.Th. Kempe's book *Criminaliteit en kerkgenootschap* (1938), which emphasizes the question of why Roman Catholics score higher on crime than members of other churches or non-churchgoers, a subject that dominated the debate in Dutch criminology for many years. Kempe places the issue within the perspective of Max Weber's thesis in *Protestant Ethics and the Spirit of Capitalism*.

Another study worth mentioning in the criminographic tradition is H. van Rooy's *Criminaliteit van stad en land: Nijmegen en omstreken* (1949). This is statistical criminological research into the factors that influence patterns of criminality in the town and the country and their development between 1910 and 1935. These studies are based on officially recorded crime. The influence of investigating and prosecuting agencies is barely discussed. This oversight, too, is a typical result of the strong ties with criminal law because criminology functions mostly within the boundaries of criminal law. This characteristic also means that there has been less empirical research than normative thinking—so distinctive in legal studies.

STIMULUS OF CRIMINOLOGY IN THE 1960s

Criminology did not expand and demand more attention until the 1960s. At that time W. Buikhuisen, a trained research psychologist, was appointed professor of criminology at the State University of Groningen. He initiated an elaborate research program in which there was much emphasis on drunken driving, drug abuse, and hidden crime. In conception, this research was still relatively within the positivist tradition. Buikhuisen started from the fact that hardly any empirical criminological research had been done in The Netherlands and that therefore the first priority was to discover the state of affairs in regard to different sorts of crime: How often does it occur? How much is discovered by the police and especially who commits it? Such questions led to a long series of publications by Buikhuisen and his assistants, some of which attracted much public interest— once or twice leading to questions in Parliament.

Criminology also developed at the other universities. In the 1970s, there were fierce debates on the starting points of criminology and on the question of what should be done with the results of criminological research. In the the 1980s, Dutch criminology has presented an extremely varied image. Thinking is deter- mined by two pairs of much discussed and opposing ideas: fundamental versus applied criminology and governmental versus nongovernmental criminology. Of late, a new subject had been added: biosocial criminology. The following is a brief discussion of the different approaches.

FUNDAMENTAL VERSUS APPLIED RESEARCH

C. I. Dessaur of the Institute of Criminology of the Catholic University of Nijmegen advocates a more fundamental criminology, as opposed to positive criminology, that is based on existing criminal law and can therefore be said to be applied criminology. (In dark-number research too, the issue is whether the existing rules of criminal law have been broken without having been recorded by the police).

According to Dessaur, criminology is not, as yet, scientifically emancipated. What criminologists do is really determined by topical social problems such as "the increase in crime," "breaches of public order," or "increasing violence." The authorities must find a solution to the problems which society believes urgent, and the criminologist is expected to provide those solutions. This, how- ever, brings him or her into the realm of application and, therefore, of ethical value-judgments: is this a good, useful, valuable solution? Fundamental crimi- nology, however, is concerned primarily with nonproblem-related analysis, un- related to ethically determined practical application. Dessaur believes that crim- inology should be a combination of two sociological disciplines: the sociology of criminal law and the sociology of deviant behavior.

At the Institute of Criminology of the State University of Groningen in 1973, R. W. Jongman succeeded Buikhuisen who had gone to the Ministry of Justice at the Hague. At the institute there is a more direct concern for the social aspects of crime, and criminological research is seen as a means of determining certain inequalities in Dutch society and of showing which changes are necessary. To this end, the institute does research on police behavior, the public prosecutor's policy of prosecution, and sentencing behavior by judges. This research centers around the relation between social class and the risk of being caught, prosecuted, and sentenced, while the emphasis is on empirical research and not on theoretical speculation regarding class-justice.

The method applied is logic-positivist, although it is recognized that as such it is open to criticism. The institute expects that the results of its research will promote more understanding of the way in which the apparatus of the criminal justice system functions. A study on the relation of social class and the risk of being sentenced by a judge, published in 1976, led first to a public outcry and then to a long debate in the Dutch journal of criminology, *Tijdschrift voor Criminologie*. The study, which concerned theft, showed that members of the lower social classes were more likely to be sentenced than others and more often.

The Bonger Criminological Institute was founded in 1973 at the University of Amsterdam, and I am the present director. This institute is not characterized by a distinct approach as are the others to some extent. It conducts research on several subjects in criminology, such as children's ideas on crime and punishment (perception) and the relation between criminality and environment. There are also studies on the historical aspects of criminality, for example, the criminalization of behavior. Much value is attached to empirical research.

In 1978, I published a collection of essays on criminality in The Netherlands called: "Onrust is van alle tijden"; the main theme was that criminality constitutes an inevitable phenomenon in human society. Because of the many contradictions in that society, crime is less easily eradicated or prevented than some criminologists, especially the more radical ones, would have us believe. The criminologist's task is to determine the state of affairs with regard to criminality: Why is certain behavior defined as such? Why is it increasing? Why do some *say* that it is increasing? What are the specific elements of the different sorts of crime? My essays refute the idea that radical and fundamental social change is the goal of science, including criminology, as is propagated by some. At most, criminology might contribute to a very slow change in society. Radical opposition to the different agencies of the criminal justice system, such as the police, the public prosecutor, and the judiciary, is more likely to lead these agencies to become increasingly inaccessible to scientific research and therefore uncontrollable and more powerful.

OPPOSITION TO "GOVERNMENT RESEARCH"

This sketch of the panorama of different approaches in Dutch criminology is still not complete. Amsterdam also has a Free University (Vrije Universiteit), founded in 1880 as a Calvinistic stronghold in the face of increasing secularization in The Netherlands. A hundred years later, as far as Dutch criminology is concerned, it is from this university that the most radical ideas have come. The criminologist H. Bianchi is radically opposed to the existing application of criminal law. He supports nongovernmental criminology. Of late, he has been the fiery advocate of the re-creation of sanctuaries such as existed in the olden days, to which those who had committed some crime could retreat for a while in order to negotiate with the (judicial) authorities or with the victim or his kin—a sort of internal asylum. According to Bianchi, operating from a more or less anarchist perspective, citizens should not allow the state to deprive them of their own conflicts.

At the Erasmus University of Rotterdam, G. P. Hoefnagels also takes a fairly radical stand. In 1973, he published *The Other Side of Criminology*, in which he emphasizes the necessity of making the labelers of crime (the power elite of society) the most important subject of criminological research. His work concentrates on the "others," rather than the perpetrators of crime. This theme is also appropriate to his interest in environmental crime (pollution) and affluent crime. By means of an artistic approach, namely, the theater, he seeks to promote understanding of the way in which a trial functions and of the rites it involves.

Criminology at the State University of Utrecht is considered part of criminal law. In this connection, the so-called Utrechtse School is famous; it has been of great importance in the humanization of criminal justice in The Netherlands. Existentialist and phenomenological ideas on freedom and responsibility (the "I-thee-relationship") led to a strong interest in the criminal as a human being and in the question of how he came to act as he did. The notion of responsibility is also important with regard to punishment in which the aspect of treatment is emphasized. For a long time, criminology at Utrecht was concerned more with penology than with anything else. At the Willem Pompe Institute for the Sciences of Criminal Law at this university, there is still much interest in the place of the prisoner in the criminal justice system and in the rights he should be accorded in the light of state power.

FIELDS OF VICTIMOLOGY AND BIOSOCIAL CRIMINOLOGY

For many years, the Institute of Criminology of Leyden was led by W. H. Nagel, initiator and editor of *Abstracts on Criminology and Penology* (previously *Excerpta Criminologica*). Long before, Nagel had already called attention to victimology, a field of research still fairly neglected in The Netherlands. In 1965, he published his book *Het voorspellen van crimineel gedrag* [*The Prediction of Criminal Behavior*], in which he breaks a lance in a valiant attempt to justify prediction studies. Still in Leyden, he later became the first Dutch criminologist to set up a cohort study, as a means of discovering whether children in elementary school show tendencies that could point to criminal careers in later life. Finally, he wrote many works on terrorism by the state.

In 1978, Nagel was succeeded by W. Buikhuisen, who announced his intention to practice biosocial criminology. The announcement alone was enough to set off a huge campaign against any such plan as being "unchristian," "fascist," and "back to Lombroso." During a parliamentary debate, the minister for justice promised that any abuse of prisoners would be impossible. In his book *Kriminologie in biosociaal perspectief* (1979) [*Criminology in a Biosocial Perspective*], Buikhuisen presents a preliminary sketch of his ideas and plans. In it, he stresses the necessity for a differential criminology. Until now, the tendency has been to explain all criminality by one single theory. The heterogeneous criminal population should be divided into homogeneous subpopulations. Moreover, there should be an interdisciplinary approach in which biological and social factors should not be regarded as operating separately. The biological substratum is influenced by environment, and vice versa. In his book, he elaborates on this idea, using three types of aggressive crime as an example: subcultural "teddy-boy" behavior and aggressiveness by "overcontrollers" and "undercontrollers." He emphasizes that a biological approach does not mean that all behavior has a biological explanation. The absolute and relative importance of biological variables will differ according to the type of behavior studied. Buikhuisen appears to be fairly optimistic with regard to the opportunities afforded by the biosocial approach. Time will tell.

The common denominator in this brief summary of the different approaches in Dutch criminology is that criminology is practiced at universities. However, criminological research is also conducted outside of the universities. The Ministry of Justice has its own Research and Documentation Center, which expanded to a large institute under Buikhuisen. The center is especially concerned with policy-related, applied research. The Ministry of Home Affairs also has a research department which is especially directed towards police studies.

At present, a debate is taking place in the world of Dutch criminology as to whether the independence of scientific research is endangered when conducted by agencies also responsible for policymaking. In some instances, a ministry may also ask a university institute to undertake a certain study, while providing the financial means. This research is important for decisions on problem-related policy. In practice, there is a fair amount of cooperation between university and nonuniversity institutes, but this could change, depending on the political climate. The Research and Documentation Center at the Ministry of Justice occupies a key position, because it advises, also in cases of pure university research, on permission for access to research material belonging to the judicial authorities (police reports, dossiers belonging to the public prosecutor's office, the courts, and so on).

Research not directly financed by a ministry is paid for out of university funds or by the Organization for the Advancement of Pure Research.

PATTERNS OF CRIMINOLOGICAL TEACHING

At Dutch universities, criminology is not only restricted to research; it is also taught. The emphasis used to be on teaching because the teachers were trained in law and had not received any specific training in research. One cannot study criminology as a major subject at Dutch universities (with the exception of the Free University of Amsterdam). Students usually choose the subject as part of another study such as Dutch law, sociology, psychology, pedagogy, or, sporadically, some other subject. One becomes a psychologist, or a criminal lawyer, with a certain specialization in criminology.

Criminology is not taught at any of the universities until after the candidate's examination. There are two important examinations in all university courses: the candidate's examination, which usually takes place two or three years after the beginning of the course; and the doctoral examination, after about five years. The doctorate is more or less comparable to the M.A. degree in the Anglo-Saxon system.

Anyone taking a course in criminology at a university does so within the framework of an academic study. Unlike the practice in some other countries, police officers in The Netherlands, for example, cannot simply take a course in criminology. There are police officers or probation officers studying at universities, but they are completing a normal university study of which criminology could be part.

In The Netherlands, criminology is a highly academic affair, but this is not to say that it is not taught anywhere else. It often appears in the curriculum at the Dutch Police Academy, a training institute for high-ranking police officers. The Central Recruitment and Training Institute of Dutch Prisons, where prison personnel receive their training, also teaches criminology at an elementary level. Finally, there are the social academies which train social workers and sometimes offer a course in criminology. These functionaries, police officers, prison guards, and probation officers are confronted with criminology because it is deemed important in the light of their profession.

OBSCURITY OF THE CRIMINOLOGIST'S STATUS

Where do those university graduates with criminology as a minor subject end up? Many of them do not find jobs in which knowledge of criminology is essential. They took the course as a matter of improving their "general knowledge," which means that they are more systematically informed about the phenomenon of crime than the man in the street. A criminal lawyer employed by the judiciary might be able to do something with his knowledge of criminology, although this is not certain; it depends on the university from which he graduated.

In The Netherlands there are no strong links between university training and one's profession, at least not as far as the social sciences are concerned. There are psychologists who have studied criminology as a minor subject and who are later engaged in personality research among criminals, but there are also psychologists engaged in the same sort of research without ever having attended a single lecture on criminology.

In the professional world of The Netherlands, a criminologist is a vague phenomenon, not clearly defined. Only at the university does he or she occupy a definite place: someone who is concerned in the widest sense with the study of the phenomenon of criminality. This somewhat marginal position is partly the result of the fact that criminology has developed only in the recent past. At the beginning of the 1960s, no more than ten people were occupied with the subject at the university level; at the beginning of the 1980s, this number had grown to around seventy, a relatively sharp increase over a twenty-year period.

BONDS AMONG SPECIALISTS IN CRIMINOLOGY

In 1974, The Nederlandse Vereniging voor Kriminologie (Dutch Society of Criminology) was founded, a fact which is in keeping with the development sketched above. In July 1979, the society had 110 members. Membership is open to people in The Netherlands whose main occupation is criminological research or teaching. They may or may not be employed within the framework of a university. The nonuniversity members include research-criminologists at the Ministries of Home Affairs and Justice; researchers or policymakers employed by the police, the prisons, and the Agency for Child Welfare; and teachers of criminology at such institutes as the Dutch Police Academy. It is therefore fundamentally a scientific society, aimed at promoting research and teaching in criminology and at applying the results of criminological research in the practice of the criminal justice system. The last-named aim has been somewhat neglected, which is hardly surprising considering the wide divergency of approaches in Dutch criminology: which results should be applied to what?

Since the society was founded, it has organized two congresses as an elaboration of the first goal: in 1975 on the theme of "Violence in Our Society," and in 1978 on "Moments of Decision in the Criminal Justice System." Moreover, the society organizes a one-day seminar each year on different subjects. The society's Committee on Teaching edited a Dutch-language study book with introductory essays on criminology, entitled *Tegen de Regels* (1977).

The *Nederlands Tijdschrift voor Criminologie* (which has appeared every two months as the *Tijdschrift voor Criminologie*, since 1977) was started in 1958 and also functions as a platform for the exchange of views and ideas. However, other scientific magazines also regularly publish articles with a criminological orientation, such as the journal for criminal law *Delikt en Delinkwent* and the *Sociologische Gids*.

Finally, it is worth mentioning that an important part of the debate on criminological issues takes place in daily and weekly newspapers to which several criminologists are attached as columnists. In the past years, criminologists have fought several battles before an audience of Dutch newspaper readers.

POLITICAL CONTEXT OF PUBLIC ISSUES

In general, Dutch criminologists differ only slightly in their views as to what their subject should encompass; they agree that it covers the study of the phenomenon of crime in the widest sense. This sphere includes the origin of rules of criminal law (definitions of criminal behavior), the transgression of those rules, and the reaction to such transgressions.

Interest in any one of these three themes is partly a question of political preference. In The Netherlands, all three, including the reaction to crime by official agencies, are subjected to research. The Netherlands is a parliamentary democracy, and to a certain extent criminological research into the functioning of such agencies such as the police, the public prosecutor, and the Child Welfare Agency is a means of public control. Research could show that police behavior is selective, or that the public prosecutor's decisions favor the middle and upper classes. Such research is possible in The Netherlands. The necessary material is available to the scientist, who is sworn to secrecy while the privacy of those concerned is guaranteed. This guarantee of privacy is a sensitive aspect since much of the debate on criminology takes place in dailies and weeklies before a general, interested audience.

The Dutch criminologist can afford to be fairly critical of the authorities' behavior, while still receiving the financial means to undertake his research. To a reasonable extent scientific freedom is guaranteed in The Netherlands, although it is frequently threatened, for example, by financial limitations. There is a tendency to reorganize the universities, shifting the emphasis to teaching and leaving the research in the lurch.

Of course, there is always the risk of science being abused for political or other ends, but that risk is somewhat minimized by the Dutch political system. A distinguishing feature of The Netherlands is the large variety of political and religious groups represented in Parliament through a system of proportional representation. There are three large groups: the Social Democrats, the Christian Democrats, and the Liberals. None of these, however, can claim a majority in Parliament so that a coalition of two of the three is the only possible means of government. In practice, this does not mean that the third party is entirely cut off from political decision-making.

Politically speaking, the Christian Democrats usually occupy the center position, with the Social Democrats to the left and the Liberals to the right. But this is not the case in all of the political issues that are important in The Netherlands. From a socioeconomic point of view, the Social Democrats are closer to the Christian Democrats than are the Liberals. In the field of law and morality, there is more agreement between the Social Democrats and the Liberals than there would be in a Liberal-Christian Democrat coalition. Bills are regularly passed by a parliamentary majority made up of representatives from both government and opposition parties.

It is impossible for a single party to usurp power completely. Moreover, several small groups are represented in Parliament alongside the three large ones. Indeed, they have often split off from the larger parties, which have to be constantly on their guard against groups of renegades. The identity of the big parties is more or less "guarded" by the small ones which take a more extreme stand. They all watch each other carefully, and there is less risk of Parliament becoming an affair where the choice is really one of six or two of threes. Each group wants to see at least part of its own program realized. This system of competitive groups, which is also reflected in sociocultural life, for example, in the radio and television system, is responsible for a reasonable and moderate public climate.

MODERATION AND MILD SANCTIONS

This moderation is especially apparent in the sentences passed by Dutch judges. Although comparison with other countries is almost impossible because of differences in penal codes and judicial policies, the sentences in Holland do appear to be milder than those of other countries. This is a popular notion in The Netherlands, often voiced by some newspapers and by "the man in the street." Rumor has it that many foreigners come to The Netherlands to commit crimes because the sentences are so mild. Bank robbers, who could expect a fifteen-year sentence in Italy, France, or Belgium, would escape with five years at the most in The Netherlands; it is, therefore, worth one's while to rob a Dutch bank. The truth of such allegations has never been examined; they remain extensions of a widespread notion that punishment in The Netherlands is too mild when compared to that of other countries. In criminological literature, it is often stated that in The Netherlands the number of prisoners per 100,000 inhabitants is the lowest in the world.

Doleschal has compared the figures for The Netherlands with those for Denmark, Sweden, and the United States.[1] The low rate in The Netherlands ("the lowest rate of imprisonment in the world") is often explained as follows. Prominent Dutchmen were incarcerated in prisons and concentration camps during the German occupation (1940-1945), and their experiences are said to have had some effect on policy so that long prison sentences have become less self-evident that they used to be.

This explanation is probably incorrect. To start with, people do not usually learn much from experiences. Furthermore, why have there not been similar developments in other countries also occupied by Germany during World War II, such as Belgium, Denmark, or Norway? Indeed, there likely is no single explanation, although the sociocultural and political system of The Netherlands is partly responsible for the low rate of imprisonment. None of the large groups important in political decision-making can afford to take an extreme stand. Moreover, neither the public prosecutors nor the judges attach much value to imprisonment as a punishment. A committee, officially appointed by the minister of justice, is seeking to design alternative penal sanctions as a means of eliminating imprisonment even further.

In this regard, the role of the press is also important, for it is fairly critical of the state's behavior. Although on occasion some newspapers write sensational and rash articles on crime, they do not do it all the time. Politicians responsible for policy are not incited daily to reintroduce capital punishment (abolished in The Netherlands except in military law, in 1870). Voices are sometimes raised in Dutch society calling for the death penalty, but not very loudly. These sporadic outbursts may become more persistent; there are no guarantees that new circumstances will not make feasible a demand for the reintroduction of capital punishment. Punishments and provisions, long vanished from criminal law, may return someday.

INCIDENCE OF CRIME IN HOLLAND

Finally, what is the state of affairs with regard to crime itself, a phenomenon with which both criminology and the criminal justice system are concerned? As in other countries, the "increase in crime" is a fairly popular subject in The Netherlands, but a particular sort of crime is seldom specified. *Crime* is increasing; *therefore*, we must have more police. Briefly, this is the topic of many conversations. The agency responsible for the regular publication of data on the state of affairs and development of recorded criminality in The Netherlands is the Central Statistics Bureau. The most enlightening statistics—notwithstanding all the limitations that apply—are those on crimes that have come to the knowledge of the police. This is the lowest level of registration.

In Dutch statistics, four main categories of crime are distinguished; these categories are based on provisions in the penal code. From the point of view of behavioral science, there should probably be other classifications, but as yet this is out of the question in Dutch criminology. In the meantime, we must make do with the classification used by the Central Statistics Bureau.

The main categories are: *crimes against property*, such as theft, burglary, and fraud; *aggressive crimes*, such as murder, manslaughter, assault and battery, and the destruction of property; *sexual crimes*, such as rape, sexual assault, and offenses against public decency; and *traffic crimes*, such as hit and run, drunken driving, and culpable manslaughter.

The population of The Netherlands numbers about fourteen million inhabitants. In 1978, a total of 561,798 crimes came to the knowledge of the police; in 1976, the figure was 519,490. The following figures show the percentage of crimes from the four different categories per 100,000 inhabitants between the ages of twelve and seventy-nine: crimes against property 3,500 per 100,000; aggressive crimes 600 per 100,000; traffic crimes 600 per 100,000; and sexual crimes 50 per 100,000 inhabitants. By far the largest category is that of crimes against property, with simple theft and burglary comprising about half of all recorded crime. The most noteworthy of the serious crimes are (attempted) murder and manslaughter; in 1978, 1,100 crimes of this nature came to the knowledge of the police. Fatalities due to aggressive crime (apart from traffic violations) number less than two hundred. Destruction of property and, to a lesser degree, assault and battery, are the most prominent aggressive crimes. When viewed over a longer period of time, sexual crime seems to be decreasing, mainly because of a change in judicial policy with regard to offenses against public decency (such as pornography). During the past years, there have been several suggestions for liberalization in this field. The crime of rape, also considered a sexual crime, is slowly increasing, although the rate of recorded instances is fairly low (735 cases in 1978). Of late, the feminist movement has aroused interest in the seriousness of this crime. Traffic crime is increasing with a certain regularity, which is linked with the growing number of car owners. The most frequent crime in this category is drunken driving; about three thousand Dutchmen are killed on the road each year.

FINAL COMMENT

In general, criminality in The Netherlands is not particularly spectacular. It more or less reflects the nature of Dutch society. Were that society to change drastically in the 1980s—because of long-term, widespread unemployment, for example, because of a change in the relationship between work and spare time, or because of tension between the Dutch and the ethnic minorities living in The Netherlands—one could expect the pattern of criminality to change too.

NOTE

1. Eugene Doleschal, "Rate and Length of Imprisonment—How Does the United States Compare with The Netherlands, Denmark and Sweden?" *Crime and Delinquency* 23 (January 1977):51-56.

BIBLIOGRAPHY

The following list of references includes works employed in the analysis of criminology in this chapter. Also included are references believed to be of special interest to readers.

The Netherlands and Criminology

Bianchi, Herman. "Social Control and Deviance in The Netherlands." In Herman Bianchi, Mario Simondi, and Ian Taylor (eds.). *Deviance and Control in Europe*. London: John Wiley and Sons, 1975. Pp. 51-57.

Goudsblom, Johan. *The Dutch Society*. New York: Random House, 1967.

Jongman, R. W., S. J. Steenstra, and G. A. van Bergeijk (eds.). *Geweld in onze samenleving* [Violence in Our Society]. 's Gravenhage: Staatsuitgeverij, 1978.

Van Dijk, J.J.M. "Attitudes Toward Crime in The Netherlands." *Victimology: An International Journal* 3 (1978):265-273.

Van Weringh, Jac. *Onrust is van alle tijden: Opstellen over criminaliteit in Nederland* [Fear Is Timeless: Essays on Criminality in the Netherlands]. Meppel: Boom, 1978.

Treatises in Criminology

Bonger, W. A. *An Introduction to Criminology*. London: Methuen and Company, Ltd., 1936.

Buikhuisen, W. *Kriminologie in biosociall perspektief* [Criminology in Biosocial Perspective]. Deventer: Kluwer, 1979.

Dessaur, C. I. *Foundations of Theory-formation in Criminology: A Methodological Analysis.* The Hague: Mouton, 1971.

Fiselier, Jan, and Ellie Lissenberg (eds.). *Tegen de Regels: een inleiding in de criminologie* [Against the Rules: An Introduction in Criminology]. Utrecht: Ars Aequi Libri, 1980.

Kempe, G. Th. *Inleiding tot de criminologie* [Introduction to Criminology]. Haarlem: Bohn, 1967.

Nagel, W. H. *Het voorspellen van krimineel gedrag* [Prediction of Criminal Behavior]. 's Gravenhage: Staatsuitgeverij, 1965.

Zwanenburg, M. A. *Prediction in Criminology.* Nijmegen: Dekker en Van de Vegt, 1977.

Conceptions of Criminology

Bianchi, Herman. *Basismodellen in de kriminologie* [Basic Models in Criminology]. Deventer: Van Loghum Slaterus, 1980.

Buikhuisen, W. "An Alternative Approach to the Etiology of Crime." In S. A. Mednick and S. G. Shoham (eds.). *New Paths in Criminology.* Lexington, Mass.: Lexington Books, 1979.

Hoefnagels, G. Peter. *The Other Side of Criminology: An Inversion of the Concept of Crime.* Deventer: Kluwer, 1973.

Landman, Richard J., and Jac. van Weringh. "De wereld van Aletrino" [The World of Aletrino]. *Tijdschrift voor Criminologie* 19 (1977):144-155.

Moedikdo, Paul. "De Utrechtse School van Pompe, Baan en Kempe" [the "Utrecht School" of Pompe, Baan and Kempe]. In C. Kelk and M. Moerings (eds.). *Recht, Macht en Manipulatie* [Law, Power and Manipulation]. Utrecht/Antwerpen: Het Spectrum, 1976. Pp. 90-154.

Nagel, W. H. "De Groningse School I and De Groningse School II" (two articles on the Heymans approach in Dutch criminology). *Nederlands Tijdschrift voor Criminologie* 8 (1966):81-93 and 122-135.

Nagel, W. H. "Politiek en kriminologie" [Politics and Criminology]. In *Waarde, Macht, Kriminologie* [Values, Power, Criminology]. Studium Generale Erasmus University Rotterdam. Den Haag: Martinus Nijhoff, 1974. Pp. 3-25.

Peters, T., and Jac. van Weringh (eds.). "De actualiteit van Bonger" [The Importance of Bonger for the Present Day]. Special issue of *Nederlands Tijdschrift voor Criminologie* 18 (1976):145-217.

Factors in Criminality

Bonger, W. A. *Criminality and Economic Conditions.* Boston: Little, Brown and Company, 1916.

Bonger, W. A. *Race and Crime* New York: Columbia University Press, 1943

Kempe, G. Th. *Criminaliteit en Kerkgenootschap* [Criminality and Church Denomination]. Utrecht: Dekker en Van de Vegt, 1938.

Van Dijk, J.J.M. *Dominantiegedrag en geweld* [Dominance Behavior and Violence]. Nijmegen: Dekker en Van de Vegt, 1977.

Van Rooy, H. *Criminaliteeit van Stad en Land: Nijmegen en omstreken* [Crime in the City and the Countryside]. Utrecht: Dekker en Van de Vegt, 1949.

Issues in Justice Administration

Fiselier, J.P.S. *Slachtoffers van delicten* [Victims of Crime]. Utrecht: Ars Aequi Libri, 1978.

Jongman, R. W. *Ongelijke kansen in de rechtsgang* [Inequality in the Criminal Justice System]. Assen: Van Gorcum, 1972.

Lissenberg, Ellie. *Kinderen spreken recht* [The Jurisprudence of Youth]. Alphen aan den Rijn: Samson, 1979.

Moerings, M. *De gevangenis uit, de maatschappij in: de gevangenisstraf en haar betekenis voor de sociale contacten van ex-gedetineerden* [Out of Prison, into Society; Prison Detention and Its Effect on the Social Contacts of Ex-prisoners]. Alphen aan den Rijn: Samson, 1978.

Moor, L. Gunther, and E. Leuw (eds.). *Beslissingsmomenten in het strafrechtelijk systeem* [Moments of Decision in the Criminal Justice System]. Utrecht: Ars Aequi Libri, 1978.

23

NEW ZEALAND

Neil Cameron

To date, criminology in New Zealand may be described as highly disorganized, with little contact between even its academic practitioners and with no central physical or intellectual focus. It exists primarily within the universities. While a few government departments make use of criminological expertise in their research and planning sections, none of the personnel involved would describe themselves as criminologists.

Even within the universities, criminology exists largely as an adjunct to other disciplines. Only two universities currently teach criminology courses as such, and in only one of these is the teaching under the auspices of an autonomous criminological institute. Furthermore, such teaching as exists is not especially research-oriented, being offered largely at the undergraduate (first-degree) level as an element of a general "liberal" education.

With one or two exceptions, research can be best characterized as criminal justice research rather than as strictly criminological. That is, it tends to focus on reactions to crime and the operation of criminal justice agencies rather than on the explanation of crime as such. It is in this sense a legal and administrative criminology—at both the university and government levels. In the university, it is heavily influenced by legal perspectives and legal research methods and orientations. In government departments, it is embedded largely within the legal/law reform structure rather than the welfare/correctional structure.

THE SETTING FOR CRIME AND CRIMINALS

New Zealand has long prided itself on being a stable, homogeneous, multicultural society with a basic commitment to the ideas of equality, social welfare, and individual liberty.[1] Until quite recently this pride was largely justified. Political conflict and dissent were muted and easily accommodated within the existing political party and labor union structures. Real poverty was rare and well concealed, and extreme wealth was nonexistent. Cultural and racial differences were largely submerged under a veneer of homogeneity achieved by the suppression of all but the rhetoric of the multicultural society.

Over the last two decades, however, this image has become somewhat tarnished. A generally worsening economic climate, the reemergence of widespread unemployment, the rediscovery of poverty and manifest inequality, and the destruction of traditional cultural and political ties—all of these developments have challenged the traditional virtues of New Zealand life.

Population

Physically, New Zealand is larger than the United Kingdom and smaller than Japan.[2] Its population of just over three million is predominantly European, drawn essentially from British emigrant stock. The indigenous Maori population makes up just over 9 percent of the total, and there are significant Chinese and Pacific Island minorities.

Until the mid-1960s, Pacific Island migration to New Zealand was very limited.[3] By the mid-1970s, in the context of a high overall immigration rate, the number of migrants from the Cook Islands, Niue, Fiji and Western Samoa had increased significantly—so much so that they had come to be seen as a "problem," at least by some politicians. Since 1976, the immigration rate has declined, largely as a result of a deliberate government policy. Indeed, since 1976, New Zealand has experienced a consistent net population loss because of emigration.

The years since 1945 have also seen significant internal changes, particularly within the Maori population. In 1945, 28.4 percent of the total population and 74.3 percent of the Maori population lived in communities with less than 1,000 inhabitants. By 1976, these figures had dropped to 17 percent and 23.8 percent, respectively, and just over 50 percent of the population lived in centers with 25,000 inhabitants or more. The largest urban area, Auckland, contained 804,000 inhabitants, just over a quarter of the total population.

Economy

Despite the continuing development of urban-based light industry and the increasing importance of manufactured goods in the export statistics, New Zealand remains heavily dependent on agriculture.[4] On average, well over two-thirds of the annual value of New Zealand's exports comes from farm and forest products, and the country is a leading world exporter of butter, wool, meat, and cheese.

Such an economy—with its heavy reliance on imported fuel, consumer goods, and technology—is very vulnerable to external changes. In recent years, and especially since the entry of the United Kingdom into the European Economic Community, New Zealand has been faced with the erosion or loss of traditional overseas markets, worldwide agricultural protectionism, spiralling fuel and transportation costs, and a rapidly rising general import bill. Domestically, these difficulties have manifested themselves in relatively high inflation and unemployment rates, a real reduction in the overall standard of living, and strenuous efforts by the government to cut spending and to encourage investment and diversification.

Culture

Although New Zealand is a Pacific nation with an economy that is dependent upon agriculture, its culture is essentially European and urban. Modern New Zealand's roots are British, and it is from the urban cultures of Britain and North America that New Zealand's cultural identity comes. Maori and Polynesian culture has had little impact on mainstream New Zealand life except as an adjunct to the tourist trade or as an interesting curiosity.

Political and Social Policy

New Zealand is a liberal democratic welfare state.[5] Its political culture emphasizes concepts of democratic representation, the rule of the law, and the open scrutiny and restriction of governmental power. Its welfare system is extensive and well funded. In 1977-1978, government expenditure on social services alone accounted for a massive 27 percent of total expenditure.[6]

The parliamentary system is built around a unicameral legislature, triennial elections, and two major political parties. Both of these parties are publicly committed to the maintenance of the welfare system, the achievement of full employment, the rapid development of such natural resources as New Zealand possesses, and the restructuring of New Zealand industry. Similarly, there is basic political party agreement on the need to protect civil liberties, maintain law and order, and preserve the egalitarian ideology that underpins much of New Zealand's cultural and political life. In spite of separate Maori representation in Parliament, government and administrative policies towards minorities have generally been overtly assimilationist.

In short, New Zealand's political and social system can probably be best characterized as that of a classic Western, liberal democratic, welfare-oriented, consensual society. The hegemony of the white, urban middle class has rarely, if ever, been subjected to serious challenge; when it has been, such challenges have been easily assimilated or defused.

A Changing Climate

Much of this picture is now changing. Urban drift and changes in migration patterns have created the beginnings of a significant Maori and Pacific Island proletariat in the major cities, especially Auckland. The last decade or so has seen the belated rediscovery of poverty and social inequality in New Zealand. Industrial conflict has intensified and has taken on increasingly political overtones. Unemployment, inflation, and cuts in government spending on medical, educational, and welfare services have inevitably fallen most heavily on the least privileged sections of the community. Economic and racial inequalities that could be concealed in times of prosperity and full employment have reemerged.

This process has been accompanied by the growth of a number of Maori groups and organizations which are beginning to provide an explicit political and cultural challenge to European society. The welfare state itself has come under increasing attack—both from the left and the right—and the two-party system has been challenged both by new party formations and by the specter of internal dissolution. At the same time, the last few years have seen a developing governmental retreat from consensus politics and at least the partial erosion of some of the traditional constitutional protections and conventions. In particular, there has been a marked decline in the status and power of Parliament vis-à-vis the executive.

CRIMINAL JUSTICE IN NEW ZEALAND

Until recently, crime in New Zealand was unremarkable. Its steady increase and social cost were deplored, and its causes and cure were considered to be mysterious but generally susceptible of discovery. Today crime is increasingly part of the political culture, with some using it as a symbol of the destruction of traditional virtues and others as a symptom of repression and inequality. Similarly, criminology in New Zealand has generally been pragmatic, liberal, and overtly apolitical. Today this status is also in the process of change, and a new, more critical perspective is emerging under the somewhat belated influence of overseas trends and in response to the manifest changes that are taking place in New Zealand society.

Criminal Law

Criminal law in New Zealand is codified. Major offenses appear in the Crimes Act of 1961, and more minor offenses in the Police Offenses Act of 1927 and in specialist legislation. It is difficult to look at the statute book without concluding that New Zealand, like many other Western nations, is inclined to see the criminal law as a panacea for most social ills and to legislate accordingly. Hence, much of the law and, more importantly, much of the enforcement activity involve minor, nuisance-type behavior. Recent efforts to decriminalize some minor offenses and to reform restrictive abortion and homosexuality laws have been singularly unsuccessful.

The Police

New Zealand has had a centralized national police force since 1886. The modern force is unarmed and is under the control of a commissioner drawn from the ranks of the force itself. While the commissioner is appointed by the government of the day and is ultimately responsible to the minister of police, his position as regards the running of the Police Department and the setting of law enforcement policy is an independent one.

Within the police, specialist sections deal with drugs, vice, juvenile offenders, fraud, terrorism, and armed offenders. The Ministry of Transport or local authority traffic departments handle traffic offenses. Training and recruitment are centralized and of a fairly high standard, with recruitment and in-service training extending well beyond the traditional police-skills courses. At the commissioned officer level, for example, the training program includes a compulsory paper in criminology. The Police Department is increasingly recognizing the need for university training for its more senior officers and for specialist personnel, and is currently sponsoring the development of a Diploma in Police Studies at one of the main universities.

The Courts

Most criminal cases are tried summarily before full-time, legally trained judges in the district court. Some traffic cases and the preliminary hearing of cases that are to be tried on indictment are heard by part-time lay justices. More serious cases may be tried on indictment before selected district court judges or, in the most serious cases, before a high court judge. Trial on indictment generally means trial by judge and jury, and in practice it is rare, with both defendants and the police preferring the summary process. In recent years, only about 2.5 percent of those eligible for jury trial have in fact selected it.[7] Jury verdicts must be unanimous.

In minor cases, prosecution is undertaken by the police themselves. In more serious cases, either Crown counsel (a local lawyer in private practice specially appointed to handle police prosecutions when called to do so), or a member of the Crown Law Office is employed. The Crown Law Office provides general legal advice and assistance to the government and to government departments and is under the control of the solicitor-general.

Legal assistance is available to the accused by way of a state-funded legal aid scheme and, at an earlier stage in the process, through the operation of a duty solicitor scheme. No offender may be imprisoned unless he has had or has been offered and refused legal representation.

Children and Young Persons

There is a distinct court structure for offenders under the age of seventeen, the children and young persons court. It is presided over by a district court judge and adopts an informal court-based form of procedure. The minimum age of criminal responsibility is ten. With the exception of homicide, children under the age of fourteen may not be prosecuted for offenses per se. Instead, they are handled either informally or before the court as children in need of care, protection, or control. Young persons between the ages of fourteen and seventeen can either be prosecuted in the children and young persons court in the usual way or dealt with by way of the care procedure provided for the younger age group. There are a number of informal screening and diversionary bodies designed to keep children and young persons out of the justice system as far as possible.

The Penal System

The New Zealand penal system is similar to the systems of most other Western nations. It is built around the prison and around a judicial sentencing structure. From time to time, New Zealand has experimented with various types of indeterminate sentences. However, such sentences—even in the heyday of positivist influence on New Zealand in the early 1900s—have always been limited in their application. Today, few vestiges of indeterminacy remain, and even the parole system is restricted to sentences of five years or more. Such sentences constitute a very small proportion of the prison sentences passed in any one year.

Apart from imprisonment, the major sentences available for adult offenders are the fine, probation, and periodic detention. Periodic detention is a comparatively recent development and involves the offender in a compulsory period of community work, generally over the weekend. Probation exists both as a sentence in its own right and as a form of after-care for prisoners released on parole and for many of those who—while not eligible for parole—are released on remission prior to the expiration of their sentences. For younger offenders, borstal and detention center training are also available. Borstal training at present involves a sentence of up to two years in a special youth institution, with earlier release at the discretion of parole board. Detention center training involves a three-month custodial sentence. Both of these sentences are currently under review and are likely to be replaced in the near future. Offenders under seventeen years of age and those found to be in need of care and control can also be placed under the supervison or care of the Social Welfare Department.

By international standards, New Zealand has a relatively high imprisonment rate.[8] In 1978, its rate was 146.9 per 100,000. In the same year, two new prisons were completed, and planning and construction continued on three more.[9]

The Ministry of Justice

The courts, law reform, and the penal system all come under the control of the Justice Department. The minister of justice generally is a lawyer and holds the post of attorney-general. The department is responsible for both the prison service—which includes borstal and detention centers—and the probation service—which supervises offenders released on both probation and parole, operates probation hostels, and runs the periodic detention scheme.

The department is also heavily involved in the task of criminal law reform. It is responsible, for example, for the Criminal Law Reform Committee which is a voluntary, part-time body made up of lawyers drawn from the universities, private practice, and the Justice and Police Departments. This committee makes reports from time to time, but by and large its work has not produced much legislative activity. In fact, law reform initiatives more commonly come from the two major government departments concerned—police and justice. In addition to a general law reform division equipped with legally trained staff, the Justice Department has a planning division with a small research section engaged primarily in criminal justice research.

PATTERNS OF CRIME AND CRIMINALITY

Since 1945, New Zealand has experienced a steady increase in all categories of crime. Politically, the most explosive issues are violence and drug offenses. For violence at least, the degree of political concern is scarcely borne out by available statistics.[10] Insofar as drug offenses are concerned, there has undoubtedly been a serious increase in the use of both "hard" and "soft" drugs over the last decade. Little explanation beyond the corrupting influence of sundry unidentified "Mr. Bigs" has been offered. Police sources suggest that the drug trade is beginning to provide a nucleus for large-scale organized crime. Whatever the reality of the situation, the perception of a growing drug "menace" has precipitated a number of legislative measures increasing police powers of search and seizure, restricting access to bail for certain types of suspects, encouraging the imposition of severe prison sentences, and restricting access to parole.

In terms of criminality, a distinctive feature of crime in New Zealand is the massive overinvolvement of Maori and Polynesian groups in crime and in the penal system. Between them these groups make up under 10 percent of the population; yet, they constitute roughly 30 percent of the cases brought before the district courts and up to 40 percent of those sentenced to imprisonment. This effect is even more marked as regards Maori and Polynesian women. It also becomes much more noticeable when one turns to the younger age groups. Thus, nearly 70 percent of those sentenced to borstal training are Maori or Polynesian, as are nearly 60 percent of those committed to the care of the Department of Social Welfare.

Socially and politically, this situation is exacerbated by popular conceptions of Maori and Polynesian culture which tend to equate the "Maori crime problem" with the problem of violence generally. Thus, one theme in the prevalent European view of Maori and Polynesian life stresses the cultural acceptability of violence within such groups and the existence of a generalized disrespect for property and other European values. Maori and Polynesian groups thus tend to be seen as undersocialized—as coming to New Zealand from the Pacific Islands or as migrating to the cities from the countryside with inadequate preparation for coping with the realities of European culture.

In fact, the basic equation between Maori and Polynesian crime and violence is scarcely supported, even by official data.[11] Nevertheless, it is a potent stereotype that provides a politically unthreatening explanation for the "problem." It shifts responsibility to the minority group itself and fits well with the general scapegoating of such minorities. It also provides part of the ideological under- pinning for the government's attempts to reduce immigration from the Pacific Islands and to expel those illegal Island immigrants whose labor is no longer needed by New Zealand's contracting economy. Furthermore, it provides an explanation that is consistent with the dominant view of New Zealand as an egalitarian, multicultural, tolerant society that treats its minorities well. Other explanations for the phenomenon—for example, those based on economic and social disadvantage and discrimination and especially on labeling—are less ac- ceptable and hence much more muted.

In recent years, Maori gangs have been defined as a further crime problem, at least as part of the political culture. This "problem" began in the mid-1960s as the so-called bikie gang. Over the last five years or so, it has developed into a much wider phenomenon, with such gangs emerging as relatively well-knit groups that are increasingly challenging the more traditional tribal and commu- nity structures in the Maori milieu. They are also beginning to articulate political grievances and to develop, in conjunction with other more overtly political Maori groups, a political and cultural challenge to European society. While such gangs only become sporadically involved in serious offenses, their general behavior is highly marginal and their publicity value immense. Their activities and their treatment by the police and the media tend to highlight the violent Maori youth stereotype discussed earlier.

Hence, the major problems of special criminological interest in New Zealand are probably: (1) Maori and Polynesian offenses; (2) drugs; (3) violence; and (4) gangs, predominantly Maori gangs. The usual interests, of course, also exist in juvenile and white-collar crime, crime rates generally, and so on. They are, however, somewhat secondary to the major political concerns.

CRIMINOLOGY AS AN OCCUPATION

New Zealand possesses few, if any, criminologists. Criminology is not a discrete discipline either in the universities or in the public service. Such crimi- nological endeavor as is performed is conducted by specialists in other fields with an interest in criminology or some branch of it, or by public servants involved in research and policy formulation. In short, while there is a steady low-level demand for criminological expertise, it is not presently sufficient to provide a significant number of people with either a full-time occupation as criminologist or with a secure criminological career structure.

The nearest that New Zealand comes to full-time criminology is in the Institute of Criminology at Victoria University, Wellington. The institute comprises a full-time director, one staff member involved almost full-time in teaching, and three research fellows. Other universities offer criminology courses both at the graduate and undergraduate level, but the personnel involved are not generally occupied in such courses or in criminological research on a full-time basis. In the public service area, a number of bodies deal in criminological research, but this work is also interspersed with other research and, often, with other duties. Hence, it, too, scarcely merits the appellation "criminology."

Criminology, then, does not constitute a separate occupational field in New Zealand. The professional criminologist can exploit openings in both the universities and the public service, but at present the jobs available tend to be defined in such a way as to inhibit an exclusive concentration on criminology. What are these openings and how attractive are they likely to be to the professional criminologist, both now and in the future? Two general areas are of importance here, the public service and the universities.

Public Service Opportunities

A number of government departments have specialized research and/or planning units that offer some chance of employment to the criminologist. In particular, the Justice Department Planning and Development Division employs a number of researchers in the general criminal justice system area. Similarly, the Social Welfare Department employs some research personnel both in its own research unit and under the aegis of a body called the Joint Committee on Young Offenders. (For a more detailed discussion of the organization and work of these bodies, see "Types of Criminological Research" below.)

In neither of these departments are the research tasks likely to be exclusively criminological, and the scope for occupational advancement beyond research officer is limited if a central interest in criminology is to be retained. Such positions are unlikely to be attractive for long to the person who views himself/herself as a professional criminologist.

Other departments—especially the Transport Department and the Department of Maori Affairs—offer some scope to criminological researchers, but the opportunities are very limited. Similarly, there may be some scope for a criminologist, or at least for criminological expertise, in bodies such as the Secretariat of the New Zealand Planning Council. This council, set up in 1977, advises the government on planning for social, economic, and cultural development. It has a full-time secretariat drawn from most branches of government, including the Justice and Social Welfare Departments.

University Opportunities

Most of New Zealand's universities offer courses on deviant behavior and/or criminology. Auckland University offers diploma and certificate courses in criminology and a range of graduate and undergraduate units. The Victoria University of Wellington has three courses in the criminological area taught by the institute, as well as a number of graduate and undergraduate units in deviance and the criminal justice system taught in the sociology, psychology, and law departments. The University of Canterbury offers criminology and deviance courses in law and sociology, respectively. Otago University has courses in deviance and the administration of criminal justice.

These bodies provide fairly extensive teaching opportunities for criminologists drawn from particular parent disciplines, especially law. Yet, only at the institute in Wellington is the teaching of criminology likely to be sustainable as a full-time interest. Elsewhere, teaching and perhaps research in other areas will also have to be undertaken. While the usual system of academic advancement applies to such a teacher, his chances of promotion qua criminologist are small; as indicated earlier, the only full-time post for a criminologist in New Zealand is that of director of the Institute of Criminology in Wellington. While the number of courses in criminology offered in New Zealand universities will probably increase over the next few years, especially at Victoria University, it is unlikely to be accompanied by any significant increase in employment opportunities for criminologists at the university level.

The undeveloped nature of criminology as an occupation in New Zealand is demonstrated further by the lack of any systematic means of communication between persons working in the field. New Zealand does not as yet have a professional association and a professional newsletter or journal, or even a criminological section within the New Zealand Sociological Association. Communication between practitioners is related more to the institution and the city in which the individual works and lives than to his or her criminological interests per se. This situation is now changing. Since late 1979, the institute in Wellington has begun to provide a focus for future association and debate; the first professional conference has already been arranged.

TEACHING CRIMINOLOGY IN NEW ZEALAND

New Zealand has no formal system for the recruitment and training of criminologists. Recruits are attracted to the university criminology scene largely on the basis of their parent discipline, lawyers with an interest in criminology teach criminology and criminal justice courses in the law schools, and so on. They are attracted to the public service area because of their research interests and skills rather than their specific criminological orientation. Public service criminologists tend to be drawn from general social science backgrounds rather than from any specifically criminological base.

At the university level, those who teach criminology—and related units such as criminal justice and deviant behavior—have received no formal criminological training or have received it at overseas universities. This situation is scarcely surprising as criminology was not really taught as a subject in New Zealand universities until the mid-1960s. Since then, instruction has been directed primarily at professional groups (social workers, police, prison officers) and at general education (second year arts courses in B.A. degrees) rather than at training criminologists.

For the future, the training of criminologists in New Zealand seems to depend on two universities, Auckland and Wellington. At present, only Auckland offers courses directly relevant to training criminologists as such, a certificate course and a diploma. The institute in Wellington currently offers a number of general courses only, but is now developing a more professionally oriented graduate degree.

The Auckland certificate course is directed primarily at students drawn from probation, the police, the prisons, and social welfare and voluntary organizations. It covers a wide range of crime and law-related subjects, with no special emphasis on criminology per se. More importantly, the university also offers a full-time diploma in criminology. This course is taught within the Law Faculty and is divided into two parts.

Students must do papers in criminal law and criminology (both taken from the basic LL.B. degree) and a number of other papers selected from approved first-year courses in sociology, anthropology, education, philosophy, or psychology. They must also do papers in criminal etiology, penal policy, crime and its prevention in New Zealand, and research methods in criminology. Candidates for the diploma with honors must in addition complete a dissertation on a topic approved by the dean of the Faculty of Law. The diploma attracts a small number of students each year. Most are currently employed or intend to make careers in either the criminal justice agencies or teaching.

In Wellington, the hope for proper professional training centers around the Institute of Criminology. This institute was set up in 1975 as an independent body within the university. It is funded partly by direct government grant and partly through the university. At present, it teaches three undergraduate courses in criminology. It does no postgraduate teaching and has no postgraduate students. Its major teaching responsibility is a full-year, second-year course in general criminology. It also teaches two half-year, third-year courses in criminal justice administration and in crime and punishment. Students cannot major in criminology. In practice, students taking the two third-year units tend to be drawn from social work, police, prison, and justice staffs.

Providing little opportunity for professional criminological training, this structure is currently under review. Over the next few years, it seems likely that it will be replaced by a properly structured M.A. in criminology and a range of undergraduate courses designed to permit students to major in the subject. There are also plans to introduce a certificate in criminology directed specifically at the needs of the Justice and Police Departments.

With the possible exception of the Auckland diploma, the teaching of criminology within New Zealand universities is somewhat piecemeal. It is generally directed either at general liberal educational ends or at providing for the needs of police, welfare, and correctional personnel. It is mostly taught within law faculties, and it often appears in the guise of courses in criminal justice or the sociology of deviant behavior. It is likely that the development of new courses at the Institute of Criminology in Wellington will improve this situation considerably, but it is also likely that for some time to come potential New Zealand criminologists will continue to get their training, or a substantial part of it, overseas.

TYPES OF CRIMINOLOGICAL RESEARCH

Criminological research in New Zealand has no distinctive form. Until now, it has followed the interests and needs of the various disciplines and government departments. The limited amount of research is usually directed at criminal justice rather than specifically criminological problems. That is, it tends to focus on the identification and processing of offenders rather than on the explanation of crime.

Some idea of the major concerns and orientations of researchers in New Zealand can be obtained from the bibliography at the end of this chapter. A clearer picture emerges if we look at the types of research currently being undertaken in various research settings and at the major sources of research funds.

Universities

At the general university level, there is a certain amount of activity in terms of research papers and theses. In terms of staff research, the only major project seems to be a study of Maori gangs and reactions to them based in the Auckland Law Faculty. Other studies on police stress and on the effectiveness of particular penal measures are also in progress.

The Institute of Criminology

This body is currently involved in historical research and in a government-funded project on violence in New Zealand. Some preliminary papers on this topic have been published over the last couple of years. This project is ending, and planning for a number of new projects is underway, including a major study of sentencing in the superior courts.

The Justice Department

The research effort of the Justice Department has recently been reorganized and now comprises two areas: fairly large-scale studies produced by the research section of the Planning and Development Division; and smaller study papers on criminal justice topics of immediate concern to the department, also produced within the division. Logically enough, the output of this division tends to be related to the everyday work of the Justice Department rather than to such areas as the etiology of crime. In addition to projects conducted by the research unit, some officers in the department's other divisions—for example, psychological services and probation—have research aspects to their work. Research currently being undertaken by the department includes a study of drug violations and the impact of recent changes in the law in this area; a study of legal needs in the community; a study of rape and the criminal justice system; and a study of probation recidivism.

The Department of Social Welfare

The research section of this department is made up of two distinct units. The first, the social unit, is concerned with research on such topics as social work, juvenile crime, and provision for children in the care of the department. The second unit, the economic unit, is concerned more with the benefits and social security aspects of the department's work.

The department also houses and services the research unit of an interdepartmental committee, the Joint Committee on Young Offenders, that was established in 1958 and comprises representatives of the Departments of Police, Justice, Education, Social Welfare, Maori Affairs, and Internal Affairs. Its general task is to coordinate the activities of the departments represented in planning, implementing, and evaluating programs to minimize delinquent behavior by children and young persons, and to promote programs by government and other agencies which will minimize such behavior. To date, the research section of the Joint Committee has produced reports on such subjects as the role of race and socioeconomic status in Maori offenses, the background characteristics of juvenile gang members, the prediction of recidivism among juvenile offenders, and sentencing in the children's court.

Even this brief list shows that the interests of the research units within the Department of Social Welfare are somewhat broader than those of the Department of Justice. It should be noted, however, that much of the work done by the social and research units of the Joint Committee is for internal consumption only and has never been published.

Other Departments

Some research with a criminological flavor is occasionally undertaken in other government departments. For example, the Department of Internal Affairs has in the past done work on work cooperatives, youth clubs, detached youth worker programs, and similar delinquency prevention schemes. Similarly, both the Transport and the Police Departments have produced some research in their own areas of expertise. Little of this work has been published.

Research Funding

In regard to the major question of funding, modest research projects usually excite a good deal of interest and are likely to be funded relatively easily.

Large-scale projects are likely to run into serious funding problems and to face further problems engendered by a lack of basic criminological expertise and research experience.

Research funds are available for suitable projects from such sources as internal university grants, interested government departments, the New Zealand Council for Educational Research, the social science research fund of the National Research Advisory Council, private charitable bodies, industry-based bodies like the Liquor Advisory Council, and special interest groups like the National Society for Alcoholism and Drug Dependence. In addition, the National Research Advisory Council funds a number of fellowships each year which may be available for criminological research. More importantly, the Justice Department is responsible for the funding of two research fellows at the Institute of Criminology, which at present comprises roughly two-thirds of that body's research manpower.

It needs to be emphasized that many of the major sources for research funds in New Zealand are directly or indirectly funded by the government. This is especially so where large-scale projects are concerned.

CONCLUSIONS: CURRENT STATUS AND PROSPECTS

As indicated at the beginning of this chapter, criminology is still in its infancy in New Zealand. Professionally, it is weak and disorganized. Academically, it is dependent on other disciplines, and its energies are dissipated by geography and by academic fragmentation. At the governmental level, its influence is weak and its practitioners scattered. Insofar as it has a distinctive character, it is pragmatic and administrative. The research that exists is dominated by legal and administrative concerns and is often tailored specifically to the needs of particular government bureaucracies. New Zealand criminologists have engendered little controversy and not much enthusiasm. They have made no significant impact beyond their own immediate students or government departments.

Much of this situation, however, may be starting to change. Specifically, the Institute of Criminology is likely to start providing a new, coherent professional leadership in terms of both teaching and research. It will accordingly begin to act as a focus around which a distinctive criminology will have some chance of emerging. New Zealand has the seeds of a professional, more critical criminology and has a social and political environment that cries out for one. Any such development will undoubtedly be very slow and will, at least for the next few years, be very much at the mercy of a rapidly changing economic, social, and political environment.

NOTES

1. Most of the material in this section was taken from the *New Zealand Official Yearbook 1979* (Wellington: Government Printer, 1979).

2. Ibid., pp. 51-68.

3. D. Bardman, "Polynesian Immigrants: Migrating Process and Distribution in New Zealand," in S. Webb and J. Colletta (eds.), *New Zealand Society: Contemporary Perspectives* (Sydney: John Wiley, 1973), p. 318.

4. *New Zealand Official Yearbook 1979*, pp. 539-587.

5. For a recent general discussion of New Zealand's political culture, see L. Cleveland, *The Politics of Utopia: New Zealand and Its Government* (Wellington: Methuen, 1979).

6. *New Zealand Official Yearbook 1979*, pp. 651-654. Overall expenditure on health, education, and social services accounted for 56 percent of total government spending.

7. *Report of the Royal Commission on the Courts* (Wellington: Government Printer, 1978), p. 369.

8. I. Waller and J. Chan, "Prison Use: A Canadian and International Comparison," *Criminal Law Quarterly* 17 (1975):47-71.

9. *Annual Report of the Department of Justice for the Year Ended 31 March 1979*, Parliamentary Paper E.5 (Wellington: Government Printer, 1979).

10. M. Schumacher, *Violent Offending*, Justice Department Research Series No. 2 (Wellington: Government Printer, 1971). Also see the *Report of the Select Committee on Violent Offending, 1979*, Parliamentary Paper I.18 (Wellington: Government Printer, 1979), pp. 8-13.

11. P. T. O'Malley, "The Influence of Cultural Factors on Maori Crime Rates," in Webb and Collette, *New Zealand Society*, p. 386. See also A. D. Trlin, "Immigrants and Crime: Some Preliminary Observations," *New Zealand Society*, p. 397.

BIBLIOGRAPHY

This bibliography covers selected books, monographs, and research reports that relate specifically to crime and criminology in New Zealand or that draw to a significant extent on New Zealand data. It does not include material published in New Zealand or written by New Zealanders in New Zealand which is concerned only with crime and criminology in general. Neither does it include references to periodical articles on crime in New Zealand or to unpublished and parliamentary material. Information on such material can be obtained from two useful reference works:

Northey, J. K. (ed.). *Index to New Zealand Legal Writing*. Auckland: Legal Research Foundation Inc., 1977; and *1977 Supplement*.
White, S., and A. Edwards. *Criminological Materials in the Parliamentary Papers of Australia and New Zealand from 1901*. Canberra: Australian National University, 1977.

The bibliography is arranged according to the source of the material and gives some indication as to how it can be obtained.

Annual Reports and Statistics

Annual Report of the Department of Justice, Parliamentary Paper E.5.
Annual Report of the Prisons Parole Board. Parliamentary Paper E.5.A.
Annual Report of the Borstals Parole Board. Parliamentary Paper E.5.B.

Annual Report of the New Zealand Police. Parliamentary Paper G.6.
Annual Report of the Department of Social Welfare. Parliamentary Paper E.12.
All of these reports are available from the Government Printer, Wellington. The various departmental reports contain statistical material and useful analyses of current policy and problems.

Justice Department Publications

BOOKS

Crime and the Community. Wellington: Government Printer, 1964.
An early discussion of the New Zealand penal system and of penal policy, with an emphasis on community involvement.

Crime in New Zealand. Wellington: Government Printer, 1968.
An overview of major offenses in New Zealand, with some discussion of relevant overseas descriptive and causal literature.

MONOGRAPHS AND STUDIES

The Research Series

No. 1. Schumacher, M. *Waipiata—A Study of Trainees in an Open Borstal Institution* (1971).
A straightforward follow-up study of a sample of youths released from a minimum security youth institution. Characteristics and "success."

No. 2. Schumacher, M. *Violent Offending* (1971).
A descriptive study of serious violent offenders tried in the high court and of general trends in violent crime.

No. 3. Roberts, J. *Self-Image and Delinquency* (1972).
A study of self-image in a sample of girls in a youth institution.

No. 4. Gibson, R. E., and C. Ma'auga. *Periodic Detention in New Zealand* (1973).
A descriptive study of youth and adult periodic detention, with some limited follow-up material on offenders released from the youth centers.

No. 5. Hampton, R. E. *Sentencing in a Children's Court and Labelling Theory* (1975) (out of print).
An application of labeling "theory" to a sample of offenders referred to and sentenced in the children's court.

No. 6. Parsons, K. R. *Violence on the Road: A Logical Extension to the Subculture of Violence Thesis?* (1978).
An attempt to analyze serious traffic offenses involving injury or death in terms of the subculture of violence hypothesis.

No. 7. Oxley, P. *Remand and Bail Decisions in a Magistrate's Court* (1979).
An analysis of the criteria used by the police and the courts in assessing eligibility for bail and of the effects of bail refusal on an accused. Sample drawn from Wellington in the early 1970s.

No. 1 in this series is available only from the Justice Department, Wellington. Nos. 2-4 and 5-7 are available from the Government Printer.

The Study Series

No. 1. *Survey of Pleas in Supreme Court Trials* (1978).
A brief survey of pleas and trends in pleas in Auckland and Wellington. Some discussion of plea negotiation and the incidence and effects of legal representation.

No. 2. *Study of Preliminary Hearing Procedure Before Committal for Trial* (1978).
An analysis of the early results of the introduction of an abbreviated procedure for preliminary hearings in serious criminal cases.

No. 3. *Study of Young Persons Remanded in Custody to a Penal Institution* (1979).
A discussion of the incidence, circumstances of, and alternatives to remanding offenders under the age of seventeen to adult prisons.

No. 4. *Periodic Detention; A Comparison of Residential and Non-Residential Centers* (1979).
A follow-up to the 1973 research report noted above. Purports to show that "success" rates for the two types of periodic detention are similar.

No. 5. *Probationers and Their Reoffending* (1979).
A study of the characteristics and recidivism of a sample of probationers.

These five studies are available from the Planning and Development Division of the Department of Justice, Wellington.

MISCELLANEOUS

Engel, P. R. *The Abolition of Capital Punishment in New Zealand, 1935-1961*. Wellington: Justice Department, 1977.
A first-class discussion of the abolition debate and of New Zealand's unique vacillation over the death penalty.

Mayhew, P. K. *The Penal System of New Zealand 1840-1924*. Wellington: Justice Department, 1959.
Written initially for internal consumption only, this book provides a useful description of and commentary on the New Zealand penal system from its inception.

Social Welfare Department Publications

RESEARCH REPORTS

No. 2. Fergusson, D. M., A. A. Donnell, and S. W. Slater. *The Effects of Race and Socio-Economic Status on Juvenile Offending Statistics* (1975).
An analysis of a prospective sample of school children seeking to isolate and distinguish the influence of racial and socioeconomic factors on court appearance before the age of seventeen.

No. 3. Fergusson, D. M., A. A. Donnell, S. W. Slater, and J. K. Fifield. *The Prediction of Juvenile Offending: A New Zealand Study* (1975).
An application of the Bristol Social Adjustment Guide to a sample of New Zealand school children.

No. 4. Fergusson, D. M., J. K. Fifield, S. W. Slater, and A. A. Donnell. *New Zealand Validity Data for the Bristol Social Adjustment Guide* (1976).
Validity data accompanying the study noted above.

No. 5. Fergusson, D. M., J. K. Fifield, and S. W. Slater. *Social Background, School Performance, Adjustment and Juvenile Offending: A Path Analytic Model* (1976).
A further analysis of data obtained in the study noted above.

All these reports are available from the Government Printer, Wellington.

MISCELLANEOUS

Fergusson, D. M., J. Fleming, and D. O'Neill. *Child Abuse in New Zealand*. Wellington: Government Printer, 1972.
A general survey of the incidence, reporting, and causes of child abuse in New Zealand.

Institute of Criminology Publications

OCCASIONAL PAPERS

No. 2. Robson, J. L. *The News Media and Criminal Justice* (1976).
A general discussion of the role of the New Zealand media as regards the reporting and discussion of crime and criminal justice matters. With examples.

No. 5. Burnett, R. *Executive Discretion and Criminal Justice: The Prerogative of Mercy: New Zealand 1840-1853* (1977).
A descriptive study of the exercise of the prerogative of mercy in early New Zealand.

No. 8. Stace, M. *Schoolboy Vandalism in the Hutt Valley: Preliminary Analysis* (1978).
A report on a small self-report study on vandalism and minor delinquency among schoolboys.

No. 9. Burnett, R. *Penal Transportation: An Episode in New Zealand History* (1978).
A descriptive study of transportation from New Zealand to Australia up to 1854.

All of these papers are available from the Institute of Criminology, Victoria University, Wellington.

General Publications

Black, W. A. M., and A. J. W. Taylor (eds.). *Deviant Behavior: New Zealand Studies*. Auckland: Heinemann Educational Books, 1979.
A collection of psychologically oriented articles reprinted from New Zealand and overseas journals. A few are of some value, and the bibliography indicates the somewhat bizarre concerns of early New Zealand criminology.

Blizard, P. J. (ed.). *Juvenile Delinquency in New Zealand*. Wellington: Wellington Social Sciences Section of the Royal Society of New Zealand, 1967.
A collection of largely descriptive essays on juvenile delinquency and its treatment in New Zealand.

Clark, R. S. *Essays on Criminal Law in New Zealand*. Wellington: Sweet and Maxwell, 1971.
Legally oriented essays on criminal law and the criminal justice system. Uneven quality and interest.

Glyn, J. F. *The New Zealand Policeman*. Wellington: Government Printer, 1975.
A general discussion of the role, both traditional and emerging, of the police in New Zealand.

Holland, K. J. *Police Unionism in New Zealand*. Student Research Papers in Industrial Relations No. 5. Wellington: Victoria University Industrial Relations Centre, 1978.
An excellent study of the development and significance of police unionism in New Zealand.

McKenzie, D. F. *While We Have Prisons*. Wellington: Methuen, 1980.
Anecdotal material on the New Zealand prison system coupled with a discussion of likely and unlikely reforms.

Nixon, A. J. *A Child's Guide to Crime*. Wellington: A. H. and A. W. Reed, 1974.
A somewhat whimsical introductory text on crime in New Zealand. Described by one reviewer as the "Monty Python of the South Pacific."

Report of the Royal Commission on the Courts. Wellington: Government Printer, 1978.
A useful survey of the development, structure, and operation of the present court system and of projected developments in caseloads. Some of the suggested reforms have now been implemented.

Seymour, J. A. *Dealing with Young Offenders in New Zealand—The System in Evolution*. Occasional Pamphlet No. 11. Auckland: Legal Research Foundations Inc., 1976.
A very useful description of the development of the juvenile justice system in New Zealand up to and including the Children and Young Persons Act of 1974. Some valuable social and political analysis.

24

NIGERIA

Oluyemi Kayode

Legal scholars and social scientists, especially sociologists, have tried to explain crime in Nigeria and have suggested measures for its control. Nevertheless, criminology is very much in its infancy in Nigeria. The country has no systematically developed publications, and its commitment to criminological investigation is rather low. Only a modest contribution has been made to undertstanding the Nigerian crime situation. Social scientists are apt to conclude, rather hastily perhaps, that policymakers are not interested in academic research findings. Such pessimism and superficial attention to a subject matter undermine the growth of an academic discipline. Time is, of course, a crucial factor in determining the maturity of a scientific pursuit; unfortunately, academic interest in crime came late in Nigeria.

This chapter deals with the Nigerian crime situation and with the development of criminology as an academic discipline. Its three main themes center on the Nigerian socioeconomic scene; the incidence of crime from about 1945 to the present; and the growth of criminology and its impact on social policy.

THE SOCIOECONOMIC SCENE IN NIGERIA

With 890,000 square kilometers of territory, Nigeria represents the largest single political entity on the West African coast. The country took its name from the Niger which, along with the Benue River, represents Nigeria's most striking physical feature. The most populous African state with 66,510,000 inhabitants,[1] Nigeria has three major ethnic groups—Hausa-Fulani, Ibo, and Yoruba—and over a hundred other linguistic groups. Military conquests and cultural assimilation have fused many groups into the three large, culturally homogeneous groups and a few prominent "minority" ones.

Political Evolution

Nigeria came into being on New Year's Day 1914 with the amalgamation of the then Colony of Lagos and the Protectorate of Southern Nigeria, on one hand, and the Protectorate of Northern Nigeria, on the other. From that date, Nigeria passed through various stages of colonial rule until 1960 when the British government granted the country its political independence. Exactly three years later to the day, Nigeria became a republic within the Commonwealth.

The euphoria generated by the swift movement toward nationhood had hardly died down when a series of political crises precipitated the intervention of the armed forces. On January 16, 1966, the Nigerian armed forces took over from the Council of Ministers that had completely lost control of the machinery for effecting law and order. But the political confusion continued with a countercoup, the expensive holocaust of a civil war, another countercoup, an unsuccessful countercoup, and persistent rumors of attempted military insurrections. The implementation of plans to return Nigeria to civil rule is at an advanced stage at this writing. If the soldiers return to their barracks as hoped, the military interregnum in Nigeria would have spanned almost fourteen years.

High but Uneven Economic Growth

The Nigerian economy has experienced tremendous growth within the last decade or so, attributable to vast petroleum resources. Between 1966 and 1975, the economy grew at a high rate of 8 percent, compared with a 4-percent growth in the 1950s and a 5-percent growth between 1960 and 1965.[2] From 1961 to 1974, the gross domestic product (GDP) tended to increase in the long term (see Table 24-1), but the trend was interrupted in fiscal years 1967-1968 and 1968-1969 when the civil war ravaged the country, reaching its peak in 1969. Government efforts to rehabilitate the war victims and to stimulate the economy explain the sharp rise in the rate of growth between 1970 and 1972.

The growth rates for 1960-1975 have varied among the main sectors of the Nigerian economy: manufacturing, building and construction, and oil and mining, in that order. The agricultural sector, on the other hand, has declined steadily. During the 1961-1962 fiscal year, agriculture, forestry, and fisheries contributed 61.7 percent of the GDP, but only 40 percent in 1973-1974, and its all-time low of 23 percent in the 1978-1979 fiscal year.

The persistent decline of these industries is due largely to the increased prominence of petroleum in the economy, but Nigerian agriculture is not prospering. The productivity of the average farmer is dropping; the weather has not always been predictable.[3] More important, however, is the factor of rural-urban population drift. Because life on the farms and in rural areas is perceived as less and less rewarding, the younger and more able-bodied quit the drudgery and placid way of village life to embrace the apparently more rewarding attractions of the cities.

TABLE 24-1
NOMINAL GROSS DOMESTIC PRODUCT FOR NIGERIA, 1961-1978

Year	GDP (in ₦Millions)	Rate of Change
1961-1962	2,362.6	—
1962-1963	2,597.6	9.9
1963-1964	2,755.8	6.1
1964-1965	2,894.4	5.0
1965-1966	3,110.0	7.4
1966-1967	3,374.8	8.5
1967-1968	2,752.6	−18.4
1968-1969	2,656.2	−3.5
1969-1970	3,549.3	33.6
1970-1971	5,281.1	48.8
1971-1972	6,650.9	25.9
1972-1973	7,187.5	8.1
1973-1974	8,452.7	17.6
1974-1975	18,553.7	119.5
1975-1976	21,326.8	14.9
1976-1977	26,956.3	26.4
1977-1978	31,992.0	18.7

Source: Federal Office of Statistics, *Annual Abstract of Statistics.*

Inflation

In recent years, prices in Nigeria have been inflationary. If 1960 is taken as the base year, Table 24-2 shows the movement of the consumer price index for the 1960-1977 period.

In this period, the general consumer index rose over 400 percent, while the price index for food rose even higher. The phenomenal increase in the two indices which started in 1970—coinciding with the end of the civil war—has continued unabated. The economic implication of this phenomenon for the average Nigerian is that it costs more to keep body and soul together. The revenue generated by petroleum resources and the determination of the federal government to speed up infrastructural development and the provision of social services are responsible for the sharp and steady increase in the money supply since 1973. In the midst of rising expectations, the relatively fixed incomes, and the increasing cost of living, the temptation to resort to any means of surviving the apparent cruelty of the economic arrangement becomes great.

TABLE 24-2
MONEY SUPPLY AND CONSUMER PRICE INDEX, 1960-1978

Year	Money Supply (in Million ₦)	Consumer Price Index (1960 = 100)	
		All Items	Food
1960	240.7	100.0	100.0
1961	243.0	106.4	109.8
1962	252.4	112.0	118.0
1963	268.6	108.9	106.7
1964	305.2	110.1	105.7
1965	316.9	114.4	110.5
1966	344.9	125.5	133.1
1967	313.4	120.8	119.3
1968	328.1	120.3	112.6
1969	426.8	132.3	133.9
1970	608.4	150.6	164.4
1971	628.9	174.1	211.4
1972	700.2	179.6	216.6
1973	827.2	189.3	223.6
1974	1,178.4	214.7	258.7
1975	2,044.1	287.4	367.2
1976	3,293.0	348.2	465.7
1977	4,794.6	423.1	592.2
1978	4,894.9	479.1	631.2

Source: Central Bank of Nigeria's *Economic and Financial Reviews.*

URBANISM AND FAILURES OF EDUCATION

Migration to urban centers is not a recent phenomenon in Nigeria, and the attractions offered by towns to rural dwellers in African societies are too obvious to demand a restatement here.[4] Closely tied to the persistent influx of young people into the cities is the serious problem of unemployment.

With an educational system geared towards acquiring literacy rather than vocational skills, Nigerian primary and high schools turn out hundreds of thousands of graduates annually who roam the streets of the major towns in search of white-collar jobs. Arikpo describes the situation in the early 1960s:

Every year a vast and growing number of primary school leavers entered the Nigerian labor market. Their seven or eight years in primary schooling have been devoted mainly to the three R's, they had acquired no practical skills by the end of the course. They had neither the training nor the desire to take up agriculture or any skilled vocation, and sought paid employment in government for which they were virtually disqualified by their level of education and in which opportunities were fast shrinking in relation to the number of qualified school leavers. *Neither the primary school leavers themselves nor their peasant parents wanted a return to the traditional subsistence farming of the rural areas with all its drudgery and physical fatigue.* [Emphasis mine.][5]

The situation of secondary (high) school leavers during the same period was just a shade better. As the economy expanded and diversified into manufacturing, mining, building, and construction in the late 1960s and beyond, this class of school graduates became increasingly unsuited for the skills that the expanding sectors of the economy required. Added to this burgeoning increase of school-leavers in urban centers is the class of persons without any formal education who subsist on the meager incomes that come their way through manual work. Lacking a skill and any educational accolade, they are the most vulnerable to seasonal fluctuations in employment.

DEVELOPMENT POLICIES AND SOCIAL INEQUITIES

Nigeria has the problem of inequalities between the relatively few wealthy persons and the mass of the society and between urban centers and the rural areas. (See Table 24-3 for evidence of the persistent inequity of income distribution.) Government policies on economic development have aggravated the problem.

TABLE 24-3
PERCENTAGE SHARES OF GROSS INCOMES GOING TO POPULATION GROUPS OF DIFFERENT INCOME LEVELS IN NIGERIA

Year	Poorest 10 Pct.	Poorest 20 Pct.	Middle 40-60 Pct.	Highest 20 Pct.	Highest 5 Pct.
1969-1970	8.5	27.0	10.0	56.0	40.0
1970-1971	8.0	27.5	11.0	57.0	41.0
1971-1972	7.5	28.0	13.5	58.0	47.0
Average	8.0	27.5	11.5	57.0	40.7

Source: E. A. Etim and F. N. Eronini, "Personal Income Distribution in Nigeria" (1975).

Rise of Elites

The exit of the colonial civil servants created a vacuum that was gradually filled by indigenous citizens. With each top position came lavish fringe benefits for the new incumbent; the Nigerian top civil servant inherited a taste for the exclusive living standards designed by the British Colonial Office for its officers in the then colony of Nigeria. An elegant house on a half-hectare plot in a fashionable area of town designated Government Reservation Area (GRA), a servant's quarter to match, an automobile acquired with government loan, a generous monthly allowance to run it, a maintenance allowance for each child, and a paid annual vacation were some of the benefits for the new senior civil servant.

Nigerian entrepreneurs, middlemen, and landlords also benefited from the policies of the immediate post-independence government. Because there was a shortage of indigenous capital for industrial and business ventures, the national and regional governments established banks, corporations, and other institutions with public funds to ensure the liberalization of credit facilities for indigenous businessmen and would-be industrialists. Thus emerged the first set of Nigerian entrepreneurs, middlemen, and landlords.

The Nigerian Enterprises Promotion Decree of 1972 gave this group of Nigerians a much-needed "shot in the arm." Conceived as a strategy of consolidating "our political independence by doing all we can to promote more participation by Nigerians in our economic life,"[6] the decree stipulated that certain categories of foreign enterprises in Nigeria should be wholly or partly owned by Nigerians. Although no thorough examination of the consequences of this decree has been carried out, its implications for social arrangements cannot be overemphasized as the most effective single instrument for the institutionalization of a powerful indigenous business class in Nigeria.

Such is the extent of inequalities in Nigeria that 5 percent of the population controls about 40 percent of the gross income. This disparity in income levels is translated into concrete and highly obvious distinctions between the "haves" and the "have nots." The most expensive automobiles grace Nigeria's rickety and pothole-ridden highways; tastefully furnished mansions dot its vast slums. Lavish social gatherings offer opportunities for ostentatious display of wealth in the presence of impoverished bystanders. In a country without mass public transportation, with an erratic supply of electricity, with hospitals short of medical personnel and drugs, and where practically "nothing works," the Nigerian rich person has frequent opportunities to distinguish himself from his less privileged compatriot.

Favoring of Urban Areas

The inequalities between urban areas and their rural surroundings stem from government policies of concentrating public institutions, industrial projects, and large-scale employment-generating agencies in urban centers. The availability of social services (electricity, pipe-borne water, paved roads) and amenities (hospitals, commercial banks) has become exclusively urban and partly explains the constant movement of people from rural to urban areas as a permanent feature of Nigerian life. Constant wage reviews and incessant clamor for better working conditions have made salaried persons and wage-earners a privileged minority when compared with the living standards of the peasant farmers and other nonurban workers.

Recognizing the dangers posed by gross social inequalities to the social order, the federal government in its Second National Development Plan (1970-1974) set as one of the objectives the establishment of "a just and egalitarian society." To achieve this objective, the government intended to take measures to "minimize existing inequalities in wealth, income and consumption standards which may tend to undermine production efficiency, offend a sense of social justice and endanger political stability."[7] The Third National Development Plan shared these sentiments; two of the plan's objectives were to achieve a more even distribution of income and a reduction of unemployment. The lofty goal of "a just and egalitarian society" has remained an elusive possibility. The yawning gap between the rich business class and senior salaried persons, on the one hand, and the low-income salaried persons, petty traders, peasant farmers, and the unemployed who together constitute the bulk of the population, on the other hand, appears to be widening. The Nigerian Enterprises Promotion Decree of 1972 and the massive salary increases early in 1975—retroactive to April 1974—have substantially contributed to income disparity.

CRIME: ITS MEASUREMENT AND PATTERNING

Now we turn to the incidence of criminal activities, their varieties, and the measures aimed at controlling them. Table 24-4 shows the annual rate of crime in Nigeria from 1947, the earliest year for which police data are available.

Limitations of Crime Data

At this point, it is appropriate to note the limitations of the figures in Table 24-4. For a number of reasons, they capture only a portion of the crimes perpetrated in the years covered.

Prior to 1968, there were two parallel police forces in the country: the Nigerian Police Force controlled by the federal government, and the Native Police Forces controlled by the then regions. Although the Nigerian Police Force had countrywide jurisdiction before 1968, the various native forces had authority to deal with certain offenses within their jurisdictions. These local forces were largely incompetent and dependent on the political leaders controlling the given region. The crime reports they sent to the Nigerian police are very suspect.

The second reason for caution stems from factors affecting public willingness to report crimes to the police: the society's level of awareness and sophistication, its level of technology (especially communication and transportation), and the vigor with which laws are enforced.

Much of the crime information that reaches the police in Nigeria is derived from a fraction of the population. A large portion of the country, geographically speaking, remains almost unpoliced; about 75 percent of the Nigerian Police

TABLE 24-4

RATE OF CRIME BASED ON OFFENSES KNOWN TO THE POLICE, 1947-1976

Year	All Offenses Against Person and Property and Miscellaneous Offenses	Offenses Against Local Ordinance (Excluding Motor Traffic Offenses)	Total No. of Offenses	Population of Nigeria (Estimates)[a]	Rate of Crime per 100,000
1947	32,540	8,722	41,262	23,745,000	173.77
1948	34,834	9,448	44,282	24,000,000	184.50
1949	46,516	9,065	55,581	24,000,000	231.58
1950	42,179	8,980	51,159	24,300,000	210.53
1951	49,451	7,180	56,631	25,000,000	226.52
1952	48,619	6,191	54,810	29,600,000	185.16
1953	42,550	5,060	47,610	35,875,000	132.71
1954	61,429	7,811	69,240	36,772,000	188.29
1955	62,424	14,356	76,780	37,691,000	203.70
1956	52,854	14,159	67,013	38,633,000	173.46
1957	60,824	13,259	74,083	39,599,000	187.08
1958	67,107	15,496	82,603	40,589,000	203.51
1959	68,354	12,534	80,888	41,604,000	194.42

Year				
1960	66,766	12,137	78,903	42,644,000	185.02
1961	75,409	11,495	86,904	43,710,000	198.81
1962	80,393	12,512	92,905	44,803,000	207.36
1963	88,668	13,490	102,158	45,923,000	222.45
1964	92,277	12,762	105,039	47,071,000	223.15
1965	105,314	11,825	117,139	48,248,000	242.78
.	.	.	.	.	.
.	.	.	.	.	.
.	.	.	.	.	.
1972	146,341	7,576	153,917	57,351,000	268.37
1973	156,696	5,106	161,802	58,785,000	275.24
1974	NA	NA	NA	NA	NA
1975	180,983	12,652	193,635	61,760,000	313.52
1976	194,063	20,223	214,286	63,305,000	338.50

Source: Annual Reports of the Nigerian Police Force; Nigeria Yearbook, mimeograph, 1976.

[a]1947-1952 figures are based on U.N. Demographic Yearbook Estimates. All the other figures are taken from O. O. Arowolo, "Growth of the Population of Nigeria" (unpublished mimeograph, 1976).

NA = not available.

Force is stationed in state capitals and other major urban centers where only 25 percent of Nigerians live. The ratio of police officer to population is roughly 1 per 1,800. Even where police posts are physically within reach, the nonavailability of telephone services is a constraint on reporting crime incidents. In addition, the average Nigerian has tremendous distrust of the police; only serious crimes are usually reported.

In spite of these limitations, the figures in Table 24-4 should provide a sufficient basis for examining the trends in criminal behavior. Fluctuations in reported offenses against local ordinances deprived the absolute number and rate of total crimes of consistent direction of change between the years 1947 and 1960. The total rate was lowest for 1953 (132.7 per 100,000 inhabitants) and highest in 1951 (226.52 per 100,000 inhabitants). After a steady increase from 1947 to 1951, the rate started to fall until 1954. Thereafter, the rate fluctuated over the years, with the period between 1960 and 1965 showing consistent increases.

There were no published official data for the years 1966 to 1971 because of the civil war and its attendant upheavals which disrupted the government machinery. With a sizable portion of the country severed from the rest politically, that area could and did not send crime returns to Lagos. Besides, the resources of the Nigerian Police Force—its strength drastically reduced by large-scale desertion in the political crisis—were stretched almost to the breaking point. Gathering crime figures under these conditions was a low priority.

The rates for 1972 and 1973 conform to the 1960-1965 trend. Although data after 1974 are not available, it appears reasonable to expect continuing increases in crime rates.

Police crime returns are rendered under four offense categories in order of importance: offenses against persons, offenses against property, offenses against local ordinances, and "other offenses." Prior to 1956, all offenses, with the exception of those against local ordinances, were usually lumped together, thus making intergroup comparisons over time difficult.

Crimes Against Property

Except for 1956 when crimes against property accounted for only 48 percent of all offenses known to the police, offenses against property have consistently accounted for over half the total offenses. The percentage has risen above the 56 percent mark four times—1961, 1962, 1972, and 1973. When figures for the period after 1974 are available, we expect the crimes against property to represent an even greater share of all offenses.

This trend appears understandable, given the socioeconomic context of criminal behavior. In a growing free enterprise economy with unchecked migration into the cities, where economic differentials between groups are growing and increasingly visible—these circumstances favor the underprivileged using theft as an illegal redistribution of wealth. Among crimes against property, thefts, burglary, housebreaking, and storebreaking account for 80 to 90 percent in a given year.

Crimes Against Persons

A post-civil war phenomenon is armed robbery, the forcible dispossession of a victim of his money or other property by an armed assailant. In the confused situation of the civil war and its abrupt ending, many sophisticated military weapons found their way to the streets through thousands of army deserters and the hurriedly assembled men of the "Biafran" army. Suddenly relieved of their military duties, these ex-soldiers took to the streets robbing persons and killing for a living. The situation became so grave that the federal government had to promulgate a decree in 1970 stipulating a twenty-one-year prison term or death by firing squad upon conviction. Subsequently, Armed Robbery Tribunals headed by high court judges were set up in each state capital to cope with the volume of cases arising from the enforcement of the decree. The public execution of condemned armed robbers has become a routine event attracting huge crowds of spectators. Whether the government's rather harsh punitive reaction has reduced the spate of violent robbery incidents has not yet been empirically ascertained.

Among the category of offenses against persons, assaults (both minor and grievous) constitute between 70 and 75 percent of the total volume in any one year. In terms of level of reportability, murder and manslaughter are the most important offenses in this group. Their contribution to the total was around 5 percent in the years 1956 to 1959, 5.23 per cent in 1956, 5.55 percent in 1957, 5.24 percent in 1958, and 4.53 percent in 1959. The percentage declined consistently, from 3.69 percent in 1964 to 2.58 percent for 1973. The situation with rape and indecent assault is slightly different; although its share of the total number of offenses against persons also showed a decrease over time, between 1956 and 1959 it experienced a vacillating trend: 3.34 percent for 1956, 4.26 percent for 1957, 3.95 percent for 1958, and 4.17 percent for 1959. Between 1960 and 1973, available figures point to a consistent decrease from 4.19 percent in 1961 to 2.42 percent in 1973.

In the absence of any systematic compilation of data on white-collar crimes, the best one can do is to speculate on the volume of such offenses over time. But such a speculation—if not very guarded and restrained—is likely to be fraught with erroneous conclusions. In a significant sense, the amount of such offenses that become known to the police is a function of the number of commissions of inquiry set up by the government to probe specific public agencies or institutions. Because such inquiries—prior to 1966 when the military took over government—were largely underpinned by political motives, the findings of such commissions call for critical assessment. The prominence given to the 1975 mass public-service purge and the sensationalism with which Nigerian newspapers are apt to report allegations of white-collar offenses have tended to confirm the impression that the incidence of this type of offense has assumed such unprecedented proportions. No doubt there is a massive amount of bribery, fraud, and corruption in Nigeria, but given the consensual nature of many of these offenses, it is extremely difficult to draw reliable conclusions from the information obtained on them.

POLICE AND LAW ENFORCEMENT

As cautioned earlier, the volume of crime known to the Nigerian police represents some unknown fraction of the total offenses actually committed. This situation is not peculiar to Nigeria. The divergence between the "actual" and the "known" is of concern to the criminologist, and the amount of this divergence is a function of the effectiveness of the police agency and the confidence the public has in its personnel.

Among the stated objectives of the Nigerian police are the prevention and detection of crimes, the apprehension of offenders, the preservation of law and order, the protection of property, and the enforcement of all laws and regulations with which they are directly charged.[8] The prevention of crimes before they are committed and the detection of those perpetrated constitute a critical aspect of police functions. Through a well-organized and coordinated patrol system, a reasonable measure of success can be achieved.

Patrol activities are so restricted, sporadic, and ineffective that a significant proportion of would-be offenders are convinced they can escape detection. The Nigerian police are severely limited by lack of facilities, equipment, and human resources. More public cooperation is needed to facilitate police investigation as a consequence of the "widespread belief that he who sincerely tries to be of assistance (in police investigation) is somehow involved in the offense."[9]

The ineffectiveness of the police in clearing offenses and recovering stolen property has been well documented. Of the 106,165 and 110,019 offenses reported to the Nigerian police in 1960 and 1961, respectively, only about 66,000 and 75,000 of them were dealt with at all. In the same period, about N3 million worth of property was reported stolen and only 15 percent was recovered; the comparable percentage for 1964 and 1965 was about 17 percent.[10] An empirical study of records for May 1969 to April 1970 at the Ibadan Center Police Station showed that, in 70 percent of the offenses known to the police, there were no suspects for the crime.[11]

With a staff of 45,000 in 1975,[12] the police are grossly undermanned; this partly explains the virtual nonexistence of community services. The acute shortage of men has reduced the police to crime-fighters to the detriment of the diversification of police functions found in Western societies. Furthermore, the Nigerian police lack equipment for achieving stated objectives: a properly equipped and maintained scientific laboratory, transport, communications, specialized and sophisticated equipment, and office accommodation.[13]

Even where citizens are in real need of police help or protection they find it impossible to reach the nearest police post because of lack of communication conveniences; and when it can be reached the average police post is miserably short of essential equipment. The chances that its own telephone is out of order are quite high; not to mention the inavailability of service-rendering or crime-fighting equipment like motor vehicles and efficient telecommunication links with neighboring units.[14]

Nigerian policemen do not carry arms except when on special assignment, and the caliber of weapons borne on such occasions is rather antiquated and ineffective. This policy may have to be revised in view of the continuously increasing sophistication of offenders. In light of the absence of a well-staffed and well-remunerated force, it will be improper to blame ineffective law enforcement solely on the Nigerian police.

SENTENCING AND PUNISHMENT

Sentencing practices in Nigeria follow the orientations of retribution, deterrence, prevention, and rehabilitation. Retribution, fairly prominent in the English legal tradition, was handed down to Nigeria by successive generations of English-trained administrators and judges. The essence of this sentencing philosophy is that "the punishment must fit the crime"; thus, while petty theft carries a maximum three-year jail term, a serious stealing charge attracts up to a seven-year prison term. Some amount of discretion is allowed the court in handing down a sentence—within the range stipulated by the law—according to the gravity of the offense and the circumstances of the accused.

Deterrence plays a prominent role in Nigerian sentencing. The faith of legislative bodies in the efficacy of deterrence is demonstrated by the permeation of much of criminal legislation in the post-1966 era by this philosophy; mandatory death sentences, severe punishment for specific offenses, minimum sentences, and the like, became a recurring feature of the Nigerian criminal code.[15]

The prevention approach emphasizes the protection of members of the society by disabling the offender, but the rehabilitation orientation is aimed at ensuring that the offender is given the opportunity within prison walls to readjust socially to the community, the norms of which he had violated. Dispositions for petty offenses include caution and discharge, binding over the offender to keep the peace, conditional or unconditional discharge, and probation.

The four orientations should be seen as interconnected aspects of the Nigerian sentencing approach, as is demonstrated by the uses made of the prison, which receives by far the majority of court convictions in Nigeria.[16] The extent to which the Nigerian prison system fulfills any of these sentencing requirements is yet to be empirically explored.

The rehabilitation of incarcerated offenders has long been one of the stated objectives of the Nigerian prison system, but more than a decade ago the director of prisons confessed: "Not much has, however, been done in connection with the rehabilitation of prisoners because both the government and the public have not been cooperative enough."[17] The director went further to blame the government for not making much needed funds available.

Low salaries limited promotion chances, and the unwillingness of policymakers to undertake reforms has raised barriers against improvements in the quality of the staff. Most of the staff is illiterate or almost so. Because the staff lacks adequate training, "the prisoner population is geting more, far more, intelligent than the staff."[18] Adeyemi and Idada, in a study of the Nigerian prison system, found that five after-care officers were provided in the prison department estimates for 1948-1949 and that twenty years later (1978) their numbers were the same.[19] The prison service finds it difficult to attract professionals like lawyers, psychologists, sociologists, and social workers; the ones who give the prison system a try soon quit for more rewarding jobs.

Prison facilities are too congested and filthy for the physical and social needs of the inmates. The food is of a low quality, and medical services are poor. The equipment available for the few trades taught in prison—carpentry, plumbing, shoemaking, and so on—is in short supply; many of the smaller prisons have no trade courses. Discharged inmates reenter the mainstream of society virtually penniless and without skills, armed only with travel fare to their hometowns. The prison service provides neither assistance in obtaining jobs nor after-care services.

Although the state of the prisons has not been improved significantly, the recidivism rate has dropped. In all Nigerian prisons for the years 1960 through 1964, the following percentages of prisoners had one or more previous convictions: 41, 52, 51, 59, and 52 percent, respectively. The percentages of inmates who were recidivists in 1973, 1974, 1975, and 1976 were 43.2, 45.4, and 38.6, respectively.[20]

The resources of the prison service are being stretched to the fullest by the federal government's plan to integrate the federal prisons and those controlled by local councils. The overcrowded and unsanitary conditions of federal prisons are bad, but the conditions are even worse in local prisons. Starved of funds and inadequately managed, the local prisons have been mere lockups for petty offenders and political opponents.

Integration of the prisons, achieved in 1975, has imposed enormous financial costs on the Prison Department. This partly explains the huge increases in budgetary allocation earmarked for prisons in the 1975-1980 Development Plan. The federal prison budget was N11 million in the 1970-1974 period and N173.065 million in the current (1975-1980) plan.[21] The phenomenal increase in allocations is not peculiar to the prisons; it reflects the sharp and unprecedented increase in government resources produced by the "boom" in oil revenue. The allocation of N173.065 million to prisons represents only 5 percent of the total budget for the defense and security sector (the army, police, and prisons). In the 1970-1974 plan, the prison's allocation of N11 million was 5.71 percent of the total for the sector.

The enormous construction work demanded of the Prison Department makes even this budgetary increase inadequate. Most prisons taken over from local authorities were to be pulled down and rebuilt. Those with sites taken over by rapid urban growth were to be relocated. The steady rise in prison population has required more cell blocks and a larger staff. The daily average population in Nigerian prisons was 25,899 in 1976, a 25-percent increase over the 1975 population.[22] With 121 regular prisons, two special penal institutions, and 229 prison lockups spread over the country, the resources at the disposal of the Prison Department are grossly inadequate.

CRIMINOLOGY AND CRIMINOLOGICAL RESEARCH

Criminological research has been rather modest and scarce. Systematic interest in criminological research is quite recent in Nigeria. Defined in the narrow legal sense of understanding and explaining the content and process of the criminal law and its relevance to understanding legal development and social change, criminology has been part of the legacy handed down by Nigerian legal scholars. Their orientation has been British because many generations of Nigerian lawyers were trained in British universities and Inns of Court. The influence of legal scholars on the development of criminology has been promoted by the establishment of law schools in Nigerian universities before the social sciences, especially sociology, arrived on the Nigerian university scene.

In light of the scope of the scientific study of crime and criminals, the sociology of law represents an integral component of Nigerian criminology. In this encompassing sense, criminology in Nigeria is about a decade old. It was offered as a course in the Sociology Department at the University of Ibadan during the 1969-1970 academic year. Five other universities now provide courses that fit this description. At the University of Lagos, criminology resides in the Faculty of Law; otherwise, the courses are in departments of sociology.

As a subsidiary to sociology and law, criminology has experienced some growth over the past decade. The post-civil war crime "wave" increased governmental interest in the social and environmental conditions conducive to crime and in the need to deal with the mounting crime problem. Perhaps for the first time in modern times, crime became a popular subject of discussion among Nigerians from all walks of life, largely because of the unprecedented dimensions of violent crimes since the end of the war. The universities—especially in departments of sociology—have enjoyed increased enrollments in courses such as criminology.

Criminology remains very much the appendage of the disciplines of sociology and law. First, there are very few criminologists in Nigeria's universities and research institutes; the bibliography at the end of this chapter attests to this assertion. Second, despite the proliferation of research centers, institutes, and agencies in Nigeria, there is no such institution for research in criminology. Criminological research efforts are restricted to a part-time activity in universities. Third, there is no organized forum for the discipline. Foreign criminological journals and Nigerian journals in the social sciences and law are the only outlets for communication of criminological research and discussions. Without an association of their own and a local journal in criminology, criminologists have yet to make a real impact on Nigerian society.

Shortage of funds inhibits the development of criminology. Heavy reliance must be placed on financial grants that universities can provide. The Nigerian Institute for Social and Economic Research (NISER) and some other government agencies have also provided funds.

Although the volume of criminological research is necessarily limited, Nigeria offers richness and variety in topics for research.[23] Areas that have attracted some attention in Nigeria include juvenile delinquency (Oloruntimehin, 1970; Bamisaiye, 1974; Odekunle, 1978), adult criminality (Asuni, 1969, Lambo et al.; Odekunle, 1978), and law enforcement (Kayode, 1976; Odekunle, 1979; Tamuno, 1970; Okonkwo, 1966). Efforts have been made in crime and judicial statistics (Oloruntimehin, 1974; Kayode 1977, 1978), the judicial process (Adewoye, 1974; Kayode, 1975; Oloruntimehin, 1978), and law and social development (Elias, 1973; Kayode, 1978). Odekunle (1979), Ohaeri (1976), and Nkpa (1976) have worked in victimology; some findings on the Nigerian prisons have been reported in the conference papers edited by Elias (1968), the work of Milner (1972), and some publications of Kayode (1978, 1979). Chambliss (1975) has reported on organized crime in Nigeria. Odekunle (1975) among others discusses some issues of policy. Theoretical treatments have been rare in Nigeria; perhaps only Odekunle (1978) and Kayode (1974) merit mention.

FINAL COMMENT

As for all forms of research, the impact of Nigerian criminology on government policy is difficult to determine. The tremendous changes and serious problems of Nigerian society are summarized above. How can one measure the effect of particular knowledge on social policy within such dynamic situations? In the fact of the great need for sound policy, government agencies have remained static.

The quantity of knowledge generated by research, modest though it has been, has not been reflected in qualitative changes of crime-control measures and mechanisms. Many Nigerian criminologists agree that only a radical improvement in resource distribution can reverse the current trend in criminal activities; journal articles, workshop papers, and conference proceedings present this conclusion. The daily pronouncements of judges, military men in political office, and high-ranking civil servants generally blame inequalities and the materialism of Nigerians as prime factors behind criminality. These individual positions, however, are not congruent with government policy and practices.

Describing the police situation, a major official publication admits the understaffing of the police organization and reports that the agency's "personnel and equipment resources are being stretched beyond their optimum capacity."[24] The government's policy for the current plan period is "therefore to significantly improve the current police/population ratio and make the services of the police available to the public at all times."[25] Infrastructural facilities are to be expanded, and modern sophisticated gadgets for fighting crime and processing crime information are supposed to be acquired. The visions are still to be translated into practice. Policemen are still short of human and material resources.

Numerous recommendations on the content of criminal law, the trial process, and general administration of justice have hardly touched the work of the judiciary. Neither have prisons gained benefits from research conclusions and conference resolutions—not even from government white papers.

Reduction of crime and delinquency—especially in a technologically developing society as Nigeria—cannot be conceived in isolation from general socioeconomic planning. The criminologist's role in such planning centers mainly on producing hard facts on crime and relating these facts to alternative solutions.

NOTES

1. This estimate is taken from O. O. Arowolo, "Growth of the Population of Nigeria" (unpublished mimeograph, 1976).

2. A. Iwayemi, "The Military and the Economy," in O. O. Oyeriran (ed.), *Nigerian Government and Politics under Military Rule, 1906-1979* (London: Macmillan, 1979).

3. A. A. Owosekun, "Structure of the Nigerian Economy," in A. A. Marciniak and A. A. Owosekun (eds.), *Forecasting Planning Systems for the Nigerian Economy: Preliminary Details* (Zaria: Center for Social and Economic Research, Ahmadu Bello University, June 1977), p. 185.

4. For a detailed discussion of the subject, see P. C. Lloyd, *Africa in Social Change* (Harmondsworth, England: Penguin, 1967), Chapter 4; also see Kenneth Little, *West African Urbanisation* (Cambridge, England: Cambridge University Press, 1965), especially Chapter 1.

5. O. Arikpo, *The Development of Modern Nigeria* (Harmondsworth, England: Penguin, 1967), p. 105.

6. General Yakubu Gowon, then Nigeria's head of state, as quoted in the *New Nigerian*, June 13, 1973.

7. Taken from Federal Republic of Nigeria's *Third National Development Plan, 1975-80* (Lagos: Central Planning Office, Federal Ministry of Economic Development), p. 16.

8. C. O. Okonkwo, *The Police and the Public in Nigeria* (London: Sweet and Maxwell, 1966), p. 4.

9. Federal Republic of Nigeria, *Public Service Review Commission: Main Report* (Lagos: Federal Ministry of Information, 1974), p. 85.

10. Femi Odekunle, "The Nigeria Police Force: A Preliminary Assessment of Functional Performance," *International Journal of Sociology of Law* 7 (1979):61-83.

11. Anne Bamisaiye, "The Spatial Distribution of Juvenile Delinquency and Adult Crime in the City of Ibadan," *International Journal of Criminology and Penology* 2 (February 1974):65-83.

12. Federal Republic of Nigeria, *Third National Development Plan 1975-80*, Vol. 1 (Lagos: Ministry of Economic Development, 1974), p. 327.

13. Federal Republic of Nigeria, *Public Service Review Commission: Main Report*, p. 86.

14. O. Kayode, "Public Expectations and Police Role Concepts: Nigeria," *Police Chief* 63 (May 1976):56-59.

15. A. Milner, *The Nigerian Penal System* (London: Sweet and Maxwell, 1972).

16. T. O. Elias (ed.), "The Prison System in Nigeria," papers submitted at the National Conference on the Prison System in Nigeria, 1968.

17. Ibid., p. 56.

18. Federal Republic of Nigeria, *The Report of the Working Party on Police and Prison Services in Nigeria* (Lagos: Federal Ministry of Information, 1967), p. 61.

19. Elias, "The Prison System in Nigeria," p. 188.

20. These figures were computed from issues of *Annual Reports of the Federal Prisons Department* (Lagos), 1964-1965, 1965-1966, and 1976; and Federal Office of Statistics, *Annual Abstract of Statistics* (Lagos), 1973.

21. Federal Republic of Nigeria, *Third National Development Plan 1975-80*, p. 331.

22. Federal Republic of Nigeria, *Nigerian Prisons Service Annual Report 1976* (Lagos: Federal Ministry of Information, 1978), p. 5.

23. The following references are found in the bibliography at the end of this chapter.

24. Federal Republic of Nigeria, *Third National Development Plan 1975-80*, p. 328.

25. Ibid., p. 328.

BIBLIOGRAPHY

Patterns of Delinquency and Crime

Asuni, Tolani. "Homicide in Western Nigeria." *British Journal of Psychiatry* 115 (October 1969):1105-1113.
Fifty-three subjects found guilty of criminal homicide in western Nigeria were interviewed. Asuni reports that the lower classes are more likely to turn their aggression outward in homicidal acts.

Bamisaiye, Anne. "The Spatial Distribution of Juvenile Delinquency and Adult Crime in the City of Ibadan." *International Journal of Criminology and Penology* 2 (February 1974):65-83.
Bamisaiye examines the relevance of the classic ecological explanation to a non-Western urban situation. Her findings suggest that the spatial distribution of adult crime and juvenile delinquency in Ibadan deviate from the Shaw and McKay zonal pattern.

Chambliss, W. J. "The Political Economy of Crime: A Comparative Study of Nigeria and the U.S.A." In Ian Taylor, et al. (eds.). *Critical Criminology*. London: Routledge and Kegan Paul, 1975.
This comparative study of Seattle (United States) and Ibadan (Nigeria) discusses the various vices common to those cities and highlights the organized nature of many criminal activities.

Kayode, O. "Towards an Explanation of Crime in Africa: A Review Article." *Nigerian Journal of Economic and Social Studies* 16 (November 1974): 519-524.
Drawing on Clifford's *Introduction to African Criminology* and Clinard and Abbott's *Crime in Developing Countries*, this paper calls attention to the task of formulating theoretical postulates to explain crime in African countries.

Kayode, O. "The State of Nigeria's Crime Statistics." *Journal of East African Research and Development* 7, no. 1 (1978).
Kayode examines the process of compiling Nigerian crime statistics, attempts to determine items of information available in official returns, and suggests reforms in data collection.

Lambo, T. A., et al. "A Survey of Criminal Homicide in Nigeria." Unpublished report. Ibadan: Behavioral Science Research Unit, University of Ibadan, undated.
A sample of five hundred cases was drawn from records of the Federal Supreme Court of Nigeria; two hundred cases were analyzed. The authors found that "the highest number of victims fell within primary group relationships." The favorite weapons were machetes and cutlasses.

Nkpa, N.K.U. "Armed Robbery in Post-Civil War Nigeria: The Role of the Victim"; and C. E. Ohaeri, "Community Responsibility and the Victim in Nigerian Society," in E. C. Viano (ed.). *Victims and Society.* Washington, D.C.: Visage Press, 1976.
Armed robbers are seen as largely products of the civil war.

Odekunle, O. "Juvenile Delinquency and Adult Crime in Nigeria." *Proceedings of National Seminar on Social Problems, Social Disorganization and Criminality, 1978.*
Some data on delinquents and criminals provide a framework for discussing Nigeria's sociolegal response to the crime problem.

Odekunle, O. "Capitalist Economy and the Crime Problem in Nigeria." *Contemporary Crises* 2 (January 1978):83-96.
The author identifies the free enterprise economic system of Nigeria as the cause of crime.

Odekunle, O. "Victims of Property Crime in Nigeria: A Preliminary Investigation in Zaria." *Savannah.* In press.
This preliminary study of criminal property victimization in Nigeria is based on a burglary-victim survey in the town of Zaria.

Oloruntimehin, O. "A Note on Juvenile Delinquency Statistics in a Nigerian City." *Ghana Journal of Sociology* 8 (July 1974).
This sharp critique of the absence of useful statistics on delinquency offers data which the author collected from Ibadan juvenile court records for 1966 to 1970.

Oloruntimehin, O. "The Role of Family Structure in the Development of Delinquent Behavior Among Juveniles in Lagos." *Nigerian Journal of Economic and Social Studies* 12 (July 1970):185-203.
The legal definition of delinquency is a starting point in the analysis of family structure as an explanation for delinquency. The author found some similarity between influence of the family on children in Nigeria and in industrialized societies.

Law and the Courts

Adewoye, O. "Courts of Law and Sociocultural Change in Southern Nigeria, 1854-1954." *Nigerian Journal of Sociology and Anthropology* 1 (September 1974):57-77.

Adewoye's main argument is that, whereas courts of law were established by the British primarily for the purpose of colonial control and administration, they have become important to the sociocultural development of southern Nigeria.

Elias, T. O. *Law in a Developing Society*. Bein City, Nigeria: Ethiope Publishing Corporation, 1973.
The central subject of this work is the relationship between the law and Nigerian economic development in the vital areas of mining, agriculture, and industry among others.

Kayode, O. "Judicial Administration in a Changing Society: Customary Courts in Western Nigeria." *Verfassung und Recht in Ubersee* 8, 3-4 Heft (1975):435-446.
The traditional system of justice among the Yoruba of Western Nigeria is used to trace the evolution of the judicial system from colonial to self-government. The place of indigenous judicial administration, in the face of the expanding influence of the Western legal system, is examined.

Kayode, O. "Measuring Performance from Limited Information: A Research Note on Two Magisterial Districts." *Nigerian Journal of Economic and Social Studies* 19 (March 1977):143-149.
Kayode calls for objective criteria for measuring the performance of judicial agencies on the basis of his effort to evaluate performance in two magisterial districts.

Kayode, O. "The Place of Law in Nigeria's Development Process." *Afrika Spectrum* 13, no. 1 (1978):67-74.
The main focus of this article is the Nigerian Enterprises Promotion Decree of 1972 as a means of ensuring a greater participation of Nigerians in economic life. It is argued that the absence of necessary supportive elements has inhibited the meaningful realization of the intentions.

Odekunle, O. "Crime and Social Defense." In E. O. Akeredolu-Ale (ed.). *Social Development in Nigeria: A Survey of Research and Policy*. Ibadan: Nigerian Institute for Social and Economic Research. In press.
This review of available knowledge on crime and reactive measures taken by the government offers suggestions to policymakers.

Oloruntimehin, O. "Operational Problems of Modern Penal Justice in Nigeria." *Ghana Social Science Journal* 5 (May 1978).
Oloruntimehin argues that the introduction of the British judicial system into Nigeria was antithetical to the traditional forms of dispute settlement and that this difficulty explains the irrelevance of the modern penal system to the sociocultural background of Nigerians.

Law Enforcement and Society

Kayode, O. "Public Expectations and Police Role Concepts: Nigeria." *Police Chief* 63 (May 1976):56-59.
This brief history of the Nigerian police examines their role and organization, public attitudes toward the police, and problems confronting law enforcement in Nigeria.

Odekunle, Femi. "The Nigeria Police Force: A Preliminary Assessment of Functional
    Performance." *International Journal of Sociology of Law* 7 (1979):61-83.
Odekunle suggests that the police fall far short of optimum standards; he examines reasons
for this failure and suggests measures for improving police performance.

Okonkwo, C. O. *The Police and the Public in Nigeria*. London: Sweet and Maxwell,
    1966.
Okonkwo discusses the organization and control of the Nigerian police; he suggests ways
of curbing police excesses and improving the public image of the police.

Tamuno, Tekena. *The Police in Modern Nigeria*. Ibadan: Ibadan University Press, 1970.
This volume is an authoritative source of the historical development of law enforcement in
Nigeria.

Penal System and Prisoners

Elias, T. O. (ed.). *The Prison System in Nigeria*. Papers submitted at the National
    Conference on the Prison System in Nigeria, 1968.
Various aspects of prisons and corrections in Nigeria were the subject of this 1968
conference.

Kayode, O. "A Survey of Male Inmates in Selected Nigerian Prisons." *Prison Service
    Journal*, no. 30, new series (April (1978):7-9, 14.
The attributes of inmates in selected prisons are compared with those of the general
population in the region where prisons are located.

Kayode, O. "Inmate Expectations and Prison Aftercare: A Study of Nigerian Prisoners."
    Joint Endeavor. Huntsville, Tex., 1979.
The expectations of prisoners prior to their discharge are believed to be the proper basis
for concrete reintegration programs.

Milner, A. *The Nigerian Penal System*. London: Sweet and Maxwell, 1972.
This book is the most comprehensive critique of the sentencing and treatment of offenders
in Nigeria. Milner makes fundamental suggestions for an integrated penal policy.

25

NORWAY

David Orrick

In any analysis of a nation's criminological output, an important question is: Is it possible to identify a distinctive criminology? For Norway, evidence of a distinctive criminology did not emerge from the wealth of criminological work examined in the preparation of this chapter. Nonetheless, the work of Norwegians must be considered in any review of international criminology. If the ordinary man is what he eats, the criminologist is what he or she produces. From this perspective, Norwegians have made important contributions because of the healthy skepticism they traditionally apply in their examinations of authorities and of widely established dogmas. Furthermore, they have a special ability to identify crucial areas of study at least as early as their counterparts in other countries.

WORLD WAR II AS REFERENCE POINT

For some, war is the ultimate crime against property and person. The conditions raised by war have lent themselves to criminological analysis. One opportunity presented itself in Denmark when the invaders removed the organized police force; in his classic monograph, Jörgen Trolle analyzes the effects of "seven months without police."[1] Norway's exposure to war has been memorialized, to Norway's embarrassment, by the addition to the international lexicon of the technical term "quisling," which denotes active collaboration with the enemy. A more responsible evaluation of the criminological effects of World War II could examine the question whether or not this Norwegian phenomenon was unique.

In his research, Christensen found that former mental patients were overrepresented among those Norwegians who sided with the Germans by joining the Nazi party.[2] Christie's original criminological research also was on a war-related issue.[3] He investigated former guards in concentration camps for his master's thesis as the beginning of a highly varied and productive career in criminology. Almost single-handedly, Eitinger looked at Jewish survivors of concentration camps,[4] with valuable time-series analysis. Eitinger has not received proper credit for his research into the psychological impact of the Holocaust and the Nazi obsession with the Jews. He has expanded his original research interest to take up analysis of Norwegians arrested by Nazis for activities they prohibited. He has gone beyond this general topic to apply a time-series methodology in an investigation of infanticide in Norway.[5]

After imprisonment for a half year (winter 1954-1955) as a conscientious objector, Galtung returned to the prison to administer questionnaires to both inmates and guards. His study, *Fengselssamfunnet* [The Prison Society], was published in 1959 in Oslo.[6] This book was a useful comparative study for Sykes's *Society of Captives* which analyzed an American prison.[7] By constructing a reaction mechanism, the book provides a valuable contrast to Sykes's paradigm which has come to be regarded as a classic. The failure of Galtung's investigation to receive its due attention suggests the insularity of Anglophone criminology at that time. Mannheim's *Comparative Criminology* has been influential in European criminology. This otherwise comprehensive publication refers to Sykes's research but not to Galtung's investigation.[8]

THE THREE NORWEGIAN "CRIMINOLOGIES"

For any nation, the literature of criminology comes from three sources: (1) scholars who publish for domestic consumption; (2) scholars who prepare articles and books for publication outside their country; and (3) foreigners, whether scholars or nonscholars, who publish materials on criminological subjects that deal with that country. Since the three sources have different perspectives and purposes, they may be thought to constitute different forms of criminology. The distinction promotes understanding of Norwegian criminology because of the particular interaction among the Scandinavian nations and because of the special importance of access to Anglophone publication opportunities for Norwegian criminologists.

Norway's *domestic* consumption must be broadly defined. At least for the purposes of this chapter, all Scandinavian publications may be included under Norway's domestic consumption. The Scandinavian countries are drawn together by the similarities of their language and histories. (Finland is considered Scandinavian in a broad sense, in spite of its fundamentally different language.) *Vernelagsnytt*, published in Oslo, no more confines itself to Norwegian material than *Nordisk Medicin*, published in Stockholm, publishes only Swedish studies of medicine, or than *Alkoholipolitikka*, published in Helsinki, limits itself to Finnish research on alcohol.

With regard to the "second criminology," Norwegian criminologists are especially likely to prepare monographs published outside of Scandinavia and written in English. Two examples are illustrative. Hauge's summary of new Norwegian legislation concerning juveniles appeared in the *International Child Welfare Review* published in Geneva, Switzerland,[9] and Kjølstad's article on group therapy for alcoholics was published by an Austrian medical journal.[10] The "third criminology" is not easily compatible with the first two because its materials usually are, at best, quite lightweight. Here Norwegian criminological matters are considered by non-Scandinavians, and the materials invariably appear in non-Scandinavian publications. As we shall see, sound research can be produced, but most non-Scandinavians are not sufficiently familiar with the Norwegian sociocultural environment and the criminological implications of this setting.

English does not always convey the precise meanings expressed in Norwegian. Two examples are relevant. In discussing the implied threat of a conditional sentence, Kolstad used the title "Riset bak speilet."[11] No three words in English convey this meaning. A rough translation would be "the birch rod in the back of the closet." The significance of the phrase would be clear to the Norwegian boy who appreciates that a rod made of birch hurts more than one of pine. Hauge examined how much a typical Norwegian would be willing to pay to avoid a month in jail.[12] The translation of his title "Tid eller penger" as "Time or Money" requires more than the conversion of a week's salary in 1968 kroner into American dollars.

Foreign publications have unusual importance to Norwegian criminologists. Since part of their output appears in Anglophone journals and books, English has of necessity become a second language for them. In fact, Norwegians are among those criminologists who seem to write more clearly in a second language than in their mother tongue. Of course, this characteristic is secondary to the quality of the ideas being expressed and the skill of the analysis. Both Nils Christie and Johannes Andenaes have received awards from the American Society of Criminology acknowledging "international recognition for their contributions in criminology."

THE "FIRST CRIMINOLOGY" AND OSLO'S INSTITUTE

To the outsider, particularly the Anglophone, criminological research in Norway since World War II has been synonymous with the Institute for Criminology and Criminal Law at the University of Oslo. Nils Christie, Johannes Andenaes, and Anders Bratholm, all of whom are very productive Norwegian criminologists, are full professors at the institute. The institute has had remarkable influence on students in its day-to-day operations. The cooperation between faculty and students, matched by few other schools in the world, resulted in the provocative book, *The Police in Norwegian Society*. The main author, Anne Marie Stokken, was a student at the time it was published.[13] Professor Christie is among its co-authors.

The impact of the book on criminal policy demonstrates the potentialities of a criminological research unit in the capital, especially in a country Norway's size. At the time of writing, the government was considering centralizing the police force. The Minister of Justice eventually recommended a decentralized organization pattern that was preferred by the authors of the book. Perhaps in this instance the institute's influence may be attributed in part to its proximity to the Parliament and the head offices of the Civil Service. Although the research staff rarely numbers more than twenty, the institute has high visibility for the mass media. Perhaps the relatively small staff has helped the institute avoid the inflexibility generally characteristic of great institutionalization.

As a creation of the law faculty of the University of Oslo, the institute reflects the traditional European pattern of identifying criminology with the study of law. However, the Oslovian/Norwegian approach is distinctive. Norway does not require either the senior or junior members of the institute to be legally trained. Christie, for example, was originally educated as a sociologist. If there is any recent trend, it is in the institute's increasing representation of a blend of legally trained and social science-trained personnel.

Other Norwegian organizations have also contributed to criminology. For example, the Institute for Social Research, directed by Professor Vilhelm Aubert and also part of the University of Oslo, has made valuable contributions to "pure" criminological research. The National Institute of Alcohol Research, based in Oslo, has been routinely involved in criminological concerns. Its current director, Ragnar Hauge, was once a senior lecturer at the Institute of Criminology and Criminal Law. The productive social science faculty at the University of Bergen has potential for criminological research, particularly in reference to deviance and the effects of Norway's new oil fields which are located near Bergen.[14]

Norwegian criminologists, as already noted, deserve much credit for their perceptiveness in dealing with important issues, often before those issues have received attention elsewhere. On the negative side, it should be pointed out that there are deficiencies in the area of the "first criminology." A most obvious omission is the failure of postwar criminological research in Norway to study the Lapplanders. A number of questions invite searching inquiry: How do these remarkable nomads deal with that phenomenon which would be considered crime in an urbanized society? How do they distinguish between deviance that is not subject to criminal sanctions and that which is punished? How does the nomadic life insulate the Lapps against criminogenic tendencies? How do the Lapps differ in such matters when compared with distinctively tight-knit minorities, such as the Nisei-Japanese in North America? Another topic, the legal issues of police detention and arrest powers in Norway, has been considered by Anders Bratholm, as we shall see, but the opportunity for fuller research has not been taken up.

Perhaps the country's foremost oversight has been its lack of a basic text in criminology. In contrast, Denmark has the classic textbook prepared by Hurwitz.[15]

One reason why Norway has not undertaken a full range of research is that only limited personnel are available. The country has so few centers of higher education that many of the abler high school graduates attend foreign colleges and universities. As a result, Norway has probably lost some potential criminologists, engineers, physicians, and the like. Nevertheless, at the same time Norwegian criminology has been enriched by the importation of concepts and findings developed elsewhere. Nils Christie is a prime example.

THE "SECOND" AND ANGLOPHONE CRIMINOLOGIES

The relevance of the "second criminology" to Norway is related to access to publication opportunities, as discussed above, and to the influence of Anglo-American social sciences in the development of Norwegian criminology. The influence is most visible at the University of Oslo where the trend has shifted from the legally trained traditions towards a more typically American institute based on social science. The influence has not been furthered by the personal efforts of American criminologists; rather, the major stimulus has been the remote control of journal articles and books. In a 1974 interview, Christie offered a more general explanation:

I am a sociologist by basic training, and I perceive criminology—at least the kind of criminology I am fond of—to be a branch of sociology. Criminology is an excellent tool for the understanding of social phenomena, and that is the way I am trying to use it—to use crime data as an indicator of what sort of society I live in. I was educated in sociology at the University of Oslo and I have had some additional education in England and the United States. Like many Norwegian sociologists, I may be unduly oriented towards the Anglo-American countries, which is natural when you realize all the other cultural relationships between the United States and England and Norway. The intellectual orientation follows trade as well as tourist traffic, and you can really figure out the international influence by looking at the number of flights between major cities. Oslo is much closer to New York than to Berlin.[16]

Christie does not mention that this criminological traffic has been excessively one-way. Comparatively few North American criminologists have even visited Norway, let alone conducted research there. The unfamiliarity of foreign scholars with Norwegian as a second language[17] has worked against the dissemination of Norwegian criminological literature in the original language. Some worthy Norwegian works remain "hidden" to the Anglophone criminologist because they have not been translated into English from one of the Scandinavian languages. The rule appears to be that these works will not be translated unless they have been first, or simultaneously, published in English. The earliest volumes of the Scandinavian Studies in Criminology, published by the Universitetsforlaget (University Press) in Oslo, provided valuable collections of current Scandinavian research. Recent volumes have tended to be thematic; for example, one volume was on policing in Scandinavia.[18] The constraints on university-sponsored publishing limit the feasibility of large-scale collections in both English and one of the Scandinavian languages.

In spite of the obstacles to the dissemination of the findings of Norwegian criminology, real progress has been made in achieving the international esteem accorded a number of the Norwegian criminologists. The work of Anders Bratholm deserves special mention as an illustration of the contributions of Norwegians outside Norway. After postgraduate study in law at New York University, Bratholm was visiting professor in the spring term of 1960 at the law school of the University of Pennsylvania. During his stay in the United States, he published four important articles on police arrest and detention privileges in Norway.[19] Bratholm has updated his analysis of what he terms the "personal integrity of the suspect."[20]

INSUFFICIENCY OF "THIRD CRIMINOLOGY"

Norway is an attractive place to academics because of the space it offers in contrast to the crowded environment they typically encounter in most urban universities of Europe and North America. Norway's sociocultural and economic systems invite comparative investigations that exceed the resources of Norwegian criminology. In addition to the relatively compact nature of Norwegian society, the national statistics are of good quality. Credit should be given the almost single-handed efforts of the late Stein Rokkan to improve those statistics. It would appear that foreign criminologists, possessing superior access to vital resources, would seize upon the opportunities the data offer for research.

Nevertheless, what little outside analysis has been undertaken has been of very varied quality. John Haines's report of his study tour has the flavor of a summary of a travel junket.[21] A similar impression is conveyed by Brinkhof's even briefer report of a Dutch study tour in 1975.[22] The Canadian report, *The Criminal Justice System: Norway*, published by the Strategic Planning Committee in Ottawa, is not much better.[23]

Some Anglophone criminologists, however, have produced more impressive works after a research stay in Norway. A leading student of the effects of long-term imprisonment, Hans Toch, surveyed inmates of two Norwegian prisons when they returned from furloughs.[24] In the late 1960s Norway's use of furloughs was on a par with that of any other nation. In 1963, Donald Cressey, in partnership with Elg Elgesen,[25] completed a report on the street behavior of Oslo policemen which compares favorably with James Q. Wilson's work on police discretion.[26]

ANALYSES OF DEVIANT BEHAVIOR

Delineation of the proper boundaries between criminology and the sociology of deviance has stimulated great international interest. Regardless of the merits of the opposing arguments, exploration of criminological research in Norway must include consideration of social issues such as alcoholism, drug abuse, and suicide. The formidable efforts to understand these deviant phenomena illustrate the special interest of Norwegian criminologists in identifying social problems that are beginning to have great impact on Norwegian society and in investigating the implications of these issues for the law and social control.

No topic has received more attention in the Norwegian criminological literature than alcoholism, with the carnage caused by drunken drivers highlighting
the issue. Tests to measure the blood alcohol level, regardless of the driver's
physical performance, predate World War II. The precision of those tests has
now been questioned. The Norwegian language has contributed the compound
term "promilleskjøring" (the act of driving under the influence of alcohol in
contravention of the 0.5 *pro mille* blood alcohol level) to the literature. (Even the
most hardened Parsonian sociologist would be delighted by the technical precision of the term.)

Among both Scandinavian and non-Scandinavian criminologists are some who
have established their reputations in part on the basis of their analyses of the 1936
legislation. The several works of H. Laurence Ross in Anglophone journals[27]
have cast him as a prominent American expert on the control of drunken driving.
In his detailed analyses, Ross provides some of the most telling empirical criticisms of Andenaes's theories on deterrence which especially drew on "promilleskjøring" legislation. Votey's analyses of that legislation, expressing his econo-
metric concerns, also deserve mention.[28]

Brun-Gulbrandsen's work on alcohol abuse, which he considers just another
aspect of "dangerous drugs,"[29] has provided useful data. Collaborating with
Irgens-Jensen in the mid-1969s, he looked at the question of alcohol abuse
among sailors.[30] (The research topic is especially interesting because it involves
one of two major stereotypes applied to Norway. There is a folk belief that
Norway is crowded with drunken sailors, a belief that is as inaccurate as the other
stereotype: that Norway is a society without crime.) Contrary to the popular
impression that life at sea explains alcohol abuse among sailors, Brun-Gulbrandsen's
findings suggest that certain personality traits of some young Norwegians com-
plicate their adjustment to their home environments and that the merchant navy is
seized upon as an escape. Those personality traits have selective impact in
differentiating those youths who go to sea from those who do not. Thus Brun-
Gulbrandsen concludes, those personality traits, rather than conditions of life at
sea, explain proneness to alcohol abuse.

That study suggests that all is not well with the mental health of a portion of
young Norwegians, in spite of their living within one of the more effective
welfare states. Other studies lend even more substantial support to that speculation. In the late 1960s, Retterstöl followed up attempted suicide patients admitted to the Department of Psychiatry, University of Oslo, over a three-year
period.[31] He found that women were disproportionately represented in the study
groups (61 percent female versus 39 percent male) and that the person attempting suicide is most likely to repeat the attempt, if at all, within the first year
after discharge from treatment. Suicides also are found among military personnel, a phenomenon not likely to be noted in recruiting drives. In the mid-1960s,
the Norwegian armed forces considered that phenomenon among peace-time
military personnel, using data extending back to the end of World War II.
Englestad reports that suicides are less likely among Norway's military person-

nel than among its civilians and that the chances are greater for officers than enlisted men.[32]

The examination of suicide patterns in a given nation is not the equivalent of cross-cultural comparative research. It appears that Norwegians are not comparatively more prone to suicide. In Faber's comparative study, Norway was included among those nations with low suicide rates, lower than Denmark's rate, for example.[33]

As other countries, Norway has been slow to give the attention to narcotic drugs that has been given to alcohol. Not until 1968 did the Norwegian criminal code include any reference to unlawful dealing in narcotics. And even this legislation was little more than an imprimatur on a closely split decision of the Supreme Court the previous year that nonmedical use of narcotics is a crime. Since then, the severity of punishment has been raised to ten years' imprisonment, in addition to a fine, for illegal import and trade.

Some Norwegian research into drug abuse predates those changes in the criminal code. Retterstöl, a psychiatrist, began collecting data in the mid-1950s on the characteristics of drug abusers admitted to the University Psychiatric Clinic in Oslo. His results were published in an important paper in 1964.[34] From his base at Gaustad Hospital, University of Oslo, Retterstöl has added to his publications in major journals of North America.

The Institute for Alcohol Research has engaged in research on other chemically active agents. When head of the institute, Brun-Gulbrandsen published his piece "How Dangerous Are Dangerous Drugs?"[35] he co-authored with Brit Bergersen Lind a chapter in *Marihuana and Hashish*[36] that raises issues limited to neither Norway nor Scandinavia. As the successor to Brun-Gulbrandsen as head of the Institute for Alcohol Research, Ragnar Hauge has edited an important volume on drinking and driving in Scandinavia.[37] In recent years, other staff members of the institute, notably Irgens-Jensen,[38] have published a number of articles in leading Anglophone journals specializing in drug issues.

In a country with relatively few university-based centers devoted to criminology, research-oriented hospitals are particularly important in conducting criminological research into physiological aspects. These activities in Norway are not limited to Oslo. Noteworthy scholars are Haug[39] at Trondheim's Ostmarka Hospital and Vaglum[40] at Solberg's Dikemark Hospital. In the best traditions of hospital-based research, Laberg analyzed the well-known abstinence program for alcoholics at Victoria A-Sentrum in Bergen. In the early 1960s, Norway was aware of the value of chemotherapy in minimizing the pains of withdrawal symptoms. Laberg's paper at the Fourth World Congress of Psychiatry (1966) in Madrid demonstrated the effectiveness of chemotherapy and identified drugs.[41]

Research in chemotherapy highlights the medical doctor's ability to contribute to criminological knowledge, but ethical questions lurk in the "sick man versus evil man" premises of medical research and forensic psychiatry. In 1962, Mathiesen[42] raised serious questions about the value of the forensic psychiatrist for adjudicative and predictive work. Langfeldt[43] reached similar conclusions about the testimony of forensic psychiatrists in a trial in Bergen of a murderer in a case that attracted great media interest. Andenaes has analyzed the role of a physician in the Norwegian court case.[44]

BEYOND THE PENAL SANCTION SYSTEM

By relating to the broader range of deviance, one must ask whether the use of penal sanctions is the most promising societal reaction to those forms of misconduct officially defined as crime. The relative deemphasis on penal sanctions in Norway is in sharp contrast with nations that are now confronting the crisis of overcrowded prisons. The usual surplus of prison bedspace in Norwegian correctional institutions violates an adaptation of Parkinson's Law which states that empty prison cells always are filled by sentencing courts. The tendency of Norwegians to minimize the use of imprisonment has offered the opportunity to do something about another social problem, drunken driving. Andenaes has pointed out that a substantial number of empty cells have been diverted to receive convicted drunken drivers for relatively short sentences.[45]

Although Norway faces a rising crime rate, alcoholism continues to hold remarkably high priority in Norwegian ranking of social problems. Alcoholism has criminogenic potential, and the modes of dealing with it suggest that alternatives to penal sanctions are available. The discussion above on chemotherapy is relevant. Yet, the Norwegian responses to alcoholism have not been successful in expressing humanitarian concerns. Christie has pointed out that Temperance Boards were created to protect their clientele—the alcoholics—from undesirable encounters with the police.[46] In reality, the objective has been compromised because most of the referrals to the boards are by the police.

The Child Welfare Board represents a typical Scandinavian alternative to the sanctions of juvenile justice. Tove Stang Dahl has traced the emergence of the child welfare law[47] and, more recently,[48] has examined the Child Welfare Board within the context of the social welfare system. Along with Nyquist's analysis of the Swedish Child Welfare Board,[49] Dahl has supplied materials appropriate to a comparison with the American juvenile court model.

Thomas Mathiesen's work has been prominent in analyses of inmate roles and in documenting the history of a noteworthy Norwegian campaign to reform the prisons. His *Defenses of the Weak*[50] is a valuable study of inmates in a medium-security, treatment-oriented institution. Perhaps even more impressive is his book, *The Politics of Abolition*,[51] in which he describes KROM—the Norwegian version of the committees in Denmark (KRIM) and Sweden (KRUM) which undertook penal reform. Mathiesen served as chairman of the Norwegian committee during some of the time he devoted to writing the book. The emotions that colored the movement seep into his analysis, but it is a useful analysis of the stormy history of this reform campaign in Scandinavia.

TRAIL BLAZERS OF INTERNATIONAL SCOPE

The "second criminology" is of special significance in any assessment of Norwegian accomplishments in the field. As already noted, publication of Norwegian works in foreign journals and books has allowed a relatively small country with a language understood by few foreigners to present a number of its scholars who have been pioneers in criminology.

Johannes Andenaes is one of the best known of these scholars. Probably no one has explored the topic of deterrence as thoroughly as he has. His first internationally acclaimed article appeared in 1952;[52] its title summarized his perspective: "General Prevention: Illusion or Reality?" Along with several other of his articles on the topic, this article was reprinted in his *Punishment and Deterrence* in 1974 published by the University of Michigan Press. (Again we see the vital importance of foreign publishers to Norwegian criminologists.) Morris, not given to excessive praise, has attested to the importance of Andenaes's book: "Serious analysis of the operation and efficacy of deterrent sanctions is essential to shaping an efficient and humane system of criminal justice. Those who approach this topic find that the writings of Johannes Andenaes tower over the work of others."[53]

The title which Andenaes chose, *Punishment and Deterrence*, provides an interesting sidelight. "Deterrence" in English is translated as "prevensjon" in Norwegian, but are the two terms equivalent? Even Andenaes has not explored the question, although the title of his 1952 paper, "General Prevention—Illusion or Reality?," conveys the healthy skepticism of Norwegian criminology.

Nils Christie is also among Norway's foremost criminological scholars. His versatility makes him a unique figure in that Norway. In his article, "At Arms with Society,"[54] Christie describes the crime situation in Norway and summarizes the sanctioning system applied against crime from 1814 to 1964. The historical criminology found in this work was in advance of the current radical interest in historical development. His paper remains the major historical analysis of crime in Norway.

Christie has also written self-report studies, another recent interest in international criminology. Along with Andenaes and Skirbekk, he took advantage of a unique opportunity offered by inductees to the Norwegian armed forces to obtain data on crimes perpetrated by the persons who reported them.[55] Free of the weaknesses of official crime statistics, their analysis has made a sound contribution to this methodologically complex sphere of criminological research.

Christie investigates juvenile gangs in Norway in his article, "Juvenile Gangs and Social Structure."[56] Here, he compares the juvenile gangs of Norway to those of Sicily, reputedly the home of the so-called Mafia. On the basis of this article, some critics have asserted that he assumes that the Mafia is a genuine phenomenon. However, the paper's title does not suggest this premise.

As suggested earlier, Christie is more versatile in his research interests than his peers. Despite this versatility, however, there is an underlying theme in all his work: skepticism towards criminal law, framed in a treatment ideology. In "Sociology of the Child Welfare Councils,"[57] Christie for the first time raised critical questions about Norway's closest equivalent to the Anglo-American juvenile courts. He questioned the capacity of ordinary penological methods to treat the offender long before the theme became popular in the early 1970s. In his latest book, *Limits to Pain*,[58] Christie asks, in a somewhat utopian fashion, whether the entire institution of punishment might be phased out. He proposes this action as the alternative to systematizing and regulating punishment.

Extraordinary achievements in the sociology of law have earned scholars, such as N. S. Timasheff,[59] the rank of a genuine pioneer. Vilhelm Aubert helped revitalize the field in the 1960s. His classic article, "Some Social Functions of Legislation,"[60] deals with the Norwegian Housemaid Law of 1948. The title conceals its relevance to criminology in its explanation of the necessity that the language of penal laws be understandable to the common citizen. Furthermore, the paper reinforces a principle of "Scandinavian realism," a version of jurisprudence not limited to a particular country: namely, that the effectiveness of a penal law depends on the spontaneous obedience of citizens because they are aware of its existence and, more particularly, are aware of the exact details of the law.

Aubert's reader, *Sociology of Law*,[61] has lent vitality to the burgeoning field of the sociology of law. He has demonstrated the interaction of this field with criminology by including two well-known criminologists, Roger Hood and Abraham S. Blumberg, among the contributors to the book of readings.

In conclusion, the distinction of "three criminologies" is useful in understanding the development of criminology in some other nations, but it is particularly appropriate for an analysis of criminological activities in Norway. This review of the accomplishments of Norwegian criminologists shows that, in some respects, they have blazed new trails in the dynamic growth of criminological theories. Their accomplishments have been possible because the issues they have raised have given them access to the publication opportunities available through the "second criminology." The "first" and "third criminologies" have not been equally effective in attracting attention to the criminological phenomenon of Norway. This deficiency must be corrected before Norwegian criminology can truly be said to be a major arm of international criminology.

NOTES

1. Jörgen Trolle, *Syv maneder uden politi* [Seven Months Without the Police] (Copenhagen: 1954).

2. Ragnar Christensen, "Sinnslidende mannlige landssvikere i Norge" [Psychotic Male Collaborators in Norway], *Nordisk Tidsskrift for Kriminalvidenskab* 41 (1953): 147-161.

3. Nils Christie, "Fangevoktere i konsentrasjonsleire" [Guards in Concentration Camps], *Nordisk Tidsskrift for Kriminalvidenskab* 40 (1952):439-458 and 41 (1953):44-60.

4. Leo Eitinger, "The Late Results of Chronic Excessive Stress on Two Different Population Groups," *Excerpta Medica Foundation International Congress Series*, No.

117 (Amsterdam), 1966 (Paper presented at the Fourth World Congress of Psychiatry, Madrid, September 5-11, 1966); Eitinger, "Jewish Concentration Camp Survivors in Norway," *Israel Annals of Psychiatry and Related Disciplines* 13, No. 4 (1975):321-334.

5. Eitinger, "Infanticider observert judicielt i Norge, 1900-1960" [Infanticides Noticed and Processed through Court in Norway, 1900-1960], *Nordisk Tidsskrift for Kriminalvidenskab* 57, Nos. 1 and 2 (1969):57-73.

6. Johan Galtung, *Fengselssamfunnet* [The Prison Society] (Oslo: Oslo University Press, 1959). Summaries of the book were published in the United States: Johan Galtung, "The Social Functions of a Prison," *Social Problems* 6 (Fall 1958): 127-140; and Johan Galtung, "Prison: The Organization of Dilemma," in Donald R. Cressey (ed.), *The Prison: Studies in Institutional Organization and Change* (New York: Holt, Rinehart and Winston, 1961), pp. 107-145.

7. Gresham M. Sykes, *Society of Captives* (Princeton, N.J.: Princeton University Press, 1958).

8. Hermann Mannheim, *Comparative Criminology* (New York: Houghton Mifflin Company, 1965).

9. Ragnar Hauge, "New Norwegian Legislation Concerning Juvenile Offenders," *International Child Welfare Review* 20, No. 2 (1966):97-101.

10. Thomas J. Kjølstad, "Gruppentherapie bei alkohollikern" [Group Therapy for Alcoholics], *Wiener Medizinische Worchenschrift* 115, No. 8 (1965):146-158.

11. Ragnar Kolstad, "Riset bak speilet" [The Birch Rod in the Back of the Closet], *Vernelagsnytt* 8, No. 4 (1964):110-113.

12. R. Hague, "Tid eller penger" [Time or Money], *Nordisk Tidsskrift for Kriminalvidenskab* 56, Nos. 1 and 2 (1953):137-140.

13. *Politiet i det Norske Samfunn* [The Police in Norwegian Society] (Oslo: Universitet sforlaget, 1974).

14. Especially noteworthy is P. Stangeland, "Controlling the Oil Industry," *Stensilserie*, No. 29, (Oslo: Institute for Criminology and Criminal Law, University of Oslo, 1978).

15. Stephan Hurwitz, *Kriminologi* [Criminology] (Copenhagen: G.E.C. Gad, 1948; 2d ed., 1951). Later editions (1968 and 1971) were greatly revised and extended with Karl O. Christiansen as co-author.

16. Annika Snare, "Dialogue with Nils Christie," *Issues in Criminology* 10 (Spring 1975):35-47.

17. For a shoulder-shrugging, almost sad, assessment of the Norwegians' acceptance of the outsiders' lack of familiarity with their language, see Donald S. Connery, *The Scandinavians* (New York: Simon and Schuster, 1966), p. 273.

18. Volume 7 (1980) with introduction by R. Hauge.

19. Anders Bratholm, "Arrest and Detention in Norway," *University of Pennsylvania Law Review* 108 (January 1960):336-354; "Police Detention and Arrest Privileges Under Foreign Law—Norway," *Journal of Criminal Law, Criminology and Police Science* 51 (November-December 1960):437-440; "Compensation of Persons Wrongfully Accused or Convicted in Norway," *University of Pennsylvania Law Review* 109 (April 1961):833-845; "Police Interrogation Privileges and Limitations Under Foreign Law—Norway," *Criminal Law, Criminology and Police Science* 52 (May-June 1961):72-73.

20. Anders Bratholm, "Police Investigations and the Personal Integrity of the Suspect in Scandinavia." in *Policing Scandinavia*, Vol. 7, *Scandinavian Studies in Criminology* (Oslo: Universitetsforlaget, 1980).

21. John Haines, "Norway—A New Look at Crime," London: Institute for the Study and Treatment of Delinquency, 1971.

22. H. Brinkhof, "Het noorse gevangeniswezen. Verslag van een veertiendaagse studiereis. deel len 2" [The Norwegian Prison System. Report on a 14-Day Study Tour. Parts 1 and 2], *Balans* (The Hague) 6, No. 2 (1975):1-4 and 6, No. 3 (1975):24-26.

23. *The Criminal Justice System—Norway*, Background Report 2, Strategic Planning Committee (Ottawa: Canadian Correctional Service, 1980).

24. Hans Toch, "Prison Inmates' Reactions to Furlough," *Journal of Research in Crime and Delinquency* 4 (July 1967):248-262.

25. Donald R. Cressey and Elg Elgesen, "The Police and the Administration of Justice," *Scandinavian Studies in Criminology*, Vol. 2 (Oslo: Universitetsforlaget, 1968), pp. 53-72.

26. James Q. Wilson, *Varieties of Police Behavior* (Cambridge, Mass.: Harvard University Press, 1968).

27. For example, H. Laurence Ross, "The Scandinavian Myth: The Effectiveness of Drinking and Driving Legislation in Sweden and Norway," *Journal of Legal Studies* 4, No. 2 (June 1975):285-310.

28. His most recent article is Harold Votey, "Scandinavian Drinking—Drinking Control: Myth or Intuition?" *Journal of Legal Studies* 11 (January 1982):93-116.

29. Sverre Brun-Gulbrandsen, "How Dangerous Are Dangerous Drugs?" *Scandinavian Studies in Criminology* 3 (1971):35-49.

30. Sverre Brun-Gulbrandsen and O. Irgens-Jensen, "Abuse of Alcohol Among Seamen," *British Journal of Addiction* 62, Nos. 1 and 2 (1967):19-27.

31. N. Retterstöl, *Long-Term Prognosis After Attempted Suicide: A Personal Follow-Up Examination* (Springfield, Ill.: Charles C Thomas, 1970).

32. Bull Englestad, "Suicides and Attempted Suicides in the Norwegian Armed Forces During Peace Time," *Military Medicine* 133, No. 6 (1968):437-448.

33. Maurice L. Faber, "Suicide and Welfare State," *American Psychologist* 18, No. 7 (1963):347 (Paper presented at 71st annual meeting of the American Psychological Association, 1963).

34. N. Retterstöl, "Drug Addiction and Habituation," *Acta Psychologica* (Scandinavia), 40 (1964):179-299 (Supplement). Also see his "Misbruk av medikamenter. Saerlig med henblikk pa arsaksforhold og forebyggelse" [Drug Addiction and Habituation, with Special Reference to Etiological and Prophylactic Aspects], *Tidsskrift for den Norske Laegeforening* 36, No. 21 (1966):1465-1472.

35. See footnote 29.

36. *Marihuana og Hasjisj* [Marihuana and Hashish] (Oslo: Universitetsforlaget, 1970).

37. *Scandinavian Studies in Criminology*, Vol. 6 (Oslo: Universitetsforlaget, 1978).

38. O. Irgens-Jensen, "The Relationship Between Self-Reported Drunken Driving, Alcohol Consumption and Personality Variables Among Norwegian Students," in H. S. Israel and S. Lambert (eds.), *Alcohol, Drugs and Traffic Safety* (Toronto: Macmillan, 1975), pp. 159-168.

39. T. Haug, "Research Note," *Psychopharmacology* 75 (1981):110.

40. P. Vaglum, "Comment," *Journal of Drug Issues* 10 (1980):505.

41. J. Laberg, "Abstinence Treatment of Alcoholics in Victoria A-Sentrum, Bergen, Norway," *Excerpta Medicia Foundation*, International Congress Series, No. 117 (1966):271-277.

42. Thomas Mathiesen, "Noen problematiske sider ved norsk rettspsykeatrisk prakis"

[Some Problematic Aspects of Norwegian Forensic Psychiatric Practice], *Vernelagsnytt* 6, No. 1 (1962):21-30.

43. G. Langfeldt, "Rettspsykiaterens medivirken i straffrettsplein" [The Position of Forensic Psychiatry Experts in Norway], *Tidsskrift for den Norske Laegeforening* 83, No. 12 (1963):1027-1030.

44. Johannes Andenaes, "The Physician's Role in Law Court Decisions," *World Medical Journal* 13, No. 5 (1966):138-140; J. Lundevall, "Legen i retten" [The Doctor in Court] *Tidsskrift for den Norske Laegeforening* 85, No. 19 (1965):1463-1465.

45. Johannes Andenaes, *Punishment and Deterrence* (Ann Arbor: University of Michigan Press, 1974).

46. Nils Christie, "Edruelighetsnomnder. Analyse av en velferdslov" [The Temperance Boards: An Analysis of a Welfare Law], *Nordisk Tidsskrift for Kriminalvidenskab* 52 (1964):89-118.

47. Tove Stang Dahl, "The Emergence of the Norwegian Child Welfare Law," *Stensilserie*, No. 1 (Oslo: Institute for Criminology and Criminal Law, University of Oslo, 1971).

48. Tove Stang Dahl, *Barnevern og Samfunnsvern* [Child Welfare and Social Welfare] (Oslo: Institute for Criminology and Criminal Law, University of Oslo, 1978).

49. Ola Nyquist, *Juvenile Justice* (London: Macmillan, 1960).

50. Thomas Mathiesen, *Defenses of the Weak* (London: Tavistock, 1965).

51. Thomas Mathiesen, *The Politics of Abolition* (Oslo: Universitetsforlaget, 1974).

52. Johannes Andenaes, "General Prevention—Illusion or Reality?" *Journal of Criminal Law, Criminology and Police Science* 43 (July-August 1952):176-198.

53. Norval Morris, Foreword to *Punishment and Deterrence*.

54. Nils Christie, "Paa kant med samfunnet" [At Arms with Society], *Glydendale Jubileumsverk* 1 (1963):235-260.

55. Nils Christie, Johannes Andenaes, and Sigurd Skirbekk, "A Study of Self-Reported Crime," *Scandinavian Studies in Criminology*, Vol. 1 (Oslo: Universitetsforlaget, 1965), pp. 86-116.

56. Nils Christie, "Ungdomsgrupper og samfunnsforhold" [Juvenile Gangs and Social Structure], *Nordisk Tidsskrift for Kriminalvidenskab* 51, Nos. 3 and 4 (1963):173-182.

57. Nils Christie, "Barevernsnemndenes sosiologi [The Sociology of the Child Welfare Councils], *Sociologiske Meddelelser* 6, No. 2 (1961):83-98.

58. Nils Christie, *Limits to Pain* (Oslo: Universitetsforlaget, 1981).

59. For example, N. S. Timasheff, *An Introduction to the Sociology of Law* (Cambridge, Mass.: Harvard University Committee on Research in the Social Sciences, 1939).

60. Vilhelm Aubert, "Some Social Functions of Legislation," *Acta Sociologica* (Copenhagen), 10 (1966):98-110.

61. Vilhelm Aubert, *Sociology of Law* (Harmondsworth, England: Penguin Modern Sociology Readings Series, 1969).

BIBLIOGRAPHY

Articles relevant to Norwegian criminology were selected to suggest the range of research interests. When the title does not indicate the contents of the article, a brief descriptive statement is provided. Emphasis is placed on recent literature.

Administration of Justice in Norway. 2d ed. (for the Royal Ministry of Justice). Oslo: Universitetsforlaget, 1980.

Ancherson, P., and K. Noreik. "Present Status of Forensic Psychiatry in Norway." *Acta Psychologica (Scandinavia)* 55, No. 3 (1977):187-193.

Ancona, L., M. Cesa-Bianchi, and F. Bocquet. "Identicazione al padre in assenza di modello paterno" [Identification with the Father in Absence of the Paternal Model]. *Archivo di Psicologia Neurologia e Psichiatria* (Milan) 24, No. 2 (1963):119-172; 24, No. 4 (1963):339-361; 25, No. 2 (1964):103-129.

A comparative survey in Italy and Norway of the psychological effects of long absences of Navy officers on their children.

Anonymous. "Norwegen: die Knastschlange" [Queuing Up for Jail in Norway]. *Fürsorger* (Thun, Switzerland) 44 (1976):47-48.

A criticism of Norway's drunk driving legislation.

Antilla, Inkeri, and P. Törnudd. *Kriminologi i ett kriminalpolitisk perspektiv* [Criminology in the Perspective of Criminal Policy]. Stockholm: 1973.

Bjenke, H. *Fengsling* [Imprisonment]. Oslo: Universitetsforlaget, 1977.

Bjornsen, B. "The Obstacles to Prison Reform in Norway." *Center Magazine* 13, No. 3 (1980):25-32.

Bødal, K. "Fakta om ungdomsfengslet" [Facts About the Youth Prison]. *Vernelagsnytt* 12, No. 1 (1968):6-13.

Bødal, K., "Jeg vil ikke til arbeidsskolen" [I Will Not Go to the Borstal]. *Vernelagsnytt* 7, No. 2 (1963):23-27.

Borch, U. "Personundersøfkelse og bevisførsel" [Social Inquiries and Their Use as Evidence]. *Vernelagsnytt* 3, No. 1 (1962):5-14.

Bratholm, Anders. "Ertatnigens plass in kriminalpolitikken" [The Place of Compensation to Victims of Crime in Criminal Policy]. *Vernelagsnytt* 12, No. 1 (1968): 22-32.

Bremer, J. "Kastrasjonsbehandling av sedelighetsforbrytere" [Castration Therapy for Sexual Offenders]. *Tidssk. Norske Laegeforen* 85, No. 4 (1965):379-384.

————. "Sinnssykdom som medisinsk og straffrettslig begrep" [Insanity as a Medical and Judicial Concept]. *Nordisk Tidsskrift for Kriminalvidenskab* 54, Nos. 1 and 2 (1966):66-75.

Chazan, Maurice. "Special Education for Maladjusted Children and Adolescents in Norway." *Journal of Child Psychology and Psychiatry*, 14, No. 1 (1973):57-69.

Dalgard, O., and E. Kringen. "A Norwegian Twin Study of Criminality." *British Journal of Criminology* 16, No. 3 (1976):213-232; also see J. Forde, "Twin Studies, Inheritance and Criminality: A Criticism of Dalgard and Kringen." *British Journal of Criminology* 18, No. 1 (1978):71-74.

Eckhoff, E., J. Gauslaa, and A. Baldwin. "Parental Behavior Towards Boys and Girls of Pre-School Age." *Acta Psychologica* (Amsterdam), 18, No. 2 (1961):85-99.

A comparative study of parental behavior in the United States and Norway.

Gammeltoft-Hansen, H. "Die Untersuchungshaft in Dänemark und Norwegen" [Pretrial Detention in Denmark and Norway]. *Zeitschrift ges Strafrechtswiss* 26, No. 2 (1976):516-556.

Halvorsen, R. "Ungdomsarrest og detention centre" [Youth Arrest and Detention Center]. *Vernelagsnytt* 2 (1962):12-16.

A consideration of the applicability of two strategies to Norway: Youth arrest as practiced in Germany and detention centers as administered in England.

————. "Work Release in Norway." *Prison Journal* 44, No. 1 (1964):26-27.

Hauge, R., and S. Halleraker. "Vaneforbrytere-tilfeldig-hetsforbrytere" [Habitual Offenders—

Occasional Offenders]. *Nordisk Tidsskrift for Kriminalvidenskab* 53, Nos. 3 and 4 (1965):216-228.

————, and H. Stabell. "Politivirksomhet i et norsk landdestrikt" [Police Functions in a Norwegian Province]. *Nordisk Tidsskrift for Kriminalvidenskab* 63, Nos. 3 and 4 (1975):269-286.

Hauge, R. (ed.). "Drinking and Driving in Scandinavia." *Scandinavian Studies in Criminology*. Vol. 6. Oslo: Universitetsforlaget, 1978.

————. "Policing Scandinavia." *Scandinavian Studies in Criminology*. Vol. 7. Oslo: Universitetsforlaget, 1980.

Holsten, F. "Repeat Follow-up Studies of 100 Young Norwegian Drug-Abusers." *Journal of Drug Issues* 10, No. 4 (1980):491-503.

Johansen, P. O. *Menstadkonflikten* [The Riot at Menstad]. Oslo: Tiden Norsk Forlay, 1978.

Kjeldsen, T. "The Cultivation of Cannabis in Norway." *International Criminal Police Review*, No. 32 (1977):86-88.

Lodrup, Peter. "Norwegian Law: A Comparison with Common Law." *St. Louis University Law Journal* 6 (Fall 1961):520-532.

Manninen, J. "Alkoholopolitikka tiumemmaksi Novjassa" [Tougher Alcohol Policy in Norway]. *Alkoholopolitikka* 45, No. 2 (1980):51-56.

Møglestue, I. *Kriminalitet og sosial bakgrunn* [Crime and Social Background]. Oslo: Central Bureau of Statistics of Norway, 1962.

Mortvedt, L. "Arbeitsformidling av kriminelle" [Work Rehabilitation for Prisoners After Release]. *Vernelagsnytt* 12, No. 1 (1968):35-37.

Nordland, E. "En undersøkelse av gutter med problematferd og stort Y-kromoson" [An Investigation of Boys with Behavior Disorders and an Extra Y Chromosome]. *Nordisk Tidsskrift for Kriminalvidenskab* 57, Nos. 1 and 2 (1969):74-92.

Norwegian Joint Committee on International Social Policy. "Treatment of Offenders in Norway." *Canadian Journal of Corrections* 2, No. 4 (1960):358-362.

Odegard, Ørnulv. "Seasons of Birth in the General Population and in Patients with Mental Disorders in Norway." *British Journal of Psychiatry* 125 (October 1974):397-405.

Olsen, L. "Mittsyn På reakjonsmatene for promillekjøring" [My View of the Public Reaction to the Law on Drunken Driving]. *Tidsskrift Edru-Spørsmaler* 30, No. 1 (1978):19.

Orfield, L. "Norwegian Law." *Temple Law Quarterly* 23 (April 1950):257-305.

Politimannen [The Policemen]. Organ of the Oslo Police Association, first volume in 1958.

Rasmussen, A. "Om sinnssyke ildspäsettere" [Insanity and Arson]. *Nordisk Tidsskrift for Kriminalvidenskab* 54, Nos. 1 and 2 (1966):22-60.

Retterstøl, N. *Medikament- og stoffmisbruk* [Medicine and Substance Abuse]. Oslo: Universitetsforlaget, 1972.

————. "Use and Abuse of Dependency-Producing Drugs in Norway." *Journal of Drug Issues* 5, No. 1 (1975):22-23.

Scandinavian Research Council for Criminology. *Crime and Industrialization*. Stockholm: Stockholms Universitet Fack, 1974.

Report of the first seminar for criminologists from socialist and Scandinavian countries.

Stang, H. "Three-Year Follow-up of 100 Vagrant Adolescent Drug Abusers in Oslo." *Acta psychologia scandinavia* 55, No. 5 (1977):381-390.

26

POLAND

Jerzy Jasiński

As in a number of other countries, criminology in Poland as an organized body of knowledge has had a relatively short history. Its beginnings can be traced back to the late 1920s or early 1930s when, until the outbreak of World War II, it accumulated quite a few promising empirical and theoretical studies pertaining particularly to penology and juvenile delinquency. As was quite common in Europe at that time, criminology in Poland was very closely related to criminal law. Criminologists, most of them jurists by education, often took a stand in debates on criminal policy issues, and in this field they also produced some studies of lasting importance.

DEVASTATING EFFECTS OF WORLD WAR II

All of the main schools of European scientific pursuit in criminology were represented in Poland. It is therefore difficult to tell what shape its further development would have taken had the war not started in 1939. Soon after invading Poland, the occupying forces brutally stopped nearly all research activities. The German invaders closed Polish universities and other scientific institutions; the period of occupation, the extermination of Polish citizens, and the fight against the intruders lasted six years.

The postwar revival of criminology was relatively slow because the country was devastated to a degree difficult to imagine. Its population was reduced by about six million, nearly one-fifth of the prewar figure. Its frontiers were changed. Previously one of the most important national cultural and intellectual centers, the capital city was almost completely destroyed. Rebuilding of the universities and other places of scientific pursuit took much time and effort. The tasks of restoration were complicated by the fact that the new postwar government did not consider itself to be a continuation of that which had existed before the war. Instead, the government was committed to undertaking a profound political and social revolution.

The revival of criminology also encountered a very important hindrance directly related to the field, that is, lack of qualified specialists. This situation prevailed in the majority of other branches of science and technology, but the effects were especially marked for criminology. The Polish criminological community had had few members; only a fraction of them was left after the war. Some of them were killed, as was Tadeusz Kuczma; some stayed abroad, as did Leon Radzinowicz.[1]

EMERGENCE OF NEW FIELDS OF INTEREST

In spite of these obstacles in the immediate postwar years, some important criminological research was accomplished or at least begun. It is not surprising that only a portion of prewar areas of interest continued to receive research attention, partly because the persons who could pursue them were missing and partly because new problems appeared to be more pressing.

The most important of the newly recognized spheres of research were the crimes against Polish citizens committed in Poland by the German invaders. These crimes included genocide, torture, so-called medical experiments performed in concentration camps, war crimes, killing in a variety of circumstances, robbery, and extortion of national and private property. These war crimes appeared to be a new phenomenon, at least in their prevalence, because they had been carried out in an organized manner by the occupying authorities and their subordinates and because the perpetrators usually did not differ from the general law-abiding population in their social or cultural background.

Research in this area was primarily descriptive and of a fact-finding nature, but some works provided insights into the development of Nazi criminals by social conditioning within the party (NSDAP), paramilitary organizations, or the army. The shaping of attitudes was favorable to acts of unimaginable cruelty with complete indifference to the suffering of other human beings. Research in this field was to continue for some time but less intensively in succeeding years.

At that time, juvenile delinquency also drew the attention of persons interested in research into crime. One is tempted to regard that research as a continuation of the prewar work, but the effects of the war were particularly germane in creating conditions for new topics for research into juvenile delinquency. The sheer magnitude of juvenile delinquency was coupled with the related problem of predelinquent children orphaned by the war.[2]

The Polish government acknowledged the seriousness of the juvenile delinquency problem by establishing a new, educationally oriented system of juvenile courts covering the whole country.[3] The establishment of juvenile courts appears to be one of the most important developments in the reform of both the criminal and civil justice systems for youth. The development has had a lasting effect on shaping the court system.

INTERRUPTION OF CRIMINOLOGY'S PROGRESS

In the first years after the war, few papers on traditional criminal offenses and on their perpetrators were published, and several new projects were started. Unfortunately, the slow but marked progress of the late 1940s was very soon brought to a halt. Criminology as a branch of scientific endeavor encountered serious impediments.

In 1950, its scholarly production, particularly when evaluated against the conditions of its situation previous to the war, was severely and unjustly criticized. Criminology was accused of being biologically oriented and scientifically ill-founded. New ideas on the purposes and subject matter of criminology were developed and promoted.[4] Crime was considered to be a transitional phenomenon, alien to the socialist social order. It was supposed to disappear as soon as the new classless communist society had been established completely. As a consequence of this belief, the need for study of the crime problem in Poland was put in doubt. The interest in crime in the capitalist countries was encouraged as a means of showing how the social conditions in those countries stimulate criminal behavior and lead to a constant growth of crime.

Developing criminology as a separate branch of science was declared unnecessary and even false. Criminal lawyers were to focus on the crime problem rather than on the content of the penal law itself. Thus, some of the problems of interest to criminologists were to be considered only by lawyers within the framework of preliminary examination of substantive criminal law.

The consequences of this perspective can be easily guessed. Empirical investigation of the crime problem was almost completely stopped. The authors of some criminal law textbooks failed to address the problems of crime. Others did consider these issues but in a rather superficial way. If these textbooks are used to evaluate the nature of Polish criminology, one is tempted to conclude that it is unworthy as a branch of science.

Despite these developments, empirical work in criminology was never entirely abandoned in Poland. The late Professor S. Batawia taught criminology first at the University of Lodz, located in the second largest industrial city of Poland where a new university was established after the war. Later, he taught criminology at the University of Warsaw where he afterwards taught forensic psychiatry only.

Batawia also guided the research activities of a small group of his colleagues. He conducted or supervised research into various topics, but the major interests were the traditional criminal offenses in postwar Poland, proceedings of courts against persons who collaborated with the German invaders and were found guilty of the wartime atrocities, and finally juvenile delinquency. Professor Batawia was also active in research in the 1960s and 1970s, becoming a full member of the Polish Academy of Science. Today he is recognized as the leading criminologist in postwar Poland.

RESURGENCE UNDER CHANGED CONDITIONS

In the mid-1950s, the general situation in the country changed dramatically. The fateful year 1956 brought developments with far-reaching political, economic, and social implications. Liberation from the Stalinist deformities was not only quick but in some areas also profound. The processes of liberation would require analysis that exceeds the space available here and would divert our attention excessively from the analysis of Polish criminology, which is our central purpose.

It suffices to mention only that one consequence of the dramatic changes was the initiation of a new period of development of the social sciences in Poland. First, Marxism had been converted into a political tool by camouflaging narrow partisanship in the wrappings of scientific objectivity. This perversion of Marxist principles was now terminated. Second, the social sciences were liberated from the rigidity of a simplified version of Marxism. That theoretical perspective became more open to absorbing a variety of approaches to issues previously considered alien to the perspective. Authorities continued to give preferential treatment to Marxism, but it ceased to be regarded as the only philosophical and methodological foundation for all branches of social science.

A new era for development of criminology stemmed from a number of conditions. Of great importance was a significant change in the attitude towards the crime problem. Crime ceased to be regarded as an embarrassing phenomenon, the existence of which could not be denied completely but should be concealed as much as possible. The authorities began to view crime as a "normal" social problem rooted in the social conditions then prevailing in the country. There was less effort to explain crime in contemporary Poland as a relic of the capitalist past or as behavior that could be attributed to subversive actions of the class enemies.

One of the most obvious results of the changed attitudes was the publication of criminal statistics. Poland's *Statistical Yearbook* provides a rather extensive body of data derived from three official sources: police statistics based on offenses known to the police, judicial statistics based on sentences, and prison statistics based on those persons confined in penal institutions.[5] These data are supplemented by information on the business of the public prosecutor and the courts, on juvenile delinquents, on judges and lay magistrates, and finally on transgressions and the disposition of transgressors. More detailed statistics have been made available to research workers. Although published primarily for internal use, the statistics are available in the major university libraries for public use.

In this new atmosphere, it is no wonder that empirical research in criminology expanded rapidly by taking up new areas for investigation, in terms of the number of research workers engaged in the study of the crime problem and in related topics, in terms of the amount of publications, and in terms of a variety of educational backgrounds among those persons attracted to criminology. As in much of Europe, criminology in Poland has been an occupational field populated predominantly by lawyers. To some extent, Polish criminologists continue to be lawyers, but in the late 1950s criminology began to benefit from the growth of interest in criminology among psychologists, sociologists, educators, and psychiatrists.

MAJOR DIRECTIONS OF CRIMINOLOGICAL RESEARCH

The foundations for contemporary criminology in Poland were set in the late 1950s, but the subsequent developments in research must be examined to understand the present-day state of the field. The main lines of that research should be considered.

For the last two and a half decades, juvenile delinquency has remained the most intensively investigated subject. A number of longitudinal studies were undertaken with the aim of exploring the life conditions of juvenile delinquents from the sociological, psychological, and sometimes also the psychiatric perspective. Papers and books were devoted to special categories of juveniles, such as young recidivists, gang members, delinquents in metropolitan areas and in rapidly industrialized towns, delinquents reared in families of heavy drinkers or alcoholics, those subjected to different measures administered by juvenile courts, and those coming to the attention of the court at a very young age.

Several studies explored hidden delinquency. As is the case in other countries, petty larcenies in Poland were found to be common among youngsters, but official reactions to them were exceptional. One investigation dealt with all youngsters born in one calendar year who were subjected to the attention of a juvenile court at any time. Only about one-third of the former juvenile delinquents engaged in further offenses during the first six years of their adulthood. More than half of them seem to have grown completely out of their former mode of deviant behavior.

Another project investigated the maladjustment of school children as manifested in behavioral disorders and in difficulties in coping with the school curriculum. One of the aims of this project has been to look more deeply into the onset of the process of becoming a juvenile delinquent who becomes known to the police and the courts. The research is still in progress.

The jurisdiction of the juvenile courts—at present falling within the general jurisdiction of the family courts—covers cases of juvenile offenders as well as those of neglected or dependent children. A recent investigation reported a number of similarities between two legally distinct groups of youngsters: first, the neglected children who usually come from broken or disturbed homes and who commit larcenies, and, second, the juvenile delinquents committing larcenies who often come from disturbed or broken homes.

Another study of juvenile delinquency gathered information about young prostitutes; a number of them were former clients of the juvenile courts. The phenomenon of prostitution, often attributed directly to conditions prevailing in the capitalist countries, was found to exist also in a socialist society. Some twenty years later, another study of young prostitutes is now in progress. Its aim is to determine what changes in this trade and in the persons engaged in it have occurred in those twenty years.

After the war, Poland experienced mass population movements because of the changes of its frontiers and the processes of rapid industrialization and urbanization. Several studies have been undertaken on the possible effect of those processes on the extent and spatial distribution of juvenile delinquency and adult crime. The impact of those processes on juvenile delinquency in the 1950s and 1960s was clearly demonstrated, but conclusions for adult crime were less clear. In nonurbanized communities experiencing rapid industrialization, the crime level was found to rise.

The spatial distribution of crime has also received attention in the studies on urban ecology carried out by town planners and sociologists. In different parts of those towns and cities investigated, the crime pattern and crime rates varied markedly. Those areas of towns and cities also differed in their social characteristics. The urban ecological studies proved that at least some of the principles in this sphere of the sociological literature are relevant to urban growth in a socialist society in spite of claims that the process of urbanization there is carried out in an organized and planned way.

Alcohol abuse and alcoholism are one of the serious social problems troubling Polish society. In the last three decades alcohol consumption has nearly trebled in Poland. Since strong beverages of the vodka type are favored in Poland, the social consequences of drinking are much more acute than in countries where wine and beer are the predominant forms of alcohol consumption. No wonder that the influence of heavy drinking and alcoholism on crime has been the subject of a considerable number of studies. The analyses have concentrated on individual offenders and on the relationships between trends in crime and alcohol consumption. The life histories of the most repetitive recidivists indicate that heavy drinking plays an important part in the careers of dedicated criminality. In the majority of cases alcohol abuse was a factor accompanying and stimulating the social degradation of offenders. Analysis of another group of recidivists suggested that criminal offenses are a consequence of heavy drinking; this group began to commit offenses while already alcohol dependent, and most of their offenses were related to their drinking habits.

Traditional criminal offenses—particularly serious types such as homicide, robbery, rape, and other crimes of violence—were much more often investigated than the most common offenses such as burglaries and simple thefts. Most of these studies were based on analysis of court records. Some were carried out, however, in the form of interviews of offenders and their families. In the latter type of studies and in research on recidivists, psychologists, and to some extent also psychiatrists, made the most important contribution.

Economic crime has peculiar significance for socialist law and economy. The criminal law intervenes in the economic aspects of social life much further than in capitalist societies, where, for example, mismanagement of a public enterprise is rarely a criminal offense. Economic criminality assumes new dimensions in socialist states because of their great concentration of power and decision-making in the economic and political spheres. The studies of economic offenses are numerous in Poland, but most of them are purely descriptive. They tell much about how these offenses are committed, about the circumstances that simplify or stimulate their perpetration, and about the formation of gangs of "law-abiding employees" committing economic offenses. However, these studies give the impression that basic questions are neither asked nor answered. To reach profound conclusions, it would be necessary to establish how the qualities of the political economy are related to economic criminality.

RESEARCH ON CRIMINAL POLICY ISSUES

Criminologically oriented lawyers have often raised criminal policy issues. Sentencing has been investigated in some depth, particularly in a study observing and analyzing the decision-making processes of reaching a verdict and of choosing the penalty. Other studies investigated trends in criminal policy in general or trends related to particular groups of offenders: young adults, recidivists, perpetrators of certain types of offenses.

These controversial issues have provoked hot disputes. Poland has had a very severe penal policy; the sentences imposed by the Polish criminal courts are much harsher than in a number of other European countries. The advocates of this penal policy and its critics have clashed many times, but the critics have not been able to claim success.

To be conclusive, research on the effectiveness of penal measures requires a great deal of sophistication, which has been lacking in most of those Polish studies. Generally speaking, these studies have demonstrated that long sentences to prison are no more effective in reducing recidivism than shorter sentences. Some studies have even showed that the offenders tended to commit crimes sooner after longer sentences than after shorter ones. Because those studies held only a few factors constant, the conclusions reached should be considered more plausible than conclusive.

In comparison with many other European countries, Poland for years has had a very high prison population, roughly three hundred per one hundred thousand inhabitants. Research in corrections in general, and on prisoners and prisons in particular, has been relatively developed. In this area, psychologists, sociologists, lawyers, and psychiatrists have made important criminological contributions. Here we offer one sphere of investigation as an example rather than an extensive description of all these studies. A number of projects examined the subcultures of prisoners in institutions for juvenile or adult offenders. These studies refute the claims that rehabilitative and reeducational efforts are successfully undertaken in penal institutions.

PREVAILING DEFINITIONS OF CRIMINOLOGY

Although individual authors formulate different definitions of criminology, in the majority of instances the disparities are in wording rather than in content.

Those authors who take a stand on the scope of criminology agree on several points: (1) Criminology constitutes an inquiry into the causes of crime, and emphasis is usually placed on causes that are of a social nature; (2) the forms of criminal behavior are investigated, and sometimes the boundaries of criminological inquiry are extended into other manifestations of deviance; (3) the ways of combatting crime are part of the subject matter of criminology; and (4) the same may be said about delinquency and crime prevention.

The ways of combatting crime are conceived in a rather narrow sense. They are restricted to the penal measures provided by criminal law, the application of those measures to offenders, and consideration of the question of their effectiveness. Only in exceptional instances is criminology considered to be a field that looks into alternatives to penal measures in dealing with offenders. Diversion from the criminal justice system is seldom discussed and then largely in connection with juvenile delinquency.

The things which these authors consider to be outside the scope of criminology are worthy of special note. Particularly significant is the failure to call for inquiry into the sphere of criminal law itself. Thus, criminology does not deal with the process of criminalization whereby a rationale emerges and exists for making particular forms of misconduct subject to criminal penalities. Similarly, the operation of the criminal justice system is not recognized as a legitimate topic for criminological research.

The formal definition may appear to provide an answer to the question of what this particular branch of learning is, but the function of the definition in this regard may be interpreted in two different ways. First, a definition may be considered a statement of what criminology should be. This is a postulative approach. Second, the definition may inform us on what is actually going on in criminology. The second approach is descriptive. Both approaches are interesting, but the latter one provides better insight into what criminologists in a given country do in a definite period of time.

The descriptive approach demands resolution of the complicated problem of defining who the criminologists are. One way of providing an answer would be to ask a large variety of persons—those doing research connected with crime and delinquency, those dealing with offenders in the work of criminal justice or crime prevention, and so on—whether they consider themselves criminologists. Because the question has not been systematically investigated in Poland, one is compelled to confine oneself to "a knowledgeable guess." Such questioning would bring negative results. Probably only very few, if any, persons engaged in such research would describe themselves as criminologists. They would rather think of themselves as lawyers, psychologists, sociologists, educators, or psychiatrists, interested mainly or only partly in crime or in problems related to it.

This secondary identification of self with the field of criminology has far-reaching consequences for the shape of criminology. First, it is hardly possible to talk in Poland of a community of criminologists. Persons doing research on aspects of the crime problem are scattered in a variety of professional groups. They feel much stronger ties with those who graduated from the same faculty than with those persons whose educational background has been different. The common involvement of this diverse group in research on a similar criminological subject is not a sufficient linkage for a firm sense of colleagueship as criminologists. In fact, the similarity of their subject matter interests is not always recognized and acknowledged.

One of the negative side-effects of this state of the art is that problems posed by crime are conceived and studied mainly within the frame of reference of a particular discipline, such as law, sociology, psychology, education, or psychiatry. Admittedly, it happens quite often that, for example, lawyers conducting a research project in criminology consider not only the legal aspects of crime but also those of a sociological or psychological nature. The main stress, however, is on the legal aspects, and the sociological or psychological aspects are usually treated in a way that is not satisfactory to a sociologist or psychologist.

Consequently, the general picture of criminology in Poland resembles more an archipelago of islands with little communication among them than a continent covered by a network of roads. This analogy becomes evident to anyone familiar with the Polish scientific literature on crime, simply by looking into the footnotes of the articles or books. The psychiatrists quote almost exclusively other psychiatrists and refer to medical books and journals. The psychologists refer to psychological literature. This pattern is also true in the case of educators and sociologists. Only lawyers writing on crime quote the literature of other professions, but this tendency does not necessarily mean that their research seriously considers aspects other than legal or criminal policy matters.

ASSESSMENT OF THE STATE OF RESEARCH

The necessity of overcoming the fragmentation in research on crime is as serious and widespread a concern in Poland as it is in other countries. The deficiency is frequently pointed out in criminological literature. Criminology has been praised for helping to reduce the fragmentation of research, but the praise is only partly justified. It is true that the crime problem attracts the attention of specialists from a number of branches of learning, but the problem of fragmentation persists in that really multidisciplinary research continues to be an exception rather than a rule.

The most common strategy for broadening the range of theoretical perspectives in a research project is to recruit teams of persons with different educational backgrounds. Undoubtedly, the most important criminological studies in Poland emerged as a result of such teamwork. The teams have originated more often in the institutes attached to the Polish Academy of Sciences or to government bodies such as the Ministry of Justice or the Attorney-General's Office, because these institutes employ persons from a variety of professions. This team approach is either less common or nonexistent at the universities where research activities are concentrated predominantly within a particular faculty.

One of the weaknesses of criminology in Poland is its relative disregard of a more general theoretical perspective. We do not lack papers and books analyzing theories of criminal behavior of historical value and present relevance. What is annoying is that the theoretical perspectives seem to have little impact on current empirical research. Only rarely does one come across studies in which questions asked are put into a broader perspective, are expected to test theoretical assumptions, or lead to the formulation of general theories. As a rule, the purpose of empirical research is descriptive and is limited to testing concrete hypotheses on relations between simple variables. The amount of available information is usually restricted.

Many studies are based on small samples derived from ill-defined universes. It is difficult to estimate the generality of the results obtained or to integrate conclusions drawn from different studies. It is not clear whether the opposing conclusions of several projects are the consequence of differences in the populations from which samples were drawn or are the consequence of the phenomenon under examination. Even the need to apply proper sampling methods is not always recognized. Finally, the methods used for testing hypotheses are usually too simple and inadequate. Only a few studies employ more advanced analytical tools, such as factor analysis or discriminant function analysis. However, slow but steady progress is noticeable in methodology.

THE FUTURE OF POLISH CRIMINOLOGY

In conclusion, one more question has to be asked, that of the future of Polish criminology. It seems certain that crime will continue to trouble Polish society in the foreseeable future. It also seems certain that its shape will change. In the sphere of traditional criminal offenses, no dramatic new developments are expected. The changes in the shape of crime will occur elsewhere.

Increases in the number of traffic offenses and in other kinds of offenses connected with the use of modern technology, whether machinery or chemicals, seem unavoidable. The latter offenses manifest themselves as culpably contributing to accidents at work or in spoiling the natural environment. With regard to road traffic, Poland is still in a period of rapid growth. The greater number of motor vehicles has been accompanied by an increase in the number of road accidents. The same pattern is true in other uses of modern technology.

The example of more developed industrial countries shows that this is a transitional period in the long-term price society has to pay for economic growth. This cost can be higher or lower, and the length of the transitional period can vary. It is generally felt in Poland that the price has been too high and the period too long. The prevailing opinion favors further criminalization and the imposition of stiffer penalties against behavior contributing to the undesirable consequences of the use of modern technology. It seems that there is ample opportunity and urgent need for criminological research testing the validity of expectations that something can be gained by criminalization of those forms of misconduct.

Economic offenses produce the greater trouble among the kinds of criminal behavior. In the present economic disarray, their scope as well as their social significance have become more and more visible, felt, and perceived as being influential in the creation and augmentation of unwarranted social inequalities. Economic crime creates a new challenge for criminology which has to be taken up despite all the difficulties it raises for sound research. Economic criminality, as it is well known, is conditioned to a large extent by the distribution and concentration of power within the society. It is difficult to examine the distribution of power in the penetrating way it deserves. If criminology is to avoid losing its social relevance, it has to expand rapidly the research into this sensitive area.

The operation of the criminal justice system should be another target of greater research, but little has been done in this area in Poland. Another area that requires serious empirical research is crime prevention, which entails a broad range of topics and approaches. The specific areas for research would range from concrete strategies of reducing the opportunities for committing offenses to the development of social and economic policy for curbing crime while building a just and sane society of the future. Apart from these spheres of prospective interests, it is likely that the present trends in research on the crime problem will continue.

NOTES

1. The extent of war losses among Polish scientists and professionals was enormous, and they are relatively little known abroad. As an example, one can cite what happened to the psychiatrists. In 1939, the Polish Psychiatric Association, in which nearly all doctors of that specialty were members, numbered four hundred, but in 1946 there were only eighty.

2. The term "orphan" refers to fatherless and motherless children because of the death of one or both parents. Here the term also refers to children of parents who could not be traced or to children parentless because the war separation led one or both parents to form a new family.

3. In prewar Poland, there had been only two juvenile courts of limited regional jurisdiction.

4. At that time, "to promote" meant mainly to stop activities that did not strictly conform to the officially declared line.

5. Poland has been the only socialist country to publish data on the prison population for the years 1955-1971. Unfortunately, in the last decade this practice was abandoned.

BIBLIOGRAPHY

With the exception of three major criminological journals, the following list presents only selected books as representative of the criminological literature of Poland.

Batawia, Stanislaw, with the collaboration of Jadwigi Sochoń and Helena Kolakowska. *Proces społecznego wykolejania sie nieletnich przestepców* [The Process of Social Maladjustment in Juveniles]. Warsaw: Państwowe Wydawnictwo Naukowe, 1958.
Part 1 discusses research on juvenile delinquents with nondelinquent brothers of similar age; Part 2 is a follow-up study of juvenile delinquents released from children's homes and from borstals.

Błachut, Janina. *Kobiety recydwistki w świetle badań kryminologicznych* [Criminological Research on Women Recidivists]. Wroclaw-Warsaw-Krakow-Gdansk-Lodz: Zakład Narodowy imienia Ossolińskich, 1981.
This is a study in the life histories of women recidivists doing their sentences in prison; research is based on personal interviews.

Bossowski, Jozef Jan. *Wiadomości z nauk kryminologicznych* [Compendium of Criminology]. Posen: Księgarnia Akademicka, 1946.
This short account discusses theories and research in the etiology of crime.

Bożyczko, Zbignie. *Kradzież kieszonkowa i jej sprawca* [Pickpocketing and Pickpockets]. Warsaw: Wydawnictwo Prawnicze, 1962.
This research study is based on personal interviews with pickpockets on their trade and way of life.

Dluźniewska, Kazimiera. *Zagarnięcie mienia społecznego w zakładzie produkcynym* [The Appropriation of Common Property in an Industrial Plant]. Warsaw: Wydawnictwo Prawnicze, 1974.
This survey of thefts in an industrial plant discusses the dimensions of the problem, the stimulating factors, and the process of disclosing the thefts committed.

Falandysz, Lech. *Wiktymologia* [Victimology]. Warsaw: Wiedza Powszechna, 1979.
This work is a general introduction to victimology.

Hołyst, Brunon. *Kryminologia* [Criminology]. Warsaw: Państwowe Wydawnictwo Naukowe, 1979.
This textbook of criminology deals with the subject of criminology and its relation to other branches of learning; basic sources of data on crime; research methods in criminology; general traits of contemporary crime and other criminogenic social phenomena; a survey of theories of criminology; determinants of crime; prognosis in criminology; and the system of crime prevention.

Horoszowski, Paweł. *Kryminologia* [Criminology]. Warsaw: Państwowe Wydawnictwo Naukowe, 1965.
This textbook in criminology presents the following topics: statistical analysis of criminality; biological and psychological factors in the etiology of crime; sociological problems of crime; and statistical methods in criminology.

Jasińska, Magdalena. *Proces społecznego wykolejenia młodocianych dziewczqt* [The Process of Social Degradation of Young Girls]. Warsaw: Wydawnictwo Prawnicze, 1967.
This study in prostitution is based on personal interviews covering the process of becom-

ing a prostitute, social stratification among prostitutes, and trade and involvement in crime.

Jasiński, Jerzy. *Przewidywanie przestepczości jako zjawiska masowego* [Forecasting Future Trends of Crime]. Warsaw: Wydawnictwo Prawnicze, 1980.
This study focuses on the foundations of forecasting future events in the social sciences; prognostic research in criminology; and a forecast of prospective changes in the scope and structure of crime in Poland.

Jasiński, Jerzy (ed.). *Zagadnienia nieprzystosowania spolecznego i przestępozości w Polsce* [Problems of Social Maladjustment and Crime in Poland]. Wroclaw-Warsaw-Krakow-Gdansk: Zakład Narodowy imienia Ossolińskich, 1978.
This collection of papers summarizes the Polish empirical literature on crime and its macrosocial determinants; alcohol abuse, alcoholism, and drug-taking; and environmental and personal factors that lead to social maladjustment and crime.

Jedlewski, Stanisław. *Analiza pedagogiczna systemu dyscyplinaro-izolecyjnego w resocjalizacji nieletnich* [The Educator's Analysis of the Disciplinary-Isolationist System in Resocialization of Juveniles]. Wroclaw-Warsaw-Krakow: Zakład Narodowy imienie Ossolińskich, 1966.
This theoretical and empirical analysis centers on the coercive educational system in borstal training.

Kaczmarek, Tomasz. *Sędziowski wymiar kary w Polskiej Rzeczypospolitej Ludowej* [Sentencing in the Polish People's Republic]. Wroclaw-Warsaw-Krakow-Gdansk: Zakład Narodowy imienia Ossolińskich, 1972.
This research in attitudes and opinions on punishment and sentencing is based on a survey carried out among judges.

Kołakowska-Przełomiec, Helena. *Przestepczość i nieprzystosowanie społeczne nieletnich w genezie przestepczości dorosłych* [Delinquency and Social Maladjustment of Juveniles and Its Impact on Their Prospective Crimes]. Wroclaw-Warsaw-Krakow-Gdansk: Zakład Narodowy imienia Ossolińskich, 1977.
This research study discusses the future social adjustment and offenses of all boys born in 1949 to whom the juvenile courts applied educational or corrective measures at the time these boys were juveniles.

Lernell, Leszek. *Zarya kryminologii ogólnej* [An Outline of General Criminology]. Warsaw: Państwowe Wydawnictwo Naukowe, 1973.
The topics of this textbook of criminology are: general information; factors in the etiology of crime: the structure and dynamics of crime in contemporary Poland; some special problems, for example, the typology of offenders, prognosis in criminology, prostitution, and crime; and problems of victimology.

Majcerzak, Irena. *Pracownicze przestępstwo gospodarcze i jego sprawca* [The Employee's Economic Offense and Its Perpetrator]. Warsaw: Wiedza Powszechna, 1965.
This sociological analysis of criminal gangs and a network of gangs in public enterprises is based on court records of criminal cases in the tanning and leather industries.

Malewska, Hanna, and Vincent Peyre, with the collaboration of Anna Firkowska-Mankiewicz. *Przestepczość nieletnich. Uwarunkowania społeczno-okonomiczne* [Juvenile Delinquency: Its Socioeconomic Causes]. Warsaw: Państwowe Wydawnictwo Naukowe, 1973.
Juvenile delinquency is examined as a side-effect of economic development and social mobility.

Mościcka, Lidia. *Przestepczość nieletnich. Podłoże, genezą, Motywy* [Juvenile Delinquency: The Background, Origin and Motives]. Wroclaw-Warsaw-Krakow-Gdansk: Zakład Narodowy imienia Ossolińskich, 1970.
Móscicka presents a psychological analysis of juvenile delinquency.

Pawełczyńska, Anna. *Przestępczość grup nieletnich* [The Delinquency of Juvenile Gang Members]. Warsaw: Książka i Wiedza, 1964.
This work focuses on a sociological analysis of juvenile gangs, the process of formation, organization, delinquencies, and functions. It is based on interviews of gang members, their parents, and neighbors.

Siemaszko, Andrzej. *Społeczna geneza przestepczości. Wokół teorii zróżnicowanych powiązań* [Social Origins of Crime: On the Differential Association Theory and Other Related Matters]. Warsaw: Państwowe Wydawnictwo Naukowe, 1979).
A critical analysis of Edwin H. Sutherland's theory of differential association is presented.

Strzembosz, Adam. *Nieletni sprawcy kradzieży w środowisku wielkomiejskim* [Juveniles Committing Larcenies in an Urban Milieu]. Warsaw: Państwowe Wydawnictwo Naukowe, 1971.
Strzembosz discusses a survey of juvenile delinquents who were referred to the juvenile court in a district of Warsaw during one year. A follow-up took place after five and eight years.

Świda, Hanna, and Witold Świda. *Młodociani przestępcy w więzienitu* [Young Adult Prisoners]. Warsaw: Wiedza Powszechna, 1961.
The authors describe an educational experiment in a prison for young adult offenders, and present a rationale and description of the progress of the experiment.

Świda, Witold (ed.). *Kryminologia* [Criminology]. Warsaw: Państwowe Wydawnictwo Naukowe, 1977.
This textbook of criminology considers the following topics: general information; research methods in criminology; structure and rate of crime; etiology of crime; juvenile delinquency; young adult offenders; alcoholism; prostitution; the influence of industrialization and urbanization on crime; research on the personality of offenders and their typology; prognosis in criminology; crime prevention; the fight against crime in Poland; and resocialization of offenders.

Szelhaus, Stanisław. *Młodociani recydywiści* [Young Adult Recidivists]. Warsaw: Państwowe Wydawnictwo Naukowe, 1969.
This study is of one hundred young adult recidivists interviewed while in prison, with a ten-year follow-up.

Szmanowski, Teodor. *Powrotność do przestępatwa po wykonanin kary pozbawienia wolności* [Return to Crime after Release from Prison]. Warsaw: Wydawnictwo Prawnicze, 1976.
This survey is of recidivism among young offenders, seventeen to twenty-three years old, sentenced to immediate imprisonment and released during one calendar year from penal institutions in Poland. A follow-up was undertaken after five and ten years to assess the effectiveness of imprisonment.

Tyszkiewicz, Leon. *Badania osobopoznawcze w prawie karnym* [Personality Assessment in Criminal Law]. Warsaw: Wydawnictwo Prawnicze, 1975.
This work is an introduction to clinical criminology.

Wąsik, Józef. *Kara dożywotniego więzienia w Polsce* [The Life Sentence in Poland]. Warsaw: Wydawnictwo Prawnicze, 1963.
The execution of life sentences passed by the courts in Poland in the years 1946-1949 is discussed.

Wójcik, Dobrochna. *Środowisko rodzinne a pozion agresywności młodzieży przestępczej i nieprzestępczej* [Family Environment and the Level of Aggressiveness in Young Offenders and Nonoffenders]. Wroclaw-Warsaw-Krakow-Gdansk: Zakład Narodowy imienia Ossolińskich, 1977.
Wójcik presents a study of the social determinants of aggressiveness stemming from family environment.

Zakrzewski, Paweł. *Zjawisko wykolejenia społecznego młodzieży na terenach uprzemysławianych: wyniki badań w Nowej Hucie* [Social Maladjustment of Youth in an Industrialized Area: The Results of a Study in Nowa Huta]. Warsaw: Wydawnictwo Prawnicze, 1969.
Zakrzewski discusses research on juvenile delinquency in a newly built industrial town.

Zawadzki, Sylwester, and Leszek Kubicki (eds.). *Udział ławników w postępowaniu karnym. Opinie a rzeczywistość* [The Participation of Lay Magistrates in Penal Proceedings: Opinions and Real Facts]. Warsaw: Wydawnictwo Prawnicze, 1970.
This work describes the results of a research project on the participation of lay magistrates in the conviction and sentencing processes in criminal cases.

Major Criminological Journals

Archiwum Kryminologii [Archives of Criminology]. Vols. 1-7 (1960-1976). Vols. 8-9 in print.
Przeglad Penitencjarny i Kryminologiczny [Prison and Criminological Review]. Quarterly that appeared in the years 1965-1975.
Studia Kryminologiczne, Kryminalistyczne i Penitencjarne [Studies in Criminology, Police Science and Prison Issues]. Vols. 1-11 (1974-1981).

27

SOUTH AFRICA

Jacob Van der Westhuizen

Criminology began in South Africa, around 1930. At that time, a South African scholar named Geoff Cronje was studying criminology in Amsterdam in The Netherlands under Willem Adriaan Bonger. What Bonger accomplished for The Netherlands, Cronje did for South Africa.

HISTORIC BACKGROUND FOR SOUTH AFRICA

Criminology gained a foothold in South Africa because of Geoff Cronje's unbounded enthusiasm, but the establishment of criminology as a scientific activity was not to come until 1954 and then as a result of the efforts of penal reformers. Criminology became a teaching subject in 1963 at the University of South Africa.

The report of the Penal and Prison Reform Commission[1] (popularly known as the Lansdown Report) was tabled in Parliament in 1947, but the report is significant to South Africa's relatively brief and recent history because it reflected the views of a host of prolific "penal reformers" who were chiefly lawyers and judges. The report highlighted the following criminological issues: the causes of delinquency and crime in South Africa, especially among juveniles and non-Europeans; the adequacy of the measures available for the prevention of crime and delinquency; the general objectives of punishment, the methods available to courts of justice for the punishment of offenders, and the applicability of such methods to particular classes of offenders; and the transition of prisoners from institutional to community life, including release on probation, and the appointment, functions, and control of probation officers.

The Lansdown Report is relevant to the development of criminology in South Africa because, among its recommendations, there was a call for research and a research body to provide information on crime, punishment, deterrence, and treatment of offenders. Furthermore, an impressive agenda for the management of crime and the reduction of recidivism was set forth in recommendations such as the following:

The general objective of punishment should be deterrence *and* treatment of offenders. Punishment should have regard to the offender's individual characteristics and to the internal and external pressures that contributed to his lawlessness. The form of detention imposed on the dangerous prisoner who has been detained as a preventive measure for the protection of society should afford maximum security and the most humane treatment practicable within such limits. Short-term prison sentences tend to have undesirable results and should be avoided, and the courts should make fuller use of provisions in certain legislation for the suspension of sentences.

Slum conditions should be eliminated. In respect to problem children, the closest cooperation is necessary between the home, the school, the child guidance clinic, and the probation officer. The granting of compensation for damage to or loss of property to a complainant in criminal proceedings should be extended.

Psychoneurotic and psychopathic conditions leading to antisocial conduct should be treated in a separate institution. Sheltered employment should be provided for the physically deformed members of society. Inebriates and drug addicts need treatment and not punishment. The idle young should be taken in hand by probation officers and the older "won't work" type dealt with in work colonies.

A classified series of institutions and an effective scheme for the allocation of certain types of prisoners to these institutions are essential to the satisfactory administration of a prison system. Training and treatment are necessary for the offender's reformation. Response to corrective treatment should result in earlier release from detention on parole. There should be a proper system for the after-care of released prisoners.

The interest created by the Lansdown Commission was kept alive by the so-called Penal Reform League of South Africa. As might be expected, many of the league's studies and suggestions revolved around the recommendations made by the Penal and Prison Reform Commission. Deputations of the league met the minister of justice from time to time to discuss important penal issues.

On one memorable occasion in 1948, a league delegation met the then minister of justice, C. R. Swart, and offered their views on crime prevention, sentencing of offenders, and after-care of released prisoners. Professor Hahlo of the Witwatersrand University "dealt with the question of research and pleaded for the creation of a chair of criminology at any one of our universities."[2] Referring to public views on crime and punishment and a lack of scientific criteria to relationalize penal measures, he went on to say:

The time has come when an Institute of Criminology should be created, whose main function should be the study of crime, the collection of proper statistics, surveys of the prison population, etc....No matter where such chair or institute functions, one is urgently needed.

From its inception as an independent science at the University of Pretoria in 1954, criminology has engaged its students in studies of crime, juvenile delinquency, the criminal, and the administration of justice. When criminology was established as a teaching subject at the University of South Africa in 1963, another study dimension—the victim of crime—was added to its curriculum.

South African pioneers made considerable efforts to widen the scope of criminology so as to include law enforcement, criminal justice, and the after-care of prisoners. The need for a discipline that could be rationalized on theoretical, methodological, and practical grounds was crucial.

Venter wrote his doctoral thesis on the general causes of recidivism shortly before he became the first professor of criminology in South Africa in 1954. In his thesis, he analyzed the causes of crime and recidivism, emphasizing the need for the scientific and humane treatment of incarcerated criminals. Subsequent works provided a general description of the incidence and gravity of juvenile delinquency and suggested how to curb it. For instance, a recommendation gaining support was "the compulsory military training of juveniles when they leave school."[3]

Van der Walt made his debut with a comprehensive description of the development of criminology as a science.[4] His subsequent analysis of the scope, content, and functions of criminology provided a sound blueprint for the future pursuit of knowledge, and the eventual recognition of police science and penology as special teaching subjects at the university level.

WHAT IS CRIMINOLOGY?

Studying criminology in South Africa means studying patterns of delinquency and crime with a view to understanding how, when and why these phenomena are generated and perpetuated within our society. Understanding the criminal means tracing the motives behind his behavior and inferring why some measures to socialize, restrain, or rehabilitate him succeed while others fail. It also implies that some model of man is used to describe the criminal's rejection of societal norms and laws and resorting to criminal means to achieve certain ends. Beyond this, South African criminology is concerned with the victims of crime and attempts to understand and account for a wide range of interactional patterns that can be described as crime-precipitating situations.

By using a wide variety of approaches, the occurrence of crime is then explained by causal, contingent, historical, purposive, structural-functional, and/or rule-following analyses. In the final analysis, providing an explanation of crime means understanding the cultural, social, legal, economic, political, and spiritual processes that take place in the country and any foreign influences or world trends that may have a bearing on the dynamics of deviant thought, emotion, and behavior.

As the pioneer criminologist of South Africa, Conje, as did Bonger for The

Netherlands, introduced a deterministic approach to the explanation of crime and deviance, thereby embracing Ferri's frame of reference:

[Crime] is the effect of multiple causes. [The causes are]...always interlaced in an indissoluble net (and are)...*anthropological* or *individual* (age, sex, status, occupation, residence, social class, education, organic and mental constitution);...*physical* or telluric (race, climate, fertility, seasons, temperature, soil);...and *social* (population, migration, public opinion, customs, religion, family, politics, economics, agriculture, industry, education, welfare, legislation, etc.).[5]

From this base fifty years ago, South African criminology has come to see itself as the science that deals with human maladaptation, its origin, development, forms, diagnosis, and correction. The accommodation of scientific methods and practical concerns can be explained by the course of history reviewed above.

Briefly, criminology is regarded as the science that deals with the crime phenomenon, criminals, victims of crime, and the administration of justice.[6] The administration of justice entails the reaction of South African society and various communities to the crime phenomenon, both before and after the event. Criminology has the following functions:

1. A description of the crime phenomenon (as well as societal reactions to it, criminals and victims of crime).
2. An explanation of the crime phenomenon.
3. The application of knowledge and insight gained through descriptions and explanations for the purposes of prediction and control of the incidence and fluctuation of the crime phenomenon.[7]

At the beginning of the 1970s, the analytical method was introduced to aid in the search for truth; to furnish a reliable and valid system of knowledge; to counteract one-sidedness; and to yield unbiased and significant research findings. Application of the analytical method in criminological research confirms the claim that criminology is unique.

The general scientific approach to the formulation and testing of theories has been positivistic in nature, applying inductive and deductive reasoning to achieve its objectives. In both approaches, the "evidence" used has been the product of descriptive investigations.

Because the concern of criminology has been to build an open system of knowledge (that is, a system that makes no claim that its methods, techniques, generalizations, and theories are indisputable), it has always been considered inappropriate to lay down a fixed procedure for every new research project. Instead, the analytical method was introduced (1) to establish a meaningful relationship between fact and theory (adaptive function); (2) to confer neutrality on the investigation, thus enabling the investigator to describe and explain his study object on the group level, individual level, or both, and giving him the opportunity of synthesizing his analyses into comprehensive generalizations and systematic theories (integrative function); (3) to respect and to preserve recognized methodological principles and accepted techniques of description, explanation, prediction, and control, yet leaving ample room for change, technical refinement, and innovation (pattern-maintenance function); and (4) to make provision for *descriptive* investigations/analyses using explanatory techniques, and *applicative* investigations/analyses using prediction and control techniques (goal-achievement function).[8]

WHAT IS CRIME? A CRUCIAL DEFINITION

One very important question which South African criminologists have sought to answer since the inception of criminology as an autonomous science at the university level in 1954 is "What is crime?" Various perspectives on the origins, nature, and functions of crime have been advanced because some conception of crime is a prerequisite for the description and explanation of the crime phenomenon and any subsequent efforts to predict and control its incidence and the way in which it fluctuates.

In his doctoral thesis, "A Sociological Classification of Crime" (1954), Van der Walt advanced the view that "crime is any serious violation of social relationships" whether interpersonal, familial, political (cultural), economic, sexual, religious, or community relations.[9] This view has enabled criminologists to come to grips with the crime problem in a positive way and to eradicate certain faulty conceptions about the causes of and the cures for crime. For instance, it has forced criminologists to reconsider their views that (1) crime and sin are synonymous; (2) a single cause can be found for all crimes; (3) all criminals are tarred with the same brush and should be treated accordingly; (4) the "cause" of crime lies with the criminal alone and external circumstances are in no way involved; and (5) the victim of the crime plays no part in causing it.

The classical approach to the definition of crime is strongly evidenced by the fact that Van der Walt's definition considers any serious (that is, sanctioned) violation of social relationships to be regarded as "crime." The legal definition of a crime as "any act that breaches an existing law" is almost synonymous with Van der Walt's definition. The only difference is that laws are viewed as various prescribed ways and means to achieve inviolate social relations.

The relativity of crime, concerning the cultural variance in definition and sanctions, led South African criminologists to examine crime and delinquency in a criminological perspective that goes beyond the content of criminal codes. This view has been confirmed by the discovery that crime is but a symptom of maladaptation.

Labeling theory, circumscribed by the notion of nominalism, is very much in evidence in South Africa. It means that crime acquires its conceptual and operational meaning and content when defined and that no meaning can be attached to any human action until it is given meaning by society. The current trend is to direct research at those processes of interaction that define behavior as criminal, either on the group level or on a personal plane. The starting point for crime analysis seems to gravitate toward the crime situation and includes descriptions and explanations of the criminal's and victim's needs, motives, background, expectations, tendencies, maladaptation, morality, and maturity; the environmental setting, mostly in regard to sociocultural, political, and climatic considerations; and the "generalized indirect victims" of the suspected crime.

The fact that criminal law gives behavior its quality of criminality can be witnessed in the overreach of the law discussed at length during an international conference on crime, law, and punishment held at the University of Cape Town in 1975. In his opening address at the conference, Justice J. H. Steyn referred to "the destructive impact which the public demand for retributive and oppressive legislation has upon our criminal justice." He emphasized that the public demand "inhibits rationality, especially in the determination of the most appropriate methods of disposition. It frustrates the application of rehabilitative techniques, and it inhibits the aftercare and resocialization of the offender into the community."[10]

KEY PROBLEMS OF CRIMINOLOGY

On the present-day South African scene, criminology attempts to formulate the principles (or laws) that govern normative adaptation or maladaptation. This means that the main problems of criminology are to describe and explain juvenile delinquency and crime on the one hand and to show on the other hand how such knowledge and insight can be applied to predict and control (correct and remedy) the incidence and fluctuation of juvenile delinquency and crime.[11]

The problems of crime fall into two main classes: first, how to detect, describe, and explain maladaptation and, second, how to deal with maladaptation and to correct maladapted members of society. The static aspect of criminology, entailing the detection, description, and explanation of maladaptation, includes problems of juvenile delinquency, adult crime, and a spectrum of deviancy that supposedly causes crime. On the other hand, the dynamic aspect of criminology displays such problems as the overreach of the criminal law; social and cultural change; progressive or retrogressive adaptation; and the evolution of law and lawlessness.

Finding an appropriate definition of normative maladjustment poses an intricate problem. In broad terms, normative maladjustment can be defined as the incompatibility of behavior expected from the individual by society, with his latent or manifested behavior—thus including individual values, needs, norms, expectations, beliefs, and desires which may or may not be observed by society. More specifically, normative maladjustment can be viewed as a violation of the moral principles held by the majority of individuals in the given person's group.

Degrees of adaptation (and maladaptation) are described by considering the person's acceptance or nonacceptance of societal norms (including legal norms) and societal values. Any crime is regarded as an explicit rejection of a norm, while persistent crime can be viewed as an implicit rejection of a specific societal value. Adapting Merton's example,[12] nine degrees of maladaptation are evident:

		+	±	−
	+	a	b	c
Societal	±	d	e	f
norms	−	g	h	i

Societal values

where	+	=	acceptance
	±	=	instability
	−	=	rejection

In attempting to apply scientific perspectives and methods to criminological issues, South African criminologists have had to depend upon a number of the natural and social sciences, that is, biology, chemistry, mathematics, computer science, philosophy, history, sociology, psychology, politics, social work, education, law, and ethics. In this regard, the findings of other sciences are treated as factual sources. This means that relevant high-order propositions are utilized to arrive at some kind of superstructure by means of which crime can be described and explained. This approach has enabled many criminologists to advance beyond the descriptive phase because the tedium associated with revalidation of previously known findings has been eliminated.[13]

The last decade has witnessed serious attempts by South African criminologists to do away with the obsolete perspective, first, that criminology is only the meeting place of a number of specialists from various disciplines; and, second, that criminology comprises a number of constituent sciences. Although criminology has to borrow some relevant principles of interpretation and methods and techniques from other sciences, it has its own unique problems, philosophy, study object, and ways and means to describe, explain, predict, and control crime. In fact, criminology is unique in the sense that so many sources are tapped to solve its problems.

Developments during the last decade have affected some of the theories of crime causation and may someday change the course of criminological thought and practice in South Africa.

First is the trend in South African criminology toward a more refined classification of crime and effective crime-specific descriptions, explanations, and predictions which may form the basis of experimental crime control. Inextricably bound up with this trend, and indeed basic to a comprehensive approach to human behavior, has been the increasing emphasis on interaction and a logical definition of crime and criminal behavior.

Inherent in Van der Walt's definition that crime is a violation of social relations is the element of social interaction and the fact that crime is defined within the limits of a dynamic behavior pattern rather than in relation to a theory or abstraction. The criminologists' increasing attention to the crime situation per se and to the victim of crime has resulted in greater understanding of the process by which crime is defined and the criminal is labeled by the group.

Second, individual case histories have been introduced and used increasingly. For instance, systematic efforts are currently being made to utilize fully the case histories of recidivists. This procedure has permitted a clearer insight into the causes of crime and has enabled criminologists to formulate prediction instruments of parole behavior.

A third development has been the rediscovery of the meaning and origin of crime. The identification of interactionary parameters ranks among the most significant of the scientific discoveries made in South Africa, because differences between human beings are viewed as differences of degree rather than of kind. Researchers are now, by their own distinctive methods and techniques—which include factor analysis, discriminant analysis, regression analysis, and signal detection analysis—attempting to identify the most significant motivating forces at work in the "maladapted" personality.

A fourth significant development has been the full-scale use of the computer to analyze criminal statistics and criminological data. This development paved the way to a conception of the criminal as a biosocial product, as a creation of society in general, and as a consequence of the crime situation in particular.

Fifth, until recently there were no specialized journals to serve as clearinghouses for students of criminology and as a rostrum for scientific views and philosophies. These needs are being met by the *South African Journal of Criminal Law and Criminology*, issued in April 1977 in its first volume. The appearance of the journal marks the beginning of a new criminological determination to straddle the gulf between fact and theory.

The last and most significant development concerns an in-depth appraisal of the crime phenomenon and a total reevaluation of the nature, structure, functions, and objectives of criminology as a behavioral science. The earlier failure of South African and overseas criminologists to define, describe, and explain the crime phenomenon in real-life terms and to identify its essential features has stimulated new attempts to discover the truth behind the so-called phenomenal world of human behavior. As a direct result of these endeavors, the view that crime is a natural phenomenon—like lightning or wind—has been invalidated. It is now asserted that crime is a symptom of maladjustment between the individual and society.

PATTERNS OF CRIME IN SOUTH AFRICA

In attempting to delineate the magnitude and patterns of crime and to explain its appearance, South African students of criminology are familiar with overseas research into biological, socioeconomic, and psychological factors. Some important efforts have been made to develop general explanations for crime and delinquency within a classical frame of reference.

During the 1950s, Louis Franklin Freed, a psychiatrist, made a thorough study of the crime problem in South Africa, utilizing the integralist approach of medical thought, in terms of which the human personality is conceived of as a "mind-body" in constant interaction with a multiplex environment and, consequently, as a final product of environmental forces. He defined the criminal as a frustrated person emerging in society as a product of disorganizing forces variously arising from the complex of his personality, or of his environment, and leading finally to a form of behavior, which insofar as it threatens the safety, security, and happiness of other persons in the community brings him into conflict with the law.

General Considerations

In *Crime in South Africa* (1963), Freed describes, first, the magnitude, character, and cost of the crime problem; second, the causality; and, third, the control of crime in South Africa.[14] Important findings and generalizations from Freed's study may be summarized as follows:

From 1912 to 1953, the crime rate increased approximately 5.1 times, while the increase in the police strength rose 2.6 times, and the increase in population 2.2 times.

Nonserious crime is responsible for 94.2 percent of all crime in South Africa. Among the serious crimes, "Class E serious crimes," or crimes relating to property, are the most frequent, constituting 36.7 percent of all serious crimes. These are followed by Class D serious crimes, relating to persons (32.9 percent); Class B serious crimes, relating to the welfare and public health of the community (16.6 percent); Class A serious crimes, relating to the state and public administration (6.8 percent); and Class C serious crimes, relating to the mining industry (0.6 percent).

The phenomenon of a progressive rise in the incidence of crime has not been peculiar to the Republic of South Africa; it is, in fact, characteristic of all European countries that have been subjected to similar sociological forces. Factors over and above the operation of a single agency—namely, functionally related sociological factors in the forms of increasing industrialization, urbanization, and rural-urban migration—were responsible for the rise in the incidence of crime.

Crime is not an independent social phenomenon; it is one of the indices of social disorganization. The problem of crime in the Republic of South Africa is not soluble in a context of disequilibrium wrought by uncontrolled sociological forces like rapid industrialization and urbanization. The magnitude of the problem of crime in South Africa will likely be very considerably reduced by virtue of the progressive social legislation that is being contemplated and is to be enacted in the immediate future.

The high crime rate in South Africa and the steady increase in the incidence of crime may be attributed to those general sociological forces operating in many parts of the world, but explanation may also be attempted in a number of ways through either single-factor or multivariable approaches. The main variables include the following: From time to time, more acts are officially defined as crimes, and more cases of outlawed deviance are discovered. More and more discovered crimes are officially reported. More mass media coverage of crime is currently in evidence. Once the media highlight any type of crime, some societal reaction becomes apparent. Of course, more crimes are in fact committed by South Africans. The operation of particular variables is evidenced in recent patterns of crimes of violence, rape, drug abuse, and theft of motor vehicles. By examining those categories, we will gain insights into the broad range of variables involved in the perpetration and in the typical reactions to crime in South Africa.

Crimes of Violence

Because of their grounding in the broad range of variables and because they hold implications for other kinds of crime, crimes of violence were the subject of the National Symposium on Crimes of Violence (1979) at the University of South Africa, where the typological description of violence in South Africa as shown in Figure 27-1 was presented.

Conflict is the common element in the legal, social, and individual realities of violence that make those crimes an invaluable opportunity for research into patterns of crime in general. On the individual level, violence arises from the person's need to reconcile discordant desires, values, and other personal needs. Legal realities interact directly with social realities because criminal law can be conceived as institutionalized societal norms. On the social level, conflict occurs between groups and between persons when specific means (norms) and ends (values) become incompatible.[15]

Speakers at the symposium demonstrated the far-ranging implications of crimes of violence by stating themes such as the following: Aggression in prisons presents a worldwide problem, but South African prison authorities have so far not had to cope with mass violence. South Africa is lagging behind a worldwide move to compensate the victims of crimes. Traffic violence is costing South Africa about eight thousand lives and seventy thousand injuries annually. The present penal system dealing with traffic violations should be modified. Punishment has limited success in preventing the recurrence of crime. Extraordinary measures should be adopted to stem juvenile delinquency. Prevention of crime at the community level is of primary importance. Strict government control of relevant information is hampering research into terrorism in South Africa. Every South African should become actively involved in the fight against crime.

As for all official statistics, the following data are subject to influences other than the perpetration of crimes per se, such as changes in police practices, the

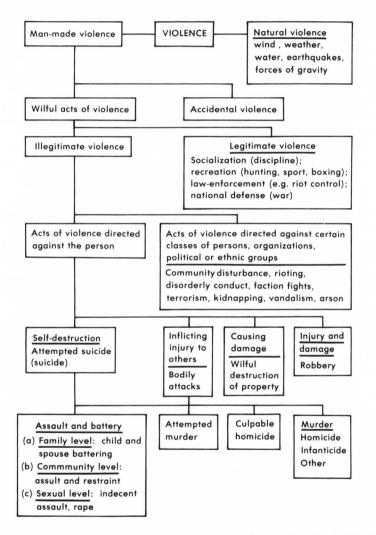

FIGURE 27-1   THE SPECTRUM OF VIOLENCE: A TYPOLOGICAL
DESCRIPTION

discretionary nature of police charges, the differential perceptions of acts of violence, and—as a sum of those influences—changes in societal reaction to violent crime.

There was an overall increase in the crime rate beginning in 1973, which has outstripped the population increase. The rate of violent crime has decreased significantly; murders declined markedly from 8,133 reported cases in 1973-1974 (or 33.1 per 100,000 population) to 5,644 reported cases in 1977-1978 (or 22.5 per 100,000 population), or a 44-percent drop.

About a third of the people convicted of crimes during 1977-1978 were under twenty-one years old, while 80 percent of all offenders were illiterate or had an elementary education. The full extent and impact of crimes of violence cannot be gleaned from official statistics. Direct violence against the person is significantly related to value conflicts inasmuch as these disagreements can be identified with the end results of friction, social conflict, and strife.

Three distinct types of social conflicts are in evidence: norm conflicts (for example, rape, robbery, and murder for gain); value conflicts (for example, family feuds leading to violence, maiming and killing of persons during faction fights, assault and murder as a result of brawling); normative and value conflicts (crimes perpetrated by disturbed individuals, psychotics, tramps, vagrants, alcoholics, drug addicts, terrorists, and family slayers). Operationally, any crime of violence is defined as the infliction of direct and indirect perceptible injury, harm, and damage to another person or group, or law and order as a result of norm and/or value conflicts and subsequent illegitimate use of force to attain certain objectives.

Alcohol and Drugs

The misuse and abuse of drugs and alcohol showed a sharp increase during the 1960s, and this phenomenon has been seized upon by legislators, criminologists, and members of the medical profession as an important "factor" in crime causation. Harsh legislation was introduced in the 1970s to stem the tide but to no avail.

Since then there has been another dramatic development. Although dagga (marijuana) is still the most widely abused drug, alcohol—which is alleged to be much more dangerous—is catching up fast. According to Dr. Sylvain de Miranda, head of the clinical services of the South African National Council on Alcoholism and Drug Dependence (SANCA), an increasing number of thirteen- and fourteen-year olds are abusing liquor. Moreover, the number of young people requiring treatment in their twenties recently doubled. This trend has been increasing for the last six years and is consistent with trends in the rest of the world. Indications are that the pressures of modern society and the breakdown in values and family and parental control could be blamed for this serious problem.

In 1980, a new country-wide survey into dagga and alcohol abuse among school children was proposed by Chris Van der Burgh,[16] a chief research officer of the South African Human Research Council in Pretoria. Results obtained by Van der Burgh in his 1975 survey indicated that about 50 percent of the school children questioned had experimented with dagga. More than 31 percent were labeled "occasional dagga smokers," while almost 19 percent admitted that they were "heavy dagga smokers." He expected the situation was worsening, but only a scientific inquiry could verify this hypothesis. Dagga confiscated by the South African police in the year ended June 30, 1979, was valued at R40.4 million. The total population on that date was estimated at 25 million.

Theft of Cars

All over South Africa car thefts have become a serious problem. In 1979, at least thirty-eight thousand cars, worth about R190 million, were stolen and eleven thousand, valued at R45 million, were not recovered. Thefts of cars and motorcycles have increased nearly 4 percent per year, according to figures submitted to Parliament by the Commission of Police in 1979.

The seriousness of the situation and the concern of the public have been reflected in sentences passed for car theft. South African magistrates have sentenced car thieves, even if they were first offenders, up to four years' imprisonment without the option of a fine. In addition, special police squads were formed to combat the theft of cars, and numerous arrests have been made, including members of gangs who smuggled the stolen cars across homeland borders. It has been estimated that between 60 and 70 percent of the stolen cars were destined for the homelands.

From time to time, the South African police advise car owners to have car alarms installed, to fit locks to steering wheels, to have codes sandblasted on windscreens, and to lock cars at all times.

Rape

More than fifteen thousand cases of rape and attempted rape (sixty cases per one hundred thousand population) are reported annually to the police. It is estimated that the total recent cases of rape in the Cape Town area exceeds the number of rapes in New York City by almost 300 percent. Ronald Graser, head of the Department of Criminology at the University of Durban-Westville, thinks that only about one-tenth of all rapes are reported to the police and that official figures reveal only the tip of the iceberg.

A nationwide reaction to rape ranges from parliamentary seminars and media discussions to the establishment of rape crisis centers in the major cities. An important aspect of the drive against rape is the determination of South African women to explode certain prevalent myths about rape which may hamper victimogenic precare, care, and after-care strategies of control. These myths are:

Good girls are never raped, and a man cannot rape a women if she does not consent. If a woman answers "no," she means "yes." Even if the woman did not provoke the rape, she enjoyed it nonetheless. A raped woman would soon forget the incident.

Males are incapable of restraining their sexual urges, and rapes are not planned in advance. Rape does not occur very often. Rape is not a crime of violence.

Pretty or "sexy" women are more likely to be preyed upon by rapists than ugly women. The way the woman was dressed made her more susceptible to the rapist's designs. Women cry rape for reasons of vengeance or fear of parental wrath.

Important recommendations were submitted to the Standing Penal Reform Committee by the Women's Legal Status Committee in 1979: extension of the definition of rape to include homosexual, oral, and instrument rape; provision for hospital facilities to treat rape victims; and restrictions on the line of questioning to which the victim is subjected in court and the omission of any personal information that has no bearing on the case. At the First National Rape Crisis Conference in Cape Town in 1980, it was proposed that the definition of rape in law be broadened to include sexual assualt and that the death sentence for rape be abolished.

REACTIONS TO CRIME:
SOCIAL CONTROL AND CRIME CONTROL

Basically, punishment is the main method of crime control in South Africa, but from a broader perspective at least six types of social control—or lines of social defense against crime and deviancy—are being applied:

1. Socializing members of society within the family, school, church, and other institutions (run-of-the-mill conditioning and learning).
2. Identifying and forestalling strain by applying mechanisms that prevent potential strain and conflict from materializing, that is, providing separate homelands and amenities for the black population, providing recreational outlets for juveniles.
3. Making socially disapproved behavior and crime difficult to commit or making it very costly (for example, security measures, perimeter barriers, drug laws, and harsh penalties for drug offenders; consistent prosecution of shoplifters).
4. Removing the criminal and deviant from the social scene through dismissal, arrest, banishment, conviction, incarceration, institutionalization, and hanging.
5. Resocializing convicts and deviants to prevent repetition of strain and conflict (for example, crime prevention campaigns, probation, diversion of juvenile delinquents, rehabilitation of incarcerated criminals, hospitalization of psychopaths, provision of parole and after-care services).
6. Channeling reactions to strain into socially accepted patterns of behavior (for example, providing education/training facilities for prisoners, juvenile delinquents, and vagrants; devising a new socioeconomic dispensation for the different races and ethnic groups).

Crime Control Measures

Crime control in South Africa places heavy reliance on criminal law as a means of enforcing morality and of achieving and maintaining socioeconomic order. Following the example of other Western-oriented countries, South Africa has created many "victimless" crimes and status offenses that are reflected in the number of prisoners in custody at any given point in time and by the number of "infringements" and offenses reported within one year. According to the *Report of the Commissioner of Prisons* of the Republic of South Africa for the period July 1, 1978, to June 30, 1979 (R.P. 36/ 1980), the expenditure on prison supplies, services, and salaries for 1978-1979 was estimated to exceed R93 million. During this period, 432,418 persons were admitted to South African prisons. About 83 percent of the prisoners had sentences of six months or less, and about 123,000 prisoners were released on parole.

In our complex society, there is some disagreement over the definition of morality, and a conflict has arisen between differing socioeconomic values and norms. The incompatibility of the areas of traditional and formal control has lent itself to normative marginality where economic needs are met by "illegal" practices such as the brewing of beer, "pirate" taxis, forging passbooks and other documents, administrative corruption, and the connivance in enforcement of many regulations, bylaws, and laws. Informal social control has thus lost much of its regulating function, while the tendency to prescribe criminal sanctions for the control of a great assortment of human behaviors has resulted in a crisis of overcriminalization.

Recommendations of the Viljoen Commission

In 1977, the findings of the Commission of Enquiry into the Penal System of the Republic of South Africa were published. The main recommendations of the so-called Viljoen Commission covered four main areas of concern: diversion and rehabilitation of offenders; noninterference with judicial discretion; depenalization; and permanent law revision.

Among others, recommendations were made for the establishment of presentence diagnostic, detoxification, rehabilitation, and after-care centers. A promising feature of its recommendations was the attempt to make the criminal justice system more humane by urging that influx control and curfew laws be converted into administrative measures, corporal punishment be drastically reduced, granting of postponements in cases of prisoners awaiting trial be limited by law, and offenders be allowed to pay fines in installments. One of the most outstanding features of the report was the commission's opposition to interference with judicial discretion and its recommendations, first, that minimum sentences as prescribed in the Dangerous Weapons Act and the Drug Act be eliminated and, second, that the suspension and postponement of whole sentences in certain specified offenses be revoked.[17]

In his appraisal of the commission's report, Nairn[18] applauded the major recommendations, especially those concerning, first, the training of sentencing officers in the lower courts in the "art" of sentencing and the production of a sentencing handbook; and, second, the establishment of presentence diagnostic centers. However, he was disappointed with the lack of depth and perspective in some recommendations. None of the fundamental flaws in the system had been identified, and no comprehensive plans for the systematic reform of the criminal justice components—legislature, police, courts, and prisons—were formulated.

Community Involvement

A number of national campaigns have been launched in South Africa to get private citizens involved in crime prevention. In 1973, a National Symposium on Crime, Punishment and Rehabilitation was held by the Department of Criminology of the University of South Africa (UNISA). One of the objectives of the meeting was to stimulate criminological research in South Africa and to bridge the gulf between theoretical criminology and criminal reality. An important resolution passed at the meeting stipulated than an institute of criminology be established at the University of South Africa.[19]

INSTITUTES OF CRIMINOLOGY, RESEARCH, AND ACTION

Over the years, criminological knowledge and expertise have largely been derived from random efforts to describe and explain the crime phenomenon and to predict and control its incidence and fluctuation. The lack of a systematic approach can be ascribed to several minor and major causes. Chief among these causes has been a lack of a feasible, operational definition of crime. South African criminologists have held to contradictory definitions of crime, delinquency, and deviance, thus inevitably adding confusion to ignorance. Moreover, appropriate descriptions of the incidence of specific crimes have been lacking, resulting in inadequate classification systems. This deficiency in turn has been reflected in many invalid explanations of crime and delinquency. Worst of all, unfounded speculations and biased predictions have characterized most of these so-called scientific analyses.

The 1970s marked the beginning of a new era in criminological research with the establishment of institutes of criminology in South African universities.

Institute for Criminology—UNISA

The establishment of the Institute for Criminology was approved by the Senate and Council of the University of South Africa in September 1975, and the institute commenced operation in 1976. It is affiliated with the Department of Criminology and is located in the Faculty of Arts of the university.

Since its inception, the institute has aimed at using empirical methods to fill the void in criminological theory. Six important research projects have been completed, and another six are underway. These projects include the prediction of parole success in South Africa, a description of suburban housebreaking in Johannesburg, the study and distribution of whorl patterns on the fingertips of violent criminals, the diagnosis and classification of juvenile delinquents in South Africa, and the development of measurement techniques for combining individual items into scales and indexes.

The institute assists the Department of Criminology at UNISA in the post-graduate field, especially in the design of research projects, data collection, computerization, formulation and testing of hypotheses, sampling, and the measurement of crime and related concepts. It also undertakes the supervision of postgraduate studies for master's and doctor's degrees.

A number of seminars and symposia are held annually to foster criminological research, education, and training within academic circles and within the divisions of the criminal justice system, including the private and public sectors concerned with crime, justice, and correction.

A national symposium on crimes of violence, mentioned above, was held October 2 to 4, 1979, and fourteen papers were read on the subject. About two hundred delegates attended the meeting.

Specialists from South Africa and abroad are regularly invited to visit the institute and to attend seminars. In 1979, Dr. Menachem Amir, director of the Institute of Criminology in Jerusalem, Israel, visited the institute and various other universities and institutions in South Africa. He gave a number of talks and lectures on rape, organized crime, and victimology.

The University Council may decide to introduce correspondence courses in security management in 1981 to assist security officers, supervisors and managers in assessing, planning, structuring, measuring, and revising existing security programs and to provide them with a working knowledge of proper physical security measures to protect assets from espionage, sabotage, pilferage, and other security hazards.

Financial assistance for research is available from a variety of sources within and without the university. The main project in which the institute is currently engaged, that is, the prediction of parole success or failure, is financed by a generous grant from the Human Sciences Research Council.

The university's library contains a very large and excellent collection of criminological, sociological, and psychological materials as well as equally large collections of study material on police science, security management, and law.

Institute of Criminology—Cape Town

The Institute of Criminology of the University of Cape Town commenced operations in 1977. As a multidisciplinary body within the Faculty of Law of the University of Cape Town, it was established for teaching and research in all aspects of criminology.

Exceptionally active in research, the institute has completed or is now involved in projects on the following topics: parole employment, assessment of attitudes of legal practitioners on the need for research; survey of courts, prison gang study, violent crime on the Peninsula, analysis of prison admissions, alternatives to traditional incarceration of young offenders, and repetitive cycles of crime.

The institute is convinced that a great deal of basic data gathering is necessary to build up an accurate picture of crime and criminality in the Western Cape area. To that end, a two-pronged approach has been followed. First, the institute has undertaken a comprehensive collection of statistics, crime reports, and other information concerning all aspects of crime. Because of a paucity of published statistics on the Western Cape area, the institute has had to mount statistics-gathering programs. Second, in-depth studies and analyses of selected populations or crime areas have been undertaken on a long-term and more extensive basis.

Human Sciences Research Council—Pretoria

The Human Sciences Research Council (HSRC) was established under the Human Sciences Research Act (Act No. 23 of 1968) as a corporate organization outside the public service. The HSRC's main source of funds is an annual grant voted by Parliament and paid by the Treasury through the Department of National Education. The HSRC is controlled by a council of a full-time president and ten other members appointed by the minister of National Education from among persons who have distinguished themselves in the human sciences and who possess special qualifications relative to the functions of the HSRC.

Previous to the founding of HSRC, research into crime and the explanations for crime was initiated by its predecessor, the National Bureau for Educational and Social Research, established in 1957. The bureau's main objective was to conduct research into juvenile delinquency and crime. Since 1957, a number of important articles and books have been published on juvenile crime; recidivism; crime statistics; ecology of crime; rehabilitation of juveniles; criminal victimization; class-based sociological theories of crime; and perceptions of crime, criminal justice, police functions, and homosexuality.

The HSRC is responsible for research and development in the human sciences. Its functions are to undertake or to aid such research as approved by the minister of National Education. The HSRC also advises the minister on the research that should be undertaken, the ways in which research may be promoted, the ways in which the country's human potential may best be developed and utilized, and the application of research findings to benefit the country. The HSRC also coordinates research; cooperates with educational institutions, individuals, and authorities to promote and conduct research; and eliminates duplication of research efforts. It cooperates with persons and authorities in other countries in connection with research in the human sciences.

The HSRC makes grants for research to universities, persons, and authorities, publishes research findings or financially supports their publication, fosters the training of persons for research work, and awards bursaries for such training. Another of its functions is to devise, standardize, and make available psychological and scholastic tests and other aids. It also evaluates educational qualifications, publishes educational statistics, and is responsible for the establishment of facilities for the collection and dissemination of information concerning the human sciences.

Most of the completed projects have been those of the Institute of Social, Demographic and Criminological Research (SDCR). A special feature of the institute's work has been the replication of studies through reexamination of some important problem areas within the institute's field of concern. This procedure has resulted in a new methodological approach to the description and explanation of deviancy and to a better understanding of the personal, social, and cultural dynamics of crime and delinquency. Briefly, the approach can be described as an in-depth inquiry into the qualities of criminal behavior, instituted to complement mass observation. As it does not purport to supersede or replace the traditional methods and techniques in any way, in-depth studies of selected cases have added significantly to our knowledge and understanding of crime in South Africa.

NICRO

According to Pegge,[20] the South African National Institute for Crime Prevention and Rehabilitation of Offenders (NICRO) has been active in the field of correction for the past sixty-eight years. Through its branch offices, the institute provides a skilled professional social work service to offenders and their dependents.

NICRO has launched a number of crime prevention campaigns designed to induce citizen involvement and awareness. The main purposes have been to create an opportunity for each branch at various major centers to identify well-defined targets and to gain increasing impact, knowledge, and public support for expansion in other fields. NICRO's campaigns are directed to three main areas of concern: social work, community education, and publicity. The constitution formally defines its role in crime prevention as follows:

2(b) To promote crime preventative activities and more particularly, but without limiting the generality of this object; to undertake and stimulate research in the causes of and social defenses against crime; to determine conditions which are criminogenic and to take all possible steps to secure the elimination or amelioration of such conditions; to determine and promote the most effective methods of the treatment of offenders; to stimulate and secure public participation in the prevention of crime; and to disseminate information relative to the incidence of crime and the prevention thereof.

2(c) To encourage and to strive for coordination and cooperation among welfare organizations and state departments so as to bring about an interdisciplinary team approach to matters pertaining to crime, crime prevention and aftercare of offenders.

Terrorism Research Center—Cape Town: The Terrorism Research Center (TRC) is an autonomous body that researches all forms of national and international terrorism. It has existed informally since January 1973 and formally since May 1978. Informal reciprocal arrangements exist or can be arranged between TRC and broadly similar institutions elsewhere in the world.

TRC also investigates matters other than terrorism: industrial security, crime statistics and tendencies, disaster case studies, and ultramodern security equipment. In these areas of concern, TRC sponsors visual, media, public and private presentations, seminars, and lectures.[21]

CRIMINOLOGY AS A TEACHING SUBJECT

Currently, criminology is taught at a number of South African universities and institutions. Among the most important centers are the University of South Africa (teletuition and periodic group meetings); the University of Pretoria; the University of Cape Town; the University of Durban-Westville; the University of Potchefstroom; the University of Zululand; the University of Witwatersrand; the University of the Orange Free State (Bloemfontein); the University of Fort Hare (Grahamstown); the South African Police Training College; and the Inservice Training Center of the Department of Justice of Pretoria.

A number of basic fields of concern are covered, including the following: crime and antisocial conduct, criminal behavior and types of criminals, victims of crime and victimization, the police, the courts, prisons, care and after-care, corrections, juvenile delinquency, crime statistics, legal control and the sociology of law, deviancy, socialization, learning and conditioning, human motivation, social relationships and interaction, and methodological issues. The methodological issues are defining crime and related concepts; delimiting the scope of inquiries; technical problems of sampling, measurement, scaling, quantification, operationalization, and techniques of description; explanation and prediction; and strategies of crime control.

In 1974, police science and penology were introduced as separate, independent majors for B.A. degree courses at the University of South Africa, and since 1976 students have been allowed to enroll for a B.A. (police science) graduate course.

If one were to observe any distinctive quality about the descriptions and explanations of crime during the last four decades in South Africa, it would be that no particular school of thought and no single explanatory theory are indigenous to South Africa. There is no absence of theory; rather, most perspectives have been borrowed from Western-oriented countries. The ease with which South African criminologists have been borrowing from European and American sources can be explained by cultural affinity and continual enculturation from abroad. Another major reason has been the constant struggle of South African criminologists to establish criminology as a teaching subject at the university level.

At the two universities where criminology had been taught, until 1965 departments of criminology considered crime and the criminal as social problems rather than as unique subjects for instruction in their own terms. Students were content to limit their knowledge to criminal anthropology, psychology, psychiatry, and law.

FUTURE OF CRIMINOLOGY IN SOUTH AFRICA

The problems facing South African criminologists in the 1980s, as in the 1970s, are multiple and complex, but the road ahead is clearly visible, despite a heavy mine field of criminological dilemmas. If "dilemma" is taken to refer to an argument in which an opponent is faced with two alternatives, both of which will be conclusive against him, the 1980s will witness renewed interest in and energetic endeavors to highlight some of the ever-present dilemmas on the South African scene.

The areas of dilemma include: legislation as opposed to decriminalization and depenalization; pre- and post-trial alternatives to imprisonment, such as diversion of juvenile delinquents, first offenders, and petty "infringers"; punishment as opposed to rehabilitation of offenders; abolition as opposed to retention of capital punishment; the proactive role of the police (and the law) in combatting ethical improprieties, petty sociocultural deviations, and public inebriation; and the civil rights of the offender as opposed to the interest of the victimized group.

When considering cultural and socioeconomic explanations for crime and delinquency in South Africa, the basic proposition is that human beings respond to various definitions of situations. Both the response to a definition and the definition itself may be learned, acquired, or conditioned. What criminologists are concerned about is whether normative or deviant South African patterns are internalized by members of society, and whether the gratification or deprivation of personal needs may have any effect upon the learning and conditioning process.

NOTES

1. *Report of Penal and Prison Reform Commission* (Pretoria: Government Printer, 1947), pp. 20-157.

2. *Penal Reform News* 8 (January 1949):7.

3. Herman Venter, *Youth at the Cross Roads* (Cape Town: HAUM, 1958), p. 57. Other works by the same author are *Residivisme* [Recidivism] (Cape Town: HAUM, 1954); *Die geskiedenis van die Suid-Afrikaanse gevangeisstelsel—1652-1958* [History of the South African Prison System—1652 to 1958] (Cape Town: HAUM, 1959); *Bantoejeugmisdaad* [Juvenile Delinquency in Black Communities] (Cape Town: HAUM, 1960); *Jeugmisdaad* [Juvenile Delinquency] (Pretoria: Crafts Pers, 1965); and *Kriminologie* [Criminology] (Pretoria: Van Schaik, 1977).

4. P. J. Van der Walt, *Die Suid-Afrikaanse Misdaadstatistiek* [South African Crime Statistics] (Potchefstroom: Pro Rege-Pers, 1954), p. 1.

5. Hermann Mannheim (ed.), *Pioneers in Criminology* (London: Stevens and Sons, 1960), p. 283.

6. P. J. Van der Walt (ed.), *Crime and Society*, Vol. 1 (Pretoria: UNISA, 1973), p. 3.

7. Jacob Van der Westhuizen, " 'n Bespreking van die analitiese metode in die kriminologie—beskrywend, verkarend en applikatief " [The Application of the Analytic Method in Criminology—Descriptively, Explanatorily and Applicatively], M.A. thesis, Pretoria: University of South Africa, 1971, p. 6.

8. Jacob Van der Westhuizen, *Measurement of Crime* (Pretoria: UNISA, 1980).

9. P. J. Van der Walt, *'n Sosiolgiese klassifikasie van misdade* [A Sociological Classification of Crime] (Cape Town: Nassau, 1963).

10. *Proceedings of the Conference on Crime, Law and the Community* (Cape Town: Juta, 1976), p. 2.

11. Jacob Van der Westhuizen and H. P. Oosthuizen, *Prediction of Parole Outcome and Maladaptation* (Pretoria: UNISA, 1980).

12. Robert K. Merton, "Social Structure and Anomie," *American Sociological Review* 3 (October 1938):672-682. See also his *Social Theory and Social Structure* (New York: Free Press, 1957), Chapters 4 and 5.

13. Jacob Van der Westhuizen, *An Introduction to Criminological Research* (Pretoria: UNISA, 1977), p. 78.

14. Louis F. Freed, *Crime in South Africa* (Cape Town: Juta, 1963), pp. 159-160 and 388-389.

15. Jacob Van der Westhuizen and T. J. Van Heerden (eds.), *Crimes of Violence in South Africa* (Pretoria: UNISA, 1980).

16. Chris Van der Burg in J. M. Lötter (ed.), *Social Problems in the RSA*, S-68 (Pretoria: HRSC, 1979).

17. R.S.A., *Report of the Commission of Enquiry into the Penal System of the Republic of South Africa* (Pretoria: Government Printer, 1977).

18. R. J. Nairn, "A Look at the Recommendations of the Commission of Enquiry into the Penal System of the Republic of South Africa," *South African Journal of Criminal Law and Criminology* 1 (April 1977):4-5.

19. P. J. Van der Walt (ed.), *Crime and Society*, Vol. 2 (Pretoria: UNISA, 1973), p. 229.

20. John V. Pegge, "Creating a Balance Between Rehabilitation and Prevention," *South African Journal of Criminal Law and Criminology* 2 (July 1978):176.

21. Michael Morris, *Security Factors* 2 (August 1979):9.

BIBLIOGRAPHY

Crime and Criminology in General

Cronje, G., et al. *Deviancy in Society—A Crimino-Pathological Approach.* Pretoria: UNISA, 1979.
This general descriptive analysis of "deviant" behavior includes, among others, prostitution, homosexuality, alcohol and drug abuse, and suicide.

Lötter, J. M. (ed.). *Social Problems in the RSA* S-68. Pretoria: HSRC, 1979.
This collection of articles and monographs focuses on a number of social issues, such as divorce, crimes of violence, prostitution, urbanization, family planning, minority groups, lesbianism, housing problems, and urban crime.

Proceedings of the Conference on Crime, Law and the Community. Cape Town: Juta, 1976.
This record of an international conference held at the University of Cape Town in April 1975 seeks to stimulate local interest in criminology.

Report of the Commission of Inquiry into the Abuse of Drugs. Pretoria: Government Printer, 1970.
This inquiry into the nature, extent, and causes of drug abuse in South Africa presents recommendations in respect of its prevention and control.

Rip, C. M. *Contemporary Social Pathology.* Pretoria: Academica, 1978.
This general textbook of social pathology deals with family pathologies (family disorganization, divorce, illegitimacy, old age); economic pathologies (unemployment, poverty); withdrawal pathologies (alcoholism, drug addiction, suicide); and formal-legal pathologies (crime, juvenile delinquency, sexual offenses).

Slabbert, Mana. *Repetitive Cycles.* Cape Town: University of Cape Town, 1980.
This analysis centers on the history of five hundred offenders who were clients of the NICRO After-Care Centre in Cape Town during the 1970s.

Slabbert, Mana, et al. *Some Implications of Tattooing in and Outside Prison.* Cape Town: University of Cape Town, 1978.
This descriptive analysis of the nature, extent, and functions of tattooing in South Africa offers some explanation for the prevalence of tattooing in prison populations.

Van der Walt, P. J., et al. *Criminology—An Introduction.* Pretoria: UNISA, 1977.
This work provides a general orientation to the nature, scope, contents, and methods of criminology.

Van der Walt, P. J. (ed.). *Crime and Society.* Pretoria: UNISA, 1979.
This book of readings covers the nature, extent, and prevention of crime in South Africa.

Dictionary

Louw, D. A., et al. *Kriminologiewoordeboek/Dictionary of Criminology.* Durban: Butterworths, 1978.
This dictionary presents definitions in Afrikaans of about one thousand commonly used terms and concepts with their equivalents in English.

Juvenile Delinquency

Cronje, G., et al. *Juvenile Delinquent in South Africa.* Pretoria: UNISA, 1976.
This work provides a comprehensive survey of studies pertaining to juvenile delinquency from a multidisciplinary point of view.

Midgley, J., et al. *Crime and Punishment in South Africa.* Johannesburg: McGraw-Hill, 1975.

This collection of articles is on South African crime, criminal justice, and correctional practice.

Midgley J. *Children on Trial*. Cape Town: NICRO, 1975.
This analysis of the South African juvenile court calls for a critical appraisal of the suitability of juvenile justice for coping with the problems of children.

Venter, H. J. *Youth at the Cross Roads*. Cape Town: HAUM, 1958.
This work is a compendium of radio talks given in the 1950s on juvenile delinquency in South Africa.

Venter, J. D. *The Incidence of Juvenile Crime in South Africa*. Pretoria: National Bureau of Educational and Social Research, 1964.
Venter discusses the *what*, *where*, *how*, and *why* of juvenile delinquency.

Willemse, W. A. *Constitution-Types in Delinquency*. London: Trubner, 1932.
This work presents practical applications and biophysiological foundations of Kretschner's types, based on experimental findings on 177 case studies of juvenile delinquents from Tokai and Houtpoort.

Willemse, W. A. *The Road to the Reformatory*. Pretoria: Van Schaik, 1938.
Willemse endeavors to uncover the general causes of maladjustment and to elucidate the personal and environmental determinants of juvenile maladjustment in South Africa.

Methodology

Van der Westhuizen, J. *An Introduction to Criminological Research* Pretoria: UNISA, 1979.
Van der Westhuizen explains the various approaches, methods, and techniques relating to descriptive, explanatory, and predictive studies in criminology.

Van der Westhuizen, J. *Measurement of Crime*. 2 vols. Pretoria: UNISA, 1980.
This in-depth analysis covers the measurement and scaling of crime aimed at reappraising the nature, scope, content, goals, and methods of criminology.

Penology

Corry, T. M. *Prison Labor in South Africa*. 1979.
This work presents a critical but constructive examination of prison labor in South Africa and elsewhere.

Rabie, M. A., et al. *Punishment—An Introduction to Principles*. Johannesburg: Lex Patria, 1979.
The authors discuss contemporary views on the theories of punishment expounded in sentencing by South African courts.

Police Science

Van der Westhuizen, J. *Descriptive Analysis of Housebreaking in the Area of the Norwood Police Station*. Pretoria: UNISA, 1979.

Van der Westhuizen analyzes 542 housebreaking cases in the jurisdiction of the Norwood Police Station from July 1, 1974, to June 30, 1975. American hypotheses are tested in respect to the spatial and temporal housebreaking pattern, discovery of crime, modus operandi, disposition of cases, and victimization.

Van Heerden, T. J. *Criminalistics*. Pretoria: UNISA, 1977.
This manual deals with the identification of persons (living and dead), examination of a corpse, toxicological examinations, disputed documents, the determination of the origin of biological, organic, and inorganic material, and print identification.

Van Heerden, T. J. *Introduction to Police Science*. Pretoria: UNISA, 1976.
Van Heerden gives a general orientation to the structural-functional aspects of policing.

Terrorism

Morris, M. *Terrorism: The First Full Account in Detail of Terrorism and Insurgency in Southern Africa*. Cape Town: H. Timmins, 1971.
This contribution to the literature on terrorism supplies details in southern Africa.

Morris, M. *Armed Conflict in Southern Africa—A Survey of Regional Terrorisms from Their Beginnings Up to the Present, With a Comprehensive Examination of the Portuguese Position*. Cape Town: H. Timmins, 1973.
Morris provides a historian account of the parameters of terrorism as they have operated in the countries of southern Africa.

28

SPAIN

Manuel Cobo del Rosal and Enrique Bacigalupo

Although the origins of Spanish criminological thought are usually traced to the work of physiognomists,[1] this chapter concentrates on the development of modern criminology as an expression of Spanish science which began in the vein of the Italian positivists (Lombroso, Ferri, and Garofalo) and of the movement of the International Society of Criminology. Furthermore, this chapter is limited to the development of Spanish criminology as a means of avoiding a diffusive analysis. Thus, we exclude the interaction of this development with movements in other countries, especially those in Europe, because an overemphasis would imply that Spanish cultural phenomena are only a reflection of foreign influence. Conversely, the conclusions offered here pertain to Spain alone and are not meant to have universal significance.

ORIGINS OF SPANISH CRIMINOLOGY

Spanish criminology has been characterized by an orientation to penology. The programming has not been formal and conscious but simply the elaboration of the purposes and orientations of research projects undertaken by those scientists who have specialized in one of the concerns of the penal sciences. Spanish criminology has reached its contemporary situation through the efforts of the penal scientists at a given time to explain rationally the circumstances they encountered. Each succeeding generation of penal scientists has adjusted its work to the situation of its time, and has built upon the ideas of its predecessors. Thus, the work of present scientist represents one moment in the evolutionary process.

The development of Spanish criminology has been determined by the course of penal-juridical ideas because generally the contributors to criminology have been jurists. The foundation for modern criminological thought was established

Translated by Muriel Nixon Canfield, Southern Illinois University.

early by the "Spanish correctional school"[2] which drew from the liberal intellectual movement nurtured by Karl Christian Krause. The Krause movement may be understood as a segment of German idealism which, in rejecting the penal theory of Kant and Hegel,[3] favors special prevention in opposition to retribution. Punishment is not identified conceptually with wrong; instead, it is expected to fulfill the positive functions of guidance and education. The behavioral sciences did not emerge until the end of the nineteenth century, and the postulates of the Krause movement stood in sharp contrast to the premises of the penal law of the time.

Opposed to the positive school was the absolute school of thought which was then especially prevalent in Germany and Italy, but Spain was more congenial to positivist penal thought.[4] A struggle against established ideas was not necessary because the Spanish correctional school was predisposed to embodying in penal science the empirical knowledge of anthropology, sociology, and psychology.[5] Nevertheless, the positivist school was not accepted uncritically in Spain, perhaps because positivism did not gain dominance as a philosophical doctrine.[6] It is clear that the willingness to be critical of positivism was part of a general skepticism toward criminology that has characterized Spanish penal science, especially after 1930, in evaluating purely descriptive works.

Spain began to demand empirical data about criminality in the eighteenth century, when King Philip V ordered the counts to report pending and completed trials. Effective in 1792 upon an order of Charles IV, the courts were required to produce an annual summary of civil and criminal trials. Criminal justice statistics were first published in 1838. These actions were only the first efforts to provide descriptions of the social facts of criminality. After 1885, serious efforts were made to improve the descriptions and even to insert more substantial theoretical foundations significant for reliable understanding.[7]

TENDENCIES IN
CRIMINOLOGICAL INVESTIGATION

Scientific Spanish criminology was a product of the first third of the twentieth century when two fundamental tendencies began to emerge: (1) a close identification of criminology with social criticism and the questioning of the scientific merits of Italian positivism, especially those of an anthropolitical bent; and, (2) as an alternative to Italian positivism, emphasis on the etiological study of crime predominantly from sociological and psychobiological perspectives and sometimes under the strong influence of Catholic moral philosophy.

The basic ideas of each tendency are analyzed here, while for the sake of clarity the shadings that separate some authors from one another are avoided. Of course, the distinctions made here are not as absolute in reality as abstract analysis makes necessary.

The scientific efforts of Spanish criminology may be categorized as either "theories of criminalization" or "theories of criminality." These categories are considered not in historical sequence, but for the purpose of delineating the theoretical position of the authors. Theories of criminalization seek to investigate the social mechanisms through which deviance becomes regarded as a crime, whereas theories of criminality are oriented to the discovery of natural laws that will explain and predict how a person becomes a criminal.

THEORIES OF CRIMINALIZATION

The work of Pedro Dorado Montero (1861-1919)[8] and of Luis Jiménez de Asúa (1889-1970) is representative of the criminalization approach. Although they emphasize very different aspects of the history of criminological thought, they are in fundamental agreement.[9]

The views of Dorado Montero can be placed within the context of broader scientific developments in criminology, principally outside of Spain.[10] His work can now be read, not from the perspective of etiological theories or of efforts to distinguish the causes of crime, but from the perspective of deviant behavior as a social reality produced by the definition of crime and by the reactions to those deviant acts defined as crimes. Thus, crimes would not be regarded as a universal and necessary phenomenon. According to this interpretation, the works of Dorado Montero are opposed to the Italian positivism represented in the writings of Lombroso, Ferri, and Garofalo. It is equally clear that Dorado Montero differs fundamentally from the German positivist Franz Von Liszt. Dorado Montero rejected both the causal explanations of the Italian school and those of the authors from which Von Liszt derived his political-criminal propositions and his theory about punishment.

Dorado Montero rejected the notion that delinquency is found only in a minority of the total population and that delinquent behavior demonstrates abnormality. "We all are immoral and unjust," he wrote,[11] "and accordingly delinquent, perpetrators of social injustices, although some may be more so than others." He denied the existence of a social morality or a social order that could be characterized as more correct than others. Instead, he saw only a diversity of social orders that lacked viability because of the homogeneity among the groups subject to the various orders. "We do not have any means through which we may know that a given value interpretation or a decisive authority is the accepted moral order and that all others are invalid," Dorado Montero said. "Moral conceptions are found in this way to have equivalent validity. No single moral order can be assumed to have the right to present itself as being a monopolistic instrument of truth."[12]

From this standpoint, Dorado Montero also rejected the classification of delinquents into a limited number of types as did Italian positivism and the German sociological school. "All classification which has to do with them [delinquents]," Dorado Montero explained, "has to be artificial because each delinquent, like men in general, is different from all others, and he constitutes therefore a category in himself."[13] He added: "Nowadays in order to distinguish delinquents from those who are not, we have no sign other than the legal sentence. Those individuals are delinquents who may have been declared such officially by means of judicial sentences; all the other individuals are reputable. But this differentiating designation is insufficient sometimes and deceiving at other times."[14] Thereby, Dorado Montero considered crime to be an "imposed" concept, that is, a matter of choice by those persons in authority.

Let us assume that whoever of the presiding officers with a given point of view succeeds in occupying a preeminent position and in having at this disposal the necessary authority to declare his criteria to be valid. From the authoritative position, he will be considered the only valid interpreter of natural laws and rationality; he will see to it that others respect, willingly or by force, the subjective conception he holds about the moral order and his penal code; his list of criminal acts, will be that which will prevail. The exterior sign, which did not exist before, has begun to exist now. Crimes, therefore, are those acts that the most powerful persons refuse to carry out and whose fulfillment are threatened with punishment. That is to say, that the concept of crime is in this way an imposed concept. In fact, it is not possible to give another definition of crime but this one: all action which the law of a state or the judgment of the powerful (as occurs with military leaders in time of war or similar circumstances) prohibits and punishes.[15]

Dorado Montero's solution to the problem of defining crime obviously places him in the sphere of criminological theories of criminalization.[16] In other words, his works do not support the view that the purposes of criminology involve the etiology, or criminogenesis, or the causes of crime; rather, his works deal with the social process whereby the agencies of social control define crime in the course of reacting to it.

With rare exceptions,[17] Spain has not followed the course of causal-explicative criminology or of classical criminology found in the rest of Europe. If we judge by the development of classical criminology in Spain, the ideas of Dorado Montero carried great power of conviction, probably more latent than manifest, in favoring skepticism about the causal-explicative approach to delinquent behavior. Until a short time ago, this approach did not consider the issues raised by the theories of criminalization.

Luis Jiménez de Asúa later developed skepticism toward the "criminology of criminality," but the concepts of "criminology of criminalization" were characteristic of Dorado Montero. The specific merit of Jiménez de Asúa's work was his definition of the orientation of the penal sciences for the years after 1930, an orientation that still survives.[18]

Jiménez de Asúa was not dedicated to advancing the investigations of Dorado Montero; instead, he broke from these concepts. From the correctional idea,[19] he tried to delineate the task of criminology as being similar to that of penal law. He repeatedly expressed serious doubts about the potentialities of the models of either causal-explicative or clinical criminology.[20] Although he attempted to blunt the optimism of his time about clinical criminology, he did not renounce criminology.

Jiménez de Asúa postulated the substitution for penal law of what apparently was clinical criminology,[21] a postulate that was implicit in the work of Dorado Montero.[22] Jiménez de Asúa argued that the potentiality of clinical criminology was dependent upon the reform of society. He would later introduce a purely special preventive system. The possibilities of crime prevention, he said, "are attainable with an absolute change, in a word, not only of political horizons but of social environments and that can only take root in a socialist system where punishment ceases to be punishment."[23] He warned that the postulates of clinical criminology, "upon adapting themselves to the prevailing regimens, are transformed into a weapon of arbitrariness and a defense of the dominant class.[24]

Jiménez de Asúa's concern about clinical criminology stemmed from Ferri's compromise in Italy with the fascist regime.[25] Jiménez de Asúa noted that reducing the guarantees of penal law would postpone the program of social reform implicit in a purely special preventive approach. "When the positive Italian school believed it had effected a great liberal conquest with its advanced principles, instead of bringing about benefits for liberty," he declared, "it caused considerable disturbance."[26]

As a logical consequence of Jiménez de Asúa's thesis, the issue of liberty is favored over the issue of special prevention.[27] The ultimate impact of that consequence was directed against criminology in the clinical and causal-explicative models. Dorado Montero had rejected these models by denying their scientific merit; Jiménez de Asúa extended the scope of that skepticism by warning of their political consequences.

In delineating a scientific course for penal science, Jiménez de Asúa departed from the premise that "the principle of liberty is protected by classicism and, on the other hand, it runs an enormous risk in the positive school."[28] When engaged in scientific activities, the jurist should be primarily dogmatic in the sense of his knowledge of positive laws.[29] That thesis has had such a profound hold on Spanish jurists that it has been expressed time after time over almost half a century.[30] In the practical order, Jiménez de Asúa's thesis opposed what he intended, although jurists recognize the relevance of criminology to legal work.[31] Furthermore, classical criminological research—in the sense of criminology of criminality and clinical investigation—has not developed in Spain.[32]

Neither has the criminology of criminalization moved beyond the level attained in Dorado Montero's work, probably for three reasons. First, it is strongly critical of established society. In the years following the Spanish Civil War (1936-1939), the government was restrictive.[33] Second, Spanish jurists have adopted the concepts of German legal science which has conservative traditions. Criticism of the established order by the legal-penal dogmatist is only slightly possible. Third, Spanish jurists have followed a "technical-legal" orientation which in practice rejects any integration of the legal and social sciences.

In assessing the trend for criminology delineated by Dorado Montero and especially Jiménez de Asúa, Antón Oneca said: "Those orientations are utopian which transcend reality and, upon passing to the plane of practice, they tend to destroy, either partially or completely, the order of things existing in a given period." Until the evolution of society makes utopia a reality, one recommends postponing criminological research suitable for theories of criminalization, as well as radical reform of the penal system urged by correctionalism.[34]

THEORIES OF CRIMINALITY

Theories of criminality contrast with the strong radicalism of Dorado Montero's criminology of criminalization. The major representatives of the criminality approach are Rafael Salillas (1854-1923), Father Jerónimo Montes (1865-1932),[35] Quintiliano Saldaña (1878-1938), and Mariano Ruiz Funes (1889-1958).

Rafael Salillas, a physician, was one of the most stimulating thinkers at the end of the nineteenth century. The first attempts to elaborate an explicit theory about the behavior of delinquents were Rafael Salillas's *Penal Life in Spain* (1888) and the *Spanish Delinquent—Underworld* (1898). In the latter volume especially, Salillas also deals with deviant behavior in general. Departing from the view that delinquency is a form of atavism, as Lambroso believed, Salillas found the delinquent type to be "defined by the standards of national sociology."[36] "The Spanish delinquent engaged in organized delinquency is only a reflection of the most characteristic national types."[37] In this way, criminal behavior is symptomatic of certain tendencies that go with living in the reality of society. "The delinquent," Salillas says, "personifies the vicious tendencies of the society which has generated delinquency."[38]

With respect to the criminal type, Salillas's central thesis differs substantially from the anthropological version proposed by Lambroso. Although Salillas does not follow the course of Dorado Montero either, his thesis conveys the theme of a critical theory of the given society. "The delinquent type is not a strange being who may correspond to an archaic period of humanity, nor is he definitely a pathological being," Salillas said in elaborating his ideas. "His nature is in concert with a part of the national character, and his imbalance is of the same kind as the society in which he lives."[39]

In his investigation of delinquent types, Salillas depended on the Spanish literature as the basis for studying the national character. His methodology was consistent with scientific standards and may have significance beyond his research interest. The basic types he delineated were the "picaresque" and the "matonesco" (a bully type). Both types manifest the state of nomadism or parasitism.[40] "These states are characterized by a lack of one's own means of substenance," he explained, "and by a kind of activity that, instead of pursuing normal procedures of production and exchange, resorts to plunder or to certain simulations designed to produce certain relationships through which one succeeds in getting the benefits one is seeking."[41] Salillas takes a strongly biological view in attempting to explain nomadism or parasitism. "The diatheses and the neuroses constitute imbalances of nutrition, with only one difference," he contends, "which is that the diatheses represent stages of nutritive imbalance, while in the neuroses the nutritive imbalance is localized in the nervous system."[42] In turn, the nomadism or the parasitism is explained by a "basic lesion which powerfully influences the constitution of the psyche and which is manifested by a series of abnormal relationships."[43]

Salillas conducted some very significant studies of the language spoken by delinquent communities. Certain elements in these studies are congenial to the development of a theory of delinquent subculture.[44]

Another proponent of theories of criminality was Father Montes whose work, *Precursors of Penal Science in Spain—Studies of the Delinquents and the Causes and Remedies of Crime* (1911), is considered an important exposition of the criminality approach. From both Dorado Montero's advanced perspective and the classical point of view, Montes opposed penal positivism which was struggling to penetrate Spain from Italy. On one hand, he defended a special preventive conception of punishment which had historical antecedents in Spain.[45] On the other hand, he made a penetrating criticism of those supposed causal chains that positivism describes as the conditioning components for crime. Montes reviewed the antecedents of Lombroso's theory of the Criminal type.[46] He saw no scientific proof of a relationship between anthropometric characteristics and the moral qualities of man,[47] nor did he see evidence for the "hereditary transmission of organic characteristics between forebears and decendants."[48] Montes questioned the atavism hypothesized by Lombroso, a criticism supported by the biological knowledge of Montes's time. Montes affirmed:

It is worthwhile to give attention to point that is still very debatable today: I refer to the limits of atavism, that is to say that the number of generations in which a determined quality or type can remain latent, until appearing again in an individuals of the descendants. It is recognized that the Lombrosian school extends atavism to thousands of generations, to the point of assuring that this very day the supposed primitive man is reproduced with frequency, a hypothesis as whimsical as necessary in order to produce from it the explanations which Lombroso makes about criminality.[49]

Father Montes insisted upon the classical position that crime is a product of the free will of man: "The immediate and essential cause of crime is not in the organic conditions of man nor in the exterior circumstances that surround him, but in his free will, and this, on the other hand, is not subject to mortal laws like the physical organism and is therefore susceptible to modifications and improvements."[50] Nevertheless, Montes did not deny the influences of the "circumstances that surround man in society," but he considered the circumstances to be only "occasional" causes "which have greater importance when it is a question of a badly directed and weak will."[51] Therefore, he would direct the special preventive function of penal law on the "improvement of will through education."[52] Montes emphasized the task of education to prevent crime and criticism of social inequality.[53] Both emphases were made from the classical point of view.

Unitl 1930, Father Montes's perspective was the agenda for criminological research into crime causation, research that employed criminal biology, criminal psychology, and classical criminal sociology. Criminal psychoanalysis had no place in this work. Yet, all of these branches of scientific criminology were developed precisely contrary to Montes's metaphysics. In trying to explain the causal determination of behavior, criminal psychology and biology found it necessary to abandon the concept of free will and even to oppose it as an inadequate point of departure for acquiring scientific knowledge.

The theories of criminality were also addressed in the works of Quintiliano Saldaña (1878-1938) which afforded no original theory, provided only a large accumulation of information, and attempted to apply the pragmatic philosophy to criminology.[54] Pragmatically, Saldaña believed that crime should not be seen as "a matter of legal infraction, but rather as a phenomenon of production and destruction, subject to the general physical and psychological laws of modification of disorder and disturbance, either for development, or for withdrawal of active and voluntary phenomena."[55] For Saldaña "pragmatic criminology" meant a "physio-sociological explanation, in the first place, but also physical-psychological, since it determines to what extent the criminal outcome, individual and social, was considered possible, not only in the objective or intention, but also in the cause, that is, in the environments where one finds the index of individual and social capacity."[56]

From this perspective, Saldaña's concrete applications referred more to the juridical definition of crime and the associated perceptions of the consequences of crime and less to an explanation of criminal behavior. Saldaña also examined criminal biotypology in summaries of a fairly lengthy series of theories and classifications of delinquents.[57] He contended that "the criminal type does not exist" because "criminals, by being physical and social misfits, are the aberrant counterfigure of the ethnic type; they are the anti-type."[58] His error here is obvious; far from denying the delinquent type as he intended, Saldaña explained the delinquent as a type different from the "normal." If it is theoretically valid to speak of an ethnic type, it would be difficult to deny the existence of a criminal type.

This search for crime causation led Spanish criminology to an attempt to apply endocrinology. The basic text using this approach is *Endocrinology and Criminality* (1929), edited by Mariano Ruiz Funez (1889-1953). His volume recommended research into the "normality of dysfunctionality of the endocrine formula of the criminal," although an ingenuous correlation between delinquent types and glandular malfunctioning was rejected.[59]

TRANSITION INTO CONTEMPORARY TIMES

Until 1930, as we have seen, the directions of criminological thought in Spain deviated from the course followed by the rest of Europe and by Latin America. Its criminological investigation programs had different purposes than those of the Italian school which had provided the initial inspiration. Dorado Montero defined a sector of research which acquired great importance with the ascendancy of the "labeling" theory. Jiménez de Asúa proposed a scheme for penal science that favored skepticism of clinical criminology from scientific and political points of view. Father Jerónimo Montes undertook investigations that supported a special preventive concept of punishment; this concept was based on ideas contrary to the positivism that inspired the birth of criminology in general.

In Spain the causal-explicative and clinical models of criminology were unable to provide the theoretical framework necessary to deal with the problems that were raised. From 1939 to 1975, however, Spain's political climate did not favor a research program that would develop highly critical theories of criminalization. Consequently, the course of criminological thought after 1930 was consistent with the literature summarized above.

Beginning with the 1940s, a few criminological works surfaced, including certain chapters in *Principles of Spanish Penal Law* by Juan del Rosal.[60] Del Rosal did not abandon the priority he assigned to penal law when he placed criminology within jurisprudence,[61] but he contended that juridical treatment of crime should not rule out penal discourse. Criminology, he said, is interested in the explanation "of the origin and motivation" of the crime.[62] As a science, criminology would participate in "the dual position of the natural and moral sciences and explicative science."[63]

This point of departure defines a criminology that is strongly influenced by moral philosophy and cultural science which oppose the notions of positivist criminology. Del Rosal supports this approach from two points of view: "The prestige of personalism in law and the moral principles of juridical-penal thought."[64] Instead of seeking causal explanations for crime, he appears to call for "a clarification and comprehension"[65] of how the law defines the punishable deed. Comprehension requires examination of the disposition of the offender and typical environment of lawbreaking.[66] From del Rosal's perspective, criminology becomes an auxiliary of penal law, offering a prognosis of the threat, since its "juridical-penal significance is the theory of penal responsibility."[67] Del Rosal maintained this position all his life, reiterating it in his *Treatise on Spanish Penal Law*.[68]

Regardless of merit, del Rosal's orientation failed to give increased emphasis to criminological research in the decades that followed. Penal scientists took up criminological questions only sporadically.[69] Among them Manuel López-Rez deserves special mention for this contributions, first, while with the United Nations and then as a visiting fellow at the Institute of Criminology in Cambridge, where he treated crime as a sociopolitical phenomenon and considered crime prevention to be an aspect of national planning. At the present time, he would reorient penal science as conceived by Dorado Montero and Jiménez de Asúa, toward empirical criminology: "getting a little into the history of Spain and its penal justice as well as into what really should be understood as criminal politics would be beneficial . . . than continuing to devote oneself preferentially to the cultivation of the juridical-penal dogmatism of the so-called technical-juridical conception of penal law."[70]

THE INSTITUTES OF CRIMINOLOGY

The institutionalization of criminology in Spain may be traced to the beginning of this century. By royal decree, the School of Criminology was established at the University of Madrid on March 12, 1903. Its activities began in 1906 under the direction of Professor Rafael Salillas. Its mission was predominantly instructional and designed to serve prison staffs. The curriculum was strongly influenced by the positivist criminology of the early twentieth century. The school was closed when royal decree prescribed new regulations for prison personnel. During the 1930s, a Laboratory of Criminology and a School of Criminal Anthropology, both directed by Quintiliano Saldaña, operated at the University of Madrid.[71]

Spanish criminology is now being institutionalized within schools of law, but its subject matter is not required in the curricula for the law degree (*Licenciatura en Derecho*), with the sole exception being at the University of Valencia. Not all the schools of law have an institute of criminology. There is an institute of criminology only at the University of Barcelona, directed by Professor Dr. Octavio Pérez Vitoria; at the University of Madrid, directed by Professor Dr. Manuel Cobo del Rosa; in the Basque province, directed by Professor Dr. Antonio Beristan, S.J.; at the University of Valencia, directed by Professor Dr. Casabó Ruiz; and at the University of Santiago de Compostela, directed by Professor Dr. Agustín Fernández Albor.

These institutes present extremely varied activities. The institute at the University of Madrid was founded by a ministerial order on June 10, 1964, and it was directed by Professor Juan del Rosal until his death in 1973. Although it is part of the School of Law, it maintains close ties with the Schools of Medicine and Philosophy. Since, 1978, when it became an institute of the university, research has been its basic function, but it continues to offer courses that are designed primarily for law enforcement agency personnel. In 1979, the admission of doctoral candidates began. The institute has a specialized library of approximately five thousand volumes. Annually, it receives more than one hundred recipients of foreign scholarships, especially from Latin America but also from Europe and Africa. Under the supervision of the director, monographs in criminology and penal law are published, now comprising twenty-four titles. Since 1977, the journal *Cuadernos de Política criminal* has been published four times a year.

The education of criminologists is carried out in the institutes, although the students are more likely to specialize in law than in sociology, psychology, or medicine. The faculty in Spanish universities frequently pursue complementary studies in other European countries. Jurists specializing in penal law usually study in the Federal Republic of Germany. Nevertheless, in spite of the progress criminology has made in the Federal Republic of Germany in the last decade, there has not been a flow of scholars interested in studying criminology outside of Spain.

In addition to the university institutes, criminological research is conducted by government departments. On October 30, 1976, the president of Spain established the Institute of Sociological Research, which includes the problems of crime and its prevention within its purview.

In 1965, the Spanish Society of Criminology was founded by Professors Juan del Rosal, Manuel Cobo del Rosal, Bernard F. Castro, and José María Vega Villa; in 1970 the society organized the Sixth International Congress of Criminology. The Institute of Criminology of Madrid published the program of that congress in 1973.[72] In 1962, the International Society of Criminology held its Eleventh Course of International Criminology on the theme of abnormal delinquents at the School of Law of the University of Madrid, sponsored by UNESCO. Professor Juan del Rosal headed the executive committee of that course.

CURRENT STATUS OF SPANISH CRIMINOLOGY

An evaluation of the level attainted by the Spanish criminology is complicated by the questionable quality of research accomplished to date. We have indicated above that the points of departure and the goals of contemporary work do not differ significantly from what criminological investigation of the last two decades has brought into question. Many contemporary critics say criminology is at point zero.[73] If this evaluation is correct—and the negative assessment is possibly no exaggeration—there would be little point to rank Spanish criminology at some point along a scale.

As noted above, serious questioning of the scientific merit of causal-explicative criminology and clinical criminology arose in Spain long before it occurred in other European countries, but the alternative perspective of correctionalism lacked a social climate that would nurture its development.

At present, one may observe a slight shift of interest of penal scientists toward criminological questions. On one hand, ambivalent relations continue to exist between the dominant model of juridical study of penal law and the more recent concepts of criminology.[74] In addition, the universities have not committed themselves to criminology and its subject matter. In other words, the realities do not support a prediction that quantitative development of criminology is in the immediate future. On the other hand, the growing interest in criminal policy, stimulated by the reform of Spanish penal law, holds favorable possibilities.

Although long-range investigations are being embodied in the scholarly assignments in criminology of degree candidates at the Institute of Criminology of Madrid, the dominant tendency is empiricist-phenomenological and does not acknowledge methodological problems in utilizing a variety of descriptive techniques to examine criminal phenomenon. Their attention is directed primarily to problems related to drug traffic, juvenile delinquency, and prostitution.

To bring research into the criminological mainstream, the Institute of Criminology of Madrid has begin to emphasize investigations that present theoretical frames of reference requiring empirical data on crime that bear concretely on the

Spanish situation. Concurrently, critical analysis is being directed toward a model of penal science that would integrate criminological knowledge with that of penal law. The latter form of knowledge is dominant at the present time; the model is more or less vague on how this integration is to be accomplished; and the practical consequences have been minimal. The most fertile area for this incipient model appears to be that of economic criminality.[75]

NOTES

1. See Constancio Bernaldo de Quirós, *Las nuevas teorías de la criminalidad* [New Theories of Criminality], 2d ed. (Madrid: Hijos de Reus, 1898), pp. 16ff.; and Jerónimo Montes, *Precursores de la ciencia penal en Espana* [Precursors of Penal Science in Spain] (Madrid: L. G. Victoriano Suareg, 1911), pp. 35ff.

2. For discussion of Spanish correctionalism, see Jiménez de Asúa, *Tratado de Derecho Penal* [Treatise on Penal Law], 3d ed., Vol. 2 (Buenos Aires: Losado, 1964), pp. 540ff.

3. Enrique Bacigalupo, *Strafrechtsreform und Rechsverglichung* (edited by Hans Lüttger) [Criminal Law Reform and Legal Comparison] (Berlin: De Gruyter, 1979), pp. 115ff.

4. See Von Bar, *Geschichte de deutschen Strafrechts und der Strafrechtstheorien* [History of German Criminal Law and Theories of Criminal Law] (Berlin: Weidmansche, Verlag, 1882), p. 95; Antón Oneca, *La utopía penal de Dorado Montero* [The Penal Utopia of Dorado Montero] (Salamanca: Editora de la universidad, 1951), p. 43; also see Bacigalupo, *Strafrechtsreform und Rechsverglichung*

5. Montes, *Precursores de la ciencia penal en Espana.*

6. See, among others, Pío Baroja, "Final del siglo XIX y principios del XX" [End of the 19th Century and Beginning of the 20th], in *Obras Completas* [Complete Works] (1951), p. 77; Gil Cremades, *El reformismo español* [Spanish Reformism] (Barcelona: Ariel, 1969), p. 267; Francisco Javier Valls, *La filosofia del derecho de Dorado Montero* [The Philosophy of Law of Dorado Montero] (Granada: Universidad, 1971), p. 11. Neither Cremades nor Valls explains the significance of the positivist influence on Dorado since their analysis emphasizes the rhetoric over the thought itself.

7. See Jimeno Agius, "La criminalidad en España" [Criminality in Spain] *Revisita de España* 101 and 102 (1885); C. Sillió y Cortés, "La crisis del Derecho Penal" [The Crisis of Penal Law], date missing, and "La criminalitá nella Spagna" [The Criminality of Spain], in *La Scuola Positiva* [The Positivist School], Vol. 2 (Milano: Fr. Vallardi, 1891); Pedro Dorado Montero, "La criminalidad en España en el periodo de la Regencia (1885-1902)" [Criminality in Spain During the Period of the Regency], *Nuestro Tiempo* (May 1902), published next in *De criminología y penología* [About Criminology and Penology] (1906); Constancio Bernaldo de Quirós, *Criminología de los delitos de sangre en España* [The Criminology of Blood Crimes in Spain] (Madrid: Ed. Internacional, 1906); Eugenio Cuello Calón, "La criminalidad infantil y juvenile en algunos países" [Child and Juvenile Criminality in Some Countries], *Revista General de Legislación y Jurisprudencia* 603 (Madrid: 1906); Jimeno Azcárate, *La criminalidad en Asturias* [Criminality in Asturias] (1900); Jimeno Azcárate and Llanas Aguilaniedo, *La mal vida en Madrid* [Low Life-Style in Madrid] (Madrid: 1901); Gil Maestre, *Los malhechores en Madrid* [Criminals in Madrid] (Madrid: 1889); Maestre, *La criminalidad en Barcelona y en las grandes poblaciones* [Criminality in Barcelona and in Large Populations] (Barcelona: 1886); Rafael Salillas, "Los locos delincuentes en España" [Insane Delinquency in Spain] *Revista General de*

Legislación y Jurisprudencia 90 (1899); Gómez Ocaña, *El Alcoholismo* [Alcoholism] (1903); Salillas, "La edad y el delito en España" [Age and Crime in Spain], *Revista de Legislación y Jurisprudencia* 100 (1902); Salillas, *El delincuente español* [The Spanish Delinquent] (1896, 1898, 1905); Constancio Bernaldo de Quirós, "El carácter de la delincia femenina" [The Character of Femine Delinquency], *Revista Iberoamericana de Ciencias Médicas* (March 1903): Quirós, *Alrededor del delito y la pena* [About Crime and Punishment] (Madrid: 1904); Ramón Albó Martí, *Corrección de la infancia delincuente* [Correction of Child Delinquency] (Madrid: 1950).

8. See bibliography of works by Pedro Dorado Montero in Jiménez de Asúa, *Tratado* [Treatise] 3d ed. Vol. 1 (Buenos Aires: Losada, 1964), p. 872. Other bibliographies appeared later: Manuel de Rivacoba y Rivacoba, "Prologo y bibliografía" [Prologue and Bibliography] in the new edition of Dorado Montero, *Bases para un nuevo Derecho Penal* [Bases for a New Penal Law] (Barcelona: José Gsallach, undated; Barbero Santos, *Homenaje a Luis Jiménez de Asúa* [Testimonial to Luis Jiménez de Asúa] (Buenos Aires: Pandille, 1970), pp. 349ff.

9. See Jiménez de Asúa *Psicoanálisis criminal* [Criminal Psychoanalyses] 5th ed. (Buenos Aires: Losada, 1959), pp. 352 ff.; Jiménez de Asúa, *Tratado* [Treatise], 3d ed., Vol. 2 (Buenos Aires: Losada, 1964), pp. 872ff.

10. Among others, see Ian Taylor, Paul Walton, and Jock Young (eds.), *Critical Criminology* (London: Routledge and Kegan Paul, 1975), p. 49; V. F. Sack, in *Kriminologischer Journal* 4 (1972):3ff.; V. F. Sack in René König (ed.), *Handbuch der emperischen Sozialforschung* [Handbook of Empirical Social Research] vol. 2 (1969): pp. 961ff.; Werner Rüther, *Abweichendes verhalten und labeling approach* [Deviant Behavior and the Labeling Approach] (Köln: Karl Heymans Verlag, 1975); Lola Anillar de Castro, *Criminología de la reacción social* [Criminology of Social Reaction] (Maracaibo: Universidad del Zulia, 1977); Franz von Liszt, *Strafrechtliche Aufsätze und Vorträge*, [Lectures and Essays in Criminal Law] Vol.1 (Berlin: J. Guttentag, 1905), pp. 121ff.

11. Manuel de Rivacoba y Rivacoba, *Bases para un neuvo Derecho Penal* [Bases for a New Penal Law] (Buenos Aires: 1973), p. 14. In regard to this interpretation, also see Émile Durkheim, *Les régles de la Méthode Sociologique* [Rules of the Sociological Method] 1st ed. (1895); Émile Durkheim, "Kriminalität als normies Phänomen" [Criminality as a Normative Phenomenon], in V. F. Sack and R. König (eds.), *Kriminalsoziologie* [Criminal Sociology] (Frankfurt: 1968); Robert K. Merton, "Social Structure and Anomie," *American Sociological Review* 3 (October 1938):672-682.

12. Dorado Montero, *Bases para un nuevo Derecho Penal*, p. 18.

13. Ibid., p. 38.

14. Ibid., p. 39.

15. Ibid., p. 21.

16. See W. Naucke, *Die Abhändigkeiten Kriminologie und Kriminalpolitik* [The Foundations of Criminology and Criminal Policies] (1977).

17. See Mario Ruiz Funes, *Endocriminología y Criminalidad* [Endrocriminology and Criminality] (Madrid: Javier Morata, ed., 1929); Funes, *Etiología del suicide en España* [Etiology of Suicide in Spain], a preliminary Spanish version of Émile Durkheim's *Suicide*; Luis Jiménez de Asúa, *Psicoanálisis Criminal*.

18. See Luis Jiménez de Asúa, *Le sentencia indeterminada* [The Indeterminate Sentence] (Madrid: Hijos de Reus Editores, 1913; 2d ed., 1948); *El estado peligroso del delincuente y sus consecueriasante el Derecho Penal moderno* [The Dangerous State of the Delinquent and Its Consequences Before Modern Penal Law] (Madrid: Hijos de Reus,

Editores 1920); *El estado peligroso* [The Dangerous State] (Madrid: Imprento Juan Pueyo, 1922); *Endocrinología y Derecho Penal* [Endrocrinology and Penal Law] (Montevideo: Imprento Nacional, 1927); *Libertad de amar y derecho a morir—Ensayo de un criminalista sobre eugenasia, eutanasia y encrinología* [Liberty to Love and Right to Die— Essay of a Criminologist in Eugenics, Euthanasia, and Encrinology] (Madrid: Historia Nueva, 1927; 6th ed., Buenos Aires, 1946); *Valor de la psicología profunda en las ciencias penales* [Value of Profound Psychology in the Penal Sciences] (1935).

19. See Jiménez de Asúa, *La sentencia indeterminada*, p. 6.

20. See Jiménez de Asúa, *Psicoanálisis criminal*, 5th ed., 1959, pp. 12ff.

21. See his *El nuevo sesago de la Criminología* [The New Slant of Criminology], in *Temas penales* (Penal Themes) (Córdoba, Argentina: Universidad Nacional, 1931), p. 63; *La teoría Jurídica del delito* [The Juridical Theory of Crime] (Madrid: Imprenta Colonial, 1931), pp. 25ff.; *Tratado de Derecho Penal* [Treatise on Penal Law] 3d ed., Vol. 1 (Buenos Aires: Losada, 1964), p. 109; and other bibliographic references.

22. See Dorado Montero, *Bases para un nuevo Derecho Penal*, pp. 65ff.

23. Jiménez de Asúa, *Problemas de Derecho Penal* [Problems of Penal Law] (Sante Fé, Argentina: Universidad Nacional del Litoral, 1931), p. 15.

24. Ibid., pp. 134 and 144.

25. Jiménez de Asúa, *Lombroso*.

26. Jiménez de Asúa, *Problemas de Derecho Penal*, p. 14.

27. "I defend subjective danger, the discretionary judgment of arbitrators, the indeterminant sentence, and many other institutions of new stamp," Asúa said, "for when the old punitive law is transformed into a protective institution for delinquents and society." *Problemas de Derecho Penal*, p. 14; also see his *El nuevo Derecho Penal* [The New Penal Law] (Madrid: Paez, 1929).

28. See his *Problemas de Derecho Penal*, pp. 14ff.

29. See his *Temas penales*, p. 62; *Tratado I*, pp. 81ff.

30. See Juan del Rosal, *Principios de Derecho Penal Español* [Principles of Spanish Penal Law] (Valladolid: C. Martin, 1945), p. 480; Enrique Gimbernat Ordeig, *Homeraje a Jiménez de Asúa* [Testimonial to Jiménez de Asúa] (Buenos Aires: Panille, 1970), pp. 87ff.; and, with reservations, Enrique Bacigalupo, *Review International de Droit Pénal* [International Review of Penal Law], 49, no. 1 (1978):15ff.

31. Among the general works are: Rodríguez Devesa, *Derecho Penal español* [Spanish Penal Law], 7th ed. (Madrid: Gráficas Caracasa, 1979), pp. 72ff.; José Cerezo Mir, *Curso de Derecho Penal español* [Course of Spanish Penal Law], Vol. 1 (Madrid: Tecnos, 1976), p. 67; José A. Sainz Cantero, *Lecciones de Derecho Penal* [Lessons of Penal Law], Vol. 1 (Barcelona, ed. Bosch: 1979), p. 87; Juan del Rosal, *Tratado de Derecho Penal* [Treatise on Penal Law] (Madrid; Imprento Aguire, 1969-1972). Translations of works in criminology written by jurists also deal with the relationships of criminology and the legalistic perspective: José Arturo Rodríquez Muñoz, *Kriminal Politik* [Criminal Policy] (1942); Juan del Rosal in Franz Exner, *Kriminologie* [Criminology], 3d ed. (Barcelona, Ed. Bosch, 1946): Devesa in Seelig, *El Tratado de Criminología*. Recently, the criminological works of Günther Kaiser and Hans Göppinger have been translated.

32. Exceptions to this statement are found in the following works: Manuel López-Rey, *Criminología* [Criminology] (Madrid: Aguilar, 1975, 2d vol., 1977); López-Rey, *La criminalidad* [Criminality], trans. by P. L. Váñez (Madrid: Tecnos, 1976); Carlos María de Landecho, S.J. "La tipificación lombrosian del delincuente" [The Lombrosian Typing

of the Delinquent], Part 1 (Madrid: Unpublished doctoral dissertation, 1976); Alfonso Serrano Gómez, *Delincuencia juvenile en Espana* [Juvenile Delinquency in Spain] (Madrid: Ed. Doncel, 1970); Gómez and José L. Fernández Dopico, *El delincuente español* [The Spanish Delinquent] (Madrid: Publicaciones del Instituto de Criminologia, 1978); Alarcón Bravo and Marco Purón, *La intelligencia en los delincuentes españoles [Intelligence Among Spanish Delinquents]* (Madrid: Imprenta T.P.A., 1968); F. Chamorro Gundín, *Resultados obtenidos con téchnicas productivas en una muestra de 200 delincuentes homosexuales españoles* [Results Obtained with Predictive Techniques in a Sample of 200 Spanish Homosexual Delinquents) (Madrid: Direccíon General de Instituciones Penitenciarias, 1970). Alarcón Bravo, Castillón Mora, García Ruiz, Gonzáles Alvarez, Marco Purón, Rodríguez Gandul, Torres Sánchez, and Velasco Escasi, *Un sistema de trabajo en el estudio de la personalidad criminal* [A System of Work in the Study of the Criminal Personality] (Madrid: 1970).

33. See López-Rey, *Criminología.*

34. Anton Oneca, *La utopía penal de Dorado Montero*, p. 86.

35. Jiménez de Asúa, *Revista de Derecho Público* 1 (September 15, 1932):257; Jiménez de Asúa, *Tratado*, Vol. 1, pp. 880ff.; Isaías Sánchez Tejerina, *Un gran penalista español el Padre Jerónimo Montes* [A Great Spanish Penologist: Father Jerónimo Montes] (Madrid: 1934).

36. Rafael Salillas, *El delincuente español—Hampa* [The Spanish Delinquent— Underworld] (Madrid: 1898), p. 375.

37. Ibid., p. 375.

38. Ibid., p. 450.

39. Ibid., p. 457.

40. Ibid., p. 412.

41. Ibid., p. 412.

42. Ibid., p. 405.

43. Ibid., p. 452.

44. Jiménez de Asúa, *Tratado de Derecho Penal*, Vol. 1, p. 871.

45. Enrique Bacigalupo, "Historia-Instituciones-Documentes" [History-Institutions-Documents] (Sevilla: June 1979), pp. 11ff.

46. Montes, *Precursores de la cencia penal*, pp. 35ff.

47. Ibid., pp. 155ff.

48. Ibid., pp. 166ff.

49. Ibid., p. 167.

50. Ibid., p. 525.

51. Ibid., p. 526.

52. Ibid., p. 526.

53. Ibid., pp. 573ff.

54. Quintiliano Saldaña, "Criminología pragmática" [Pragmatic Criminology] in *Trabajos del Laboratorio de criminología de la Universidad de Madrid* [Works of the Laboratory of Criminology of the University of Madrid], no. 3 (1936), pp. 7-62.

55. Ibid., p. 10.

56. Ibid., p. 10.

57. See "Biotipología criminal" [Criminal Biotypology], in *Trabajos del Laboratorio de criminología de la Universidad de Madrid*, no. 2 (1935), pp. 93-181.

58. Ibid., p. 147.

59. With respect to this type of investigation, see Gregorio Marañón, "La endocrinología

y la ciencia penal" [Endocrinology and Penal Science], in *Trabajos del Laboratorio de Criminalogía de la Universidad de Madrid*, no. 2 (1935), pp. 81ff.; the article indicated the limits of conclusions possible to obtain.

60. Juan del Rosal, *Principios de Derecho Penal Español*, pp. 473ff.
61. Ibid., p. 480.
62. Ibid., p. 482.
63. Ibid., p. 533.
64. Ibid., p. 484.
65. Ibid., p. 532.
66. Ibid., p. 580.
67. Ibid., p. 580.
68. See Juan del Rosal, *Tratado de Derecho Penal Español*, 2d ed., revised and corrected by Manuel Cobo del Rosal (Madrid: 1976), pp. 65ff.
69. See Marino Barbero Santos, *Estudios de Derecho Penal y Criminología* [Studies of Penal Law and Criminology] (Valladolid: 1971; Antonio Beristain, *Questiones Penals y Criminólogicas* [Penal and Criminological Questions] (Madrid: Ed. Reus, 1979).
70. Manuel López-Rey, *La justicia penal y la política criminal en España* [Penal Justice and Criminal Policy in Spain] (Madrid: Instituto de Criminología, 1979), p. 18.
71. With reference to the School of Criminology, see Jiménez de Asúa, *Al servicio del Derecho Penal* [At the Service of Penal Law] (Madrid: Ed. Morata, 1930), pp. 131ff.
72. *Memoria del VI Congreso Internacionale de Criminología* [Account of the Sixth International Congress on Criminology], 1973.
73. See Günther Kaiser, *Kriminologie* 3 [Criminology], 3d ed. (Karlsrhue, Müller, 1976), p. 2 and material from Katschinsky, "Sociological Aspects of Deviance and Criminality," in *Collected Studies in Criminological Research* 9 (1972), pp. 9-99.
74. See "Actes de premier coloque régional espagnol sur politique criminelle et droit pénal" [Acts of the First Regional Spanish Congress on Criminal Policy and Penal Law] in *Revue International du Droit Pénal* 1 (1978); and "Diskussionsbericht der Fachgruppe 'Schuldelemente'" [Discussion of the Special Group, "Elements of Guilt" in Kurt Matlener, Dietrich Papenfuss, and Wolfgang Schönne, *Strafrecht und Strafrechtsreform* [Criminal Law and Criminal Law Reform] (Köln: Carl Heymanns, 1974), p. 334, where it is recommended to include the results of criminological investigation in the dogma and system of penal law.
75. See Miguel Bajo Fernández, *El Derecho Penal Economico. Un Estudio de Derecho Positivo Español* [The Economic Penal Law, A Study of Spanish Positive Law] (Madrid: Ed. Civitas, 1978); also in *Cuadernas de política criminal* 5 (1978): 3ff.; and in his *Derecho Penal económico* [Economic Penal Law] (Madrid: Ed. Civitas, 1978), pp. 47-85.

BIBLIOGRAPHY

Aramburu y Zuloaga, Félix. *La nueva ciencia penal* [The New Penal Science]. (Madrid: Fe, 1887.

Aramburu y Zuloaga, Félix. *La neuva orientación del Derecho Penal y la lucha contra el delito* [The New Orientation of Penal Law and the Struggle Against Crime]. Madrid: 1910.

Arenal, Concepción. "El reo" [The Criminal]; "Estudios penitenciarios" [Penitentiary Studies]; "La carcel llamado modelo" [The Jail Called "Model"]; and "Las colonias penales in Australia y la pena de deportación" [The Penal Colonies in Australia and the Penalty of Deportation], in *Obras Completas* [Complete Works]. Madrid: Sucesores de Rivadaneyra, 1894.

Beristain, Antonia. *Cuestiones penales y criminológicas* [Penal and Criminological Questions]. Madrid: Reus S. A. 1979.

Calón, Eugenio Cuello. *Penología* [Penology]. Madrid: Reus, 1920.

Calón, Eugenio Cuello. *La nueva penología* [The New Penology]. Barcelona: Bosch, 1958.

de Asúa, Luis Jiménez. *Endocrinología y Derecho Penal* [Endocrinology and Penal Law]. Montevideo: Impr. Nacional, 1927.

de Asúa, Luis Jiménez. *Libertad de amar y derecho a morir—Ensayos de un criminalista sobre eugenesia, eñtanasia y endocrinología* [Freedom to Love and the Right to Die—Essays of a Criminologist on Eugenics, Euthanasia and Endocrinology]. Madrid: Historia Nueva, 1928.

de Asúa, Luis Jiménez. *Cronica del Crimen* [Chronicle of Crimes]. Madrid: Historic Nueva, 1929.

de Asúa, Luis Jiménez. "Nuevo sesgo de la Criminología" [The New Start of Criminology], in *Temas Penales* [Penal Themes]. Santa Fe, Argentina: Instituto Social de la Universidad del Litoral, 1931.

de Asúa, Luis Jiménez. *Psicoanálisis Criminal* [Criminal Psychoanalysis]. [Buenos Aires: Losado, 1942; 5th ed., Buenos Aires: Losado, 1959.

de Landecho, Carlis Mariá. *Körperbau, Charakter und Kriminalität* [Body Build, Character and Criminality]. Bonn: Röhrscheid, 1964.

de Los Ríos, Francisco Giner. "Tutela penal" [Penal Guardianship]. In *Resumen de Filosofia del Derecho* [Resume of the Philosophy of Law]., Madrid: Suárez, 1898.

de Quirós, Constancio Bernaldo. *El alcoholismo* [Alcoholism], Barcelona: Gilli, 1903.

de Quirós, Constancio Bernaldo. *Las nuevas teorías de la criminalidad* [The New Theories of Criminality]. Madrid: Reus, 1892, 2d ed.; Havana: Montero, 1946, 3d ed.

de Quirós, Constancio Bernaldo. *Criminologiía* [Criminology]. Puebla, Mexico: Cajica, 1948.

del Rosal, Juan. *Principios de Derecho Penal* [Principles of Penal Law]. Valladolid: Librería Lara, 1948.

del Rosal, Juan. "Algunos aspectos de la criminalidad contemporánea" [Some Aspects of Contemporary Criminality]. *Revisita de Derecho y Ciencias Poliíticas*. Universidad de San Marcos, Lima, Peru, 1951.

del Rosal, Juan. *La personalidad del delinquente en la téchnica penal* [The Personality of the Delinquent in the Penal Method]. Valladolid: Seminarios de la Facultad de Derecho de la Universidad de Valladolid, 1949, 2d ed., 1953.

Funes, Mariano Ruiz. *Endocrinología y Criminalidad* [Endocrinology and Criminality]. Madrid: Morata, 1929.

Funes, Mariano Ruiz. *Estudios criminológicas* [Criminological Studies]. Havana: Montero, 1952.

Serrano Gómez, Alfonso, and José L. Fernandez Dopico. *El Delincuente español* [The Spanish Delinquent]. Madrid: Instituto de Criminología de la Universidad Computense, 1978.

Lopez-Rey, Manuel. *Criminología* [Criminology]. Madrid: Aguilar, 1975.

López-Rey, Manuel. *La criminalidad* [Criminality]. Madrid: Tecnos, 1976.

Montero, Pedro Dorado. *Estudios de derecho penal preventivo* [Studies of the Law of Penal Prevention]. Madrid: Reus, 1900.

Montero, Pedro Dorado. *Bases para un nuevo Derecho Penal* [Bases of a New Penal Law]. Barcelona: Manuales Soler, 1902.

Montero, Pedro Dorado. *De Criminología y Penología* [Criminology and Penology], Madrid: Vda. de Rodriguez Serra, 1906.

Montero, Pedro Dorado. *La Psicología criminal en nuestro derecho legislado* [Criminal Psychology in Our Enacted Laws]. Madrid: Reus, 1910.

Montero, Pedro Dorado. *El derecho protector de las criminales* [Laws that Protect the Criminals]. 2 vols. Madrid: Suárez, 1916.

Montes, Jerónimo. *Precursores de la ciencia penal en España.Estudio del delincuente y las causas y remedios del delito.* [Precursors of the Penal Science of Spain. Studies of Delinquency and the Causes and Remedies of Crime]. Madrid: Suárez, 1911.

Saldaña, Quinitiliano. *Los orígines de las criminología* [The Origins of Criminology]. Madrid: Suárez, 1914.

Saldaña, Quintiliano. *La antropología criminal y la justicia penal* [Criminal Anthropology and Criminal Justice]. Madrid: Reus, 1915.

Salillas, Rafael, *El delincuente español: Hampa—Antropología picaresca* [The Spanish Delinquent: Underworld—Picaresque Anthropology]. Madrid: Suárez, 1898.

Salillas, Rafael. *Evolución penitenciaria española* [Evolution of Spanish Penitentiaries]. 2 vols. Madrid: Clásica Española, 1919.

Salillas, Rafael, "Sentido y tendencias de las últimas reformas en Criminología". [The Direction and the Tendencies of the Latest Reforms in Criminology]. *Asociación para el progreso de las ciencias, Congreso de Zaragoza* 5 (1909):153ff.

Barbero Santos, Marino. *Estudios de Criminología y Derecho Penal* [Studies of Criminology and Penal Law]. (Valladolid: Universidad, 1972).

SWITZERLAND

Martin Killias

Criminology in Switzerland has made remarkably little progress since World War II. This is the conclusion Marshall Clinard reached after his study of crime in that country.[1] To elaborate on that conclusion, this chapter examines the conditions that have shaped Swiss development of the social sciences, especially those conditions that have inhibited the emergence of a viable and independent criminology. Analyses of these circumstances and of their effects will provide important insights for studies of the development of criminology in other settings. Switzerland is all the more valuable as a case study because it is one of the few developed nations to have notably low official crime rates.

DEVELOPMENT OF SCIENCE AND RESEARCH

Switzerland is a small country with a highly developed technical industry and considerable economic power. With a population of only about 6.3 million, the gross national product per capita is the world's highest.[2] The combination of a small population and the role of being an international financial center requires certain adaptations within the Swiss society which also influence the position of science and research.

The adaptation involves extreme specialization in a few externally directed economic activities and simultaneously less specialization in internally oriented sectors.[3] Those branches of the Swiss economy that are directed toward export are highly specialized in activities that require much capital but only a small labor force; examples of such activities are the manufacture of machines, watches and instruments, chemical derivatives and pharmaceutical products, and the provision of services as in banking. This specialization allows the Swiss economy to withstand international competition. Conversely, the domestically oriented sectors are less differentiated; the small population base and the available educational resources do not permit the degree of specialization found in other highly developed societies. Thus, for example, political functions and military functions are performed almost entirely by nonprofessionals.

These conditions favor investment in applied research in the natural sciences because they are relevant for the export industries. Basic research and those studies that are significant for the planning and interpretation of social development tend to be neglected. This is true most of all for the social sciences, which in Switzerland have been encouraged only since the 1960s, but even now corporate, government, and university investments are only modest when compared to Swiss investments in other research fields and investments of other countries in the social sciences.

The possibility of sociology developing criminology as a subfield, for example, has been and continues to be remote. Sociological research concentrates on those issues that draw most attention in current politics.[4] Publications of the last ten years have been predominantly Xn immigration,[5] the structuring of opportunities in the educational system,[6] the social integration of youth,[7] and so on. Crime received little relative notice from the public or from sociologists before 1973.[8]

CRIME TRENDS IN SWITZERLAND

Switzerland has a low crime rate in comparison with other highly developed countries, such as the United States of America, Sweden, and the Federal Republic of Germany.[9] This conclusion is supported by comparisons of official statistics and by victimization surveys.

The validity of official statistics and victimization data may be questioned, but Table 29-1 does lend support to the thesis that conventional criminality occurs much less frequently in Switzerland than in the Federal Republic of Germany and the United States. As an international center of finance, Switzerland would be more likely to have commercial and fiduciary transgressions (white-collar crimes) than other countries, but comparative data are lacking.

The crime rate in Switzerland remains remarkably stable except for robbery and burglary (see Tables 29-2 and 29-3). In his especially valuable analysis of official crime statistics in Switzerland, Clinard finds that the absence of nationally collected police data raises major problems for research, but he reports any increases in the amount of crime to be small.[10]

INSTITUTIONALIZATION OF CRIMINOLOGY

The relatively low crime rate and the general situation for science and research may be one explanation of the modest development of Swiss criminology.

Research and Teaching

Diverse institutes of legal medicine and an institute for criminalistics exist, but they do not concern themselves with criminology in the usual sense. In fact, no

TABLE 29-1
**RATES PER 100,000 POPULATION FOR SELECTED SERIOUS CRIMES
IN ZÜRICH, SWITZERLAND; STUTTGART, WEST GERMANY; AND AN
AVERAGE OF EIGHT AMERICAN CITIES[a]**

Offense Category	Zürich	Stuttgart	U.S. Cities
Consummated homicides, attempts excluded (1973, police data)	0.75	6	19
Consummated burglaries (1973, survey data)	5,400	7,100	10,400
Auto thefts, consummated and attempted (1973, survey data)	1,000	2,300	4,100
Robberies, consummated and attempted (1973 survey data)	1,000	2,200	1,900

Sources: Marshall Clinard, *Cities with Little Crime: The Case of Switzerland* (Cambridge: Cambridge
University Press, 1978), p. 68 (data on homicides); and Egon Stephan, *Die Stuttgarter
Opferbefragund* [The Stuttgart Victimization Survey] (Wiesbaden: 1976), pp. 329-331.

[a]Atlanta, Baltimore, Cleveland, Dallas, Denver, Portland, (Oregon), Newark, and St. Louis.

TABLE 29-2
**CONVICTIONS FOR SELECTED CRIMES OF VIOLENCE
PER 1 MILLION POPULATION, 1954-1977**

Year	All Offenses Against Safety of Person	Homicides	Robberies	Forcible Rapes (Criminal Sex Assault Included)
1954	498	6.1	13	23
1958	521	6.2	15	19
1962	486[a]	6.2	24	30
1966	393	4.3	19	24
1970	441	6.6	19	25
1973	421	4.2	20	25
1974	383[a]	5.7	25	21
1975	415	5.5	27	17
1976	362	8.4	39	20
1977	371	6.6	32	24

Sources: *Die Strafurteile in der Schweiz* [Criminal Convictions in Switzerland] (Bern: Eidgenössisches
Statistisches Amt, 1954); and *Statistisches Jahrbuch der Schweiz 1979* [Statistical Yearbook
of Switzerland, 1979], edited by Eidgenössisches Statistisches Amt (Basel: 1979), p. 31.

[a]After 1960 and 1973, certain minor offenses ceased to be registered.

TABLE 29-3
SERIOUS CRIMES REPORTED TO POLICE IN ZÜRICH
PER 100,000 POPULATION, 1973-1978

Year	Homicides Including Attempts	Forcible Rape, Including Attempts	Robbery	Burglary	Auto Thefts
1973	2.2	13.2	17.2	971	289
1974	4.8	8.1	25.5	931	298
1975	3.1	7.7	29.3	1,220	291
1976	3.9	8.9	31.3	1,214	309
1977	2.6	9.5	53.5	1,364	313
1978	2.7	11.7	45.4	1,452	224

Source: Statistisches Jahrbuch der Stadt Zürich 1978 [Statistical Yearbook of the City of Zürich, 1978] (Zurich: Statistisches Amt der Stadt Zürich, 1980), p. 377 (police data) and p. 38 (population data).

institutions in Switzerland specialize in criminology.[11] None of the ten universities of Switzerland has a chair of criminology, and, when courses in criminology are offered, they usually are within the programs of the law faculties. They are conducted irregularly and mainly by foreign teachers.[12] Unlike the situation in the Federal Republic of Germany, the study of criminology is not an optional field in the training of lawyers. Social work education in Switzerland includes courses in criminology, but courses in social work are not offered at the universities. Since criminology is not taught at the universities, few persons active in governmental or criminal justice occupations have had systematic training in criminology.

Professionalization and Criminology

Although there are persons in Switzerland who are interested in criminology, the criminologist has not gained an independent status among the professions. Those persons engaged in criminological research are employed in some related discipline, mostly in jurisprudence; some are in the social sciences and in psychology. From these disciplines they derive their professional identities: primarily as jurists, sociologists, psychologists, and so on. Frequently, they have demonstrated an incidental interest in criminology while pursuing postgraduate studies in some related subject; often it is only a passing interest. Consequently, a large proportion of the Swiss publications in criminology are academic dissertations, which are the sole contributions of many scholars to the field.

Perhaps the absence of an autonomous status for criminology holds advantages for its future. The diffusion of scarce resources into allied social and behavioral sciences will strengthen criminological knowledge when adherents of the other disciplines recognize the possibilities of criminological issues for developing their own fields. However, the development of criminology per se is retarded by the irregularity of communication among those scholars whose interests in criminology are secondary to their primary career commitments and by the very limited use of criminological knowledge in nonacademic occupations and research.

Even if these difficulties were to be overcome, the development of a full-fledged professional status for criminologists would be inhibited by the language diversity which has effects on communication among all university scholars.[13]

Although its several languages have been cited as an opportunity for Switzerland to function as Europe's linguistic mediators, Swiss criminologists tend to ignore publications in other linguistic regions. This explains the failure in Switzerland, until recently, to recognize developments in modern Italian criminology.

Nevertheless, progress has been made in overcoming language barriers to establish communication among those Swiss who have interests in criminology. To be mentioned first is the Schweizerische Arbeitsgruppe Kriminologie (Swiss Criminological Association), founded by the Zürich psychologist W. T. Haesler and reconstituted in 1978 as the union of Swiss criminologists. Its meetings have been attended by important foreign criminolgists,[14] and since 1975 its journal *Kriminologisches Bulletin* has published pertinent Swiss articles. Criminological articles have also been published in the *Revue Suisse de Sociologie* in French and German since 1975, in *Der Strafrollzug in der Schweiz*, edited by the Swiss Association for Prison Administration and Parole (Schweizerischer Verein für Straf-, Gefanguiswesend und Schutzaufsicht founded in 1867), and *Déviance et Société* published in French since 1977. The last-named journal is edited by Christian-Nils Robert, professor of criminal law in Geneva, and is directed toward all French-speaking countries. The bilingual *Revue Pénale Suisse*, founded in 1888, is now edited by Hans Schultz, professor of criminal law in Bern. The *Revue International de Criminologie et de Police Techique* was founded in 1947 and was edited by Jean Graven, professor of criminal law in Geneva, until 1970; this journal is directed to all French-speaking countries.

The series of monographs published in Switzerland includes *Berner Kriminologische Untersuchungen*, issued by Professor Hans Schultz in German since 1963. The series *Der Schweizerische Strafvollzug* has been published since 1976 in French and German by the following professors of criminal law: Ph. Graven of Geneva, P. Noll of Zürich, H. Schultz of Bern, and G. Stratenwerth of Basel. The series *Déviance et Société*, issued in Geneva since 1976, has Christian-Nils Robert as co-editor. The bilingual *Schweizerische Criminalistische Studien* was issued from 1946 to 1966 by O. A. Germann, in which Erwin Frey's chief work appears.[15]

Because the institutionalization of criminology has lagged in Switzerland, as expected there have been limited contacts with the criminologists of other European countries. Although François Clerc, professor of criminal law in Neuchâtel, belonged for years to the Comité Européen pour les Problemes Criminels, Switzerland has not been represented for many years at the meetings in Strasbourg of the directors of criminological institutes.[16] But in recent years Swiss interest in such events has increased. In the field of criminal law, however, there have long existed informal contacts between Swiss and foreign scholars. Teachers of criminal law in German-speaking Switzerland have concerned themselves with reform of the criminal law in the Federal Republic of Germany. Professors H. Schultz from Bern, G. Stratenwerth from Basel, and P. Noll from Zürich were co-authors of the so-called alternative draft (in contrast to the official drafts) for reform of the German Criminal Code.[17] The French-speaking Swiss have cooperated with professional colleagues of other French-speaking countries.[18]

CRIMINOLOGICAL RESEARCH, 1945 TO 1979

The inadequate institutionalization of criminology has resulted partially from a failure to attract scholars from the disciplines in which they have become established. Zürich professor of criminal law Erwin R. Frey claimed this failure was ultimately an advantage in that criminology functioned as a "clearinghouse" for its related disciplines rather than an autonomous discipline defining its own topics for research.[19]

For a long time, criminological research in Switzerland followed this model. The contributions of jurists were more numerous than those of psychiatrists, psychologists, and sociologists. Because most of these publications were produced in the course of attaining an academic degree, they conformed to the perspective and expectations of disciplines other than criminology per se. Most of them were either small empirical studies or reviews of foreign literature. The first real examination of the crime situation in Switzerland—that of Marshall Clinard in 1973—was carried out by an American scholar and with financial support from the United States. Switzerland has yet to produce, from the Swiss perspective, a textbook and a comprehensive review of criminology.

Research from the Perspective of Criminal Law

As in most European countries, criminology in Switzerland has been the almost exclusive domain of the scholars of criminal law.[20] Because of the many connections between the scholars of German-speaking Switzerland and those of Germany—Franz Exner, Wilhelm Sauer, Hans von Hentig, Karl-Siegfried Bader[21]—Germany has had a strong influence on Swiss criminology. In the 1950s and 1960s, this influence was apparent in numerous studies that focused on biological concepts, the multiple factor approach, and nonhypothetical empiricism.[22] Etiological studies examined special types of crime or criminals: fraud (Leemann, 1972), shoplifting (Stephani, 1968, and Rust, 1972), mistreatment of children (Lechleiter, 1971), sexual offenses (Reinhardt, 1967), escape from prisons (Giger, 1959), abortion (Alexandrow, 1947, and Siegrist, 1971), crime among foreign workers (Neumann, 1963) and among old people (Fopp, 1969), and so on.[23] The best known of these studies was Frey's research on young recidivists;[24] he was influenced by Exner and the Gluecks in the development of prognostic tables which he persistently recommended for use in criminal proceedings.

In the 1970s, this pattern of research was increasingly superseded by sociological analyses inspired by American investigations of criminal justice and penology. A group of Swiss doctoral candidates have been studying the operations of diverse Swiss penal establishments by evaluating the officially proclaimed goals of resocialization.[25] The administration of justice has been examined by a limited number of research projects: namely, the relationship between the social status of the arrested person and the use of pretrial detention in the Canton of Geneva;[26] the evaluation of the defendant's earlier life as a factor in sentencing;[27] knowledge of law among citizens;[28] and the effect of social change on the definition of sexual offenses.[29]

Research from the Perspective of Psychiatry

Before World War II, Swiss legal psychiatry had achieved a great international reputation, thanks to the fundamental works of Auguste Forel[30] and Eugen Bleuler.[31] The problems of penal responsibility and the concept of guilt in psychiatry and criminal law were studied predominantly; Binder[32] offers a major example. Since then, the emphasis has been displaced toward the problem of the adequacy and the effectiveness of penal sanctions. J. Bernheim, professor of legal psychiatry in Geneva, and M. Gschwind, the Basel psychiatrist in Göttingen, Germany, have published various works concerning the reform of penal institutions and the procedure of sentencing.[33] Legal psychiatry has also followed an etiological tradition by seeking the social psychiatric causes of various forms of deviance.[34]

Traditionally, the role of legal psychiatrists determining the defendant's responsibility in criminal proceedings was undisputed. In the last several years, this function has become the subject of debate. A conference on this issue resulted in a publication.[35] Various articles have also been published.[36]

Research from the Perspective of Psychology

Paul Reiwald (1895-1951), who taught in Switzerland after World War II, was one of Europe's most important criminologists in his day. Originally an attorney-at-law and a lecturer in criminal psychology in Berlin, he fled to Brussels in 1933 and later to Geneva, where he taught at the University until his death.[37] He was allied theoretically with other contemporary criminal psychologists influenced by Freud, namely, Franz Alexander, Hugo Staub, and some others. During his teaching in Switzerland, he developed a comprehensive psychological theory of crime, whose general applicability stretched beyond the limited framework of other psychoanalytical criminologists. He anticipated some aspects of the labeling approach. Reiwald postulated that the conformist needs the transgressor as a target for the projection of his own deviant tendencies; thereby, the criminal represents essentially a product of his society.[38] At first, Reiwald's theses were not recognized in Switzerland or elsewhere. Only recently have his ideas been rediscovered, mainly because of the republication in Germany of his principal work by Herbert Jäger and Tilmann Moser in 1973 and because of the publications of Eduard Naegeli in Switzerland.

In the 1950s and 1960s, Swiss criminal psychology abandoned the search for comprehensive theories of crime. Foremost were the studies on criminal responsibility,[39] on the instrumentalization of psychology to serve the prosecution,[40] and, sometimes under the influence of the "défense sociale,"[41] on the means of treating certain types of offenders as, for example, juvenile delinquents[42] or sexual offenders.[43]

In the 1970s, Eduard Naegeli, professor in Saint Gallen, sought to establish more general psychological theories of crime.[44] Similarly, Rüdiger Herren, who teaches in Freiburg, West Germany, has examined the influence of psychoanalysis upon criminology.[45]

Research from the Perspective of Sociology

In 1957, before sociology had developed in Switzerland, René König, then professor of sociology in Köln (Cologne), and his Swiss colleague Peter Heintz, who then also was teaching in Köln, published *Soziologie der Jugendkriminalität* (Sociology of Juvenile Delinquency). Among others, leading American criminologists contributed to the volume, which included a review of the development of American criminology since 1930.[46] The book contributed to the introduction of sociological thinking into European criminology, but it had little effect in Switzerland. Swiss criminology remained largely untouched by sociological theories and methodology until the end of the 1960s.[47] The skepticism toward sociology held by Swiss jurists, who were most numerous among criminologists in Switzerland, was probably the crucial factor in this delay.

The gap between sociology and criminology did not diminish until the mid-1970s when the labeling approach made considerable progress. Swiss studies endeavored to establish a linkage with international criminological research that followed the ideas advanced by Becker, Lemert, Goffman, Garfinkel, and others. Recent Swiss studies, such as those of Malherbe (1977), Fischer (1976), Besozzi (1976), Robert (1977), and others,[48] reviewed the "classical" works of the labeling approach. Only a few authors (for example, Schultz,[49] and Bühler and Niederberger[50]) tried to relate the labeling approach to its predecessors, namely, anomie theory and differential association. Until now, little attention has been given to the development of the labeling approach in the Federal Republic of Germany where its recognition came some years earlier than in Switzerland.[51] French-Swiss criminology especially is oriented almost exclusively toward the Americn labeling approach and toward the newer research literature of other French-speaking countries.[52]

Since 1975, the increased Swiss interest in criminology has been expressed in theoretical considerations more than through empirical studies. Among the few empirical contributions are studies on the social history of crime[53] and penal institutions,[54] the influence of school pupils on the delinquent behavior of their fellows,[55] the interdependence of sociostructural factors and socially determined variables of personality in pecuniary and property crimes,[56] and the impact of mass media upon the perception of and attitudes toward criminality.[57] Not completed yet is a project financed by the Swiss National Fund. It deals with the sociostructural conditions of the genesis and social effects of the contacts of juveniles with social control events. The research is being conducted by the Sociological Institute of the University of Zürich and the Swiss Office for Problems of Alcoholism (Schweizerische Fachstelle für Alkoholprobleme).

Peter Heintz,[58] who has been teaching in Zürich as professor of sociology since 1966, has not intervened in criminal-sociological discussions since 1957. But his contributions to the further development of structural-theoretical approaches in sociology are having increasing effect on Swiss criminal sociology. Hypotheses that are especially fruitful for the analysis of deviant behavior may be derived from his theory of structural and anomic tensions.[59] His highly abstract theory has general application to analyses of very different social problems.[60] It may be that Heintz's influence will lead Swiss criminology in a direction similar to that of the British "new criminology."[61] Recently, two students of Heintz[62] vigorously criticized the failure of the labeling perspective to account for the impact of social structure. Their criticism may give strong impetus to the integration of the labeling and structural perspectives,[63] even if in Switzerland, as elsewhere, the labeling approach is the "current orthodoxy."[64]

Perhaps these recent developments are tentative signs of an eventual emancipation of Swiss criminology. At least, they are evidence that the allied disciplines are becoming more interested in criminological topics. In either sense, criminology in Switzerland appears to be entering a period when the restraints of its setting will be eased.

NOTES

1. Marshall Clinard, *Cities with Little Crime: The Case of Switzerland* (Cambridge: Cambridge University Press, 1978).

2. In 1977, Switzerland had the world's highest per capita GNP if only the countries with a population of 1 million or more are considered. See *World Bank Atlas 1978*, edited by World Bank, Economic Analysis and Projections Department, Washington, D.C., 1978.

3. See Samuel N. Eisenstadt, "Sociologische Merkmale und Probleme kleiner Staaten" [Sociological Characteristics and Problems of Small Nations], *Revue Suisse de Sociologie* 3 (Spring 1977):67-85; Hans Geser and François Hopflinger, "Probleme der Strukturellen Differenzierung in kleinen Gesellschaften" [Problems of Structural Differentiation in Small Societies], *Revue Suisse de Sociologie* 2 (1976):27-54.

4. See *Index of Sociological Research Projects, 1976-1977*, edited by Société Suisse de Sociologie, Lausanne, Switzerland, 1978.

5. For example, Hans-Joachim Hoffman-Nowotny, *Soziologie des Fremdarbeiterproblems* [Sociology of the Problem of Foreign Workers] (Stuttgart: 1973).

6. For example, Roger Girod, *Inégalité-Inégalités* [Inequality-Inequalities] (Paris: Presses Universitaires de France, 1977).

7. For example, R. Blancpain and E. Haüselmann, *Zur Unrast der Jugend* [On Restlessness of Youth] (Frauenfeld, Switzerland: 1974): P. Arnold, et al., *Jeunesse et Société* [Youth and Society] (Lausanne, Switzerland: 1971).

8. Before 1973, crime was not regarded as an important issue, and very few questions were raised about it in Parliament in the 1950s and 1960s. See Clinard, *Cities with Little Crime*, pp. 12-33.

9. Ibid.

10. Ibid., pp. 34-52.

11. Ibid., p. 2.

12. See *Kriminologisches Bulletin* 4 (Fall 1978):88. Also see Bauhofer (1980) under "Criminology and Theories" in the bibliography.

13. Twenty percent of Switzerland's population speak French, 75 percent German, 4 percent Italian, and 1 percent Romansh (data from *Almanach der Schweiz* [Almanac of Switzerland], ed. by the Sociological Institute of the University of Zürich, Bern, 1978). In five of Switzerland's ten universities, teaching is predominantly in German, at four universities predominantly in French, and at one university in French and German. The official languages at the national level are German, French, and Italian.

14. See the following Congress reports: W. T. Haesler (ed.), *Neue Perspektiven in der Kriminologie* [New Perspectives in Criminology] (Zürich: 1975); Jorg Rehberg (ed.), *Probleme des Gerichtspsychiatrischen und psychologschen Gutaschens* [Problems of Forensic and Psychological Expertise] (Diessenhofen, Switzerland, 1976); and *Kriminologische Aufgaben de Polizei*, 1978.

15. Erwin R. Frey, *Der früchkriminelle Rückfallverbrecher* [The Criminal Recidivist] (Basel: 1951).

16. See lists of participants in *Conférences des Directeurs d'Instituts de Recherche Criminologiques, 1963-1976* (Strasbourg: Council of Europe).

17. See *Alternativ-Entwurf eines Strafgesetzbuches, Allgemeiner Teil* [Alternative Draft of Penal Code, General Part] (Tübingen, Germany: 1966-1977), 5 vols.

18. In connection with the periodicals *Revue Internationale de Criminologie et de Police Technique*, Geneva, since 1947 and *Déviance et Société*, Geneva, since 1977.

19. Frey, *Der frühkriminelle Rückfallverbrecher*, p. 67.

20. For German criminology, see Günther Kaiser, *Kriminologie* [Criminology], 3d ed. (Karlsruhe-Heidelberg: 1976), p. 20; for French criminology, see Jean Pinatel, *Criminologie* [Criminology] (Paris: Dalloz, 1963), p. 4.

21. Bader was professor in the Law Faculty of the University of Zürich from 1953 to 1973. Although he was teaching the history of law, many doctoral dissertations in criminology were written under his direction.

22. See the brilliant critique of this method by Albert K. Cohen, "Multiple Factor Approaches," in Marvin E. Wolfgang, Leonard Savitz, and Norman Johnston, (eds.), *Sociology of Crime and Delinquency*, 2d ed. (New York: Wiley, 1970), pp. 123-126.

23. Urs Leemann, "Der junge Betrüger und seine kriminelle Entwicklung: Eine phänomenolvgische Untersuchung von verunteilten Betrügern" [The Young Defrauder and His Criminal Career: A Phenomenological Analysis of Convicted Defrauders], Law Dissertation (Zürich: 1972); Rolf Stephani, "Die Wegnahme von Waren in Selbstbedienungsgeschäften durch Kunden" [Shoplifting from Supermarkets by Customers], Law Dissertation (Bern: 1968); Paul Rust, "Ladendiebstahl und 'Selfstjusting' " (Shoplifting

and 'Private Justice'), Law Dissertation (Zürich: 1972); Georg Lechleiter, "Das Kind als Gegenstand und Opfer krimineller Misshandlung" [The Child as an Object and Victim of Criminal Battery], Law Dissertation (Bern/Frankfurt: 1971); Heinz Reinhardt, "Die Bestrafung der Unzucht mit Kindern, unter besonderer Berücksichigung des Verhaltens und der Persönlichkeit des Opfers" [The Punishment of Statutory Rape, with Special Reference to the Behavior and the Personality of the Victim], Law Dissertation (Bern: 1967); Hans Giger, "Kriminologie der Entweichung" [Criminological Analysis of the Prison Escape], Law Dissertation (Winterthur: 1959); Wladimir Alexandrow, "Unterschungen über die Persönlichkeit der passiven Abtreiberin" [Studies in the Personality of Women Who Have Undergone an Abortion], Law Dissertation (Bern: 1947); Harold Siegrist, "Der illegale Schwangerschaftsabbruch aus kriminologischer Sicht" [The Illegal Abortion from the Criminological Point of View], Law Dissertation (Hamburg: 1971); Jürg Neumann, "Die Kriminalität der italienischen Arbeitskräfte im Kanton Zürich" [Criminality of the Italian Foreign Workers in the Canton of Zürich], Law Dissertation (Zürich: 1963); and Elizabeth Fopp, "Die Straftaten des alten Menschen" [The Offenses of Old People], Law Dissertation (Bern: 1969).

24. Frey, *Der frühkriminelle Rückfallverbrecher*.

25. The director of this project is Professor Günther Stratenwerth of Basel. The conception of the project is outlined in Günther Stratenwerth and Peter Aebersold, *Der schweizerische Strafvollzug: Programm, Methode und Durchfurung einer empirischen Untersuchung* [Switzerland's System of Penal Institutions: A Program, Methods and Development of Empirical Analysis] (Aarau/Frankfurt: 1976). Up to the present (July 1979), seven doctoral dissertations on individual prisons have been completed: Paul Baumann, "Die Straf- und Verwahrungsanstalt Thorberg (BE)" [The Punishment and Custody Institution of Thorberg, Bern], Law Dissertation (Aarau/Frankfurt: 1978); Martin Clerc, "Die Strafanstalt Basel-Stadt" [The Penal Institution Basel City], Law Dissertation (Aarau/Frankfurt: 1977); Andrea Haemmerle, "Die Strafanstalt Solothrun/Oberschöngrün [The Penal Institution of Solothrun/Oberschöngrün], Law Dissertation (Aarau/Frankfurt: 1976); Jürg Hofer, "Die Strafanstalt Wauwilermoos (LU)" [The Penal Institution at Wauwilermoos, Luzern], Law Dissertation (Aarau/Frankfurt: 1978); Claude-François Janiak, "Die Anstalten in Witzivil (BE)" [The Institution at Witzivil, Bern], Law Dissertation (Aarau/Frankfurt: 1976); Pierre Joset, "Les établissements de la Plaine de l'Orbe Bochuz (VD)" [The Penal Institutions in the Orbe Valley/Bochuz, Vaud], Law Dissertation (Aarau/Frankfurt: 1976); and Martin Lucas Pfrunder, "Die Strafanstalt Lenzburg" [The Penal Institution of Lenzburg], Law Dissertation (Aarau/Frankfurt: 1978). All the dissertations were published in the monograph series *Der Schweizerische Strafvollzug* (Swiss Correctional System).

26. Christian-Nils Robert, "La détention preventive en Suisse Romande et Notament a Geneve" [Preventive Detention in French-Speaking Switzerland and Especially in Geneva] (Geneva: 1972). Robert found a positive relationship between the specification of the preconditions of imprisonment on remand in the pertinent laws and the frequency of detention pending trial.

27. Peter Schneider, "Strafzumessung: Glatteis für Straftater" [Sentencing: A Trap for Offenders], Law Dissertation (Zürich: 1979).

28. Rainer Bressler, "Rechtskenntnis der Bevölkerung am Beispiel des Strafrechts" [Legal Knowledge of the Population: The Example of Criminal Law], Law Dissertation (Zürich: 1978).

29. Martin Killias, "Jugend und Sexualstrafrecht. Eine rechtssoziologische und

rechsvergleichende Untersuchung" [Adolescence and Sexual Criminal Law Analysis], Law Dissertation (Bern: 1979).

30. Forel's publication influenced legislation rather than criminology.

31. Eugen Bleuler, *Der geborene Verbrecher—eine kritische Studie* [The Born Criminal: A Critical Study] (München: 1896); Eugene Bleuler, "Zur Behandlung Gemeinsgefährlicher" [On the Treatment of Offenders Dangerous to the Public], *Monatsschrift für Kriminalpsychologie und Strafrechtsreform* 1 (1904-1905):92-99. Bleuler was the author of a well-known textbook on psychiatry: *Lehrbuch der Psychiatrie* [Textbook of Psychiatry] (Berlin: Springer, 1st edition in 1916 to 13th edition in 1975.

32. See Binder (1964) under "Psychiatry and Psychology" in the bibliography.

33. See Bernheim (1975) and Gschwind (1975) under "Treatment: Crime and Delinquency" and Gschwind (1969) under "Criminology and Theories" in the bibliography.

34. Ambros Uchtenhagen, "Abweichendes Verhalten bei jugendlichen—psychiatrische Beiträge zur Identifikation von Risikofaktoren" [Deviant Behavior of Juveniles—Psychiatric Contributions to the Identification of Risk Factors], *Rue Suisse de Sociologie*, no. 1 (1976):37-61; and Ambros Uchtenhagen, "Psychiatrische Ansätze zur kriminologischen Forschung" [Psychiatric Approaches in Criminological Research], *Kriminologisches Bulletin*, no. 1 (1977):47-51.

35. Rehberg, *Probleme des gerichtspsychiatrischen und psychologischen Gutachtens*.

36. Robert (1977), Bernheim (1978), and Ernst (1979); see "Psychiatry and Psychology" in the bibliography.

37. See W. Bernsdorf and H. Kospe (eds.), *Internationale Soziologenlexion*, 2d ed. (International Directory of Sociologists), Vol. 1 (Stuttgart: 1980).

38. See Reiwald (1948) under "Criminology and Theories" and Reiwald (1948) under "Psychiatry and Psychology" in the bibliography.

39. See Walder (1962) under "Psychiatry and Psychology" in the bibliography.

40. See Walder (1952) under "Psychiatry and Psychology" in the bibliography. Walder urged the use of Szondi's psychology in criminal investigations.

41. Hans Zulliger, *Helfen statt strafen* [Help Instead of Punishment] (Stuttgart: 1956).

42. Hans Zulliger, "Hintergründige Triebfedern von Eigentumsdelikten" [Unconscious Motives of Property Offenders], in Peter Heintz and René König (eds.), *Soziologie der Jugendkriminalität* [Sociology of Juvenile Delinquency], 6th ed. (Opladen, West Germany: 1974), pp. 132-155; and Julia Schwarzmann, *Die Verwahrlosung der weiblichen Jugendlichen: Entstehung und Behandlungsmöglichkeiten* [The Disturbed Female Delinquent: Development and Treatment Possibilities] (Munchen/Basel: 1971).

43. See Haesler (1970) under "Treatment: Crime and Delinquency" in the bibliography.

44. As an example of his work, see Eduard Naegeli, *Die Gesellschaft und ihre Verbrecher* [Society and Its Criminals] (Zürich: 1972).

45. Herren (1973) is listed under "Psychiatry and Psychology" in the bibliography.

46. David J. Bordua, "Hauptrichtungen in Theorie und Erforschung der Kriminalität in den U.S.A. seit 1930" [Main Trends in Theory and Research in Criminality in the United States Since 1930], in Heintz and König, *Soziologie der Jugendkriminalität*, pp. 156-188.

47. "First swallows that do not make a summer" were the sociologists Pradervand and Cardia (1966) in Geneva and the Genevan sociologist Ribardy (1969) who was then teaching in Montreal, Canada. They adopted the cultural conflict theory for the study of crime among Italian immigrants. (See references in "Crime in Switzerland" and "Criminology and Theories" in the bibliography.)

48. In the bibliography, Malherbe (1977) is under "Criminology and Theories," Fi-

scher (1976) under "Criminal Justice System," and Besozzi (1976) and Robert (1977) under "Juvenile Delinquency."

49. Schultz (1974) in "Research and Evaluation" in the bibliography.

50. Bühler and Niederberger (1976) in "Juvenile Delinquency" in the bibliography.

51. Although such temporal fixing should be regarded with caution, one could trace the beginning of the labeling approach in West Germany in 1968 with the appearance of the reader, F. Sack and H. König (eds.), *Kriminalsoziologie* [Criminal Sociology] (Frankfurt, 1968; 2d ed., 1974).

52. It is remarkable how rarely French-speaking Swiss criminologists refer to the recent developments of labeling theory in West Germany and in Scandinavia, when one considers the amount of empirical research conducted in those countries.

53. See Graf (1979) in "Crime in Switzerland" in the bibliography.

54. Roth (1977); see "Criminal Justice System" in the bibliography. The most famous analysis of the relationship between punishment and social structure was conducted by G. Rusche and O. Kirchheimer, *Punishment and Social Structure* (New York: Columbia University Press, 1939). In 1964, a professor of social and economic history published an article on this topic, but it has made little impression on Swiss criminologists: Wilhelm Bickel, "Strafe und Gesellschaftsstruktur" [Punishment and Social Structure], in Erwin R. Frey (ed.), *Schuld—Verentwortung—Strafe* [Guilt—Responsibility—Punishment] (Zürich: 1964), pp. 125-149.

55. Meili (1977) is based on the theory of differential association. See "Juvenile Delinquency" in the bibliography.

56. Killias and Zwicky (1978) appears under "Categories of Crime" in the bibliography.

57. Martin Killias, "Wahrnehmung und Bewertung von Kriminalität als Produkt von Massenmedien-Konsum. . ." [Perception of and Attitudes Toward Criminality as a Product of the Impact of Mass Media. . .], Unpublished dissertation (Zürich: Sociological Institute of the University of Zürich, 1978). This study follows the assumptions derived from a version of Robert K. Merton's anomie theory that allows for the current critiques of Merton's original statement.

58. See Peter Heintz, *Einführung in die Soziologische Theorie* [Introduction to Sociological Theory], 2d ed. (Stuttgart: 1968), pp. 280-299.

59. For example, the theory of Heintz served as the theoretical framework for a study of immigration in Switzerland by Hoffman-Nowotny; see Note 5 above.

60. This conclusion was also expressed in Hans Hartwig Bohle, *Soziale Abweichung und Erfolgschancen. Die Anomietheorie in der Diskussion* [Social Deviance and Chances of Success. The Anomie Theory under Discussion] (Neuwied-Darmstadt: 1975). The Killias and Zwicky study (see Note 56) is largely based on Heintz's theoretical work.

61. See I. Taylor, P. Walton, and J. Young, *The New Criminology: For a Social Theory of Deviance* (London: Routledge and Kegan Paul, 1973).

62. Buchmann and Held (1979); see "Criminology and Theories" in the bibliography.

63. For an example of a similar convergence in German criminology, see Werner Ruther, *Abweichendes Verhalten und Labeling Approach* [Deviant Behavior and the Labeling Approach] (Köln/Bonn/Berlin/München, 1975).

64. This term was used to characterize the state of American criminology some years ago by Malcolm Spector, "Labeling Theory in Social Problems: A Young Journal Launches a New Theory," *Social Problems* 24 (October 1976):69-75.

BIBLIOGRAPHY

Since a full-fledged bibliography of Swiss criminology has not been provided previously, the following list is more comprehensive than usual for this kind of volume. Items were selected to be representative, without duplicating sources used in the body of the chapter.

Crime in Switzerland

Clinard, Marshall B. *Cities with Little Crime: The Case of Switzerland.* Cambridge: Cambridge University Press, 1978.

Frey, Jorg. "Die Kriminalität in Zeiten des Wohlstandes. Eine Untersuchung der schweizerischen Kriminalität von 1951-1964" [Criminality in the Times of Prosperity. An Analysis of Switzerland's Criminality from 1951 to 1964]. Law Dissertation. Zürich: 1968).

Graf, Erich O. "Kriminalität und sozialer Wandel: Eine soziologische Untersuchung der Kriminalität im Kanton Zürich zwischen 1850 und dem ersten Weltkrieg" [Crime and Social Change: A Sociological Analysis of Crime in the Canton of Zürich Between 1850 and the First World War]. Unpublished dissertation. Zürich: Sociological Institute of the University of Zürich, 1979.

Jordi, Urs. "Statistische Untersuchungen zur Kriminalität des Kantons Bern" [Statistical Analysis of Crime in the Canton of Bern]. Law Dissertation. Bern: 1975.

Pradervand, Pierre, and Laura Cardia. "Quelques aspects de la délinquance italienne a Genève. Une enquête sociologique" [Some Aspects of the Delinquency of Italians in Geneva. A Sociological Analysis]. *Revue internationale de criminologie et de police technique* 20 (1966):43-58.

Schultz, Hans. "Die Bedeutung der Wirtschaftskriminalität in der Schweiz" [The Relevance of White-Collar Crime in Switzerland]. In H. Göppinger and H. Walder (eds.), *Wirtschaftskriminalität—Beurteilung der Schuldfähigkeit* [White-Collar Crime—Criminal Responsibility]. Stuttgart: 1978. Pp. 53-66.

Weidmann, Max. "Das Drogenverhalten von Basler Schülern" [Drug Abuse Among Basel School Children]. Sociological dissertation. Basel: 1977.

Criminology and Theories

Bader, Karl-Siegfried. *Soziologie der deutschen Nachkriegskriminalität* [Sociology of German Post-War Criminality]. Tübingen, West Germany: 1949.

Bauhofer, Stefan. "Kriminologie in der Schweiz—Stand und Entwicklung" [Criminology in Switzerland—Its Present State of Development]. *Revue pénale suisse* 97 (1980):145-174.

Bosshard, Peter. "Bildung als kriminologischer Faktor" [Education as a Criminological Factor]. Law Dissertation. Zürich: 1968.

Buchmann, Marlies, and Thomas Held. "Zur Strukturblindheit der heutigen Devianzsoziologie" [On the Structural Blindness of the Present-Day Sociology of Deviance]. *Revue suisse de Sociologie* 5 (Spring 1979):5-19.

Frey, Erwin R. "Kriminologie—Programm und Wirklichkeit" [Criminology: Program and Reality]. *Revue pénale suisse* 66 (1951):49-73.

Gasser, Rudolf. "Victimologie. Kritische Betrachtung zu einer neuen kriminologischen Begriff" [Victimology: A Critical Examination of a New Criminological Concept]. Law Dissertation. Chur, Switzerland: 1965.

Gschwind, Martin. *Die Wertfunktion des Menschen: Ein Betrag zur kriminologischen Grundlagenforschung* [The Functional Value of People: A Contribution to Basic Criminological Research]. Mainz, West Germany: 1969.

Malherbe, Nelly. "Les tendences récentes de la sociologie de la déviance aux Etats-Unis" [Recent Trends in the Sociology of Deviance in the United States]. *Revue suisse de Sociologie* 3 (Summer 1977):145-184.

Reiwald, Paul. *Die Gesellschaft und ihre Verbrecher* [Society and Its Criminals]. Zürich: 1948. Republished by Herbert Jäger and Tilmann Moser. Frankfurt, West Germany: 1973.

Ribardy, François-X. "L'elignment psycho-sociologique dans l'analyse de la criminalité des migrants: L'exemple de la migration italienne au Canada" [The Psychosociological Alienation in the Analysis of Crimes Committed by Migrants: The Example of Italian Emigration to Canada]. *Revue internationale de criminologie et de police technique* 23 (1969):263-284.

Zwicky, Heinrich, and Martin Killias. "Peter Heintz und die Kriminalsoziologie: Zum Verhältnis der Devianzforschung zur allgemeinen Soziologie" [Peter Heintz and the Sociology of Deviance: On the Relationship Between Deviance Research and General Sociology]. In G. Hischier, R. Levy, and W. Obrecht (eds.). *Weltgesellschaft und Sozialstruktur* [World Society and Social Structure]. Diessenhofen, Switzerland: 1980. Pp. 533-554.

Psychiatry and Psychology

Bernheim, Jacques. "Justice pénale et délinquants mentalement anormaux: les expertises de responsabilité en psychiatrie légale" [Penal Justice and the Mentally Abnormal Delinquent: Expertise on the Responsibility of Legal Psychiatry]. *Revue pénale suisse* 95 (1978):337-349.

Binder, Hans. *Die Urteilefähigkeit in psychologischer, psychiatrischer und juristischer Sicht* [The Competency to Judge in the Psychological, Psychiatric and Judicial Views]. Zürich: 1964.

Binswanger, Herbert. *Leitfaden der forensischen Psychiatrie* [Guide to Forensic Psychiatry]. Zürich: 1945.

Ernst, Klaus. "Was antwortet der Psychiater dem Strafrichter?" [How Does the Psychiatrist Answer the Criminal Court Judge?]. *Revue pénale suisse* 96 (1979):45-66.

Herren, Rüdiger. *Freud und die Kriminologie* [Freud and Criminology]. Stuttgart, West Germany: 1973.

Reiwald, Paul. "Verbrechensverhütung als Teil der Gesellschaftspsychohygiene" [Crime Prevention as a Part of Society's Psychological Hygiene]. In Heinrich Meng (ed.). *Die Prophylaxe des Verbrechens* [The Prophylaxis of Crime]. Basel: 1948.

Robert, Christian-Nils. "Le verdict psychiatrique: de la responsabilité de l'inculpé aux responsabilités de la psychiatrie" [The Psychiatric Verdict: From the Responsibility of the Defendant to the Responsibility of the Psychiatrist]. *Déviance et société*, no. 2 (1977):239-251.

Walder, Hans. *Triegstruktur und Kriminalität: Kriminalbiologische Untersuchungen* [Drives and Crime: A Criminological-Biological Analysis]. Bern/Stuttgart: 1952.

Walder, Hans. "Bewusstes und Unbewusstes in der Genese verbrecherischen Verhaltens" [Conscious and Unconscious in the Development of Criminal Behavior]. In *Kriminalbiologische Gegenwartsfragen (Neue Folge)*. Vol. 5. Stuttgart: 1962.

Wyrsch, Jakob. *Gerichtliche Psychiatrie: Ein Lehrbuch für Juristen und Mediziner* [Forensic Psychiatry: A Textbook for Lawyers and Physicians]. 2d ed. Bern: 1955.

Law and Criminology

Marangopoulos-Yotopoulos, Alice. "Les mobiles du délit: Etude de criminologie et de droit pénal" [Criminal Motives: A Criminological and Criminal Law Analysis]. Law Dissertation. Paris: 1973.

Murbach, Ruth. "Das medizinische Modell der Delinquenz. Entwicklung und Auswirkungen am Beispiel der nordamerikanische Sexualpsychopathengesetze" [The Medical Model of Crime: Its Development and Consequences, Illustrated by the Example of the American Sexual Psychopath Laws]. Law Dissertation., Zürich: 1980.

Research and Evaluation

Haefely, Markus H. "Das Verhalten von 200 Insassen der Arbeitserziehungsanstalten Uitikon a.A und Witzwil nach ihrer Entlassung..." [The Behavior of 200 Inmates After Their Release from the Juvenile Institutions of Uitikon and Witzwil...]. Law Dissertation. Bern: 1962.

Robert, Christian-Nils. "Quelles recherches et quelles criminologies en Suisse?" [Which Research and Which Criminology in Switzerland?]. *Kriminologisches Bulletin* 3 (Spring 1977):10-22.

Schultz, Hans. "Von der dreifachen Bedeutung der Dunkelziffer" [On the Threefold Meaning of the Dark Figure of Crime]. In Claus Roxin (ed.). *Grundfragen der gesamten Strafrechtswissenschaft: Festschrift fur Heinrich Henkel* [Basic Issues in Criminology and Criminal Law]. Berlin: 1974. Pp. 239-251.

Categories of Crime

Aebersold, Theo. "Die fahrlässige Tötung im Strassenverkehr. Eine kriminologische Untersuchung" [Negligent Homicide in Road Traffic: A Criminological Analysis]. Law Dissertation. Bern: 1968.

Bickel, Walter. "Zur Kriminologie des Autodiebstahls und verwandter Delikte. Nach Akten der Kantons- und Stadtpolizei Zürich" [On the Criminology of Automobile Theft and Related Offenses. From the Files of the Canton and City Police of Zürich. Law Dissertation. Zürich: 1972.

Burki, Peter. "Die Stellungnahme von Vermögensdelinquenten zu ihrer strafrechtlichen Verurteilung" [The Attitude of Property Offenders Toward Their Sentence]. Law Dissertation. Bern: 1963.

Buettikofer, Klaus. "Die falsche Zeugenaussage aus kriminologischer Sicht" [Perjury from a Criminological Point of View]. Law Dissertation. Zürich: 1975.

Condrau, Felix. "Die Kriminalität der körperlich Behinderten" [The Criminality of the Physically Handicapped]. Law Dissertation. Zürich: 1971.

Jenny, Rolf. "Drogenkonsum und Drogenhandel in der Sicht des Kriminologen..." [Drug Abuse and Drug Traffic from a Criminological Point of View...]. Law Dissertation. Zürich: 1973.

Killias, Martin, and Heinrich Zwicky. "Sozialstruktur, Persönlichkeit und Bereicherungs-delinquenz" [Social Structure, Personality and Profit-oriented Property Crimes]. *Revue suisse de Sociologie* 4 (Summer 1978):129-162.

Mazurczak, Eric. "Persönliche Verhältnisse angetrunkener Fahrer" [Personal Backgrounds of Drunken Drivers]. Law Dissertation. Zürich: 1972.

Mueller, Hugo-Roman. "Zur Kriminologie der Verkehrsdelinquenz unter besonderer Berücksichtingung des Problems der Ueberforderung im Strassenverkehr" [A Criminological Analysis of Road Traffic Offenses with Special Reference to Problems of Stressful Situations]. Law Dissertation. Winterthur: 1975.

Schaufelberger, Jürg, "Die 'offentlichen unzuchtigen Handlungen': Eine kriminologische Darstellung" [The "Public Obscenity Offense": A Criminological Analysis]. Law Dissertation. Zürich: 1973.

Sigg, Alfred. "Begriff, Wesen und Genese des Beziehungsdelikts. Ein kriminologischer Beitrag aus daseinsanalytischer, tiefenpsychologischer und juristischer Sicht" [Concept and Causes of Crime Between Acquaintances: A Contribution from the Viewpoints of Criminology, Psychoanalysis and Criminal Law]. Law Dissertation. Zürich: 1967.

Juvenile Delinquency

Besozzi, Claudio. "L'interprétation sociale de la déviance juvénile dans la vie quotidienne" [The Social Interpretation of Juvenile Delinquency in Daily Life]. *Revue suisse de Sociologie* 2 (Spring 1976):63-91.

Bühler, Doris, and Josef Martin Niederberger. "Ansätze zu einem integralen Konzept der Jugenddevianz" [Inception of an Integral Concept of Juvenile Delinquency]. *Revue suisse de Sociologie* 2 (Spring 1976):125-137.

Decurtins, Liliane. "Film und Jugendkriminalität" [Film and Juvenile Delinquency]. Law Dissertation. Zürich: 1961.

Heintz, Peter. "Ein soziologischer Bezugarahmen für die Analyse der Jugendkriminalität" [A Sociological Framework for the Analysis of Juvenile Delinquency]. In Peter Heintz and René König (eds.). *Soziologie der Jugendkriminalität* [Sociology of Juvenile Delinquency]. Opladen, West Germany, 1st ed., 1957; 6th ed., 1974.

Meili, Bernhard. "Familie, Schule, Freunde und Jugenddelinquenz" [Family, School, Friends and Juvenile Delinquency]. *Kriminologisches Bulletin* 3 (Fall 1977):22-39.

Pesch-Fellmeth, B. "Verwarlosung und Jugendkriminalität" [Wayward and Delinquent Juveniles]. Unpublished Philosophy Dissertation. Zürich: 1959.

Robert, Christian-Nils. "Fabriquer la délinquance juvénile" [Producing Juvenile Delinquency]. *Revue suisse de Sociologie* 3 (Spring 1977):31-65.

Staub, Sylvia. "Ursachen und Erscheinungsformen bei der Bildung jugendlicher Banden" [Causes and Phenomenology of the Organization of Juvenile Gangs]. Law Dissertation. Zürich: 1965.

Veillard-Cybulska, Henryka. "L'application des mesures psychosociales et éducatives aux délinquants mineurs: Etude de l'activité de la Chambre des mineurs du Canton de Vaud (Suisse), complétée par l'analyse de cent cas" [The Application of Psychological and Educational Measures to Juvenile Delinquents: A Study of the Activities of the Children's Division of the Canton of Vaud (Switzerland), an Analysis of 100 Cases]. Law Dissertation. Nyon, Switzerland: 1971.

Criminal Recidivism

Bigler-Eggenberger, Margrith. "Zum Problem der Spätresozialisierung von frühkriminellen Rückfallsverbrechern" [On the Problem of Late Resocialization of the Young Criminal Recidivist]. Law Dissertation. Zürich: 1959.

Blaser, Annemarie. "Rückfall und Bewährung straffälliger Jugendlicher im Kanton Luzern" [Recidivism and Rehabilitation of Adolescent Offenders in the Canton of Luzerne]. Law Dissertation. Bern: 1963.

Brueckner, Christian. "Der Gewohnheitsverbrecher und die Verwahrung in der Schweiz. . ." [The Habitual Criminal and the System of Custody in Switzerland. . .]. Law Dissertation. Basel/Stuttgart, 1971.

Treatment: Crime and Delinquency

Bernheim, J. "Un projet d'institution pour traiter certains délinquants mentalement perturbés [A Projected Institution for the Treatment of Certain Mentally Disturbed Offenders]. In W. T. Haesler (ed.). *Neue Perspektiven in der Kriminologie* [New Perspectives in Criminology]. Zürich: 1975.

Bleuler, Manfred. "Richter und Arzt" [Judge and Physician]. *Revue pénale suisse* 58 (1944):1-23.

Engeler, Wilfried Johann. "Das Verhalten der Strafgegangenen und ihre soziale Prognose" [The Behavior of Convicted Offenders and Their Social Prognosis]. Law Dissertation. Bern: 1968.

Feigel, Sigmund. "Der Erziehungszweck im schweizerischen Strafvollzug" [The Educational Approach to the Execution of Sentences in Swiss Prisons]. Law Dissertation. Zürich: 1949.

Gschwind, Martin. "Die Kriminologischen Voraussetzungen zur Einweisung in eine Sozialtherapeutische Anstalt" [The Criminological Prerequisites of Placing Offenders in a Social Therapeutic Institution]. In Haesler, *New Perspectives in Criminology.*

Haesler, W. T. "Psychotherapeutische Behandlung von Sexualdelinquenten" [Psychotherapeutic Treatment of Sexual Delinquents]. *Kriminologische Gegenwartsfragen (Neue Folge).* Vol. 9. Stuttgart: 1970.

Kuentz, Peter. "Die Behandlung der Gewohnheitrinker nach Art. 44 StGB: Eine Untersuchung über die schweizerische Gerichtsund Vollzugspraxis in den Jahren 1964-1969" [The Treatment of the Habitual Alcoholic According to Section 44 of the Swiss Penal Code: An Analysis of Court Decisions in the Years 1964-1969]. Law Dissertation. Bern/Frankfurt: 1975.

Schuh, Jörg. "Zur Behandlung des Rechtsbrechers in Unfreihelt. Möglichkeiten und Grenzen der Therapie in geschlossenem Milieu" [Treatment of Offenders in Confinement: Practicability and Restrictions]. Law Dissertation. Diessenhofen, Switzerland: 1980.

Criminal Justice System

Fischer, Werner. "La 'déviance' et l'autonomisation du système des instances" ["Deviance" and the Autonomisation of the Social Control System]. *Revue suisse de Sociologie* 2 (Spring 1976):93-123.

Kelterborn, Hans. "Die Basler Schutzaufsicht. . . [Basel's Parole Department]. Basel: 1975.

Kriminologische Aufgaben der Polizei [Criminological Tasks of the Police]. Edited by Schweizerisches Nationalkomitee für geistige Gesundheit, Arbeitsgruppe Kriminologie [Diessenhofen, Switzerland: 1978].

Roth, Robert. "Prison-modèle et prison-symbole: l'exemple de Genève au xixème siecle" [Model Prisons and Symbolic Prisons: The Example of Geneva in the Nineteenth Century]. *Déviance et société*, No. 4 (1977):389-410.

Schaeuble, Jean-Pierre. "Die Untersuchungshaftpraxis im Kanton Tessin. . ." [The Use of Detention Pending Trial in the Canton of Tessin. . .]. Unpublished Law Dissertation. Basel: 1977.

Stieger-Gmuer, Regula. "Gerechtigkeit im Strafrecht durch Individualisierung? Ein theoretischer und empirischer Beitrag zum Problem der Rechtsfindung im schweizerischen Jugendstrafrecht" [Justice in Criminal Law Through Individualization? A Theoretical and Empirical Contribution to the Administration of Swiss Juvenile Criminal Justice]. Law Dissertation. Diessenhofen, Switzerland: 1976.

TURKEY

Sulhi Dönmezer

As a combination of the old and the new, Turkey is a worthy subject for criminological examination. Turkish society is ancient, but the Turkish Republic was established only in 1923. As a developing country, contemporary Turkey is experiencing the upsetting effects of modernization, but traditional values are deeply rooted in its people, with the consequence that the crime associated with industrialization and urbanization has not been as evident in Turkey as in other developing nations. Criminology itself is relatively new in this nation, but, as is discussed below, the combination of the old and the new already has stimulated the creation of a body of research.

FROM EMPIRE TO REPUBLIC

To lend substance to the criminological implications of this merger of the ancient and the modern, it is necessary to examine the cultural and political history that reaches back through the centuries, to summarize briefly the demography, and to refer to the sociocultural changes unleased in recent decades.

Turkish society and culture are among the oldest in the history of humanity. Starting from the frontiers of Yugoslavia to the borders of China, the traveler will encounter peoples using only the Turkish language. Turkish groups are scattered all over Balkan countries, the Soviets, Iran, Mongolia, India, and Pakistan; they share the same language, culture, and religion with slight differences. Nobody knows, for example, the exact number of Turks living in the Soviet Union, but the total number of Turks in the world would be well over 300 million.

The Turkish Republic is now the only independent Turkish state; it has a population of about 45 million. Founded in 1923, the republic gained its constitution in 1924 under the guidance of the great Kemal Atatürk, the father and founder of the new Turkish state.

The republic is the last remnant of the Ottoman Empire, one of the largest empires in world history, that had established *pax ottomana*, based on a common culture, within the Mediterranean basin and the Middle East for several centuries. In a sense, the republic is a transformation of that empire, representing a survival that was salvaged from the ruins of World War I.

POLITICAL SYSTEM: TRANSITION AND TENSION

Continuous cultural change has had impact on Turkish society, beginning in the nineteenth century, through the effects of many changes that may be summarized under the terms "modernization" and "Westernization." New schools, new state organizations, and institutions were modeled mostly after French institutions.

The rate of change was intensified throughout the nineteenth century when the sultan, the head of state, was not only an absolute secular authority but also the caliph, supreme chief of the religion. His double role must be taken into account in assessing every attempt to adapt Western institutions, based on a Christian culture, to Turkish traditions. Formidable obstacles had to be overcome to adjust these institutions to the centuries-old Turkish traditions, customs, and mores deeply rooted in Islamic values. Rebellions of reactionary forces cost the lives of open-minded sultans like Selim IV.

In an effort to create a rule of law, the French Penal Code of 1810 was accepted almost in its entirety, but even in the first article it was mentioned that the Turkish adaptation was only prescriptive in its basis on the right of "tazir" given the caliph by Islamic law. The same article specified that the preservation of the rights of citizens emanates from *Sharia*. This duality of criminal law was clarified during the foundation of the new republic; the constitution expressed the principle that secularization would be one of the most significant characteristics of the state. The Criminal Code in Article 163 supports the principle by prohibiting all sorts of progaganda against the principle.

The present Turkish Criminal Code was enacted by Parliament in 1926 and is still in effect with substantial modifications made in various years.[1] The main source of the Turkish Penal Code is the Italian Code of 1889 (Code Zanardelli). Code Zanardelli is based on the ideas of liberalism and individualism.

The individualistic character of the Italian Code does not correspond to the dominant attitude of the Turkish people, but the Italian Penal Code was evaluated at the end of the nineteenth century as a progressive juridical creation, well grounded in logic and technique and consistent with the democratic traditions of the century. The Italian Code was not oriented to the principles of scientific criminology and is not consistent with the requirements of today's criminal policy. Even today the purposes and concepts of the Italian Code are an uncertain platform for conducting research in light of the complexities of accommodating the diverse theories of our era.[2]

The Turkish Penal Code also has had no such particularity, and it departs from the Code Zanardelli in the general severity in the style of applying sanctions. Penalties, especially prison sentences, are much heavier than provided for by the

Italian Code and codes of other European countries. The Turkish Code grants only a minimum level of discretion to judges. Research has not evaluated the deterrent influence of this philosophy of severity, but the courts' imposition of harsh penalties is usually not enforced, since laws of amnesty are periodically passed. Under these conditions, reliable evaluation of deterrent sentencing is almost impossible.

Since 1965, progress has been made toward mitigating the severity of the sanctioning system and providing an improved setting for criminological research as a resource for criminal policy. The new Act on the Enforcement of Penalties, Number 647,[3] published in 1967 by the Parliament, modified almost all the prescriptions concerning sanctions of the Penal Code. This act gave rather large discretionary power to the courts for substituting fines for prison sentences, employing security measures, and using probation and parole. Nevertheless, prisons continue to be crowded with all their well-known shortcomings.

DEVELOPMENTS IN THE POLITICAL SECTOR

A system of one-party politics was practiced from the early days of the republic until 1946. In these years of political, social, and economic changes, a road towards democracy and a multiparty system was gradually followed. Several other political parties were established in 1946 in a society that had lacked political activities and opposition for about twenty years. Even the simplest citizens wanted to take part in the political arena; in a rather short time, almost every aspect of life has been politicized.

Westernization implies political and social changes producing clashes between traditional and emergent values, culture conflicts, loss of common direction, and antagonisms between groups supporting new ideas and groups loyal to traditional values. Those processes contributed to the appearance of deviant behavior among members of the new society. From the early days of the republic until 1950, those processes were operating, but, within the framework and under the pressure of a disciplined one-party system and limitations on freedoms, formal control mechanisms were rather strong and effective.

In 1950, a new era of political liberties emerged, culminating in the constitution of 1961. Turkish society finds itself with a democratic parliamentarian regime which guarantees its citizens basic freedoms and human rights. The formal control mechanisms have become less effective in maintaining compliance, and the processes of normative dissensus have increased the visibility of deviant behavior.

Beginning particularly with the 1950s, rapid industrialization and urbanization took place in Turkey. The many effects on a traditional society undergoing profound changes began to appear.[4] In a very short time, industrial relations became the main concern of the new society. Labor unions of opposite ideological persuasions flourished, and the leaders of ultra-left organizations began to use their labor management power with the purpose of supplanting the democratic regime with a proletarian dictatorship. They tried diligently to establish an alliance with other legal and illegal leftist organizations, associations, student groups, and political parties at home and abroad. This trend was particularly evident in the 1970s until the intervention of the armed forces on September 12, 1980.

That movement cultivated a social climate favorable to the increase of general criminality and the escalation of terrorist activities to the point that an average of more than twenty persons were killed in ideological militant fights each day. Terrorism in Turkey is now a subject worthy of criminological investigation. Turkey remains traditionally a law-abiding society. The bulk of the citizens are indeed respectful to the state authority, referring to the state as the "father state."

Nevertheless, social crises have produced clandestine national and international seditious forces—identified primarily with some members of the youthful generation—that have challenged the state's legitimacy by killing, bombing, damaging properties, destroying public utilities, and stopping factory operations. Among the inherent topics worthy of criminological examination is the Turkish family, which is the strongest instrument of social control in Turkey and has rather abruptly encountered difficulties in managing some of its younger members.

IMPACT OF SOCIOCULTURAL CHANGE

Since the 1950s, the rate of urbanization has increased rapidly, with the great internal migration more of a factor than the birth rate,[5] although there are approximately 1 million births each year. Almost half of the general population consists of teenagers who are particularly influential in affecting the outcomes of ideological struggles between traditional and emergent values in a time of rapid sociocultural change. These ages contribute more than their share of the criminal population.

Urbanization as a Criminogenic Factor

The migration from rural areas to the cities continues at an explosive pace. Transition from a rural village economy to a market economy has accelerated this process. The unplanned growth of certain cities exceeds their capacity to absorb new residents and aggravates the inefficiency—even causes the lack—of public utilities and other public services.

Problems created by unplanned urban growth are very evident in the functioning of the criminal justice system. The inadequacy of the number and efficiency of the police and the organization and resources of public prosecutor's offices and courts are always behind the obvious needs. The Criminal Code is becoming something of a paper tiger. The percentage of criminals who are detected leaves too much to be desired.

Criminal areas in big cities, in the form of shanty towns erected by newcomers from villages, may be considered important sources of crime. Excessive unemployment and decreased management of children must also be considered. In a village setting, parents do not have to watch their children continuously because of the vigilance of relatives and neighbors. Urban conditions disrupt the benevolent control system when village families move to the city. Cultural change, conflict, and differential association promote the expansion of juvenile delinquency.

Industrialization and a Turkish Community

Nevertheless, traditional values are so deeply rooted and internalized that the crime-producing mechanisms of urban areas have had less effect in Turkey than one might expect. Turkey experienced high rates of industrialization, urbanization, and other social changes between 1955 and 1966, but the upsurge in crime did not match these rates except for violent crimes. Criminality in general rose slightly, and the proportion of fraudulent crimes remained the same.[6]

The social values, Islamic customs, and very strong family structures established over the centuries are still functioning as social control mechanisms to muffle the effects of social changes on criminality. Economic development in Turkey has brought a general increase in criminality, but crimes of violence for the sake of profit or for other forms of economic gain have not exceeded the traditional crimes of violence.

In one research study,[7] the relationship between delinquency and urbanization in Ereğli, a new, small town created through industrialization,[8] is examined. The changes observed in Western societies undergoing industrialization were not repeated here. This conclusion is based on an analysis of changes in the incidence of delinquency over a five-year period (1964-1968).

The Turkish experience with industrialization, as illustrated by Ereğli, differs fundamentally from that experience usually cited to predict increased criminality as the inevitable result of rapid industrialization. The latter expectation rests on the assumption that the characteristics of the traditional community gradually vanish to be replaced by a new form of social structure that might be called a "complex industrial society." The traditional grounding of the community in kinship gives way to specialized economic, political, religious, and educational organizations that become the elements of urban-industrialized societal organization. A high rate of spatial mobility, the process of urbanization, and the effects of developing technology generate new institutions based on new norms and eliminate old ones. The interest groups of an industrialized society express norms that emphasize their special interests. Conflicts with traditional norms stimulate normative dissensus which is a fertile field for deviance.

This scenario is not inevitable for all industrializing societies. The effects in terms of increased criminality are dependent on the normative order of the society, the socioeconomic conditions, and the strength of the people's perceptions of the proper moral order.

In these terms, Ereğli resisted the tendency toward significantly greater deviance because, as an example of the village structure in Turkey, its traditional norms and social system were so deeply rooted that the accommodations to change were accomplished without serious weakening of sociocultural integration.

Economic Development and Criminality

One cannot be certain how long Ereğli will continue to benefit from its "moral capital." We can only guess that the pressures of industrialization and urbanization will mount in the coming years. The demands on the formal control structure, including the agencies of criminal justice, are likely to increase. Nevertheless, aware of the events associated with industrialization elsewhere, Turkey may be in a position to husband that "moral capital" to counter trends toward increasingly serious criminality by easing the process of achieving a new social integration.

The relationship between economic development and criminality has always been a very important subject for research, mostly in developing countries including Turkey. The economic system is the most significant part of the whole social structure because economic development produces changes influencing the etiology and structure of crime. If it is possible to explain crime by assessing the type of economic order of Turkey, what kinds of change-related crime will occur in the Turkish society in the process of rapid economic development?

In a comparison of national statistics of Turkey with those of other countries,[9] a close relation was found between the qualities of economic development and crime that indicates Turkish society faces increasing difficulty in managing criminality. Resources reserved for the control of crime may therefore be considered an important contribution to the national economy. In setting up the plan of economic development, serious consideration should be given to matters relating to criminological problems.

CRIMINOLOGY: ITS NATURE AND ACTIVITIES

Criminology is a young science in Turkey, compared to its development in Western Europe and the United States. In the last sixty or seventy years, this sphere of scientific activity has been a part of the curricula of Western universities, but its teaching in Turkey as a university discipline only began in 1953 in the Law School of the University of Istanbul.

Criminology and Instruction in Law

Previous to 1953, a well-rooted tradition was established to give considerable attention to the problems of theoretical criminology in the teaching of criminal law. In the course of studying different notions and institutions of law, criminological matters and problems also are explained. The tradition was consistent with the proposal expounded by Gabriel Tarde at the First International Congress of Anthropology that the teaching of criminal law be completed by dealing with criminology. The same view was presented at the International Union of Criminal Law Congresses of 1895 in Linz and of 1925 in London. The tradition is still followed in various law schools of Turkey.

In 1943, an institute of criminology was founded first in the Law School of

Istanbul University and another later in the Law School of Ankara University.[10] Since then, the Institute of Criminology of Istanbul has been particularly active in research within the limits of its budget and the capacity of its staff and resources.[11] Conferences and symposia are sponsored at the national and international levels. A rather satisfactory library of criminological literature has been assembled. The institute may be considered the center of the science of criminology in Turkey.

A Conception of Criminology

Since 1953, the only textbook of criminology used in the higher education institutions of Turkey was written by the author of this chapter.[12] The book offers a description and analysis of crime patterns. Although it is mainly policy oriented, the textbook summarizes and evaluates different theoretical approaches with due recognition of the major critiques made over recent years. This textbook is the basis for the following discussion of theoretical perspectives prevalent in Turkey.

Criminology is a science of synthesis; its subject matter is directed toward explanations of deviant behavior. Understanding requires investigation of the traits and roots of personality through biological, psychological, and psychiatric criminology. Deviant behavior as a whole is a social phenomenon that involves society's structural components. Thus, criminology is a science of synthesis, with the purpose of explaining the crime problem. It is an autonomous science that makes use of data and knowledge drawn from the other sciences in accordance with its own method. The contribution of sociology in this venture is of prime importance, much more than other sciences.

In addition to mobilizing a multidisciplinary battery of theoretical concepts, criminology has to be at the same time an applied science—a science of social defense—that studies criminal behavior and responses to crime in action. The police, courts, prisons, and other institutions reacting to crime are investigated in action as facets of social control.

Textbook materials are oriented primarily to students of criminal law; hence, a single theoretical approach is not likely to be followed. The functional approach to criminal behavior in the Mertonian sense is the most desirable one. Crime is considered unavoidable in any ideological and social system, and, strangely, it is an aspect of system maintenance and survival. However, my textbook also devotes considerable space to the opposing arguments of Marxian theory as a means of providing a basis for comparative evaluation of different existing theories.

Publications in Criminology

In the last twenty-five years, some significant criminological monographs have been published in Turkey. Later sections of this chapter deal with some of them as examples.

Scientific articles on criminological matters are published in the *Hukuk Fakültesi Mecmuasi* (Review of the Faculty of Law of Istanbul) which is now fifty years old, in the journals of the bar associations of Istanbul and Ankara, and in the *Review of the Ministry of Justice* which is chiefly concerned with law but also publishes articles on criminological topics. The *Review of the Institute of Criminal Law and Criminology* specializes in reports of research undertaken by that institute. *Annals of the Faculty of Law of the University of Istanbul*, published in foreign languages, gives space to criminological articles.

Publications in theoretical criminology—pure theory, methodology, and model-building—are quite rare. The tendency is to be concerned only with empirical data, with readers left largely free to draw their own interpretations from the research data. There are publications concerning the volume of crime; crime statistics; "dark crime"; prison populations; specific types of crime, especially road accidents; recidivism; and the functioning of criminal justice as a control system. Legal scholars have been predominant among the authors, but since 1970 psychologists have shown greater interest in crime problems, particularly juvenile delinquency.

REVIEW OF SELECTED AREAS OF RESEARCH

In reviewing the criminological literature of Turkey, the discussion is limited to works issued since 1950, in accordance with the scheme of this book. Furthermore, the review concentrates on the areas of juvenile delinquency, the criminality of Turkish "guest workers" who migrated temporarily for jobs in foreign countries, traffic offenses, and murders and vendettas. Because of the diverse topics relevant in Turkey, it may be said that the chief characteristic of Turkish research is that the authors are chiefly from academia and that the reports are mostly descriptive and comparative. Research of Western countries, particularly that of the United States, is usually the basis for comparison with the situation in Turkey.

Juvenile Delinquency

Studies of juvenile delinquency have always been a favorite subject of scholars in Turkey. Even though the rate of juvenile delinquency is not high, any upsurge in the rate excites concern in a country where the family institution is particularly strong. Studies are mainly statistical and descriptive and are conducted by social scientists and lawyers.[13] But some research follows the psychological and cultural points of view. Two of them are mentioned here.

In 1977, Professor Halûk Yavuzer studied 214 young male convicts in the treatment schools of Ankara, Izmir, and Elaziğ to determine their level of intelligence and factors concerning the environment and personality traits.[14] The control group was made up of 150 nonconvict boys. The research instruments were personality tests (Alexander), practical capacity tests (Cornell Index and Eysenck

Personality Inventory), and a questionnaire of 180 items. They measured the effects of psycho-pedagogical, socioeconomic, and cultural factors in developing deviant behavior. The young inmates were divided into three groups according to the crimes committed. According to Yavuzer, the level of intelligence is not the most significant cause of delinquency, although it might be considered a secondary influence. He concluded that inmate and noninmate groups differed in personality traits: lack of adaptation, psychopathic symptoms, anxiety, nervousness, and hypochondria.

In another study, Nephan Saran dealt with the sociocultural particularities of the children under eighteen years of age who were involved with the police of Istanbul in the years 1958-1963.[15] Theft, violence, sexual crimes, smuggling, and pickpocketing were the most prevalent crimes. Delinquency was especially concentrated in the sixteen- to eighteen-year-old group. According to the author, the delinquency of members of the study population was associated with crowded families, poor housing, unemployment, and culture conflict. There were no gang and organized crime activities among these children.

Criminality of Turkish Migrant Workers in Foreign Countries

Since the 1960s, one of the most crucial social problems faced by Western European countries has been, no doubt, the phenomenon of migrant workers, mostly in economic but also in criminological terms. The criminality of "guest workers" has been the subject of research in the last twenty years.[16]

Emigration from Mediterranean and Eastern Europe raises problems that differ from those of Canada and the United States in earlier decades. Migrant workers in Europe are bound to return to their homeland after a period of hard work, whereas the migrants to North America usually established permanent residence in their new countries. Many of those going to North America took their families with them; this pattern is not true of the guest workers. These differences have produced a two-sided problem of adaptation of migrants to the new foreign working conditions and, on their return, readaptation to their original community. The problem is much more crucial for the children of those migrant workers who establish their families in the host country; they are likely to become a semisocialized generation only partially adept in the mother language and culture and those of the host country.

Research published by Orhan Tuna[17] is an example of the investigations carried out in Turkey. He deals with the problem of criminality of the Turkish migrant workers in West Germany. Between 1960 and 1965 in West Germany, there were 3,525 sentences after conviction for various crimes committed by Turkish migrant workers. Criminality for males and females was concentrated in the twenty-five to twenty-nine age group. The males were dominant; females convicted of crimes represented 2.6 percent of all female migrant workers. Penalties were mostly fines and imprisonment, but the majority of the prison sentences averaged less than a month. Of the male crimes, 71.3 percent involved traffic violations. In the male criminality, assault (8.8 percent) was the second most prevalent offense. Murder represented 0.2 percent of all offenses.

Theft was most frequent among females—a pattern that is noteworthy when one considers that in Turkey, especially in rural areas,[18] crimes against property are not prevalent, particularly for females. Yet, among female members of the migrant families, there is a rather high percentage of crimes committed against property, and these are mainly theft and shoplifting. This pattern might be explained by the influence of European supermarkets on Turkish peasant women.

In evaluating the offenses of Turkish migrants, one also has to take into account the severe and discriminatory attitude of local authorities against the *Gastarbeiter* (guest workers). Anomie appears to be an apt theoretical explanation because the Turkish migrant workers constitute the "new Negroes" of Europe. As an aspect of exploitation of an important labor force, especially in times of economic stagnation, host countries do not establish health and social programs, especially for the children of migrant workers. The theories of culture conflict, differential association, and stigmatization through labeling may be relevant.

The years of hard work and discriminatory treatment of migrant workers are inconsistent with their contributions to the economic power and wealth of the Western countries. Experiencing discrimination has its effects on the attitudes of migrant workers; it undermines their respect for law and order in the societies that deny them the benefits of compliance with norms not necessarily familiar to them. Furthermore, the natives of the host country tend to exaggerate the extent of criminality among migrant workers. When there is a perceptible rise in crime rates, especially when economic difficulties occur, the "strangers" are likely to be the major personification of evil. This judgment arises even in the face of statistical evidence that the crime rate of migrant workers does not exceed that of the native residents.

Murders and Vendettas

Upon its establishment in 1944, the Institute of Criminology and Criminal Law of Istanbul took up investigations of murder as the first item on its research agenda. The study, published in 1948 in Turkish and French, covered 6,386 persons convicted of murder, and it is still considered a main source in that subject.[19] Additional investigations have been published, but only two of them are cited here as samples.

In a study on the effects of weather (climate) on murders and assaults[20] published in 1967, Ümram F. Çölaşan states that there is a correlation of 75 percent between high temperature and the occurrence of murders and assaults. His data covered the years 1960-1966. He found that the increase in temperature was accompanied by an increase in crime, particularly in summer days of maximum heat. The number of murders and assaults also rose significantly. My textbook summarizes a number of criticisms of this kind of research which are applicable to Çölaşan's claims.[21]

In his study published in 1972, Mahmut Tezcan deals with the problem of the vendetta[22] and tries to explain it in terms of sociological factors present in some parts of Turkey. The author treats the political, juridical, and educational dimensions of the problem and suggests several preventive measures.

A vendetta usually begins with a conflict over land property rights, intensified by unemployment. The idleness of unemployment directs their attention to those conflict situations, reviving old hatreds. Other social dimensions are abduction of girls for a marriage, the instigations of relatives, and intimacy of living in close proximity. To take vengeance is considered a duty owed to one's neighborhood. The choice is to kill enemies or to leave in shameful exile.

Traffic Offenses

Turkey has a very high rate of casualties resulting from road accidents. Among the many publications on this topic is the paper of Duygun Yarsuvat.[23]

His research covers 2,260 judgments of the district court, traffic court, and justices of the peace of Istanbul for 1968. Of the total population of Istanbul, 52 percent reside within the jurisdiction of these courts. The jurisdiction is patrolled by 215 traffic policemen.

The offenses were examined in regard to types of vehicle, months of the year, days of the week, and seasons. Traffic offenses were at a minimum on weekends. Twenty-three percent of the offenses were associated with a traffic accident. Speed was found to be the major factor in traffic accidents. Vigilant traffic control by the police increased the official rate of driving under the influence of alcohol which had a marked relationship with hit and run cases. Drivers of private cars, as opposed to professional drivers, were most frequently detected for drunken driving.

The research also deals with attributes of the offenders: age, sex, professional standing, and so on. The offense rate was particularly high for eighteen to thirty year olds and for professional drivers. The examination of sentences revealed a court policy of leniency.

FUNCTIONING OF CRIMINAL JUSTICE

As is true in other countries, public opinion in Turkey has expressed increasing dissatisfaction with the criminal justice system in the last twenty years. Several scholars have applied themselves to the assessment of and proposing solutions for the shortcomings of the system.

In a 1972 study of the criminal justice system,[24] among the facets of the crisis of justice in Turkey, attention was given to the delay in justice administration. Several evils resulted from it. Nine major causes of delay were summarized, and twelve policy measures were proposed to correct the problem.

Concentrating on the criminal justice system of Istanbul, the largest city in Turkey, Duygun Yarsuvat presented the hypothesis that urbanization in Turkey has not yet had a noticeable effect on the functioning of the criminal justice system, although it is not as efficient as one would desire from social control institutions.[25] He concluded, first, that the work load of the criminal courts in Istanbul is less than that of more developed countries. Second, he found that the period of trial in justice of peace courts is shorter than that of other criminal courts.

It would seem that the lower work load would enable Istanbul courts to avoid the tendency of judges to give insufficient attention to cases by processing them rapidly and to grant acquittals too frequently as a hedge against erroneous decisions. However, inefficiency may stem from factors other than an excessive work load. Defense attorneys aggravate the procedural delays. The lack of trained staff and of sufficient administrative resources—conditions found in Turkish courts—also contribute to trial delay and other forms of inefficiency. The introduction of modern management techniques is a serious need to correct the haphazard operation of courts and their inadequate relationships with other offices. Thus, the judges would be able to perform more effectively.

Urbanization alone does not have a direct effect on the administration of criminal justice, but population growth and industrialization will create the heavy burden on criminal justice agencies in Turkey that has affected more developed nations. As discussed earlier in this chapter, planning for economic development must give heed to criminal justice.

CONCLUDING COMMENT

Until the 1960s, criminality was not considered a serious nuisance in Turkey. Thereafter and especially in 1968, the situation began to deteriorate rather rapidly. Violence became more visible; ideological and political terrorism has become a more serious concern. Fear of crime has gradually become widespread among all strata of society.

In a law-abiding society that has to husband resources essential for economic development, one can understand the marginal interest in Turkey in criminological studies in the years before 1960. The devastating effects of terrorism have been the most obvious pressures for a new interest in criminological matters in the last twenty years. Demands for reform have centered on the police, the courts, and prisons.

There is increased awareness of the crucial role criminological research can play in lending substance and direction to the framing of criminal justice policy. It is important to tie those aspects of policymaking activities with the broader efforts toward economic development that are dedicated to meeting the needs of the people of Turkey. Younger social scientists, especially those with positions in institutions of education, are turning their attention increasingly to criminological issues. Evidence is accruing that the future will bring a richer array of publications that will demonstrate the potential of criminology.

NOTES

1. Sulhi Dönmezer, "Le Cinquantenaire du Code Pénal turc et les Problemes de l'Evolution de la Politique Criminelle Moderne" [The Fiftieth Anniversary of the Turkish Penal Code and the Problem of the Modern Policies Toward the Criminal], *Archives de Sciences Criminelles*, no. 2 (1977):203.

2. Jean Pinatel, "La Criminologie au Regard de l'Avant—Projet de Code Pénal" [Looking to the Future of Criminology—Project of the Penal Code], *Revue Internationale de Droit Pénal*, 1er et 2ème trimestre (1980):73.

3. Sulhi Dönmezer, "La Loi sur l'Exécution des Peines" [Concerning the Execution of Penalties], *Annales Internationales de Criminologie*, 1er semestre (1967):30.

4. Sulhi Dönmezer, *Sosyoloji* [Sociology], 7th ed. (Istanbul: ITIA Press, 1978), p. 239.

5. Çetin Özek, "Main Characteristics of Urbanization in Turkey and the Problems It May Cause from the Point of View of Criminal Justice," *Annales de la Faculté de Droit d'Istanbul*, no. 39 (1975):93-158.

6. Sulhi Dönmezer, "Criminality and Economic Development," *Journal of the Regional Cultural Institute, Iran, Pakistan, Turkey* 3 (1970):65-74.

7. Sulhi Dönmezer, "Criminality in a Small Community of Rapid Urbanization and Industrialization, the Ereğli Project," *Annales de la Faculté de Droit d'Istanbul*, no. 38 (1974):55-71.

8. During the 1960s, Ereğli was the scene of the establishment of the largest iron-steel industrial enterprise in Turkey. Located on the coast of the Black Sea, this community experienced rapid urbanization, population growth, and increased population mobility. Here we can observe the effects of cultural change, conflict, and the weakening of local mores and customs and of informal controls under the impact of a new way of life.

9. For further discussion, see Dönmezer, "Criminality and Economic Development."

10. "Summary of the Report Presented by Sulhi Dönmezer," in *The University Teaching of Social Sciences: Criminology* (Paris: UNESCO, 1957).

11. For publications of the Institute of Criminal Law and Criminology, see the Bibliography at the end of this chapter.

12. Sulhi Dönmezer, *Kriminoloji* [Criminology] (Istanbul: Hukuk Fakültesi Press, 1976).

13. See the bibliography for the publications of the Institute of Criminal Law and Criminology of the University of Istanbul.

14. Halûk Yavuzer, *Ankara, İzmir ve Elaziğ Çocuk Ceza ve Islâh Evindeki Suçlu Çocuklarin Zekâ, Yakin Çevre ve Kisilik Özellikleri Yönüden İncelenmesi Konusunda Deneysel Bir Arastirma* [An Experimental Research on the Intelligence, Environment and Personality Traits of Juvenile Delinquents Who Are in the Treatment Schools of Ankara, Izmir and Elaziğ] (Istanbul: Edebiyat Fakültesi Press, 1977).

15. Nephan Saran, *Istanbul Sehrinde Polisle İlgisi Olan Onsekiz Yaşindan Küçük Çocuklarin Sosyo-Kültürel Özellikleri Hakkinda Bir Arastirma* [Sociocultural Particularities of the Children under 18 Who Were Involved with the Police of Istanbul] (Istanbul: Edebiyat Fakültesi Press, 1968).

16. For a comprehensive international bibliography on this subject, see Franco Ferracuti, "La Criminalité Chez les Imigrants Européens" [Criminality in European Immigrant Society], in *Etudes Relatives à la Recherche Criminologique* [Studies Relative to Criminological Research], Vol. 3 (Strasbourg: Council of Europe, 1968).

17. Orhan Tuna, *Federal Alanya' da Galisan Türk İşçilerinin İsledikleri Suçlarin Tahlili*

[Analysis of Crimes Committed by Turkish Migrant Workers in Germany] (Istanbul: Prime Minister's Office, 1966).

18. See the statement of Sulhi Dönmezer in *Tenth Conference of Directors of Criminological Research Institutes on Violence in Society* (Strasbourg: Council of Europe, 1973), p. 62.

19. *Statistique Criminologique Relative aux Condamnés pour Homicide en Turquie* [Criminal Statistics in Regard to Those Condemned for Homicide in Turkey] (Istanbul: Turk Kriminoloji Enstitüsü Press, 1948).

20. Ümran F. Çölaşan, *Meteorolojik Faktörlerin Cinayet ve Yaralama Olaylarina Etkileri* [The Effects of Meteorological Factors on Homicides and Assaults] (Ankara: Devlet Meteoroloji Genel Müdürlüğü Press, 1967).

21. See Dönmezer, *Kriminoloji*, p. 170.

22. Mahmut Tezcan, *Kan Gütme Olaylari Sosvolojisi* [Sociology of Vendetta Cases in Turkey] (Ankara: Ankara University Press, 1972).

23. Duygun Yarsuvat, *Trafik Suçlari* [Traffic Offenses] (Istanbul: Hukuk Fakültesi Press, 1972).

24. Sulhi Dönmezer, *Ceza Adaletinde Reform İlkeleri, Ceza Adalet Reformu İlkeleri Sempozyumu* [Orientations of Reform of the Criminal Justice System of Turkey] (Istanbul: Ceza Hukuku ve Kriminoloji Enstitüsü Press, 1972), p. 1.

25. Duygun Yarsuvat, *Türkive' de Sehirlesme ve Ceza Adaleti, Sehirlesmenin Doğurduğu Ceza Adaleti Sorunlari Sempozyumu* [Urbanization and Criminal Justice System in Turkey] (Istanbul: Ceza Hukuku ve Kriminoloji Enstitüsü Press, 1973), pp. 297-300.

BIBLIOGRAPHY

Representative works mentioned in the body of the chapter are supplemented by the following items drawn from the Turkish literature on criminology.

Crime and Criminology in General

Dönmezer, Sulhi. *Kriminoloji* [Criminology]. Istanbul: Istanbul Hukuk Fakültesi Press, 1976.

Evrim, Selmin. *Psikoloji Acisindan Suclulun Sorunu ve Psikolojik İzahi* [The Problems of Criminality from the Point of View of Psychology and Its Psycho-Sociological Explanation]. Istanbul: Istanbul University Press, 1970.

Yucel, Mustafa T. *Kriminolojik Notlar, Toplum Suclu ve Ötesi* [Criminological Notes, Society, Criminal and Beyond]. Ankara: Ankara Training School Publication, 1971.

Conferences and Data on Crime, Law, and the Community

Akil Hastalarina Karşi Cemiyetin Müdafaasi Mevzuunda Kollokyum: Raporlar [Colloquium on the Protection of the Society against Mentally Ill, Reports]. Istanbul: Ceza Hukuku ve Kriminoloji Enstitüsü Press, no. 8, 1958.

Değişen Toplum ve Ceza Hukuku Karşisinda Türk Ceza Kanununun 50. Yili ve Geleceği [Symposium on the Five Decades of the Turkish Penal Code Facing Changing Society and Criminal Law, Evaluations for the Future. Reports and Proceedings]. Istanbul: Ceza Hukuku ve Kriminoloji Enstitüsü Press, no. 19, 1977.

Enquête Criminologique Concernant 894 Cas de Suicide [Criminological Survey on 894 Suicide Cases]. Istanbul: Turk Kriminoloji Enstitüsü Press, no. 5, 1954.

Juvenile Delinquency

Ağaoğlu, Tezer Taşkiran-Samet. *Suçlu Cocuklarimiz: Ankara Çocuk Islâh Evinde bir Araştirma* [Our Delinquent Children: A Research in the Ankara Training School]. Ankara: 1943.

Dönmezer, Sulhi. *Garp Memleketlerinde ve Memleketimizde Çocuk Sucluluğunun Umumî Inkişaflari* [General Development of Juvenile Delinquency in Turkey and Western Countries]. Istanbul: İş Mecmuasi, Çocuk Sayisi, 1943):96-126.

974 Suclu Cocuk Hakkinda Kriminolojik Anket [Criminological Survey on 974 Juvenile Delinquents]. Istanbul: Ceza Hukuku ve Kriminoloji Enstitüsü Press, no. 4, 1953.

Report of a Working Group on the Prevention and Treatment of Juvenile Delinquency in Turkey. Istanbul: Ceza Hukuku ve Kriminoloji Enstitüsü Press, no. 2, 1953.

Suçlu Çocuklar Hakkinda Kriminolojik Araştirma [A Criminological Survey on Juvenile Delinquency]. Istanbul: Ceza Hukuku ve Kriminolojo Enstitüsü Press, no. 12, 1964.

Murders and Vendettas

Dönmezer, Sulhi. *Konya'da Adam Öldürme Cürümleri* [Murders in Konya]. Istanbul: Istanbul Üniversitesi Press, 1946.

Dönmezer, Sulhi. "Kriminoloji Açisindan Kan Gütme Saikiyle İşlenem Suçlar" [Crime and Vendetta: A Criminological Appraisal]. *Istanbul Hukuk Fakültesi Mecmuasi* 40, nos. 1-2 (1974):1-13.

Terrorism

Dönmezer, Sulhi. "Milletlerarasi Tedhişçilik" [International Terrorism]. *Istanbul Hukuk Fakültesi Mecmuasi* 44, nos. 1-4 (1980):55-70.

Ergil, Doğu. *Türkive' de Terör ve Şiddet* [Terror and Violence in Turkey]. Ankara: Turhan Kitabevi Press, 1980.

Türkiye' de Terör, Abdi İpekçi Semineri [Reports and Proceedings of the Seminar Convened in Memory of Abdi İpekçi—Terror in Turkey]. Istanbul: Gazeteciler Cemiyeti Press, 1980.

Urbanization, Industrialization, and Crime

Özek, Çetin. "Main Characteristics of Urbanization in Turkey and the Problems It May Cause from the Point of View of Criminal Justice." *Annales de la Faculté de Droit d'Istanbul* no. 39 (1976):93-158.

Şehirleşmenin Doğurduğu Ceza Adaleti Sorunlari Sempozyumu [Symposium Related to the Problems Created by Urbanization for the Administration of Criminal Justice], Istanbul: Ceza Hukuku ve Kriminoloji Enstitüsü Press, no. 18, 1974.

Türkive' de Trafik Problemleri, Semineri [Seminar on Traffic Problems in Turkey]. Istanbul: Ceza Hukuku ve Kriminoloji Enstitüsü Press, no. 14, 1967.

Yarsuvat, Duygun. "Urbanization and Administration of Justice in Turkey." *Annales de la Faculté de Droit d'Istanbul*, no. 38 (1972):393-414.

Drugs

Enquête Criiminologique Concernant 121 Toxicomanes [Criminological Survey of 121 Drug Addicts]. Istanbul: Ceza Hukuku ve Kriminoloji Enstitüsü Press, no. 9, 1958.

Dönmezer, Sulhi. "Uyuşturucu Maddelerin Hukuk ve Kriminoloji ile ilgili bazi Yönleri" [Some Legal and Criminological Aspects of Drugs]. *Istanbul Huku Fakültesi Mecmuasi* 36, nos. 1-4 (1971):1-14.

Günal, Yilmaz. *Uyuşturucu Madde Suçlari* [Offenses of Drug Abuse]. Ankara: Kazanci Press, 1976.

Köknel, Özcan. *İnsanlik Tarihi Boyunca Uyuşturucu Maddeler Sorunlari* [The Problems of Drugs Throughout Human History]. Istanbul: Gelişim Press, 1976.

Uvuşturucu Maddeler Mevzuunda Kollokyum [Colloquium on Drugs]. Istanbul: Ceza Hukuku ve Krminoloji Enstitüsü Press, no. 6, 1957.

Migrant Workers

Abadan, Nermin. *Bati Almanya'daki Türk İşçileri ve Sorunlari* [Turkish Workers in West Germany and Their Problems]. Ankara: Başbakanlik Devlet Plânlama Teşkilâti, 1964.

Alpaslan, M. Sükrü. "Yabanci İşçilerin Suçluluğu" [Criminality of Migrant Workers]. *Istanbul Hukuk Fakültesi Mecmuasi* 41, nos. 1-2 (1975):109-131.

Economic Crimes

Erman, Sahir. *Doviz Suclari* [Offenses Violating Foreign Currency Regulations]. Istanbul: 1978.

Tosun, Oztekin. *Fiat Nizamini Ihlal Suclari* [Offenses Against Regulations on Price Control]. Istanbul: Ceza Hukuku ve Kriminoloji Enstitüsü Press, no. 11, 1960.

Criminal Justice System

Ceza Adalet Reformu İlkerleri Sempozyumlari, 24 Şubat, 1972; 26-28 Nisan 1972, Raporlar ve Tartişmalar [Reports and Proceedings of the 1st and 2d Symposia on the Orientation of the Reform of the Criminal Justice System]. Istanbul: Ceza Hukuku ve Kriminoloji Enstitüsü Press, Vol. 1, 1972, Vol. 2, 1973.

Dönmezer, Sulhi. "Some Reflections on the Introductory Reports Submitted to the Regional Symposium Organized by the United Nations and the Dutch Government." April 14-27, 1980. In press.

Sokullu, Füsun, "Bir Karakolun Tanitilmasi" [Evaluation of Police Station Work in Istanbul]. *Ceza Hukuku ve Kriminoloji Enstitüsü Dergisi* 1, no. 1 (1979):105-110.

Tosun, Öztekin. *Suçlularin Gözlemi* [Examination of New Convicts]. Istanbul: Ceza Hukuku ve Kriminoloji Enstitüsü Press, no. 13, 1966.

UGANDA

James S.E. Opolot

The study and application of criminology in Uganda can be looked at in several ways, all of them useful. It is possible, for example, to answer the question "Who was responsible for the development of criminology in Uganda?" by examining the role of law-appliers relative to that of the academicians. Or we might wish to look at the social forces responsible for the emergence of criminology in Uganda as an academic subject. Or, again, we might try to define criminology in Uganda by its products: What kind of claims does it make? What kind of propositions does it generate?

Regardless of the approach taken, an understanding of criminology in Uganda, as an intellectual enterprise, requires study of the basic problems it confronts, the intellectual ends it seeks, and the kind of propositions that emerge. The study of criminology anywhere can never take place in a vacuum. The interrelations of criminology with history, geography, anthropology, sociology, law, political science, and economics are inextricably close. Therefore, this review of criminology in Uganda must briefly examine other disciplines.

This examination is especially appropriate because criminology in Uganda is in too early a stage of development to justify serious debate about whether or not it is an independent discipline or whether or not it should include practitioners within the ranks of full-fledged "criminologists." This chapter is a report on a version of criminology that is at an early period of institution-building and for a nation that provides and will provide a fascinating environment for criminological research.

PRE-1950 FOUNDATIONS OF SOCIAL SCIENCES

Although the social sciences were present earlier in Uganda, as elsewhere in Africa, they began to emerge as a basis for both practical and academic research after World War II. The social sciences developed somewhat differently in Uganda than they did in the West. Sociologists, psychologists, and, to a lesser degree, political scientists pioneered the use of the survey in the United States and Europe; it was primarily the anthropologist who introduced the systematic survey in Uganda.

In the period between the two world wars and subsequently, a new breed of colonial administrator-anthropologist was attracted to Uganda. That is, social science research in Africa was associated for the most part with the needs of the colonial governments for certain basic demographic statistics for planning and administrative purposes. Academic researchers were sometimes engaged to conduct or to supervise the administration of government-sponsored projects. Nearly every British territory (of which Uganda was one), for example, employed a government sociologist. Not infrequently, social anthropologists were also retained to work on specific projects. The next three sections of this chapter elaborate on these points.

Survey Studies

The most common social science investigations were survey studies conducted to provide information for social and economic planning. For example, survey research was conducted in East Africa on aspects of labor immigration related to colonial economic developments. Northcott, a labor management expert, studied the social and economic conditions of the more than six thousand Africans who worked on the construction of the Kenya-Uganda Railway.[1] In another survey relevant to economic changes, Sofer and Sofer examined the hydroelectric complex around the Uganda industrial town of Jinja.[2]

Case and Field Studies

Prior to 1950, other social science research techniques were employed, notably case and field studies and descriptive studies. Case and field studies are very similar. Case studies usually examine one person, group, project, institution, or agency. They are basically intensive investigations of the factors that contribute to characteristics of the case under scrutiny. In a sense, when a legal investigator or social anthropologist investigates the significance of a tribal law, he is conducting a case study. In Uganda, prominent examples include the investigations of Roscoe[3] and Driberg.[4]

Field studies are virtually indistinguishable from case studies except for the researcher's point of view. Specifically, researchers who conduct case studies tend to be practitioners who are interested in understanding a condition so that it can be treated or altered in some way. Those who conduct field studies tend to be more interested in fostering a general understanding of the phenomena involved and may have little interest in changing the status of the case under study.

Descriptive Studies

The term "descriptive research" is used here to denote a broad range of activities that have in common the purpose of describing situations or phenomena. These descriptions may be necessary for decision-making or to support broader research objectives. Descriptive research was also conducted to advance the broader aims of science. In this context, it was usually performed to develop knowledge on which the problems and explanations of subsequent research would be based. Again Roscoe's and Driberg's works qualify in this category.

A later generation of anthropologists, such as L. A. Fallers,[5] N. Dyson-Hudson,[6] and W. Goldschmidt,[7] worked primarily as independent academic anthropologists. They were interested not only in traditional enthnographic descriptions of tribal structure but also in the relation between customary law and the national legal system. Thus, these scholars made important contributions in providing primary data useful to the criminologist for secondary analysis and for outlining issues for future in-depth analysis. In the latter instance, all of these scholars have touched on the critical relationships between formal and informal controls in modern Uganda. These relationships have important implications for evolution of an integrated criminal justice system relevant to the culture of Uganda.

CONTRIBUTIONS OF LEGAL RESEARCH

The previous section gave a general sketch of the foundations and shape of social sciences in colonial Uganda adequate enough to bring into focus the tremendous potential contribution to criminological analysis and thought. In this section, an attempt is made to give an account of legal research in terms of its rationale, focus, and contributions to criminological analysis and thought.

Legal research, relative to that of the anthropologists, came later and was a response to the need to change the colonial legal system before independence. It was considered essential to "modernize" the legal systems: codifying or integrating customary law, making the necessary changes in it, tightening rules of evidence and procedure or types of punishments. For example, the Bushe "Committee" of Inquiry into the Administration of Justice in Kenya, Uganda, and Tanganyika Territory in Criminal Matters included a judge from Uganda, the attorney-general of Kenya, the secretary for native affairs in Tanganyika, and, as chairman, the legal advisor of state for the colonies. It was charged with the task of finding out not only how colonial penal sanctions were faring in the light of customary law, but also what recommendations would be appropriate.[8] In other words, legal research was directed towards systematization of rules, the mechanism for implementing recommendations, and so on. It was more policy-oriented than the anthropological research; and those who conducted it evinced a much greater faith in the instrumentalism of law than in anthropological research.

There were important differences in the methodologies of legal research and anthropological research. Anthropologists are committed to field work, case studies, and descriptive studies, and studied the actual operation of the courts and specific aspects of the relationship between law and society. Most of the lawyers focused on more general questions (for example, the role of customary law) and on problems of the formal, written legal system, such as the place of received law in the legal system of the nation-to-be.[9] A few of the lawyers did show an interest in more direct observation and detailed study of the effect of law on social relations.[10] But these efforts were limited in scope, were not based on questionnaires, and tended to ignore such rich data as local court decisions.

With the establishment of faculties of law in the University of Dar es-Salaam and the University of Makerere and the Law Department Center[11] in Kampala, there has been some work on the national statutory laws.[12] There has been a significant increase in the number of native law teachers and researchers; a few law periodicals and a number of monographs and books have been written.

The lawyers have continued doctrinaire research. There has been a great deal of concern among Ugandan scholars about the relevance of the legal system to encouraging institutional development. Indeed, today it is scarcely possible to discuss Ugandan law without reference to development. Unfortunately, this emphasis has thwarted to an important extent the type of analysis and thought criminologists or students of sociology of law would entertain, namely, to study the crime problem and the criminal justice system on the basis of empirical research. There is some support for the latter type of research,[13] but attempts in that direction failed to bring the social sciences to bear on the study of law.

DEVELOPMENT OF CRIMINOLOGICAL PERSPECTIVES

Let us now turn to Uganda's colonial background from which criminological analysis and thought in Uganda are becoming increasingly distinctive and influential. The colonial authorities neglected criminological analysis and thought partially because there were few criminologists, even in England.

The only social research of direct criminological relevance was carried out towards the end of the colonial era by R.E.S. Tanner, a foreigner. Basically, Tanner constructed a typology of inmate adaptation to an African prison in terms of conformity, innovation, ritualism, withdrawal, rebellion, and manipulation. He found that African inmates did not suffer from deprivation, as would ordinarily be the case in Western society, because living standards in the African prison were higher than those in the free community. In other words, the African prison provided more material amenities than the free community. In addition, Tanner claimed to have found that imprisonment may have carried little social stigma.[14]

In the post-colonial period, criminological analysis and thought fell into two broad categories: research and instruction. An analysis of each category now follows.

Criminological Research

Tanner has continued to build upon his previously mentioned work, in terms not only of East Africa but also the new states of Africa as a whole. His prominent publications include *Three Studies in East African Criminology* and "Some Problems of East African Crime Statistics"; both works are descriptive and analytical. In another article, entitled "Penal Practice in Africa: Some Restrictions on the Possibility of Reform,"[15] Tanner outlines critical obstacles to penal reform in the post-colonial period.

Among the new, prominent foreign researchers are the United Nations teams of experts and Professor M. B. Clinard and his associate, D. J. Abbott, whose work in Uganda centers on the growing adult crime and juvenile delinquency in the late 1960s.[16] Armed robbery and vigilantism in particular had become quite a menace.

In 1969, the Uganda government invited the most prominent United Nations team from the Research Institute in Rome to conduct exploratory research. Its findings are embodied in a monograph entitled *Social Defense in Uganda: A Survey for Research.*[17] This document outlines the social defense-criminal justice system, as well as those areas that require further research.

Clinard and Abbott[18] were attracted to conduct research in 1969 because the crime problem and other social problems made Uganda an ideal setting to test sociological theories such as differential association (Edwin Sutherland)[19] and differential opportunity (Richard Cloward and Lloyd Ohlin).[20] This research was reported in *Crime in Developing Countries: A Comparative Perspective*, which turns out to be descriptive, too.

Meanwhile, the work of Ugandan criminologists began to emerge, sometimes in collaboration with non-Ugandans. For example, Eric Kibuka at Makerere University worked with the United Nations experts in their research. On his own he embarked upon a descriptive field study of juvenile delinquency in Kampala for his doctoral dissertation.[21] Sociologist Tibamanya Mwene Mushanga conducted another descriptive study on homicide in his home region for his master's thesis.[22] I have undertaken extensive library study for purposes of analyzing and making recommendations in regard to alternative ways of dealing with offenders in Africa in general and Uganda in particular.[23]

Instruction of Criminology

Criminological research in Uganda, as in many parts of the Third World, has preceded the organization of courses in the local institutions of higher learning, such as Makerere University in Kampala. "Stray" criminological research and cognate research projects preceded by almost a decade the organization of instruction and helped provide a perspective for theoretical courses.

Criminology, as taught in Makerere University, is suited to graduate study more than as a supportive "foundation" study, like law, agriculture, or medicine.

It is a study of considerable complexity, involving a great mass of subject matter that may be ordered in certain ways and that is capable of being supplemented, analyzed, and manipulated by techniques that someday may reach the rigor found in many social sciences. The academic pursuit of criminology at Makerere has already gone far beyond the empirical descriptions typical of the "package tour" method.

Fabian Okware's Role

Criminological developments in Uganda cannot be analyzed without mention of the contribution of the late Fabian Okware, the first indigenous commissioner of prisons and a self-taught criminologist. Okware acted as a catalyst between local investigators (such as Kibuka and Mushanga) at Makerere University and among penal administrators, on one hand, and foreign investigators such as Tanner, Clinard, and their associates on the other.[24] Okware encouraged others to recognize the interrelationships between theory and practice—a recognition seldom found among the new states of Africa.

Born in eastern Uganda, the approachable Okware was educated in the neighboring Catholic secondary school, Tororo College. Thereafter, he joined the Uganda Prisons Service as a chief jailer and rose through the ranks to the highest position held by a Ugandan previous to the gaining of independence. During his career, he became dedicated to the field of criminology. This interest perhaps developed in the course of his experiences while representing Uganda in various international conferences, many of which were sponsored by the United Nations. Certainly, he was induced to learn more and more about criminology.

Okware was also a forward-looking, imaginative man who realized man's limitations.[25] These qualities were demonstrated in his program development, particularly the recruitment of "new blood" personnel (university-bound students) to be trained in middle management locally as well as in Great Britain, India, Australia, and Canada. (Thereby, Andre Kayiira and I became involved in penal work and came to the United States for academic studies.) By the time Obote's government was overthrown, Okware had made the Ugandan penal system one of the best in Africa.[26]

The significance of Okware's contributions to Ugandan criminology is that his life and prison administration straddled the regimes of Milton Obote and Idi Amin; his accomplishments were made in the years when this emergent nation was engaged in political competition among various factions.[27] In this period, the progress reported above was achieved. In 1971, the coup of Idi Amin brought these developments to a halt, and criminology and criminal justice administration shared the heavy costs of despotism until April 1979 when Amin's regime was terminated. Now the future course of criminology will be determined in large measure by the further development of Ugandan society and its institutions because, as stated earlier, the study of criminology anywhere can never take place in a vacuum.

SUMMARY AND CONCLUSIONS

This introduction to criminological development in Uganda has focused on its background, the social forces influencing it, and prominent actors in its history. Criminological analysis and perspectives have stemmed from a general social science development, especially that of anthropology in Africa in general and in Uganda particularly. Trends in legal research have also been important to criminology as one of the aspects of influences on the present and future structure of Ugandan society. Codification and systemization of codes may be seen as a process toward integration of social control in Uganda.

Social changes unleashed by urbanization and industrialization are primary in explorations for a remarkable upsurge of adult and juvenile delinquency in Uganda, especially in the late 1960s. Contemporary Uganda offers rich opportunities for investigations to add to the intellectual resources of criminology that began to accumulate through the work of foreign researchers, studies sponsored by the Uganda government, and indigenous researchers. The role of Fabian Okware in this regard has earned him a place in the history of Ugandan criminology.

Criminological analysis and thought has begun to move beyond mere descriptive research toward analytical research, but much remains to be done in theory (or model) construction. The sociological focus will probably be prominent because the majority of researchers, whether foreigners or Ugandans, are educated in sociology.

The contemporary uncertainty about the future direction of the nation increases the risk for any prediction as to whether or not an authentic Ugandan criminology will emerge. The empirical purposes of legal and anthropological research in the past give some comfort to those who would believe that the urgent national needs for economic development and building of indigenous social institutions will favor opportunities for strengthening educational and research programs essential to a stable foundation for criminology. Already available are at least four criminologists—Kibuka, Kayiira, Mushanga, and myself—as a cadre. With the ending of eight years of tyranny, Uganda faces the travail of national reconstruction, but with every reason to know ultimately the costs of the criminogenic society that Amin created. The examination of this creation of a dictator is, in itself, a unique opportunity for criminological inquiry.

NOTES

1. C. H. Northcott, *African Labor Efficiency Survey* (London: His Majesty's Stationery Office, 1949).

2. C. Sofer and R. Sofer, "Recent Population Growth in Jinja," *Uganda Journal* 17 (1953):38-50; "Jinja Transformed: A Social Survey of a Multi-racial Township" (Kampala, Uganda: East African Institute of Social Research, 1955). See also C. Sofer, "Urban African Social Structure and Working Group Behavior in Jinja, Uganda," in *Social Implications of Industrialization and Urbanization in Africa South of the Sahara* (Lausanne: UNESCO, 1956), p. 602.

3. J. Roscoe, *The Baganda* (London: Macmillan, 1911).

4. J. H. Driberg, *The Lango: A Nilotic Tribe of Uganda* (London: T. Fisher Unwin, Ltd., 1923).

5. L. A. Fallers, *Law Without Precedent* (Chicago: University of Chicago Press, 1969).

6. N. Dyson-Hudson, *Karimojong Politics* (Oxford: Oxford University Press, 1969).

7. W. Goldschmidt, *Sebei Law* (Berkeley, Calif.: University of California Press, 1967).

8. See H. F. Morris, *Some Perspectives of East African Legal History* (Uppsala: Scandinavian Institute of African Studies, 1970); see also H. F. Morris and J. S. Read, *Uganda: The Development of Its Laws and Constitution* (London: Stevens and Sons, 1966).

9. W. Twinning, "The Place of Customary Law in the National Legal Systems of East Africa," Lecture delivered at the University of Chicago Law School, April and May, 1963.

10. H. F. Morris, "Report of the Commission on Marriage, Divorce, and the Status of Women," *Journal of African Law* 10 (1966):3-7; "Marriage Law in Uganda: Sixty Years of Attempted Reform," in J. Anderson (ed.), *Family Law in Asia and Africa* (London: 1968).

11. The Law Development Center Act, 1970, provides in S.2, in respect of law reform that the center shall have the functions of:

(f) assisting any Commissioner who may be appointed in the preparation and publication of a revised edition of the Laws of Uganda;
(g) assisting in the preparation of reprints of Acts of Parliament in accordance with any law for the time being in force;
(h) assisting the Law Reform Commission in the performance of its functions;
(i) undertaking research into any branch of the law.

12. For example, the Law Development Center produced draft bills for a new Magistrates Courts Act, Prevention of Corruption Act, the Penal Code (Amendment) Act, and the Criminal Procedure (Amendment) Act. The legislation on these topics became operative in 1970 and 1971. Several drafts have been submitted to the attorney-general which are still pending appropriate action. It is hoped that since Idi Amin is no longer in the picture in Uganda, the center's activities will pick up. It is also hoped that criminological concerns will become new dimensions of the center.

13. L. L. Kato, "Methodology of Law Reform," in G. F. Sawyer (ed.), *East African Law and Social Change* (Nairobi, Kenya: East African Institute of Social and Cultural Affairs, 1967); "Rethinking Anti-Witchcraft Legislation in East Africa," University of East Africa, University of Social Sciences Council Conferences, Makerere University, Kampala, Uganda, December 30, 1978-January 3, 1979.

14. R.E.S. Tanner, "The East African Prison Experience of Imprisonment," in A. Milner (ed.), *African Penal Systems* (New York: Frederick A. Praeger, 1969), pp. 294-315.

15. R.E.S. Tanner, *Three Studies in East African Criminology* (Uppsala: Scandinavian Institute of African Studies, 1970); *Some Problems of East African Crime Statistics* (Kampala, Uganda: Institute of Social Research, 1964 (mimeographed); "Penal Practice in Africa: Some Restrictions on the Possibility of Reform," *Journal of Modern African Studies* 10, no. 3 (1972):201-218.

16. Of course, the growing crime problem has been a continent-wide problem. The phenomenon is in itself new, but it has been without precedent and speed. Before coloni-

zation, crime as understood in the West was almost unknown. In the early 1960s, virtually every new African state began to feel the impact of the crime problem attributed to rapid social change—urbanization, industrialization, and urban migration.

17. *Social Defense in Uganda: A Survey for Research* (United Nations Social Defense Institute in Rome, Publication No. 3, 1970).

18. M. B. Clinard and D. J. Abbott, *Crime in Developing Countries: A Comparative Perspective* (New York: John Wiley, 1973).

19. E. Sutherland and D. Cressey, *Criminology* (Philadelphia: Lippincott, 1970), pp. 77-100.

20. R. Cloward and L. Ohlin, *Delinquency and Opportunity* (Glencoe, Ill.: The Free Press, 1960), pp. 17-20.

21. E. Kabuka, "Sociological Aspects of Juvenile Delinquency in Kampala, 1962-1969," Ph.D. dissertation, University of East Africa, 1972.

22. T. M. Mushanga, "Criminal Homicide in Uganda," M.A. thesis, Makerere University, Kampala, Uganda, 1970.

23. J.S.E. Opolot, "The Treatment of Offenders in Uganda," M.S. thesis, Southern Illinois University, Carbondale, 1972; and J.S.E. Opolot, *Criminal Justice and Nation-Building in Africa* (Washington, D.C.: University Press of America, 1976).

24. The now defunct Uganda Criminology Society was formed in the late 1960s at the encouragement of Okware. One of its purposes was to facilitate communication between academicians and practitioners.

25. Unlike the commissioner of police and his associates, Okware fought hard to ensure that his young men and women received the best possible education and training. In this way, the Uganda Prisons Service did not receive massive resignations of university-bound officers that the police force experienced.

26. G. E. Berkley, M. W. Giles, J. F. Hackett, and N. C. Kassoff, *Introduction to Criminal Justice* (Boston: Holbrook Press, 1976), p. 504.

27. Uganda had its first direct elections for African representatives on the Legislative Council in 1958. In March 1961, elections were held in which the Democratic party won forty-three seats, and the Uganda People's Congress (UPC), led by Dr. Milton Obote, won thirty-five seats. The Buganda region, however, boycotted this election, even though the Democratic party originated inside Buganda, reflecting the Catholic groups, as distinct from the majority Protestants. In October 1961, the majority Buganda peoples formed a party called Kabaka Yekka (KY), which allied with the UPC, and this coalition won the national elections in April 1962. (The UPC won forty-three out of ninety-one seats.) In November 1964, there was another election—the "lost counties" referendum—and by December 1965 the UPC majority had increased to sixty-seven out of ninety-one seats. In February 1966, Prime Minister Obote deposed the president, Sir Edward Mutessa II, the Kabaka of Buganda, and put an end not only to Bugandan autonomy, but also that of the other three kingdoms. The Kabaka died in exile in November 1969. Following the assassination of Dr. Obote in December 1969, all the opposition parties were banned. The military government banned all parties after the January 1971 coup of Idi Amin. Amin himself was toppled in April 1979 after a bloody rule.

BIBLIOGRAPHY

Clinard, M. B., and D. J. Abbott. *Crime in Developing Countries: A Comparative Perspective.* New York: John Wiley, 1973.

The volume makes a strong case for comparative criminology—testing of theories developed in Western countries in the context of developing countries and relevant literature on adult crime and juvenile delinquency in developing countries, especially Uganda. It outlines the legal dilemmas and attempts to resolve them in the developing countries.

Fallers, L. A. *Law Without Precedent*. Chicago: University of Chicago Press, 1969.
As an in-depth study of the anthropology of law, the text provides rich material on customary law and the interplay between customary law and state (national) law, even though the study was conducted in the 1960s.

Goldschmidt, W. *Seibei Law*. Berkeley, Calif.: University of California Press, 1967.
This book is also an in-depth study of the anthropology of law conducted in the late 1950s and early 1960s.

Kibuka, E. "Sociological Aspects of Juvenile Delinquency in Kampala, 1962 to 1969." Ph.D. dissertation, University of East Africa, 1972.
Kibuka provides a fairly extensive review of literature on juvenile delinquency in Africa in general and in Uganda in particular. He also provides useful insights into the problems of conducting field interviews in an African setting.

Morris, H. F. *Indirect Rule and the Search for Justice*. Oxford: Clarendon Press, 1972.
This historical overview presents an introduction to colonial law in East Africa in general and Uganda in particular.

Mushanga, M. T. "Criminal Homicide in Uganda," M.A. Thesis, Makerere University, Kampala, Uganda, 1970.
The thesis is a descriptive (case) study that provides insight into victim-offender relationships, including dispute resolution in some cases.

Opolot, J.S.E. *Criminal Justice and Nation-Building in Africa*. Washington, D.C.: University Press of America, 1976.
A descriptive (case) study of colonial law, the book also deals with post-colonial attempts to forge new, relevant legal structures in Uganda by focusing on the law of murder.

Sawyer, G. F. *East African Law and Social Change*. Nairobi, Kenya: East African Institute of Social and Cultural Affairs, 1967.
Several articles are studies of law reform in East Africa in general and Uganda in particular. The article by L. L. Kato on "Methodology of Law Reform" articulates the relationship between social science (that is, criminological) research and legal research.

Social Defense in Uganda: A Survey for Research. United Nations Social Defense Institute in Rome, Publication No. 3, 1970.
This monograph is an exploratory and descriptive study of the structure and operation of the Uganda criminal justice (social defense) system.

Tanner, R.E.S. "The East African Prison Experience of Imprisonment." In A. Milner (ed.). *African Penal Systems*. New York: Frederick A. Praeger, 1969.
This chapter is a comparative analysis of penal policy and practice.

UNION OF SOVIET SOCIALIST REPUBLICS

Vladimir K. Zvirbul

Soviet criminology as a branch of science studying human behavior has developed into an independent discipline. It studies the social regularities that determine the appearance, development, and commission of crimes; the social reactions to crime under different socioeconomic structures; and the regularities that determine the formation of the offender's personality and his interactions with the conditions of life and education, with a definite criminological situation and the prevention system. Among the subjects of Soviet criminology are a study of crime; its state, structure, dynamics, and causes; separate types of crime and circumstances contributing to them; offender's personality; classifications of offenders; and ways, means, and systems of crime control and prevention, including classification of types and measures of prevention.

GENERAL NATURE OF SOVIET CRIMINOLOGY

The subject matter of Soviet criminology encompasses the phenomena usually studied by criminology generally: crime, the offender's personality, and the social reactions to crime. The processes, phenomena, and factors examined in criminology appear in conjunction where social, sociopsychological, legal, and other aspects of human behavior interact. The specific character of criminological purposes determines the methodology of the studies that should always have a compound nature.

Soviet criminology is also noted for its general historical and materialistic approach. Within the framework of historical and dialectical materialism, Soviet criminology considers crime to be a historically determined phenomenon and not an eternal one, depending on the stage of development of the humanity where contradictions between personal and social interests result in violations of laws and the community order. The root causes of such violations, as defined by V. I. Lenin, are "the exploitation of the masses, their want and their poverty. With the removal of this chief cause, excesses will inevitably begin to 'wither away.' We do not know how quickly and in what order, but we know that they will inevitably begin to 'wither away.' "[1] Historical and social studies of Soviet criminologists justify the statement that, simultaneously with the general causes of crime, each socioeconomic formation possesses its own determinants of the structure, dynamics, and trends of crime and consequently shapes the specific measures of crime prevention and control.

Soviet criminology focuses on socially determined phenomena, rooted in the living conditions of society which is divided into antagonistic classes, with its inevitable attributes such as mass unemployment, growing social conflicts, individualistic psychology, and contradictions between personal and social interests. All elements of this doctrine point to the fact that an elimination of social antagonisms; improvement of living conditions; education and culture of all strata of the population; and harmonization of personal and social interests may lead to a decline in the crime rate and, ultimately, the liquidation of crime as a mass phenomenon within a reasonable period of time.

PREVENTION CRUCIAL IN THE WAR ON CRIME

That is why crime prevention has been chosen as the main direction of the war against crime in the Soviet Union. Correspondingly criminology faces the necessity of analyzing the needs and interests that characterize society and of providing knowledge for the elimination of existing contradictions. The strategies and tactics of the war against crime are based on these analyses that are aimed at a gradual elimination of conflict situations from society.

Soviet criminology regards crime prevention as a peculiar sphere of behavior regulation, functioning within the framework of the Soviet control system. The main premise of the Soviet doctrine on crime prevention is that the struggle against crime should concentrate on (1) the elimination or neutralization of the processes and phenomena that have a negative impact on personalities and (2) on the conditions that cause changes in the ways of living of certain persons that contradict in any way the societal norms. In this connection, decisive significance is attached to the growth of material well-being, the raising of the cultural level and the consciousness of citizens as necessary prerequisites for crime prevention, and, in historical perspective, the eradication of crime as a social phenomenon.

From this perspective, the effectiveness of the war against crime is determined by large-scale measures undertaken to improve socioeconomic and educational activities, to lay the groundwork for the adoption of proper attitudes by society's members, and their realization of demands and requirements of the society in their way of living. In other words, crime prevention is envisaged as a series of separate aspects of the social life organization at different levels. Meanwhile, the system of prevention is enriched and its effectiveness strengthened by the growth of the socioeconomic and moral potentiality of the society and by the elimination of the factors interfering with the normal forming and functioning of personalities.

The protective and educative impact of the system on an individual and his environment acquires great significance in order to prevent possible distortions in a person's consciousness and behavior. At the same time, criminology as a science stresses the necessity of directing a combination of measures that have corrective impact on personalities in the course of the war against crime that positively changes and enriches the environment. As confirmed by criminological research, this approach creates opportunities for preventing the acquisition of criminal behavior by more than half of the potential offenders.

RELEVANCE OF THE GENERAL SYSTEM OF PLANNING

Management of economic and social life is achieved on the grounds of planning thanks to the prevalence of social property under socialism. Accordingly, the elaboration of measures for the fight against crime is realized in the framework of the general system of a state, regional, and departmental planning from top to bottom. The system of planning distinguishes corresponding tasks and functions applicable to the responsibilities, respectively, of each organ of power and administration, enterprise, educative establishment, and primary collective. Peculiar complexities exist in the coordination of these organs as elements of the system of planning.

The war against crime is regarded as a task of the entire nation. Accordingly, great attention is attached to the interaction of the criminal justice system with the organs of state power and management, economic organizations, educational establishments, and trade unions and youth organizations in the development and realization of complexes of preventive measures. These several forms of interaction operate on the national, regional, and branch or enterprise level.

In the USSR, economic and social development planning creates considerable opportunities for making use of the management of social processes in the area of crime prevention. The management of social processes pertains to socialist formation primarily through the creation of conditions contributing to economic and social development. The fight against negative phenomena is accomplished by creating situations opposing their appearance, and that purpose calls for sound analysis and prognosis which determine the structural and temporal aspects of the causes of antisocial behavior. Thus, purposeful and persistent effort may be directed toward eliminating structural and temporal aspects.

The legal education of the population is an important means of cultivating citizen reactions to crime, and research can increase the effectiveness of this education. Some efforts are being made to keep the people constantly and systematically informed about new legislation as a means of enhancing their readiness to behave consistently with the requirements of law and the rules of socialist community life. In addition, through legal education, it is hoped that those persons who have committed crimes will regain their legal and moral consciousness.

In the fight against crime, the widespread participation of social organizations and autonomously formed entities—people's druzhines, comradeship courts, sections of order, and so on—is essential in the prevention of violations and the education of offenders.

SOVIET CRIMINOLOGY: TWO MAJOR SECTIONS

Soviet criminology is usually divided into two large sections: (1) a general section, which deals with the subject, methodology, system, and history of the discipline, its principal notions, the characteristics of the state, structure, and dynamics of crime, the offender's personality, and the system of crime prevention and its major elements; and (2) a special section, which includes an examination of separate categories of crime and of their causes; and the undertaking of other specific studies that include topics of prevention. The categories of crime are as follows: violent crimes, violent mercenary crimes, mercenary crimes, official crimes, casual crimes, juvenile and young adult crimes, recidivist crimes, and so on.

This classification of criminology permits the combination of the tasks of differentiation and complex elaboration of crime prevention measures. In this connection, Soviet criminology searches for ways and means of increasing the effectiveness of individual prevention. Criteria are applied for personality evaluation and prognosis to predict possible future behavior and in the methods for correcting offender behavior.

Soviet criminology studies the development of personality through the interaction of its genetic properties (physiological, intellectual, and psychical), social macro- and microenvironments, and concrete crime-prone situations. In a narrower sense, the key problem defined here is the study of the issues of criminal motivation. In Soviet criminology, personalities are studied from the point of view of the clarification of the social essence of a man, expressed in his position in the system of social relations, and in the roles and contacts with other people, which is ultimately social life itself. A complex approach to the personality issue, typical for Soviet criminology, thus consists of a dialectical integration of social and other elements of this notion.

Criminology studies the preventive-educational aspect of criminal punishment, its role in the rehabilitation of an offender, and its provision of a positive social alternative. Simultaneously, research is being carried out on the development of state and social patronage over persons who have served criminal punishments through measures for their employment, housing accommodations, social help, and control.

The major tasks of Soviet criminological research are to analyze the processes and phenomena connected with crime and to elaborate measures for their neutralization and liquidation within the general regularities immanent in the development of socialist society.

A combination of juridical, sociological, and sociopsychological approaches is characteristic of Soviet criminology. Whether an analysis of a specific crime, the personality of a concrete offender, the causes of a crime, or preventive measures, criminal justice agencies accomplish the study of criminal cases and of the procedures carried out in decision-making. A psychological methodology permits penetrating investigation of the features of the offender's personality and the identification of differences from positive social behavior.

To study crime and other broad categories of behavior, a sociological methodology is necessary to deal precisely with a complex of criminological variables involved in the interaction of economic, sociopsychological, legal, and other processes. From the sociological perspective, an offender's personality is regarded as a complex of moral and psychological properties; aspirations and values; and cultural, educational, and sociodemographic features. Considering that criminal tendencies and particular crimes are linked in terms of the general and special dimensions of criminology as outlined above, it is necessary that analysis take into account the objective and subjective parameters. The necessity means that social phenomena are studied in terms of their impact on the personality in its individual peculiarities as expressed in aspirations, interests, behavioral norms, personal wants, and so on. Preventive measures are couched in consideration of the given person's individual peculiarities.

RECENT HISTORY OF SOVIET CRIMINOLOGY

Rather than being an independent discipline from its beginning, Soviet criminology developed in several distinguishable stages. The first stage was marked by works that examined the problems of crime and its causes in the course of the creation of the Soviet law enforcement agencies and the development of legislation. In those years, the issues received the most complete elaboration in articles by F. E. Dzerzhinsky, P. I. Stŭcka, D. I. Kursky, N. V. Krylenko, and M. I. Kozlovsky.

In the 1920s, independent criminological establishments began to appear; examples are the Center for Studies of Crime and Offender's Personality, the Criminal Clinic at the Kiev Institute of People's Economy, and the Center of Criminological Studies at the Belorussian State University. Some aspects of criminological problems are investigated at the Center of Criminal Etiology and Statistics, and the Center of Criminal Anthropology at Moscow State University.

On March 25, 1925, the State Institute of Studies of Crime and Criminals was founded by a decision of the Government of the Russian Federation. Criminological centers in Moscow, Leningrad, and Rostov-on-the-Don became affiliated with it. The State Institute prepared annual statistical surveys, along with monographs. In 1931, the State Institute was transformed into the Institute of Criminal and Corrective Labor Policy.

Research projects conducted by the State Institute were described in the periodical *Problems of Criminal Policy*. In 1936, this institute merged with the All-Union Institute of Juridical Sciences, and criminological research then was limited to the analysis of the struggle against crime within frameworks useful for the functioning of criminal justice agencies. Some theoretical questions of criminology were considered in studies of criminal law issues. Among the most important publications of the 1930s and 1940s were the monographs prepared by M. I. Hernet, A. A. Hertzenson, and A. A. Piontkovsky.

The intensive development of criminology—enlarging its contribution to the practices opposing crime—was renewed after the Twentieth Congress of the Soviet Communist party in 1956, in keeping with a series of party decisions.

At the end of the 1950s, major law institutes engaged in scientific research began to include criminological problems in their working plans. Some chairs in law schools started to elaborate these problems. In 1963, the All-Union Institute for the Study of Causes and the Elaboration of Measures for Crime Prevention was established to coordinate and direct criminological studies on a nationwide basis. In a decision—"Further Development of Juridical Sciences and Improvement of Juridical Education in the Country" (1964)—the Central Committee of the Communist party of the Soviet Union emphasized the importance of incisive investigation of the causes of crime, called attention to the importance of the elaboration of a scientific approach to crime prevention, and envisaged specific measures for developing criminological research and training personnel.

From 1964 to 1965, the new discipline of criminology was introduced in law schools, with special chairs created at some schools. In its decision "Measures of Further Development of Social Sciences and Strengthening Their Role in the Communist Instruction" (1967), the Central Committee of the Communist party of the Soviet Union played an important part in activating criminological research projects and in broadening their theoretical potential. One of the main directions of the legal studies was set as the elaboration of measures for the prevention and liquidation of crime and other forms of lawbreaking.

The *Manual of Criminology of 1979* is an outstanding achievement in current Soviet criminology because it presents a comprehensive elaboration of its theoretical foundations according to the tasks of each of the following contributors: A. A. Hertzenson, "Introduction to Soviet Criminology" (1965) and "Criminal Law and Sociology" (1970); A. B. Sakharov, "Offender's Personality and Causes of Crime in the USSR" (1961); H. M. Minkovsky, V. K. Zvirbul, and others, "Crime Prevention" (1962); I. I. Karpets, "Problems of Crime" (1969) and "Contemporary Problems of Criminal Law and Criminology" (1976); V. N. Kudriavtsev, "Causality in Criminology" (1968) and "Causes of Law Infractions" (1976); A. M. Yakovlev, "Crime and Social Psychology" (1970); V. K. Zvirbul, "Procurator's Office Activities on Crime Prevention" (1971); G. A. Avanessov, "Theory and Methodology of Criminological Prognosis" (1972); A. S. Shliaposhnikov, "Soviet Criminology at Present" (1973); and some works by groups of authors, such as "Offender's Personality" (1971, 1975) and "Theoretical Grounds for Crime Prevention" (1977).

During 1975-1978, scientific research projects were carried out on complex planning schemes of crime prevention.[2] Monographs described investigations into particular types of crime: property misappropriations, violent crimes and violent mercenary crimes, casual crimes, juvenile and adult crimes, recidivism, and others. General aspects of those studies were the materials for the first Soviet (and Russian) manual, *Criminology*.[3]

ANALYSES OF CRIMINALITY

Among criminological studies generally, investigations of crime and its causes predominate, and they are carried out by both scientific establishments and units of the Procurator's Office and the Ministry of Interior. Analyses have examined criminality in the 1920s, the postwar period, and the 1970s. The research has been conducted at the national, territorial, regional, and district levels; special types of crimes and of offenders have been investigated.

Since 1945, the prevalence of offenses has been insignificant. When the growth of the nation's population is compared with the crime rate, we find that, from 1926 to 1976, the population increased by 117 million and the 1976 crime rate was one-third of the 1926 rate. The level of the decline has varied over time and among regions of the country.

The frequency of the perpetration of crimes varies among the legal categories of offenses: crimes against persons, casual crimes, and official crimes. When the commission of crimes by individuals is considered along a continuum from most frequent to less frequent, we find this order: mercenary, mercenary-violent, violent, abuse of professional position, and casual offenses.

Crimes against the state, mass disorders, and banditry are almost nonexistent; the occurrence of such cases is singular. About half of the cases of especially dangerous state crime deal with the cruelties of the Hitler invaders during World War II.

With scientific and technical advances, prevention and control become more important in dealing with casual crimes connected with technological and environmental considerations.

MULTIDISCIPLINARY ORIENTATION
OF CRIMINOLOGY

Criminological investigations have specificity of purpose and implications that extend into the specialized interests of many disciplines. These two features of criminological inquiry explain its absorption of the data and methods of other sciences, transforming criminological research into a complex exercise in the methodology of dealing with the phenomena being studied.

Broad generalizations at the societal level involve criminology in economic, social, sociopsychological, and demographic analyses and prognoses that are elaborated by economic science, sociology, social psychology, and demography. Research on the personality level is based on the premises of psychology, exposing psychic processes that form the offender's criminal behavior in concrete situations. Working out in detail the issues of individual prevention entails information on the genetics of the given persons, as well as psychology, pedagogies, and medical science. Improving the crime prevention activities also includes the concepts of management and system analysis.

The battle against crime in the USSR is based upon strict observance of the law, making compulsory the criminologists' close cooperation with the juridical science. The connection between criminology and the sociology of criminal law deserves special notice, because sociology studies the influence of social factors on criminal law and the effectiveness of criminal law in its practical applications. The research findings by criminal law specialists are relevant to criminological examination of the impact of the findings on the effectiveness of the crime-prevention system and of the efforts to correct offenders' behavior. Criminology makes wide use of research into criminal procedure, procurator's supervision, and criminalistics in the general area of identifying and eliminating the causes of particular crimes.

Criminology and the corrective labor science share a sphere of research interests—recidivist crimes and their impact on acquiring the morals and customs of the criminal world. Statistical indices underlie the criminological analyses of offenses; these analyses are promoted by the science of criminal law statistics. Probing the problems of prevention turns criminologists to a consideration of the state and administrative laws that offer insights into the tasks and responsibilities of state bodies and social organizations.

CRIMINOLOGISTS: TRAINING AND WORK LOCALES

A new professional has emerged in the USSR—the criminologist—combining juridical and sociological education with knowledge in psychology and other behavioral sciences. The criminologist's principal quality is the ability to think and approach his research in a complex manner. The criminologist should strive to elaborate optimum measures of actual crime prevention. Soviet criminologists generalize the practice of research and of crime prevention to help agencies improve their work. In this connection, V. N. Kudriavtsev suggests that criminological practice be included in the subject matter of criminological science.

The constitution of the USSR stipulates that legality is one of the main principles of state and social life. Combatting crime can be conducted only within the framework of legality. Such a position determines the leading role of lawyers in crime studies and in elaborating measures of crime prevention and control.

Criminology is being taught in all higher educational establishments. The intensive special training of criminologists is accomplished in postgraduate courses. During the last twenty years, a few hundred criminologists took postgraduate courses at the All-Union Institute of the Study of Causes and Elaboration of Measures of Crime Prevention, the academy of the Ministry of the Interior, the All-Union Scientific-Research Institute of the Ministry of Interior, and other scientific and higher educational establishments. Employees of the Procurator's Office and the Ministry of Interior are involved in crime analysis, generalizations of the results of crime combatting, preventive work, and criminological training.

This contingent is educated at the Institute of Advanced Training of Leading Personnel of the Procurator's Office of the USSR.

Scientific and educational establishments award scientific degrees (candidate and doctor of sciences) and scientific titles (senior researcher, docent, or professor) in criminology. The responsibilities of the criminologists who conduct scientific research are defined clearly. Research problems are selected considering the demands of practice, the logic of science development, and the specialized interests of researchers and teachers in higher educational establishments. The work is accomplished in coordination with the plan of each scientific or educational institute and university departments.

A special crime prevention service is operated by the Ministry of Interior. Personnel in the service accomplish criminological duties predominantly within individual crime prevention. Officials of the Procurator's Office and the Ministry of Interior conduct research and crime prevention work simultaneously with other responsibilities of their respective official positions. The introduction of an independent criminologist position in some agencies of the Procurator's Office and Ministry of Interior is at the stage of broad consideration. All criminologists in the USSR are state employees.

The greatest influence of criminology in the USSR is manifested in expanding the scientific foundations for combatting crime in socialist society. In this connection, the social prestige of criminology is quite high.

At present, criminological insights are being especially directed toward elaborating crime prevention measures, conducted at the levels of labor collectives and places of residence.

Criminological establishments carry out studies in some regions and enterprises, the findings of which are used for positive experience, generalization, elaboration of recommendations, and introduction of proposals for organizing legal regulations in the field of prevention. With regard to crime prevention measures at the regional and labor collective levels, the criminologists participate by applying a considerable portion of their research to preventive activities by strengthening the linkages with criminological theory. Law enforcement agencies are planning to introduce scientific achievements into crime-combatting practices.

The data and findings of criminological research are widely used in preparing new legislation and in elaborating economic and social development plans. These contributions are accomplished by criminological sections, laboratories, and departments of scientific institutions of the Procurator's Office, the Ministry of Interior, the Ministry of Justice, and scientific institutions of the republics.

INTERACTION AMONG CRIMINOLOGISTS

Exchange of information among criminologists in the USSR is rather extensive. Periodically, all-union, republican, and local conferences are held for discussions of criminological problems. The All-Union Institute for Study of Causes and Elaboration of Measures for Crime Prevention coordinates criminological studies in the Soviet Union. Issues of crime-combatting practices are systematically discussed at coordination meetings of law enforcement agencies.

The journal *Issues on Crime Combatting* is published regularly, and articles by criminologists are printed in legal and sociological magazines and special editions issued by the Ministry of Interior and the Procurator's Office of the USSR. Monographs are published primarily by the Yuridicheskays Literature and Nauka printing houses. Local, republican, and regional periodicals publish articles by local criminologists.

Since the great majority of criminologists are lawyers, the question of creating a special criminologists' association has not been raised.

Soviet criminologists have close contacts with criminologists of other socialist countries. These contacts are maintained in various forms: joint research, exchange of specialists, information on research findings, practical experience in crime combatting, seminars, and conferences. Once in four or five years a regular congress of criminologists for socialist countries takes place. The Fifth Congress took place in 1978 in Zakopane, Poland, when issues of public participation in crime prevention were discussed. Juvenile delinquency, recidivist crime, and other issues were discussed at previous congresses.

Soviet criminologists are increasingly participating in the United Nations' criminological activities, notably in preparing surveys and reference materials about crime combatting in the USSR and through participation of experts. Soviet criminological institutions take part in the activities of the International Association of Criminal Law, the International Society for Criminology, and the International Society of Social Defense. In addition, international colloquiums on casual crime, criminal policy planning, and other topics have recently taken place in the USSR.

Soviet criminologists constantly analyze the published data and reports on criminological research in other countries, primarily those of the United States, France, the Federal Republic of Germany, Japan, and similar countries.

SUMMARY: CRIMINOLOGY IN THE USSR

Criminology in the USSR reflects the peculiarities of the country's socioeconomic and political structure, historical conditions, specificities of morals, traditions and customs, cultural character, legal system, and level of scientific knowledge. In this sense, Soviet criminology reflects the peculiarities of the functioning of a mature socialist society, its attitude toward crime, and the role of science in administering the social processes.

The aims of Soviet criminology are to eliminate crime as a phenomenon alien to socialist society and to eradicate all causes contributing to crime, while concentrating on crime prevention. Science occupies a leading place in solving the crime problem. Its role was impressively characterized by decisions of the Twenty-sixth Congress of the Communist party of the USSR. The congress drew attention to the growth of science as significant in solving urgent social problems and to the necessity of practical applications of scientific achievements. The congress renewed the advanced development of fundamental sciences and increased effectiveness of applied research. All the recommendations fully referred to criminology, since its major fundamental problem is clarification of ways, mechanisms, and means of crime eradication. Applied research primarily emphasizes the optimization of crime prevention at both social and individual levels.

Soviet criminology has accomplished complex research into the causes of crime in the USSR and their classification. Intersecting philosophy, sociology, psychology, and other branches of science, criminology has contributed to the study of causes at the general social level and at the individual and group level. For a long time, the study of the state of crime has been carried out in the Soviet Union as a whole and in the Union Republics, with special attention given to any peculiarities of the geography of crime.

One of the principal directions of criminological research is analysis of the offender's personality and its typology. The data collected in recent years have provided a generalized picture of the offender's personality structure, its sociodemographic and moral characteristics. Thereby, the principal criteria have been identified for a classification of offenders. At present, the scope of sociopsychological research is broadening. Certain attention is being paid to victimology, with research focused primarily on the properties and qualities of the victim's personality and behavior.

The present stage of Soviet criminology development is characterized by the system-structural approach to exploring theoretical problems in crime prevention. The problems of crime prognosis, planning, and coordination of crime combatting are being solved by complex efforts.

Increased attention is now being given to using the mathematical methods of analysis in order to obtain information vital to crime combatting and to expose the extent of latent crime. In August 1979, a long-term, multi-goal program was introduced to improve the legal order and to strengthen the campaign against crime. Its essence is expressed in a complex approach to strengthening all aspects of crime prevention.

NOTES

1. "The State and Revolution," in *The Essentials of Lenin in Two Volumes*, Vol. II (London: Lawrence and Wishart, 1947), p. 203.
2. See *Criminology* (Moscow: 1979), pp. 40-41.
3. The manual has been published in four editions (1966, 1968, 1976, and 1979).

BIBLIOGRAPHY

The most general view of the present state of Soviet criminology is expressed in law school manuals. Four editions of these manuals have already been issued, and almost all leading criminologists of the USSR participated in their preparation. The first edition in 1966 was directed by A. A. Hertsenson, I. I. Karpetz, and V. N. Kudriavtsev, and the fourth edition by V. K. Zvirbul, N. F. Kuznetsova, and H. M. Minkovsky.

A historical view of Soviet criminology's development may be obtained from the monograph by A. S. Shliapochnikov, *Soviet Criminology at Present* (Moscow: 1973).

Research projects and other studies of crime and its causes and the personality of the offender are covered in the following monographs: A. B. Sakharov, *An Offender's Personality and Causes of Crime in the USSR* (Moscow: 1961); V. N. Kudriavtsev, *Causality in Criminology* (Moscow: 1968) and *Causes of Offenses* (Moscow: 1976); I. I. Karpets, *Problems of Crime* (Moscow: 1969); N. F. Kuznetsova, *Crime and Criminality* (Moscow: 1963); A. M. Yakovlev, *Crime and Social Psychology* (Moscow: 1970); M. I. Kovalev, *Fundamentals of Criminology* (Moscow: 1971); N. S. Leikina, *Offender's Personality and Social Danger* (Leningrad: 1968); and V. N. Kudriavtsev, H. M. Minkovsky, A. B. Sakharov, et al., *Offender's Personality* (Moscow: 1975).

Studies of crime prevention are described in: H. M. Minkovsky, V. K. Zvirbul, et al., *Crime Prevention* (Moscow: 1962); G. S. Sarkissov, *Social System of Crime Prevention* (Erevan: 1975); A. E. Zhalinsky, *Social Crime Prevention* (Lvov: 1976); K. E. Igoshev, *Social Control and the Prevention of Offenses* (Gorky: 1976); V. K. Zvirbul, V. V. Klochkov, H. M. Minkovsky, et al., *Theoretical Fundamentals of Crime Prevention* (Moscow: 1977).

Problems of criminological prognosis and formulation of plans are dealt with in the monograph by G. A. Avanessov, *Theory and Methodology of the Criminological Prognosis* (Moscow: 1972); and by V. K. Zvirbul, *Social Planification and Its Role in the Prevention of Law Violations* (Moscow: 1977).

The criminal justice role in crime prevention is described in the following monographs: G. G. Zuikov, *Causes and Conditions Contributing to Crime Commissions Revealed During the Investigation and Measures Taken to Eliminate Them* (Moscow: 1964); G. F. Gorsky, *Causes of Crime as Exposed During Preliminary Investigation and Their Studies* (Voronezh: 1964); V. K. Zvirbul, *Scientific Fundamentals of the Procurator's Office Activities in Crime Prevention* (Moscow: 1971); N. A. Struchkov, *Soviet Corrective Labor Policy and Its Role in Crime Combatting* (Moscow: 1970); and S. S. Ostroumov, *Soviet Criminal Statistics* (Moscow: 1976).

YUGOSLAVIA

Zvonimir Paul Šeparović

From its early start at the beginning of this century, Yugoslav criminology has followed a variety of theoretical directions. It has responded recently to the worldwide trend of expanding the traditional study of the etiology of criminal behavior, of the removal of its causes, and of correctional programs—as emphasized traditionally—to the total field of crime control, including the study of operational agencies and their impact on criminal behavior. The field of crime control directs special attention to the specifics of the so-called self-protection system in Yugoslav society as a special form of state and self-management (social) control.

This chapter deals mainly with the key perspectives and themes that have dominated and continue to dominate Yugoslav criminology and secondarily with the social and cultural context of its development.

In Yugoslavia, the term "criminology" refers exclusively to academic, didactic, and research-oriented activities and does not include administrative and professional practice within criminal justice agencies. However, before taking up these criminological matters in detail, it is necessary to review briefly the development of modern Yugoslavia.

DEVELOPMENT OF MODERN YUGOSLAVIA

Those who wonder at the dramatic resurgence of "tribal nationalism" earlier in 1971 of Kosovo and Croat nationalism tend to forget that modern Yugoslavia was born only in 1918 on the ruins of the Austro-Hungarian monarchy, when the unification of South Slav nations in the Kingdom of Serbs, Croats, and Slovenes was accomplished.

Up to that time the country's economic, political, and cultural development had evolved along different lines. Yugoslavia's fractured personality goes back to 395 A.D., when the Roman Empire was divided by a border running through the heart of the nation's present boundaries. The modern-day republics of Croatia and Slovenia adopted the Roman Catholic religion and the Latin alphabet; historically, these people have considered themselves part of the West. Economically advanced, this population has a living standard that approximates that of Austria and Italy. On the other side of the earlier dividing line, the people eventually adopted either the Orthodox or the Muslim religion and the Cyrillic alphabet; they have traditionally looked toward the Slavic East. Less developed economically, this area now forms the republics of Serbia (with the autonomous provinces of Kosovo and Vojvodina within it), Bosnia-Herzegovina, Montenegro, and Macedonia.

In 1941, Yugoslavia was occupied by German and Italian armies. Until 1945, the Yugoslav nations were engaged in a harsh struggle with occupying forces on one hand and in a struggle for a socialist revolution on the other hand. Human and material losses were enormous in the fratricidal strife of 1941-1945 that took almost a million lives. The partisan guerrilla movement tied down twenty-six Axis divisions.

The Socialist Federative Republic of Yugoslavia emerged after the liberation in several stages. At the beginning, the peoples of Yugoslavia set out to rebuild their devastated country and economy. Large power and industrial projects were built, and the social structure began to change rapidly. The dispute, and ultimate break, with the USSR and the Eastern Bloc countries in 1948 impeded but did not halt Yugoslavia's development. Broad-based national creativity received fresh impetus with the introduction of worker's self-management (1950) and the adoption of the constitution in 1953.

The subsequent constitutional reforms were designed to advance self-management and to consolidate direct democracy. The so-called Yugoslav road to socialism is really a unique series of experiments in industrial self-management and administrative decentralization through the devices of worker's councils and communes. The socioeconomic system is based on freely associated labor, socially owned means of production and self-management. In furthering the process of decentralization, the constitution of the Socialist Federative Republic of Yugoslavia transferred to the republics and provinces many functions formerly within the jurisdiction of the federation.

Unlike the period between 1953 and 1963—which can be characterized as a decade of stable social development—the years 1964 to 1974 were a time of crises and reforms. The democratic and liberal trends in the internal and external policies were hampered by the centrally organized state security service. The so-called Brioni plenary session of 1966 therefore condemned the excesses of the security police and discussed necessary reforms of this service. In the early 1970s, this turbulence was reflected in the relationships between nations within Yugoslavia, each expressing strongly the sentiments of nationalistic chauvinism. Several extremist groups operating in exile have launched campaigns of terrorism. These extremist groups go by various names, but most are successors of the fascist Ustashi ("insurgents"), who set up a puppet Croatian government under Nazi protection during World War II. Among the acts of violence were the assassination of a Yugoslav ambassador in Stockholm and placing a bomb in the baggage compartment of a Yugoslav airliner, killing twenty-seven persons.

DEMOGRAPHY AND THE ECONOMY TODAY

Yugoslavia is situated in the southeast portion of Europe, mainly on the Balkan Peninsula and partly belonging to Central Europe (the region north of the River Sava, on the northwest side of the country). According to the latest population census, Yugoslavia had over 22.5 million inhabitants in 1981. The territorial distribution of the population is uneven. The northern regions are densely populated, and the central ones are most sparsely populated.

A considerable number of Yugoslavs live abroad where they went many years ago fleeing the invading Turks, or in more recent times, as economic migrants. Around 2 to 3 million Yugoslavs live in different parts of the world, mostly in Western Europe and overseas, especially in the United States and Australia.

After World War II, the country's industrialization resulted in a strong population shift from villages to towns and a decline in the number of people engaged in farming. It is reckoned that today about one-third of the population earns a living from agriculture, placing Yugoslavia among the nations with a medium level of industrial development.

Yugoslavia's system of factory management is new to socialist countries. In most communist countries, a gargantuan state bureaucracy runs all economic enterprises. In contrast, Yugoslavia has turned control over to the workers themselves in the form of elected worker's councils, which have full power to hire and fire managers as well as other employees; set wages, prices, and production goals; and borrow money from banks. Each factory is autonomous and must compete with its rivals, such as for private firms in the West. In spite of this competitive feature, there is much disorder in Yugoslavia's economy. There are signs of worker dissatisfaction, protest, and alienation; there were more than two thousand strikes in the last fifteen years.

In a small but vigorous free enterprise sector, private entrepreneurs operate building and trucking concerns, restaurants, small hotels, and retail stores. Many make more money than their socialist rivals. Peasants, who account for more than a third of the population, are allowed to own land up to twenty-five acres. Indeed, 85 percent of the arable land is in private hands. There are also underdeveloped regions, as a consequence of uneven economic development in the past, especially in the Kosovo Province.

PATTERNS OF CRIMINAL BEHAVIOR

The official statistics of Yugoslavia refer to convicted persons, and, as frequently noted by criminologists around the world, these data fail to cover all the volume and facets of criminality. The official data do not capture the full realities of crime because of the "dark figure" of crime, changes in legislation and prosecution policy, availability of staff and their efficiency, the duration of criminal proceedings, and changes in the jurisdictions of criminal courts.

It has been said that there is nothing new in human behavior itself, although some new trends and certain new forms of criminality have been noted. As opposed to murder, fraud, and theft as forms of "conventional" criminality, there are new forms of criminal behavior like white-collar crime, highjacking and terrorism, and traffic offenses.

In order to evaluate the trends in the number of recorded offenses, it is necessary to compare the frequency rates in addition to considering the absolute numbers. The frequency rate represents the number of recorded offenses per one hundred thousand inhabitants. It expresses more exactly the danger which crime poses.

In the years following World War II, the general rate of crime has been lower than that of the prewar years. In analyzing this time series, Bayer draws attention to the influence of legislative and economic changes, administrative changes, and the increased efficiency of institutions dealing with offenders.[1]

From the end of World War II to 1947, there were no reliable crime statistics. However, it is believed that the major offenses were connected with the war and collaboration with the enemy, as well as those criminal acts involving the defense of the state and the social order. After 1947, criminal offenses against the state (political offenses) consistently declined. On the other hand, offenses against life and limb, against civil liberties and rights, and against the family remained at the same level. Other offenses steadily increased, especially offenses against property, against official duty, against honor and reputation, against the administration of justice, and against public order and legal transactions. Similar trends can be observed in juvenile delinquency with offenses against property dominant.

According to Vodopivec, the main social and political changes can be traced by comparing the dynamics of the structure of adjudicated persons by main offenses.[2] The time series of the offense categories in Table 33-1 is much more influenced by legislative changes, especially for petty offenses, and reflect the macrosocial and political changes only indirectly. In the second and third periods (1957, 1967), violent offenses suddenly increased. The most prominent characteristic of that period was the sudden decrease in offenses against the national economy.

The relative number of persons convicted for political offenses declined sharply because the political and social orders have been stabilized. In addition, the law on amnesty (1962) had a strong influence by clearing all persons who had committed war crimes except those persons who were organizers, initiators, or commanders. The offenders convicted of offenses against honor and reputation have represented as much as 25 percent of all convicted persons in Yugoslavia, but their proportional representation has declined because reconciliation councils were set up in 1960 to deal with these and other minor offenses. Offenders convicted of sex offenses—mostly rape—comprise only 1 percent of all convicted persons, but rape has become relatively more frequent. Offenses against

TABLE 33-1
DISTRIBUTION OF OFFENSE CATEGORIES BY SELECTED YEARS

Offenses against:	Percentage Distribution by Year			
	1947	1957	1967	1977
The state	7.7	0.4	0.1	0.5
Life and limb	12.7	22.3	26.8	18.9
Honor and reputation	10.9	23.4	27.4	14.5
Property	19.1	22.3	18.4	24.8
Economy	35.6	7.9	6.4	7.0
Official duty	1.6	6.7	2.7	3.7
Safety (traffic offenses)	—	—	8.9	18.5
Other offenses	12.4	17.0	9.3	12.1
Total	100.0	100.0	100.0	100.0

Source: Statistical Yearbooks (Belgrade: Federal Statistical Office).

private and social property are among the most frequent. Offenses against the safety of persons and property have increased remarkably, along with the development of road traffic.

As can be seen from Table 33-2, the total number of convicted persons decreased during the years reported. The general trend from 1947 through 1975 has been downward for both the absolute number of adjudicated adults and the frequency rates. For crimes of violence and some other serious offenses over the long term, the rates have either decreased or remained steady. Nevertheless, the crime problem in Yugoslavia is still serious. There are about six hundred willful homicides a year. The number of offenses causing willful bodily harm stirs great concern.

Comparisons of Yugoslav crime patterns with those of other countries are exceedingly difficult, of course, because of transnational differences in statutes, reporting procedures, and cultural interdicts. Criminal statistics are the most frequent means of such analyses, but their usefulness depends on data that approach the standards for comparability. The efficiency of crime detection and the systems of data collection vary from country to country, but the most intricate difficulty is that of the differences among the legal definitions of crimes. Only for crimes with identical definitions—at least similar definitions—can there be meaningful international comparisons.

To deal with these problems, some Yugoslav experts in the field, notably M. Bayer,[3] have undertaken research to determine the comparability of available crime statistics of a number of selected countries. They have endeavored to identify those methodological difficulties involved when data from only a few countries are employed. The central focus has been on dissimilarities among the definitions of crime. Several comparative studies deserve special mention. Skaberne and Šelih[4] have examined young offenders in Poland and Yugoslavia. Criminal-

TABLE 33-2
NUMBER OF ADULT OFFENDERS AND RATES PER
100,000 POPULATION BY SELECTED YEARS

Year	Number of Adjudicated Adult Offenders	Rate per 100,000 Population
1947	136,873	1,528
1950	92,843	940
1955	139,105	1,242
1960	107,940	909
1965	113,877	911
1970	101,915	758
1975	115,649	790

Source: Statistical Yearbooks (Belgrade: Federal Statistical Office).

ity rates for selected property offenses have been compared by Bayer[5] for Austria, Poland, and Yugoslavia.

In comparing sentences served in France and Yugoslavia, Brinc found no significant differences;[6] in both countries, more than three-quarters of all convicts were serving sentences of less than five years. The relative number of prison sentences imposed, however, is considerably greater in Yugoslavia. As of January 1, 1977, France had an imprisonment rate of 38 per 100,000 inhabitants, compared with a rate of 101 for Yugoslavia. France is among the European nations with comparatively low rates, while Yugoslavia is among those with the highest rates. The number of prisoners is increasing gradually in both countries. Increased crimes have brought a harsher sentencing policy in France as revealed by numerous documents. In Yugoslavia, reports on the incidence of crime do not support any interpretation that crime is a social problem requiring a revision of public policy toward increasing the rigor of sentencing.

CRIMINOLOGY AS A THEORETICAL FIELD

Criminology in Yugoslavia went through periods of speculative studies before the comparatively recent development of criminology as a scientific field engaged in incisive investigations of crime and criminals drawing the attention of scholars from many disciplines. In Yugoslavia, these scholars and scientists have been drawn primarily from jurists and much less from psychologists and physicians. Only recently have social scientists given serious attention to the crime problem. Almost all universities offer criminology as a standard course, primarily in law schools. All widely used textbooks in criminology are written by jurists. Only rarely and sporadically is the subject taught in other schools, such as the postgraduate course for psychiatrists taught by the Faculty of Medicine,

University of Zagreb, and at the schools for law enforcement, social work, or pathology.

In the countries that are now a part of Yugoslavia, criminology has had a relatively long tradition. The decades of the late nineteenth and early twentieth centuries produced analyses of criminal policy issues and treatises on juvenile delinquency, short-term sentencing, probation, criminal careers, and similar topics. The modern criminal justice system was emerging at this time. Although beginning as simple formulations only a step from folklore, criminology was increasing its capacity to understand criminal behavior. The influences from abroad were especially marked in regard to the so-called sociological school of Von Liszt, Prins, and Van Hamel. The Italian positivists (Lombroso, Ferri, and Garofalo) were also influential.

The beginning of criminology in Croatia may be connected with the small book, *Kriminala sociologija* [Sociological Criminology] written in 1909 by A. Biankini. The full-scale textbooks in Yugoslav criminology appeared rather late, from 1946 to 1981.[7] Only a handful of persons were teaching courses in criminology before the first of the textbooks appeared, but the instruction expanded markedly in the period after 1960.

Between the two world wars, teaching and research in criminology had been present in the law schools in Zagreb[8] and Ljubljana, and courses have been taught in the law school in Belgrade since 1946. Since World War II, criminology has become a special teaching subject at all the eighteen law schools of Yugoslavia. Nevertheless, it has never been possible to take a university or college graduate program or to earn a degree in criminology exclusively. Some doctoral dissertations have dealt with the subject matter of criminology, such as recidivism and juvenile delinquency.

Several journals specialize in publishing criminological articles: *Revija za kriminalistiko in kriminologijo* [Review for Criminalistics and Criminology] published in Ljubljana; *Jugoslavenska revija za krivicono pravo i kriminologiju* [Yugoslav Review of Criminal Law and Criminology] in Belgrade; and *Penologija* [Penology] in Belgrade. Criminological articles are also published in the journals of law schools and the journals devoted to sociology and psychiatry.

Although heavily dependent on the other disciplines, criminology has been considered an autonomous science. Yugoslav authors have given special attention to the social functions of penal legislation for society as a whole. Criminal law may be considered an instrument of political authority according to the circumstances involved in safeguarding human rights and liberties.[9] From this perspective, penal laws are reflections of the level of culture, civilization, and social relationships attained by the given society.

To understand the behavior of the criminal, one must understand his social environment. Criminologists for the most part have been inclined to look for the causes of criminal behavior in the sociocultural milieu and the person's response to it. The biological or psychological makeup of criminals is not excluded as a factor in certain types of criminals and crimes. Nevertheless, we can emphasize that criminology in Yugoslavia has been centered on sociological criminology. Criminology courses are most often being offered in law schools by professors— such as M. Milutinović—who identify themselves as sociologists specializing in criminology.

The more complex approach of Zlatarić, Vodopivec, Separović, and others suggests that criminal behavior is the result of various personal and environmental circumstances and the dynamic interrelations underlying them. We do not want the study of criminality to be restricted by absolute determinism. On the contrary, "we regard man as a free and equal producer and creator. Therefore, a dynamic approach to criminology could yield better results than a static and factorial one."[10]

Initially, the subject matter of criminology was almost exclusively oriented to the criminal offense and the offender. The traditional, legal definition concentrates on the criminal who broke the law and is sentenced by the court as such. This approach is thought to be inadequate because other sociopathological phenomena interact with criminality. It is not possible to limit the subject matter to the changing penal norms. Several authors began to define criminology as a science that examines criminal offenses as well as other sociopathological phenomena.[11] According to Vodepivec, approximately 14 percent of all research has dealt with other sociopathological phenomena, for example, alcoholism, suicide, and drug abuse. The first analysis of the sociopathological phenomena in Yugoslavia has been done by Stampar, Geric, Bavcon, Šeparović, Zvonarevic, and Najman.[12] Ecological aspects of the problem were studied by Šelih and Pečar,[13] and a theoretical approach was undertaken by Jakovljevic that suggests an integral approach to social pathologies.[14] Yet, other disciplines, such as sociology and education, have thereafter dominated the investigations of such topics.

THE STUDY OF SOCIAL DEVIANCE

The investigation of deviance has attracted increasing attention in Yugoslavia. Two perspectives are noteworthy. First, in peacetime only destructive behavior is included within the sphere of deviance.[15] Second, the concept of deviance has been expanded to refer to behavior directed against human life and progress in socioeconomic development.[16] There also has been comparative research on perceptions of deviance among citizens of several countries, carried out in 1970 in India, Indonesia, Iran, Italian-Sardinia, Yugoslavia, and the United States, published by Newman.[17] The best study in the field of social deviance is the recent study by Janković and Pešić.[18] They present a critical approach to the sociopathological approach in analyzing problems from the standpoint of interactionist and radical criminology.

Jambrek[19] presents deviant behavior in terms of conflict and innovation. First, the concept of legitimacy is questioned on grounds that social groups are internally split into mutually opposing parts, each pursuing its own interests and thus creating its own normative order. Common acceptance of only one set of norms thus masks the reality of the ability of one subgroup to give its own interests and norms the appearance of societal consensus. Second, the main source of behavior labeled "deviant" is seen to be conflict among different normative orders internal to a group. Various sources of normative conflict are also identified and interpreted in terms of anomie theory. Third, some latent functions of deviance are considered, especially those that contribute to the maintenance of the existing normative order and the corresponding vested interest.

Taking into consideration the notions of stigmatization and social deviance and the major problems of contemporary research in criminology, Vodopivec has called attention to the dilemmas of modern criminological science.[20] The penetration of European criminological thought by the American sociological orientation, through Great Britain and the Scandinavian countries, has greatly expanded the subject matter of criminology by pushing the clinical aspects of the offender into the background. Although yet to be synthesized, two views on the offender prevail in the criminological science. The first view defines the offender as a deviant personality; the second considers him as a normal personality adapted to a particular subculture. In principle, criminological science pleads for the limitation of the definitions of offenses and for the development of other services, for example, health and social services. However, the tendency is hindered by the slow and unequal development of such services in different countries and by the unsolved problem of the threat by compulsory intervention to the protection of liberty and personal integrity. Judicial and police systems are intended to protect the social order, the victims of criminal offenses, as well as criminal offenders against the primitive vengeance of people. Being an instrument for execution of legal definitions of crime, the judicial system might thereby accelerate the stigmatization of the individual, consolidate the structures of subcultural systems, and impede general social progress.

Interactional theory (also called labeling theory) was first mentioned in Yugoslav literature in 1971. In 1973, Milutinovic[21] denied that it makes any contribution to explaining the etiology of criminality. Rather, he considered it useful in calling attention to stigmatization as an effect of social control possibly damaging the development of personality.

BIOLOGICAL AND OTHER EXPLANATIONS OF CRIME

Despite the overwhelming sociological orientation of Yugoslav criminality, some criminologists have questioned the adequacy of explanations that make no room for biological influences. Sociological explanations of social actions will continue to be incomplete and inadequate unless the biological bases of behavior are incorporated into them. Psychiatrists argue that biologically based mental defects and pathology weigh heavily in criminality. Regardless of the merits of this argument, the importance of individual personalities and psychological forces in deviance and criminality is obvious.[22]

So-called sociobiology has been echoed in Yugoslavia too. Wilson's basic proposition is that there must be some link between man's genetic inheritance and his culture.[23] As originally formulated, sociobiology made the mistake of making the link too simple and rigid. Excited by discoveries about animal behavior in the wild, by the Darwinian principles of natural selection, and by the mathematics of population genetics and games theory, sociobiologists equated culture with instinct. Genes influence some aspects of human behavior, but culture is unique to the human animal. In culture, the rules of behavior are more flexible, and the individual can reflect on alternatives. The incest taboo, for example, is one of the most widespread of cultural rules. An individual may break the rule, but very few people actually do so.

Modern behaviorist psychology, which pays minimal attention to the influence of genes, stands at the opposite extreme of sociobiology. Concentrating on the outward manifestation of behavior, it sees behavior as being conditioned by the environment and studies how this conditioning operates. In principle, behaviorism contends, the conditioning of—say, pigeons—(Skinnerian researchers' frequent object for experimenting) is no different from that of humans. Aćimović[24] has surveyed behaviorism, its range within criminology, and the contributions of those psychologists who have applied this approach to understanding and coping with criminality. Emphasizing that behaviorism cannot give profound explanations for criminality, Aćimović holds, nonetheless, that this theory can produce considerable results in preventing crime and in the process of resocialization, although such solutions would be only partial.

Aćimović has also written on the psychoanalytic explanation of criminality.[25] He holds that psychoanalysis and Marxism are not in contradiction. It is assumed that psychoanalysis will contribute to the better explanation of certain forms of criminality. Psychoanalytic interpretations risk errors, he says, and psychoanalysts differ in opinions, but these faults are found in other professions as well.

The so-called frustration theory was followed in the first empirical research dealing with delinquent youth in Slovenia. It found that 90 percent of offenses were against property.[26] This theoretical perspective has also been followed in some investigations of adult offenders, especially recidivists.[27]

Social psychology and social psychiatry have had strong impact on Yugoslav scientists through evolving intellectual movements from Freud and Fromm to Laing, Erikson, Szasz, and Skinner. It has been stressed that this orientation is compatible with the general orientation of dialectical materialism,[28] which tends towards a distinctly revolutionary orientation of the social sciences, notably criminology. Criminology, according to Zupancic, would have a critical relationship toward society as a whole—especially towards the political structure—and would actively participate in the oncoming transformation and in altering the present value structure of consumer society toward the new morality of aspiration. Criminality itself, he believes, is a function of society's incoherencies and can therefore be abolished only as a by-product of some basic change in the society by applying its perspective to demonstrate that criminality is a symptom and an index of the need for change. Alleviation of the individual's difficulties and coping with the more general consequences of social pathology are only secondary functions of criminology.

THEORY OF ALIENATION AND MARXIST APPROACHES

The Yugoslav literature defines criminology as a science of social reality as opposed to the policy sciences that deal with social goals. Since this reality must be evaluated, criminology is an "engaged science" rather than only positivist in nature. It has been considered an autonomous science.

Yugoslav criminology has been dominated by efforts to elaborate the theoretical Marxist explanation of the crime problem. Yugoslav authors have employed the alienation theory in the Karl Marx sense that offenders are alienated from possibilities for human creativity because of the effects of disorganization in society.[29] Disorganization has been especially identified with issues related to economic development, industrialization, and migration of people.[30] A greater number of authors suggest a more eclectic approach because they see criminality is not a homogeneous social phenomenon that can be explained by a single theory. They say that the relevance of a given theory depends on the subject under consideration.[31]

East German scholars Erich Bucholz, Richard Hartmann, John Lekschas, and Gerhard Stiller have been dealing with the socialist interpretation of crime, in both capitalist and socialist countries. Criminality in socialist nations has been attributed to various "survivals" and "relics" of capitalism:

Criminality in socialist society is no longer a product of objectively insoluble situations. Instead, it is an individual's specific conflict—conditioned by certain social and personal circumstances—with society, with the state, with minor collectives, or with other individuals, a conflict in which the lawbreaker violates the elementary norms of social behavior.[32]

Some Yugoslav authors have been fighting this naive Stalinistic "explanation" of the crime problem in socialist countries expressed by Eastern European criminologists. There has been bitter discussion between a group of authors with the socialist criminology perspective and a group of authors from Yugoslavia. The Yugoslav authors maintain that deviance, as a specific social phenomenon, is characterized by conflict in a given situation. As early as 1958, it was stressed that criminality is not simply a residue of social organization found in earlier (capitalist) societies but also persists in a new, socialist society because of contradictions thrown up by the process of social development.[33] Thus, the authors reject the thesis that a socialist society emerges without contradictions and that it is a nonconflict society. On the contrary, socialist societies generate their own conflicts, stemming from the social problems and individual disorders to which a new society is not immune.

According to Willem Bonger, the Dutch criminologist, crime must be defined in relation to the social organization within which it takes place. In his very generalized way, he considers economic arrangements to be the basis of all social values and social structures. Capitalism produces a society that encourages egoism, and therefore crime among all classes, Bonger said, and the sweeping away of capitalism will eventually sweep away crime. He attributes not only property crimes and crimes of violence, but also drunkenness and sex crimes to the conditions and assumptions under which the various classes are reared.

The supplanting of capitalism has not swept away crime. On the contrary, besides all the "classical" forms of crime (such as crimes against property and against persons), there are new forms of deviant behavior specific to socialist countries. Among those new forms of deviance are types of offenses against the so-called social property and counterrevolutionary attacks on the state and social organization.

The official Soviet explanation is oversimplified and false in attributing criminality in the USSR to two general causes: first, as a result of capitalist surroundings and, second, as remnant/remains/residue of capitalism in the people's consciousness. This explanation is by no means a scientific approach; rather, it is an ideological approach that ignores the fact that criminality is a result of social disorganization, or "anomy" as it has been called by Durkheim.

The criminological approach to the crime problem in Yugoslavia is more sophisticated and less ideological. The main criminological concepts are present in Yugoslav sociology and criminology.

CRIMINOLOGICAL RESEARCH IN YUGOSLAVIA

The number of criminological institutes in Yugoslavia has increased in the last twenty-five years. In this respect, research has a relatively short history, but an impressive collection of empirical research has been accumulated to provide a foundation for contemporary criminology. The research sometimes comes from a single researcher but more frequently from a team of scientists working together in an interdisciplinary way. Criminological research is financed mainly by funds made available in each republic for all research branches or made available by agencies involved in the administration of justice and other social control responsibilities.

Among the several criminological institutes in Yugoslavia, one was established at the law school in Ljubljana and another in Sarajevo in 1954. In 1961, the Institute of Criminological and Criminalistic Research was founded in Belgrade as the federal institute. In 1962, a state research office was created in Skopje. The institutes in Belgrade and Skopje were merged recently with the local institute for sociology. Lawyers are dominant in the personnel of all these research organizations, but the research teams also include sociologists, psychologists, and psychiatrists.

In 1960, the National Association for Penal Law and Criminology was established and, along with the institute in Belgrade, has organized yearly conferences for the whole country. Meetings and seminars have also been organized by the state institute and state associations established in 1977 in particular republics. Criminological themes were prevalent in the years before 1973. The new Association for Penal Law and Criminology of Croatia discussed the problem of violent crime in 1979 and traffic offenses in 1981; both topics were discussed in terms of research findings.

Methodological Problems

Studies have been largely descriptive and therefore make fewer demands on methodology, but the trend is toward increasing sophistication of design and more collaboration with statistical experts.

The essence of any science lies in its characteristic manner of interpreting reality. The Marxist, dialectic method is characterized by its observation of phenomena in terms of (1) their mutual connection and conditional relations, (2) the processes of their changing, regenerating, and developing, (3) the transformation of quantitative changes into essential, qualitative changes, and (4) internal discrepancies characteristic of certain phenomena. In these respects, the dialectic method brings under observation the struggle between the old and the new, the struggle between what constitutes dying and being born.

It is impossible to separate the method from the practical problem being investigated. The aim of research is not cognition itself, but cognition for the purpose of active change of reality. The humanities in general and criminology in particular, a more recently emerging discipline, seem to be lagging behind the natural sciences in regard to methodology. The whole question is reduced to the degree of exactness required of the humanities relative to the purposes and subject matter of this field of study. Criminology shares a concern that Socrates expressed by saying that, only by facing the man and his situation, can one get to know him well. As a science, however, criminology is opposed to the speculative theoretical orientation. Notable in criminology is a tendency toward empirical methodologies and an interest in quantifying all relationships and social phenomena. The possible excesses of these tendencies, however, are suggested by critics who refer to the "measuring mania" of "sociometry."

A handful of investigations has been made available in Yugoslav criminology. A selected portion of them is presented below without implying either that they provide final conclusions or that further research is unnecessary. Some spheres of research have been scarcely touched, and the brief summary presented here does not include all investigations into recidivism, women offenders, alcoholic and drug-use delinquents, psychotic cases, suicides, violent offenses, economic crimes, traffic offenses, the efficacy of capital punishment, and so on.

As already mentioned, Yugoslav criminology is based on the concept that it is an applied science and has a role to play in criminal policy and in solving serious social problems. It is probably for that reason that violent crimes, economic and traffic offenses, juvenile delinquency, and recidivism have most frequently been investigated and have engaged public discussion. Some of the research on these topics is reviewed in the following sections.

Violence and Tradition

Several investigations have been conducted on violence, its causes and solutions. One of the best is the study of violence in Croatia.[34] Despite severe penalties provided for violent crime (the death penalty or imprisonment up to twenty years for murder), the number of homicides remains high.

The study of homicide in Yugoslavia,[35] conducted by the Institute of Criminology in Belgrade, found that offenders were mainly from the low-income group. Among them, 24 percent had no property and mostly lived in villages as casual laborers for wealthier farmers. The number of murders committed directly for profit was low. It is assumed that murders committed out of animosity and revenge often originate in quarrels over property. Disturbed marital and family relations are another frequent reason, often stemming from the alcoholism or idleness of the murderer or some other member of the family, financial difficulties, or jealousy and adultery. Chronic and acute alcoholism, as in other offenses, represents one of the main causes of homicide.

In his study *Homicide in Slovenia*,[36] Uderman found that 85 percent of the offenders were workers with only an elementary education. Most of the offenders were in the age groups twenty to twenty-nine and forty to forty-nine years, and 35 percent already had a court record. Half of them had already committed homicide. A larger proportion of the offenders (38 percent) was found to be mentally disturbed, and the degree of alcohol intoxication at the time of the offense was extremely high (53 percent).

Pešic[37] found that over 80 percent of offenders were men. The majority of them were sanguinary in temperament; aggressiveness and primitivism were particularly marked. The general tolerant attitude towards homicide also contributes to the commission of this crime.

Social and cultural factors in homicide are evident effects of the history of Yugoslavia which has been the scene of many wars and internal disputes when killing was a common occurrence. Easy provocation to violence is unevenly distributed in a country that shows sharp contrasts and rather different cultural backgrounds. In Dalmatia and other southern parts of Croatia along the Adriatic Coast, homicide is extremely rare; if it takes place at all, it is usually committed by mentally disturbed and other unusual persons.

An ancient blood-feud tradition among Albanians, requiring a death for a death to uphold honor, continues to resist official sanctions in the autonomous Yugoslav province of Kosovo. The usual pattern for a murder of vengeance is for the killer, often designated by tribal leaders, to encounter his victim in a public place, preferably the marketplace, where all can see vengeance exacted. After a fusillade the killer turns himself over to the police to accept punishment. To flee is considered dishonorable. Fears of falling victim to an avenger's bullet have confined about eight thousand Kosovo inhabitants to walled, fortress-like households. Families suffer from the long confinement, malnutrition, lack of medical attention, and nervous strain.

The feuds, an anachronism in a society emerging from isolation and backwardness, hinder ambitious socioeconomic efforts to improve conditions in the province. The authorities are combatting the tradition with harsh punishment, involving the death penalty or prison terms up to twenty years, and with a combination of propaganda and conciliation. The deterrent effect of punishment is doubtful, but in 1977 the new Criminal Code of Kosovo provided stricter sanctions. Although education and economic development have made great strides since World War II, blood-feud killings have increased.[38]

Psychiatrists are showing greater interest in the problem of homicide.[39] Various studies of pathological homicides have shown that schizophrenics commit the greatest proportion of criminal homicides by the mentally sick.[40] The social danger posed by the mentally sick is no longer determined by nosologic principles but by the structure of psychopathologic syndromes and manifestations and by developmental stages of the pathologic process. Comparative studies have shown, according to Krstic, that the depersonalization phenomenon can often be found in the psychopathology of schizophrenic murderers. The difference is statistically significant.

Since only a minority of mentally ill persons shows violent behavior, the psychiatric literature has asked why only this small share of patients with psychopathologic traits commits criminal acts. The question is becoming even more important in light of the present-day sociopsychiatric processes and "extramural" treatment of mental patients, especially in cases of murder. The earlier literature sought to find the causes of murders committed by mentally ill persons, relative to the nature, kind, and intensity of the mental disorder or a psychopathologic syndrome. When these attempts failed to give the desired answers, the more recent literature turned to the premorbid mental structure of the murderer, the field of victimology, and the role of various psychosocial provoking factors:

In endogeno-psychotic murderers anxiety is expressed to a considerable extent. Among paranoid ideas, the idea of jealousy is very pronounced. Among hallucinations, the existence of imperative auditory hallucinations is striking. Alcoholics-murderers are characterized by impulsiveness; they are mentally very labile, hypersensitive, and aggressive. What characterizes murderers with old age mental disorders is that they commit murders in the state of a "mild organic psychosyndrome;" their paranoid symptomatology is nearing a statistical significance. The role of premorbid mental factors in mentally sick murderers is considerable; it is particularly pronounced in murderers-alcoholics and in persons with old age mental disorders. The share of psychosocial factors in mentally sick murderers is also considerable and most pronounced in alcoholics and persons with old age mental disorders, but also in endogenous psychotics (sometimes up to 40 percent). Victimological analyses have shown that the more seriously the murderer is psychopathologically changed, the more the victim is nearer the family circle, while, on the other hand, if in the dynamics of the crime also social factors are combined with the psychopathologic ones, then the circle of victims is enlarged.[41]

Economic Crime

As a detrimental social phenomenon, economic crime is an acute social handicap to Yugoslav society. Despite two decades of research work[42] in the field, there is no agreement either about the concept of economic delinquency and the definition of economic or business crime or about the notion of economic criminal law. Economic offenses can be classified in two main groups. The first group includes the "classical" offenses perpetrated for the purpose of acquiring illegal material or other gain. The second group includes offenses perpetrated to acquire illegal material gain for the criminal's economic organization, for another economic or social organization, or for the community.

The conditions directly related to the crime and circumstances indirectly favoring it are in many respects peculiar to each group. Conditions of particular importance to the second group of offenses are, above all, the following: the relative prevalence of localism and particularism, weak legal discipline, shortcomings in the functioning of the self-management entities, and so on. Adequate attention has not been paid to the problem of setting up a suitable system of social control.

The new forms of criminality call for a reconsideration of the so-called collective responsibility of particular executive authorities within an enterprise, as well as of the individual responsibility of their members. It has been stressed that the existing structure of moral consciousness is not adequate in regard to the protection of social property.[43] Moral, political, and legal consciousness, respectively, are at an insufficiently high level, to countervene deviant behavior in the economic sphere. It is believed to be crucial that moral consciousness be increased in proprietorship relations, particularly in socioproprietorship relations.

The police detect those individuals appropriating social property and those enterprises with unlawful profits. The most frequent offense is bribery, which is very difficult to detect. The enterprises acquire unlawful profits, especially in connection with foreign trade. Abroad, the enterprises provide opportunities to conceal violations of criminal law, of laws on foreign trade, and of other codes. In the past, the courts applied mild sentences to those offenders; they have not exercised a positive influence on the potential offenders. In contrast, administrative sanctions applied to enterprises for duty and foreign currency infringements have been very severe.[44]

When dealing with economic deviance, researchers, depending on their starting point, use the notions of economic crime and of white-collar crime interchangeably. When sociological approach is concerned, they usually adopt the term "white-collar crime," and when the question is managed within the framework of legal norms, they use the expression "economic crime." In a comparison of economic malpractice and crime in Yugoslavia with white-collar crime,[45]

Pečar states that these phenomena in Yugoslavia spring from similar motives, are carried out in similar ways and means, and, above all, are to be found among the same high social strata as in the United States where the term "white-collar crime" was invented. Because of their social status and economic and political power, the offender can also weaken the effectiveness of social control agencies.

Inefficiency in clearing up white-collar crime entails unjustified social differentiation that poses the problem of justice in general and challenges the principle of the equality of man before the law. There have been numerous specific investigations into business deviance,[46] the criminological aspects of foreign trade,[47] the criminal offense of "plunder" in the new criminal legislation,[48] and penal policy in regard to economic crimes.[49]

Traffic Delinquency

Among the very intricate problems for criminal law and social control agencies is traffic delinquency. Various aspects of the general problem, including those of particular criminological importance, have been the subject of more or less successful investigations:[50] traffic offenders and their basic characteristics, specific psychophysiologic characteristics of road traffic offenses, difficulties of identifying the causes of traffic delinquency and framing appropriate penal policy, driving while under the influence of alcohol, and so on. Since alcoholism is one of the major health and social problems in Yugoslavia, a certain proportion of alcoholics is to be expected in the population of drivers and applicants for driving. Drinking contributes to a large number of fatal and other accidents.

A mass seasonal migratory process on a worldwide scale, tourism has recently undergone rapid development which has had explosive effects throughout Yugoslav society. Tourist criminality involves, first, crimes committed by tourists and, second, criminal damages inflicted on tourists, hotels, and catering organizations serving them, or public property used in tourism. One research project in the Dalmatian region concentrates on the structure and dynamics of tourist criminality.[51]

Traffic delinquency is related to individual deviance in the forms of aggressive personalities, so-called accident-prone persons, and faulty driving by abusers of drugs and alcohol, but the individual-oriented approach does not offer a sufficient explanation.[52] From an overall perspective, traffic accidents must be placed within the context of the invasion of the natural environment by human technology. The automobile is a source of great energy, holding risks for life and property. In a continuum from complete safety to grave risk in the use of this great energy, the automobile illustrates the interaction between technological development and the increased opportunities for releasing behavior that violates safety as a fundamental human requirement. In analyzing the social irresponsibility of persons who perpetrate traffic delinquency, the most promising theory appears to be that of modern man's alienation. Accordingly, punishment and repression appear to be inferior as accident-prevention policies when compared with efforts to strengthen a sense of responsibility and to increase awareness of the potential danger of expressing anger through driving. Traffic safety also hinges on the development of defensive measures by individuals, self-managing organizations, and communities.

Recidivism

The serious and complex problem of recidivism has been thoroughly explored. The first investigations were conducted by the Institute of Criminology in Ljubljana,[53] in Zagreb,[54] and in Belgrade where the Thirteenth International Course in Criminology in 1971 provided the opportunity for Yugoslav authors to report on their research.

Polič and his colleagues told of investigations into the temporal and temporal-space symbolism within a group of recidivists.[55] Musek and others dealt with concepts differentiating the crucial attitudes found in a group of recidivists.[56] In research with a sociological orientation, Milosavljević[57] found that recidivism is characteristic of the middle-aged population and of crimes such as property offenses, white-collar crimes, and violent crimes; and that recidivists are involved in 12 percent of the total criminal activity. Arnaudovski and others have published an impressive work on recidivism and recidivists in Macedonia and on primary criminality as well.[58]

DRUGS IN YUGOSLAVIA AND THE FUNCTIONS OF SOCIAL CONTROL

In Yugoslavia, as in other parts of the world, drug use and drug traffic have increased, although, as yet, not to an alarming extent. Organized drug traffic has already appeared, and the structure of drug use and the kind of drugs used have changed. Drug use has reached a broader circle of otherwise nondeviant youth, who most frequently use hashish, LSD, and cannabis.

In the years 1970-1974, Milcinski and Grilc[59] analyzed the drug use patterns of 212 addicts who were outpatients of a psychiatric clinic. The researchers differentiated three groups—moderate consumption, excessive consumption, and dependency—on the basis of the intensity of drug use. The kind of drugs used was also categorized: opiate consumers who may or may not use other drugs; consumers of soft hallucinogenics who may or may not take other drugs with the exception of opiates; consumers of analgetics who do not take opiates and/or hallucinogenics. Of all the addict outpatients, 93.9 percent fell within those three categories; the remaining 6.1 percent were addicted to drugs not mentioned above.

In an epidemiological study of drug use among youths, Spadijer-Dzinić[60] traced the regional distribution of drug abuse, examined the influence of various sociocultural environments on the volume of drug use, described the demographic characteristics of addicts, and otherwise considered the distinctive features of drug abuse. Other investigations have probed the knowledge about and attitudes toward drug abuse among youth,[61] the rehabilitation and resocialization of addicts,[62] outpatient treatment,[63] and the Yugoslav laws relative to prevention of drug addiction.[64] One of the best studies on drugs, juveniles, and crime is that of Singer.[65]

International comparisons of narcotic usage are complicated by the lack of reliable information on usage in earlier periods of history, the exclusion of one kind of narcotic by the use of another kind, the effects of social factors in temporarily inflating usage rates, and the possibility that severe sanctions will strengthen the commitment of initially casual users to drug subcultural groups. Considering the economic, social, and cultural aspects of Yugoslavia's development, Vodopivec[66] predicts that narcotics usage is likely to increase but not in mechanical conformity to quantitative dimensions of trends in some other countries. A carefully developed rationale for prevention, therefore, appears to be appropriate. The Yugoslav press usually treats alcoholism and drug addiction as distinct vices. This distinction may rest on commonly accepted value judgments rather than on any objectively determined differences in the intrinsic nature and consequences of the two vices. In these respects, the existing norms are not relevant to the newly appearing vices that a people have come to tolerate.

MIGRATION: CRIMINOLOGICAL AND VICTIMOLOGICAL RESEARCH

According to Pečar, criminological research and criminal policy in Yugoslavia have rather neglected the intensive migration of the last two decades.[67] Political, economic, and organizational considerations of the increased population movement have not given sufficient attention to the crime proneness and crime victimization of migrants coming to Slovenia in search of employment. The general consequences are similiar for that internal migration and for Yugoslavs who go to other countries. The conception of the migrant as a victim has emerged only in recent years as a perceived social problem and subject for scientific research.[68]

There are no reliable data about Slovene migrants abroad or for foreign workers in Slovenia, but it appears that migrants are generally no more deviant than the native population. Nevertheless, they are particularly likely to engage in some form of misconduct, being conditioned by ethnopsychological and other factors. Alienation, segregation, anomie, loneliness, personal distress, and other difficulties induce them to deviate as a result of being different from the native population and being pushed into a marginal status. They suffer difficulties in maintaining stable relationships with their families and children and in achieving cultural assimilation within a foreign environment. External and internal conflicts and inconveniences lead migrants to avoid formal social control.

There are widely held and persistent notions that the immigrants have disproportionately high crime rates and that the foreign-born have a higher rate of crime than the native-born. Research into the immigrant crime rate in Australia found it to be lower than the per capita rate for native-born Australians.[69] Reports by Frances and Dovey[70] support this conclusion for immigrants, including those of Yugoslav origin.

RESEARCH ON JUVENILE DELINQUENCY

There have been quite a number of studies on juvenile delinquency.[71] A research group from the Institute for Criminological and Sociological Research in Belgrade has completed several studies: "Juvenile Delinquency in Yugoslavia," "Juvenile Delinquency in Industrial Settlements," and "Juvenile Delinquency in Belgrade." These studies examine juvenile delinquency primarily to determine basic phenomenological dimensions, its scope in the observed period, its structural characteristics, particularly the policy for reacting against juvenile delinquents, and the relationships between the qualities of juvenile personalities and educational and therapeutic measures.[72]

Research into juvenile delinquency, runaways, and truants[73] has focused on economic development as a direct or underlying influence on the primary groups that either promote or impede the socialization of minors. The investigation calls attention to the importance of ultimately establishing an association between some indicators of economic development in the residential areas of the juveniles and the functions of the family, school, and peer groups as primary groups. The intersections between economic development and many social and psychological variables are identified as being relevant to the more serious forms and incidence of delinquent and other antisocial behaviors. Rapid economic development brings greater migration, social mobility, and sociocultural change. The impact on the family magnifies tensions among members, weakens child-parent contacts, and otherwise reduces chances for parental influence. Incentives for schooling are reduced to the detriment of educational achievement and to favor truancy. Minors are more likely to run away from home and perhaps to engage in serious crimes, especially when certain personality traits are present.

In another research project,[74] an observed group of hooligans (siledjije) provided legal, social, and psychological data, including their treatment in a special institution. Hooligans are a special category of delinquents who, while committing petty offenses, express disregard for the community's interests and are prone to recidivism that increases the chances for further threats to public law and order, the peace of citizens, or public morals.

Promising new research[75] is concerned with juveniles less than fourteen years of age who are delinquents. It seeks to extend insights on the kind of threat these youngest of all offenders pose for society and what countermeasures would be appropriate. This investigation was continued into 1981 for followup of what happens to these children as they become older.

A crosscultural study has examined data on the relationship between schools and delinquency in the United States and Yugoslavia.[76] The specific question is whether or not the schools generate juvenile delinquency. Most interpretations derived from anomie theory argue that deviant behavior is most likely to appear among lower class juveniles. In challenging this simplistic explanation, the data suggest that social classes are transformed when the school challenges their values and assumptions. The research findings include key variables in delinquency that are remarkably similar for the two countries when differences between the countries are noted.

Research on juvenile delinquency can be grouped around certain themes. The etiology of delinquency has been treated in regard to the influence of constitutional factors[77] and of social and psychiatric problems.[78] Books by Singer and Hirjan, Todorović, and Jašović have dealt generally with different aspects of the complex problems of delinquency.[79] Cultural variables are emphasized in investigations on mass culture and juvenile delinquency,[80] on new "religions" among youth and their ethnic sources,[81] and on subcultural theory and juvenile gangs.[82] Social institutions have been related to delinquency in regard to family disorganization,[83] juvenile perceptions of crime and the relevance of educational countermeasures,[84] runaways from educational institutions,[85] recreational activities as a source and preventive of delinquency,[86] and juvenile gangs.[87] A number of research reports have concentrated on various aspects of responses to delinquency: adjudication of adults for delinquencies they perpetrated as juveniles,[88] the feasibility of treatment of delinquents,[89] the functions of social workers' reports in criminal proceedings taken in behalf of juveniles,[90] disposition of the petty offenses of juveniles and children,[91] and recidivism among juveniles and children.[92]

Skalar and Kambovski[93] have examined the treatment programs of penal institutions. Rejecting the efficacy of deterrence through categoric punishment and rejecting the techniques of behaviorism, Skalar favored therapeutic support of persons in distress and psychodynamic therapy oriented to the active cooperation and receptivity of the clients. His recommendations are consistent with the findings of an experiment in an institution for maladjusted youth where group methods of communication were employed.[94] It was concluded that, in light of the realities of the institution's environment and the level of staff competence, barriers against staff-inmate communication could be overcome only through formidable effort.

RESEARCH INTO THE WORKINGS OF CRIMINAL JUSTICE

Theoretical and applied research overlaps at many points, but none is more important than the common interest in the "dark figure" of crime. Yugoslav writers have emphasized the importance of research into the differences between the magnitude of crime in reality and what is reported officially.[95] That research is especially important to the evaluation of criminal justice administration and to dependable public policy.

The sentencing process of courts has been the subject of several investigations.

The first one was carried out by the Institute of Criminology in Ljubljana.[96] Another research project on this topic used the written justifications for sentences as its data.[97] Cotič examined regional differences in penal policy in regard to the proportion of sentences that were suspended.[98] In a dissertation, Horvatić evaluated previous research on the choice of penalty and offered his own findings.[99]

Several minor studies have dealt with the diagnoses of defendants and convicted persons, evaluating their usefulness and potentiality for unnecessary stigmatization. Other research has considered judicial control over the execution of sanctions, the methods and effectiveness of assistance to released prisoners, training of the custodial staffs of prisons, short-term imprisonment, psychic tension of murderers serving prison sentences, voluntary work of nonprofessionals, and other topics. Vodopivec has investigated correctional institutions for persons serving sentences of one year or less and those for long-term prisoners.[100] Šuković and Arnaudovski have considered conditional release.[101] Mrs. Špadijer-Dzinić, one of the leading penologists in the country, has studied the prison subculture, publishing an excellent book, *Zatvoreničke društvo* [Convict's Society].[102]

In Yugoslavia, the death penalty may be imposed for forty-five different offenses. Much of classical socialist doctrine rejects the death penalty, but it has been in use throughout the history of Yugoslavia and Eastern European countries. Penal and criminological theory tends to give preference to corrections and to reeducation (resocialization) over punishment. Several scholars have made public their opposition to capital punishment.[103] Some research has stressed that psychopaths committing the most heinous crimes are frequently vulnerable to execution, although their mental normality is questionable.[104] In many cases, the death sentence is imposed when the courts are not in a proper position to decide whether or not the defendant is sane.

The goal of rehabilitation was granted priority in Yugoslavia by the beginning of the 1960s. With the support of the social and criminological sciences and the movement called social defense, a new law emphasized the rehabilitative ethos. Abandonment of revenge and retribution has turned attention toward individual prevention and treatment. The classification of adult criminals in Yugoslavia is carried out according to age, recidivism, sex, term of sentence, need for a specific treatment, and capacity for self-discipline. Prison overpopulation has favored a penological philosophy of reduced use of prison sentences.[105]

In 1968, the Association for Penology of Yugoslavia was founded; since 1973, its periodical *Penologija* [Penology] has been published twice a year, with B. Čejović its first editor and Obrad Perić the editor thereafter. All leading criminologists and penologists have contributed papers. For example, Loncar critically has reviewed the assumptions of prisoner self-management.[106] He outlines the forces in correctional institutions that hinder the development of self-rule activities of prisoners, but self-management in prisons has been recommended as a means of encouraging the prisoners' rehabilitation after release from prison.

VICTIMOLOGICAL RESEARCH AND CONCEPTS

The recent growth of victimology has included Yugoslavia. In his work, Makra has studied interpersonal relationships in criminal homicide.[107] Pečar has studied the role of the victim in criminal homicide,[108] victimological components of self-service stores,[109] women as victims of criminal offenses,[110] and victims of criminal offenses and formal control.[111] Selih has studied the victims of illegal abortions.[112]

Yugoslavs have participated in international disputes among scholars over conceptual issues and the dimensions of victimology, especially at the Third International Symposium in Münster in 1979. The main contribution of these deliberations was a call for a general victimology and for new theoretical guideposts. The general victimology recommended would deal not only with the victims of punishable acts but also with the victims of other events such as earthquakes, drugs, ignorance, poverty, and technology. The boundaries of a general victimology must be defined more clearly than they have been, but an independent victimology would not refuse to accept relevant contributions by other fields. Many victimologists believe that the major contributors will be criminologists. It was made clear that a victimology mainly attached to criminological thought must accommodate the victimization of corporations, white-collar crimes, and similar organization-oriented crimes. Victimology has grown and flourished by focusing first on homicide and then on traffic victims, child abuse, victimization of the elderly, and transgressions in the practice of medicine.

FINAL COMMENT

In summary, the years since 1945 have been particularly eventful in the history and sociopolitical development of Yugoslavia as a country. The relevance of this development to the incidence of crime and to Yugoslav criminology and its activities is illustrated here. Yugoslav scholars are taking part in criminological activities, associations, and institutions on the international plane. Yugoslavia has been the host country for a number of international gatherings of criminologists, social psychiatrists, specialists in criminal and comparative law, and the like.

Criminology emerged in Yugoslavia during the 1960s. In the last decade, parallel disciplines—victimology, penology, social pathology, and social psychiatry—have also emerged. All of them fit into the family of the social sciences, along with such other disciplines as sociology and psychology. A look ahead will show that Yugoslavia is going to create an all-embracing conception of the crime problem or safe human living.

NOTES

1. M. Bayer, "Kretanje i sastav sudski utvrdenog kriminaliteta u Hrvatskoj" [Trends and Structure of the Crime Established by Courts in Croatia], *Nasa zakonitost* 1 (1957):46-70, 176-183.

652   ZVONIMIR PAUL ŠEPAROVIĆ

2. K. Vodopivec, "Vergleichende Kriminologie: Jugoslawien" [Comparative Criminology: Yugoslavia], in *Die Psychologie des 20. Jahrhunderts* [Psychology of the Twentieth Century] (Zürich: Kindler Verlag, 1981), pp. 1051ff.

3. M. Bayer, *Uporedna studija o nekim vrstama imovinskog kriminaliteta u Jugoslaviji, Austriji i Poljskoj* [Comparative Study of Crime Against Property in Yugoslavia, Austria and Poland] (Ljubljana: Institut za kriminologijo pri Pravni fakulteti, Publication 15, 1972).

4. B. Skaberne and A. Šelih, "Obravnovanje mladinske kriminaliteta na Poljskem in v Jugoslaviji" [Dealing with Juvenile Delinquency in Poland and Yugoslavia], *Revija za kriminalistiko in kriminologijo* 15, no. 4 (1964):216-223.

5. Bayer, *Uporedna studija o nekim vrstama imovinskog kriminaliteta u Jugoslaviji, Austriji i Poljskoj.*

6. F. Brinc, "Uporaba prostostnih kazni v Franciji in Jugoslaviji" [The Use of Prison Sentences in France and Yugoslavia], *Revija za kriminalistiko in kriminologijo* 31, no. 2 (1980):112-122.

7. J. Tahović, *Kriminologija* [Criminology] (Belgrade: Odbor za objavljivanje predavanja na Pravnom fakultetu, 1946); A. Maklecov, *Uvod v kriminologijo s posebnim ozirom na kriminalno politiko* [Introduction to Criminology with Special Regard to Criminal Policy], Vol. 1 (Ljubljana: Tipkopis, 1947); M. Milutinović, *Kriminologija* [Criminology] (Belgrade: Savre mena administracija, 1969, 1976, 1979); K. Vodopivec, et al., *Kriminologija* [Criminology] (Zagreb: Narodne novine, 1966); R. Kupčević-Mladenovic, *Kriminologija* [Criminology] (Sarajevo: Univerzitet u Sarajevu, 1978); Z. Horvatic, *Elementarna kriminologija* [Elementary Criminology] (Zagreb: Liber, 1981); Z. Šeparović, *Kriminologija i socijalna patologija* [Criminology and Social Pathology] (Zagreb: Pravni fakultet, 1982).

8. Through E. Miller, the law school in Zagreb had been active since 1907.

9. B. Zlatarić, "Stav suvremenog zakonodavca prema novim tendencijama moderne kriminologije i kriminalne politike" [Contemporary Legislature's Attitudes Toward New Tendencies of Modern Criminology and Criminal Policy], *Revija za kriminalistiko in kriminologijo* 11, no. 4 (1960):247-249.

10. Ibid.

11. Šeparović, *Kriminologija i socijalna patologija*; K. Vodopivec, "Kriminologija in socialna patologija" [Criminology and Social Pathology], *Zbornik znanstvenih razpray* 39 (1973):1-15.

12. A. Stampar, *Socijalna medicina* [Social Medicine] (Zagreb: Institut za socijalnu medicinu, 1925); R. Geric, *Socijalna medicina (Opsti deo)* [Social Medicine, General Part] (Belgrade: Zavod za izdavanje udzbenika SRS, 1964); L. Bavcon, et al., *Socialna patologija* [Social Pathology] (Ljubljana: Mladinska knjiga, 1969); V. N. Najman, *Sociopatologija u socijalističkom društvu* [Social Pathology in Socialist Society] (Belgrade: Vuk Karadzic, 1973); Šeparović, *Kriminologija i socijalna patologija*; M. Zvonarevic, *Socialna psihologija* [Social Psychology] (Zagreb: Skolska knjiga, 1972).

13. A. Šelih, "Nekaj misli o prostorskem raziskovanju socialnopatoloških pojavov" [Some Reflections on Ecological Research on Socialpathological Phenomenon], *Revija za kriminalistiko in kriminologijo* 18, nos. 3-4 (1967):140-142; J. Pečar, "Odklonskost porajalna območja v urbani Ljubljani" [Areas Within the City of Ljubljana Breeding Deviance], *Revija za kriminalistiko in kriminologijo* 26, no. 2 (1975):109-124.

14. V. Jakovljevic, *Uvod u socijalnu patologiju* [Introduction to Social Pathology] (Belgrade: Naučna knjiga, 1971).

15. K. Vodopivec, "Naučno istraživanje i kriminalna politika" [Scientific Research and Criminal Policy], *Jugoslavenska revija za kriminologiju i krivično pravo* 9, no. 2 (1971):209-232.

16. Najman, *Sociopatologija u socijalističkom društvu.*

17. G. Newman, *Comparative Deviance: Perception and Law in Six Cultures* (New York: Elsevier, 1976).

18. I. Janković and V. Pešić, *Društvene devijacije—kritika socijalne patologije* [Social Deviance—Critic of Social Pathology] (Belgrade: Visa skola za socijalne radnike, 1981).

19. P. Jambrek, *Družbeno soglasje o pravu in sodstvu* [Social Agreement on Law and Justice] (Ljubljana: Pravna fukulteta-DDU Univerzum, 1979), pp. 52-96.

20. Vodopivec, "Naučno istrazivanje i kriminalna politika."

21. M. Milutinovic, "Osnovne tendencije u savremenoj kriminologiji" [Basic Tendencies in Modern Criminology], *Jugoslavenska revija za kriminologiju i krivično pravo* 11, no. 3 (1973):353-376.

22. Zvonarevic, *Socijalna psihologija*; Z. Šeparović, "Lombroso i biologizam danas" [Lombroso and Biological Theories Today], *Zbornik Pravnog fakulteta u Zagrebu* 30, no. 3 (1980):329-336; M. Aćimović, "Hromosomi i kriminalitet" [Chromosomes and Criminality], *Jugoslavenska revija za kriminologiju i krivično pravo* 10, no. 1 (1972):38-52.

23. E. O. Wilson, *Sociobiology: The New Synthesis* (Cambridge, Mass.: Belknap, 1975).

24. M. Aćimović, "Biheviorizam u kriminologiji" [Behaviorism in Criminology], *Jugoslavenska revija za kriminologiju i krivično pravo* 13, no. 2 (1975):219-232.

25. M. Aćimović, "Psihoanalitica objasnjenja kriminaliteta" [Psychoanalytical Explanations of Criminality], *Jugoslavenska za kriminologiju i krivično pravo* 10, no. 4 (1972):563-579.

26. M. Kobal in Vodopivec, et al., *Kriminologija*; S. Saksida, "O motivacijskih mehnizmih in frustrackjskih stereotipih" [On Motivation Mechanism and the Frustration Stereotype], *Kriminalistična družba* 10, no. 2 (1957):103-114.

27. M. Kobal, "Eksperimentalno proučevanje osnovnih osebnostnih značilnosti povratnikov" [Experimental Studies of Basic Personal Traits of Recidivists], *Revija za kriminalistiko in kriminologijo* 15, no. 3 (1964):171-190.

28. See Z. Šeparović, "O drustvenoj funkciji psihijatrije" [On Social Functions of Psychiatry], *Nase teme* 21, no. 2 (1977):396-406.

29. Milutinovic, *Kriminologija*; P. Kobe, "Znanstevna revolucija in kazensko pravo" [Scientific Revolution and Criminal Law], *Revija za kriminalistiko in kriminologijo* 20, no. 4 (1969):238-245; I. Josifovski, *Kriminalitet i drugi slični oblici devijantnog ponašanja kao izraz otudenja čovjeka* [Criminality and Other Similar Forms of Deviant Behavior as an Expression of Alienated Behavior] (Skopje: Disertscija, 1965); Bavcon, *Socijalna patologija.*

30. A. Todorović, et al., *Malojetnička delinkvencija u Beogradu* [Juvenile Delinquency in Belgrade] (Belgrade: Institut za kriminologija i kriminalistička istraživanja, 1970); M. Petrović and D. Radovanovic, *Maloljetni delinkventi, bijeg od kuce bezanje od skole* [Juvenile Delinquent, Runaway from Home and School] (Belgrade: Institut za kriminologija i kriminalistička istraživanja, 1977).

31. Šeparović, *Kriminologija i socijalna patologija*; K. Vodopivec, "Sodobne sociološke teorije o socijalno ptakoških pojavih" [Contemporary Sociological Theories of Social Pathological Phenomenon], *Revija za kriminalistiko in kriminologijo* 23, no. 3 (1972):140-150; Acimovic, *Pravci kriminalne psihologije.*

654 ZVONIMIR PAUL ŠEPAROVIĆ

32. E. Buchholz, et al., *Sozialistische Kriminologie* [Socialist Criminology] (Berlin: Staatsverlag der DDR, 1971).

33. L. Bavcon, *Kriminalna politika in njene tendence v socijalisticki druzbi* [Criminal Policy and Its Tendencies in Socialist Society] (Ljubljana: Cankarjeva zalozba, 1958).

34. M. Singer, "Neki modaliteti kriminalnog nasilja" [Some Aspects of Crimes of Violence], *Defektologija* 15, no. 1 (1979):9-44.

35. V. Pešić, *Ubojstva u Jugoslaviji* [Homicides in Yugoslavia] (Belgrade: Institut za kriminoloska i socioloska istraživanja, 1972).

36. B. Uderman, "Uboji v Sloveniji" [Homicide in Slovenia], *Revija za kriminalistiko in kriminologijo* 23, no. 1 (1972):13-20.

37. Pešić, *Ubojstva u Jugoslaviji.*

38. In the last ten years, several studies have been directed to blood feuds.

39. B. Kapapamadija, *Ubistvo, psihopatologija i sudska psihijatrija* [Homicide, Psychopathology and Forensic Psychiatry] (Novi Sad: Matica Srpska, 1981).

40. Kusej has found that psychopathic persons represent 6 percent of all murderers, but their share of the total population is estimated to be between 3 and 8 percent: M. Kusej, "Psihiatricni pogledi obravnavanja storilcev ubojev" [Psychiatric Aspects of Dealing with Perpetrators of Criminal Homicide], *Revija za kriminalistiko in kriminologijo* 23, no. 1 (1972):91-97.

41. A. Sila, "Psihopatološka obilježja počinitelja krivičnog djela ubojstva" [Psychopathological Traits of Murderers], *Socijalna psihijatrija* 5, no. 1 (1977):3-87.

42. P. Kobe, "Meje represije na području gospodarskih deliktov" [Repression's Limit to Economic Offenses], *Revija za kriminalistiko in kriminologijo* 24, no. 4 (1973):275-286.

43. S. Pihler, "Problem odredivanja pojma kriminaliteta i utvrdivanja njegove dinamike i strukture" [The Problem of Definition of Crime and Its Dynamics and Structure], *Jugoslavenska revija za kriminologiju i krivično pravo* 8, no. 3 (1969):396-405.

44. A. Stezinar, "Nevarne oblike gospodarske kriminaliteta" [Dangerous Forms of Economic Offenses], *Revija za kriminalistiko in kriminologijo* 24, no. 2 (1973):152-159.

45. J. Pečar, "Kriminaliteta belong ovratnika in druzbeno nadzorstvo" [White-Collar Crime and Social Control], *Revija za kriminalistiko in kriminologijo* 24, no. 1 (1973):25-38.

46. J. Pečar, "Podjetniskoskupinska/gospodarskoposlovna/odklonost" [Corporate/Business/Crime], *Revija za kriminalistiko in kriminologijo* 30, no. 4 (1979):270-282.

47. M. Deisinger, "Gospodarski kriminal v zunanji trgovini" [Business Crime Within the Foreign Trade], *Revija za kriminalistiko in kriminologijo* 25, no. 1 (1974):14-19.

48. J. Buturovic, "Krivicno delo pljacke u novom krivicnom zakonodavstvu" [The Criminal Offense of Plunder in the New Criminal Law], *Jugoslavenska revija za kriminologiju i krivično pravo* 15, no. 3 (1977):57-70.

49. D. Atanacković, "Kaznena politika u oblasti privrednog kriminaliteta" [Sentencing Policy for Economic Crimes], *Jugoslavenska revija za kriminologiju i krivično pravo* 11, no. 1 (1973):69-90.

50. A. Makra, *Ugrožavanje sigurnosti cestovnog saobracaja* [Endangering Road Traffic Safety] (Zagreb: Ured za kriminalisticka vjestacenja, 1967); V. Vasilijević and M. Radovanovic, *Saobracajni prestupnici* [Traffic Offenders] (Belgrade: Institut za kriminologija i kriminalistička istraživanja, 1975); Z. Šeparović, "Sigurnost i odgovornost u prometu" [Safety and Responsibility in Traffic] (Sisak: Jedinstvo, 1969).

51. A. Carić, "Kriminalitet i turizam" [Crime and Tourism] *Jugoslavenska revija za kriminologiju i krivič pravo* 15, no. 2 (1977):65-82.

52. Šeparović, "Sigurnost i odgovornost u prometu."

53. M. Bayer, et al., *Problemi povrata* [Problems of Recidivism] (Ljubljani: Institut za kriminologijo pri Pravni fakulteti v Ljubljani, 1962).

54. T. Marković, "O recidivizmu" [On Recidivism], *Narodna milicija*, nos. 11-12 (1958):78-90.

55. M. Polič, et al., "Časovni in časovno prostorni simbolizem pri skupini delinkventov povratnikov [Temporal and Temporal-Space Symbolism Within a Group of Recidivists] *Revija za kriminalistiko in kriminologijo* 22, no. 4 (1971):266-270.

56. J. Musek, et al., "Prostorsko razločevanje pojmov kot kazalnik kritičnih stališč pri skupini prestopnikov-povratnikov" [Space Differentiation of Concepts as an Indicator of Critical Attitudes in a Group of Recidivists], *Revija za kriminalistiko in kriminologijo* 22, no. 3 (19710:188-192.

57. M. Milosavljević, *Izmedu neslobode* [Between Prisons] (Belgrade: "Ideje," 1975).

58. L. Arnaudovski and V. Caceva, *Provtorot i povtornicite* [Recidivism and Recidivists] (Skopje: Institut za Socioloski i politicko-pravni istraživanje, 1979).

59. L. Milcinski and A. Brilc, "Uzivalci drog—poskus prakticne klasifikacije" [Drug-users—An Essay of Practical Classification], *Revija za kriminalistiko in kriminologijo* 26, no. 4 (1975):251-259.

60. J. Špadijer-Dzinić (ed.), *Droga i mladi* [Drugs and Youth] (Belgrade: Savremena administracija, 1980).

61. M. Petrović in Špadijer-Dzinić, *Droga i mladi*.

62. J. Bukelić in Špadijer-Dzinić, *Droga i mladi*.

63. S. Petrović in Špadijer-Dzinić, *Droga i mladi*.

64. O. Peric in Špadijer-Dzinić, *Droga i mladi*.

65. M. Singer, *Drogs, omladina i kriminalitet* [Drugs, Youth and Crime] (Zagreb: Sveučiliste u Zagrebu, 1975).

66. K. Vodopivec, "Uloga društvene kontrole i represije u sprecavanju uzivanja opojnih droga" [The Role of Social Control and Repression in Combatting Drug Use], *Jugoslavenska revija za kriminologiju i krivično pravo* 8, no. 3 (1970):470-488.

67. J. Pečar, "Kriminološki pogledi na migracije" [Criminological Views on Migration], *Revija za kriminalistiko in kriminologijo* 31, no. 2 (1980):113-123.

68. Šeparović, *Kriminologija i socijalna patologija*, pp. 127-134.

69. Z. P. Šeparović, "Migrant and Crime," in *Third International Symposium on Victimology* (Münster: 1979) (Berlin and New York: W. de Gruyter, 1981).

70. R. D. Frances, *Migrant Crime in Australia* (St. Lucia: University of Queensland Press, 1981).

71. M. Bayer, et al., *Perpetrators of Criminal Offenses Under the Age of Fourteen (Final Report)* (Zagreb: Zagreb University School of Law, Department of Criminal Law, 1974); Z. B. Jasovic, *Kriminologija maloletnicke delinkvencije* [Criminology of Juvenile Delinquency] (Belgrade: Naucna knjiga, 1978); O. Peric, *Krivicnopravni polozaj maloljetnika s posebnim osvrtom na jugoslovensko i francusko pravo* [Juvenile Delinquent in Criminal Law with Special Regard to Yugoslav and French Law] (Belgrade: Institut za kriminoloska i socioloska istraživanja, 1975); O. Matić, *Ispitivanje licnosti maloletnih delinkvenata* [Research on the Personality of Juvenile Delinquents] (Belgrade: Institut za kriminoloska istraživanja, 1974).

72. A. Todorović, *Prestupnistvo maloletnika u Beogradu* [Juvenile Delinquency in Belgrade] (Belgrade: Institut za kriminoloska i socioloska istraživanja, 1970); A. Todorović, *Prestupnistvo maloletnika u industrijskim naseljima* [Juvenile Delinquency in Industrial Settlements] (Belgrade: Institut za kriminoloska i socioloska istraživanja, 1966); D. Lazarevic,

Prevencija maloletnicke delinkvencije [Prevention of Juvenile Delinquency] (Belgrade: Institut za kriminoloska i socioloska istraživanja, 1971).

73. M. Petrović and D. Radovanovic, *Prestupnistvo maloletnika, bezanje od kuće, bezanje od skole* [Juvenile Delinquency, Runaways, Truancy] (Belgrade: Institut za kriminoloska i socioloska istraživanja, 1977).

74. O. Matić, et al., *Siledjije* [Hooligans] (Belgrade: Institut za kriminoloska i socioloska istraživanja, 1966).

75. M. Bayer, *Perpetrators of Criminal Offenses Under the Age of Fourteen*.

76. D. E. Frease, "Sole in mladinsko prestupnistvo v Jugoslaviji in ZDA" [The Schools and Juvenile Delinquency in Yugoslavia and the United States], *Revija za kriminalistiko in kriminologijo* 22, no. 1 (1971):11-19.

77. A. Kos-Mikus, "Vloga konstitucionalnih dejavnikov pri razroju negativnih vedenjskih oblik otrok in mladoletnikov" [The Role of Constitutional Factors in the Development of Behavioral Disorders in Children and Juveniles], *Revija za kriminalistiko in kriminologijo* 24, no. 2 (1973):115-120.

78. Jasovic, *Kriminologija maloljetnicke delinkvencije*.

79. M. Singer and F. Hirjan, *Maloljetnicko krivicno pravo* [Criminal Law for Juveniles] (Zagreb: Informator, 1979); A. Todorović, "Teorija subkultura i maloljetnicke bande" [Theory of Subculture and Juvenile Gangs], *Jugoslavenska revija za kriminologiju i krivično pravo* 11, no. 1 (1973):54-67.

80. A. Todorović, *Masovna kultura i maloletničko prestupništvo* [Mass Culture and Juvenile Delinquency] (Novi Sad: 1971).

81. L. Milcinski, "Pojav novih 'religij' med mladimi in njihovo etiogenetako ozadje" [New "Religions" Among the Young and Their Ethiogenetic Background], *Revija za kriminalistiko in kriminologijo* 24, (1973):213-218.

82. Todorović, *Teorija subkultura i maloljetnicke bande*.

83. A. Šelih, "Dezorganizacija družine in njen vpliv na mladinsko delinkvenco" [Disorganization of the Family and Its Influence on Juvenile Delinquency], *Revija za kriminalistiko in kriminologijo* 22, no. 4 (1971):251-257.

84. T. Brejc, "Mladoletnikovo vrednotenje kazenskega postopka in izvrševanje kazenskih sankcij" [Juvenile's Perception of Criminal Procedure and Implementation of Educational Measures], *Revija za kriminalistiko in kriminologijo* 4 (1972):246-255.

85. B. Skaberne, "Pobegi gojencev iz vzgojnih zavodov" [Escapes from Educational Institutions], *Revija za kriminalistiko in kriminologijo* 25, no. 4 (1974):285-295.

86. Jasovic, *Kriminologija maloljetnicke delinkvencije*.

87. A. Šelih, "Moznosti za obravnavanje mladinskega prestopnistva" [Possibilities for Treating Juvenile Offenders], *Revija za kriminalistiko in kriminologijo* 25, no. 2 (1974):85-94.

88. F. Brinc, "Sojenje polnoletnim osebam za kazniva dejanja, storjena v mladoletnosti" [Judging of Adults for Criminal Offenses Perpetrated When They Were Juveniles], *Revija za kriminalistiko in kriminologijo* 25, no. 3 (1974):169-177.

89. A. Šelih, "Možnosti za obravnavanje mladinskega prestopništva."

90. K. Vodopivec, "Vloga poročil socialno varstvenih organov v kazenskem postopku protiv mladoletnikom" [The Role of Social Worker's Reports Within the Criminal Proceedings on Behalf of Juveniles], *Revija za kriminalistiko in kriminologijo* 25, no. 1 (1974):3-13.

91. A. Šelih, "Prekrski mladoletnikov in nacin njihovega obravnavanja" [Juvenile's

Petty Offenses and Their Disposal], *Revija za kriminalistiko in kriminologijo* 24, no. 3 (1973):219-227.

92. D. Davidović, "Recidivizam maloletnika i dece" [Recidivism in Youth and Children], in *Problemi povrata* [Problems of Recidivism] (Belgrade: Institut za kriminoloska i socioloska istraživanja, 1971).

93. V. Skalar, "Kazen ali tretman" [Punishment or Treatment], *Revija za kriminalistiko in kriminologijo* 26, no. 4 (1975):274-284; V. Kambovski, "Resocijalizacija i klasna suština krivicnog prava" [Resocialization and Class Meaning of Penal Law], *Jugoslavenska revija za kriminologiju i krivicno pravo* 14, no. 3 (1976):307-332.

94. K. Vodopivec, et al., *Eksperiment u Logatcu* [Experiment in Logatec] (Belgrade: 1974); also see K. Vodopivec (ed.), *Maladjusted Youth: An Experiment in Rehabilitation* (London: Saxon House, 1974).

95. Šeparović, *Kriminologija i socijalna patologija*.

96. M. Bayer and B. Uderman, *Kriteriji za odmjeravanje kazne od strane sudova u Sloveniji* [Criteria in the Sentencing Practice of the Slovene Courts] (Ljubljana: Institut za kriminologiju, 1967).

97. L. Bavcon, et al., *Individualizacija kazni v praksi naših sodisc* [Individualization of Punishment in the Courts' Practice] (Ljubljana: Institut za kriminologijo, 1968).

98. D. Cotič, et al., *Uslovna osuda, sudska opomena i oslobodenje od kazne* [Conditional Sentence, Admonition and the Exempt Form of Punishment] (Belgrade: Institut za kriminoloska i socioloska istraživanja, 1975).

99. Z. Horvatić, *Izbor kazne u jugoslavenskom krivicnom pravu i sudskoj praksi* [Option of Punishment in Yugoslav Penal Law and Court Practice] (Zagreb: Pravni fakultet, 1980).

100. Vodopivec, *Kriminologija*.

101. M. Šuković, *Uslovni otpust* [Parole] (Belgrade: Institut za kriminoloska i socioloska istraživanja, 1971).

102. J. Špadijer-Dzinić, *Zatvoreničke društvo* [Convict's Society] (Belgrade: Institut za kriminoloska i socioloska istraživanja, 1973).

103. B. Zlatarić, "O sistemu represivnih mjera prema odraslima po jugoslavenskom krivicnow zakonodavstvu" [The System of Repressive Measures in Yugoslav Criminal Law], *Jugoslavenska revija za kriminologiju i krivično pravo* 4, no. 2 (1966):195-216; Z. Šeparović, "Smrtna kazna u svijetu nasilja" [Death Penalty in the World of Violence], in M. Zurl, *Na smrt osudeni* (Zagreb: A. Cesarec, 1976); I. Jankovic, "O kazni i protiv smrtne kazne" [On Punishment and Against the Death Sentence], *Socioloski pregled* 14, nos. 3-4 (1980):97-112.

104. Z. Šeparović, "Psihopatske (sociopatske) licnosti i smrtna kazna" [Psychopaths—Sociopaths—Personality and the Death Penalty], *Pitanja* 4, no. 10 (1972):2047-2060.

105. F. Brinc, "Uporaba prostotnih kazni v Franciji in Jugoslaviji" [The Use of Prison Sentence in France and Yugoslavia), *Revija za kriminalistiko in kriminologijo* 31, no. 2 (1980):102-112.

106. R. Loncar, "Kriticki osvrt na samoupravu osudenih i osnovne pretpostavke za njeno uspesno funkcionisanje" [Critical Review of Prisoner Self-Management and Basic Suppositions for Its More Successful Functioning], *Penologija* 6, nos. 1 and 2 (1978): 29-42.

107. A. Makra, "Interpersonalni odnosi kod ubojstva," *Prilog* 4 (1961):10-13.

108. J. Pečar, "Vloga žrtev pri ubojih na Slovenskem" [The Role of the Victim in

Criminal Homicide in Slovenia], *Revija za kriminalistiko in kriminologijo* 21, no. 4 (1971):258-265.

109. J. Pečar, "Viktimološke sestavine samopostrezne trogovine" [Victimological Components of Self-Service Stores], *Revija za kriminalistiko in kriminologijo* 29, no. 4 (1978):264-274.

110. J. Pečar, "Ženske kot zrtve (kazenskih dejanj)" [Women as Victims of Criminal Offenses], *Revija za kriminalistiko in kriminologijo* 31, no. 4 (1980):289-300.

111. J. Pečar, "Žrtve kaznivih dejanj in formalno nadzorstvo" [Victims of Criminal Offenses and Formal Control], *Revija za kriminalistiko in kriminologijo* 30, no. 3 (1979):192-202.

112. A. Šelih, "Žrtve pri nedovoljenem splavu in homoseksualnosti" [The Victims of Illegal Abortion and Homosexuality], *Revija za kriminalistiko in kriminologijo* 22, no. 2 (1972):73-79. See also Z. Šeparović, "Victimology: A New Approach in the Social Sciences," in *Victimology: A New Focus*, Vol. 1 (Toronto and London: Lexington Books, 1974), pp. 15-25; Z. Šeparović, "Some Reflections on the Victim, Law Enforcement, and the Rights of the Victim in the United States of America," in *Victimology: A New Focus*, Vol. 2 (Toronto and London: Lexington Books, 1974), pp. 29-41.

BIBLIOGRAPHY

Carić, A. et al., *Turistički kriminalitet i njegova prevencija* [Touristic Criminality and Its Prevention]. Split: Pravni fakultet Split i Naša zakonitost, 1981.
The great and sudden expansion of tourism in Yugoslavia has produced a seasonal upsurge in crime and various sociopathological phenomena. This work reports on research (1971-1975) in the Dalmatian region where some 96 percent of offenses are against property. The research gives special attention to the personalities of offenders and victims and to preventive and repressive measures. "Touristic delinquency" includes crimes, other punishable acts, and sociopathological phenomena in the tourist season and connected with the aggregate of relationships involving travel and the stay of visitors.

Davidović, D., O. Matić, B. Vukacinović, and B. Vucinić. *Kategorizacija kazneno-popravnih domova i klasifikacija osudenih lica u Jugoslaviji* [Categorization of the Penal Corrective Houses and Classification of Convicted Persons in Yugoslavia]. Belgrade: Institut za kriminoloska i socioloska istraživanja, 1970.
Classification systems for convicted persons in Yugoslavia is compared with those in the United States and the Soviet Union. Yugoslav legislation provides the basis for a modern system, but it has not been implemented. Each penal institution has a variety of treatment reactions to inmates without giving much attention to their actual needs.

Milutinović, M. *Kriminologija sa osnovima kriminale politike* [Criminology with Elements of Criminal Policy]. Belgrade: Savremena administracija, 1976.
The leading Yugoslav criminologist with a Marxist-sociological orientation, the author draws from the literature of both the East and the West in this textbook that connects basic criminology with elements of criminal policy. His textbook has been used in all Yugoslav universities.

Petrović, M., et al. *Droga i mladi* [Drug Abuse and Youth]. Belgrade: Privredna štampa, 1980.

The contributors to this volume take differing approaches to the drug problem: the epidemiology of drug abuse, the regional and sociocultural distribution of drug abuse among youth, the social and demographical characteristics of addicts, the level of knowledge of drug addiction among youth, their attitudes toward drug use, the methods of the hospital-based programs of rehabilitation and resocialization for drug-dependent adolescents, outpatient treatment, penal measures associated with obligatory treatment, and the relationship between Yugoslav law and the prevention of drug addiction.

Spomenica prof. Bogdanu Zlatariču [Memorial to Professor Bogdan Zlatarić]. *Zbornik Pravnog fakulteta* 28, nos. 3 and 4 (1978).
This memorial edition of the journal of the Law School, University of Zagareb, is dedicated to the late Bogdan Zlatarić (1912-1977), professor at the University of Zagreb and a prominent expert in criminal law, international law, and other penal sciences including penology and criminology. Drawn from Yugoslavia and abroad, the contributors deal with many topics: the sentencing process, politics of crime prevention, mentally disturbed offenders, international and comparative penal policy, comparison of the execution of penal sanctions in the United States and Mexico, determination of punishments in criminal law, rehabilitation, capital punishment, ecology, juvenile penal law, international penal law, socialist penal law, protection of privacy, criminal expertise, European criminal law, and a review of criminological themes treated in Zlatarić's scientific work.

Vasilijević, V., and D. M. Radovanović. *Saobraćajni prestupnici* [Traffic Offenders]. Belgrade: Institut za kriminologija i kriminalistička istraživanja, 1975.
As a consequence of the rapid growth of highway transportation, traffic offenses have increased rapidly in Yugoslavia. The personality characteristics of traffic offenders were studied to reveal five basic factors: (1) general abilities, (2) the asthenic syndrome, (3) the conversion syndrome, (4) the sthenic syndrome, and (5) the adjusted-nonadjusted factor. These offenders were found to be average in general intellectual capacities. They exhibited rigidity in reactions and handling of vehicles, constant apprehension, and hypertension. Those features were coupled with aggressive tendencies. Sixty percent had been under the influence of alcohol. Consumption of alcohol was more frequent while driving in their residential area than elsewhere.

Vodopivec, K., "Kriminologija in socijalna patologija" [Criminology and Social Pathology]. *Zbornik znanstvenih razprav* 39 (1980):1-15.
In her article, Dr. Vodopivec sees criminology and social pathology being enriched by the theoretical contributions of social deviance as a third field. The content of criminology has been enlarged. The effects for social pathology have followed a different course by first conceiving "social problems" and then restricting itself to "social deviance." She recommends limitation of subject matter to homogeneous units but analyzed dialectically to take all social conflicts and antagonisms into account. The scientist would be expected to declare openly his criteria for including a certain social fact in the content of social deviance. All social strata would be considered in dialectical interpretation of selected social facts.

INDEX

ABOUT THE CONTRIBUTORS

INKERI ANTTILA: LL.D., criminal law (1946); licentiate of political sciences (1954); Pol. Dr. H.C., Helsinki (1977); Jur. Dr. H.C., Uppsala (1979). Anttila was director of the school for prison officials (1949-1959); professor of criminal law, University of Helsinki (1961-1979); director of the Finnish Research Institute of Legal Policy, since 1974, on leave of absence; and minister of justice and member of the cabinet (1975). She has been a member of the Scandinavian Research Council for Criminology (1959 to date); vice-president of the International Penal and Penitentiary Foundation (1965 to date); member of the Board of the International Association of Penal Law (1969 to date); and chairman of the Board of the International Center of Comparative Criminology, Montreal (1977 to date). She has written eleven books and about one hundred articles on criminal law, criminology, and crime control.

ENRIQUE BACIGALUPO: Doctorate from the University of Buenos Aires (1969), followed by studies at Tulane University and the University of Bonn. Bacigalupo has been professor of penal law, University of Buenos Aires (1970-1974); visiting professor, University of Bonn (1974-1978); and now professor in the School of Law, University of Madrid. He served as secretary of state for the federal government of Argentina. Among his publications are *Improper Crimes of Omission* (1970), *Type and Error* (1974), *Insolvency and Crime* (1970), and *Features of the Theory of Crime* (1974 and 1978).

ISRAEL L. BARAK-GLANTZ: Ph.D. in sociology, Ohio State University (1978). Barak is assistant professor of sociology at Wayne State University in Detroit. His primary interests are in deviance, criminology, and corrections. His publications include many technical research reports and papers. The first volume of *Israel Studies in Criminology* carried his paper "Personality Characteristics of First-Time Offenders." With Simon Dinitz and John Conrad, he is co-author of *The Dangerous Offender in Custody.*

JAMES P. BRADY: Doctor of criminology, University of California at Berkeley (1974). Brady has been visiting professor at Sheffield University, England, and Cabot College, International University in Rome. His publications have been on law and social change in China, Cuba, and the United States. He is a member of the Boston Radical Criminology Collective. Currently, he is studying the "Social Legacy of the Viet Nam War" under a grant from the National Endowment for the Humanities.

NEIL CAMERON: LL.B. with Honors and LL.M. London (1968). Cameron is senior lecturer in law, Victoria University of Wellington, New Zealand. His professional experience includes service with the Home Office Research Unit in London. His articles in law and criminological journals reflect his interest in criminal law, the sociology of law, and police and penal systems.

DUNCAN CHAPPELL: LL.B., First Class Honors, University of Tasmania (1962); Ph.D., University of Cambridge (1965). Chappell's positions on university faculties include the University of Sydney; John Jay College of Criminal Justice; City University of New York; School of Criminal Justice, State University of New York at Albany; University of Washington at Seattle; La Trobe University, Melbourne; and now Simon Fraser University, Burnaby, British Columbia. Until recently, he was a member of the Australian Law Reform Commission. He has published extensively.

SULHI DÖNMEZER: Doctorate of law, University of Istanbul. Dönmezer became a member of the Faculty of Law in 1941 and attained the status of Professor Ordinarius in 1957, dean of the Faculty of Law (1953-1955), and director of the Institute of Criminology in 1955. He was a visiting scholar at the University of Illinois (1946-1948) and a member of the Scientific Criminological Council, Council of Europe (1975-1980). He has lectured in France, Holland, Portugal, Iran, and Pakistan and has published books and articles in Turkish, French, and English.

SAIED EWIES: M.A. (1954) and Ph.D. (1956) in sociology and anthropology at Boston University. Ewies's research in delinquency prevention and treatment began in 1939 and has continued since he joined the National Center for Social and Criminological Research, Cairo, in 1956. He was awarded the State Prize in Sociology and the Decoration of Sciences and Arts, First Grade, in Egypt and a United Nations fellowship to study institutions in Yugoslavia. He has participated in many national and international conferences and has studied criminological activities in the United Kingdom, the USSR, Switzerland, Scandinavia, and the United States. Among his professional publications are fourteen books.

JÁNOS FEHÉRVÁRY: D. Jur., University of Graz (1972); scholarship at the Max Planck Institute for Foreign and International Criminal Law, Freiburg,

Federal Republic of Germany (1973-1976). At the Max Planck Institute, Fehérváry studied the functions of the German state prosecutor, white-collar crime, juvenile delinquency, and official reactions to child abuse. Since 1977 he has been security chief, Vienna Police Department, and criminological and legal advisor to the Ministry of Justice.

FRANCO FERRACUTI, M.D.: Professor of criminological medicine and forensic psychiatry in the Medical School of the University of Rome. Ferracuti was formerly a staff member of the Social Defense Section of the United Nations and consultant to the Social Defense Research Institute of the United Nations. He has published 150 papers and monographs in criminology and forensic psychiatry. Dr. Ferracuti received the Sellin-Glueck Award of the American Society of Criminology.

KATALIN GÖNCZÖL: Gönczöl is associate professor, Department of Criminology, Faculty of Law and Political Science, Eotvos Lorand University in Budapest. She obtained her law degree in 1968, her diploma in 1971, and was awarded the degree "candidate of political and legal sciences" in 1978. Her dissertation was on "The Typology of Recidivists." She is co-author of the university textbook in criminology at Eotvos Lorand and of a monograph, *Violent Crimes and Their Perpetrators*. She has been active in international seminars on comparative law and criminology; five of her thirty published papers have been in English.

JERZY JASIŃSKI: the Faculty of Law, University of Warsaw, in 1954; Ph.D. degree (1961) and LL.D. degree (1976), Institute of State and Law, Polish Academy of Sciences. In 1979, Dr. Jasiński was a visiting professor at Kyoto University, Japan, and in 1981, a visiting fellow at the Institute of Criminology, University of Cambridge, United Kingdom. In addition to papers on criminology and social pathology, his publications include *Problems of Social Maladjustment and Crime in Poland* (1978), of which he was editor as well as contributor, and *Forecasting Future Trends* (1980). His major fields of interest are criminology, criminal policy, and social pathology.

ELMER H. JOHNSON: Ph.D. in sociology, University of Wisconsin (1950). Johnson has served from assistant professor to professor, North Carolina State University at Raleigh (1949-1966); assistant director of the North Carolina Prison Department on academic leave (1958-1960); and professor of sociology and criminal justice, Center for the Study of Crime, Delinquency, and Corrections, Southern Illinois University at Carbondale (1966 to date). Author of *Crime, Correction, and Society*, 4th ed. (1978) and *Social Problems of Urban Man* (1973), he has published considerably on correctional issues, criminological theory, the community and criminal justice, and comparative criminology.

GÜNTHER KAISER: Kaiser is director of the Max Planck Institute for Foreign and International Criminal Law, Freiburg, Federal Republic of Germany. His academic credentials are law studies at the Universities of Göttingen and Tübingen (1951-1956); Jr. D. (1962); and habilitation in criminology and penal law (1969). He has been honorary professor at the University of Freiburg since 1971. Among his numerous publications in criminology and law are *Criminological Research Trends in Western Germany*, with Th. Würtenberger as co-editor (1972); *Juvenile Law and Juvenile Delinquency* (1973); *Genetics and Crime* (1973); *Factory Justice—Studies on the Social Control of Deviant Behavior in Factories*, with G. Metzger-Pregizer as co-editor (1976); *Criminology and Penal Procedure*, with H. Göppinger as co-editor (1976); *Society, Youth, and the Law* (1977); *Juvenile Delinquency* (1977); and *Criminology: Introduction and Foundations*, 4th ed. (1979).

KOO CHIN KANG: LL.B. (1964) and LL.M. (1966) degrees, School of Law, Seoul National University; LL.M. and S.J.D., Harvard Law School. Kang is professor of law at Seoul National University. His experience in law in Korea includes private practice, public prosecution, and service as judge in several district courts. His publications have been two books on criminal law and articles in professional journals.

OLUYEMI KAYODE: M.A. in criminology (1970) and Ph.D. in sociology (1973), University of Pennsylvania. Kayode is now lecturer, Grade I, in the Department of Sociology, University of Ibadan. He was awarded the University of Ibadan Postgraduate Scholarship (1968-1969), a Rockefeller Foundation Scholarship for graduate study in the United States (1969-1973), and a Barclays Bank Scholarship to the International Teachers Program in France (1978). Dr. Kayode was a lecturer in sociology at Lincoln University in Pennsylvania (1971-1973). In addition to his publications, some of which are listed in the bibliography for his chapter on Nigeria, he is conducting research on remand homes, the Nigerian prison system, and the methodology for collecting crime statistics in Nigeria.

MARTIN KILLIAS: Master's degree (lic. phil.) in sociology and social psychology and a doctoral degree (Dr. jur.) from the University of Zürich. Killias is now associate professor of criminology and penology at the University of Lausanne, Switzerland. As a visiting scholar, he conducted research and taught at the School of Criminal Justice, State University of New York at Albany. He has published in criminology and the sociology of law.

GUENTER LEHMANN: Law degree, Karl Marx University in Leipzig and studies in the economy, College of Economy, Berlin-Karlshorst. Professor in ordinary of political law and criminology at the German Democratic Republic's Academy of State and Law at Potsdam-Babelsberg. Lehmann has had many years of judicial practice. He is the head of the Working Group on Crime

Prevention and Combatting of the Council of Research in the Field of State and Law of the GDR Academy of Sciences. His two hundred scientific publications have been directed primarily toward the workings of justice, their greater social effectiveness, and the theory and practice of crime prevention.

JIŘÍ NEZKUSIL occupies the chair of criminology, Law Faculty of Charles University in Prague. Since 1973, he has been director of the Criminological Research Institute attached to the Office of the Prosecutor General of the Czechoslovak Socialist Republic. He is chairman of the Council for the Coordination of the Investigation of Criminality Causes and Prevention in Czechoslovakia, which is an advisory board of the Scientific Council for State and Law in Czechoslovakia. His professional activities have focused on scientific studies of criminal law and criminology in works dealing with methodological issues, economic offenses, and causes of crime and crime prevention in Czechoslovakia. He is co-author of the first Czechoslovak textbook on criminology, *Czechoslovak Criminology: Fundamental Problems*.

D.N.A. NORTEY is senior lecturer and head of the Prison Administration Unit, Department of Sociology, University of Ghana in Legon. He studied at the Presbyterian Teachers' Training College, Akropong, Ghana; at the School of Social Welfare, Accra, University of Ghana; and, for postgraduate studies, at the University of Sussex, England. He has been headmaster, Presbyterian High School at Osu, a senior assistant welfare officer, a probation and prison after-care officer, a probation officer in London, England, a member of the panel of Juvenile Court Magistrates in Accra, and a member of the Prison Service Council of Ghana.

JAMES S.E. OPOLOT: While on leave of absence as senior penal administrator in Uganda's Prison Service, Opolot obtained a Ph.D. in sociology (criminology) at Southern Illinois University at Carbondale. Since receiving his doctorate, he has been a member of the faculties of Mississippi State University, the University of Alabama in Birmingham, the University of Alaska, and the Criminal Justice Institute at Atlanta University. He is the author of *Criminal Justice and Nation-Building in Africa* (1976), *Introduction to Modern Criminal Justice Systems* (1977), *Organized Crime in Africa* (1980), and *World Legal Traditions* (1980).

DAVID ORRICK is head of the Criminal Justice Program, Norwich University, Northfield, Vermont. He has an Ll.D (Honors) in law, University of Southampton, England; a Master's of Philosophy in Criminology, University of Cambridge, England; and a Master's of Arts in Criminal Justice, State University of New York at Albany. Under a Tennant Fund Scholarship, University of Cambridge, he studied in Norway where he graduated from Nansenskolen Folkhoyskole. His latest publication will be a chapter on Norwegian penology for a forthcoming book edited by John Dussich.

LODE VAN OUTRIVE: Doctor of law sciences and doctor in political and social sciences; professor of criminology and industrial sociology in the Department of Criminology, Penal Law, and Sociology, Catholieke University of Leuven. Outrive's extensive scholarly publications have been in the areas of the theory of criminological sociology, the administration of justice, police functions, and prison systems.

DANIELLE QUANTEN: Licentiate in criminology from the Catholic University of Louvain and in social work from the Higher Institute for Social Work in Antwerp. She has had social work experience in public service. Currently, she is director of the Provincial Youth Service in Hasselt, Limburg, Belgium.

PHILIPPE ROBERT holds degrees in sociology, law, political science, and criminal science from the University of Bordeaux where he obtained his doctorate in 1967. He heads the Service d'Etudes Penales et Criminologiques, a research center under the auspices of the Centre Nationale de la Recherche Scientifique and the Ministry of Justice. Dr. Robert teaches at the School of Advanced Studies in the Social Sciences in Paris, at the Institute of Criminology of the University of Paris, and at the University of Bordeaux. He is co-editor of the criminal sociological division of *Année Sociologique*. His publications include *Adolescent Gangs, A Theory of Segregation*, with Pierre Lascoumes as co-author (1966, 1974); *Treatise on Juvenile Law* (1969); *The Image of Collective Rape and Objects Reconstruction*, Thibault Lambert and Claude Faugeron as co-authors (1976); *The Cost of Crime or the Economy in Pursuit of Crime*, Thierry Godefray as co-author 1977); and *Justice and Its Public or the Social Representations of Penal Justice*, Claude Faugeron as co-author (1978).

MANUEL COBO DEL ROSAL: Professor of penal law and dean of the Law Faculty, University of Loguna (1967-1971); professor of penal law, dean of Law Faculty and rector, University of Valencia (1971-1978); now professor, director of Institute of Criminology, and undersecretary at University of Madrid. Cobo del Rosal has studied at the University of Madrid, the University of Rome, and the University of Bonn. He is a founding member of the Spanish Society of Criminology. Among his publications are *Spanish Penal Law*, with Juan del Rosal and Gonzalo Rodriguez Mounullo as co-authors (1963); "Technical-Juridical Considerations Regarding the Concealment of Minors" in *Yearbook of Penal Law and Penal Sciences* (1963); "Magistrate Interview and Origin of Guilt" in *Yearbook of Penal Law and Penal Sciences* (1965); revision of Juan del Rosal, *Treatise on Penal Law*, general part (1968); "Discovery of Secrets Without Disclosure. . . ." in *Yearbook of Penal Law and Penal Sciences* (1971); "Prevention and Social Danger in the Law of August 4, 1970" in *Collection of Studies of the Institute of Criminology of the University of Valencia* (1975).

HARJIT S. SANDHU: Ph.D., Punjab University (1962); master of social work, Ohio State University (1959). Sandhu served in several posts in Punjab and New

Delhi prisons (1942-1964), retiring as principal of the Prison Staff School and superintendent of an experimental prison. He was a Fulbright Scholar (1957). His publications include *A Study of Prison Impact* (1968), *Modern Corrections* (1974), and *Juvenile Delinquency* (1977). He has a special interest in the effectiveness of correctional programs.

PARVIZ SANEY: LL.B. ("License"), Tehran (1957); master's in comparative law, Columbia University (1959); doctorate in law (J.S.D.), Yale University (1963). Saney has taught in Iran and in the United States at Seton Hall University, Vermont Law School, and Columbia University. Among his publications are *Law and Society*, 2 volumes; *Sociology of Values*; and *Readings on Population for Law Students* with T. Lee as co-editor.

GILDA SCARDACCIONE: Ph.D.; researcher in criminological medicine and forensic psychiatry at the Medical School of the University of Rome. Scardaccione has conducted research on correctional treatment and juvenile delinquency.

ZVONIMIR PAUL ŠEPAROVIĆ is professor of law and criminology, Faculty of Law, University of Zagreb. In addition to his doctoral studies in Yugoslavia, he has studied as a Humboldt scholar at the Max Planck Institute of Foreign and International Criminal Law at Freiburg, Federal Republic of Germany, and on a Fulbright-Hayes scholarship in the United States. His three books and professional articles have been in the fields of criminal law, medical law, criminology, and victimology.

RICHARD F. SPARKS received the B.A. degree from Northwestern University in 1954 and the Ph.D. degree from Cambridge University in 1966. From 1964 to 1967, he was lecturer in criminal law and criminology in the Faculty of Law, Birmingham University. From 1967 to 1974, he was an assistant director of research at the Institute of Criminology, University of Cambridge. Since 1974, he has been professor at the School of Criminal Justice, Rutgers University, Newark, New Jersey. He is also director of the Center for the Study of the Causes of Crime for Gain. His publications include *Key Issues in Criminology* (with R. G. Hood, 1970); *Local Prisons* (1971); *Surveying Victims* (with H. G. Genn and D. J. Dodd, 1977); *Studying the Victims of Crime* (1982); and *Methodological Problems of Retrospective Social Surveys* (1982).

C. D. SPINELLIS: Doctorate, School of Law, University of Chicago (1964). From 1965 to 1969, Spinellis taught sociology courses at Pierce-Deree College in Greece. Since 1976, she has been a lecturer in juvenile delinquency, criminology, and penology and has served as assistant chair of criminology and penology at the Law School, University of Athens. Dr. Spinellis also teaches criminology in in-service programs of the Ministry of Justice and the School for Police. Her current research is on general deterrence and social control.

OLDŘICH SUCHÝ is engaged in the Institute of Criminology of Charles University in Prague, the Law Faculty in Brno, and the Faculty of Criminology of the National Security Corps. He is also scientific secretary and vice-director of the Criminological Research Institute of the Office of the Prosecutor General. After extensive practical experience as a prosecutor, Dr. Suchý began a career of many years as a scholar in criminal law and criminology. Among his numerous scholarly works are monographs on recidivism and prisoner after-care, co-authorship of a work on youth and criminality, and a Czechoslovakian textbook of criminology prepared by a team of authors. His extensive international activity has included lectures in the universities of Sweden, Poland, and other countries.

KAZUHIKO TOKORO: Professor of law and criminology, School of Law and Politics, Rikkyo University, Tokyo; member of Board of Directors of the Japanese Association of Criminal Sociology and the Japanese Association of the Sociology of Law; bachelor of law, University of Tokyo (1957); assistant professor at Rikkyo University effective 1959; Fulbright research fellow, University of California at Berkeley (1967-1969). Tokoro's publications include "Public Participation in Crime Control," *Keiho Zasshi* 18, nos. 1-2 (1971): 125ff; "Bureaucracy, Profession and Political Models of the Judiciary," *Hoshakaigaku*, no. 26 (1973): 7ff; and "Criminology and Conflict Resolution," *Japanese Journal of Sociological Criminology*, no. 1 (1976): 31ff.

JAC VAN WERINGH studied sociology and criminology at the University of Groningen. After his military service, he worked at the Institute of Criminology of this university. In 1970, he was appointed professor of criminology at the University of Amsterdam. In 1973, the Criminological Institute "Bonger" was founded as a part of the Faculty of Law of this university. He was chairman of the Dutch Society of Criminology (1976-1978) and one of the editors of the (Dutch) *Journal of Criminology* (1970-1978). His latest book is *Fear Is Timeless, Essays on Criminality in the Netherlands* (1978). He is now working on a book on criminology in Hitler-Germany.

JACOB VAN DER WESTHUIZEN is professor of criminology at the University of South Africa and director of the Institute for Criminology in Pretoria. He is the author of a number of articles and books on crime, security, and corrections. Currently, he is working in close collaboration with private and public enterprises in South Africa to introduce a course in security management and to establish a degree course in "securiology," the science of security education, at the University of South Africa.

PREBEN WOLF: LL.M., University of Copenhagen (1945); assistant public prosecutor in Copenhagen (1945-1946), holding governing positions and administrative posts within the prison service (1946-1967); deputy chief of section from 1962; part-time researcher at the Sociological Institute, University of Copenhagen (1958) and at the Institute for Criminal Sciences (1963). Wolf was appointed reader in sociology in 1964 and associate professor in 1967. He served as project director for the Scandinavian Research Council for Criminology (1971-1973). Among his books and articles on sociological and criminological matters, his main criminological works have been *Crime in a Welfare Society*, 4th ed., with E. Høgh (1975) and *Violence in Denmark and Finland* (1972).

VLADIMIR K. ZVIRBUL: Doctor of law and professor, Zvirbul is the author of more than 160 scientific works, including four books on criminology and four manuals on supervision by procurators. His career includes service as investigator and procurator (1948-1962); for ten years, deputy director, All-Union Institute for Study of Causes and Elaboration of Measures for Crime Prevention; and, at present, professional chair, Institute of Advanced Training of Leading Personnel of the Procurator's Office of the USSR. He has served as vice-president of the Scientific Committee and on the Board of Directors, International Society of Criminology; and now serves on the Board of Directors of the USSR-USA Society and the Soviet Democratic Lawyers' Association.

DR. JOAB NJEKHO MESHAK WASIKHONGO
(April 19, 1946-July 24, 1979)

Editor's note: While preparing the chapter on Kenya that was to be in this volume, Dr. Wasikhongo died in Madison, Wisconsin. His wife—Professor Freida High-Wasikhongo of the Department of Afro-American Studies, University of Wisconsin at Madison—agreed to prepare the following statement which is offered here to commemorate his contributions to African criminology.

In 1972, a young scholar of sociology left his Kenyan home to continue studies in the United States. With a bachelor of science degree earned in 1972 from Makerere University in Uganda, he entered the University of Wisconsin to obtain a master of science (1974) and doctor of philosophy (1979), with Dr. Marshall B. Clinard his major professor. While there, he was a Rockefeller Foundation scholar.

In his relatively brief career as a criminologist, Dr. Wasikhongo had already expressed both theoretical and practical concern for comparative studies in the West and in Africa. His works include: "Uniformities in Aggravated Assaults in St. Louis (MO) and Mombasa (Kenya): A Cross-cultural Replication," *International Journal of Criminology and Penology* 4 (February 1976):9-24 and "The Role and Character of Police in Africa and Western Countries: A Comparative Approach to Police Isolation," *International Journal of Criminology and Penology* 4 (November 1976):383-396; and *African Crime and Western Theory* (East African Literature Bureau, 1980). His seminar papers were "Armed Robbery in Africa—A Research Agenda," at the University of Nairobi in Kenya, May 26, 1977; "Trends and Issues in Capital Punishment—A Lesson for Africa," Seminar on the Death Penalty in Africa, Lusaka, Zambia, October 3-8, 1977; the same paper at the Amnesty International Conference, sponsored by the All-Africa Conference of Churches and held in Stockholm, Sweden, December 10-11, 1977. As a consultant to the United Nations Defense Research Institute, he worked particularly on the project, "Monitoring of Crime Trends and Criminal Justice Information," 1977-1979.

He is mourned by his mother, Mrs. Efamanjeri Nerima, his many brothers and sisters, relatives, his two sons Comfort Meshak and Odalo Magruder, and his wife Professor Freida High-Wasikhongo.